Guide to Parallel Operating Systems with Windows 10 and Linux

Third Edition

Ron Carswell

Mary Ellen Hardee

Shen Jiang

Amita Mahajan

Troy Touchette

CENGAGE
Learning·

Australia • Brazil • Mexico • Singapore • United Kingdom • United States

CENGAGE
Learning·

Guide to Parallel Operating Systems with Windows 10 and Linux, 3rd Edition

Ron Carswell, Mary Ellen Hardee, Shen Jiang, Amita Mahajan, Troy Touchette

SVP, GM Skills & Global Product Management: Dawn Gerrain

Product Director: Kathleen McMahon

Product Team Manager: Kristin McNary

Associate Product Manager: Amy Savino

Senior Director, Development: Marah Bellegarde

Product Development Manager: Leigh Hefferon

Managing Content Developer: Emma Newsom

Senior Content Developer: Natalie Pashoukos

Product Assistant: Abigail Pufpaff

Vice President, Marketing Services: Jennifer Ann Baker

Marketing Coordinator: Cassie Cloutier

Senior Production Director: Wendy Troeger

Production Director: Patty Stephan

Managing Art Director: Jack Pendleton

Software Development Manager: Pavan Ethakota

Associate Program Manager: Divya Divakaran, Lumina Datamatics Ltd.

Cover Image(s): winui/Shutterstock

For product information and technology assistance, contact us at
Cengage Learning Customer & Sales Support, 1-800-354-9706

For permission to use material from this text or product,
submit all requests online at **www.cengage.com/permissions**.
Further permissions questions can be e-mailed to
permissionrequest@cengage.com.

Library of Congress Control Number: 2016946381

ISBN: 978-1-305-10712-0

Cengage Learning
20 Channel Center Street
Boston, MA 02210
USA

Cengage Learning is a leading provider of customized learning solutions with employees residing in nearly 40 different countries and sales in more than 125 countries around the world. Find your local representative at **www.cengage.com**.

Cengage Learning products are represented in Canada by Nelson Education, Ltd.

To learn more about Cengage Learning, visit **www.cengage.com**.

Purchase any of our products at your local college store or at our preferred online store **www.cengagebrain.com**.

Printed in the United States of America
Print Number: 03   Print Year: 2017

Brief Contents

Table of Contents

Preface

Welcome to *Guide to Parallel Operating Systems with Windows 10 and Linux, 3rd edition*. This book offers real-world examples and more than 100 hands-on activities that reinforce key concepts and help you prepare for a career in the information technology (IT) field.

This book offers in-depth study of the functions and features of two important operating systems: Microsoft Windows 10 and Red Hat CentOS 7. The book emphasizes how the two operating systems are used by computer programmers, database administrators, and network administrators. The book assumes that students have previously used a personal computer with either Windows or Linux.

Guide to Parallel Operating Systems uses a unique approach to explain operating systems. After a brief introduction to each concept, the book demonstrates virtualization, which allows students to switch instantly between the two operating systems and complete the numerous hands-on activities. Such activities reinforce the similarities and differences of the two operating systems.

The appendices provide setup instructions to use three popular virtualization software applications: Microsoft Hyper-V, Oracle VirtualBox, and VMware Workstation.

Because numerous colleges are integrating Windows and Linux into their curricula, this text provides a vehicle to learn about both operating systems in one course. This text is also designed to meet the needs of a wide range of disciplines, including programming, networking, and database administration. To succeed in class work and the workplace, students need to be competent in both Windows and Linux.

Throughout the book, detailed activities provide firsthand experience with Windows 10 and CentOS 7. Review Questions reinforce the concepts introduced in each chapter, and Case Projects prepare you to manage real-world situations in an IT environment.

Intended Audience

Guide to Parallel Operating Systems is intended both for students who are getting started in IT and for users who have experience with Windows 10 or CentOS 7 in a school or corporate environment. To best understand the material in this book, you should have a working knowledge of one of these operating systems.

Chapter Descriptions

This book has 12 chapters, as follows:

Chapter 1, "Hardware Components," introduces virtual machine technology—the vehicle that permits Microsoft Windows 10 and CentOS 7 to operate in parallel. Chapter 1 also provides an overview of the components that make up a PC system and concludes with useful information for PC care.

Chapter 2, "Software Components," covers the functions and characteristics of the two operating systems.

Chapter 3, "Using the Graphical User Interface," explains how to interact with a PC by manipulating visual elements such as icons and windows.

Chapter 4, "Installing and Configuring Applications," covers the access of Help information, use and configuration of a Web browser, and the installation of ActiveState Perl.

Chapter 5, "File Systems," describes the use of file systems supported by the two operating systems.

Chapter 6, "Directory Commands," introduces various commands and techniques for working with directories.

Chapter 7, "Files and File Attributes," covers the files used by various applications and search techniques used to locate files.

Chapter 8, "The Command Line," explains how to use the command-line interface in the two operating systems. The chapter also introduces Windows PowerShell.

Chapter 9, "Text Editors," covers text editors that are used by the two operating systems. The chapter also describes the use of PowerShell Integrated Scripting Environment as a text editor.

Chapter 10, "Scripting in Windows 10 and CentOS 7," explains Windows PowerShell and CentOS 7 scripting.

Chapter 11, "Local Network Access," explains networking terminology, viewing TCP/IP settings, accessing network resources, and viewing folder and file sharing permissions.

Chapter 12, "Operating System Management," explains how to manage processes executed on a PC, how to measure factors that indicate PC performance, and how to monitor reliability.

Appendix A, "Numbering Systems and Data Representation," explains how to convert numbers from one base to another, how data is represented by ASCII characters, and the representative storage of data in memory.

Appendix B, "Working with Hyper-V Virtualization," provides the setup instructions to use Windows 10 and CentOS 7 virtual machines with Microsoft Hyper-V virtualization.

Appendix C, "Working with VirtualBox," provides the setup instructions to use Windows 10 and CentOS 7 virtual machines with Oracle VirtualBox.

Appendix D, "Working with VMware," provides the setup instructions to use Windows 10 and CentOS 7 virtual machines with VMware Workstation.

Features and Approach

Guide to Parallel Operating Systems differs from other OS books in its unique integration of Windows 10, CentOS 7, and virtualization. To help you understand how to use both operating systems, the book covers them in parallel. In the interest of brevity, some references are missing from command descriptions throughout the text.

- **Chapter Objectives**—Each chapter begins with a list of the concepts to be mastered. This list provides a quick reference to the chapter's contents and can be a useful study aid.

- **Activities**—Activities are incorporated throughout the text to give you a strong foundation for carrying out tasks in the real world. Because the activities tend to build on each other, you should complete the activities in each chapter before moving to the end-of-chapter materials and subsequent chapters.

- **Chapter Summaries**—Each chapter's text is followed by a summary of concepts introduced in the chapter. These summaries provide a helpful way to recap and revisit the chapter's ideas.

- **Key Terms**—All of the terms that are introduced in boldface text in a chapter are listed together after the Chapter Summary. This list lets you check your understanding of the terms.

- **Review Questions**—The end-of-chapter assessment begins with a set of questions that reinforce the ideas introduced in the chapter. Answering these questions helps ensure that you have mastered important concepts.

- **Case Projects**—Each chapter closes with a section that asks you to evaluate real-world situations and decide on a course of action. This valuable tool helps you sharpen your decision-making and troubleshooting skills, which are important in IT.

Text and Graphic Conventions

Additional information and exercises have been added to this book to help you better understand what is being discussed in the chapters. Icons throughout the text alert you to these materials:

Notes present additional helpful material for the subject being discussed.

Activity icons precede each activity in this book.

Case Project icons mark the end-of-chapter case projects. These scenario-based assignments ask you to independently apply what you learned in the chapter.

Instructor Resources

Free to all instructors who adopt *Guide to Parallel Operating Systems* for their courses is a complete package of instructor resources. These resources are available from the Cengage Learning Web site, *www.cengagebrain.com*. Go to the product page for this book in the online catalog and choose "Instructor Downloads." Resources include:

- **Instructor's Manual**—This manual includes course objectives and additional information to help your instruction.

- **Solutions**—Solutions are provided for Review Questions and Case Projects.

- **Cengage Learning Testing Powered by Cognero**—A flexible, online system that allows you to import, edit, and manipulate content from the text's test bank or elsewhere, including your own favorite test questions; create multiple test versions in an instant; and deliver tests from your LMS, your classroom, or wherever you want.

- **PowerPoint Presentations**—A set of Microsoft PowerPoint slides is included for each chapter. These slides are meant to be used as a teaching aid for classroom presentations, to be made available to students for chapter review, or to be printed for classroom distribution. Instructors are also at liberty to add their own slides.

- **Figure Files**—Figure files allow instructors to create their own presentations using figures taken from the text.

- **Student Files**—All of the scripts and data files are available from the Cengage Web site. Download instructions are presented in the appendices for each virtualization application.

Minimum Lab Requirements

To install the three software components, you must have the following minimum hardware configuration:

Component	Requirement
CPU	Intel or AMD 2 Core 2.0 GHz (4 Core 2.4 GHz or more is recommended) 64-bit processor
BIOS	Intel VT or AMD-V virtualization available
Memory	At least 4 GB of RAM (6 GB recommended)
Disk space	At least 24 GB of free space (30 GB recommended)
Drives	CD-ROM and USB drive
Networking	Network interface card

Virtual Machine Setup

To complete the lab activities in this text, special attention to setup is required:

- Windows 10 Professional or Education and CentOS 7 are required for the two virtual machines. The following figure provides an overview of the required environment.
- Windows 8 Pro 64-bit Edition, Windows 8.1 Pro 64-bit Edition, Windows 10 Professional, or Windows 10 Education is recommended for the host operating system.

A recommended source for Windows 10 is DreamSpark, a Microsoft program that supports technical education by providing access to Microsoft software for learning, teaching, and research purposes.

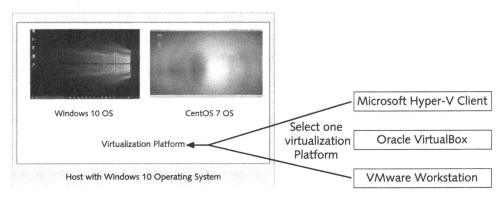

Choose one of the following three virtualization applications; the lab activities have been tested with each:

- Microsoft Client Hyper-V
- Oracle VirtualBox
- VMware Workstation

Specific instructions to set up the virtualization environments are provided in the appendices.

Author Team

Ron Carswell has more than 20 years of computer experience with both small and large organizations. Ron holds a bachelor's degree in business administration from the University of Texas and a master's degree in business administration from Baylor University. He has received A+, Network+, CTT+, MCSA, MCSE, CCNA, MCDST, MCITP, and MS:Server Virtualization with System Center certifications. He is currently a professor emeritus at San Antonio College, where he teaches MCSA and MS:Server Virtualization certification courses. Ron has written numerous textbooks for Cengage Learning. In addition, Ron authored *Test Drive the Microsoft Private Cloud* for Cengage PTR.

Mary Ellen Hardee has worked in the IT field for over 16 years and has extensive hands-on Linux/UNIX experience. She has written many technical documents that are still used in the industry. She has taught IT-related classes to many different types of students. She currently holds the following certifications: CCNA, Network+ and Security+, EC Council Certified Ethical Hacker, and Rackspace Certified OpenStack Technician. She has a bachelor of science degree in Computer Information Systems with an emphasis in networking from Regis University.

Shen (Sharon) Jiang has 11 years of experience with large organizations. Sharon holds a master's degree in Computer Information Systems from South Dakota State University and a master's degree in linguistics from Jilin University. She is currently an assistant professor at San Antonio College, where she instructs in all levels of database courses, CISCO, Program Logic and Design, basic programming, and fundamentals of networking. She has earned Oracle9i and Oracle10g certifications. She co-authored *Guide to Parallel Operating Systems with Windows and Linux, 2nd edition*.

Amita Mahajan has over 14 years of computer experience in different industries. Amita holds a master's degree in Information System Security from the University of Colorado and a master's degree in system administration. She has received the MCSE, CNA, and CCNA certifications and has presented at many technical conferences. Recently she acquired her PMP certification. She is currently working as a network analyst with Alamo Colleges and is an adjunct professor at San Antonio College and Northwest Vista College, where she teaches Microsoft certification courses.

Troy Touchette has 19 years of computing experience both in public and private organizations. He earned a bachelor of science degree in electrical engineering and a master's of engineering degree from McNeese State University. He also received the Committee on National Security Systems (CNSS) Senior Systems Managers CNSSI 4012 certificate from Texas A&M University-San Antonio. He is currently a professor and department chair of the Computer Information Systems department at San Antonio College, where he has taught since 1999.

Acknowledgments

Ron Carswell

First and foremost, I give thanks to God for the mental skills and health to complete this work. Next, I want to give a well-deserved pat on the back to our authors: Amita, Mary Ellen, Shen, and Troy. Also, I want to thank the staff at Cengage Learning, especially our senior content developer, Natalie Pashoukos, for her patience and help. Thanks to our developmental editor, Dan Seiter, for providing the inspiration to mold our thoughts clearly and concisely. And, of course, thanks to our technical editor, David Acosta, for the time and effort to verify the technical accuracy of the text and activities.

I also thank my wife, Coleen, for patience and support during many nights of writing and editing in the man cave.

Mary Ellen Hardee

I want to thank Ron and the staff at Cengage Learning for giving me an opportunity to work on this book. I also want to thank the other authors, Troy, Amita, Ron, and Shen, but especially Troy for being patient with me and working through all the issues. Thanks to our developmental editor, Dan Seiter, for pointing out where my text needed additional massaging, and to David Acosta for the time and effort to verify the technical accuracy of the text and activities.

I also thank my husband, Manuel, for patience and support during many nights and days of writing and editing, even while on vacation.

Shen Jiang

Thanks to Ron for the patience and leadership he showed to keep us on track and meet the deadline, and to the team for the group work. The team at Cengage Learning was very supportive and helped us persevere. Special thanks go to Dan Seiter for showing us how we could make the text even better and more consistent. Thanks to my husband for being understanding, patient, and supportive.

Amita Mahajan

I would like to express my gratitude to the many people who made this possible—first and foremost to Ron for believing in me and for the opportunity. I also want to thank my husband Sunil and my daughters Ankita and Smridhi for encouraging me and dealing with me while I was working on chapters and needed solitude. My acknowledgement would be incomplete without thanks and gratitude to all the Cengage Learning staff for compiling our text clearly and concisely. A big thank you to all who contributed to the making of this book in any way. You all are great!

Troy Touchette

First, I give thanks to God for the health and resources to complete this work. I also appreciate the teachers, colleagues, friends, and family who have guided me over the years and allowed me to reach this point. Thank you to the staff at Cengage Learning for the opportunity. And a special thank you, to my wife, Victoria, and our children for all of your support.

Reviewers

We are indebted to the following people for their contributions of perceptive feedback on the chapter-by-chapter reviews of the text:

- David Acosta, Technical Editor, San Antonio College, San Antonio, Texas
- Mark Turner, Central Piedmont Community College, Charlotte, North Carolina

Special Thanks

The authors wish to thank the Editorial and Production teams at Cengage Learning. Their diligent and professional efforts greatly enhanced the final product:

- Natalie Pashoukos, Senior Content Developer
- Dan Seiter, Developmental Editor
- Kristin McNary, Product Team Manager
- Amy Savino, Associate Product Manager

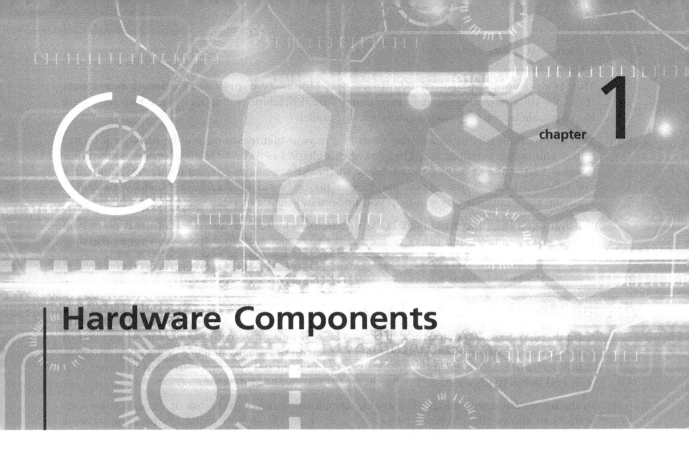

## chapter 1

Hardware Components

After reading this chapter and completing the exercises, you will be able to:

- Explain the use of virtual machine technology to run multiple operating systems concurrently
- Describe the hardware components of a personal computer system
- Describe the peripheral components that may be attached to a personal computer system
- Describe the preventive maintenance for a computer system

This text covers the use of Windows and Linux—two prevalent operating systems (OSs) for the personal computer (PC). Using virtual machine technology, these two seemingly incompatible operating systems can work in parallel.

You will undoubtedly purchase numerous PCs in your lifetime. Some will be for your job, and others will be for personal use. The goal of this chapter is to provide an overview of the components that make up a PC system. Some of these components are within the PC, and some are attached to it. Whether you purchase a major brand or decide to "build your own," knowing these components will help you understand the day-to-day workings of your OS.

When using a PC, proper maintenance is important. This chapter provides information to help you care for your PC and offers guidance on the proper way to dispose of it when the time comes.

Virtual Machine Technology

Virtualized systems—systems that appear to be real but are actually simulations—are used in many environments. Airline pilots use flight simulators for flight practice and testing, whereas computer games like SimCity let the player create a virtual city in a game environment that feels real but actually exists in the hardware and software of the game.

In the information technology (IT) world, **virtualization** refers to the use of virtualization software that allows the physical hardware of a single PC to run multiple operating systems simultaneously in **virtual machines** (**VMs**). The virtualization software simulates enough hardware to create an environment that allows an unmodified **guest operating system** (the one running inside a VM) to be run in isolation on a **host operating system** (the one running on the physical computer system).

This text uses examples of virtual machine technology, which allows multiple operating systems to run concurrently on a single PC. With virtual machine technology, you can run various Microsoft Windows operating systems as well as Linux within another host operating system. In this text, you will work with both Windows and Linux in a virtual environment. Figure 1-1 shows Windows 10 and Linux images on the Windows 10 desktop within Microsoft Hyper-V virtualization software. Hyper-V requires the Windows 10 desktop operating system. Both Windows and Linux can be used as a guest operating system. This text uses the CentOS 7 distribution of Linux.

Virtualization means that you can concurrently operate seemingly incompatible operating systems in one hardware environment, as shown in Figure 1-2. Consider the following:

- The host computer—in this case a laptop—is running Windows 10 with one hard drive, 4 GB of memory, and a network adapter, keyboard, touch pad, and liquid crystal display (LCD) screen.
- The first virtual machine is running Windows 10 with three hard drives, 1 GB of memory, and a network adapter, keyboard, mouse, and monitor. (All hardware is virtualized.)
- The other virtual machine is running CentOS 7 with three hard drives, 1 GB of memory, and a network adapter, keyboard, mouse, and monitor. (Again, all hardware is virtualized.)

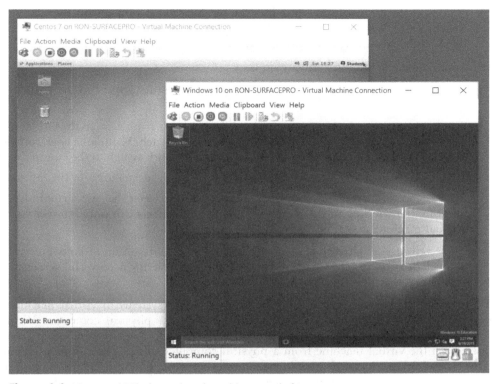

Figure 1-1 Linux and Windows virtual machines on desktop

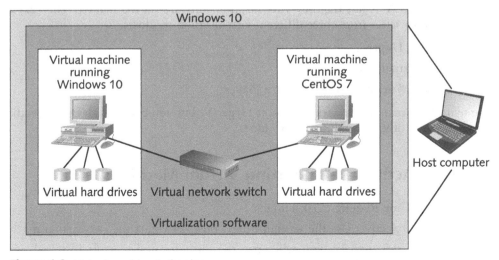

Figure 1-2 Virtual machine technology

- The virtualization software provides the hardware environment for the two virtual machines for a total of six hard drives, 2 GB of memory, two network adapters, two keyboards, two mice, and two monitors.

How does the virtualization software do this?

- The six hard drives are six files on the laptop; these files appear to the virtual machines as real hard drives.

- The two network adapters appear as virtualized network adapters to the virtual machines. These adapters are connected to the virtual network switch. Within the host, software exists to provide network connections from the virtual network switch to the laptop's network.

- The 2 GB of memory comes from the 4 GB of physical memory on the laptop.

- The keyboards, mice, and monitors are switched between the two virtual machines by clicking the window of the desired virtual machine. You can only interact with one virtual machine at a time.

Of course, given enough memory and processor cycles, virtualization software will scale to run more than two virtual machines. It is not unreasonable for a powerful server to run 100 or more virtual machines.

To summarize, you can install multiple guest operating systems in virtual machines, which look like any other applications you would use on your physical computer. Virtualization software mimics physical PCs so closely that the operating systems installed in them do not distinguish the virtual machine from a physical computer. Instead of installing operating systems on multiple costly computers or creating unwieldy multiboot installations, you can install the operating systems in multiple inexpensive virtual machines. Another benefit is that changes you make in virtual machines do not affect your physical computer. Snapshots of the virtual machine's state can also be saved. This allows you to revert back to a previous point in time, reversing any changes made inside the guest operating system since that snapshot.

Microsoft Hyper-V is not the only virtualization software on the market. This text is written to allow you to select from three different virtualization products:

- Microsoft Hyper-V
- Oracle VirtualBox
- VMware Workstation or VMware Player

The text of the main book uses Microsoft Hyper-V, but you can consult the appendices to see how to use the other virtualization products.

Activity 1-1: Starting Virtual Machines

Time Required: 10 minutes

Objective: Use the virtualization console to start the two virtual machines.

Description: In this activity, you will open the virtualization console installed on the host computers that you will use in your class, and then you will start the two virtual machines. Recall that you will use one of the three virtualization solutions.

1. If necessary, log on to your host PC with **user01** and a password of **Pa$$w0rd.**

   If you are not sure which virtualization software you are using, ask your instructor.

2. Start your virtualization software by selecting one of the following choices:

   - To start Microsoft Hyper-V, click the **Manage Virtual Machines** icon on the desktop (the icon has two green servers).
   - To start the Oracle VM VirtualBox console, click the **Oracle VM VirtualBox** icon on the desktop (the icon is a blue cube).
   - To start the VMware console, click **Start**, point to **All Programs**, and then double-click **VMware Workstation**.

   Wait for the PowerShell script to start the virtual machines and display a connection window. Steps 3 and 4 are not required when Hyper-V virtualization is installed.

3. To start the CentOS 7 virtual machine, double-click the **CentOS 7 Virtual Machine** icon.

4. To start the Windows 10 virtual machine, double-click the **Windows 10 Virtual Machine** icon.

5. To log on to the Windows 10 virtual machine, click the **user01** icon within the Windows 10 virtual machine window, type **Pa$$w0rd,** and then press **Enter.**

6. To switch to the CentOS 7 virtual machine, click within the CentOS 7 virtual machine window.

7. To log on to the CentOS 7 virtual machine, click the **User01** icon within the CentOS 7 virtual machine window, type **Pa$$w0rd,** and then press **Enter.**

8. Leave the virtual machines logged on for future activities.

Hardware Components of a PC System

A desktop computer is a PC that is designed to fit conveniently on a typical office desk. The desktop computer typically contains several devices that are assembled in a computer case:

- Power supply—Provides the necessary voltages
- Cooling system—Removes the heat generated by the PC
- System board—The main circuit board for the PC
- Microprocessor—The central processing unit (CPU) for the PC
- Memory—The electronic holding area for programs and data
- Firmware—Computer programming instructions in read-only memory, used to test and start the PC
- Ports—Used to connect external devices to the PC
- Adapters—Cards that provide capabilities to the PC

These components are explained in more detail in the following sections.

Cases

In a PC, the case houses and protects the main electronic components. You may purchase a PC in various sizes and shapes. The **form factor** is the size, configuration, or physical arrangement of a computer case or one of its internal components, such as a system board (which contains basic electronic circuitry and components).

The IBM XT PC set an early, de facto standard for case configuration. The desktop computer has since evolved through the ATX (advanced technology extended) model, the Micro-ATX, and the small-footprint PC. Some configurations include horizontal or flat desktop, vertical or tower, and rack-mounted. Later improvements reduced the size of the PC for laptop, notebook, and tablet computers. All-in-one desktop designs integrate the monitor into the same case as the PC components. Figure 1-3 illustrates various form factors.

The style of PC case that you purchase determines a number of factors. For example, what system board will be supported by the case?

A portable computer is a PC designed to be easily transported and relocated. The earliest portable computers were simply called *portables*. As the size and weight of most portables decreased, they became known as laptop or notebook computers. Eventually, keyboards could be replaced with touch-screen interfaces, which led to tablet computers.

A laptop computer is a battery- or AC-powered PC, generally smaller than a briefcase, that can be used on airplanes, in libraries, in temporary offices, at meetings, and so on. A laptop typically weighs less than five pounds.

Netbooks are a smaller, lightweight, inexpensive version of notebook computers suited for both general PC and Web-based applications. Typically, Netbooks have smaller displays, less memory, and less powerful processors. Tablets are similar in function to laptops, but they use a touch-screen interface that eliminates the need for a keyboard. Tablets usually weigh less than two pounds.

Laptops usually come with displays that use LCD-screen technology. Laptops use several approaches for integrating a mouse into the keyboard, including the touch pad and the trackball. Your laptop computer may not possess the same ports as a desktop computer; for example, laptops may be restricted to using video and USB ports. However, many laptops have built-in network adapters and wireless access. CD-ROM and DVD disc drives may be built in or attachable. This is explained in the following sections.

Desktop   Tower box   Laptop   Tablet   All-in-one

Figure 1-3 Form factors

Power Supplies

Your computer's power supply, as shown in Figure 1-4, is a sealed metal box that contains power conversion hardware. The power supply converts the 110-volt alternating current (AC) in your office or household (220 volts in some countries) to the various direct current (DC) levels required by your PC. The power supply provides clean power feeds to the components in your computer: the system board, disk drives, cooling fans, and so on. Power supplies have standardized plugs that work with all kinds of components; if you use a plug that fits the device, you are sure to get a correct voltage. PC power supplies often have an input voltage selector that can be set to 115 volts (for 110 volts) or 230 volts. In the United States, 115 volts is usually set by default by the manufacturer before shipping.

Do not open the power supply! The internal components are not user-serviceable.

Older computer power supplies are not very efficient. 80 PLUS is an initiative to promote more electrical energy-efficient computer power supplies; it certifies products that have more than 80 percent energy efficiency at rated loads. That is, units that waste 20 percent or less electric energy as heat at the specified load reduce electricity use. Multiple levels of certification have been established for higher efficiency, including bronze, silver, gold, platinum, and titanium.

Cooling Systems

Computers generate heat—lots of it. A PC's microprocessor produces 75 to 100 watts of heat, which is as much as a regular household incandescent lightbulb. Other internal computer components generate more heat; in sum, your desktop PC could generate more than 300 watts. Poor heat dissipation can cause many problems ranging from mysterious system crashes to major hardware damage. Overheating increases the risk that your computer's components will fail prematurely.

Figure 1-4 Power supply

Air is circulated within the case to dissipate the heat generated by the computer's electronic components. Air enters the case and is pulled out with one or more fans in the front or back of the case. Although most PCs rely on the circulated air to remove the generated heat, some faster PCs resort to liquid cooling for the microprocessor.

The microprocessor in your PC has a **heat sink** attached to dissipate the generated heat. Generally, your microprocessor's temperature should not run in excess of 130 to 140 degrees Fahrenheit (hot even for south Texas) while under a full load. The heat sink is attached to the microprocessor chip, is usually made of aluminum, and has extended fins. Thermal paste is used between the microprocessor and heat sink during installation to ensure proper heat transfer. An active heat sink is one that comes with a fan; it is sometimes called a *heat sink/ fan (HSF) combo*.

System Boards

The **system board** is the main circuit board inside a PC case. It contains the processor socket, memory slots, hard drive connectors, expansion slots, and other components. Additional boards, called *daughter boards*, can be plugged into the system board (see Figure 1-5).

The following sections explain the numerous components of a system board.

Microprocessor   The heart of the PC system is the **microprocessor** (see Figure 1-6). It contains the logic circuitry that performs the instructions of a computer's programs. Microprocessors were once known as central processing units; today, a microprocessor is a CPU on a single chip. This "electronic engine" is activated when you turn on your computer. The microprocessor contains a set of instructions designed to perform such tasks as

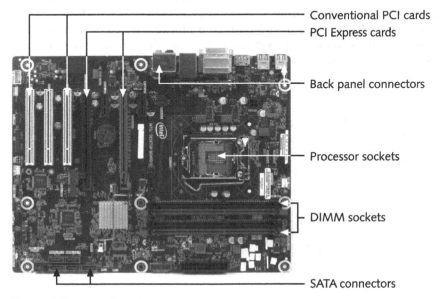

Figure 1-5 System board

1

Figure 1-6 AMD microprocessor

Source: AMD

arithmetic (adding, subtracting), logic operations (comparing two numbers), and transferring numbers from one register to another. A **register** is a small amount of high-speed memory.

Buses The **bus** is a set of circuits on the system board through which data is transferred from one part of a computer to another. You can picture the metaphor of data hopping aboard a bus to travel within a computer. The term *bus* usually refers to an internal bus that connects all the internal computer components to the microprocessor and main memory. In addition, an expansion bus permits adapter boards to access the microprocessor and memory.

All buses consist of two parts: a data bus and an address bus. The data bus transfers actual data, whereas the address bus transfers information about where the data should go.

The size of a bus—known as its width—is important because it determines how much data can be transmitted at one time. For example, a 32-bit bus can transmit 32 bits (4 bytes) of data, whereas a 64-bit bus can transmit 64 bits (8 bytes) of data.

Memory **Memory** is an electronic holding area for your programs and data. Memory usually contains the main parts of the OS and some or all of the applications and related data that are being used. Memory is often used as a shorter synonym for random access memory (RAM). This kind of memory, as shown in Figure 1-7, is located in the memory slots on the system board. You can think of RAM as an array of boxes, each of which can hold a single byte of information. A computer that has 4 GB of memory can hold about 4,096 million bytes (or characters) of information.

Several types of memory can be used in your PC:

- **RAM** (random access memory)—The term *RAM* refers to read-and-write memory, meaning that you can write data into RAM and read data from it. Most RAM is volatile—it requires a steady flow of electricity to maintain its contents. When power is turned off on the PC, any data that was in RAM is lost.

Figure 1-7 Memory module

- **ROM** (read-only memory)—A PC almost always contains a small amount of ROM that holds instructions for starting the PC. Unlike RAM, you cannot write to ROM.

- **PROM** (programmable read-only memory)—A PROM is a memory chip on which you can store a program. Once the PROM has been used, you cannot erase it and store something else on it. Like ROMs, PROMs are nonvolatile.

- **EPROM** (erasable programmable read-only memory)—An EPROM is a special type of PROM that you can erase by exposure to ultraviolet light.

- **EEPROM** (electrically erasable programmable read-only memory)—An EEPROM is a special type of EPROM that you can erase by applying an electrical charge.

Firmware ROMs, PROMs, EPROMs, and EEPROMs that contain recorded programs are called firmware. **Firmware** is a combination of software and hardware.

The **BIOS** (basic input/output system) is firmware that supports the PC during start-up. In addition, the BIOS contains the program code required to control the keyboard, display text on the screen, read from disk drives, and perform a number of miscellaneous functions.

The BIOS is typically placed in a firmware chip that comes with the computer; it is often called a *ROM BIOS*. This placement ensures that the BIOS will always be available and will not be damaged by disk failures; it also enables a computer to start itself. PCs have a flash BIOS, which means that the BIOS has been recorded on a flash memory chip (normally an EEPROM) that can be updated if necessary.

Input/Output Ports

A PC typically comes with standard input-output ports, as shown in Figure 1-8. These ports are often called *I/O* (pronounced *eye-oh*) *ports*. A system board groups these I/O ports on the back of the board, so the ports are called *back panel connectors*. Serial ports are used for modems, digitizer tablets, and other devices. Serial ports have fallen into legacy status and may not be installed on new PCs. Almost every peripheral that is connected via serial ports is now available as a USB device. Extra USB ports are often present on the front of the case.

Connectors are identified by gender. When copper pins are exposed in the connector, its gender is male. In Figure 1-8, the serial connector is a male connector. The parallel connector is female because holes are present.

These I/O ports are discussed in the following sections.

Serial Ports A serial port transfers data in or out one bit at a time. Throughout most of the history of PCs, this transfer was accomplished using **RS-232** (short for *recommended standard-232*), a standard interface approved by the Electronic Industries Alliance (EIA) for transferring data over simple cables that connect the computer to a device. Serial ports are legacy hardware but are used for connecting to other devices, such as switches or routers for maintenance.

You can identify the serial ports on the back of a PC by checking for male connectors. If you check your BIOS settings, you may see that your PC has allocated the serial ports as COM1, COM2, and so on.

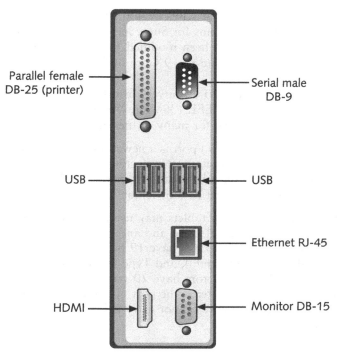

Figure 1-8 Back of computer showing I/O ports

Universal Serial Bus The Universal Serial Bus (USB) was developed to simplify the connection of peripheral devices to the PC. Almost every peripheral that once could be connected via a serial or parallel port is now available with a USB connector. The major goals of USB were to make it inexpensive to add peripherals to a PC and as easy to connect as a telephone to a wall jack. USB originally featured a minimum bandwidth of 1.5 Mbps (megabits per second) for low-speed devices such as mice and keyboards, and a maximum bandwidth of 12 Mbps for higher-speed devices such as Web cameras, printers, scanners, and external CD-RW drives. You can connect up to 127 USB peripherals with five levels of hubs to a single USB host controller.

In a quest for additional speed, USB 2.0 and then USB 3.0 were introduced. The maximum speed of the connection jumped from 12 Mbps on USB 1.1 to 480 Mbps on USB 2.0 to SuperSpeed (5 Gbps) on USB 3.0. USB 2.0 is both forward and backward compatible with USB 1.1, but USB 3.0 is not. The USB connectors and cables are identical for USB 2.0 and 1.1, but USB 3.0 ports are noted by a blue coloring. USB 2.0 is backward compatible to USB 1.1, but USB 3.0 is not. USB 2.0 devices plugged into a legacy USB 1.1 port simply operate at reduced throughput. Both Hi-Speed USB 2.0 and original USB 1.1 peripherals can operate on a PC at the same time. The new USB 2.0 expansion-hub design manages the transition of data rates between the high-speed host and lower-speed USB peripherals while maintaining full bandwidth utilization. If you have a digital camera, you can take advantage of this increased speed to transfer larger pictures with higher densities.

USB 3.0 devices featured the "SuperSpeed" bus, which provided a fourth transfer mode at 5.0 Gbps (gigabits per second). The raw throughput was 4 Gbps, and the specification considered it reasonable to achieve 3.2 Gbps (0.4 GBps or 400 MBps) or more after protocol overhead. To accommodate the additional pins for SuperSpeed mode, the physical form factors for USB 3.0 plugs and receptacles have been modified from those used in previous versions. USB 3.1 increased the transfer data rate to 10 Gbps and was called *SuperSpeed+*.

FireWire Sometimes called *IEEE 1394*, **FireWire** is a very fast digital input/output system that provides transfer rates of up to 3.2 Gbps. IEEE 1394 FireWire is a standard for a high-performance serial bus (HPSB) and can be used for many of the same applications as USB.

The HDMI (High-Definition Multimedia Interface) port is a newer addition to computers that allows them to be connected to a television, monitor, or projecting device. The HDMI port is used to transfer both audio and video in a digital format that provides a high-definition display. The HDMI port can also transport Ethernet data or remote control signals.

In addition to HDMI, some computers such as tablets may use DisplayPorts. Both HDMI and DisplayPorts can send high-definition digital video and audio from a source device to a display. So what is the difference? HDMI connectors have 19 pins and are most commonly seen in three sizes: Type A (standard), Type C (mini), and Type D (micro). Of these, Type A is by far the most common. DisplayPort connectors have 20 pins and are available in two sizes: DisplayPort and Mini DisplayPort (the latter is the port of choice for Microsoft's Surface Pro tablet). On the other hand, DisplayPort cannot carry Ethernet data, and the standard does not have an audio return channel.

Expansion Cards

An **expansion card** is a printed circuit board that you can insert into a system board to add functionality to a PC. One edge of the expansion card holds the contacts that fit into the expansion slot on the system board, establishing contact between the card's electronics (mostly integrated circuits) and the system board.

An expansion card could add more USB ports to a desktop computer. Laptop designs do not allow for expansion cards because of the compact placement of internal components.

You might refer to an expansion card as an adapter card that allows one system component to connect to and work with another. An adapter is often a simple circuit that converts one set of signals to another; however, the term often refers to devices that are more accurately called *controllers*. For example, display adapters (video cards) and SCSI (small computer system interface) adapters perform extensive processing, but they are still called *adapters*.

These adapters are plugged into slots that vary according to the slot type. Most system boards provide a conventional **PCI slot** (32-bit legacy PCI) to support older adapter cards. The newer **PCI Express** specification allows slots to have different physical sizes depending on the number of lanes connected to the slot. The specification provides for x1, x4, x8, and x16 lanes, which reduces the amount of space needed on the system board. For example, if a slot with an x1 connection is required, the system board can use a smaller slot to save space. PCI Express x16 slots are used mostly for graphics cards, although they can be used with any PCI Express card. Sound cards, for example, are typically PCI Express x1 devices.

Video Adapters You would plug a **video adapter** board, as shown in Figure 1-9, into a PC to give it display capabilities. These capabilities, however, depend on both the logical

Figure 1-9 Video adapter

circuitry and the display monitor. Each adapter offers several video resolutions (pixel densities).

Modern video adapters contain memory so that the computer's RAM is not used for storing displays. With larger amounts of memory, you can display greater resolutions with a larger number of colors. To save money, the manufacturer of your PC may use the system memory for text and graphics. While using part of the main system memory may save costs, it may also result in poor performance.

In addition, most adapters have their own graphics processing unit (GPU) for performing graphics calculations. Your computer will render graphics faster if it uses a graphics card with a fast GPU and enough video RAM.

Sound Adapters A sound adapter, which is also called a *sound board* or *sound card*, is an adapter card that records and plays back sound, as shown in Figure 1-10. Sound adapters support both digital audio and Musical Instrument Digital Interface (MIDI) formats. Sound cards provide an input port for a microphone or other sound source and output ports for speakers and amplifiers.

As an alternative to a sound adapter, your PC may have integrated sound circuits provided by a chipset on the system board. If you need to install a separate sound card, the integrated sound circuits can be disabled. An example of integrated audio is AC' 97, which was introduced in 1996 by Intel, or the updated Intel High Definition Audio specification. AC' 97 provides audio with six channels, which is comparable to the sound on a home theater system. Intel HD Audio provides up to eight channels.

Disk Drive Controllers

A disk drive controller manages the transfer of data from a system board to a disk drive and vice versa. In PCs, the controllers are often single chips. When you purchase a computer, it comes with all the necessary controllers for standard components, such as disk drives.

Figure 1-10 Sound adapter

However, if you add disk drives, you may need to insert new controllers that come on expansion boards.

Controllers must be designed to communicate with a computer's expansion bus. There are three standard controller architectures for PCs—the ATA, SATA, and SCSI. Therefore, when you purchase a disk drive, you must ensure that it conforms to your computer's controller architecture.

ATA Controllers (Parallel) ATA, or Advanced Technology Attachment, is a disk drive implementation that integrates the controller on the disk drive itself. An enhanced version of the ATA interface transfers data at rates up to 133 MBps; these enhancements are called *ATA/133*.

ATA is also called **PATA**, or Parallel ATA. Parallel controllers transfer data bits over multiple data lines in parallel. (Contrast Parallel ATA with Serial ATA, or SATA, in the next section.) In PATA, which is also known as Integrated Drive Electronics or IDE, each system board controller supports one or two devices, which could be hard drives or CD-ROM drives. Your computer system most likely has two IDE controllers—a primary and secondary controller. Each controller supports two drives—a master and a slave. Using ATA technology, you can attach up to four drives.

SATA Controllers (Serial) SATA, or Serial Advanced Technology Attachment, is an evolution of the Parallel ATA physical storage interface. Serial ATA is a serial link—a single cable with a minimum of four wires that creates a single connection between the controller and the drive. Transfer rates for SATA range from 1.5 Gbps (187.5 MBps) to 16 Gbps (2 GBps); the latter rate is much faster than PATA. Besides faster transfer rates, the SATA interface has several advantages over the PATA interface. For example, SATA drives each have their own independent bus, so there is no competition for bandwidth, as there is with PATA. SATA cables are more flexible, thinner, and less massive than the ribbon cables required for PATA hard drives, resulting in less air flow restrictions. **eSATA** allows a SATA device to be connected externally. Newer laptops and desktop computers may have eSATA connectors that allow you to attach a drive that performs at the speed of internal drives.

SCSI Controllers SCSI (pronounced *skuzzy*), or small computer system interface, is a parallel interface standard used for attaching peripheral devices to PCs. If your PC does not have a SCSI controller, you can add a SCSI adapter card and attach disk drives. The speeds for SCSI adapters meet and may exceed the speeds of SATA controllers, but they tend to be more expensive. Although you are limited in the number of devices you can attach to a SATA controller, SCSI allows you to connect up to 15 peripheral devices to a single SCSI controller. Note, however, that the lack of a single SCSI standard means that some devices may not work with some SCSI boards. Although SCSI is a standard of the American National Standards Institute (ANSI), it has many variations, so two SCSI interfaces may be incompatible. For example, SCSI supports several types of connectors. Ultra SCSI and Serial Attached SCSI (SAS) are only two examples of modern variations on SCSI.

Storage Devices

Storage devices refer to various devices for storing large amounts of data. Modern mass storage devices include all types of disk drives and tape drives. Mass storage is distinct from RAM, which refers to temporary storage areas within the computer. Unlike RAM, mass storage devices retain data even when the computer is turned off.

The main types of storage devices are:

- Hard drives—These disks are very fast and have large capacities. Some hard drive systems are portable (with removable cartridges), but most are not.

- Optical drives—Unlike hard drives, which use electromagnetism to encode data, optical disc systems use a laser to read and write data. Optical drives have very large storage capacity, but they are not as fast as hard drives.

- Tape drives—These drives are relatively inexpensive and often have very large storage capacities, but they do not permit random access of data.

- USB drives—These small, portable drives use flash memory or external hard drives to store data for backup or transfer between PCs.

Hard Drives A **hard drive** uses rigid rotating platters to read and write on magnetic media. A typical hard drive design, as shown in Figure 1-11, consists of a spindle on which the platters spin at a constant speed. Moving along and between the platters on a common armature are the read/write heads, with one head for each platter face. The armature moves the heads radially across the platters as they spin, allowing each head access to the entirety of the platter. Some hard drives known as solid-state drives (SSDs) use electronic circuits for

Figure 1-11 Hard drive

storage and do not have moving parts, which allows faster access to data. SSDs have several advantages, including lower power consumption, which can improve battery life in portable computers.

Hard drives are cabled to a disk drive controller. Depending on the configuration of the PC you purchase, these hard drives might be connected to SATA or SCSI hard drive controllers. It is also possible to connect external hard drives to USB ports.

Optical Drives Figure 1-12 shows an **optical drive** storage device that uses light produced by lasers instead of magnetism to store data on optical discs. These discs include CDs (COMPACT discs), DVDs (digital versatile disks), and BRDs (Blu-ray disks), which

Figure 1-12 Optical drive

are made up of millions of small bumps and dips. Lasers read these bumps and dips as ones and zeroes, which the computer can understand.

Common types of optical drives include CD-ROM, CD-RW, DVD-ROM, DVD-RW, BR-ROM, and BD-RE drives. CD, DVD, and Blu-ray writers or burners use lasers both to read and write data on the discs. The laser used for writing data is much more powerful than the other laser because it must "burn" the bumps and dips into the disc. Although optical drives can spin discs at very high speeds, they are still significantly slower than hard drives, which store data magnetically. However, because optical media are inexpensive and removable, they are a common format used for distributing computer software.

Tape Drives A **tape drive** is a device that stores computer data on magnetic tape, especially for backups (see Figure 1-13). Like an ordinary tape recorder, a tape drive records data on a loop of flexible celluloid-like material that can be read and erased. Tapes have a large capacity for storing data and are less expensive than hard drive storage. A disadvantage is that tape drives store data sequentially rather than randomly (as hard drives do), and the user can only access specific data by starting at the beginning and rolling through the tape until the desired data is located. The most common use of tape drives is to make backup copies of data for offline archival storage.

USB Drives A **USB drive** is a small, portable flash memory device (see Figure 1-14) that plugs into any computer with a USB port and functions as a portable drive with up to 1 TB

Figure 1-13 Tape drive

Figure 1-14 USB drive

of storage capacity. USB flash drives are easy to use and can be carried in a pocket. USB flash drives are also called jump drives, thumb drives, pen drives, key drives, or simply USB drives. These drives have less storage capacity than an external hard drive, but they are smaller and more durable because they have no internal moving parts.

A USB drive may also refer to a portable hard drive or optical drive that plugs into a computer's USB port. A portable hard drive is a disk drive that is plugged into an external port on a computer, normally a USB port. Typically used for backup, but also as secondary storage, such units rival internal drives in capacity. You can use a USB drive to transport data files between computers in the office.

Communications Devices

Communications devices support transmission of data from one PC to another, or from one device to another. For example, modems, network interface cards, and wireless adapters are all communications devices.

Modems Modem is short for *modulator-demodulator*. With the proliferation of cable TV, broadband communications became readily available for the transmission of digital data. A **cable modem**, as shown in Figure 1-15, is designed to operate over cable TV lines. Because the coaxial cable used by cable TV provides much greater bandwidth than telephone lines, your cable modem enables extremely fast access to the World Wide Web.

Network Interface Cards A **network interface card (NIC)**, as shown in Figure 1-16, is an expansion board that you insert into a computer so that it can be connected to a local area network (LAN). A network card can be either an expansion card that plugs into a computer's bus or an interface on the system board. You use a LAN to interconnect desktop computers in a workgroup and share files within an office.

Wireless Adapters A **wireless adapter**, as shown in Figure 1-17, permits a mobile user to connect to a LAN through a wireless (radio) connection. Access is similar to NIC access, but a wireless adapter allows more freedom of movement. Many newer laptop computers have wireless adapters built into the system board. Traveling sales personnel can use a wireless connection to access their office Web site and determine product specifications and prices.

Figure 1-15 Cable modem

Figure 1-16 Network interface card

Figure 1-17 Wireless adapter

Peripheral Devices

Peripheral devices are external to the PC. For example, keyboards, pointing devices, printers, and external disk drives are common peripheral devices that are not part of the PC but are used in conjunction with it.

In the sections that follow, you will learn about input and output devices.

Input Devices

Input devices feed data into the PC. Examples include keyboards, pointing devices, biometric devices, and digital/video cameras. Although storage devices can provide input, this section is restricted to devices that you use to enter data yourself.

Keyboards Computer keyboards are similar to electric-typewriter keyboards, but they contain additional keys. Keyboards are designed for text entry and to control the operation of the computer. The standard U.S. keyboard has 105 keys. In addition to the 26 letters and 10 digits, special character keys extend the character set. Additional keys are used to control the computer.

Pointing Devices You use a pointing device to move the pointer on the screen, choose commands, click buttons, select text, create drawings, and so on. Examples of pointing devices include mice, trackballs, and touch pads.

A **mouse** consists of a metal or plastic housing, a sensor on the bottom of the housing that is moved across a flat surface, and one or more buttons on top of the housing. As the mouse is moved over the surface in any direction, the sensor (which could be LED or laser based) sends impulses to the computer, causing a mouse-responsive program to reposition a visible indicator (called a *cursor* or *pointer*) on the display screen. The positioning is relative to a variable starting place. By viewing the cursor's present position, the user can readjust the position by moving the mouse. The mouse buttons are used to select text or options on the screen.

Essentially, a **trackball** is a mouse lying on its back. To move the pointer, you rotate the ball with your thumb, your fingers, or the palm of your hand. A trackball usually has one to three buttons next to the ball; you use them just like mouse buttons. You may prefer a trackball to a mouse because the trackball is stationary and does not require much space to use.

A **touch pad** is a small, touch-sensitive pad used as a pointing device on some laptop computers. By moving your finger along the pad, you can move the pointer on the display screen. You click by tapping the pad or pressing the button below the touch pad. A **touch screen** is incorporated into a display device; it allows you to provide input by touching the screen with a finger or stylus.

Biometric Devices Biometrics is the science and technology of measuring and statistically analyzing biological data. In information technology, biometrics usually refers to technologies for measuring and analyzing human body characteristics—such as fingerprints—for authentication purposes.

A **fingerprint scanner** (see Figure 1-18) has two basic jobs—recording an image of your finger and determining whether the pattern of ridges and valleys in the image matches the pattern in a previously scanned image. When the image matches, you are permitted to access the PC. Fingerprint scanners are included with a number of high-end laptop computers.

In addition to scanning fingerprints, biometric devices control access by measuring the retina and iris of the eye, voice patterns, and facial characteristics.

Digital/Video Cameras A **digital camera** stores images digitally rather than recording them on film. Typically, the image is stored on a flash card. After a picture is taken, it can be downloaded to a PC and then manipulated with a graphics program and printed. Unlike photographs on film, which have extremely high resolution, digital photos are limited by the amount of memory in the camera.

A **digital video camera** stores frames on digital tape or a digital card. After you record or shoot a video movie, you can download it to a PC and then manipulate it with a video-editing program.

Figure 1-18 Fingerprint scanner

Output Devices

Output devices such as monitors and printers provide output from a PC. Although storage devices can also provide output, this section is restricted to devices that you use to view information yourself.

The most important aspect of a monitor is its screen size. Like televisions, monitor screen sizes are measured in diagonal inches—the distance from one corner to the opposite corner diagonally. Typical sizes run from 17 to 20 inches, but monitors are available in larger sizes. The resolution of a monitor indicates how densely packed the pixels are. In general, more pixels produce a sharper image. Most modern monitors can display 1366 by 768 pixels. Some high-end models can display 2560 by 1440 pixels, or even higher.

LCD Panels LCD is short for *liquid crystal display*, a type of display used on laptop computers. LCD displays use two sheets of polarizing material with a liquid crystal solution between them. An electric current passed through the liquid causes the crystals to align so that light cannot pass through them. Each crystal, therefore, is like a shutter, either allowing light to pass through or blocking the light. Multiple monitors may be used for a single computer.

CRT Monitors CRT is an abbreviation for *cathode ray tube*, the technology used in older televisions and computer display screens.

Printers A printer is a device that prints text or illustrations on paper. Many different types of printers are available. In terms of the technology used, printers fall into the following categories:

- Dot matrix—Creates characters by striking pins against an ink ribbon. Each pin makes a dot, and combinations of dots form characters and illustrations.

- Inkjet—Sprays ink at a sheet of paper. Inkjet printers produce high-quality text and graphics.

- Laser—Uses the same technology as copy machines. Laser printers produce high-quality text and graphics.

An inkjet printer may be your best choice when color printing is required. You should consider a shared laser printer when you need high volumes of black-and-white output in an office environment.

Virtual Machines and Virtualized Devices

In this text, you will work with two virtual machines. The virtualization software provides devices for use by the operating system running within the virtual machine.

You can see which hardware is provided to the virtual machine by reviewing its settings in the management program for the virtualization software. Figure 1-19 shows the settings for a Windows 10 virtual machine running in the Microsoft Hyper-V virtualization software.

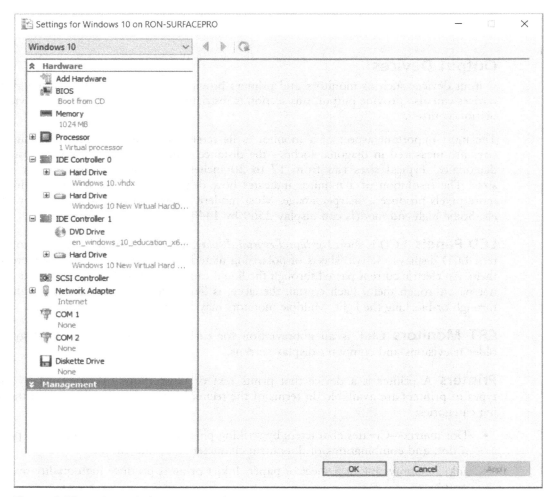

Figure 1-19 Settings window in Microsoft Hyper-V

Source: Microsoft Windows 10

The configuration for this virtual machine consists of the following settings, from top to bottom:

- BIOS—The boot sequence for the virtual machine; in this case, the .iso image is booted from a virtual DVD.

- Memory—The amount of physical memory, 1,024 MB, reserved for the virtual machine. Additional memory improves the performance of the virtual machine.

- Processor—One virtual processor. The addition of more virtual processors improves the performance of processor-bound applications running in virtual machines.

- **IDE controller** 0—An ATA controller with two virtual hard drives: the drive for the Windows 10 OS and an additional drive for data storage.

- IDE controller 1—An ATA controller with two virtual hard drives: the DVD drive for the Windows 10 ISO and an additional drive for data storage.

- SCSI controller—No SCSI drives are used by the virtual machine.

- Network adapter—A virtualized network adapter provides Internet access.

- COM 1—The first virtualized communications port.

- COM 2—The second virtualized communications port.

- Diskette drive—A diskette drive is not used by the virtual machine.

Activity 1-2: Reviewing System Information for Windows 10

Time Required: 10 minutes

Objective: Use the System Information program to review which components are available on the Windows 10 virtual machine.

Description: In this activity, you open the System Information window and review the available components on your PC.

1. If necessary, start your virtual machines using the appropriate instructions in Activity 1-1.

2. To open the System Information window, type **msinfo32** over "Search the web and Windows" in the search box, and then click **System Information**.

3. To review component information, expand the **Components** folder.

4. To review the input components, expand the **Input** folder.

5. To review information about the pointing device, click **Pointing Device**.

6. To review information about the network adapter, expand **Network** and then click **Adapter**.

7. To review information about drives, expand **Storage** and then click **Drives**.

8. To review information about disks, click **Disks**.

9. Close the System Information window.

10. Leave the virtual machine logged on for future activities.

Activity 1-3: Reviewing System Information for CentOS 7

Time Required: 10 minutes

Objective: Use the System Information program to review which components are available on the CentOS 7 virtual machine.

Description: In this activity, you open the System Information window and review the available components on your CentOS 7 virtual machine.

1. If necessary, start your virtual machines using the appropriate instructions in Activity 1-1.

2. To open the terminal console, right-click on the desktop and select **Open in Terminal**.

3. To open the System Information window, type **hardinfo** and press **Enter**.

If you see a "Command not found" message, contact your instructor.

4. To review component information, click **Summary**.

5. To review operating system information, click **Operating System**.

6. To review processor information, click **Processor**.

7. To review the input components, click **Input Devices**.

8. To review storage information, click **Storage**.

9. Close the System Information window.

10. Leave the virtual machine logged on for future activities.

Activity 1-4: Reviewing the Devices on your Windows 10 Virtual Machine

Time Required: 10 minutes

Objective: Use the Device Manager program to review which devices are available on your Windows 10 virtual machine.

Description: In this activity, you open the Device Manager and review the available devices on your PC.

1. If necessary, start your virtual machines using the appropriate instructions in Activity 1-1.

2. To open the System applet, click **Start** and type **Device Manager**.

3. To open the Device Manager, click **Device Manager**.

4. If a Device Manager warning appears, read it and then click **OK**.

5. To review information on the disk drive, double-click the **Disk drives** folder to expand it.

6. Repeat Step 5 for the remaining folders.

7. Close the Device Manager window.

8. Leave the virtual machine logged on for the next activity.

Activity 1-5: Closing the Virtual Machines

Time Required: 3 minutes

Objective: Properly close the virtual machines.

Description: In this activity, you will log off and shut down the two virtual machines. The virtual machines must be properly shut down; otherwise, damage may occur to the virtual hard disks that support the virtual machines.

1. If the screen saver was activated on the Windows 10 virtual machine, log on to the Windows 10 virtual machine, type **Pa$$w0rd**, and then press **Enter**.

2. To shut down the Windows 10 virtual machine, click **Start**, click **Power**, and then click **Shut Down**.

3. If the screen saver was activated on the CentOS 7 virtual machine, move the mouse up on the screen to return to the login screen, type a password of **Pa$$w0rd**, and then click **Unlock**.

4. To shut down the CentOS 7 virtual machine, click **User01** in the upper-right corner. Select **Power Off**, and then click **Power Off** again.

5. Ask your instructor if the host machine should be left on or shut down at the end of the lab.

Preventive Maintenance

When you own or use a PC, you may be responsible for its maintenance. For example, you might need to regularly clean the unit, which can extend its life. You also need to know that a number of potential hazards, including static electricity, can damage the PC. And what will you do with your PC when you no longer need it? This section addresses all of these topics.

Cleaning

Your PC's mortal enemy is excessive heat, which accelerates the deterioration of its delicate circuits. The most common causes of overheating are dust and dirt: Clogged vents and CPU cooling fans can keep heat-dissipating air from moving through the case, and even a thin coating of dust or dirt can raise the temperature of PC components.

In most locations, such as dusty offices, your system may need a cleaning every few months. Most cleaning requires only a can of compressed air, lint-free wipes, cotton swabs, and a few drops of a mild cleaning solution in a bowl of water.

Always turn off and unplug the system before you clean any of its components. Never apply liquid directly to a component. Spray or pour the liquid on a lint-free cloth, and wipe the PC with the cloth.

Cleaning the Outside Start by cleaning the outside of the case and attached peripherals. Wipe the case with a mild cleaning solution. Clear the ventilation openings of any obstructions. Use compressed air, but do not blow dust into the PC or its optical drives.

Turn the keyboard upside down and shake it to clear any crumbs from between the keys. If that does not suffice, blast it briefly with compressed air.

Wipe the monitor case and clear its vents of obstructions without pushing dust into the unit.

Be careful when cleaning LCD panels. These surfaces should only be cleaned with a nonabrasive, lint-free cloth and water. Avoid using glass cleaner and any cleaning solution that contains ammonia, as it will damage the plastic surface of the screen.

Dirty optical discs should be cleaned carefully using a soft, dry, lint-free cloth. Hold the disc by its outer edges or center hole, and then gently wipe outward from the center hub toward the outside edge. Stubborn fingerprints or stains can be removed using a soft, dry, lint-free cloth lightly moistened with water. Never wipe a disc in a circular motion.

Cleaning the Inside Continue your cleaning with the inside of the case. Before cleaning the components in the case, take precautions to ground the static electricity before you touch any of the internal components. You should ground the static electricity by touching the internal metal frame of the computer's case while the computer is plugged into an electrical socket. The static electricity will be discharged and grounded because the electrical circuit is grounded via the AC outlet. Be sure to unplug the power cord before you clean the inside of the case.

Use antistatic wipes to remove dust from inside the case. Avoid touching any circuit board surfaces. Pay close attention to the various fans. Spray these components with a blast of compressed air to loosen dust. To remove the dust rather than rearrange it, you should use a small vacuum.

If your PC is more than four years old, or if the expansion cards plugged into its system board are exceptionally dirty, remove each card, clean its contacts with isopropyl alcohol, and reseat it. If your system is less than two years old, just make sure each card is firmly seated by pressing gently downward on its top edge without touching its face. Likewise, check your power connectors and other internal cables for a snug fit.

Electrostatic Discharge

Electrostatic discharge (ESD) is the rapid discharge of static electricity from one conductor to another conductor of a different potential. An electrostatic discharge can damage integrated circuits in the PC. Whenever the PC case is opened and its internal workings are exposed (for example, to add an adapter card), you could damage the computer with the buildup of static electricity that your body holds.

The internal workings of a computer, and especially the hard drive, are extremely susceptible to static electricity. Human beings are not able to perceive static electricity until it has reached about 1,500 volts. (Walking across a rug can produce up to 12,000 volts of static electricity.) Although it is not life-threatening to people, even a very low voltage of static electricity can seriously damage a hard drive or a system board.

To avoid zapping internal computer components, be sure to ground the static electricity before you touch them, as described in the previous section.

To be on the safe side, always handle electronic circuitry on its insulated areas; avoid touching the circuits themselves. This advice applies to handling the system board, video card, modem, sound card, and hard drive, as well as any other internal components.

Hazards

While electrical problems can damage your PC, many hazards can injure you, including high-voltage shocks. You need to be aware of these hazards and know how to prevent them.

High Voltages in Capacitors
The interiors of PC power supplies, monitors, and laser printers contain capacitors that may retain a charge long after power is removed from a circuit; this charge can cause damage to connected equipment and shocks (even electrocution). You should not attempt to service equipment that contains large or high-voltage capacitors.

Power Supplies
Whenever you repair or perform maintenance on your PC, you must unplug it after discharging any static electricity. Modern PC system boards have a small voltage running when the PC is plugged in.

You should not attempt to repair a power supply. The safest choice is to replace it.

CRT Monitors
While CRTs are becoming a rarity, it is important to know that the voltages inside a CRT monitor can kill you! Recall that capacitors can retain a charge long after power is removed from a circuit; this charge can cause shocks and even electrocution. Another dangerous part of the monitor is the **flyback transformer**, which generates up to 20,000 volts.

Fires
You may never have a PC fire, but an electrical fire can strike your office or home. The smoke can harm you as well as your PC. You should use a type C or type ABC fire extinguisher on an electrical fire. Never spray or throw water on an electrical fire; the electrical current could travel up the water stream into you!

Disposal

Many PC components contain harmful ingredients and toxins, including lead, mercury, arsenic, cadmium, selenium, and hexavalent chromium. About 70 percent of the heavy metals (mercury and cadmium) in landfills come from electronic waste. These toxins can cause allergic reactions, brain damage, and cancer.

You must make prudent decisions when disposing of PCs and peripherals.

- Batteries contain toxic chemicals (lithium, mercury, nickel cadmium) and should not be thrown in the trash. You can take batteries to a recycling depot. In some cases, you can send the batteries back to the manufacturer.

- CRTs contain lead. If you toss them in the trash, the lead will end up in a landfill. For this reason, CRTs must be recycled or turned over to a hazardous waste program.

- Significant amounts of gold, silver, copper, steel, aluminum, wire, cable, and other resources can be extracted from computers. Many of these materials are recyclable.

You can drop off used computer equipment at participating Goodwill donation centers. It is free, and you will be given a receipt for tax purposes. At the same time, you will help protect the environment and benefit your community.

Identifying and Connecting PC Components

You should know how to "cable up" a PC. In this section, you will learn to identify the cables and connectors of a typical desktop or laptop system.

USB Cables

You can use USB cables to connect many devices to your computer, including flash memory devices, portable media players, and digital cameras. You can also connect accessories such as mice, keyboards, portable hard drives, BRD-DVD-CD drives, and microphones. Web cameras, printers, scanners, and speakers can also be connected to the computer through the USB ports.

The Standard USB connector, called a *USB-A*, is a rectangular connector found on every USB cable; it connects to your computer. The other end of the USB cable may have a variety of connectors, including the USB-B, a square connector used with printers, portable drives, and larger peripheral devices. USB-C has a 12-pin reversible plug design. Smaller connectors such as the Mini-USB and Micro-USB are commonly used with smaller portable devices, including media players and cameras. Figure 1-20 shows a variety of USB cables with their connectors.

Video Cables

One of the most common video connectors for computer monitors is the 15-pin VGA cable. For example, you can use this cable to connect a PC to a projector. Figure 1-21 shows some common video cables.

If you recently purchased a PC, you may have a Digital Visual Interface (DVI). Newer, thinner laptops use smaller versions of the DVI, such as the Mini-DVI and Micro-DVI. A DVI

USB A/B cable   USB A/Mini-B cable   USB A/Micro-B cable

Figure 1-20 USB cables with common connectors

VGA cable   DVI cable   HDMI cable   DVI/HDMI cable

Figure 1-21 Video cables

cable has 29 pins, although some connectors may have fewer pins. DVI's signal is compatible with HDMI; cables can convert between the two formats.

Sound Cables

The most common sound cable is the standard headphone jack. While it is available in several sizes, the 1/8-inch mini-audio cable (shown in Figure 1-22) is used with computers.

Data Cables

Figure 1-23 shows the most common data cables: FireWire and eSATA. FireWire, also known as IEEE 1394, is commonly used for connecting digital camcorders and portable drives. FireWire cables typically have six pins, although a four-pin variety is common as well.

While SATA cables are used internally to connect SATA drives to disk controllers, eSATA cables are designed for portable hard drives. The eSATA connector is larger than the internal SATA cable and has more shielding.

Figure 1-22 Sound cable

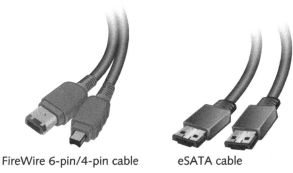

FireWire 6-pin/4-pin cable   eSATA cable

Figure 1-23 Data cables

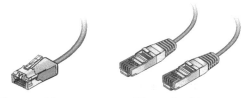

Phone cable   Ethernet cable

Figure 1-24 Networking cables

Networking Cables

The phone cable, known as the RJ-11, is still used to connect modems to phone jacks for Internet connectivity. The connector has four pins and a retaining clip (see Figure 1-24).

Ethernet is the standard for wired networking. The Ethernet connector, otherwise known as the RJ-45, is attached to an eight-wire twisted pair cable. It looks like a phone plug but is thicker and wider. It has a retaining clip to maintain a tight connector.

Chapter Summary

- Virtual machine technology allows multiple operating systems to run concurrently on a single PC. With virtual machine technology, you can run various Windows operating systems as well as Linux within a host operating system.

- Many hardware components make up a PC. The case houses and protects the main electronic components. The power supply is a sealed metal box that contains power conversion hardware. The system board, or main circuit board, contains the microprocessor, bus, memory, and expansion slots. The BIOS is firmware that supports the PC during start-up. VGA, USB, and other ports permit the connection of devices. Video and sound expansion cards permit graphical and audio communication with the user. Disk drive controllers (such as PATA, SATA, and SCSI) allow the connection of hard drives and optical drives. Communication with other devices is permitted by modems, network interface cards, and wireless adapters.

- Peripherals include input devices such as keyboards, mice, trackballs, touch pads, fingerprint scanners, and digital cameras, which permit input and communication from the user. Output devices include monitors, speakers, and printers.

- Preventive maintenance is the responsibility of the PC's owner. To avoid heat damage, keep the PC clean. Clean the inside and outside of the case and the attached peripherals.

- Many hazards can injure a PC user or damage the PC. For example, electrostatic discharge can damage a PC's internal components. Capacitors in power supplies and CRT monitors retain high voltages. Use a type ABC or type C fire extinguisher on electrical fires.

- Some PC components are not internal but are connected to the PC. Common connectors such as USB simplify the connection of these components. Connect components starting with the connector that is farthest from the power supply connector.

Key Terms

ATA An acronym for *Advanced Technology Attachment*; the disk drive standard commonly known as Integrated Drive Electronics (IDE).

biometrics The science and technology of authenticating a person's identity by measuring physiological features.

BIOS An acronym for *basic input/output system*; the set of essential software routines that test a PC at start-up and start the OS.

bus The set of hardware lines used to transfer data among the components of a PC.

cable modem A device that sends and receives data through coaxial cables.

CRT An acronym for *cathode ray tube*; the basis for the standard PC display screen.

digital camera A type of camera that stores photographic images electronically rather than on film.

digital video camera A camera that captures and stores images on a digital medium. Also known as a camcorder.

EEPROM An acronym for *electrically erasable programmable read-only memory*; a type of EPROM that can be erased with an electrical signal.

electrostatic discharge (ESD) The discharge of static electricity from an outside source—such as human hands—into an integrated circuit, often damaging the circuit.

EPROM An acronym for *erasable programmable read-only memory*; a type of memory chip that can be reprogrammed after manufacture.

eSATA An external connector that provides fast data transfer for external SATA hard drives.

expansion card A circuit card that is plugged into a PC's bus to add extra functions.

fingerprint scanner A scanner that reads human fingerprints for comparison to a database of stored fingerprint images.

FireWire A PC and digital video serial bus interface standard offering high-speed communications. FireWire is also known as IEEE 1394.

firmware Software routines stored in read-only memory (ROM).

flyback transformer A transformer in a CRT monitor that generates up to 20,000 volts.

form factor The physical size and shape of a device. The term is often used to describe the size of PC cases.

guest operating system The operating system running within a virtual machine.

hard drive A device that reads data from and writes data to one or more inflexible platters.

heat sink A device that absorbs and dissipates heat created by an electronic device, such as a microprocessor.

host operating system An operating system running on a physical machine that executes virtualization software.

IDE controller See *ATA*.

LCD An acronym for *liquid crystal display*; a type of display that uses a liquid compound with a polar molecular structure sandwiched between two transparent electrodes.

memory An area where data can be stored and retrieved.

microprocessor A central processing unit (CPU) on a single chip.

modem Short for *modulator/demodulator*; a communications device that enables a PC to transmit data over a standard telephone line.

mouse A common pointing device.

network interface card (NIC) An expansion card used to connect a computer to a local area network.

optical drive A disk drive that reads and may write data to optical (compact) discs.

PATA An acronym for *Parallel Advanced Technology Attachment*. PATA is the same as ATA, which was renamed when SATA was introduced.

PCI Express A connector on a system board that provides 1 to 16 interface lanes. This slot saves space on the system board.

PCI slot A connector on a system board used to insert an adapter card.

PROM An acronym for *programmable read-only memory*.

RAM An acronym for *random access memory*; semiconductor memory that can be read or written by the microprocessor or other devices.

register A small amount of high-speed memory.

ROM An acronym for *read-only memory*; a semiconductor circuit in which data is permanently installed by the manufacturer.

RS-232 An industry-accepted standard for serial communications.

SATA An acronym for *Serial Advanced Technology Attachment*, which transfers data serially to and from the hard drive.

SCSI An acronym for *small computer system interface*. It is used to connect SCSI devices to PCs.

sound adapter An expansion card that supports the recording and playback of sound.

system board The main circuit board that contains a PC's primary components.

tape drive A device for reading and writing data on magnetic tapes.

touch pad A pointing device that responds to movement of a finger on a surface.

touch screen A screen that allows you to provide input by touching it with a finger or stylus.

trackball   A pointing device with a stationary housing that contains a ball you roll with your hand.

Universal Serial Bus (USB)   A serial bus that connects devices to a PC. USB supports hot plugging.

USB drive   A small, portable flash memory card that plugs into a PC's USB port and functions as a portable hard drive with smaller capacity.

video adapter   Electronic components that generate the video signal sent to a video display.

virtual machine   A software implementation of a machine (that is, a computer) that executes programs like a physical machine.

virtualization   A technology that permits one or more guest operating systems to run on an operating system.

virtualized systems   Systems that appear to be real but are actually simulations.

wireless adapter   A device that supports a wireless connection through a radio connection to a wireless LAN.

Review Questions

1. With virtual machine technology, you move from one OS to another by _____.
    a. restarting the system
    b. pressing the F2 key
    c. clicking the other OS window
    d. logging off the system

2. Which of the following operating systems can be used with virtual machine technology? (Choose all that apply.)
    a. Windows 10
    b. CentOS 7
    c. Macintosh
    d. physical
    e. logical
    f. emulated
    g. free

3. Microsoft Hyper-V mimics physical PCs so closely that the applications you install in them do not distinguish the virtual machine from a(n) _____ computer.
    a. supported
    b. emulated
    c. guest
    d. physical

4. The _____ is the size, configuration, or physical arrangement of the PC hardware.

   a. system board

   b. controller board

   c. form factor

   d. none of the above

5. A power supply _____. (Choose all that apply.)

   a. provides clean power feeds to PC components

   b. is a sealed metal box

   c. has standardized plugs that work with all kinds of components

   d. is user-serviceable

6. The _____ is the main circuit board inside a PC.

   a. system board

   b. controller board

   c. form factor

   d. none of the above

7. _____ is the electronic holding place for programs and data.

   a. EPROM

   b. RAM

   c. EEPROM

   d. ROM

8. Which of the following memory types could be used to hold the BIOS firmware? (Choose all that apply.)

   a. EPROM

   b. RAM

   c. EEPROM

   d. ROM

9. Which of the following are considered I/O ports? (Choose all that apply.)

   a. serial

   b. eSATA

   c. USB

   d. FireWire

10. Which Microsoft Hyper-V virtual machine settings could be allocated for ATA virtual hard drives? (Choose all that apply.)

    a. Processor

    b. IDE controller 0

    c. IDE controller 1

    d. Network adapter

11. The _____ was developed to simplify the connection of peripheral devices.

    a. serial port

    b. parallel port

    c. universal serial bus

    d. none of the above

12. Which of the following could be used as hard drive controllers? (Choose all that apply.)

    a. ATA

    b. PATA

    c. SATA

    d. SCSI

13. The main types of data storage are _____. (Choose all that apply.)

    a. hard drives

    b. optical discs

    c. tape

    d. USB jump drives

14. Which of the following are small and portable with flash memory? (Choose all that apply.)

    a. jump drives

    b. pen drives

    c. key drives

    d. USB drives

15. Which of the following are communications devices? (Choose all that apply.)

    a. modem

    b. network interface card

    c. wireless adapter

    d. graphics adapter

16. Which of the following are input devices? (Choose all that apply.)

    a. keyboard

    b. mouse

    c. trackball

    d. fingerprint scanner

    e. touch pad

17. _____ is the mortal enemy of a PC.

    a. Dirt

    b. Dust

    c. Heat

    d. Grime

18. Wipe the case with a(n) _____ solution.

    a. alcohol

    b. arsenic

    c. mild cleaning

    d. selenium

19. A person cannot perceive static electricity until it has reached _____ volts.

    a. 110

    b. 1,500

    c. 12,000

    d. 25,000

20. Computers contain which of the following toxic ingredients? (Choose all that apply.)

    a. lead

    b. mercury

    c. arsenic

    d. cadmium

Case Projects

CASE PROJECTS

Case 1-1: Using Virtual Machine Technology

Your boss has been reading about virtual machine technology. He has received a request for 10 new PCs to run a Linux application for the Engineering Department. The engineers have one-year-old PCs that run Windows 10 with 8 GB of memory, 500-GB hard drives, and the fastest processors available.

Your boss knows that you are using virtualization technology in your operating systems course at a local community college. He wants you to write a one-page report on the possibility of using Microsoft Hyper-V on the existing Windows 10 OS to run Linux and the Linux application. He expects your report to explain the potential cost savings of using virtualization technology. Because the engineers are technically savvy, your report must provide the technical reasons for your recommendation. Write the report.

Case 1-2: Configuring a PC

You have a budget of $500. Using the Web site of a major PC manufacturer, configure a PC. Provide a report indicating the configuration and component costs.

Case 1-3: Keeping the PC Clean

Your boss has asked you to develop a procedure to keep the PCs in your work area clean and working. Provide detailed information about the use of various cleaning agents. Include precautions regarding inappropriate actions that could damage components.

## chapter 2

Software Components

After reading this chapter and completing the exercises, you will be able to:

- Describe historical milestones for popular operating systems
- Describe the architecture of common PC operating systems
- Describe the functions of an operating system
- Describe the interaction between an operating system and its components
- Describe utilities that are available for Windows 10 and CentOS 7
- Describe applications that are available for Windows 10 and CentOS 7

A PC is made up of hardware and software. You learned about hardware in Chapter 1, and you will learn about software in this chapter. The traditional definition of hardware is "something you can touch"; the traditional definition of software is "the instructions that make the PC work."

The **software components** that enable a PC to accomplish tasks are the operating system, **utilities** (programs that perform system-related tasks and maintenance on the operating system), and **applications** (programs that perform user-related tasks). To use the software on a PC effectively, you need to know the characteristics of all three types of components. In addition to describing these components, this chapter provides a brief history of operating system milestones, explains the functions of an operating system, and explains the interaction between an operating system and applications.

To be able to choose an operating system for your PC, you need to know the characteristics of two prevalent operating systems—Windows and CentOS (Community Enterprise Operating System) Linux.

Common Operating Systems

Many different operating systems run on PCs. You may not have even heard of operating systems such as MINIX, Mach, XNU, MorphOS, EROS, Chorus, and Amoeba. Many of the more popular operating systems grew out of research at major universities, including Mac OS X, Linux, and Microsoft Windows. In this text, you will use the command-line interfaces within Microsoft Windows 10 and CentOS 7.

You might be wondering why you should learn to use the command line, but there are several reasons. For example, the command line is useful for accomplishing such tasks as copying a large number of files between hard drives or changing file attributes. If you are studying to become an administrator, you need to perform your tasks as efficiently as possible. Using the command line is efficient once you learn the commands; on a Microsoft Windows server, the command-line interface is sometimes the proper tool.

 Later in this chapter and throughout the book, you will enter commands in the Activity exercises.

With Windows 10, Microsoft provides **PowerShell,** which supports OS commands. Windows PowerShell is a task automation and configuration management framework; it consists of a command-line shell and associated scripting language built on the .NET Framework, a programming environment that provides the base for Microsoft operating systems and applications. This book describes the use of PowerShell.

Windows 10 Operating System

Microsoft Windows is a range of environments and operating systems for PCs that was introduced in 1985 to counter Apple's new system, the Macintosh, which used a **graphical user**

2

interface (GUI). Both Apple and Microsoft followed in the footsteps of the OS developed at Xerox PARC (Palo Alto Research Center). Xerox PARC is best known for essentially creating the modern PC GUI. Microsoft continued Windows with the development of Windows NT (New Technology); the company hired Dave Cutler, a chief architect of Virtual Memory System (VMS) at Digital Equipment Corporation (DEC), to develop NT into a more capable operating system. Cutler had been developing a follow-up to VMS at DEC, called *Mica*; when DEC dropped the project, he brought his expertise and some engineers with him to Microsoft.

Microsoft has cornered more than 80 percent of the desktop OS market. Windows is proprietary closed-source software, meaning that Microsoft owns the software's copyright and controls its distribution.

Microsoft has released many versions of Windows; the first versions were DOS-based and culminated with Windows Me. The Windows NT thread started with Windows NT 3.1 and continues today with Windows 10 and Windows Server 2012 R2. The timelines for these two versions of Windows sometimes overlap.

The Windows timeline appears in the following list:

- November 1985—Windows 1.0 implements a graphical interface. The selection of applications is sparse, however, and Windows sales are modest.
- October 1987—Windows 2.0 adds icons and overlapping windows. Windows/386 provides the capability to run multiple DOS applications simultaneously in extended memory.
- May 1990—Windows 3.0 is a complete overhaul of the Windows environment. It can address memory beyond 640K and has a much more powerful user interface.
- July 1993—Windows NT 3.1 is intended for use in network servers, workstations, and software development machines. It is based on an entirely new OS kernel.
- December 1993—Windows for Workgroups 3.11 (code name Janus) is the first integrated Windows and networking package offered by Microsoft. It provides peer-to-peer file and printer-sharing capabilities that are highly integrated into the Windows environment.
- September 1994—Windows NT 3.5 (code name Daytona) provides improved performance and reduced memory requirements.
- August 1995—Windows 95 (code name Chicago) is a 32-bit system providing full preemptive multitasking, advanced file systems, threading, and networking.
- July 1996—Windows NT 4.0 (code name Cairo) contains advanced security features, advanced network support, a full 32-bit operating system, advanced multitasking, and user administration.
- June 1998—Windows 98 (code name Memphis) gives the desktop a browser-like interface. New hardware supports the latest technology, such as DVD, FireWire, and USB.
- February 2000—Windows 2000 (NT 5.0) provides an impressive platform of Internet, intranet, extranet, and management applications that integrate tightly with Active Directory.
- September 2000—Windows Me (code name Millennium, short for Millennium Edition) is aimed at the home user. It is basically an upgrade to the DOS-based code on previous Windows 98 versions.

- October 2001—Windows XP (code name Whistler, NT 5.1) contains the 32-bit kernel and driver set from Windows NT and Windows 2000.

- April 2003—Windows Server 2003 (code name Whistler Server, NT 5.2) is a multi-purpose OS capable of handling a diverse set of server roles. It provides security, reliability, availability, and scalability.

- April 2005—Windows XP 64-bit is designed to use the expanded 64-bit memory address space provided by the x86-64 architecture.

- January 2007—Windows Vista (code name Longhorn) includes an updated GUI and visual style dubbed Aero. Vista aims to increase the level of communication between machines on a home network, using peer-to-peer technology to simplify sharing files and media between computers and devices. The **exFAT** file system enables transfer of disk files on external media such as USB drives.

- February 2008—Windows Server 2008 (code name Longhorn Server) is built from the same code base as Windows Vista; therefore, it shares much of the same architecture and functionality. Microsoft introduces Windows PowerShell.

- October 2009—Windows 7 (code name 7) includes a number of new features, such as advances in touch and handwriting recognition, support for virtual hard disks, improved performance on multi-core processors, and improved boot performance.

- October 2009—Windows Server 2008 R2 (code name Windows Server 7) includes new virtualization capabilities and supports up to 64 physical processors or up to 256 cores per system.

- September 2012—Windows Server 2012 (code name Windows Server 8), unlike previous versions, is available with all six role services available for installation.

- October 2012—Windows 8 (code name 8) includes a totally new interface, including the "tile" interface for Windows desktops and a Start screen with tiles that connects people, files, and apps. It introduces the Windows store built into the Start screen. Windows 8 streamlines file management.

- October 2013—Windows 8.1 (code name 8) includes more Start screen personalization options and a Start button to navigate between the Start screen and the desktop.

- October 2013—Windows Server 2012 R2 introduces many security features in Active Directory, including multi-factor access control and multi-factor authentication (MFA).

- July 2015—Windows 10 (code name 10) includes numerous new features. The Start menu is back—it is more personal, better organized, and on a single desktop. From the Store, you can shop for music, videos, games, and apps. Cortana, your personal assistant, is right on your desktop. A favorites feature and search-based organization aid in the location of folders. Microsoft ditched the old Internet Explorer Web browser for Microsoft Edge.

CentOS Linux

Linux refers to the family of UNIX-like computer operating systems that use the Linux **kernel** (the essential center of a computer operating system). It is the result of the free and open source software collaboration from the Linux community around the world. Typically, all the underlying source code in open source software can be used, freely modified, and redistributed, both commercially and noncommercially.

The basic idea behind open source is simple: When programmers can read, redistribute, and modify the source code for a piece of software, the software evolves. People improve it, adapt it, and fix bugs in it, often at astonishing speeds compared with the slow pace of conventional software development.

Linux is usually packaged in a format known as a Linux distribution for desktop and server use. A Linux distribution is built on top of the Linux kernel. A typical Linux distribution comprises a Linux kernel, GNU tools and libraries, additional software, documentation, a window system (the most common being the X Window System), a window manager, and a desktop environment.

CentOS Linux owes its parentage to UNIX, which was created by Ken Thompson and Dennis Richie. Interestingly, the acronym UNIX does not actually stand for anything. The original OS was called *UNiplexed Information and Computing System* (Unics)—a pun for the larger Multics OS—and the name was later changed to UNIX.

Prior to the creation of Linux, a number of significant UNIX releases occurred, as shown in Table 2-1. The first edition included more than 60 commands, many of which are still in use today.

Linus Torvalds developed the Linux kernel while he was a student at the University of Helsinki in Finland. He began his work on the kernel in 1991 and released version 1.0 in 1994.

Richard Stallman began working on the GNU project while working at the Massachusetts Institute of Technology (MIT) artificial intelligence lab. Today, this project includes assemblers, command processors, compilers, debuggers, interpreters, shells, text editors, and many other utilities needed to support development. GNU is short for "GNU's Not UNIX."

Linux uses the X window system for graphical displays. The X (or X11) system was developed at MIT in 1984 by Jim Gettys and Bob Scheifler. It was originally designed as a

Date	UNIX release
November 1971	First edition
December 1972	Second edition
February 1973	Third edition
November 1973	Fourth edition
June 1974	Fifth edition
May 1975	Sixth edition
January 1979	Seventh edition
February 1985	Eighth edition
September 1986	Ninth edition
October 1989	Tenth edition

Table 2-1 UNIX software releases

platform-independent graphics system so that students could use computers from many different vendors.

The CentOS Project is a community-driven free software effort focused on the goal of providing a rich base platform for open source communities to build upon. Since March 2004, CentOS Linux has been a community-supported distribution derived from sources freely provided to the public by Red Hat for Red Hat Enterprise Linux (RHEL). Being a Linux distribution that is a 100% compatible rebuild of the RHEL, CentOS is for people who need the stability of an enterprise-class operating system without the cost of certification and support.

The initial CentOS release on May 14, 2004 (CentOS version 2) was based on RHEL version 2.1AS. A new CentOS version is released approximately every two years with periodic updating. The build of the latest CentOS release (CentOS 7.1-1503) in April 2015 is derived from Red Hat Enterprise Linux 7.1. There are approximately 600 Linux distributions today. According to the Web site DistroWatch, CentOS was the eighth most popular Linux-based operating system as of June 2015.

A desktop is the main workspace in a GUI. The electronic desktop is a metaphor for the top of an actual desk, where one finds files, folders, and writing instruments. CentOS 7 by default has two user-selectable desktop environments: the GNOME desktop, which was created by Miguel de Icaza and some of his friends from universities in Mexico; and the KDE Plasma Workspace, which began as KDE Desktop in Germany in 1996. In this text, you will use the GNOME desktop. You will learn more about the CentOS 7 desktop in Chapter 3.

Common Operating System Architectures

For an operating system to be a useful and convenient interface between the user and the hardware, it must provide certain basic services, such as the ability to read and write files, allocate and manage memory, and make access control decisions. These services are provided by a number of routines that collectively make up the operating system. Applications invoke these routines through the use of specific system calls. This underlying structure and its design are called the *system architecture*.

You will learn about three operating system architectures—DOS, Windows 10, and CentOS 7—in the following sections.

DOS Architecture

The **Disk Operating System (DOS)** is a real-mode operating system, which means all program modules share the same address space. The DOS user interface is a **command-line interface (CLI)**, meaning you must type text-based commands and view responses when interacting with the OS. The Windows 10 OS has replaced DOS.

Windows 10 Architecture

A simplified view of the Windows 10 architecture is shown in Figure 2-1. Notice the horizontal line that divides the user mode and the kernel mode. The kernel mode modules shown

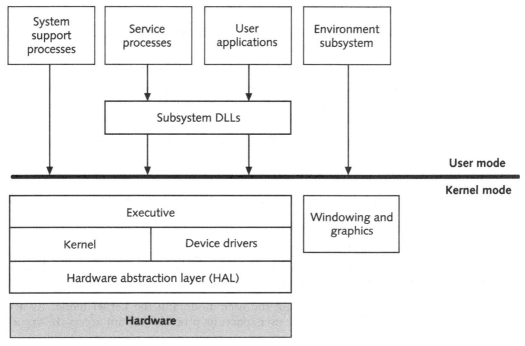

Figure 2-1 Simplified Windows 10 architecture

below the line share a common address space—the system space. All four basic types of user mode processes execute in protected-mode address spaces and thus reside in their own private address space.

The basic types of user mode processes are:

- System support processes—Processes such as logons (Winlogon) and the session manager that are not service processes
- Service processes—Host services such as the Task Scheduler and print spooler services; these processes are started by the service control manager
- User applications—Win32 and Win64 applications
- Environment subsystem—Exposes native OS system services to user applications

Notice the Subsystem DLLs box in Figure 2-1. User applications do not call the native Windows 10 OS services directly. The calls are passed through one or more dynamic link libraries. A **dynamic link library (DLL)** is a library of common routines or data that supports the development of Windows applications. Microsoft provides this library of common routines that reduce the time required to develop applications. When developing applications, programmers point to these DLLs instead of rewriting code line by line. However, a DLL can also just contain data; in this case, the DLL translates the documented function into the appropriate internal function in the Windows 10 kernel mode, thus insulating the kernel mode from the user applications.

The kernel mode components of Windows 10 include:

- Executive—Provides basic OS services, such as memory management, process and thread management, and security
- Kernel—Provides low-level OS functions, such as thread scheduling
- Device drivers—Translates user I/O requests into specific hardware I/O requests; in Windows 10, only the kernel mode can communicate directly with hardware through the hardware abstraction layer
- Hardware abstraction layer (HAL)—Insulates the kernel and device drivers from the intricacies of hardware; only the HAL interfaces with the hardware layer
- Windowing and graphics—Implements the windowing interface or GUI

For additional information related to these components, see the "Functions of an Operating System" section later in this chapter.

CentOS 7 Architecture

The CentOS 7 kernel is a monolithic kernel with device drivers configured as loadable kernel modules. A simplified view of the CentOS 7 architecture is shown in Figure 2-2.

Notice the horizontal line separating the user mode and the kernel mode. As a user, you associate with the OS by way of the user space; its processes do not access the kernel directly.

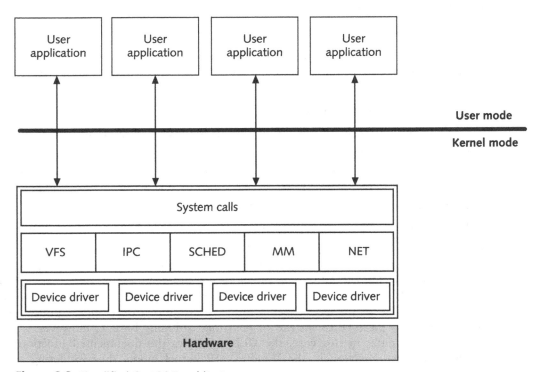

Figure 2-2 Simplified CentOS 7 architecture

Processes interact by way of system calls that reside at the outermost layer of the modules defined by the kernel. For example, hardware management takes place within the kernel space. Within the kernel, modules call on other modules to gain additional granularity.

The subset of modules that are not visible to the user mode is made up in part by device drivers and kernel subsystem functions. The CentOS 7 kernel is composed of five main subsystems:

- Virtual file system (VFS)—The VFS abstracts the details of the various hardware devices by presenting a common file interface to all devices. In addition, the VFS supports several file system formats that are compatible with other operating systems.

- Interprocess communication (IPC)—The IPC supports several mechanisms for process-to-process communication on a single CentOS 7 system.

- Process scheduler (SCHED)—The SCHED controls process access to the processor. The scheduler enforces a policy that ensures processes will have fair access to the processor, while ensuring that necessary hardware actions are performed by the kernel on time.

- Memory manager (MM)—The MM permits multiple processes to securely share the machine's main memory system. In addition, the memory manager supports virtual memory that allows CentOS 7 to support processes that use more memory than is available in the system. Unused memory is swapped out to persistent storage using the file system and then swapped back in when needed.

- Network (NET)—The NET provides access to several networking standards and a variety of network hardware.

CentOS 7 provides dynamically loadable device drivers that permit the inclusion of system code without having to compile the kernel code to include a device driver. This allows device drivers to be loaded and unloaded in real time without having to restart the OS.

Related information about these components is included in the next section.

Functions of an Operating System

The operating system's job is to manage all available resources on the computer. In fact, the OS should maximize the use of available resources, as shown in Figure 2-3.

These functions are described in the following sections.

Processor Management

The Microsoft disk operating system was a single-user, single-tasking OS that used a CLI. A single-tasking OS allows only one program to run at a time. In other words, if you are working in a spreadsheet and you want to write a report, you must shut down the spreadsheet application before you start the word processor. This is unproductive, especially if you need to quote some data from the spreadsheet in your report.

Newer operating systems like Windows 10 and CentOS 7 were designed to allow multiple programs to run at the same time, a process called **multitasking**. In this process, programs

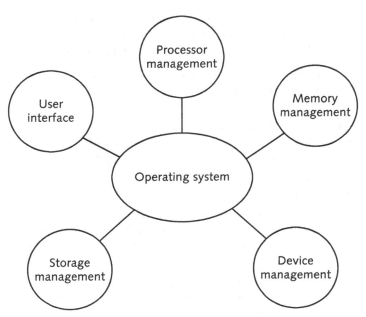

Figure 2-3 Functions of an operating system

take turns using the processor. Multitasking allows a single user to have a spreadsheet and word processor open at the same time.

You may be tempted to think of a process as an application, but this would paint an incomplete picture of how processes relate to the operating system. The application you see is certainly a process, but the application may cause one or more threads to begin for such tasks as spell checking or printing.

Also, numerous processes run without ever giving direct evidence that they exist. For example, Windows 10 and CentOS 7 can have dozens of background processes running to handle memory management and disk management.

The OS creates a process for the purpose of running a program, and every process has at least one thread. A **thread** is short for a "thread of execution," or a sequence of instructions. In this context, the term is analogous to the way that threads are interwoven to make a piece of fabric. With **multithreading** (multiple threads executed in parallel), a program splits into two or more tasks that run simultaneously. A common use of threads is to have one pay attention to the GUI while others do a long calculation in the background. As a result, the application more readily responds to a user's interaction. All modern operating systems support multithreading and multitasking.

Because the threads spawned by a process share the same address space, one thread can modify data used by another thread. This is both good and bad; it facilitates easy communication between threads, but a poorly written program may cause one thread to inadvertently overwrite data used by another thread. Sharing a single address space is one reason that multithreaded programming is usually considered more difficult and error prone than single-threaded programming.

The heart of managing the processor comes down to ensuring that each process and application receives enough of the processor's time to function properly. The key to allocating processor cycles is the scheduling of processes or threads.

Multitasking allows the OS to schedule multiple tasks, seemingly at the same time. However, task execution is switched very rapidly among each program, giving the impression of simultaneous execution. This process is also known as task switching. On single-processor machines, multitasking is implemented by letting a process own the processor for a while (a time slice), and then replacing the process with another, which then owns the processor.

The two most common methods for sharing CPU time are:

- **Cooperative multitasking**—Running applications must work together to share system resources, which requires that tasks voluntarily cede control to other tasks at programmer-defined points.

- **Preemptive multitasking**—The OS executes an application for a specific period of time, according to its assigned priority. When the time expires, the task is preempted, and another task is given access to the processor for its time slice. Preemptive multitasking prevents a single thread from monopolizing a processor.

To illustrate the differences between cooperative and preemptive multitasking, consider a young mother with two small children: Jerry is six and Carol is eight. Carol is by far the more talkative of the siblings. When asked how school was that day, Carol takes the floor and begins to talk. When Carol winds down, several minutes later, Jerry is permitted to talk. This is an example of cooperative multitasking; the program must reach a stopping point for Mom—the operating system—to gain control.

Now consider the same mother and two children in a preemptive multitasking system. Mom asks the two children about their day at school. As before, Carol goes first. After a preset interval, Mom interrupts Carol and allows Jerry to talk for his interval. Mom then cycles between the two children, allowing each a time slice. When Jerry has finished his say, Carol could get consecutive time slices, if need be. In this situation, Mom—the operating system—remains in control of the schedule.

On PCs with multiple processors, multiprocessing is implemented. **Multiprocessing** is traditionally known as the use of multiple concurrent threads in a system, as opposed to a single process, at any one instant. Like multitasking, which allows multiple processes to share a single CPU, multiple CPUs may be used to execute multiple threads within a single process. In **symmetric multiprocessing** (**SMP**) systems, several CPUs execute programs and distribute the computing load over a small number of identical processors. For multiprocessing, Windows 10 and CentOS 7 support two or more processors.

Processors were originally developed with only one core. The **core** is the part of the processor that actually reads and executes instructions. Single-core processors can only process one instruction at a time.

A multi-core processor is a system composed of two or more independent cores. One can describe it as an integrated circuit to which two or more individual processors (called *cores* in this sense) have been integrated. A dual-core processor contains two cores, a quad-core processor contains four cores, and a hexa-core processor contains six cores.

Multiuser operating systems allow multiple users to share a computer and run programs at the same time. Windows 10 supports multiple users and PC sharing through **Fast User Switching**. With this feature, if you need to use the PC, the previous user does not have to close applications first.

CentOS 7 is designed to support more than one independent user at a time on the same computer, permitting multiple users to interact with the OS. This means that you can log on using multiple user accounts and that each account can have a separate console.

Memory Management

Memory management is the act of handling computer memory. In its simpler forms, this management provides ways to allocate portions of memory to programs at their request and to allocate free memory back to the system for reuse when it is no longer needed.

Memory management is one of the most important parts of Windows 10 and CentOS 7. With the size of applications today, systems sometimes need more memory than what exists physically in a computer. Virtual memory makes the computer appear to have more memory than it actually does by storing unneeded data and instructions on the hard drive. When the data or instructions are needed, the OS fetches them from the hard drive.

In virtual memory, all addresses are **virtual addresses,** which are memory locations that intervening hardware and software map to physical memory. These addresses should not be confused with **physical addresses,** which are numbers that identify an actual storage (memory) location in the physical memory on a computer. The amount of memory that can be addressed by the processor is called *physical memory*. The virtual addresses that a process uses do not represent the actual physical location of an object in memory. Instead, the OS maintains a page map for each process; this internal data structure is used to translate virtual addresses into corresponding physical addresses. Each time a thread references an address, the OS translates the virtual address to a physical address.

To maximize its flexibility in managing memory, the OS can move pages of physical memory to and from a paging file onto a disk. When a page is moved into physical memory, the OS updates the page maps of the affected processes. When the OS needs space in physical memory, it moves the least recently used pages of physical memory to the paging file. Manipulation of physical memory by the OS is completely transparent to applications, which operate only in their virtual address spaces.

In Windows 10, you can control the size and location of the paging file. To locate this information, begin typing "Control Panel" in the search box on the taskbar, click Control Panel in the menu that appears, click System and Security, and then click System. Click Advanced system settings on the left side of the System window. The System Properties window appears. Click the Advanced tab, which contains options for Performance settings, User Profiles, and Startup and Recovery settings. Click the Settings button under Performance. In the Performance Options window that appears, click the Advanced tab to view the paging file settings. If you need to change these settings, click the Change button. The virtual memory settings are displayed, as shown in Figure 2-4.

The default settings permit Windows 10 to automatically manage the size of the paging files. If you receive warnings that your virtual memory is low, increase the size of the paging file.

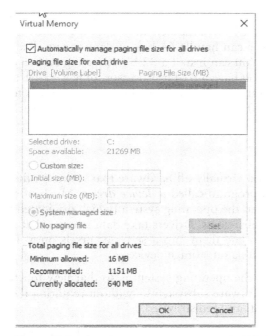

Figure 2-4 Virtual memory management in Windows 10

Source: Microsoft Windows 10/Control Panel

Windows 10 sets the initial minimum size of the paging file to the amount of random access memory (RAM) installed on your computer plus 300 MB. The maximum size is set by default to three times the amount of installed RAM. If you receive warning messages, increase the minimum and maximum sizes.

From the Advanced tab on the Performance Options dialog box, you can change the way memory is used between data caching and instruction storage. The default option, Programs, permits your PC to run faster than when memory is set aside to optimize data caching.

If you use multiple physical hard drives in Windows 10, you can increase performance by moving the paging file to a hard drive other than the one that contains the Windows 10 OS.

Memory management is quite complicated in any operating system, and CentOS 7 is no exception. Several differences exist between memory management in Windows 10 and CentOS 7; for example, you can make more detailed decisions in CentOS 7 about how memory is managed. You should only make modifications after carefully considering what you have to work with and what you want to accomplish. Other differences are that with CentOS 7, you can look at the source code and know exactly how memory is being managed, you can know exactly which algorithms are being used, and you can use the source code to expand your knowledge of memory management.

In CentOS 7, it is possible to use a whole partition of the hard drive for virtual memory. Though you can use a file for swapping, you should use a separate partition because it eliminates fragmentation, which reduces performance when swapping.

Modern operating systems like Windows 10 and CentOS 7 are available in 32-bit and 64-bit versions. The difference between 32-bit and 64-bit computers lies with the processor and how it manages information. A 64-bit processor can handle 64 bits of data at one time, while a 32-bit processor can only handle 32 bits. You can install a 32-bit operating system on a system with a 64-bit processor. However, if you have a 32-bit processor, only a 32-bit operating system can be installed. Another consideration is the memory limitation of 4 GB for 32-bit operating systems (actually closer to 3.2 GB due to other hardware allocations such as graphics card memory).

Device Management

The path between the operating system and virtually all hardware that is not on the computer's system board goes through a special program called a *device driver*. Much of a driver's function is to translate data streams between the operating system (which originated with the application programs) and the hardware subsystems. Drivers take data streams that the operating system has defined as a file and translate them into a series of pixels on a display or into streams of bits placed in specific locations on storage devices.

One reason that drivers are separate from the operating system is so that new functions can be added to the driver—and thus to the hardware subsystems—without requiring the operating system itself to be modified, recompiled, and redistributed.

One way to view device management is to consider a familiar task such as printing. In the Windows 10 approach, the OS provides a device driver for the printer. These device drivers meant that applications like Lotus no longer had to deal with printer drivers themselves, but only had to provide an interface to a Windows component called the **graphical device interface** (**GDI**). Within the OS, a device driver connects the GDI to a printer (shown in Figure 2-5). The application speaks Windows language to the GDI, which talks to the printer driver, which in turn controls the printer. The GDI possesses additional capabilities—for example, it allows applications to talk to all display devices, including graphics cards. In this scheme, the printer drivers are the responsibility of the printer manufacturer, although Microsoft wrote some of these drivers for the manufacturers.

In CentOS 7, the flow for the print model is essentially the same. The application produces **PostScript**—a page description language developed and marketed by Adobe Systems—which goes to **Ghostscript**, a suite of free software based on an interpreter of the Adobe PostScript and Portable Document Format (PDF) page description languages and a set of C procedures. In turn, the flow is passed to the device driver. Ghostscript converts the PostScript to the printer formatting commands required by the printer and prints PostScript files to non-PostScript printers. The OS provides the printer driver for every printer that it supports.

The basis of a printing system in a modern OS is the spooler, as shown in Figure 2-6. *Spool* is an acronym for *simultaneous peripheral operations online*. The spooler manages queues of print jobs. A queue is usually associated with a single printer, and jobs submitted by users are processed on a first-come, first-served basis. For Windows 10, the application generates output that is passed to a module, such as the GDI. The module then calls the printer driver to render the output. The output is then passed to the print monitor, which controls the transfer to the printer. The printing is done in the background while the user interacts with other applications in the foreground.

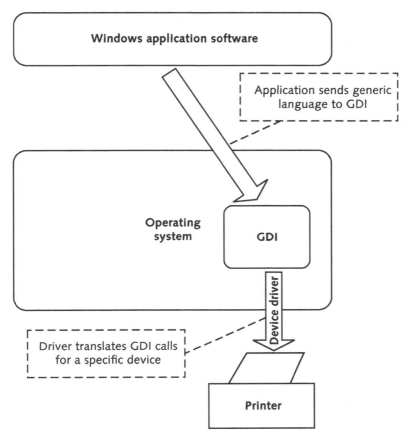

Figure 2-5 Operating system support for printing

Storage Management

A modern OS provides the tools to manage the storage areas on the PC's hard drives. In Windows 10, Disk Management is a system utility for managing hard drives and the partitions they contain. With Disk Management, you can initialize disks, create partitions, and format volumes with file systems such as exFAT, FAT32, or NTFS. You will learn to use these file systems in Chapter 5. Disk Management enables you to perform most disk-related tasks without restarting the system or interrupting users; most configuration changes take effect immediately.

Starting with Windows Server 2012, Microsoft released the **Resilient File System (ReFS)**, which is designed as a "next-generation" file system for Windows. While ReFS has some great new features that NTFS doesn't, it lacks some of NTFS's capabilities. As of this writing, you cannot boot Windows from an ReFS volume. Limited support exists for ReFS in Windows 10.

CentOS 7 supports ext3, ext4, global file system 2, XFS, NFS, and FS-Cache file systems. You will learn to use some of these file systems in Chapter 5. In Linux, you use the `fdisk` and `makefs` commands to create partitions and install file systems.

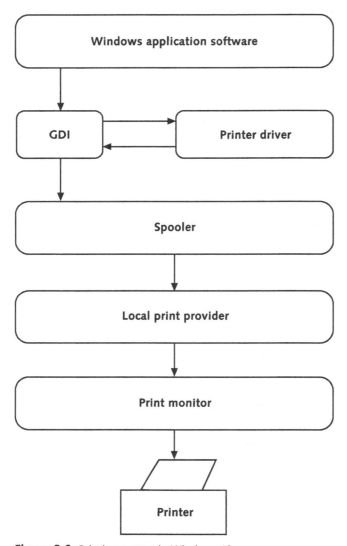

Figure 2-6 Printing system in Windows 10

User Interface

In DOS, you enter textual commands using the CLI, a method of interacting with a computer from the keyboard. In its simplest form, the computer displays a prompt, you type a command with the keyboard and then press the Enter key, and the computer executes the command.

The GUI (usually pronounced *GOO-ee*) is a graphical interface for using a computer rather than a purely textual interface. Windows 10 is an example of a GUI interface, as shown in Figure 2-7. From the GUI interface, you can still use a CLI, such as PowerShell.

Likewise, CentOS 7 provides a GUI interface. **GNOME** (pronounced *guh-nome*) is part of the GNU project and part of the free software, or open source, movement (see Figure 2-8).

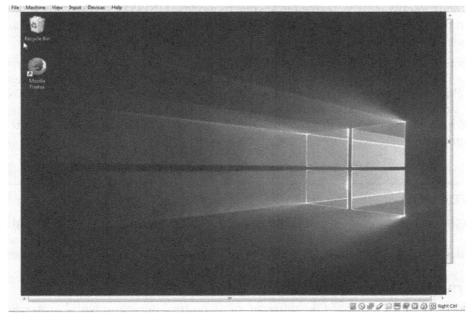

Figure 2-7 Windows desktop in Windows 10

Source: Microsoft Windows 10

Figure 2-8 CentOS 7 GNOME desktop

Source: Red Hat CentOS 7/GNOME

Open source software is available for anyone to modify. GNOME is a Windows-like desktop system that works on CentOS 7. GNOME's main objective is to provide a user-friendly suite of applications and an easy-to-use desktop.

By default, CentOS 7 configures six different types of consoles for use. You may not even realize that these consoles are available. Typically, a system administrator is logged on to a machine on several different consoles (maybe with several different user IDs) at the same time. You can easily switch between consoles by simultaneously pressing the Alt and F keys of the console in use. This allows you to work efficiently on several tasks at the same time.

OS Interaction

An OS is designed to interact with the major components of a PC—hardware and applications. You need to know how the OS controls the hardware and what valuable services it provides to applications used on the PC. This section covers both types of interaction.

Interaction with Hardware

Windows 10 and CentOS 7 take different views on the interaction with hardware in a PC. All versions of Microsoft Windows after Windows 95 have implemented the **Windows Driver Model (WDM)**. WDM is a technology developed by Microsoft to create drivers that are source-code compatible for a number of Windows operating systems, including Windows 10. WDM works by channeling some of the work of the device driver into portions of the code that are integrated into the operating system. The WDM device driver becomes more streamlined with less code and works at greater efficiency. CentOS 7 divides devices into three major categories: character devices, block devices, and network devices. Each approach has merit.

The Windows View of Hardware There are three kinds of WDM drivers:

- **Bus drivers**—Drive an I/O bus and provide per-slot functionality that is device-independent. In the context of WDM, a bus is any device to which other physical, logical, or virtual devices are attached. Windows 10 contains WDM support for the following buses: PCI, dynamic Plug and Play serial I/O buses (including USB and IEEE 1394), SCSI, NDIS, and Remote NDIS (RNDIS).

- **Function drivers**—Drive an individual device; Windows 10 contains WDM support for USB device classes, such as the Human Interface Device (HID) class, cameras/scanners, video capture over IEEE 1394, audio, and USB and IEEE 1394 storage devices.

- **Filter drivers**—Filter I/O requests for a device, a class of devices, or a bus; for example, a file system filter driver intercepts requests targeted at a file system. By intercepting the request before it reaches its intended target, the filter driver can extend the functionality provided by the original target of the request. An antivirus agent uses a filter driver to intercept files that contain viruses.

The CentOS 7 View of Hardware CentOS 7 divides hardware devices into three major categories:

- **Character devices**—Can be accessed as streams of characters; examples include the **standard input device** (the keyboard) and the **standard output device** (the screen or monitor). Other examples of character devices are serial ports and PCMCIA memory cards.

- **Block devices**—Handle input/output operations one or more blocks at a time; a block is normally 512 bytes, but it can be any larger power of two. Examples of block devices are disk drives, DVD drives, and loop devices.

- **Networking devices**—Handled differently by the kernel than character devices or block devices; with character and block devices, the kernel uses read and write calls to deal with input and output. With networking devices, the kernel must deal with **packets** (units of information transferred over a network, or network data).

Interaction with Applications

Operating systems provide a software platform on top of which other programs, called application programs, can run. These application programs require support from the operating system. The following sections explain important OS interactions with applications:

- Installing applications
- Running applications
- Managing disks and files
- Connecting to a network
- Printing documents

Installing Applications When you obtain a software application, you must install it before you can use it. Most applications today are downloaded and installed from a product Web site, unless they are purchased with the computer itself. When requested, the OS installs the application, copying the program files to the hard drive, creating an entry on a start menu or application menu, and configuring the application for your use.

The **Microsoft Windows Installer** is an installation and configuration service that ships as part of the Microsoft Windows 10 operating system. Using the Windows Installer, administrators keep software up to date by efficiently installing and configuring products and applications.

CentOS 7 uses **YUM** (Yellowdog Updater, Modified), which is the most common utility for installing and configuring software on CentOS Linux systems such as CentOS 7. YUM is an automatic updater and package installer/remover for RPM packages. The name **RPM** (**Red Hat Package Manager**) refers to the software packaged in this format. It automatically determines how to safely install, remove, and update RPM packages. YUM efficiently and easily retrieves information on any package installed or available in a repository.

Running Applications What happens when you type a command or click a program icon? The OS performs a series of steps:

- When you logged on to your PC, your privileges and group membership(s) were determined by the OS. These group memberships are used to control access to the resources on the PC. Whenever a thread or process interacts with a file or tries to perform a system task that requires privileges, the OS checks to determine your level of authorization.

- The OS provides an address space (a range of available memory addresses) for the program. The address space has a specific range of values; the limits of this range restrict the amount of memory available to the executing process.

- The OS loads the program into the address space and schedules the process or thread for execution.

- The OS monitors the execution of the thread or process.

- The OS shares the processor resources by multitasking—that is, concurrently running all active processes and threads on the system.

- When the executing program requests it, input/output operations are queued for execution. The OS opens the requested device and reads the requested data or writes data to the indicated device.

- When the program requests termination, connections to the devices are closed and the address space is released.

Managing Disks and Files The OS provides an organized storage system to aid in the location of files. Data files are arranged in a hierarchy according to standards that vary by operating system. You need to understand this arrangement to efficiently store the data you generate with various applications.

Windows 10 implements a folder structure to store and organize files, just as you use manila folders to organize information in a filing cabinet, as shown in Figure 2-9.

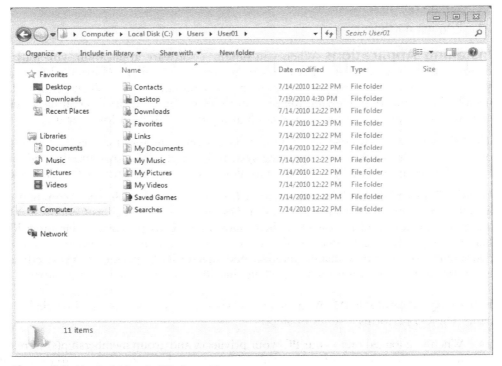

Figure 2-9 User's folders in Windows 10

Source: Microsoft Windows 10/File Explorer

CentOS 7 organizes files in a hierarchical structure similar to Windows 10, but uses the term *directories* instead of folders. A new file system structure is introduced in CentOS 7. The directories /bin, /sbin, /lib, and /lib64 are now nested under /usr. In Windows 10, you view the folder structure and file attributes with Windows File Explorer. CentOS 7 provides a number of tools to view the directory structure and filenames. For example, you will learn to use the `ls` and `tree` commands in Chapter 6.

You also need to be aware of the concept of a **home directory**, which the OS provides for a user to store data. In CentOS 7, you use the /home directory. In Windows 10, the "home" folder is named after the user's logon. Each user has a set of personal folders, as shown in Figure 2-9. The home folder has a number of subfolders to store files by file types.

In either case, the OS creates the home directory when the user account is created. When you log on to the PC, the OS points to the home directory, where you can access your data files.

Windows 10 also supports the use of **libraries** to help you manage your documents, music, pictures, and other files. In some ways, a library is like a folder. For example, when you open a library, you will see one or more files. However, unlike a folder, a library gathers files that are stored in multiple locations, as shown in Figure 2-10. This is a subtle yet important difference: libraries do not actually store files. Windows 10 monitors folders that contain your files, and lets you access and arrange the files in different ways. For example, you could have your music files stored on both the internal disk drive and a USB external drive and access your files at once from the music library.

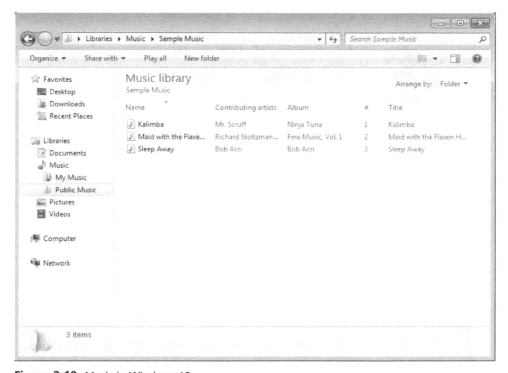

Figure 2-10 Music in Windows 10

Source: Microsoft Windows 10/File Explorer

Connecting to a Network Your applications can use files that are shared and stored in a central repository, such as a file server. The OS provides the necessary support for file sharing. You need to understand file sharing because it provides access to files, data, and information from multiple computers.

You can set up your PC to share the directories or folders on your hard drive with other PCs on a network, as shown in Figure 2-11. You can grant access to desired users and keep other users out. This sharing of resources is not limited to files. To save costs, for example, you could share a laser printer with several others on your network.

Windows-based operating systems support file-sharing traffic across a network by using the **Server Message Block (SMB)** communications protocol. CentOS 7 provides equivalent access capabilities using **Samba**.

Windows 10 provides the **Network folder** in File Explorer to locate and connect to shared folders on networked computers. With CentOS 7, you connect to the remote share by using the Network command within File Browser.

You will continue to learn more about network connections in Chapter 11.

Printing Documents The primary output for most documents is the printed page. The OS provides access to local and network printers. Windows 10 provides the **Add Printer Wizard** to make a printer available for your applications. In CentOS 7, you use the printer administration tool **system-config-printer** to set up your printer. Once the printer is installed and configured, you use it as indicated by your application.

To a great extent, your choice of an OS determines the applications you can use. Prior to selecting an OS, you should review the support requirements for the one you want to use.

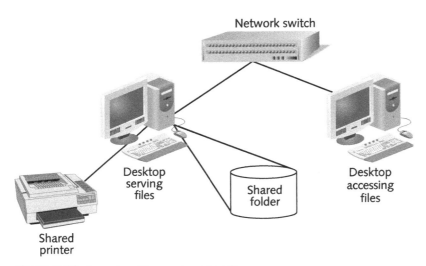

Figure 2-11 Accessing files over a network

System Utilities

You use system utilities to perform various tasks on your PC. Key utilities include text editors, configuration editors, and system information monitors, as explained in the following sections.

Text Editors

A **text editor** allows you to enter, modify, and delete data in a text file. Text files are used for many purposes; for example, you can write source code for a program in a text editor. In fact, most source code is stored in text files. As a network administrator, you may write many PowerShell scripts, most of which will be stored in text files. You will learn to use text editors in Chapter 9.

Most system utilities only know how to deal with text files. In Windows, the `type` command lists the contents of a text file within the command prompt window, as shown in Figure 2-12. For example, you can use the `type` command in Windows PowerShell to show the contents of the hosts TCP/IP configuration file.

In CentOS 7, the `cat` command performs the same function as the `type` command. For example, you can use the command to display the contents of the hosts file on the standard output device (the computer monitor). See Figure 2-13.

Files in other formats normally require specific programs to handle them.

Operating System Configuration

As an administrator, you may need to update many PC configuration entries. Within Windows, you may need to make entries to the **Registry**, a hierarchical database that

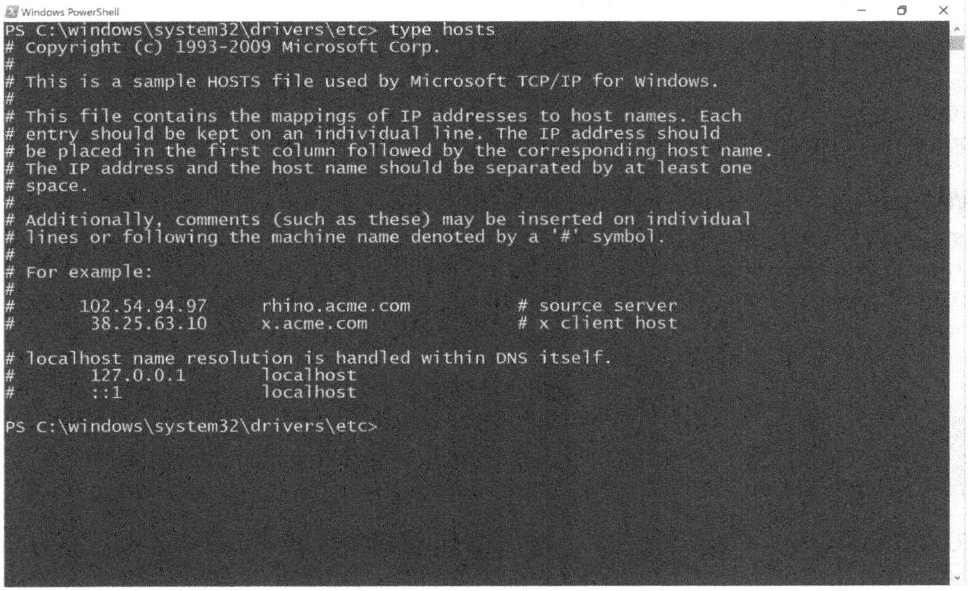

Figure 2-12 Text file listed with Windows `type` command

Source: Microsoft Windows 10/PowerShell

```
root@CentOS7:~                    _  □  ×

File  Edit  View  Search  Terminal  Help
[root@CentOS7 ~]# cat /boot/grub2/grub.cfg
#
# DO NOT EDIT THIS FILE
#
# It is automatically generated by grub2-mkconfig using templates
# from /etc/grub.d and settings from /etc/default/grub
#

### BEGIN /etc/grub.d/00_header ###
set pager=1

if [ -s $prefix/grubenv ]; then
  load_env
fi
if [ "${next_entry}" ] ; then
   set default="${next_entry}"
   set next_entry=
   save_env next_entry
   set boot_once=true
else
   set default="${saved_entry}"
fi

if [ x"${feature_menuentry_id}" = xy ]; then
  menuentry_id_option="--id"
else
  menuentry_id_option=""
fi

export menuentry_id_option

if [ "${prev_saved_entry}" ]; then
```

Figure 2-13 Text file listed with the `cat` command

Source: Red Hat CentOS 7/Terminal

contains configuration entries. Most of the configuration files in CentOS 7 that control a computer system are stored as text files.

Windows 10 Configuration Regedit is a special utility that allows a system administrator to edit Registry entries (see Figure 2-14). Microsoft uses the Registry in Windows to hold a tremendous amount of information that is critical to the normal operation of your PC. You need to be exposed to the Registry, but do not attempt to edit it in any manner.

 Editing the Registry is an advanced skill that most normal users should not attempt. One small mistake in editing the Registry can be fatal to your PC.

Rather than using a Registry like Windows 10, CentOS 7 maintains most configuration settings in text files within the /etc directory. If necessary, these text files can be edited with the Vim text editor. You will learn about this editor in Chapter 9.

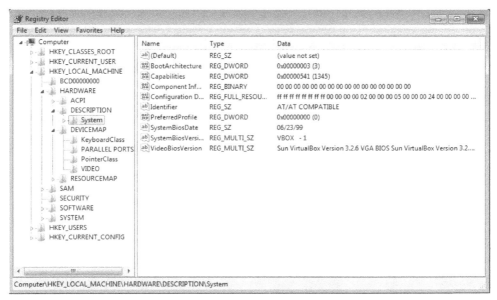

Figure 2-14 Registry entries displayed with Regedit

Source: Microsoft Windows 10/Regedit

 You must take great care when editing the text files in the /etc directory. If you make errors during editing, you could disable your computer.

System Information

You can view information about your PC by using the information tools provided by the OS. In Windows 10, you can use the System Information tool for information about your system. In CentOS 7, you can use the System Settings utility.

Windows 10 System Information The System Information tool provides summary information and configuration information about the computer. To access and use this tool, see Activity 2-1. Figure 2-15 shows the System Summary window of the System Information tool.

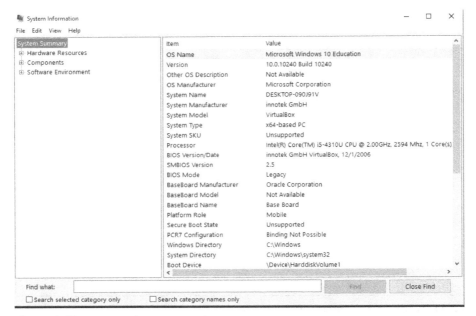

Figure 2-15 System Information tool

Source: Microsoft Windows 10/System Information

Activity 2-1: Reviewing System Information

Time Required: 10 minutes

Objective: Review information about your PC's processor.

Description: In this activity, you start the Windows 10 virtual machine and review its system information. This activity is useful if you want to obtain system information.

1. Start your virtual machines using the appropriate instructions in Activity 1-1. On the taskbar, notice the "Search the web and Windows" box. This new feature in Windows 10 is a component of your "personal assistant" named Cortana.

2. Begin typing **System Information** in the search box. Cortana displays System Information Desktop app as the first option. Click it.

3. Review the system information that appears. Review each listed topic for more information.

4. Close the System Information window after you have reviewed it.

5. Leave the virtual machine logged on for future activities.

CentOS 7 System Settings To see what type of CPU your computer uses, click Applications, point to System Tools, and click Settings. To review the system summary and information about removable media and default applications, click Details in the System category. The summary is shown in Figure 2-16.

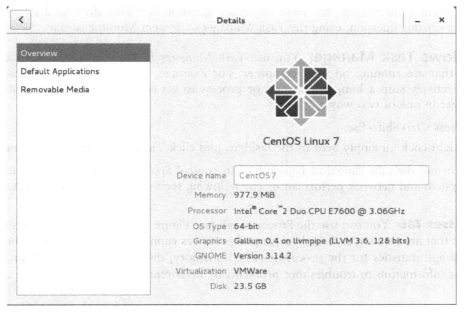

Figure 2-16 CentOS 7 system settings

Source: Red Hat CentOS 7/System Profiler

Activity 2-2: Using the CentOS 7 System Settings

Time Required: 15 minutes

Objective: Use the CentOS 7 System Settings utility to review summary information about the system. Note that you cannot perform this activity until you install the hardinfo program, as described in Appendix C.

Description: In this activity, you start the CentOS 7 virtual machine and then review system information. This activity is useful if you want to review system details and information about default applications on your virtual machine.

1. If necessary, start your virtual machines using the appropriate instructions in Activity 1-1.
2. To open the System Settings utility, click **Applications**, point to **System Tools,** and then click **Settings**.
3. Click **Details** and review the system information.
4. Close the window.
5. Leave the virtual machine logged on for future activities.

System Monitors

To help you identify problem areas and obtain the best service possible, it is important that you know exactly what is happening in your PC. As a system administrator, you use many tools to perform daily tasks. In Windows 10, you can use the **Task Manager** to see useful information about system performance; in CentOS 7, you use **System Monitor**.

To a system administrator, the most important question is "What do I need to do?" Once you answer this question, using the Task Manager or System Monitor is easy.

Windows Task Manager   You use Task Manager to monitor applications and processes that are running on your computer. For example, when using Task Manager, you can selectively stop a hung application or process to get out of a jam. You can start Task Manager in one of two ways:

- Press Ctrl+Shift+Esc.
- Right-click an empty area of the taskbar, and click Task Manager from the menu.

You can use the tabs shown in Figure 2-17 to control applications and processes as well as view system and network performance. The following sections discuss many of these tabs.

Processes Tab   You can use the Processes tab (see Figure 2-17) to view the names of applications that are running and the background processes running on the computer. The tab displays usage statistics for the processor (CPU), memory, disks, and networks. You can then use this information to troubleshoot problems by determining which programs are using the

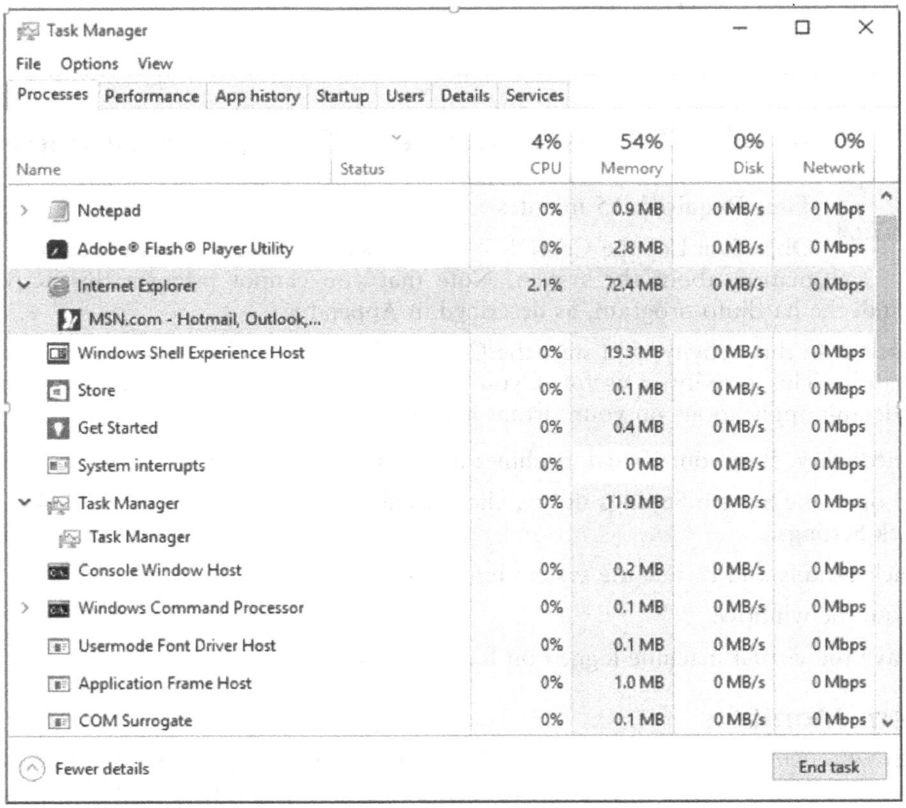

Figure 2-17   Processes tab of Windows Task Manager

Source: Microsoft Windows 10/Task Manager

most resources, such as processing or memory. A program with an abnormally high CPU value could be hung. A program with an extremely large amount of memory usage might have a memory leak—memory usage of a process grows without bounds. To stop a process, select the program and click the End task button. On this tab, you can sort any column of data by clicking the column name.

 By ending a process, you could render your computer unstable or lose valuable data in memory! Be careful.

Performance Tab From the Performance tab (see Figure 2-18), you can quickly review your computer's usage of CPU, memory, disk, and network resources. Select each resource to see the details. A high CPU usage (consistently over 90 percent) indicates that the processor speed is inadequate. A high rate of page file activity indicates that the computer needs additional RAM. To access more detailed information, click the Open Resource Monitor button.

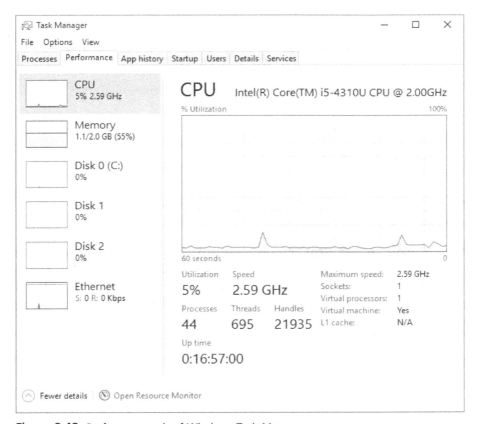

Figure 2-18 Performance tab of Windows Task Manager

Source: Microsoft Windows 10/Task Manager

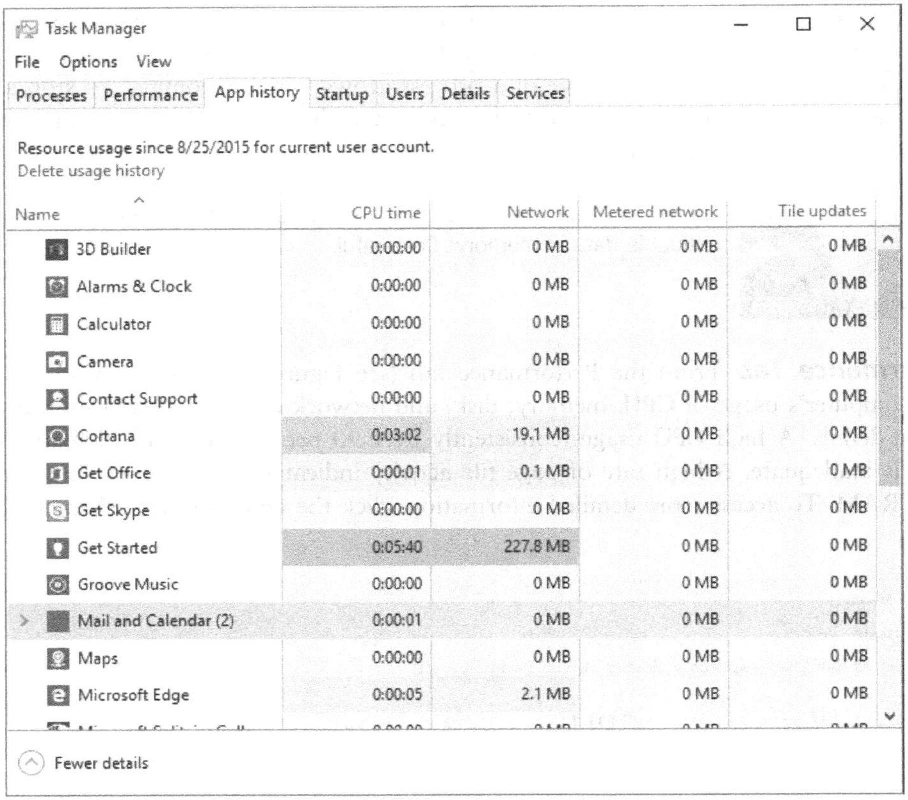

Figure 2-19 App history tab of Windows Task Manager

Source: Microsoft Windows 10/Task Manager

App History Tab You can use the App history tab shown in Figure 2-19 to view the computer's history of application utilization.

Windows Resource Monitor You can click the Open Resource Monitor button on the Performance tab to monitor the usage of four critical resources: CPU, hard disk, network, and memory. Resource Monitor automatically opens to the Overview tab. Figure 2-20 shows an overview of resource usage. In addition, four graphs appear along the right side; click one of the four chevrons to display more detailed information. Click the CPU, Memory, Disk, or Network tab for additional information and statistics for each component.

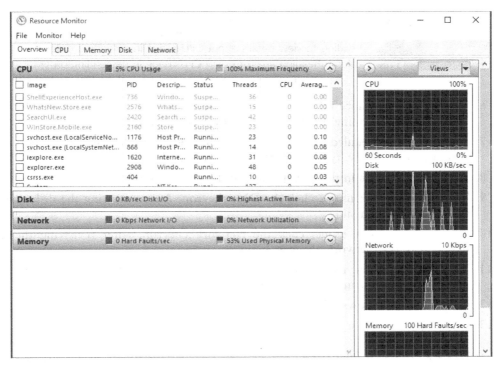

Figure 2-20 Resource Monitor showing CPU details

Source: Microsoft Windows 10/Task Manager

Activity 2-3: Using the Windows 10 Task Manager

Time Required: 15 minutes

Objective: Use the Windows 10 Task Manager to see how the PC is performing.

Description: In this activity, you open the Processes tab of the Task Manager to review the applications and processes running on the PC in Windows. To quickly review CPU performance on the PC, click the Performance tab. Below the performance chart, you can review a number of key counters to determine the number of active objects (handles), threads with all processes, and processes. You will also explore the Resource Monitor for additional information. This activity is useful if you want to review system tasks and the performance of your PC.

1. If necessary, start your virtual machines using the appropriate instructions in Activity 1-1.
2. To start the Task Manager, right-click the taskbar and then click **Task Manager**. At the bottom of the screen, click **More details** if necessary to view the details.
3. To determine which applications have run on the system, click the **App history** tab, if necessary.
4. Review the applications listed.
5. To determine which processes are running and review them, click the **Processes** tab. All resources are listed on the left side.

 To review information about a particular resource in the Processes tab, click the resource heading. For example, you can click the CPU column heading to view details about CPU usage in ascending order. Click the column heading again to view CPU usage in descending order.

6. Click the **Performance** tab. To review the utilization, speed, threads with all processes, and processes, examine the data at the bottom of the graph.

7. To obtain more detailed information, click **Open Resource Monitor** at the bottom of the window. If necessary, type **Pa$$w0rd** to proceed and click **Yes**.

8. Review the process in the CPU pane, and then click the **CPU** chevron.

9. To review the disk usage, click the **Disk** chevron. After reviewing the disk usage, click the **Disk** chevron again.

10. To review network usage, click the **Network** chevron. After reviewing the network usage, click the **Network** chevron again.

11. To review memory usage, click the **Memory** chevron. After reviewing the memory usage, click the **Memory** chevron again.

12. Close all the windows within the Windows 10 virtual machine.

13. Leave the virtual machine logged on for future activities.

CentOS 7 System Monitor You can use System Monitor to review process activity in real time. The utility displays a list of the most CPU-intensive tasks on the PC. Figure 2-21 shows the process activity sorted by percentage of CPU usage. To sort by the % CPU column, click its column heading. By default, the display is updated every five seconds.

System Monitor contains more tabs than just the Processes tab. As shown in Figures 2-22 and 2-23, it also contains Resources and File Systems tabs. From the Resources tab (see Figure 2-22), you can review real-time information about the following performance measures:

- CPU History—The graphics show CPU usage and current percentage of CPU usage.
- Memory and Swap History—The graphics show memory and swap space usage.
- Network History—The graphics show network activity in terms of bytes received and sent.

Figure 2-23 shows the File Systems tab in System Monitor; the tab displays the total space, free space, and available space for each allocated partition.

Process Name	User	% CPU ▼	ID	Memory	Priority
gnome-system-monitor	User01	1	26948	13.1 MiB	Normal
gnome-shell	User01	1	22341	149.4 MiB	Normal
gnome-keyring-daemon	User01	0	22047	808.0 KiB	Normal
gnome-session	User01	0	22097	2.0 MiB	Normal
dbus-launch	User01	0	22105	144.0 KiB	Normal
dbus-daemon	User01	0	22106	1.4 MiB	Normal
gvfsd	User01	0	22171	628.0 KiB	Normal
gvfsd-fuse	User01	0	22175	2.7 MiB	Normal
ssh-agent	User01	0	22243	572.0 KiB	Normal
at-spi-bus-launcher	User01	0	22269	568.0 KiB	Normal
dbus-daemon	User01	0	22273	616.0 KiB	Normal
at-spi2-registryd	User01	0	22278	636.0 KiB	Normal
gnome-settings-daemon	User01	0	22287	10.1 MiB	Normal
pulseaudio	User01	0	22307	2.8 MiB	Very High
gsd-printer	User01	0	22325	1.5 MiB	Normal
ibus-daemon	User01	0	22374	4.1 MiB	Normal
ibus-dconf	User01	0	22379	696.0 KiB	Normal
ibus-x11	User01	0	22382	3.9 MiB	Normal
gnome-shell-calendar-server	User01	0	22384	2.5 MiB	Normal
evolution-source-registry	User01	0	22393	3.4 MiB	Normal
mission-control-5	User01	0	22402	3.5 MiB	Normal

Figure 2-21 Process activity shown in CentOS 7 System Monitor

Source: Red Hat CentOS 7/System Monitor

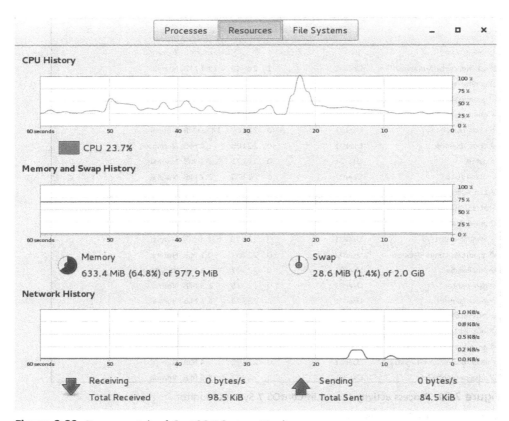

Figure 2-22 Resources tab of CentOS 7 System Monitor

Source: Red Hat CentOS 7/System Monitor

Device	Directory ▼	Type	Total	Available	Used		
/dev/mapp: /		xfs	18.7 GB	13.0 GB	5.7 GB		30 %
/dev/sda1 /boot		xfs	520.8 MB	312.0 MB	208.8 MB		40 %
/dev/sdb1 /mnt/sdb1		xfs	2.1 GB	2.1 GB	33.8 MB		1 %
/dev/sdc1 /mnt/sdc1		vfat	2.1 GB	2.1 GB	4.1 kB		0 %

Figure 2-23 File Systems tab of CentOS 7 System Monitor

Source: Red Hat CentOS 7/System Monitor

Activity 2-4: Using the CentOS 7 System Monitor

Time Required: 15 minutes

Objective: Use the CentOS 7 System Monitor to review the performance of the virtual machine.

Description: In this activity, you open System Monitor in CentOS 7. From the Processes tab, you sort by percentage of CPU usage to locate the active processes. Use the other tabs to view important information about your system. This activity is useful if you want to review processes and the performance of your virtual machine.

1. If necessary, start your virtual machines using the appropriate instructions in Activity 1-1.
2. To open System Monitor, click **Applications**, point to **System Tools**, and then click **System Monitor**.
3. To review the processes, click the **Processes** tab.
4. To determine the most active processes, click the **% CPU** button until the chevron points down.
5. To see the graphs for system resources, click the **Resources** tab.
6. To determine the amount of free disk space, click the **File Systems** tab.
7. Close the System Monitor window.
8. Leave the virtual machine logged on for future activities.

Applications

You use many applications on your PC, including word processors, spreadsheets, presentation software, a Web browser, an e-mail client, games, and graphics software. It is not unusual for an application to be made up of many smaller programs that work together. Applications are the reason that people use computers.

Microsoft Office is a suite of programs developed for the Windows OS. Its components include:

- Microsoft Word—A word processor that is considered the main program in Office 2013; it possesses a dominant share of the word-processing market. Its proprietary DOC format is considered a de facto standard, although its most recent version also supports an XML-based format.
- Microsoft Excel—A spreadsheet program; like Microsoft Word, it possesses a dominant market share. It was originally a competitor to Lotus 1-2-3, but it eventually became the de facto standard.
- Microsoft PowerPoint—A popular presentation program; it is used to create slideshows composed of text, graphics, movies, and other objects. The slides can be displayed on screen or printed on transparencies or slides.

LibreOffice

LibreOffice is a free and open source office suite developed by The Document Foundation, a nonprofit organization. It was based on OpenOffice.org in 2010. LibreOffice has significantly improved the ability to import Microsoft Office documents into Linux. All Linux distributions bundle it by default. Its components include:

- Writer—A word processor that has a similar look and feel to Microsoft Word and offers a widely overlapping range of functions and tools. It can save to .docx, the default format for saving Word documents beginning with Office 2007. Writer allows you to create or export to PDF files with no additional software.

- Calc—A spreadsheet that is similar to Microsoft Excel and has a similar range of features; Calc also provides features that are not present in Excel, including a system that automatically defines series for graphing, based on the layout of the user's data. It can save to .xlsx, a file extension for an open XML spreadsheet file format used by Microsoft Excel. Calc can also write spreadsheets directly as PDF files.

- Impress—A presentation program that is similar to Microsoft PowerPoint; Impress can export presentations to Macromedia Flash (SWF) files, allowing them to be played on any computer that has the Flash player installed. It also supports export to XHTML, HTML, and vector graphic formats (SVG, EPS). You also can create PDF files with Impress.

If you are running the CentOS 7 OS, LibreOffice is an excellent choice. (Figure 2-24 shows the default components in the LibreOffice suite.) For Windows 10 users, LibreOffice is free. However, if you are a student who shares documents with users running Microsoft Office, the Office Home and Student Edition would be a better choice for Windows 10.

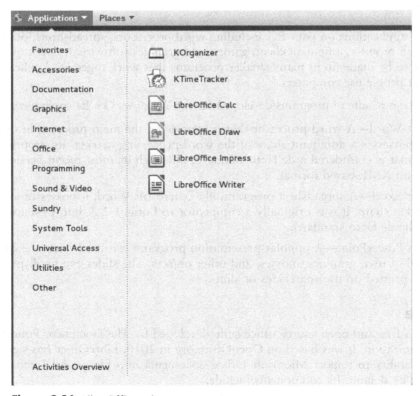

Figure 2-24 LibreOffice suite components

Source: Red Hat CentOS 7/The Document Foundation

The number of business applications supported by CentOS 7 continues to grow. Table 2-2 lists various categories of applications and the offerings for Windows 10 and CentOS 7 in each category.

Category	Windows 10	CentOS 7
Web browser	Microsoft Internet Explorer	Firefox, Opera, Google Chrome
E-mail client	Outlook Express	Evolution, Thunderbird
Project management	Microsoft Project	Phabricator
Diagramming	Microsoft Visio	Pencil
Image editing	Adobe Photoshop	GIMP, Shotwell Photo Manager
PDF reader	Adobe Acrobat	Document
Database	Microsoft Access	LibreOffice Base
FTP client	GlobalSCAPE CuteFTP	gFTPFileZilla

Table 2-2   Business applications

Freeware for Windows 10

Freeware is software that is available free of charge for personal use. Freeware is frequently distributed on the Web. Although it is available at no cost, the author retains the copyright, which means that it cannot be altered or sold. See Table 2-3 for examples of freeware that is available for Windows 10.

Category	Freeware product	Web site for downloading
Web browser	Firefox	www.mozilla.org/products/firefox/
Antivirus software	AVG	http://free.grisoft.com/
Firewall	Zone Alarm	www.zonelabs.com/store/content/company/products/znalm/freeDownload.jsp
Office suite	OpenOffice	www.openoffice.org/
Text editor	Metapad	www.liquidninja.com/metapad/

Table 2-3   Freeware for Windows 10

Activity 2-5: Using the Windows WordPad Application

Time Required: 15 minutes

Objective: Use the WordPad application to write a short note.

Description: In this activity, you use the WordPad application to write a short paragraph detailing your experiences with Windows 10 and CentOS 7. (WordPad is an example of a

Windows application that is installed by default.) This activity is useful if you want to type a short note while working on your PC.

1. If necessary, start your virtual machines using the appropriate instructions in Activity 1-1.

2. To start WordPad, begin typing **WordPad** in the search box on the taskbar, and then click **WordPad** in the menu that appears.

3. Type a short note about your experiences with Windows 10 and CentOS 7.

4. Click the **Save** icon in the upper-left corner of the WordPad window, type **Note*fml*** (where *fml* represents your initials), and then click **Save**.

5. Close all the windows within the Windows 10 virtual machine.

6. To shut down the virtual machine, click **Start**, click **Power**, and then click the **Shut Down** button.

7. Wait a moment for the Windows 10 virtual machine to completely shut down.

8. Leave the PC logged on for the next activity.

Activity 2-6: Using the CentOS 7 LibreOffice Application

Time Required: 15 minutes

Objective: Use the LibreOffice application to write a short note.

Description: This activity is similar to Activity 2-5, but this time you use a CentOS 7 application—LibreOffice Writer—to write a short paragraph detailing your experiences with Windows 10 and CentOS 7. (LibreOffice Writer is an example of a CentOS 7 application that is installed by default.) This activity is useful if you want to type a short note with a CentOS 7 application.

1. If necessary, start your virtual machines using the appropriate instructions in Activity 1-1.

2. To start LibreOffice Writer, click **Applications**, point to **Office**, and then click **LibreOffice Writer**.

3. Based on your reading so far in this text, type a short note about whether you might prefer to use Windows 10 or CentOS 7.

4. Click the **File** menu, click **Save As**, type **Note*fml*** (where *fml* represents your initials), and then click **Save**.

5. Close the LibreOffice Writer window.

6. To shut down the virtual machine, click **User01**, click **Power Off**, and then click the **Power Off** button.

7. Wait a moment for the CentOS 7 virtual machine to completely shut down.

8. Close any remaining open windows, log off, and shut down your PC.

2

Chapter Summary

- The software components of a PC are used to perform a variety of tasks. All components work together, many without a user's knowledge. Each component plays a specific role in the PC's overall performance, and no component is less important than another. PC resources are managed by many programs working within the operating system.

- The first OS for the PC was DOS. The core of a PC's operating system is the kernel, which is where the hardware is secured and each application is serviced.

- The OS manages resources by controlling the processor, memory, devices, storage, and the user interface. Modern operating systems support preemptive multitasking, multithreading, and virtual memory.

- The OS interacts with both hardware and applications. For example, the OS interacts with applications by installing and running them. The OS provides disk and network access as well as printing.

- Many operating systems exist for PCs. The most common are DOS, Windows, and CentOS 7. Each has evolved from its inception to allow users to work with editors, graphical user interfaces, and peripheral devices such as printers, keyboards, monitors, and disk drives. The best operating systems are stable, secure, and scalable products.

- The operating system works with different system utilities to perform various tasks on your PC. Operating systems use different terminology and utilities to perform these tasks. For example, to update a configuration file, you need a configuration editor. When using Windows 10, you use Regedit to update a Registry file. When you need to monitor your system, you use Task Manager in Windows 10 and System Monitor in CentOS 7. Different types of editors are used depending on whether the Registry or configuration file refers to the operating system, utilities, or applications.

- You use many applications on your PC, including word processors, spreadsheets, and a Web browser.

Key Terms

Add Printer Wizard   A wizard used in Windows 10 to make a printer available for your applications.

application   A program that helps users perform tasks on a PC, such as creating a spreadsheet.

block device   A device that moves information in blocks or groups of bytes instead of characters. An example is a disk drive.

bus driver   A WDM driver for an I/O bus. It provides per-slot functionality that is device driven.

character device   A device that transmits or receives information as streams of characters, one character at a time. An example is a keyboard.

command-line interface (CLI)   A program you use to give commands to an operating system.

cooperative multitasking   A form of multitasking in which each process controls the length of time it maintains exclusive control over the CPU.

core   The part of the processor that actually reads and executes instructions.

Disk Operating System (DOS)   A generic term for any operating system that is loaded from disk devices when the system is started or restarted.

dynamic link library (DLL)   A library of executable functions or data that can be used by a Windows 10 application.

exFAT   A Windows 10 file system developed for external drives.

Fast User Switching   A feature in Windows 10 that allows users to switch between user accounts on a single PC without quitting applications and logging out.

filter driver   A WDM driver that filters the I/O requests for a device, a class of devices, or a bus.

freeware   Software that is available free of charge for personal use. Freeware is frequently distributed on the Web.

function driver   A WDM driver that drives an individual device.

Ghostscript   A suite of free software based on an interpreter of the Adobe PostScript and Portable Document Format (PDF) page description languages.

GNOME   The default desktop for Red Hat's distribution of CentOS 7.

graphical device interface (GDI)   The display language interface for Microsoft Windows systems.

graphical user interface (GUI)   An interface that allows users to interact with computers through graphical icons and visual indicators.

home directory   A directory associated with a user account under CentOS 7.

kernel   The core of an operating system. The kernel manages memory, files, and peripheral devices, as well as starting applications and allocating system resources.

libraries   File structures that help you manage your documents, music, pictures, and other files.

Linux   Refers to the family of UNIX-like computer operating systems that use the Linux kernel.

Microsoft Windows Installer   An installation and configuration service that ships as part of the Windows 10 operating system.

multiprocessing   The simultaneous execution of instructions by multiple processors within a single computer.

multitasking   Concurrently running all active processes and threads on the PC.

multithreading   Running several processes in rapid sequence (multitasking) within a single program.

Network folder   A folder used to locate and connect to shared folders on networked computers.

networking device   A category used by CentOS 7 for network devices. The CentOS 7 kernel uses packets with these devices.

packet   A unit of information transferred as a whole from one device to another on a network.

physical address   A number that identifies an actual storage (memory) location in the physical memory on a computer.

PostScript   A page description language developed and marketed by Adobe Systems.

PowerShell   An automation platform and scripting language for Windows. PowerShell harnesses the power of the .NET Framework, providing rich objects and a massive set of built-in functionality.

preemptive multitasking   A multitasking process in which the OS ensures that all active threads have the opportunity to execute. Preemptive multitasking prevents a single thread from monopolizing a processor.

Regedit   An application that allows the user to edit the entries in the Registry.

Registry   A central hierarchical database used by Windows 10 to store information that is needed to configure the system for one or more users, applications, and hardware devices.

Resilient File System (ReFS)   A file system designed as a "next-generation" file system for Windows.

RPM (Red Hat Package Manager)   The CentOS 7 manager that provides installation services for applications.

Samba   A communications protocol used by CentOS 7 to support resource sharing across a network.

Server Message Block (SMB)   A communications protocol used by Windows-based operating systems to support resource sharing across a network.

software components   A collection of applications that make up and relate to the operating system.

standard input device   A computer device used for data input, such as a keyboard.

standard output device   Another term for a computer monitor.

symmetric multiprocessing (SMP)   A system that distributes tasks among CPUs using a load-sharing method.

system-config-printer   In CentOS 7, an administration tool used to set up a printer.

System Monitor   A utility in CentOS 7 that lets you review process activity in real time.

Task Manager   An application used to track the progress of and provide necessary resources for separate tasks running on a Windows computer.

text editor   A program that allows a user to create or edit text files.

thread   The basic unit of program execution. A process can have several threads running concurrently, each performing a different job.

utility   A program that performs system-related tasks and maintenance on the operating system.

virtual address   A memory location that intervening hardware and software map to physical memory.

Windows Driver Model (WDM)   A 32-bit architecture for creating Windows device drivers.

YUM   An installation and configuration service that ships as part of CentOS 7.

Review Questions

1. Which of the following are considered an operating system kernel's job? (Choose all that apply.)

   a. making certain that the application is serviced properly

   b. managing all the resources in a computer system

   c. installing all hardware for a computer system

   d. securing the hardware

2. Which of the following management tasks are functions of an operating system? (Choose all that apply.)

   a. processing

   b. memory

   c. devices

   d. storage

   e. applications

3. The type and cat commands are used to _____.

   a. enter text into text files

   b. display the contents of a text file

   c. modify text files

   d. modify scripts

4. To edit the Windows Registry file, you need to use _____.

   a. Windows Regedit

   b. the CentOS 7 vim command

   c. a regular text editor

   d. Microsoft Word

5. To edit the configuration settings in text files within the /etc directory, a CentOS 7 system administrator would use _____.

   a. Notepad

   b. the Vim editor

   c. the cat command

   d. the type command

6. To view detailed system usage information in Windows 10, you would use _____.

   a. System Settings

   b. Windows Task Manager

   c. Windows Regedit

   d. the visudo command

7. Which of the following are considered applications? (Choose all that apply.)
   a. spreadsheet
   b. Web browser
   c. Internet
   d. word processor
   e. graphics software

8. The reason most people use computers is to _____.
   a. learn about operating systems
   b. repair them
   c. build additional computers at home
   d. use application software

9. How many consoles are installed with CentOS 7?
   a. 2
   b. 1
   c. 4
   d. 6

10. Which of the following tabs are displayed by the Task Manager? (Choose all that apply.)
    a. Processes
    b. Services
    c. Performance
    d. Networking

11. Which of the following are categories of drivers for Windows? (Choose all that apply.)
    a. bus drivers
    b. block drivers
    c. function drivers
    d. filter drivers
    e. network drivers

12. Which of the following are categories of devices for CentOS 7? (Choose all that apply.)
    a. function devices
    b. network devices
    c. bus devices
    d. character devices
    e. block devices

13. A _____ is an example of a CentOS 7 character device.

    a. keyboard

    b. DVD drive

    c. packet

    d. disk drive

14. A _____ is an example of a CentOS 7 block device.

    a. serial port

    b. disk drive

    c. packet

    d. keyboard

15. Which of the following are examples of Windows devices that are controlled by a bus driver? (Choose all that apply.)

    a. PCI

    b. USB

    c. SCSI

    d. keyboard

16. Microsoft Windows Installer _____.

    a. needs to be purchased separately

    b. needs to be installed by the user

    c. does not exist as of the printing of this text

    d. ships as part of the Microsoft Windows 10 operating system

17. The protocol used for file sharing in Windows 10 is _____.

    a. Samba

    b. Add Network Places

    c. the mount command

    d. SMB

18. To share files in CentOS 7, you need to use _____.

    a. the mount command

    b. Add Network Places

    c. SMB

    d. Samba

19. Which freeware application suite can be used in place of Microsoft Word and Microsoft Excel?

    a. Firefox

    b. AVG

    c. OpenOffice

    d. MetaPad

20. Which of the following are applications of LibreOffice? (Choose all that apply.)

    a. Word

    b. Calc

    c. Excel

    d. PowerPoint

    e. Impress

Case Projects

Case 2-1: Viewing the Performance of a PC

Your boss is concerned that several Windows 10 and CentOS 7 computers are running near capacity. What tools could help you gain additional insight into this problem? Create a short report for your boss that details how to obtain and interpret this information.

Case 2-2: Comparing Word-Processing Applications

You see an opportunity to save your company money by adopting the LibreOffice suite for the new PCs in the Engineering Department. Your boss is interested in your suggestion but wants to see a list of pros and cons of using the Microsoft Office system versus the LibreOffice suite. Prepare the list.

Case 2-3: Discussing the Functions of an Operating System

You have been selected to present a short talk on the functions of an operating system for the weekly tech meeting. To support your talk, you must prepare a handout for the attendees. The handout should include a summary outline of the information that you have learned about this topic.

Case 2-4: Discussing How Applications Interact with Operating Systems

You have been asked to prepare a short lecture for users in the Accounting Department. They have expressed interest in learning more about how the operating system supports the applications they use. Your boss would like to review your lecture notes prior to the class, so you need to save them to a document. Your notes should provide details of your lecture.

## chapter 3

Using the Graphical User Interface

After reading this chapter and completing the exercises, you will be able to:

- Describe the desktop
- Use the Start menu and Applications menu
- Tailor the desktop
- Access data on your computer

A graphical user interface (or GUI, sometimes pronounced *gooey*) is a method of interacting with a PC by manipulating visual elements such as icons and windows. Xerox developed the first GUI as the primary interface for its Alto computer in 1973, and most modern GUIs are derived from it. Besides icons and windows, a GUI consists of such graphical elements as menus, radio buttons, and check boxes, and employs a pointing device such as a mouse or trackball to manipulate these elements. Microsoft used many of these ideas in its first version of Windows.

One benefit of using GUIs is that they standardize how you use computer programs. In other words, once you become proficient with a GUI, you can pick up other GUI programs more quickly and reduce your learning curve.

In this chapter, you will learn about some key aspects of GUI interfaces. Specifically, you will learn about the Windows Start menu and the Applications menu in the GNOME desktop environment of CentOS 7. You will also learn how to tailor the desktop and how to access local and network data resources. Access to local resources is easy when you use a GUI.

Describing the Desktop

Like a physical desk, you use a computer desktop to store your electronic work equipment and give yourself easy access to current projects. The desktop is the main screen in Windows 10 and CentOS 7. In this section, you get an overview of the organization of the Windows 10 and CentOS 7 desktops.

The Windows 10 Desktop

It has been about 30 years since Microsoft launched the first version of Windows. With Windows 3, the first Windows OS to support multitasking, Microsoft garnered extensive support from the software development community. Windows 95 gave you the Start button, which would stick around for years to come. Microsoft called Windows 98 the first version of Windows designed specifically for consumers. Windows Millennium Edition (ME) was launched in September 2000; it was the last operating system released in the Windows 9x series and the last Windows edition based on MS-DOS. Windows XP, one of the most popular versions of Windows, ditched the plain gray color scheme for blues and greens. Windows 7 brought a more refined look and a trimmed-down user interface that remains today. Microsoft made an aggressive move with Windows 8; it had a new interface and a tiled Start screen, but it came with a steep learning curve that prompted a backlash from some users. Windows 8.1 was a free upgrade to Windows 8; enhancements included an improved Start screen and the restoration of a Start button on the taskbar. Windows 10 is the latest from the software giant, as shown in Figure 3-1.

The CentOS 7 Desktop

In Linux installations, unlike Windows 10, the GUI part of the installation is really just a "skin" for the underlying Linux operating system. Therefore, it is not as integral to the operating system as the GUI is to Windows 10. You can select from many different GUI desktop environments with CentOS 7, such as GNOME or KDE. GNOME (pronounced *guh-nome*) is a desktop environment that is composed entirely of free and open source software. GNOME is an acronym for *GNU Network Object Model Environment*. KDE is a common open source desktop environment provided on a number of Linux distributions. When configuring a Linux installation, you can select one of these desktop environments. The default CentOS 7 workstation installation comes with the GNOME 3.12 or GNOME 3.8 desktop environment, depending on which version of CentOS 7 is installed. Each desktop environment has a different look

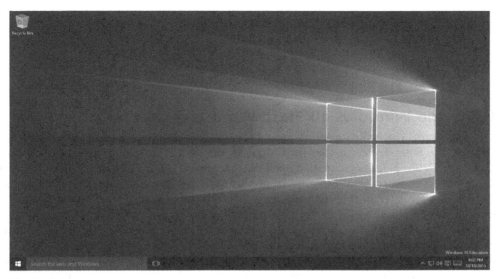

Figure 3-1 Windows 10 desktop

Source: Microsoft Windows 10

and feel and behaves differently. You will perform the activities in this book with the default CentOS 7.2 installation of GNOME 3.12. (See Figure 3-2.)

Figure 3-2 CentOS 7 desktop

Source: CentOS 7

Using the Start Menu and Applications Menu

The Windows **Start menu** and the **Applications menu** in CentOS 7 are launching pads for applications because both contain pointers to programs stored on the hard drive. These pointers are called **shortcuts**. In the following sections, you will learn to use and tailor these menus.

Using the Windows 10 Start Menu and Taskbar

You can access the most useful programs and documents on your Windows 10 computer by clicking the Start button in the lower-left corner of the screen to open the Start menu, as shown in Figure 3-3. (You can also open the Start menu by pressing the Windows key on your keyboard.) The Start menu has a list of applications on the left side and tiles on the right side. As you will see later in this chapter, you can customize much of the Start menu. The default installation of Windows 10 includes shortcuts for the most used applications, recently added applications, File Explorer, Settings, Power, and the All apps list on the left side of the Start menu. File Explorer gives you access to the file system and emphasizes commonly used files, like your documents. The Settings icon contains system settings that you can change to configure the operating system. Click Power if you want to shut down your computer, restart it, or put it in "sleep" mode. You can configure other options to appear. Clicking the All apps icon displays a list of shortcuts to all the applications installed on the system (see Figure 3-4). If a shortcut contains a right-facing arrow, you can click it to reveal a jump list. Jump lists frequently contain a list of recently used documents, tasks, or other items that are related to the application. The current user's name is displayed at the top of the menu. Click the username to change account settings, lock the screen, and sign out of the account.

The right side of the Start menu contains tiles that serve as shortcuts to applications; these tiles can be customized. Tiles, also known as *live tiles*, often display dynamic information even when the underlying application is not running.

Figure 3-3 Windows 10 Start menu

Source: Microsoft Windows 10

Figure 3-4 Windows 10 Start menu with all applications displayed

Source: Microsoft Windows 10

The taskbar at the bottom of the screen can also be used to run applications, and it contains an icon for each application pinned to it. Running applications are indicated on the taskbar as icons, but they are underlined to differentiate them from pinned applications. You can further distinguish an active window in the taskbar by placing your mouse cursor over its icon. Click a different icon on the taskbar to switch to another window.

Using CentOS 7

The CentOS 7 GNOME 3.0 main window features a "Top Bar" that helps you navigate and use the system (see Figure 3-5). The major difference between this bar and the Windows taskbar is the appearance of the program icons. By default, the bar appears at the top of the desktop.

The left side of the Top Bar displays menu options—for example, as CentOS 7 starts, two default menus are listed: the Applications and Places menus. The Applications menu is similar to the Windows Start menu in terms of the functions it generally provides. The Applications menu provides access to the applications installed on the system. When you install a new application, it is automatically added to the Applications menu. The Places menu provides a list of locations that open in File Browser windows when selected. This menu is similar to the File Explorer section of the Windows Start menu. The specific locations listed in the menu will be covered later in the chapter. Another menu is sometimes shown to the right of the Places menu; this optional menu indicates the active program on the screen and shows different options for the active program in the workspace.

By default, the right side of the Top Bar displays icons for sound, networking, the battery, the date and time, and the name of the current user. The bottom desktop bar in GNOME 3.0 has three elements. The left part of the bar is like the Windows taskbar. It lists all of the running programs on the system for the current workspace. The next section of the bar indicates which workspace you are working in (see Figure 3-6). The default installation of

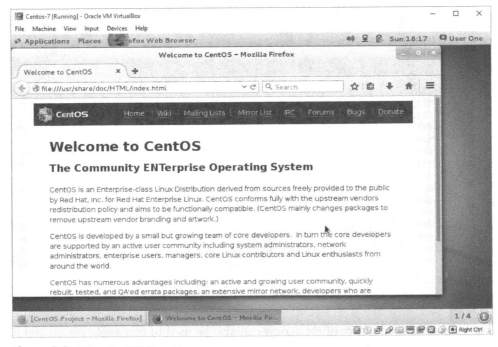

Figure 3-5 Using CentOS 7

Source: CentOS 7/Mozilla Firefox

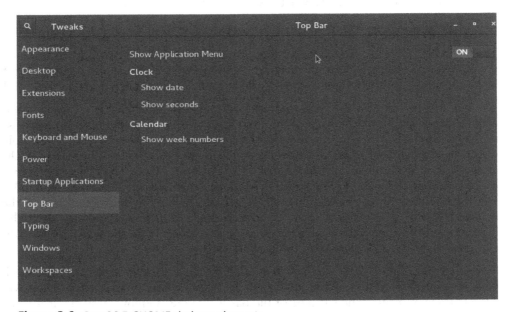

Figure 3-6 CentOS 7 GNOME desktop elements

Source: CentOS 7/GNOME

CentOS 7 has four workspaces you can switch between, but the number of workspaces is configurable. The right part of the bar lists any messages about the system.

GNOME 3.0 has an additional feature called the **Activities Overview**, which is accessible from the bottom of the Applications menu or by pressing the Windows key on the keyboard. The Activities Overview brings up an additional workspace that is like the Windows 10 Start menu. This workspace displays icons of favorite and running programs. You can open any of these programs by clicking their icons or dragging them to a specific workspace. The middle area of the window lists all currently running programs and the right side shows each of the different workspaces (see Figure 3-7). You can start a program from this workspace by typing its name and then selecting the icon when it is displayed.

Customizing Menus and Navigation Bars

This section explains how to customize the Start menu and taskbar in Windows 10. It also explains how to customize the Applications menu and desktop environment of CentOS 7.

Windows 10 Start Menu Views As you saw in Figure 3-3, the default Start menu appears when you start Windows 10 for the first time.

Illustrations of the Start menu in this chapter may look slightly different from the default Start menu on your computer. These small discrepancies occur because all live tiles were turned off for illustration purposes.

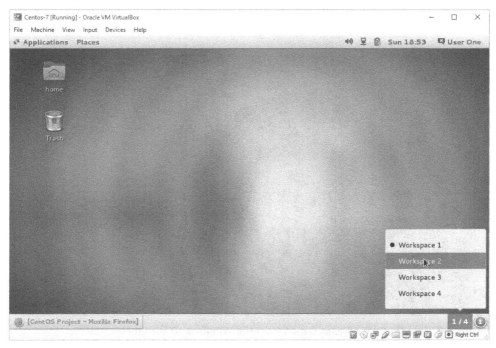

Figure 3-7 CentOS 7 GNOME workspaces

Source: CentOS 7/GNOME

To see additional programs on the Start menu, click All apps. Figure 3-8 shows that an alphabetized list of applications has replaced the default menu items. Groups appear on the list and can be expanded to display all items in them when you click the chevron that appears to the right of a group. For example, Figure 3-8 shows Windows Accessories as an unexpanded group with a chevron (a downward-facing arrow) and Windows PowerShell as an expanded group with a caret (an upward-facing arrow). Click the Back option at the bottom of the menu to close the All apps menu and return to the default menu.

The Get Started option, which appears initially at the top of the Start menu (see Figure 3-3), starts an application that contains information about features of the operating system, including videos on various topics like customizing the Start menu.

Customizing the Start Menu Applications on the left side of the Start menu can be added as tiles on the right side if you right-click an application and click Pin to Start on the context menu. Figure 3-8 shows the context menu with the Pin to Start option after Windows PowerShell was right-clicked. To remove a tile from the Start menu, right-click it and select Unpin from Start. The same tile context menu also contains options to resize tiles, turn live tiles on or off, and pin or unpin from the taskbar.

Context menus are also known as *popup menus* because they appear or "pop up" on the item you click. They provide a menu based on the context of the currently selected item. For instance, if a tile is already pinned, the context menu will contain an unpin option.

Complete Activity 3-1 to use some of the customization options available in the Windows 10 Start menu.

Figure 3-8 Selecting the All apps option from the Windows 10 Start menu

Source: Microsoft Windows 10

Activity 3-1: Customizing the Windows 10 Default Start Menu

Time Required: 10 minutes

Objective: Customize the Start menu.

Description: In this activity, you change the default Start menu to personalize your display of applications. This activity is useful if you want to control the display options on the Start menu.

1. If necessary, start your virtual machines using the appropriate instructions in Activity 1-1.
2. To display options for personalizing the Start menu, click the **Start** button, click **Settings**, click **Personalization**, and then click **Start** (see Figure 3-9).
3. Click the **Show most used apps** toggle switch to set it to **Off**.
4. Click the **Show recently added apps** toggle switch to set it to **Off**.
5. Click **Choose which folders appear on Start**, click the **Documents** toggle to **On**, click the **Personal Folder** toggle to **On**, and then click the **X** to close the Settings window.
6. Click **Start** to open the Start menu. Notice that the most commonly used and most recently used applications are not displayed. Notice that the Documents and Personal Folder shortcuts are displayed.

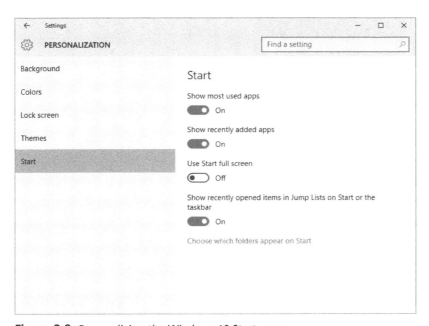

Figure 3-9 Personalizing the Windows 10 Start menu

Source: Microsoft Windows 10/Settings

7. Click **Start,** click **All Apps,** and then click the letter **A** near the top of the menu just above *Alarms & Clock*. A list of menu divisions appears, separated by the letters of the alphabet. Click the letter **W** to move to that part of the menu, and then click **Windows Accessories** to expand that group. Right-click **Notepad,** and then click **Pin to Start.** Notepad appears as a tile on the right side of the Start menu.

8. Click **Start,** right-click the **Notepad** tile, hover over **Resize,** and click **Small.**

9. Click **Start,** and then click the group area **Play and explore.** Notice that the group title is now editable. Click the blank group area above the Notepad tile, type **Accessories** as a group title, and then press **Enter.**

10. Leave the virtual machines on for the next activity.

Customizing the GNOME Applications Menu You access most of the installed programs in CentOS 7 by clicking the Applications menu on the Top Bar. The resulting menu displays folders on the left side; the right side displays program shortcuts found under each of the folders. By default, the Applications menu displays the Favorites folder and program shortcuts associated with it. The default installation of the GNOME desktop lists five program shortcuts under the Favorites folder: Firefox Web Browser, Files, Application Installer, Help, and Terminal (see Figure 3-10).

Click Activities Overview in the lower-left corner of the screen to display a new window you can customize to meet your needs.

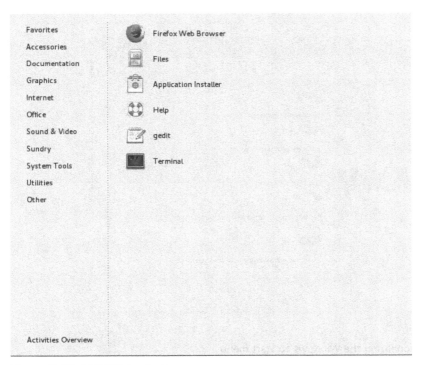

Figure 3-10 GNOME Applications menu

Source: Red Hat CentOS 7/GNOME

Activity 3-2: Customizing the Activities Overview in GNOME

Time Required: 10 minutes

Objective: Customize the Activities Overview.

Description: In this activity, you customize the default Activities Overview to add a new program icon and then launch the program in a new workspace.

1. If necessary, start your virtual machine for CentOS 7 using the appropriate instructions from Activity 1-1.

2. To display the Activities Overview, click the **Applications** menu, and then click **Activities Overview**.

3. Look for the area in the middle of the screen that contains a magnifying glass. Type **gedit** over "Type to search."

4. An icon for the gedit program is displayed. Click the icon and move it to the dash. Notice that the dash disappears when you type in the search bar, but it reappears when you start moving the icon.

5. Verify that the **gedit** icon is displayed in the icon dash.

6. To start gedit, click and hold the icon and then drop it into Workspace 2. The program starts in Workspace 2.

7. Leave the virtual machines on for the next activity.

Using the Taskbar in Windows 10
By default, the taskbar appears at the bottom of the Windows screen, but it can be customized to appear at any edge of the screen. The taskbar is a key element in using the Windows 10 interface.

From left to right, the taskbar contains the following functions:

- Start menu—This menu is discussed earlier in the chapter.
- Search box—Allows you to search for local applications, settings, Windows Store applications, and online results.
- Task view—Displays and allows switching between open application windows and different desktops.
- App icons—Displays pinned and running applications.
- Notification area—Displays icons for the clock, volume, network, Action Center, and other system or application settings.
- Show Desktop button—Minimizes all open windows so you can view the desktop.

Auto-Hiding the Taskbar Windows 10 includes a feature that can make the taskbar disappear when you are not using it, which permits you to have the entire desktop available as a maximized application window. To turn on this feature, right-click a blank area of the taskbar, click Properties, and then click the "Auto-hide the taskbar" check box, as shown in Figure 3-11. To view the hidden taskbar, move the mouse pointer to the thin line at the edge of the screen.

Figure 3-11 Windows 10 taskbar properties

Source: Microsoft Windows 10/Taskbar

Moving and Resizing the Taskbar You can increase the size of the taskbar and change its location on the screen. To increase its size, position the mouse pointer over the taskbar's outer edge and drag the pointer. To move the taskbar, click an empty area in it and drag it to the desired location. You will move and resize the taskbar in Activity 3-3.

If you cannot resize or move the taskbar, it might be locked to prevent changes. If so, right-click an empty area of the taskbar and clear the Lock the taskbar check mark.

Changing the size of the icons on the taskbar also alters its size. To do this, right-click the taskbar, click Properties, and click the "Use small taskbar buttons" check box.

Task View You can use the Task view to switch between application windows or desktops. This option is enabled on the taskbar by default. It can be hidden by right-clicking the taskbar and clicking the Show Task View button option to remove the check mark. You can also use the Task view from the keyboard with the Windows+Tab key combination. You can add and access new desktops from the Task view. You can switch between applications on a desktop or even migrate running applications to a different desktop.

Using Toolbars on the Taskbar You can add special toolbars for Web addresses, links, and desktop options to the taskbar if you right-click it and select Toolbars. For example, the Links toolbar holds links to your favorite Web sites. You can also drag any icon to this toolbar, including those for files, folders, drives, and programs, to turn them into one-click buttons. These icons are only shortcuts; you can delete them, rename them, and move them around on the toolbar.

Here are a few possibilities you might consider for toolbar shortcuts:

- Three or four of the programs you use the most
- Documents you use each day
- Folders that you frequently access for files

The Desktop toolbar provides access to the icons on your desktop; this option is convenient if you need to access an icon while a program occupies the entire desktop. The toolbar also provides access to other frequently used items, such as your personal folder, Libraries, Network folders, and the Control Panel (see Figure 3-12).

Grouping Programs on the Taskbar The taskbar can become crowded with buttons when you work with multiple instances of a given program at the same time, so Windows provides a grouping feature to help you manage multiple open documents. As shown in Figure 3-13, all documents opened with a particular program are combined into one button.

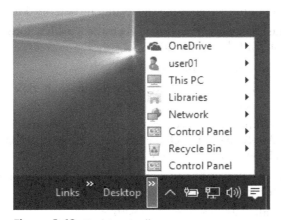

Figure 3-12 Desktop toolbar

Source: Microsoft Windows 10

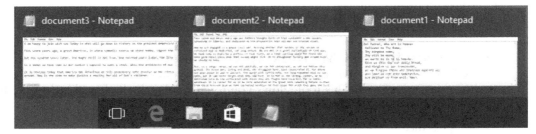

Figure 3-13 Grouping programs on the taskbar

Source: Microsoft Windows 10/Notepad

In addition to the default taskbar behavior (Always combine, hide labels), you have two other choices for the behavior of taskbar buttons: Combine when the taskbar is full, or Never combine. To access these options, right-click an empty area of the taskbar, click Properties, and then click the Taskbar buttons list box.

Activity 3-3: Working with the Windows 10 Taskbar

Time Required: 10 minutes

Objective: Manipulate the taskbar in Windows 10.

Description: In this activity, you work with the taskbar on the Windows 10 desktop. This activity is useful if you want to move or resize the taskbar or pin applications to it.

1. If necessary, start your virtual machines using the appropriate instructions in Activity 1-1.

2. Right-click an empty area of the taskbar and uncheck the **Lock the taskbar** option, if necessary.

3. Position the mouse pointer over an empty area of the taskbar, and then click and drag it to another location. You can move the taskbar to the top of the screen or to its left or right edge.

4. Move the taskbar back to the bottom of the screen using the technique described in Step 3.

5. Right-click an empty area of the taskbar, click **Properties**, click the **Taskbar location on screen** chevron, click **Left** in the list, and then click **OK**.

6. Repeat Step 5 to select the Right, Top, and Bottom locations.

7. Grab the edge of the taskbar with the mouse and stretch it to make it taller. Next, shrink the taskbar back to its original size.

8. Right-click an empty area of the taskbar, click **Properties**, click the **Use small taskbar buttons** check box, and then click **Apply**. Note the change in the taskbar icons. Uncheck the **Use small taskbar buttons** check box, and then click **OK**.

9. To pin the Calculator application to the taskbar, click **Start**, type **Calculator** in the search box, right-click the Calculator icon, and select **Pin to taskbar**.

10. To open the Calculator, click the **Calculator** icon on the taskbar.

11. To unpin the Calculator from the taskbar, right-click the **Calculator** icon, and select **Unpin this program from taskbar**.

12. Close all open windows.

13. Leave the virtual machine logged on for the next activity.

Customizing the GNOME Desktop Environment in CentOS 7
To customize your GNOME desktop environment, you use a special tool called the *GNOME Tweak tool*, as shown in Figure 3-14. This tool allows you to customize the look and feel of the following areas in the GNOME desktop environment:

- Appearance
- Desktop

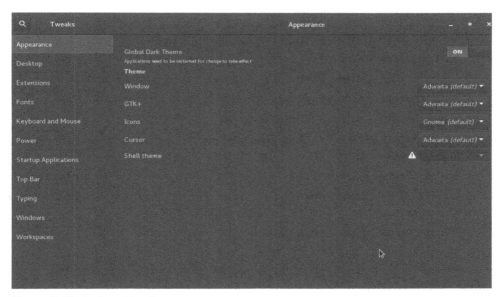

Figure 3-14 GNOME Tweaks menu

Source: Red Hat CentOS 7/GNOME

- Extensions
- Fonts
- Keyboard and Mouse
- Power
- Startup Applications
- Top Bar
- Typing
- Windows
- Workspaces

Activity 3-4: Working with the GNOME Tweak Tool

Time Required: 10 minutes

Objective: Manipulate the GNOME desktop environment with the Tweak tool.

Description: In this activity, you will work with the GNOME Tweak tool to change the overall appearance of GNOME. This activity is useful in customizing how GNOME looks and feels.

1. If necessary, start your virtual machines using the appropriate instructions in Activity 1-1.

2. Click the **Applications** menu, select **Utilities,** and then select **Tweak Tool.**

3. In the left column, click **Shell**.

4. Check the **Show Date** box.

5. Check the **Show seconds** box.

6. In the left column, click **Theme**.

7. Change the Current theme setting to **Bright** in the drop-down list.

8. Change the GTK+ setting to **HighContrast**.

9. Change the Icons setting to **HighContrast**. Notice that the screen changes to black and white and high-contrast colors.

10. Click the **Tweak Tool** menu in the Top Bar, and then click **Reset to Defaults**.

11. Click **OK** to confirm your selection. Notice that the date, seconds, and colors revert to their original settings.

12. Leave the virtual machine logged on for the next activity.

Tailoring the Desktop

Like a physical desk, you use a computer desktop to store your electronic work equipment and give yourself easy access to current projects. The desktop is the main screen in Windows 10 and CentOS 7; you can put icons on both screens to serve as shortcuts to important programs. The following sections explain how to tailor the Windows 10 and CentOS 7 desktops. First, however, you will learn about some Windows 10 desktop features.

Using the Windows 10 Desktop Features

Snap, a desktop feature that has been available since Windows 7, is a quick and fun way to resize open windows simply by dragging them to the edges of your screen. Depending on where you drag a window, you can make it expand vertically, take up the entire screen, or appear side by side with another window. Snap makes it easy to read, organize, and compare windows.

Windows 10 also has a new notification feature called *Action Center*, which you access by clicking the "speech bubble" icon just left of the time and date on the right side of the taskbar. Notifications from the system or from applications appear in Action Center and are also stored in case you missed them. Action Center also contains actions at the bottom that you can use to quickly change system settings, like enabling or disabling Wi-Fi, Bluetooth, or Airplane mode.

Two additional features are Peek and Shake. Peek appears to give you the power of X-ray vision—you can peer past all your open windows and peek at the Windows desktop. Simply click or point to the Show desktop button, a small vertical bar just right of the time and date in the far right corner of the taskbar. Any open windows fade from view, revealing the desktop. To make the windows reappear, move the mouse away from the Show desktop button or click it again.

The Shake feature lets you cut through a cluttered desktop and quickly focus on a single window. Just click the desired window's title bar and give your mouse a shake; every open window except the selected one instantly disappears. Jiggle the mouse again, and the other windows reappear. See Activity 3-5 for more information on the Peek and Shake features.

Tailoring the Windows 10 Desktop

If you have difficulty reading text on the screen, you can customize the display fonts. In the following sections, you will learn to customize the desktop display fonts, choose the appearance of desktop icons, and set the display resolution—the total number of pixels displayed horizontally and vertically.

Increasing the Size of Windows Text Fonts
If the text on your screen is too small for easy reading, you can increase the size of the fonts used in Windows menus, headings, and icon labels. Click Start, click Settings, click System, click Display, and then drag the slider for "Change the size of text, apps, and other items" to select the desired size (see Figure 3-15).

Choosing the Appearance of Desktop Icons
With prolonged activity in Windows, the desktop can become cluttered. Windows 10 offers a number of ways to manage desktop clutter. To keep your desktop neat, consider the following options:

- Icon size—Choose from Large, Medium, or Small.
- Auto arrange icons—All icons are aligned in an invisible grid and arranged in a set manner.

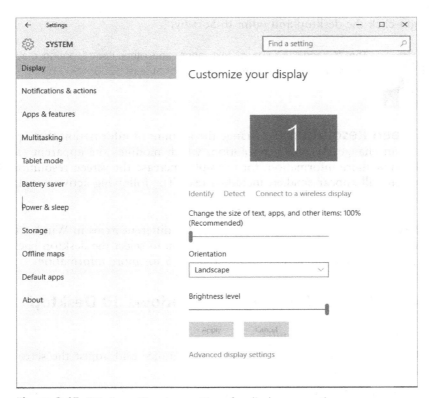

Figure 3-15 Windows 10 system settings for display properties

Source: Microsoft Windows 10/System

- Align icons to grid—All icons jump to the invisible grid.
- Show desktop icons—Hide or display desktop icons. For example, you should consider hiding desktop icons when using your laptop for a presentation.

To access these options, right-click the desktop and point to View. The choices are shown in Figure 3-16.

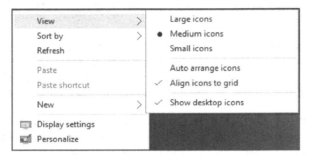

Figure 3-16 Desktop menu

Source: Microsoft Windows 10

Desktop icons can also be sorted by name, size, item type, or date modified. To access sorting options, right-click the desktop and point to Sort by.

 The "Change the size of text, apps, and other items" option may be disabled if your screen resolution is not at least 1200 × 900 pixels.

Changing Screen Resolution To change the amount of information that appears on the screen, you can change the screen resolution, which modifies the apparent size of the screen fonts. To view more information, for example, increase the screen resolution. Everything on the screen will appear smaller, including text. The following activity explains how to adjust the screen resolution.

Personalization You can change the appearance of different items in Windows by configuring personalization options. These settings allow you to select the desktop background, colors, themes, and other customizations. See Activity 3-5 for more information.

 ## Activity 3-5: Tailoring the Windows 10 Desktop

Time Required: 10 minutes

Objective: Customize the desktop's appearance and adjust the screen resolution in Windows 10.

Description: In this activity, you change the desktop background, the accent color, and the screen resolution. This activity is useful if you want to customize your screen display.

1. If necessary, start your virtual machines using the appropriate instructions in Activity 1-1.

2. To change the background, right-click the desktop and click **Personalize**. Under the Background settings, click the drop-down box under the **Background** label and select **Solid color**. Under the **Background colors** label, click a color box to select a color.

3. To change the accent color, click **Colors** on the left side of the Personalization Settings screen, and then click one of the colors under **Choose your accent color**. Look at the preview or click the **Start** button to see the color changes.

4. To change the theme, click **Themes** on the left side of the Personalization Settings screen, and then click **Theme settings**. When the personalization window opens, click the **Windows 10** theme under Windows Default Themes.

5. Close all windows.

6. To change the screen resolution, right-click an empty area on the desktop, click **Display Settings**, click **Advanced display settings**, note the resolution displayed, click the **Resolution** drop-down box, click 800 × 600, click **Apply**, and then click **Keep Changes**.

 Changing to a lower screen resolution might mean that some items will no longer fit on the screen.

7. Repeat Step 6 to change the screen resolution back to the original setting.

8. To enable the Peek feature, right-click an empty space on the taskbar, click **Properties**, click **Use Peek to preview the desktop**, and then click **OK**.

9. To open an application on the Windows desktop, type **Notepad** over "Search the web and Windows" and then click **Notepad** in the menu. Repeat this step to open **WordPad**.

10. To peek at the desktop, point to the **Show desktop** button.

11. To minimize the Notepad window, click the WordPad window and shake the mouse.

12. To return to the Notepad window, click the WordPad window and shake the mouse.

13. Close all the open windows.

14. Leave the virtual machine logged on for future activities.

Tailoring the CentOS 7 Desktop

The CentOS 7 desktop can be customized in several ways. To change the background of the desktop, you can use the Tweak tool, as you saw earlier, or you can right-click the desktop and select Change Desktop Background from the **desktop context menu** that appears. To create new folders on the desktop, right-click the desktop and select New Folder, as shown in Figure 3-17. An Untitled folder appears on the desktop; name the folder as needed. You can also create a folder by opening a Terminal window, changing the directory to /home/user1/desktop, and then creating a new directory in this directory, which will show up on the desktop. Any short-cuts, files, or folders you put in the desktop directory will also appear on the desktop.

Fonts, icons, and window size are all configurable with the GNOME Tweak tool. Windows can be made to stretch or be centered; fonts can be changed to any font installed on the system and to any size.

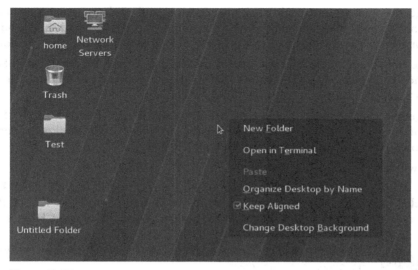

Figure 3-17 Customizing the CentOS desktop

Source: Red Hat CentOS 7/GNOME

Activity 3-6: Modifying the CentOS 7 Desktop

Time Required: 10 minutes

Objective: Modify the desktop using the desktop context menu in CentOS 7.

Description: In this activity, you open the desktop context menu, select Change Desktop Background, and modify the desktop. This activity is useful if you want to modify the appearance of the CentOS 7 desktop.

1. If necessary, start your virtual machines using the appropriate instructions in Activity 1-1.
2. To open the context menu on the desktop, right-click an empty area of the desktop.
3. To open the window that allows you to make changes to the desktop, click **Change Desktop Background**.
4. To select a new background for the desktop, click the **Background** icon.
5. Scroll through the background selections. Click the backgrounds you might like and observe the sample display.
6. To apply the selected background, click the background thumbnail and then click **Select**. Close the Settings window.
7. To change fonts and font sizes, click the **Applications menu**, click **Utilities,** and then click **Tweak Tool**.
8. Click **Fonts** in the left column.
9. Select a different font for the Windows Title, and increase the font size to 15. Then, click the **Select** button. Notice the changed appearance of the Windows Title.
10. Select a different font for the Default font, and increase the font size to 15. Click the **Select** button, and notice the changed appearance of fonts in the Tweak tool.

11. Close the Tweak tool window.

12. Leave CentOS 7 logged on for the next activity.

Changing Display Settings The Display Settings window contains various options for customizing your display, including screen resolution, color depth, and monitor type. When you select the monitor type, the available screen resolutions are constrained by the monitor's actual resolution and color depth. To open the Display Settings window, click the Applications menu, click Settings, and then click Displays. Changes to the display settings require you to log out and log on again.

Activity 3-7: Modifying the CentOS 7 Display Settings

Time Required: 10 minutes

Objective: Modify the screen resolution using the Display Settings window in CentOS 7.

Description: In this activity, you open the Display Settings window to change the resolution. This activity is useful if you want to modify the appearance of the CentOS 7 display.

1. If necessary, start your virtual machines using the appropriate instructions in Activity 1-1.

2. Click the **Applications** menu, click **System Tools**, click **Settings**, and then click **Displays**.

3. To change the screen resolution for the desktop, click the **Resolution** drop-down menu.

4. Click **800 × 600**, and then click **Apply**.

5. If your computer supports the 800 × 600 setting, accept it; if not, revert to the old setting.

6. To log out, click **User01** on the left side of the Top Bar. In the drop-down menu, select **Log Out** twice.

7. Log on to CentOS 7 by clicking **User01** and entering a password of **Pa$$w0rd**.

8. Click the **Applications** menu, click **Settings**, and then click **Displays**.

9. To select a monitor type, click the **available display icon** button, select **Generic LCD Display**, click **LCD Panel 1024 × 768**, click **Select**, and then click **OK**.

To prevent damage to the monitor, you need to select a monitor type after the resolution is reduced.

10. Read the displayed message and then click **OK**.

11. Log out by clicking **User01** on the Top Bar and then selecting **Log Out**.

12. Log on to CentOS 7 with a password of **Pa$$w0rd**.

13. Leave CentOS 7 logged on for the next activity.

Accessing Data on Your Computer

Using GUI tools, you can access the hierarchical structure of files, directories, and drives on your computer. In the following section, you will learn about the file access tools in Windows File Explorer. You will also learn to use File Browser in CentOS 7 to access local data on your computer.

Using Windows File Explorer

Windows File Explorer (see Figure 3-18) is a utility in Windows that enables you to locate and open files and folders. You can open it by clicking File Explorer on the Start menu. If you are familiar with previous versions of Windows, you may remember the Computer icon on the desktop or the Start menu that also ran Explorer. You can use this version of File Explorer in Windows 10 by clicking Start, All apps, Windows System, and then This PC.

This section explains how to use Windows File Explorer. You will work with File Explorer in Activity 3-8.

 Your computer might have fewer drives than those shown in Figure 3-18, or it might have slight differences in customization.

The functions of the address bar are summarized in Figure 3-18; the contents list requires further explanation. This list shows the file path to the current folder. For example, Figure 3-19 shows the contents list to the photos in the Saved Pictures folder. The path to this folder is indicated by > symbols, which are actually pop-up menus. Point to the symbol to see the contents of the associated folder; you can point to the symbol for any folder in the path.

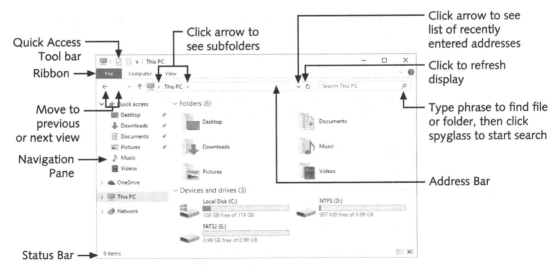

Figure 3-18 Windows File Explorer

Source: Microsoft Windows 10/File Explorer

Figure 3-19 Windows File Explorer list to Saved Pictures folder

Source: Microsoft Windows 10/File Explorer

These symbols are a type of **breadcrumb**—navigation aids used in an address bar and other parts of the GUI to help keep track of your locations. The term comes from the trail of crumbs left by Hansel and Gretel in the classic fairy tale.

The Quick Access toolbar contains buttons you can use to examine file properties or create new folders. The toolbar can also be customized to have Undo, Redo, Delete, and Rename buttons, and to be shown above or below the Ribbon.

The Ribbon in Windows File Explorer contains many functions and settings and is similar to the Ribbon in Microsoft Office. The Ribbon is context sensitive, meaning that it displays options that apply to the current selection. In Figure 3-20, for example, a text document is selected, and the Home, Share, and View tabs are displayed at the top of the Ribbon. Each tab contains items grouped by function and organized into panels. The Home tab in Figure 3-20 displays the Clipboard, Organize, New, Open, and Select panels. Each panel contains a set of related items. In Figure 3-20, the Clipboard panel displays Copy, Paste, Cut, Copy path, and Paste shortcut function buttons.

The preview pane can be shown on the right side of the File Explorer window. As you click common types of files, they are previewed in this pane. For example, click a graphics file to display a scaled-down version of the image within the preview pane. Click a text file to display the text in the preview pane. To enable or disable this preview, click the View tab on the Ribbon and then click the Preview pane button to toggle it on or off.

The navigation pane appears on the left side of the File Explorer window, as shown in Figure 3-18. If you have used a previous version of Windows, you should be familiar with the navigation pane. In Windows 10, it works like a master map to the files and folders on your computer or on the network.

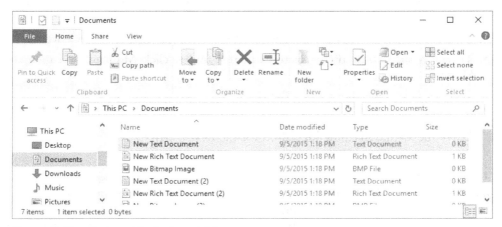

Figure 3-20 Windows File Explorer Ribbon

Source: Microsoft Windows 10/File Explorer

Activity 3-8: Using Windows File Explorer

Time Required: 10 minutes

Objective: Use the tools in Windows File Explorer.

Description: In this activity, you will use Windows File Explorer. This activity is useful if you want to locate and view information about files and folders.

1. If necessary, start your virtual machines using the appropriate instructions in Activity 1-1.
2. To create some files to work with, click **Start**, type **Paint** in the search box, and press the **Enter** key.
3. Click and drag the mouse within the Paint application to create a happy face or other drawing.
4. To save the drawing, click **File**, click **Save**, type **happy**, and click **Save**.
5. Modify your drawing by clicking and dragging.
6. To save the changes to your drawing as a different file, click **File**, click **Save As**, type **joyful**, and then click **Save**. Close Paint.
7. To view the picture files, click **Start** and then click **File Explorer**.
8. To display the contents of the C: drive, expand **Local Disk (C:)** in the navigation pane on the left side of the window.
9. To navigate to the Pictures folder, double-click **Users**, double-click **user01**, and then double-click **Pictures**. Notice how the breadcrumbs change in the address bar.
10. To add a preview pane to the layout, click **View** on the Ribbon, and then click **Preview pane**.
11. Click the picture icon of your choice. Notice the preview in the preview pane.
12. To add a details pane to the layout, click **View** on the Ribbon, and then click **Details pane**. Notice the information that appears for the selected icon.
13. To view the File Properties window for the selected icon, click **Properties** on the Quick Access toolbar. Note the creation date and other properties.
14. To close the File Properties window without making changes, click **Cancel**.
15. To run a slide show of the pictures in this folder, click **Manage**, and then click **Slide Show**.
16. To cancel the slide show, press **Esc**.
17. Close the open windows in the virtual machine.
18. Leave the virtual machine logged on for the next activity.

Files in CentOS 7

One of the major differences between the Windows and Linux operating systems is the way the file systems work. The highest level of the Linux file system is called *root*. All other directories branch off the root directory like a tree. It is important to understand how a Linux file system works at a basic level and that a visual representation of the file

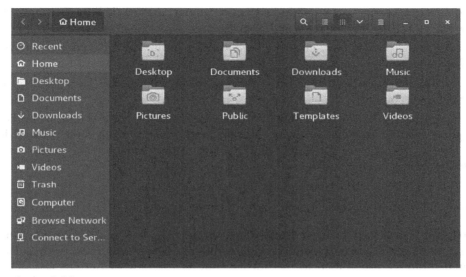

Figure 3-21 GNOME Files menu

Source: Red Hat CentOS 7/GNOME

system is displayed in the **Files** program. You can open this program by selecting the Applications menu, then Favorites, and then Files. The program starts in your home directory, as shown in Figure 3-21.

You can change the way files and folders are displayed by selecting different options. Click the button that contains three rows of dots and a line to display all the files and folders in a list format with different column options. Click the button with nine dots to display the files and folders as a grid of icons. The arrow-down button brings up a menu that changes depending on which type of display is chosen; the menu allows you to further customize your display of files and folders. The last button, which contains three lines, brings up a menu for manipulating files, folders, and searches.

Activity 3-9: Using CentOS 7 Files

Time Required: 10 minutes

Objective: Use CentOS 7 to navigate the file system.

Description: In this activity, you will use files in CentOS 7. This activity is useful if you want to locate and view information about files and folders.

1. If necessary, start your virtual machines using the appropriate instructions in Activity 1-1.
2. To create some files to work with, click the **Applications** menu, click **Graphics,** and then click **LibreOffice Draw**.
3. Add some more scribbles to the file.
4. To save the drawing, click **File,** click **Save As,** type **happy,** and then click **Save**.
5. Modify your drawing by clicking and dragging.

6. To save the changes to your drawing as a different file, click **File**, click **Save As**, type **joyful**, and then click **Save**. Close LibreOffice Draw.

7. To view the picture files, click the **Applications** menu, click **Favorites**, and then click **Files**.

8. Click **Documents** either in the left column or in the window on the right to see the two documents you created.

9. Change the layout of the window by toggling between the two file buttons in the upper-right corner. To display file details, click the button that contains three rows of dots and a line. To display icons for files, click the button that contains nine dots. Observe the differences between using the two options.

10. Close the open windows in the virtual machine.

11. Leave the virtual machine logged on for the next activity.

Using the Personal Folder in Windows 10 The Personal folder contains many user subfolders, including Documents, Downloads, Music, Pictures, and Videos. The Personal folder can be added to the Start menu, as you saw in Activity 3-1. The documents you create or save are stored by default in your own Documents folder, separate from other users who might also save files on the computer. As you use Windows applications, you should store all your files in the Documents folder and associated subfolders. User accounts individualize Windows 10 for each person who shares a computer or network server; your Documents folder is tied to your account. You need administrator privileges to access the Documents folders of other users. Music, pictures, and videos may be stored in the subfolders of the same names within your personal folder.

Home Directory in CentOS 7 The home directory in Linux is owned by the user. Figure 3-22 shows the folders that are loaded by default in the home directory of CentOS 7: Desktop, Documents, Downloads, Music, Pictures, Public, Templates, and Videos. Any files or folders put in the Desktop folder will be displayed on the desktop. The Documents folder is the default location for saving documents created by most programs. The Downloads folder is the default location of any file downloaded to the computer, either from e-mail or the Web. The Music, Pictures, and Videos folders are self-explanatory. The last two folders are used for sharing files and creating templates for reuse.

Using the Recycle Bin in Windows The Recycle Bin gives you a second chance to retrieve deleted files or folders and restore them to their original location on the hard drive. You access the Recycle Bin (see Figure 3-23) by clicking its icon on the desktop. As the Recycle Bin fills with material you have deleted, older items are removed automatically to make room for newer items. More recently deleted items remain available until you decide to delete them permanently by emptying the Recycle Bin. If you are running low on hard drive space, you should empty the Recycle Bin.

Some files might be too large to delete using the Recycle Bin; you must delete such files immediately. To do this, right-click the filename, hold down the Shift key, click Delete, and then click Yes. By default, the Recycle Bin can only hold 10 percent of the hard drive's capacity.

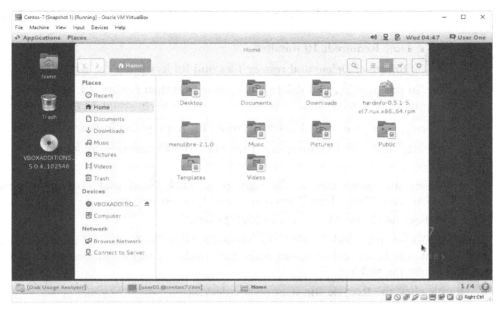

Figure 3-22 GNOME home directory

Source: Red Hat CentOS 7/GNOME

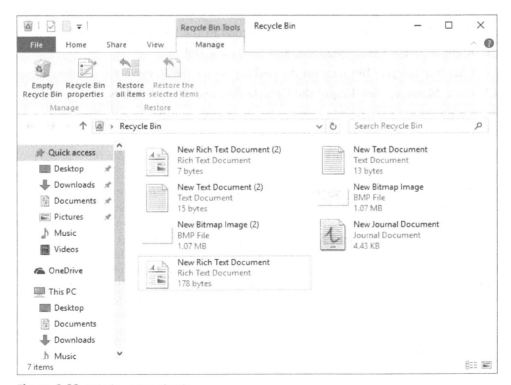

Figure 3-23 Windows Recycle Bin

Source: Microsoft Windows 10/File Explorer

Activity 3-10: Managing the Recycle Bin in Windows

Time Required: 10 minutes

Objective: Delete and restore files and folders using the Recycle Bin.

Description: In this activity, you delete a document and then restore it from the Recycle Bin. Next, you empty the Recycle Bin. This activity is useful if you want to recover deleted files.

1. If necessary, start your virtual machines using the appropriate instructions in Activity 1-1.

2. Click **Start**, click **File Explorer**, and then click the **Documents** folder in the navigation pane.

3. Right-click an empty area in the right pane, click **New**, click **Text Document**, type **Delete Me** over "New Text Document," and then press **Enter**.

4. Right-click the **Delete Me** icon, and click **Delete**.

5. In the Documents window, click the **Minimize** button—the first of the three buttons on the right side of the title bar—to make the window temporarily disappear and become an icon on the taskbar.

6. Double-click the **Recycle Bin** icon on the desktop.

7. Right-click the **Delete Me** icon, and then click **Restore**.

8. Click the **Minimize** button in the Recycle Bin window.

9. Click the **File Explorer** icon on the taskbar to see the Documents window again.

10. Verify that the **Delete Me** icon has returned to the **Documents** folder.

11. Right-click the **Delete Me** icon, and then click **Delete**.

12. Click the **Recycle Bin** icon on the desktop to see the Recycle Bin window again.

13. Click **Manage**, click **Empty the Recycle Bin**, and then click **Yes**.

14. Verify that the **Delete Me** icon no longer appears in the Recycle Bin folder.

15. Close any open windows in the virtual machine.

16. Leave the virtual machine logged on for the next activity.

Using the Trash in CentOS 7 The **Trash** option in CentOS 7 gives you a second chance to retrieve deleted files or folders and restore them to their original location on the hard drive. There are two different ways to access the Trash. One is to click the trash can icon on the desktop, which opens the Files program. The other option is to open the Files program from the Applications menu; in the left column, double-click the Trash icon (see Figure 3-24). Any files or folders displayed here have been deleted. These files or folders can be restored by highlighting them and clicking the restore button. If you are running low on hard drive space, you should empty the trash to remove deleted items.

Items that you delete from external drives or network drives are deleted permanently and are not sent to the Trash.

Figure 3-24 Using the Trash in CentOS 7

Source: Red Hat CentOS 7/GNOME

Activity 3-11: Managing the Trash in CentOS 7

Time Required: 10 minutes

Objective: Delete and restore files and folders using the Trash.

Description: In this activity, you delete a document and then restore it from the Trash. Next, you empty the Trash. This activity is useful if you want to recover deleted files.

1. If necessary, start your virtual machines using the appropriate instructions in Activity 1-1.
2. Click the **Applications** menu, click **Files**, and then double-click **Documents**.
3. Right-click an empty area in the right pane and select **Open in Terminal**.
4. At the command prompt, type **vi Delete**.
5. Within vi, type **: wq!** to close and save the file.
6. A new file named Delete appears in the vi editor. Click the **Delete** icon to highlight it and then press the **Delete** key on the keyboard.
7. Click the **Trash** icon in the left column of the **Files** program.
8. Highlight the **Delete** icon, and then click the **Restore** button. The file should disappear from the Trash window.
9. Click the **Documents** icon in the left column. Verify that the **Delete** icon has returned to the Documents folder.
10. Highlight the **Delete** icon again, and then click the **Delete** key on the keyboard.
11. Click the **Trash** icon in the left column.
12. Click the **Empty** button, and then click the **Empty Trash** button. Verify that the **Delete** icon no longer appears in the Trash folder.

13. Close any open windows in the virtual machine.

14. Leave the virtual machine logged on for the next activity.

Searching from the Start Menu   You can use the Windows 10 Search feature when you need to locate a file or folder. For example, you can use it when:

- You are looking for common file types.
- You remember all or part of a filename.
- You know when you last changed a file.
- You know a word or phrase in the file.

You will use the Search option from the Start menu in Activity 3-12.

Start your search for files, folders, and programs by opening the Start menu. Type your search information in the Search box. The search results start appearing as you type, and they change as you type additional characters. These changing results are called an *interactive search*. For example, if you are looking for the Paint application, typing *p* and then *pa* or *pai* will converge upon the application of interest. The results menu lists every file, folder, program, picture, movie, music file, and Web bookmark that contains your search information, regardless of filename or folder location. Depending on the applications installed, the search also includes data stored in Microsoft Office documents (Word, PowerPoint, Excel, and Outlook), e-mail messages, address book entries, and calendar appointments.

Again, Windows is not just searching file and folder names; it is searching the contents of files and folders, and it is searching metadata, which is descriptive information about file attributes. Attributes are descriptive and defining information about a file that can include data such as height, width, size, creator, title, author, created date, and last modification date.

If you see the entry you want in your search results, click the entry to open it. If you choose an application or a picture, it opens on the screen. Windows will usually know which associated program is required to open and display the file, but occasionally a pop-up window asks you to locate the proper program.

Windows usually displays about 10 search results depending on the size of your monitor. Windows attempts to display the most likely matches to your search request, and groups them in categories such as Apps, Settings, Folders, Documents, and Web. Figure 3-25 shows the results of a sample search request. You can click the See more results link at the bottom of the results list to see additional matches, but not matching programs and Control Panel items.

To help locate your file, you might want to add the preview pane by clicking Organize, clicking Layout, and then clicking Preview pane. When you click an entry, such as a picture, sound, or text in a WordPad file, the file contents are shown in the preview pane. This helps you locate the file you want from the available candidates.

Two additional icons appear at the bottom of the Search Results window to help you repeat a search locally using the My stuff option or perform a Web search.

Figure 3-25 Windows search results

Source: Microsoft Windows 10

Searching from the File Explorer Window The Search box in File Explorer is located at the right of the address bar. As with the Start menu, you type your search request into the Search box, but there is a big difference between the two: From the Start menu, you search your entire computer, but a search in File Explorer is limited to the displayed Explorer window. You will perform a search from the File Explorer window in Activity 3-13.

There are other differences between the two types of searches. A File Explorer search is not limited to a certain number of entries, as it is in the Start menu. If a search returns a large number of results, you see a large scrollable window.

Another difference between the two searches is the Search tab on the Ribbon of File Explorer, which you can use to filter your search results. For example, clicking Date Modified presents a list of date-related criteria, such as today, yesterday, this week, and other items that you can select to refine your search. You can also filter searches by file type, file size, and other properties.

You may be amazed at how quickly Windows displays results when you type a search request, and at how quickly the requests change as you type additional characters. Windows works in the background to add information to its indexes about the contents of files on your computer. Think of the **index** as a card catalog to the files on your hard drive. Recall that Windows examines your files for words and metadata. As you type a search request, Windows searches the index entries for data that matches your criteria. At the installation of Windows, the index is built in 15 to 30 minutes. As you add files, Windows adds information to the index.

Activity 3-12: Searching from the Windows 10 Start Menu

Time Required: 10 minutes

Objective: Search for files from the Windows 10 Start menu.

Description: In this activity, you will search for a program file. This is useful if you want to locate a file in an unknown location.

1. If necessary, start your virtual machines using the appropriate instructions in Activity 1-1.
2. To open the Start menu, click **Start**.
3. To search for a program file when you know part of the application name, type **step** and then click **Steps Recorder**.
4. To start recording steps, click the **Start Record** button.
5. Open the calculator application by clicking **Start** and then clicking **Calculator**. Close the Calculator window.
6. To stop recording, click **Stop Record**. Note the steps recorded in the Steps Recorder application. You can save these steps for later use or to provide step-by-step instructions.
7. Close any open windows in the virtual machine.
8. Leave the virtual machine logged on for the next activity.

Activity 3-13: Searching from Windows File Explorer

Time Required: 10 minutes

Objective: Search for files in Windows 10 File Explorer.

Description: In this activity, you will search for system picture files. This is useful if you want to find a file in an unknown location.

1. If necessary, start your virtual machines using the appropriate instructions in Activity 1-1.
2. To open File Explorer, click **Start** and then click **File Explorer**.

3. To search for files on the entire PC file system, click **This PC** in the navigation pane on the left side of the window.

4. To search for a picture file, click in the Search text box, and then type **.jpg**.

5. To narrow the search, click the **Search** tab on the Ribbon, click **Size**, and then click **Large (1–16 MB)**.

6. To find the location of one of the pictures, right-click a picture icon, and then click **Properties**. Note the filename and the location.

7. To cancel the search, click the **X** in the Search text box.

8. Close any open windows in the virtual machine.

9. To shut down the Windows virtual machine, click **Start**, click **Power**, and then click **Shut down**.

10. Leave the PC logged on for the next activity.

Searching for Files in CentOS 7 To search for files and folders in Linux within the GNOME desktop environment, open the Files program and then click the magnifying glass icon. The search bar opens; it has a box for entering the text you want to search for. The next button shows the folder that was selected when you clicked the search button; you can use the button to search through all files and folders on the computer. The last option on the bar is a button that contains a plus sign (+). When you click this button, an additional bar opens that allows you to create search criteria.

Activity 3-14: Searching with File Browser in CentOS 7

Time Required: 10 minutes

Objective: Search for files with File Browser.

Description: In this activity, you will search for a file that contains specific words. This activity is useful if you want to locate a file based on its content.

1. If necessary, start your virtual machines using the appropriate instructions in Activity 1-1.

2. To open gedit, click the **Applications** menu, click **Accessories**, and then click **gedit Text Editor**.

3. Type **Test for File Browser Search**, and then press **Enter**.

4. Type **Nautilus** and then press **Enter**.

5. To save the file, click **File**, click **Save As**, type **Nautilus** in the Name text box, click **Documents** in the left window pane if needed, and then click **Save**. Close the file by clicking the **X** in the upper-right corner.

6. To begin the search, click **Places** and then click **Home**.

7. Click the magnifying glass icon to bring up the search bar.

8. Type **Nautilus** in the search bar, and then press **Enter**.

If you do not see the Nautilus file in the view pane, contact your instructor.

9. Close the open windows in the virtual machine.

10. To shut down the virtual machine, click your account name in the upper-right corner of the desktop, and then click **Power Off** twice.

Chapter Summary

- The graphical user interface (GUI) has many menus that you use to work with applications. Use the Start menu to begin applications in the Windows GUI environment; use the Applications menu to begin applications in CentOS 7.

- You can tailor the GUI desktop in both Windows 10 and CentOS 7. Besides modifying the appearance of the desktop, you can control icon placement and the behavior of windows, menus, and cursors. Each operating system has different methods for modifying the desktop.

- You have many options for accessing locally stored data in Windows 10 and CentOS 7. If you do not know a file or folder's exact location, use a search utility. As long as you have not cleaned out the Recycle Bin or the Trash, you can retrieve deleted files and folders from Windows and CentOS 7, respectively. In Windows 10, you use Windows File Explorer to organize and view files; in CentOS 7, you use Files to perform these tasks.

Key Terms

Activities Overview   A window in CentOS 7 that has a shortcut bar for applications and that shows active windows and workspaces.

Applications menu   A menu in the CentOS 7 GNOME GUI that opens applications and utilities.

breadcrumbs   Navigation aids used in an address bar and other parts of the GUI to help keep track of your locations.

desktop context menu   The submenu that appears when you right-click an empty area on the CentOS 7 desktop.

Files   A utility program in CentOS that enables you to locate and open files and folders.

index   A large collection of information references on your hard drive that helps Windows to return search results.

Recycle Bin   A folder that holds files and folders you delete from a hard drive in Windows 10. You can restore the deleted files and folders, if necessary. The Recycle Bin is represented by a trash can icon.

shortcuts   Desktop icons that you can click to immediately access applications, text files, folders, and Web pages in a GUI environment.

Start menu   A menu in Windows 10 that you use to select applications, utilities, and commands. This menu appears when you click the Start icon in the lower-left corner of the screen.

Trash   In CentOS 7, a folder of deleted files and folders.

Windows File Explorer   A Windows utility that enables you to locate and open files and folders.

3

Review Questions

1. To start applications in Windows 10, use the _____.

   a.   Applications menu

   b.   Start menu

   c.   Launch menu

   d.   Control Center

2. To add an application as a tile to the Windows Start menu, click _____.

   a.   Add to Start

   b.   Pin to Start

   c.   Add to Taskbar

   d.   Pin to Taskbar

3. To start applications in CentOS 7, use the _____.

   a.   Applications menu

   b.   Start menu

   c.   Launch menu

   d.   Configure menu

4. You can use the taskbar to _____. (Choose all that apply.)

   a.   monitor current tasks

   b.   quickly move between open applications

   c.   change the configuration of the Start menu

   d.   modify the current taskbar settings

5. If you cannot move the taskbar, _____.

   a.   do not worry; the taskbar cannot be moved

   b.   unlock it by right-clicking an empty area of the taskbar and clicking Lock the taskbar to clear the check mark

   c.   double-click it

   d.   unlock it by right-clicking an empty area of the taskbar and clicking Unlock the taskbar

6. Menus are customized to _____. (Choose all that apply.)

    a. provide shortcuts to frequently used applications

    b. remove applications that are infrequently used

    c. change fonts, color schemes, and window behaviors

    d. group applications by use

7. The Windows 10 default Start menu is divided into _____ part(s).

    a. 1

    b. 2

    c. 3

    d. 4

8. Which of the following items are commonly found on the Windows 10 taskbar? (Choose all that apply.)

    a. Start button

    b. File menu

    c. Clock

    d. open applications

9. Which of the following options appear on the Windows 10 Start menu by default? (Choose all that apply.)

    a. Computer

    b. File Explorer

    c. Music

    d. Power

10. In CentOS 7, the taskbar is commonly referred to as a _____.

    a. menu

    b. taskbar

    c. Top Bar

    d. file

11. You can tailor the desktop to provide _____. (Choose all that apply.)

    a. quick access to running applications

    b. shortcuts to frequently used applications

    c. an organized workspace

    d. privacy

12. What is the default GUI application in CentOS 7?

    a. KVM

    b. GNOME

    c. Lollypop

    d. Windows

13. What is the default number of workspaces in CentOS 7?

    a. 3

    b. 1

    c. 4

    d. 6

14. Which of the following actions permits more information to appear on the screen? (Choose all that apply.)

    a. increasing the size of text

    b. decreasing the size of text

    c. increasing the screen resolution

    d. decreasing the screen resolution

15. A utility that locates and opens files in Windows 10 is _____.

    a. Control Center

    b. File Browser

    c. the Search box

    d. Internet Explorer

16. A utility that locates and opens files in CentOS 7 is _____.

    a. Files

    b. Control Center

    c. File Browser

    d. Search

    e. Windows Explorer

17. When you delete files from a folder, where do they go? (Choose all that apply.)

    a. Recycle Bin

    b. Trash

    c. File Manager

    d. the Delete folder

18. To filter a search in File Explorer in Windows 10, you can use the _____ option. (Choose all that apply.)

    a. Kind

    b. Date modified

    c. Size

    d. Date deleted

19. As an aid to organization in Windows 10 or CentOS 7, files are grouped by _____. (Choose all that apply.)

    a. places

    b. folders

    c. libraries

    d. partitions

20. Windows 10 desktop features include _____. (Choose all that apply.)

    a. Jump lists

    b. Snap

    c. Peek

    d. Shake

Case Projects

Case 3-1: Customizing the Windows Start Menu

George requested your help to customize his Windows 10 Start menu. He needs to access a limited number of applications quickly and locate previously used files. Write a short note for George with your suggestions. Create a document in the format of a note.

Case 3-2: Recovering Deleted Files in CentOS 7

You get an e-mail from Susan, who has deleted a case project by mistake. She wants to know how to recover the deleted file. What instructions will you include in your e-mail? Create a document in the format of an e-mail message.

Case 3-3: Searching for Files

You need to help your friend locate a file on his computer, but he does not recall the name of the file. Prepare a list of suggestions that could help your friend. Create a document that provides the list of suggestions.

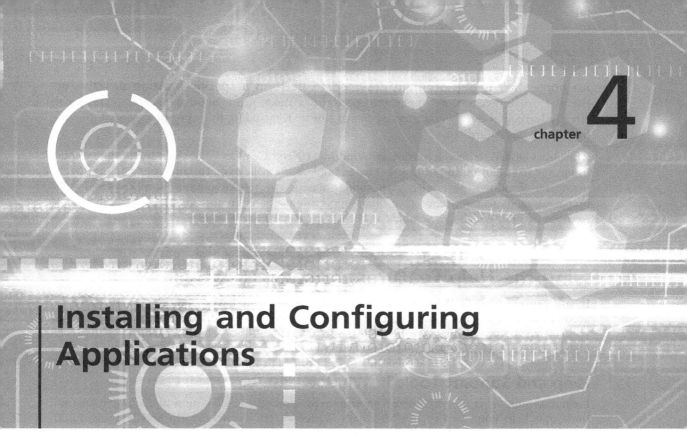

Installing and Configuring Applications

After reading this chapter and completing the exercises, you will be able to:

- Access Help information
- Use and configure a Web browser
- Install the ActiveState Perl application and test the installation with a test script

An application is any program designed to perform a specific function directly for the user. In some cases, an application performs a function for another program. You have already learned about several applications in this text, including the word processors LibreOffice Writer and WordPad.

After learning to use the Help tools in Windows 10 and CentOS 7, you will learn more about using and configuring applications. For example, you will learn to configure and use Web browsers. Windows programs have similar menus, so working with these browsers will prepare you to use and configure other applications. Later in this chapter, you will install ActiveState Perl, which is available for both Windows 10 and CentOS 7.

Accessing the Help Features

If you are working in Windows 10 or CentOS 7 and you have a question about how to accomplish a task, you should check the helpful resources at your fingertips before asking your instructor or classmate for help. In the following sections, you will learn to use the GUI Help features in Windows 10 and CentOS 7.

Help and Support Tools in Windows 10

Help and Support is a comprehensive resource for practical advice, tutorials, and demonstrations that help you learn to use Microsoft Windows 10. To open Help and Support, click Start and then click Get Started. Each item on the opening screen is a link to further information or assistance (see Figure 4-1). For example, "Get to know Windows 10," as shown in Figure 4-2, is a good link if you want to know how to set up and personalize your Start menu. Click the star icon on the left side of the screen to learn about new features in Windows 10. For examples of the wide range of information available in Get Started, click each icon on the left side of the screen to learn about the various topics each link covers. You might no longer be a neophyte, but "Get Started" is a good link for new users of Windows.

You can also press the F3 key to open the Start menu. If it does not open, click the desktop and press F3 again.

Use the Search box in the taskbar to locate a topic by keyword. For example, type *help* to see help information topics for Windows settings, applications in the Microsoft store, and the Web. You will learn more about using Help and Support in Activity 4-1.

System Information The System Information tool (see Figure 4-3) provides summary information for your computer. You learned about the System Information tool in Chapter 1.

In this chapter, you will learn more about the System Information tool. For example, you can use it to confirm your system configuration. To access this tool, type *system information* in the Search box. The first option that appears is "system information," which is a desktop application. Click to open the System Information link.

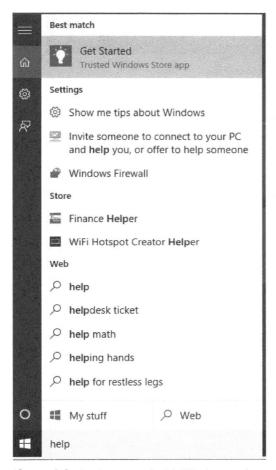

Figure 4-1 Getting started with Windows Help

Source: Microsoft Windows 10

Hardware Resources From the Hardware Resources section of the System Information tool, you can find information to help resolve a hardware resource problem. Click the + icon to expand Hardware Resources. For example, click Conflicts/Sharing to see hardware resources that are used by more than one device, as shown in Figure 4-4. You will learn more about using hardware resources in Activity 4-2.

The information in the Conflicts/Sharing area varies depending on the virtualization software installed on your computer.

Components Expanding the Components section of the System Information tool provides a detailed list of information about the hardware components on your computer system. For

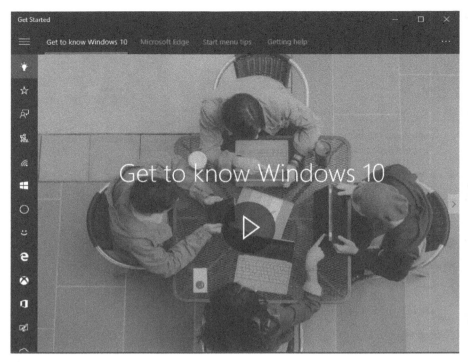

Figure 4-2 Getting to know Windows 10

Source: Microsoft Windows 10

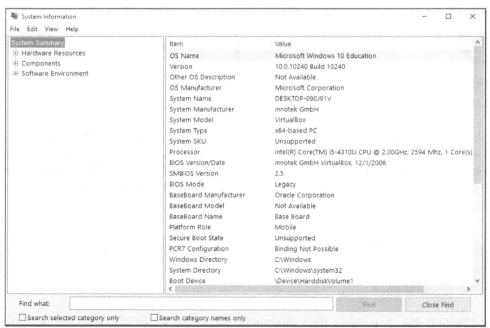

Figure 4-3 System Information tool

Source: Microsoft Windows 10

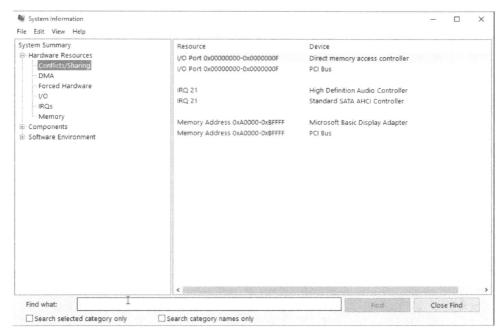

Figure 4-4 Hardware conflicts and sharing information

Source: Microsoft Windows 10

example, to find information about the CD-ROM drive in your computer, click CD-ROM. Figure 4-5 shows information about the CD-ROM drive in the Windows 10 virtual machine running in VirtualBox. You will learn more about this in Activity 4-2.

Software Environment If you need information about the software environment on your computer, expand Software Environment in the System Information tool. This section provides details about your operating system and applications. To view the programs running on your computer, click Running Tasks. The programs running in the Windows 10 virtual machine are shown in Figure 4-6. You will learn more about this in Activity 4-2.

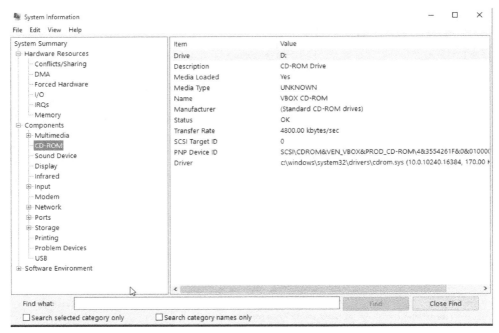

Figure 4-5 CD-ROM information in Windows

Source: Microsoft Windows 10

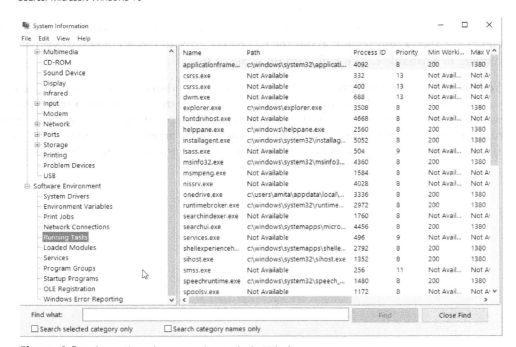

Figure 4-6 Information about running tasks in Windows

Source: Microsoft Windows 10

Activity 4-1: Using Help and Support in Windows 10

Time Required: 10 minutes

Objective: Examine the Windows 10 Help and Support.

Description: In this activity, you use the Windows 10 Help and Support. This activity is useful if you need to learn about a particular Windows 10 feature.

1. Start your virtual machines using the appropriate instructions in Activity 1-1.
2. To open Help and Support, click the **Start** menu and then click **Get Started**. If this option is not available, type **Get Started** in the "Search the web and Windows" box and then click the menu item to open it.
3. To play a video that explains how to get help and search for topics, click the **Getting help** link at the top of the screen. Click the center of the Getting help video to play it. After the video plays, click the star icon on the left side of the screen to open the What's new window.
4. Open and read one or more topics of interest under "What's new" in Windows 10.
5. To return to the initial window, click the left arrow in the upper-left corner.
6. To get familiar with various help topics, click the three-bar icon in the upper-left corner. Click any topic of interest to read and get help in setting your PC for that feature. Close the Get Started window.
7. Click the **Search the web and Windows** search box on the taskbar.
8. To determine the amount of memory on the Windows 10 virtual machine, type **Memory** and then click **View RAM info**.
9. Locate the **Installed RAM** entry.
10. Close the System window.
11. Leave the virtual machine logged on for the next activity.

Activity 4-2: Viewing System Information in Windows 10

Time Required: 10 minutes

Objective: View general system information on a PC.

Description: In this activity, you view your virtual machine's system information. This activity is useful if you need to see system information to resolve problems.

1. If necessary, start your virtual machines using the appropriate instructions in Activity 1-1.
2. To open the System Information link, click **Start,** and then type **sy** in the "Search the web and Windows" search box. Notice that Windows 10 lists items containing the characters **sy**.
3. Click the **System Information** link. Wait for the information to appear.
4. Review the System Summary page.
5. To see the subcategories for hardware resources, expand **Hardware Resources**.

6. To view the interrupt requests (IRQs) assigned, click **IRQs.**

7. Wait for the system to refresh and the information to appear.

8. To view the memory areas assigned, click **Memory.**

9. To view the available hardware components, expand **Components.**

10. Open and read one or more topics that interest you.

11. To view the software environment, expand **Software Environment.**

12. Open and read one or more topics that interest you.

13. Close any open windows.

14. Leave the virtual machine logged on for future activities.

Using the CentOS 7 Help Center and System Information

There are two ways to access the CentOS 7 Help Center (see Figure 4-7). One way is to click Applications, point to Favorites, and then click Help. The other way is to click Applications, move the cursor to Documentation, and then click Help. Next, select the link for the information you need. For example, to locate information about using the GNOME desktop, click Getting Started with GNOME.

CentOS 7 provides a System Information tool that resembles the one in Windows 10. You learned about this tool in Chapter 1. Activity 4-4 introduces additional features of the CentOS 7 System Information tool.

Figure 4-7 CentOS 7 Help Center

Source: CentOS 7

Activity 4-3: Accessing Help with the GNOME Help Browser

4

Time Required: 10 minutes

Objective: Access support information in the Help Center.

Description: In this activity, you access and investigate the Help Center for CentOS 7. This activity is useful if you need to access Help in CentOS 7.

1. If necessary, start your virtual machines using the appropriate instructions in Activity 1-1.
2. To access the Help Center, click **Applications,** point to **Favorites,** and then click **Help.**
3. Click **Networking, web, email & chat,** and read some of the online help information.
4. Close any open windows.
5. Leave the virtual machine logged on for the next activity.

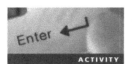

Activity 4-4: Viewing System Information in CentOS 7

Time Required: 10 minutes

Objective: Access system information with the System Information tool.

Description: In this activity, you access and investigate system information with CentOS 7. This activity is useful if you need to access system information in CentOS 7.

1. If necessary, start your virtual machines using the appropriate instructions in Activity 1-1.
2. To open the terminal console, click **Applications,** point to **Favorites,** and then click **Terminal.**
3. To open the System Information window, type **hardinfo** and press **Enter.**

If you see a "Command not found" message, contact your instructor.

4. To review the summary, click **Summary.**
5. To review operating system information, click **Operating System.**
6. To review processor information, click **Processor.**
7. To locate CPU resources, scroll down under **Devices** and click **Resources.**
8. Review the I/O ports in the right pane.
9. Scroll and review the memory information in the right pane.
10. To review the input devices, click **Input Devices.**
11. To review the mounted drives, click **Storage.**
12. Close any open windows.
13. Leave the virtual machine logged on for future activities.

Using and Configuring Web Browsers

A Web browser is a software program that you use to access and navigate the Web. The first widely used browser, called *NCSA Mosaic*, was developed at the National Center for Supercomputing Applications in the early 1990s. Mosaic's point-and-click interface helped popularize the Web.

Browsers provide tools that allow you to travel effortlessly from one Web site to another. If you want to visit the same site repeatedly, you can bookmark it.

In this section, you will learn to use two Web browsers—Microsoft Edge and Mozilla's Firefox. Windows 10 introduced the new Edge browser (see Figure 4-8). By default, it is the preferred browser in Windows 10. It provides a new way to search the Web and even allows you to write on the Web.

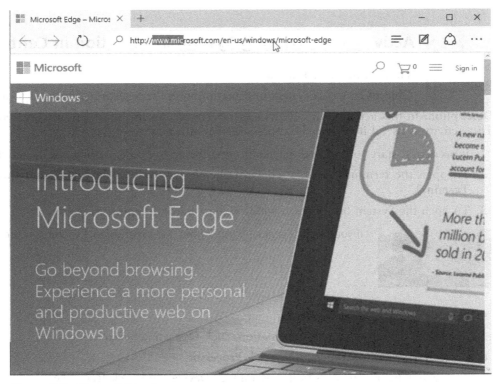

Figure 4-8 Microsoft Edge browser

Source: Microsoft Windows 10/Microsoft Edge browser

Using the security features and privacy options in Edge, you can create a secure environment that protects your personal information as you surf the Web.

Browsing the Web with Microsoft Edge

Each page on the Web is designated by an Internet address known as a **Uniform Resource Locator (URL)**. In other words, a URL identifies the location of any Web site. Figure 4-9 shows the Edge toolbar and the address bar, where you can type a URL and go to a new Web site.

Portal Site A **portal site** is a Web site that serves as a gateway to the Internet. A portal is a collection of links, content, and services designed to guide users to interesting information, news, weather, entertainment, commerce sites, chat rooms, and so on.

4

The default URL for Edge is *www.msn.com*, which is Microsoft's portal to introduce the new browser.

You can go to a Web site by typing an address in the address bar. You can also use the Back and Forward buttons on the toolbar to move backward and forward through the sites you have visited during your current browsing session. You can move from one Web page to another by clicking **hyperlinks** (usually called *links*) within the pages. A hyperlink takes you

Figure 4-9 Edge toolbar and address bar

Source: Microsoft Windows 10/Microsoft Edge browser

to a different URL that indicates a different location on the Web. The link could take you to a different Web site or to a different spot on the same page.

When you move your mouse pointer over a link, Edge detects the link and changes the pointer to a pointing finger. Hyperlinks are usually underlined or displayed in a different color to indicate text that is "hot," or clickable. Clickable links typically change their appearance when the pointer moves over them.

You can also use tabs in Web browsing and Web searches. Tabs permit more than one Web page to be displayed and allow you to switch rapidly between Web pages.

Randomly moving around the Web is easy, but finding your way to specific information can be trickier. When you read a book, the text flows from page to page. On the Internet, however, you must actively decide where to go next, which is why people often speak of "browsing" the Web, as if they were in a library browsing the shelves.

The Edge browser has a new feature called the *Hub*, which keeps track of your favorites, searches, browsing history, and downloads. To access the Hub, click the distinctive three-bar icon in the upper-right corner of the address bar. Figure 4-10 shows the Favorites bar within the Hub. The other Hub options look like the Favorites bar.

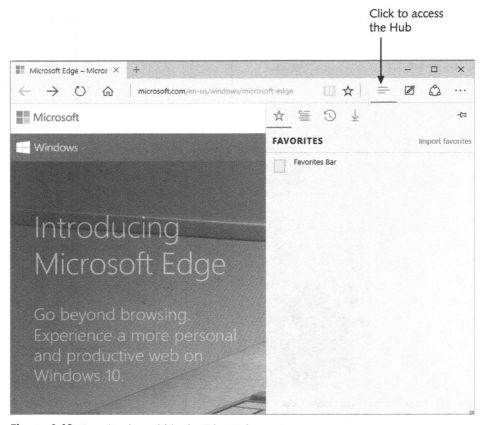

Figure 4-10 Favorites bar within the Edge Hub

Source: Microsoft Windows 10/Microsoft Edge browser

Click the star icon on the address bar to add the current Web site to your favorites list or to the reading list for later use and easy access. To save the current Web site to your list of favorites so that you can return quickly to it in the future, click the Favorites button and then click Add.

To help you locate information in cyberspace, Edge provides a search utility: the default Bing search engine. When you type a few words into it about a topic of interest, Bing presents a list of suggestions that you can click. Figure 4-11 shows the results from a search; these results are listed from the Web and from your browsing history. If no suggestions appear, click the spyglass icon in the upper-right corner of the search window.

4

Spyglass icon

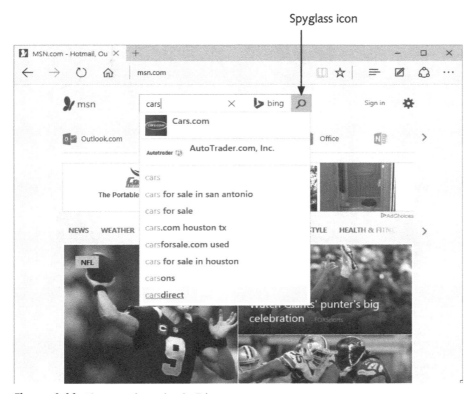

Figure 4-11 Bing search engine in Edge

Source: Microsoft Windows 10/Microsoft Edge browser

Edge allows you to write on the Web, make your own notes, highlight content on the Web, draw on Web pages, and share your notes with others. On the Web page where you want to highlight content, click the "Make a Web note" icon under the right side of the address bar. (The icon looks like a pencil and paper, as shown in Figure 4-12.) The Web page becomes editable, and new icons appear in the upper-left corner to help you start editing. Use the first icon to write on a Web page. With the successive icons, you can highlight, erase, comment, or clip content on the Web page (see Figure 4-13). When you finish editing or making notes, you can either save your work for future reference or share your work with others. To save your work, click the familiar floppy icon in the

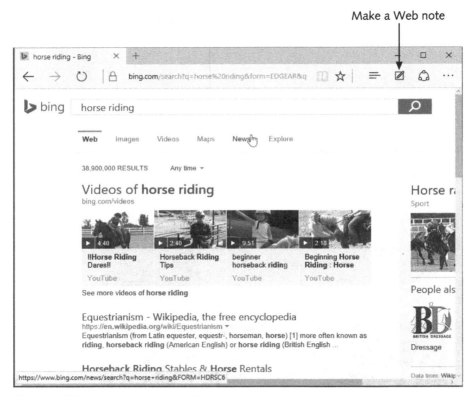

Figure 4-12 Creating a Web note in Edge

Source: Microsoft Windows 10/Microsoft Edge browser

Use these tools to
mark on a Web page

Figure 4-13 Marking on a Web page in Edge

Source: Microsoft Windows 10/Microsoft Edge browser

upper-right corner (see Figure 4-14). You have options to save in OneNote, in your favorites folder, or to your reading list. To share your work, click the share icon (the circle with three faces); you then have options to share your work via e-mail or in OneNote. When you finish, click the Exit icon to close the editable Web options.

The Edge browser has a new icon that leads to a menu with more options; the icon contains three dots and is shown in the upper-right corner (see Figure 4-15). Click this icon to open a content menu. From this menu, you can perform a number of tasks:

- Open a new window.
- Enlarge (zoom) or reduce the content on a page.
- Open an **InPrivate** window, which enables you to surf the Web without leaving a trail.
- Make changes to Edge browser settings.

Edge also gives you the option to open your Web page using Internet Explorer, an older Windows Web browser. You learn more about these topics in future sections.

Figure 4-14 Saving your work in Edge

Source: Microsoft Windows 10/Microsoft Edge browser

Click for additional options

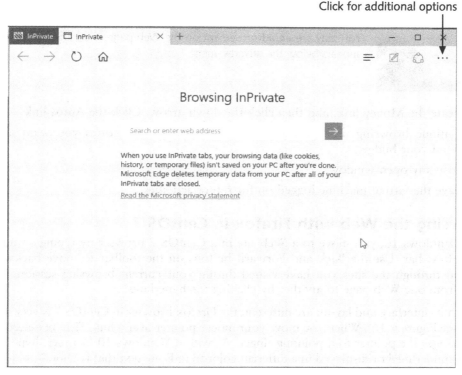

Figure 4-15 Private browsing in Edge

Source: Microsoft Windows 10/Microsoft Edge browser

Activity 4-5: Browsing the Web with Edge

Time Required: 15 minutes

Objective: Browse the Web with Edge.

Description: In this activity, you access a portal site on the Web to locate information about automobile features and pricing. This activity is useful because it shows you how to find information on the Web.

1. If necessary, start your virtual machines using the appropriate instructions in Activity 1-1.

2. To start Edge, type **Edge** in the search box on the taskbar. Click the **Microsoft Edge** link.

3. Type **www.msn.com** over "Search or enter web address" in the address bar, and then press **Enter**.

If you are trying to access a Web site whose URL ends in *.com*, type the unique part of the URL (such as *msn*) and then press Ctrl+Enter. The *www* and *.com* will be attached to the name that you typed in the address bar.

4. Click **Money** in the menu at the top of the page.

You may see an advertisement on the Web page. If so, the Money link appears below the advertisement.

5. Locate the **Money** link, and then click the down arrow. Click the **Autos** link.

6. Continue browsing until you locate a car that has the features you want and stays within your budget.

7. Close any open windows.

8. Leave the virtual machine logged on for future activities.

Browsing the Web with Firefox in CentOS 7

As in Windows 10, you move to a Web site in a CentOS 7 browser by typing an address in the address bar. Use the Back and Forward buttons on the toolbar to move backward and forward through the sites you have visited during your current browsing session. You can move from one Web page to another by clicking the hyperlinks.

Though its interface and layout are different, the Firefox browser in CentOS 7 is very similar to Edge (see Figure 4-16). When you move your mouse pointer over a link, Firefox detects the link and changes the pointer to a pointing finger. As with a Windows 10 browser, hyperlinks are usually underlined or displayed in a different color to indicate text that is "hot," or clickable.

You have several options for accessing Web sites in Firefox. For example, you can use the Web Search option by typing search keywords in the Search text box or you can use the Bookmarks menu to store, manage, and access frequently used URLs. You can also use the History menu by clicking the Open menu button in the upper-right corner of the browser. If you click the History button and then click View History Sidebar, you can view your search history without leaving the current Web page. The sites are organized by the number of days, weeks, and months since you visited them. You can view the information By Date and Site, By Site, By Date, By Most Visited, and By Last Visited. The By Most Visited option can be very helpful when you need to access a previously visited Web site for which you did not create a bookmark. The Show All History option displays all your bookmarks.

Figure 4-16 Firefox browser in CentOS 7

Source: CentOS 7/Mozilla Firefox

Activity 4-6: Browsing the Web with Firefox

Time Required: 15 minutes

Objective: Browse the Web with Firefox.

Description: In this activity, you access a portal site on the Web to locate information about a topic. This activity is useful because it shows you how to access catalogued information on the Web.

1. If necessary, start your virtual machines using the appropriate instructions in Activity 1-1.

2. To open Firefox, click **Applications**, point to **Internet**, and then click **Firefox Web Browser**.

3. To start your search for an electronic device, type **www.amazon.com** in the address bar and then press **Enter**.

4. Point to the **Departments** drop-down box, which is under the **amazon** logo. Point to **Electronics & Computers**, and then click the category of your choice.

5. Continue browsing to locate an electronic device that you like.

6. Close any open windows.

7. Leave the virtual machine logged on for the next activity.

Activity 4-7: Bookmarking a Page in Firefox

Time Required: 10 minutes

Objective: Create bookmarks in Firefox for future reference.

Description: In this activity, you use Firefox to bookmark two popular Web sites.

1. If necessary, start your virtual machines using the appropriate instructions in Activity 1-1.

2. To open Firefox, click **Applications**, point to **Internet**, and then click **Firefox Web Browser**.

3. Type **www.amazon.com** in the address bar, and then press **Enter**.

4. When the Web page appears, click the **Star** icon next to the **Search** text box. A blue star jumps to the **Show your bookmarks** icon on the right, and the Star icon's color changes to blue.

5. Right-click the **Show your bookmarks** icon, and then select **Menu Bar** to display menus at the top of the browser screen.

6. Click **Bookmarks** in the menu bar, and then select **Edit This bookmark**.

7. Type **Amazon book store** in the Name field, and then click **Done**.

8. Type **www.dogpile.com** in the address bar, and then press **Enter**.

9. When the Web page appears, click the **Bookmarks** menu and then click **Bookmark This Page**.

10. Type **Dogpile search engine** in the Name field, and then click **Done**.

11. Click the **Bookmarks** menu, and note the two bookmarks you added.

12. Close any open windows.

13. Leave the virtual machine logged on for future activities.

Searching the Web with Edge

If you are looking for information on the Web that fits neatly into an obvious subject or category, go first to a Web directory. Think of a Web directory as a subject catalog—something like the catalog in your college library. Directories such as Yahoo, the Open Directory (dmoz), and the Google Directory organize the Web by dividing it into such topics as Arts, Science, Health, Business, News, and Entertainment.

Search engines use automated software programs to survey the Web and find the information you want. These programs retrieve and analyze documents that match your search criteria, and the data collected from each Web page is then added to the search engine's database. When you enter a query at a search engine site, your input is checked against the search engine's index of all the Web pages it has analyzed. The best URLs are then returned to you as "hits," with the best results listed at the top.

You need a search engine for the same reason you need the card catalog in a library. The library contains a lot of useful information, but it is impossible to examine all the books personally. Likewise, not even the most eager Web surfer could hyperlink to all the documents on the Web. Billions of Web pages are available online, and more are posted every day.

To examine the many documents on the Web, search engines use software programs known as *bots*, *spiders*, or *crawlers*. A **bot** is a piece of software that automatically follows hyperlinks from one document to the next around the Web. When a bot discovers a new site, it sends information back to its main site to be indexed. Because Web documents are one of the most dynamic forms of publishing, bots also update previously catalogued sites.

To rank the items in the search index, search engines use closely guarded ranking algorithms; search engine companies want to protect their methods from competitors, and they want to make it difficult for Web site owners to manipulate their rankings. A Web page's relevance ranking for a specific query depends on three factors:

- Its relevance to the words and concepts in the query
- Its overall link popularity
- Whether it is being penalized for abuse, such as linking a lot of sites to each other in a circular scam to artificially drive up the number of "hits"

A search engine has only a limited ability to understand what you want. It looks within its indexes for occurrences of the keywords or phrases you specify, but it does not understand what your keywords mean or why they are important to you. To a search engine, a keyword is just a string of characters. Read the Help files and take advantage of options that let you refine a search. Use phrases if possible.

If you are searching on a noun, keep in mind that most nouns are subsets of other nouns. Use the smallest possible subset that describes what you want. In other words, be specific. Try to help the search engine by refining your search before you begin. For example, if you want to buy a car, do not enter the keyword *car* if you can enter the keyword *Ford*. Better yet, enter the phrase *Ford dealerships* and the name of the city where you live.

Use the + character to include other keywords that you would expect to find in relevant documents, and use the – character to exclude items. Excluding text is particularly important as the Web grows and more documents are posted. If necessary, you can run your query several times, each time adding refinements to focus your list of relevant hits. For example, if you want to find out about hypertension, try querying on *hypertension* AND *treatment*. If you want to learn about lifestyle changes that could minimize the occurrence of hypertension, try entering *hypertension* AND *exercise* AND *diet* AND NOT *treatment*.

Activity 4-8: Searching the Web with Edge

Time Required: 15 minutes

Objective: Search the Web with Edge.

Description: In this activity, you access a search site using Edge to locate information about a topic. This activity is useful because you need to be able to search the Web for information, such as where to purchase a car.

1. If necessary, start your virtual machines using the appropriate instructions in Activity 1-1.

2. To start Edge, type **Edge** in the search box on the taskbar. Click the **Microsoft Edge** link.

3. To start your search for your new Ford Mustang, type **www.google.com** in the search bar and then press **Enter**.

4. When the Google Web site appears, type your search string and then click the **Google Search** button. For example, to find pricing information for a Ford Mustang, type **Ford Mustang New Prices** and then press **Enter**.

5. Refine your search by trying additional keywords.

6. Close any open windows.

7. Leave the virtual machine logged on for future activities.

Searching the Web with Firefox

Because search engines are resident on the Internet and the Firefox browser is simply a tool to access the Web, the process for searching in Firefox is very similar to that in Edge. The Boolean syntax and phrasing of search queries are the same.

To access the search function from the Firefox browser, you can simply enter your search keywords in the Search text box and then press Enter. You can also enter a search engine's URL in the address bar and perform a search from the Firefox home page.

You can define the search engine you want to use by following these steps:

1. Click the Open menu icon in the upper-right corner of the browser and then click Preferences.

2. Select Search in the left panel. Click the down arrow in the Default Search Engine section, and then choose the preferred search engine. Google is selected by default.

Activity 4-9: Searching the Web with Firefox

Time Required: 15 minutes

Objective: Search the Web with Firefox.

Description: In this activity, you access a search site using Firefox to locate information about a topic. This activity is useful because you need to be able to search the Web for information.

1. If necessary, start your virtual machines using the appropriate instructions in Activity 1-1.

2. To open Firefox, click **Applications**, point to **Internet**, and then click **Firefox Web Browser**.

3. To start your search on CentOS 7, type **CentOS 7** in the Search window and press **Enter**.

4. When the search results appear, scroll up and down to look at the links.

5. Close any open windows.

6. Leave the virtual machine logged on for future activities.

Configuring Edge

Although you may assume that the default settings of Edge will suffice and that you do not need to configure the browser, that is not necessarily true. For example, if you never use the default home page that appears when you open the browser, you should select a different home page. Sometimes you might not want to leave any traces of your Web browsing on the computer you are using, such as when checking e-mail on a friend's computer or shopping for a gift on a family PC. You should also know how to regain disk space by occasionally deleting temporary Internet files that are copied to your hard drive.

Configuring Safety Settings in Edge The New InPrivate Browsing feature in Edge helps protect data and privacy by preventing the browsing history, temporary Internet files, form data, cookies, user names, and passwords from being stored or retained locally by the browser, leaving virtually no evidence of the user's browsing or search history.

You can start InPrivate Browsing by clicking the More actions menu (the three-dot icon in the upper-right corner) and then selecting New InPrivate window. A new Edge window will open with a blue and white InPrivate indicator displayed to the left of the address (see Figure 4-17). To end an InPrivate session, simply close the browser window.

To continue configuring Edge, click the More actions menu and then select Settings. You can customize Edge to open with a Light or Dark theme by clicking the Choose a theme drop-down box (see Figure 4-18). The next option lets you customize the Edge browser to always show your Favorites bar by selecting On with the toggle switch. If you display the Favorites bar, you can save all your bookmarked pages to it. The next time you open your browser, your favorite marked pages will be just a click away.

Under Settings, you can also choose to import favorite Web sites from another browser. You can set your startup page to be a specific page, a page that you previously opened, or a new tabbed page.

In Activity 4-10, you customize the following settings in Edge:

- Home page—The home page is the Web page that appears every time you open your browser.

- StartUp—This setting gives you the option to open your browser by preloading the last Web pages you accessed or to open the browser to your home page.

- Browsing history—You can regain disk space by deleting files and cookies that were stored on the computer during recent Web sessions. The History list shows all the Web pages you have visited in previous days and weeks; the list appears below the address bar as you type a Web address. When the list becomes too long, it may be difficult to find the Web site you want. **Cookies** are small files that collect and store personal information about you and your Web surfing preferences.

- Tabs—Change how Web pages are displayed in tabs.

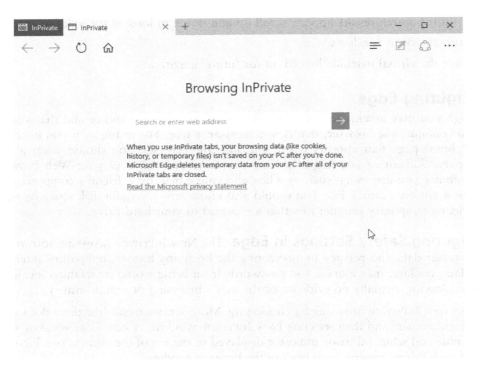

Figure 4-17 InPrivate settings in Edge

Source: Microsoft Windows 10/Microsoft Edge browser

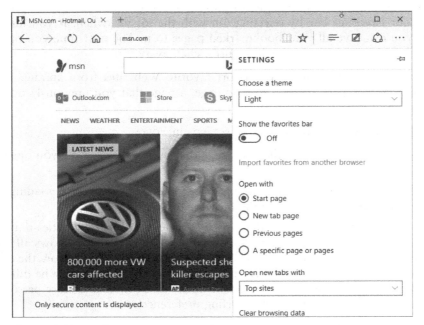

Figure 4-18 Configuring settings in Edge

Source: Microsoft Windows 10/Microsoft Edge browser

Activity 4-10: Selecting General Settings in Edge

Time Required: 15 minutes

Objective: Configure the settings in Edge.

Description: In this activity, you set the home page and the startup page in Edge. Depending on your usage, you might also need to clean up cookies, saved Internet files, and your history of recently visited Web sites. This activity is useful because it shows you how to perform basic configuration tasks for Edge.

1. If necessary, start your virtual machines using the appropriate instructions in Activity 1-1.

2. To start Edge, type **Edge** in the search box on the taskbar. Click the **Microsoft Edge** link.

3. Click the **More actions** menu (the button with three dots in the upper-right corner), and then click **Settings**.

4. To set *www.google.com* as the home page, click **A specific page or pages** under "Open with."

5. To start the customization for the initial page, click the drop-down box below "A specific page or pages." Click **Custom**. To remove the about:start option, click **X**.

6. To add a site as your startup page, type **www.google.com** over "Enter a web address." Click the **+** button.

7. To choose whether new tabs will open to top sites or blank Web pages, click the drop-down box below the "Open new tabs with" option, and then click **A blank Page**.

8. To begin the process of deleting your browsing history, scroll and locate **Clear browsing data** and then click **Choose what to clear**.

9. Review the check boxes, check the desired items, and then click **Clear**. A "Clearing Data" message appears briefly, followed by "All Clear!"

10. Close any open windows.

11. Open the browser again to verify your settings. Google.com should appear as your home page.

12. Leave the virtual machine logged on for the next activity.

Advanced Settings in Edge The Advanced settings in Edge offer an easy and flexible method for managing your privacy settings, pop-ups, and other services. To access these settings, click the More actions menu, click Settings, scroll down, and click View advanced settings. You can use these options to implement security and privacy settings.

Edge has the following Advanced settings:

- Show the home button—You can choose to display a button for your home page by turning its display on or off with a toggle switch. If you choose to show your home page, you can select a Web address that you want to set as your home page. By default, the home page is about:start, which is a blank page. Type the URL that you want to open when you select the home icon on the browser.

- Block pop-ups—This setting allows you to switch between blocking and allowing pop-ups.

- Always use Adobe Flash Player—This option is enabled by default. You can choose to turn it off.

- Use caret browsing—The caret is also known as the *text cursor*. This setting allows you to use the keyboard for navigating and selecting text instead of the mouse. When this setting is on, the mouse pointer becomes a text insert cursor. Place the cursor before any text that you want to copy, and then hold down the Shift key and click the down arrow on the keyboard to select the text line by line.

Privacy and Services Settings in Edge Using the privacy features in Edge, you and your organization can create a secure environment that protects personal information on the Internet. When you use the Internet, you need the assurance that other people cannot intercept and read the information you send and receive. You do not want other users to get your passwords or other private information, and you do not want Web sites to access your personal information without your knowledge. To set privacy for your Web browsing, turn the "Offer to save passwords" option on or off.

You also have an option to save form entries. By default, you automatically share information about your Web browsing session with the Web site's content provider, as shown in Figure 4-19. If this setting is On, Web sites track your browsing and manage the sites for you. If you choose to turn this setting Off, a "Do not track" request is sent to the Web sites.

Advanced settings in Edge allow you to set your search engine; by default, Bing is selected. Use the Advanced settings to enable or disable specific security and privacy options:

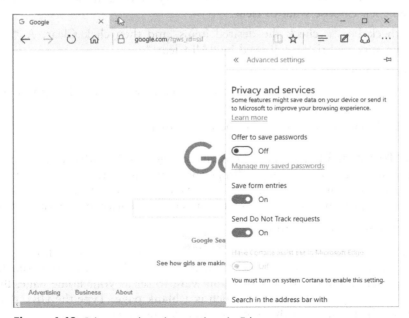

Figure 4-19 Privacy and services settings in Edge

Source: Microsoft Windows 10/Microsoft Edge browser

- Show search suggestions—When this option is enabled, Edge will recommend Web sites and search items based on your favorites, previous browsing sessions, and most popular search terms.
- Cookies—A cookie is a small piece of text sent to the browser by the Web site. It enables you to make your browsing session faster and customizable. Web sites use two types of cookies to collect and store personal information about you and your Web surfing preferences. These cookies are saved on your computer:
  - Session cookies are deleted when you close your browser.
  - Persistent cookies are more permanent. An expiration date in the cookie indicates when the browser can delete it.

Another important distinction when discussing cookies is the difference between first-party cookies and third-party cookies. First-party cookies are stored by a Web server from the same Internet domain; third-party cookies are stored by a Web server from a different domain. For example, many Web pages that contain advertising obtain it from a third-party site. Edge allows you to specify if you want to block all cookies, block only third-party cookies, or not to block any cookies.

Edge offers other advanced settings:

- Let sites save protected media licenses on my device—A user can download any type of media while using an Internet browser. Web sites that are capable of streaming use **digital rights management (DRM)** to protect against copying streamed content. If this setting is enabled, Web sites save DRM on your computer. When you visit the site that hosts protected content, this information is retrieved, which allows you to access the content. This setting is turned on by default in Edge. Use the toggle switch to enable or disable this setting.
- Use page prediction to speed up browsing—This setting is similar to search suggestions. Edge uses your browsing history data to predict and suggest sites, which are then loaded in the background for a faster browsing experience. You can disable this setting by clicking the toggle switch to turn it off.
- Help protect me from malicious sites and downloads with the SmartScreen Filter—This option blocks malicious sites and downloads from infecting your computer. By default, this setting is enabled in Edge; the filter is built into the Windows 10 operating system. This allows you to screen for files that can cause damage to your computer. The SmartScreen Filter sends information about every application that is downloaded to Microsoft's servers. This information is then analyzed and compared with a database of malicious applications. If the application is found to be malicious or is not found at all, Edge prevents you from running that application.

Activity 4-11: Configuring Privacy Settings in Edge

Time Required: 20 minutes

Objective: Configure the privacy settings in Edge.

Description: In this activity, you review and specify your home page, and then set privacy and services settings. This activity is useful if you need to select privacy settings for your browsing session.

1. If necessary, start your virtual machines using the appropriate instructions in Activity 1-1.

2. To start Edge, type **Edge** in the search box on the taskbar. Click the **Microsoft Edge** link.

3. To open the advanced settings, click the **More actions** menu, click **Settings**, scroll down, and click **View advanced settings**.

4. If necessary, turn on the home button by clicking the toggle switch or the **Off** setting below "Show the home button."

5. To set a default home page, type **cnn.com** over "about:start" and then click **Save**.

6. To set privacy settings, scroll down to **Privacy and services**.

7. To disable tracking, click the toggle switch or the **Off** option below "Send Do Not Track requests."

8. To open a new Web tab in the Edge browser, click the **+** sign after the last browser tab.

9. Type **google.com** over "Search or enter web address," and then press **Enter**.

10. To access the Edge privacy settings, click the **More actions** menu, click **Settings**, scroll down, and click **View Advanced settings**.

11. Scroll and locate the "Search in the address bar with" option. Click the down arrow, and then click **<Add new>**.

12. Click **www.google.com**, and then click **Add as default**.

13. Verify that your selection appears in the box.

14. To manage cookies, scroll and locate **Cookies**, and then verify that the option **Don't block cookies** is selected.

15. Verify that **Let sites save protected media licenses on my device** is enabled.

16. To speed up browsing, verify that **Use page prediction to speed up browsing** is enabled.

17. Verify that **Help protect me from malicious sites and downloads with SmartScreen Filter** is enabled.

18. Close any open windows within the Windows 10 virtual machine.

19. Leave the virtual machine logged on for the next activity.

Configuring the Firefox Browser

Like many applications you have used in CentOS 7, you can customize Firefox according to your own preferences. For example, Firefox opens to the default home page *file:///usr/share/doc/HTML/index.html*, but you can select any home page you want. The following sections explain your options for customizing Firefox.

Customizing Text Size and Toolbars Using the View Menu You can use the
View menu in Firefox to customize toolbars, sidebars, text size, page styles, and other particulars:

- Toolbars—Display or hide the menu bar and the bookmarks toolbar in Firefox.

- Status Bar—Display or hide the status bar at the bottom of the browser window; the status bar indicates the status of requested Web pages.

- Sidebar—Display or hide sidebars on the left side of the browser window; you can display sidebars that list bookmarks of frequently used Web sites, a history of recently visited Web sites, and various add-ons.

- Text Size—Increase or decrease the default text size of Web pages; you cannot change the text size if it was **hard coded** when the Web page was developed. You can choose to zoom text only.

- Page Style—Display the Web page in different themes that change the appearance of the page. You can select No Style to remove specialized fonts, colors, and other visual effects in the current tab or window. The other option, Basic Page Style, displays the current page in the way you want; the default option is Basic Page Style.

- Full Screen—Make the Web page take up the entire screen.

Customizing General Settings in Firefox To customize the General settings in Firefox, click the Edit menu, and then click Preferences (see Figure 4-20). You can also click the Open menu icon in the upper-right corner of the browser, and then select Preferences.

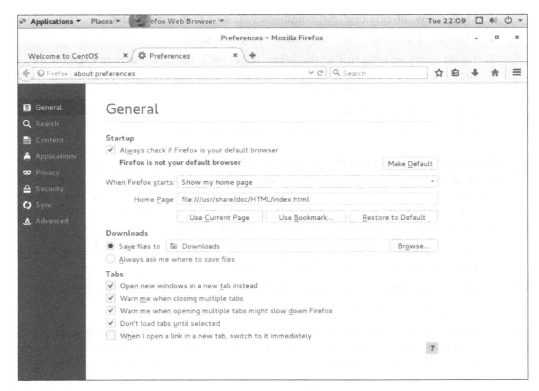

Figure 4-20 Customizing settings in Firefox

Source: CentOS 7/Mozilla Firefox

The General settings have the following options:

- Startup section—Specify whether to show the home page or a blank page when Firefox starts. You can also select the home page you want to display whenever you open Firefox.

- Downloads section—Specify whether to show the Downloads window when downloading a file, where to save downloaded files, and whether to prompt the user to choose the download destination.

- Tabs section—Specify preferences for the tabs.

Activity 4-12: Selecting General Settings in Firefox

Time Required: 15 minutes

Objective: Configure and note general settings for customizing Firefox.

Description: In this activity, you set the home page to a recently visited Web site.

1. If necessary, start your virtual machines using the appropriate instructions in Activity 1-1.
2. To open Firefox, click **Applications**, point to **Internet**, and then click **Firefox Web Browser**.
3. Type **www.mozilla.org** in the address bar, and then press **Enter**.
4. Click the **Edit** menu, and then click **Preferences**.
5. To set *www.mozilla.org* as the home page, click the **Use Current Page** button, and then click the **Home** icon in the upper-right corner of the browser. Notice that *www.mozilla.org* becomes the home page.
6. Close any open windows.
7. Leave the virtual machine logged on for the next activity.

Protecting Your Privacy in Firefox The privacy options in Firefox let you manage caches designed to protect your computer. You should clear these caches periodically to improve performance and security. Large, outdated caches can slow down your Web surfing, and storing personal information such as passwords can be a security risk; hackers may be able to read and steal your sensitive information.

To set the privacy options in Firefox (see Figure 4-21), click the Edit menu, click Preferences, and then click Privacy in the left panel.

You can manage the following items to protect your privacy when using Firefox:

- Tracking—Tell Web sites that you do not want to be tracked.

- History—Instruct Firefox to Remember history, Never remember history, or Use custom settings for history; you can also choose to clear your recent browsing history and remove individual cookies. You learned about cookies earlier in this chapter.

- Location Bar—Display a site's Web address (URL). The location bar is also called the *URL bar* or *address bar*. It remembers your browsing history, guesses your intended sites, and displays a list of suggested sites for easy selection.

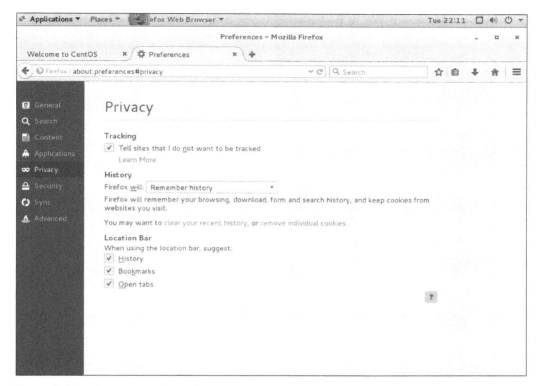

Figure 4-21 Privacy options in Firefox

Source: CentOS 7/Mozilla Firefox

If you choose "Use custom settings for history," you can prohibit all cookies or allow cookies for certain Web sites by clicking the Exceptions button (see Figure 4-22). You can also allow cookies only from "originating" Web sites; sometimes Web sites refer to other sites to load software, which you might consider a security risk. You might choose to allow cookies only for an amount of time you specify in the Keep until menu. Cookies usually expire in 30 days if you keep them. To remove cookies, click the Show Cookies button. When the Cookies screen appears, specify the cookie and click the Remove Cookie button. You can also click the Remove All Cookies button to delete all the cookies stored in the Web browser.

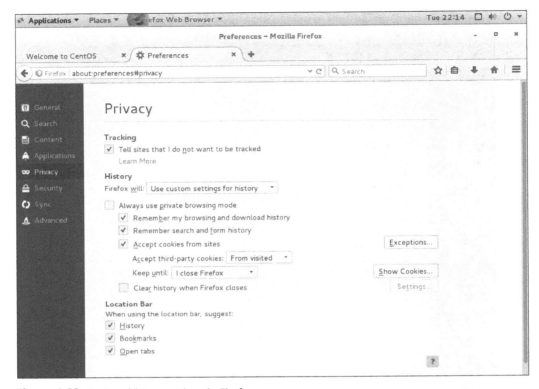

Figure 4-22 Custom history settings in Firefox

Source: CentOS 7/Mozilla Firefox

Activity 4-13: Setting Privacy Options in Firefox

Time Required: 15 minutes

Objective: Set Firefox privacy options and clear all of your browser history records.

Description: In this activity, you set privacy options in Firefox and clear the history. This activity is useful if you want to protect your privacy while using Firefox.

1. If necessary, start your virtual machines using the appropriate instructions in Activity 1-1.
2. To open Firefox, click **Applications**, point to **Internet**, and then click **Firefox Web Browser**.
3. To open the privacy options, click the **Edit** menu, click **Preferences**, and then click the **Privacy** icon.
4. To empty the history cache, click the **Firefox will** chevron, click **Remember history**, click the **clear your recent history** link, click the **Time range to clear** chevron, click **Today**, and then click **Clear now**.

5. To block a Web site from storing cookies, click the **Firefox will** chevron, click **Use custom settings for history**, click the **Exceptions** button, and then type **www.fcc.gov** (or some objectionable site of your choice).

6. To block *www.fcc.gov*, click **Block**; the URL moves to the Site and Status window.

7. To remove the site, click to highlight **www.fcc.gov**, click **Remove Site**, and then click **Close** to exit the window.

8. Close any open windows.

9. Leave the virtual machine logged on for future activities.

Customizing Content in Firefox The Content options in Firefox let you set behavior rules for Web sites to protect your computer. To set these rules in Firefox (see Figure 4-23), click the Edit menu, click Preferences, and then click Content in the left panel.

You can configure the following items:

- Pop-ups—Selecting the check box for "Block pop-up windows" stops annoying pop-up windows from appearing. Not all pop-up windows are ads, so you can indicate allowed sites by using the Exceptions button.

- Fonts & Colors—Click the Advanced or Colors buttons if you need to assign special color and font combinations to see Web pages better.

- Languages—Click the Choose button to set the default language and character encoding for Firefox.

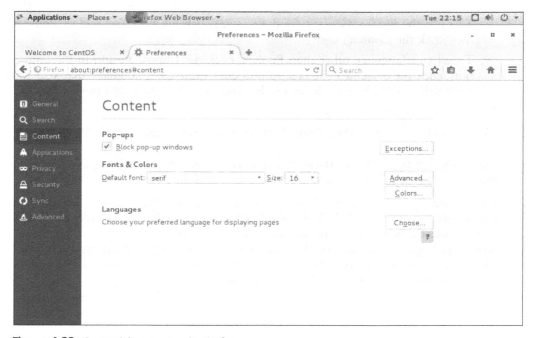

Figure 4-23 Customizing content in Firefox

Source: CentOS 7/Mozilla Firefox

Activity 4-14: Setting Content Features in Firefox

Time Required: 10 minutes

Objective: Open the Firefox Content window and set several options.

Description: In this activity, you set options for enabling and disabling pop-ups, and for display fonts and languages. This activity is helpful if you need to know more about the Content features in Firefox.

1. If necessary, start your virtual machines using the appropriate instructions in Activity 1-1.

2. To open Firefox, click **Applications**, point to **Internet**, and then click **Firefox Web Browser**.

3. To open the Content window, click the **Edit** menu, click **Preferences**, and then click the **Content** icon.

4. To block pop-up windows, click the **Block pop-up windows** check box or verify that it is already checked.

5. To set the minimum font size, click the **Advanced** button in the Fonts & Colors section, click the **Minimum font size** chevron, click **20**, click **OK**, and then click **Close**. Verify that the text in the Web page is much larger.

6. To open the Firefox Content window again, click the **Edit** menu, click **Preferences**, and then click the **Content** icon.

7. To delete the minimum font size, click the **Advanced** button in the Fonts & Colors section, click the **Minimum font size** chevron, click **None**, click **OK**, and then click **Close**.

8. To open the Firefox Content window again, click the **Edit** menu, click **Preferences**, and then click the **Content** icon.

9. To select a language other than English, click the **Choose** button in the Languages section, click the **Select a Language to add** chevron, click a language that you want to use for displaying Web pages from another country, click **Add**, and then click **OK**.

10. Close the Firefox windows.

11. Leave the virtual machine logged on for future activities.

Setting Security Features in Firefox To set the Security options in Firefox, click the Edit menu in the browser, click Preferences, and then click Security in the left panel.

Firefox manages the passwords you type as you access Web sites. Click the "Remember passwords for sites" check box to have Firefox prompt you to save passwords. If you want to set a master password to protect the other saved passwords, check "Use a master password" and specify the password in the pop-up screen. You can view saved passwords by clicking the Saved Passwords button. From this window, you can show passwords, remove a single password, or remove all your passwords.

Activity 4-15: Setting Security Features in Firefox

Time Required: 10 minutes

Objective: Set Firefox security options and clear all of the caches.

Description: In this activity, you set security options in Firefox and clear the caches. This activity is useful if you want to save your passwords while using Firefox.

1. If necessary, start your virtual machines using the appropriate instructions in Activity 1-1.

2. To open Firefox, click **Applications**, point to **Internet**, and then click **Firefox Web Browser.**

3. To open the Security options, click the **Edit** menu, click **Preferences**, and then click **Security** in the left panel.

4. To view a saved password, click the **Saved Passwords** button, click the Web site, and then click the **Show Passwords** button. Sites with associated user names and passwords appear in the window. The window might also be blank.

5. Click **Close**, and then close any open windows.

6. Leave the virtual machine logged on for future activities.

Choosing Advanced Options in Firefox The Advanced options in Firefox refer to navigation and security features; these concepts were explained earlier in this chapter in the Microsoft Edge sections. To select the Advanced options in Firefox (see Figure 4-24), click the Edit menu, click Preferences, and then click Advanced in the left panel. Five tabs are displayed on the Advanced options screen: General, Data Choices, Network, Update, and Certificates.

The following options are listed under the General tab:

- Accessibility—Select options that improve the accessibility of Firefox.

- Browsing—Select settings to make browsing more convenient, including automatic scrolling, smooth scrolling, hardware acceleration when available, and spell-checking.

The Data Choices tab provides the option to Enable Firefox Health Report. If the report is enabled, it will help you understand the performance of the current Firefox browser and share data with Mozilla about your browser's health.

The Network tab has three sections:

- Connection—Configures how Firefox connects to the Internet.

- Cached Web Content—Displays the current Web content cache use of disk space and provides the option to override automatic cache management. The Firefox cache temporarily stores images, scripts, and other parts of Web sites while you are browsing. You can specify a cache size in megabytes.

- Offline Web Content and User Data—Displays the current application's cache use of disk space and provides the option to inform you when a Web site asks to store data for offline use. To clear the cache, click the Edit menu, click Preferences, select the Advanced panel, and then click the Network tab. In the Offline Web Content and User Data section, click the Clear Now button.

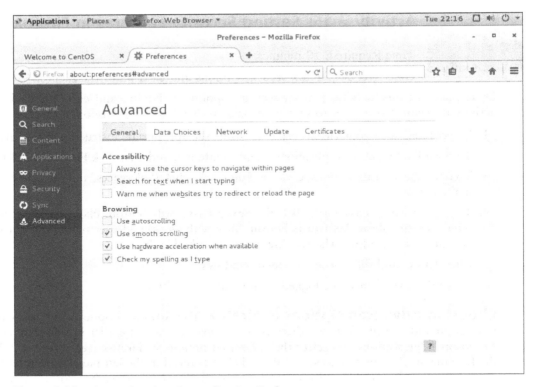

Figure 4-24 Advanced options for configuring Firefox

Source: CentOS 7/Mozilla Firefox

The Update tab specifies options for automatic search engine updates for Firefox. The automatic update for search engines is enabled by default.

The Certificates tab manages certificate information, identity authentication, and security devices. It allows you to decide whether to let the certificate be selected automatically or to prompt you for specific permission when a server requests your personal certificate. In addition, you can choose to query OCSP responder servers to confirm the current validity of certificates.

Activity 4-16: Using General and Advanced Options in Firefox

Time Required: 10 minutes

Objective: Use General and Advanced options in the Firefox browser.

Description: In this activity, you use General and Advanced options in Firefox. This activity is useful, for example, if you want Firefox to be your default browser.

1. If necessary, start your virtual machines using the appropriate instructions in Activity 1-1.

2. To open Firefox, click **Applications,** point to **Internet,** and then click **Firefox Web Browser.**

3. To open the Advanced options, click the **Edit** menu, click **Preferences,** and then click **General** in the left panel.

4. To check whether Firefox is the default browser, check **Always check if Firefox is your default browser** in the Startup section and then click **Make Default,** as shown in Figure 4-25. If Firefox is the only Web browser installed on your computer, you will not see this option.

5. To change the size of the cache space, click **Advanced** in the left panel, click the **Network** tab, and type **600** in the **Limit cache ... MB of space** text box. To clear the caches, click the **Clear Now** button.

6. Close any open windows.

7. Leave the virtual machine logged on for future activities.

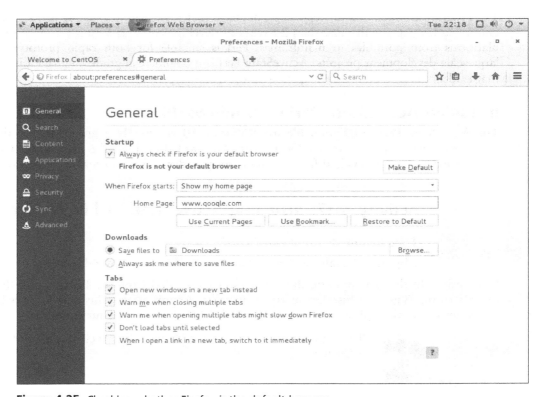

Figure 4-25 Checking whether Firefox is the default browser

Source: CentOS 7/Mozilla Firefox

Installing an Application

After you purchase or download an application, you must install it. You learned about the Microsoft Windows Installer and the Red Hat Package Manager (RPM) in Chapter 2; these installers typically automate most of the following tasks in an installation routine:

- Prepare the PC and complete any preinstallation steps, such as creating required directories.
- Uncompress the application. Most applications are compressed to reduce the size of the setup file.
- Run the setup or installation program to place the program modules in the proper directories and prepare them for use.
- Configure the program.
- Clean up and remove the files that are no longer needed.

The following sections provide information for installing ActiveState Perl, one of many applications you can use in both the Windows and Linux operating systems. After you install ActiveState Perl, you will use it to interpret a test script in each OS.

The Program Extraction and Reporting Language (Perl) is a highly capable, feature-rich programming language with more than 20 years of development. Perl 5 runs on more than 100 platforms from portables to mainframes. Perl is suitable for both rapid prototyping and large-scale development projects. **ActiveState Perl** is a commercial-grade language distribution that is ideal for community developers with open source projects.

Installing ActiveState Perl in Windows 10

The ActiveState Perl installation file for Windows 10 is actually a group of files that are stored together in a compressed file format. You will download the installation file. The installer extracts the individual files to a temporary folder and then runs the setup program.

Activity 4-17: Installing ActiveState Perl in Windows 10

Time Required: 15 minutes

Objective: Install the ActiveState Perl application in Windows 10.

Description: In this activity, you download ActiveState Perl from the Internet and then use the Microsoft Windows Installer utility to install the application. This activity is helpful if you want to install applications from downloaded files for use on your computer.

This activity requires an active Internet connection during the installation.

1. If necessary, start your virtual machines using the appropriate instructions in Activity 1-1.
2. To start Edge, type **Edge** in the search box on the taskbar. Click the **Microsoft Edge** link.

3. Type **ActiveState Perl download** in the search text box, and then press **Enter.**

4. Click the **ActivePerl Downloads–Perl Binaries for Windows, Linux** link. Use the link that accesses the *downloads.activestate.com* Web site.

5. Locate the **Download Perl: Other Platforms and Versions** table.

6. Click **Windows Installer (MSI)** in the top row to select the latest version for Windows (64-bit, x64). See Figure 4-26. The download process should start automatically.

7. Wait for the download to complete, and then click **View Downloads.**

8. Click the **Open Folder** button in the upper-right corner. Double-click the download package, click **Run,** and then click **Next.**

9. Click **I accept the terms in the License Agreement.** Click **Next** three times, and then click **Install.**

10. When the User Account Control window appears, click **Yes.**

11. Wait for the installation to complete, and then click **Finish.**

12. Close the Edge browser window. When asked, "Do you want to close all tabs?", click **Close all.**

13. Leave the virtual machine logged on; you will continue to work with ActiveState Perl in later activities.

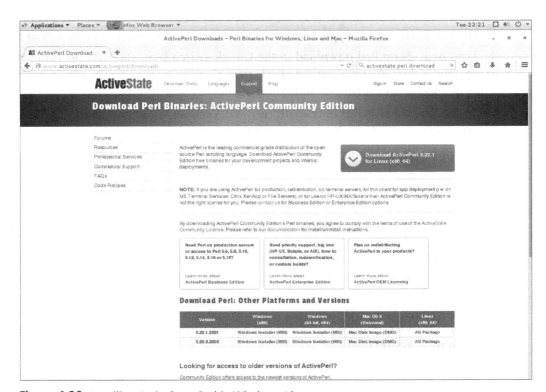

Figure 4-26 Installing ActiveState Perl in Windows 10

Source: CentOS 7/Mozilla Firefox

Installing ActiveState Perl in CentOS 7

Many applications are available for use in both the Windows 10 and Linux operating systems, but their installation routines can vary depending on which OS you use. As with Windows, you download the installation files from a Web site, but CentOS 7 has different installation options. In Chapter 2, RPM is introduced as an installation method. In this chapter, due to the limitation of the download source from ActiveState Perl's official Web site, a Linux archive handler called *GNU tar* is required to extract the ActivePerl tarball before installation.

Activity 4-18: Installing ActiveState Perl in CentOS 7

Time Required: 30 minutes

Objective: Install the ActiveState Perl application in CentOS 7.

Description: In this activity, you download and install ActiveState Perl by first using GNU tar to extract the ActivePerl tarball into the file system. The generic installer is used for the installation.

This activity requires an active Internet connection during the installation.

1. If necessary, start your virtual machines using the appropriate instructions in Activity 1-1.

2. To open Firefox, click **Applications,** point to **Internet,** and then click **Firefox Web Browser.**

3. Type **ActiveState Perl download** in the Google search box, and then press **Enter.**

4. Click the **ActivePerl Downloads** link. Use the link that accesses *www.activestate.com /activeperl/downloads.*

5. At the **Download Perl: Other Platforms and Versions** table, click **AS Package** in the top row—the latest version for Linux (x86_64).

If you are unsure about the current release number, ask your instructor.

6. When the Opening ActiveState Perl window appears, click the **Save File** radio button, and then click **OK.**

7. In the **Enter name of file to save to** screen, make sure to select the **user01** directory instead of **Downloads,** and then click the **Save** button (see Figure 4-27). Wait for the download to complete.

8. Click **Applications,** and then click **Terminal.** When the Terminal screen appears, type **ls** and press **Enter.** You should see the download package in the list. The package name starts with ActivePerl.

9. Type **tar zxf ActivePerl,** press the **Tab** key to invoke the autocomplete feature for the version numbers, and then press **Enter.** When you see the prompt again, type **ls** and then press **Enter.** You will see that a new directory has been created with the same name as the download package.

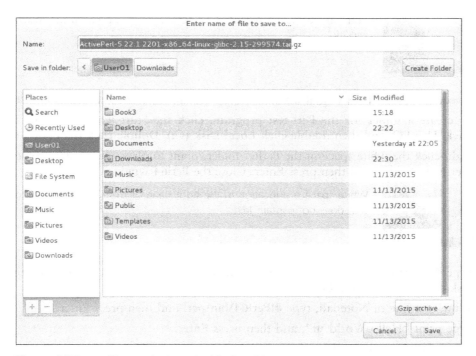

Figure 4-27 Installing ActiveState Perl in CentOS 7

Source: CentOS 7

10. Type **cd ActivePerl,** press the **Tab** key, and then press **Enter.**

11. Type **sh install.sh,** and then press **Enter.** Type **yes** two times. Type **/home/user01 /ActivePerl** as the top-level installation directory, and then press **Enter.**

12. Press **Enter** twice. Wait for the installation to finish.

13. Close any open windows in the virtual machine.

14. Leave the virtual machine logged on for future activities.

Activity 4-19: Testing the Installation of ActiveState Perl in Windows 10

Time Required: 10 minutes

Objective: Create a Perl script to test the installation of ActiveState Perl.

Description: In this activity, you use a text editor to create the Hello World script and then test the script using ActiveState Perl. This activity is useful if you need to test the installation of ActiveState Perl.

You must complete Activity 4-17 before you can perform the following activity.

1. If necessary, start your virtual machines using the appropriate instructions in Activity 1-1.
2. To create a folder for the Perl test program, click the **Start** icon. Click **File Explorer**. Click **This PC**, and then double-click **Local Disk (C:)**. Double-click the **Perl64** folder.
3. Right-click the white space of the Perl64 folder, point to **New**, click **Folder**, type **TestPerl** over New Folder, and then press **Enter**. Close the Perl64 window.

White space is a location in the right pane of the File Explorer window that does not contain text.

4. Type **Notepad** in the **Search the web and Windows** search box at the bottom of the desktop, and then press **Enter**.
5. In the first line of Notepad, type **#!Perl64\bin\perl** and then press **Enter**.
6. Type **print "Hello World \n"**, and then press **Enter**.
7. To save the file, click **File**, and then click **Save As**.
8. Click **This PC**, scroll and double-click **Local Disk (C:)**, double-click **Perl64**, and then double-click the **TestPerl** folder. Click the **Save as type** chevron, click **All Files**, type **hello.pl** in the File name text box, and then click **Save**.
9. To open a Command Prompt console, type **CMD** in the search text box and click **Command Prompt desktop app**.
10. To change to the TestPerl folder, type **cd C:\Perl64\TestPerl** at the CMD prompt and then press **Enter**.
11. Type **hello.pl**, and then press **Enter**.
12. Verify that "Hello World" appears.

If "Hello World" does not appear, contact your instructor.

13. Close any open windows in the virtual machine.
14. To shut down the virtual machine, click **Start**, and then click the **Shut Down** button.
15. Wait a moment for the Windows 10 virtual machine to shut down completely.
16. Leave the PC logged on for the next activity.

Activity 4-20: Testing the Installation of ActiveState Perl in CentOS 7

Time Required: 10 minutes

Objective: Create a Perl script to test the installation of ActiveState Perl.

Description: In this activity, you use a text editor to create the Hello World script and then test the script using ActiveState Perl. This activity is useful if you need to test the installation of ActiveState Perl.

4

You must complete Activity 4-18 before you can perform the following activity.

1. If necessary, start your virtual machines using the appropriate instructions in Activity 1-1.
2. To open gedit, click **Applications**, point to **Accessories**, and then click **gedit Text Editor**.
3. Type **#! /home/user01/ActivePerl/bin/perl**, and then press **Enter**.

In Step 3, you enter a space between ! and /home/user01/ActivePerl /bin/perl. The remainder of the line contains no other spaces.

4. Type **print "Hello World \n"**, and then press **Enter** (see Figure 4-28).

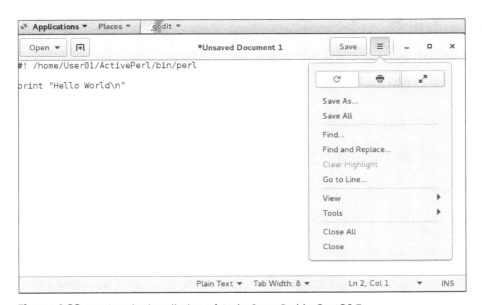

Figure 4-28 Testing the installation of ActiveState Perl in CentOS 7

Source: CentOS 7/gedit

5. To save the file, click **File**, click **Save As**, and type **hello.pl** in the **Name** text box. Double-click the **user01** directory in the right panel. Press the **Create Folder** button, type **testPerl** as the folder name, press **Enter**, and then click **Save** (see Figure 4-29).

6. To open a Terminal console, click **Applications**, point to **Utilities**, and then click **Terminal**.

7. To change to the testPerl directory, type **cd ~/testPerl** and then press **Enter**.

8. To mark the perl script as executable, type **chmod 755 hello.pl** and then press **Enter**.

9. Type **./hello.pl**, and then press **Enter**.

 In the previous step, enter a period and then a slash before hello.pl.

10. Verify that "Hello World" appears.

 If "Hello World" does not appear, contact your instructor.

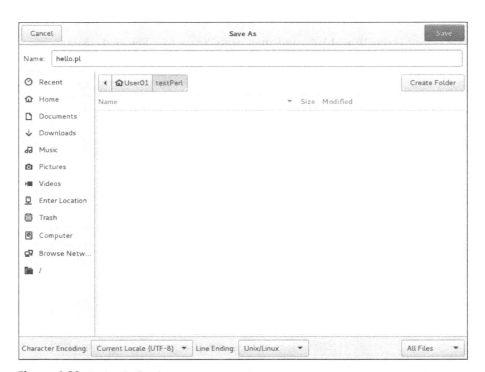

Figure 4-29 Saving hello.pl

Source: CentOS 7

11. To shut down the virtual machine, click your account name in the upper-right corner of the desktop, and then click **Power Off** twice.

12. Wait a moment for the CentOS 7 virtual machine to shut down completely.

13. Close any remaining open windows, log off, and shut down your PC.

Chapter Summary

■ You can obtain Help information using the Help and Support Center in Windows 10 and the Help Center in CentOS 7. Each application has Help files that are organized by topic and that contain glossaries and indexes. Tutorials in the Help Center can help new users learn new tools quickly.

■ Microsoft Edge and Mozilla Firefox are browsers that offer access to the Internet. Each browser has features that help you perform Internet searches, access information on the Web, and effectively manage Internet searching and URLs.

■ ActiveState Perl is one of the many applications you can install in both the Windows 10 and Linux operating systems. The installation routine is different depending on which operating system you use. After you install ActiveState Perl, you should test the installation by coding and running a small test script.

Key Terms

ActiveState Perl   The leading commercial-grade distribution of the open source Perl dynamic programming language; ActiveState Perl is available for Windows, Linux, and Mac OS X.

bot   A program that performs a repetitive or time-consuming task on a network or the Internet. On the Internet, for example, a bot might search Web sites and newsgroups for information and then index them in a database or another record-keeping system; also called a *spider*.

cookies   Blocks of data that a Web server stores on a client system to identify visitors to a Web site. When a user returns to the same Web site, the browser sends a copy of the cookie back to the server. Cookies can also instruct the server to send a customized version of a requested Web page, submit account information to the user, and serve other administrative purposes.

digital rights management (DRM)   Various access control technologies that restrict the use of proprietary software, hardware, or content.

hard coded   Data in a program or application that is designed to handle a specific situation. Data that is hard coded into a program makes it dependent on specific values rather than on values a user can enter.

hyperlink   A word, phrase, symbol, or image that you click to move from one Web location to another. A hyperlink can take you to a different part of the same Web site or to a different Web site. Hyperlinked text is usually underlined or displayed in a different color from the rest of the text.

InPrivate   A feature in Windows Web browsers that prevents others from seeing what sites and content you look at on the Web.

portal site   A Web site that serves as a gateway to the Internet. A portal is a collection of links, content, and services designed to guide users to interesting information, news, weather, entertainment, commerce sites, chat rooms, and so on.

search engine   An Internet program that searches for keywords and phrases in Web files, newsgroups, and archives. Some search engines are dedicated to a single Web site. Others search multiple sites, using agents such as spiders to gather lists of available files and databases and store them for user searches.

Uniform Resource Locator (URL)   An address used in a Web browser to locate a resource on the Internet.

Review Questions

1. An application can be a _____. (Choose all that apply.)

   a. text editor

   b. word processor

   c. text document

   d. game

2. You can use the Windows 10 Help and Support Center to _____. (Choose all that apply.)

   a. take a tutorial

   b. obtain the latest information from Microsoft

   c. search for help on a given topic

   d. seek tips for playing computer games

   e. determine the hardware and software configuration

3. The System Information tool provides _____. (Choose all that apply.)

   a. detailed information for the computer

   b. summary information for the computer

   c. a Help and Support option

   d. information on browsers

4. The CentOS 7 equivalent of the Windows 10 Help and Support Center is _____.

   a. Support

   b. Help and Support

   c. How To

   d. Help Center

5. Mozilla Firefox and Windows Edge are both known as _____.

    a. toolbars

    b. menus

    c. Web browsers

    d. Web sites

6. URL is an acronym for _____.

    a. United Reform Language

    b. Uniform Reform Locator

    c. United Resource Locator

    d. Uniform Resource Locator

7. A URL is used to _____.

    a. identify the location of any Web site

    b. begin the browser

    c. access applications on your desktop

    d. access the browser on the desktop

8. A hyperlink is _____.

    a. used to access applications on your desktop

    b. used to identify the location of any Web site

    c. used only within browsers

    d. used to access Web sites on the Internet

9. Portal sites are _____. (Choose all that apply.)

    a. pages with links to a variety of information

    b. useful tools for getting around the Internet

    c. guides to what's available on the Internet

    d. used at Web sites such as *www.yahoo.com* or *www.msn.com*

10. You can access Web sites by using _____. (Choose all that apply.)

    a. links

    b. the browser's History option

    c. bookmarks

    d. the Web Search tool

11. Search engines are used to _____. (Choose all that apply.)

    a. survey the Web and build their Web page databases

    b. examine many documents on the Web

    c. find information from only one specific source

    d. secretly write programs

12. Other terms for search engine programs include _____. (Choose all that apply.)

    a. worms

    b. crawlers

    c. bots

    d. spiders

13. InPrivate browsing protects you from _____. (Choose all that apply.)

    a. others from seeing the URLs that you accessed

    b. seeing what you looked at on the Web

    c. seeing what files you edited

    d. using the Safety tab

14. RPM is an acronym for _____.

    a. Real Program Manager

    b. Resource Program Management

    c. Red Hat Package Manager

    d. Red Hat Program Manager

15. Caches should be cleared because _____. (Choose all that apply.)

    a. they are too convenient

    b. site requests and displays can be slowed down by large outdated caches

    c. stored passwords could be stolen by hackers

    d. form information can be a security risk

16. Cookies are used by Web sites _____.

    a. to earn money for new servers

    b. to maintain information and settings, such as your surfing preferences

    c. to keep browsers from closing

    d. to keep browsers from accessing sites

17. A file that has a zip extension _____. (Choose all that apply.)

    a. contains one or more files that have been compressed or stored

    b. needs to be processed with an archive utility to extract the files

    c. is much larger than the original file that was used to create it

    d. is generally smaller than the original file or files that were used to create it

18. Application installers are used to _____. (Choose all that apply.)

    a. prepare the PC and complete any preinstallation steps

    b. uncompress the application

    c. run the setup or installation program to place the program modules in the proper directories and prepare them for use

    d. configure the program

19. Microsoft Windows Installer and Red Hat Package Manager are known as _____.

    a. compression utilities

    b. compilers

    c. object-oriented programming languages

    d. application installers

20. ActiveState Perl _____. (Choose all that apply.)

    a. runs on both Windows and Linux operating systems

    b. stands for Program Extraction and Reporting Language

    c. is a feature-rich programming language

    d. can be tested with the "Hello World" script

4

Case Projects

CASE PROJECTS

Case 4-1: Using Microsoft Help and Support

A friend asks you to examine her computer, which has Windows 10 installed. You need to know what hardware and software are installed on the computer. Your friend logs on to the computer with administrative rights. What is the quickest way to get the "big picture" of your friend's computer? Write a short report detailing how you would do this.

Case 4-2: Configuring Edge

You volunteer to support a small nonprofit organization whose network consists of 10 computers, all of which have Windows 10 Professional installed. Users connect to the Internet through an Internet firewall. The manager is concerned about protecting the privacy of employees when they access Web sites. How will you configure Microsoft Edge to meet the manager's concerns? Express your written answer in business terms rather than technical terms.

Case 4-3: Configuring Firefox

Your boss has asked you to prepare a short presentation on Firefox security. To support your presentation, prepare a short outline of the security features in Firefox to hand out.

## chapter 5

File Systems

After reading this chapter and completing the exercises, you will be able to:

- Describe the characteristics of four Windows 10 file systems
- Describe the characteristics of three CentOS 7 file systems
- Create a file system in Windows 10 and CentOS 7
- Mount a file system in Windows 10 and CentOS 7
- Manage file systems in Windows 10 and CentOS 7

A file system refers to the overall structure in which files are named, stored, and organized. File systems consist of files, directories (or folders), and the information needed to locate and access them. To prepare to use current and future operating systems, you should develop skills for using the various file systems in Windows 10 and CentOS 7. This chapter explains how.

Before storing data on a PC's hard drives, you must prepare them to accept the files. In this chapter, you will learn to create **storage areas**—areas on a disk that can be allocated and formatted for a file system—and then place a file system within a storage area. In addition, you will learn to manage file systems with standard tools in Windows 10 and CentOS 7.

File System Characteristics in Windows 10 and CentOS 7

Before you can make intelligent decisions about selecting and using a file system in Windows 10, you must know how to implement the file system. Specifically, you need to know the following information, which is explained in this section:

- Allocation of storage areas on the hard drive
- Assignment of drive letters, which are used to access storage areas
- Characteristics of available file systems

To implement the CentOS 7 file systems, you need to know the following information, which is explained in this chapter:

- Allocation of the partitions on the hard drive
- Creation of file systems on the partitions
- Creation and management of directories and files on the file systems
- Characteristics of available file systems

The file system format in Linux looks like a tree or root system and is very different from the Windows file system. The file system starts with the root level, which is denoted with a "/". Within the file system, the root level is the highest level of a path. Linux has **partitions**, but they are not prominent because of how they are used. Unlike the Windows operating system, which attaches a letter to each partition, thus limiting the number of partitions to 26, Linux and UNIX allow you simply to "mount" as many partitions as you want. The mount command serves to attach the file system to the file tree.

In the default installation of CentOS 7, two partitions are "auto-mounted" on the system. The first partition is the primary partition, which holds the files and directories associated with the operating system. The other partition is a swap partition, which is used by the computer to extend the RAM memory. Other types of partitions can be created, but the only other one covered in this chapter is the extended partition. Each partition can be formatted with different types of file systems, but the default installation of CentOS 7 formats the drives as Ext4.

Disk Partitions in Windows 10

Figure 5-1 shows the BIOS settings for the three SCSI-controlled drives represented by virtual hard drives in the VMware virtualization software. Oracle VirtualBox and Microsoft Hyper-V provide access to BIOS settings through menus available in the virtual software interface.

Figure 5-2 shows that each controller supports devices that could be a hard drive or CD-ROM drive when Oracle VirtualBox virtualization software is used. For purposes of illustration, consider a virtual machine with three physical hard drives and a CD-ROM drive on the same SATA controller.

Next, consider how the same virtual machine's drives might be separated into partitions. These hard drives and their partitions are shown in the Disk Management console, as indicated in Figure 5-3. (The allocation of drive letters is covered in the next section.)

Windows 10 has two types of storage: basic and dynamic. Basic storage is most commonly used with Windows. Using **basic disk** storage, you can allocate primary partitions in Windows 10.

A **primary partition** normally contains an OS, such as Windows 10. The active primary partition contains the files that start an OS. You can have up to four primary partitions per physical hard drive, or three if you use an extended partition. You can only create an extended partition after creating three primary partitions.

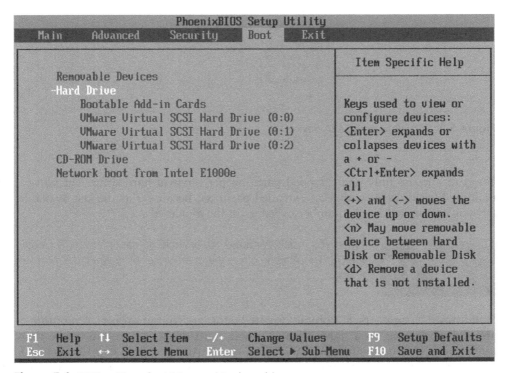

Figure 5-1 BIOS settings for VMware virtual machines

Source: VMware/Phoenix

Figure 5-2 VirtualBox with SATA devices

Source: Oracle VirtualBox

You can allocate only one extended partition per physical hard drive, but you can allocate multiple logical drives within an extended partition. Because Z is the last available drive letter, you are limited by the number of letters in the alphabet.

 When you install Windows 10, a single primary partition is created for the OS. This scheme offers the greatest flexibility when defining storage areas.

Windows 10 supports a volume-oriented storage configuration. A **volume** is a fixed amount of storage on a hard drive. A single hard drive can contain more than one volume, and a volume might span more than one hard drive. You can initialize a hard drive as a **dynamic disk,** where storage is divided into volumes rather than partitions. Dynamic disks are better suited for the vast data storage requirements of Windows Server 2012 or Windows Server 2016, and are therefore beyond the scope of this text.

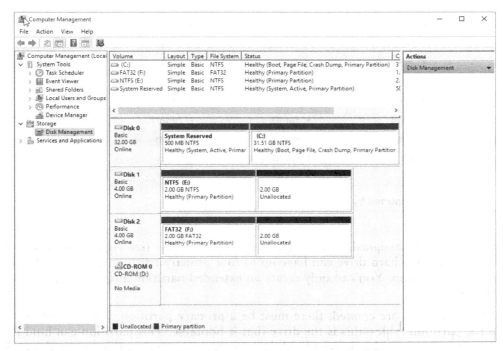

Figure 5-3 Disk Management view of three partitions and CD-ROM drive

Source: Windows 10/Computer Management

Disk Partitions in CentOS 7

This section shows how the hardware configuration you saw in Windows 10 will look within CentOS 7. Hard drives are listed in CentOS 7 in a directory called /dev, the same way they are listed in all Linux- and UNIX-based installations. This directory holds all physical and virtual devices on the computer. The physical hard drives are listed as sda, sdb, sdc, and so on; each new hard drive is assigned the next letter in line. Each drive

```
                              user01@centos7:/dev
File  Edit  View  Search  Terminal  Help
[user01@centos7 dev]$ ls -l | grep sd
brw-rw----. 1 root    disk      8,    0 Nov 11 18:34 sda
brw-rw----. 1 root    disk      8,    1 Nov 11 18:34 sda1
brw-rw----. 1 root    disk      8,    2 Nov 11 18:34 sda2
brw-rw----. 1 root    disk      8,   16 Nov 11 19:58 sdb
brw-rw----. 1 root    disk      8,   17 Nov 11 20:09 sdb1
brw-rw----. 1 root    disk      8,   32 Nov 11 20:16 sdc
brw-rw----. 1 root    disk      8,   48 Nov 11 19:02 sdd
[user01@centos7 dev]$
```

Figure 5-4 List of hard drives in CentOS 7

Source: CentOS 7

• adfs	• affs	• autofs	• cifs	• coda
• coherent	• cramfs	• debugfs	• devpts	• efs
• ext	• ext2	• ext3	• ext4	• hfs
• hfsplus	• hpfs	• iso9660	• jfs	• minix
• msdos	• ncpfs	• nfs	• nfs4	• ntfs
• proc	• qnx4	• ramfs	• reiserfs	• romfs
• squashfs	• smbfs	• sysv	• tmpfs	• ubifs
• udf	• ufs	• umsdos	• usbfs	• vfat
• xenix	• xfs	• xiafs		

Table 5-1   File systems supported by CentOS 7

partition will be assigned a number, such as sda1 and sda2 (see Figure 5-4). Like Windows systems, a single hard drive can have up to four primary partitions, or three if you use an extended partition. You can only create an extended partition after creating three primary partitions.

When partitions are created, there must be a primary partition, which is set as "Active" in the partition table—this is the drive that is bootable. This partition can hold the operating system or not, but it must hold the files that contain the information about all partitions on the system and which one holds the operating system. CentOS 7 also uses the GRUB program to manage partitions on the system instead of using the master boot record (MBR) on the hard drive. CentOS 7 natively supports the file systems listed in Table 5-1.

After a hard drive is added to the system, the drive can be partitioned and formatted using the Disks utility in the GNOME GUI, or using the `fdisk` or `parted` command on the command line. After being partitioned and formatted, the drive can be mounted and used.

Drive-Lettering Conventions for Windows 10

Windows 10 tends to follow the drive-lettering conventions that were established years ago for the earliest hard drives. You need to assign a letter to each hard drive and optical drive installed in your PC.

Each physical drive could have one or more partitions or volumes allocated. For example, when you installed Windows 10, you were asked to indicate the partition in which you wanted to install the OS. For most installations, this would be the first partition on the first physical hard drive or the master drive on the first controller. This partition was assigned to be the C drive. During installation, this partition was indicated as a primary partition and marked as active. An active partition contains an OS; by being marked as active, the PC will load the OS from this partition. The active partition also contains the files required to boot the computer. The letters A and B are reserved for two floppy drives that do not exist on most modern PCs.

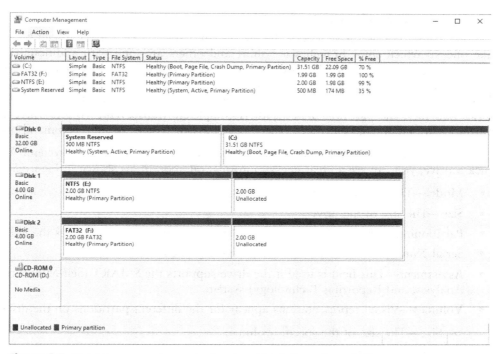

Volume	Layout	Type	File System	Status	Capacity	Free Space	% Free
(C:)	Simple	Basic	NTFS	Healthy (Boot, Page File, Crash Dump, Primary Partition)	31.51 GB	22.09 GB	70 %
FAT32 (F:)	Simple	Basic	FAT32	Healthy (Primary Partition)	1.99 GB	1.99 GB	100 %
NTFS (E:)	Simple	Basic	NTFS	Healthy (Primary Partition)	2.00 GB	1.98 GB	99 %
System Reserved	Simple	Basic	NTFS	Healthy (System, Active, Primary Partition)	500 MB	174 MB	35 %

Figure 5-5 Disk Management console showing drive letters after additions

Source: Windows 10/Disk Management

Windows 10 assigns drive letters as you create the various partitions and logical drives. You should create multiple storage areas to separate the OS from data. For example, the partitions and logical drives in Figure 5-5 were created in the following sequence:

- The System Reserved partition, placed on the Disk 0 hard drive to facilitate system recovery, did not receive a drive letter.
- The first primary partition on the first physical drive, Disk 0, was assigned drive letter C. This partition was selected during the installation of Windows 10.
- The CD-ROM drive that was available during installation received drive letter D.
- The next primary partition, which is on Disk 1, was assigned drive letter E.
- The primary partition on the remaining drive, Disk 2, received the drive letter F.

You can view the letters assigned to drives and change the CD-ROM drive letter using the Disk Management console, as shown later in Activity 5-3.

You might be annoyed that Windows 10 assigns the letter D to the CD-ROM drive when Windows 10 is installed. If you create another partition, it is assigned drive letter E, when you probably want the disk drive letters to be C and D. To address this issue, you can assign the letter R to the CD-ROM drive before allocating space for the second partition.

Mounting a Partition in CentOS 7

CentOS 7 does not use drive letters; the file system is set up like a tree and can be visualized like one, in which some branches are short and others are long with additional branches. Figure 5-6 gives you a general idea of how the tree looks, but it is not an actual representation of the CentOS 7 file system. Any partitioned file system can be mounted at any point within the tree. As you switch between different directories, the tree simply looks like directories and files; the partition underneath is completely transparent. To see where different partitions are mounted, you can use the Disks utility or type df from a command prompt.

Using the Disks utility, you can see how many drives are connected to the system. When you click a drive, you can see a great deal of information about it, as shown in Figure 5-7.

- Model—The type of drive.
- Size—The size of the drive.
- Partitioning—This field contains information only if the drive contains the MBR.
- Serial Number—The serial number assigned to the drive.
- Assessment—This field is used if the drive supports the SMART (Self-Monitoring, Analysis, and Reporting Technology) system.
- Volumes—Visual representations appear for the different partitions on the drive.
  - Size—The size of the specific volume.
  - Device—The device name of the volume.
  - Partition Type—If applicable, this field shows the partition type (for example, Linux), and whether the drive is bootable.
  - Contents—How the volume is formatted and where it is mounted.

After a partition is created, mounting it is a very simple process. You need to create a directory that will be used as the mount point. Then, from a command prompt, type the following command:

```
mount "partition path" "directory path"
```

If you mount a partition in a directory that has files and other directories, they will be hidden until the partition is "unmounted." Mounting partitions in this way allows you to create very large partitions to house logs or a great amount of data without taking the risk of filling up the drive that contains the OS and crashing the system.

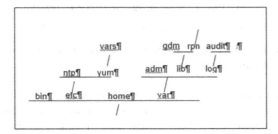

Figure 5-6 Linux tree example

Source: CentOS 7

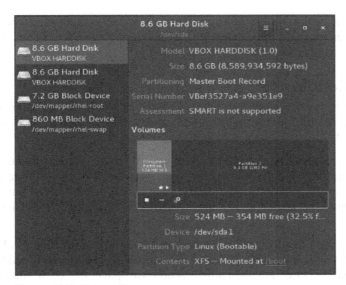

Figure 5-7 Disks utility

Source: CentOS 7/GNOME

Types of File Systems in Windows 10

The **file allocation table (FAT)** is a file system that was originally developed for early PCs running DOS. The FAT file system is relatively uncomplicated and is supported on a number of operating systems, including Windows 7, Windows 10, and Linux.

FAT32 File System—Windows 10

To support larger hard drives, Microsoft implemented the **FAT32** file system with Windows 95 OSR 2. This file system uses 32-bit cluster numbers (of which 28 bits are currently used). In theory, the 28-bit **sector** address should permit about 268,435,438 **clusters,** which allows drive sizes of approximately 2 **terabytes** (about 2 trillion bytes). However, Microsoft chose to limit the cluster count. For Windows 10, the partition limit is 32 GB for the primary partition. FAT32 continued the use of **subdirectories** and long filenames.

exFAT File System—Windows 10

Using an external flash drive among Apple, Linux, and Windows computers can be a hassle because you constantly have to reformat it to match the operating system you are using. If you use the Microsoft platform-independent **exFAT** file system, you can share files between different operating systems.

Essentially, exFAT is a file system that is both readable and writable on any modern Apple, Linux, or Windows OS. Just format the drive on a Windows machine and you are ready to use your USB drive:

1. Open Windows Explorer, right-click your drive in the left pane, and then click Format.
2. Click the File System chevron, and then click exFAT.
3. Click the Start button, and then close the window when finished.

The drive should now work well among Apple, Linux, and Windows operating systems. It will not work with older versions of Linux unless you install Linux's exFAT drivers, but for most people, exFAT is an excellent file system.

NT File System—Windows 10

NTFS (**New Technology File System**) was introduced with the first version of Windows NT. NTFS is a completely different file system from FAT32, and is the file system used for new installations of Windows 10.

When using basic disks, NTFS supports volumes as large as 2 terabytes. This is an enormous amount of hard drive space; for example, a database that contains all of the satellite photos taken by the United States and the Soviet Union during the Cold War requires about 2 terabytes. NTFS uses clusters that are similar in size to those in FATs: 512 bytes to 64 KB, with 4 KB being the default.

While FAT file systems use the file allocation table for managing access to files, NTFS uses the **master file table (MFT)**, which contains information about all the files and folders on the NTFS volume. The MFT allocates a certain amount of space for each file record. A file's attributes are written to the allocated space in the MFT. Elements such as the file's name, its security information, and even its data are all file attributes. Small files (typically 1,500 bytes or smaller) can be entirely contained within the MFT record. Fast access is assured by the use of a binary tree rather than the linear structure of FAT; NTFS does not search linearly through all table elements to find a needed file, but instead uses the **binary search** algorithm, a programming technique for locating an item quickly in a sequential list.

At the file level, NTFS supports many options that are not available in FAT32 file systems. The most notable options are:

- Journalizing—Provides a fail-safe mechanism by using transactions to ensure that data is written to the hard drive.

- Compression—Reduces the space needed to store a file.

- Encryption—Keeps files safe from intruders who might gain unauthorized physical access to sensitive, stored data (for example, by stealing a laptop computer).

- Security—Restricts data access to users who have permission to access the files.

- Auditing—Tracks the access or attempted access to files.

- Quotas—Limits the total size of files that an individual user can store on the hard drive.

These options are explained in the following sections. You need this information to use NTFS effectively.

If you are running Windows 10 and CentOS 7, it is important that you find a file system that is compatible with both systems. If formatting a drive connected by USB, you should use ExFAT so that the drive can be seen by Linux.

Journalizing—Ensuring That Data Is Written A file system that uses journalizing maintains data integrity for the hard drive if the OS crashes or stops abnormally. NTFS provides a fail-safe file system that can correct itself against a hard drive sector corruption or a power loss during hard drive writes. NTFS uses transactions, which means that the write action is either accomplished or canceled, that there are no incomplete hard drive writes, and that you will not lose data during a hard drive write.

If Windows 10 detects during a write operation that a sector is damaged, Windows 10 marks the sector as damaged and writes the data in another sector.

The case of a power loss is more complex. If data is being written and a power loss occurs, the OS restarts and discovers that the transaction was not completed. The transaction is then processed and the write operation is completed, ensuring that the power loss did not result in data loss.

5

Compression—Saving Space The Windows 10 OS supports **compression**, a means of reducing the amount of space needed to store a block of data. With compression technology, you do not need additional software to reduce the size of files on your hard drive. For example, word-processing documents contain considerable white space and other repetitive characters, and usually yield good compression. Compressed files must be **decompressed** when they are accessed, and then must be recompressed prior to rewriting to the hard drive. This decompression and recompression requires processor cycles that can reduce the performance of your PC. For this reason, you should reserve compression for infrequently used files and folders.

Encryption—Protecting Data When you use NTFS **encryption**, only you as the file creator can view the contents of a file. Anyone else who tries to view the file will see gibberish and will be denied access. For you, the file looks normal; it is automatically decrypted when accessed by an application.

Under normal circumstances, not even an administrator can view an encrypted file. In an emergency, however, an administrator can decrypt a file. In Windows 10, a file can be encrypted or compressed on a hard drive, but not both.

 You may feel that the inability to view other users' files is a little severe, but Windows 10 is specifically designed this way for security reasons. For example, you may have heard stories of employees leaving their laptops in airports; encryption keeps others from being able to view sensitive files.

Security—Restricting Access Just as you would place valuables in a locked box to guard against theft, Windows 10 controls access to files and folders. To open the locked box, you would need the key that fits the lock. Windows 10 controls the keys (user accounts) and the locks (permissions).

In Windows 10, you need a user account and a password to access the PC. Before you can access a file, Windows 10 determines if you have permission by comparing your user ID to users who have the correct permissions to access the file (such as read, write, and modify).

When a match occurs, access is permitted. As you may expect, if a match does not occur, Windows 10 displays a message indicating that access was denied.

Windows 10 is designed to provide security for files and folders accessed on an NTFS. While you may never need to specify these permissions (this is the administrator's job), you must be aware that such a security system exists to protect data on the PC.

Auditing—Tracking Access Windows 10 deploys **auditing** to keep track of previous attempts to access data in NTFS. Because auditing requires significant processing resources and hard drive space, it is not turned on by default.

When auditing is enabled, you can configure Windows 10 to keep track of certain events. When any of these events occur, Windows 10 makes an entry in a security log. Each entry indicates information about an access event, including the type of event, the date and time that it occurred, which user triggered the event, and other relevant information.

Unless you are an administrator or another user who has been granted permission to access the security log, you will not be able to read it. However, you need to be aware that an administrator may have enabled auditing to track access to sensitive data on your work PC.

Quotas—Limiting Storage When a PC is shared by several users, Windows 10 can be configured to enforce **quotas**, which are limits on the amount of data that each user can store on each storage area on the hard drive. Quotas are set for individual users and individual storage areas (in other words, an administrator cannot limit space for a group of people). Users who attempt to store data beyond their quota will receive an error message indicating that the hard drive is full. By reviewing the log file, the administrator can determine who has reached the quota limit or the warning limit.

Optical Media File Systems

You are probably familiar with CD-ROMs, which are a form of optical disc. For example, you may have used a CD-ROM to install an OS or an application. An optical disc is a computer storage medium that operates using digitized beams of light. Windows 10 supports two file systems for optical media:

- UDF (Universal Disk Format) was developed by the Optical Storage Technology Association. It was designed for read-write interoperability among the major operating systems and for compatibility between rewritable and write-once media. DVDs and Blu-ray discs are based on UDF; it is also an option for CD-Rs and CD-RWs. The specifications for UDF are contained within ISO/IEC 13346.

- Compact Disc File System (CDFS) is not an independent file system; instead, it is a loosely used alias for ISO 9660, the CD-ROM file system standard intended to make CD-ROMs readable by many different platforms.

Optical media may be used as a file with virtual machines in the form of a virtual disk image, which is also known as an *ISO image*. ISO image file names end with a file extension of .iso.

File Systems in CentOS 7

Just like Windows 10, CentOS 7 supports a number of file systems. In this section, you will learn about the CentOS 7 file systems.

Ext2—CentOS 7

Ext2, the Extended 2 file system (ext2fs), is an older file system used by Linux implementations. Ext2fs provides the same functionality as NTFS does for Windows 10:

- Compression—Reduces the space needed to store a file.

- Encryption—Keeps files safe from intruders who might gain unauthorized physical access to sensitive, stored data (for example, by stealing a laptop computer).

- Security—Restricts data access to users who have permission to access the files.

- Auditing—Tracks the access or attempted access to files.

- Quotas—Limits the total size of files that an individual user can store on the hard drive.

Ext3—CentOS 7

Ext3, the Extended 3 file system, is the most widely used Linux file system; it adds robustness through its addition of journalizing to the functionality of ext2. Journalizing provides a failsafe mechanism, using transactions to ensure that data is written to the hard drive, as NTFS does for Windows 10.

Ext4—CentOS 7

Ext4, the Extended 4 file system, adds robustness through a greater implementation of journalizing, faster time-stamping, faster file system checking, and inode structure extents, which replace the traditional block mapping scheme used by the ext2 and ext3 file systems, and afford even less chance of fragmentation than other Linux systems. Ext4 also offers larger file system support—a 48-bit block as opposed to ext3's 32-bit block.

If you are working with digital media, you need to know about the file systems CentOS 7 uses with CDs and DVDs. The ISO 966 file system is used by most CD-ROMs, and the UDF file system is meant for use with CD-RWs and DVDs.

The following activity assumes that the three-disk setup from the appendix has been completed.

Activity 5-1: Finding File System Information in Windows 10

Time Required: 10 minutes

Objective: Locate information about the file systems in Windows 10.

Description: In this activity, you log on to your virtual machine and view information about file systems. This activity is useful if you need to make a decision about a file system.

1. Start your virtual machines using the appropriate instructions in Activity 1-1.

2. To open the Control Panel, right-click the **Start** button in the lower-left corner of the screen and then click **Control Panel.**

3. To open the Administrative tools, click the **System and Security** link and then click the **Administrative Tools** link.

4. To run Computer Management as an administrator, right-click **Computer Management,** click **Run as administrator,** type **Pa$$w0rd,** and then click **Yes.**

5. To see the partitions for your virtual machine, click **Disk Management** in the left pane under **Storage.**

To see all four disks, locate and click the bar below the horizontal slider, and then drag the bar up.

6. View the information about Disk 0. Note that the installation of Windows 10 occupies the entire disk. Note the size of Disk 0.

7. View the information about Disk 1, and note that a 2-GB NTFS partition was previously allocated by your instructor. Also note that 2 GB of the disk has not been allocated and can be used for future allocations.

8. View the information about Disk 2 and a FAT32 partition.

9. Verify that a disk was assigned for use by CD-ROM media.

The CD-ROM drive is most likely empty.

10. Close the Computer Management window.

11. Leave the virtual machine logged on for future activities.

Activity 5-2: Finding Partition Information in CentOS 7

Time Required: 10 minutes

Objective: Locate information about the partitions in CentOS 7.

Description: This activity is useful if you want to review information before making a decision about a file system in CentOS 7.

1. Start your virtual machines using the appropriate instructions in Activity 1-1.

2. To open the Disks utility, click **Applications,** click **Utilities,** and then click **Disks.**

3. View the information about sda. For example, notice next to Partitioning that this drive contains the MBR and is mounted at "Filesystem Root," which means it contains the root file system.

4. View the information about sdb and notice that this drive does not have a file system, nor is it mounted.

5. Close the Disks utility window.

6. Leave the virtual machine logged on for future activities.

File System Creation

Before you can read or write to a hard drive, you must place a file system on the disk. This act, called **formatting**, prepares a storage area for use. Formatting creates the root of the directory structure and the file system for use. Prior to installing a file system, you must create a storage area.

In Windows 10, you use the Disk Management console to create the storage area and install the file system. In Linux, you use the `parted`, `fdisk`, and `mkfs` utilities at a command prompt or from the GUI Disks program to perform the same tasks. Next, you use the file system tools in both operating systems to set up storage areas for the data to be stored on your hard drive.

This section explains how to create file systems in Windows 10 and Linux, and includes activities to take you through the individual steps.

Windows 10 File System Creation

In Windows 10, you use the Disk Management console to create a storage area and then install the file system in it. When creating the storage area, you start with an unallocated area on a physical disk. An unallocated area is one that does not contain a primary or extended partition; within an extended partition, an unallocated area does not contain a logical drive. Figure 5-8 shows areas on Disk 1; the area on the right is the unallocated area where you can add a partition.

Use the New Simple Volume wizard to start the allocation process. Right-click the unallocated area, and then click New Simple Volume. Read the information in the next window, and click the Next button.

In the next dialog box, you indicate the amount of storage to set aside for the simple volume. For example, if you want to use the remainder of the virtual disk drive, you can leave the default value in the "Simple volume size in MB" field, as shown in Figure 5-9.

Windows has a number of wizards to guide you through the process of configuring various options. These wizards have a set of buttons to help you navigate through the windows. Click the Next button to accept the settings in a window and move to the next window. Click Back to return to previous windows and revise settings. Click the Finish button in the last window when you have selected and approved all the settings.

Disk 1	NTFS (E:)	
Basic		
4.00 GB	2.00 GB NTFS	2.00 GB
Online	Healthy (Primary Partition)	Unallocated

Figure 5-8 Disk Management console showing unallocated space

Source: Windows 10/Disk Management

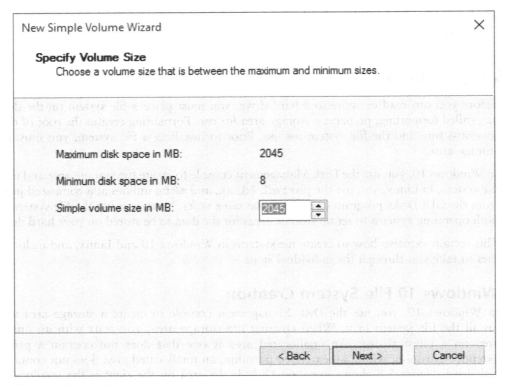

Figure 5-9 Specifying a partition size for a simple volume

Source: Windows 10/New Simple Volume Wizard

In the next dialog box, you can assign a letter to the drive, as shown in Figure 5-10.

You have three options in the Assign Drive Letter or Path dialog box:

- Assign the following drive letter—To assign a letter to a drive, click this option and then select a letter from the list box.

- Mount in the following empty NTFS folder—With this option, you can reference the partition or logical drive from a folder in another partition. This mount option is like the mount process in Linux. For example, you can click a folder on the C drive that links to the logical drive in an extended partition. If you intend to mount this folder, note that it should not contain any data files; they will be lost while the mount point is used. You will mount a drive in Activity 5-6.

- Do not assign a drive letter or drive path—If you want to delay the assignment of a drive letter or path, click this option. This is useful when you want to change an existing drive letter before assigning one to a partition or logical drive.

Finally, you must format the partition before you can use it. In the next dialog box, Format Partition, you can configure a number of options, as shown in Figure 5-11:

- Do not format this volume—Click this button to select a file system later.

- Format this volume with the following settings—Click this button to establish any or all of the following settings for the partition.

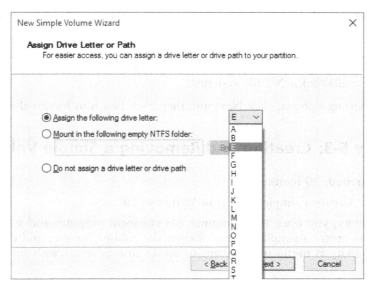

Figure 5-10 Assigning a drive letter to a volume

Source: Windows 10/New Simple Volume Wizard

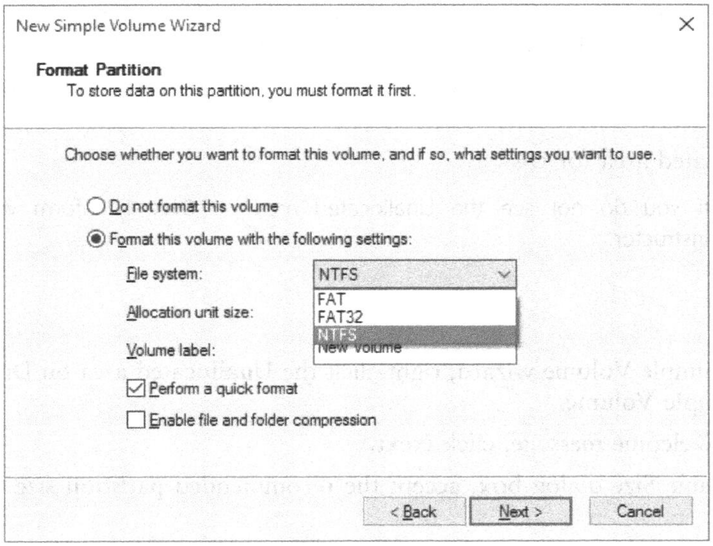

Figure 5-11 Partition formatting options

Source: Windows 10/New Simple Volume Wizard

- File system—Select a file system from FAT, FAT32, or NTFS.

- Allocation unit size—Specify the cluster size to use (it is best to let Windows 10 make this decision).

- Volume label—Type the volume label that you want to appear in reference to this partition.

- Perform a quick format—Speed up the formatting operation; you should only use this option on previously formatted partitions that are known to be in good condition.

- Enable file and folder compression—Indicate that files and folders are automatically compressed (only available for NT file systems).

After selecting the formatting options, click Next and then click Finish to format the drive.

Activity 5-3: Creating and Removing a Simple Volume

Time Required: 20 minutes

Objective: Create a simple volume in Windows 10.

Description: In this activity, you open the Computer Management program and select Disk Management. Next, you create a simple volume, format the volume for use, and delete the simple volume. This activity is useful if you want to create storage areas with file systems in Windows 10.

1. If necessary, start your virtual machines using the appropriate instructions in Activity 1-1.

2. To open the Computer Management program, click the **Start** button and then type **Computer Management.**

3. When Computer Management appears in the search results, right-click **Computer Management**, click **Run as administrator**, type **Pa$$w0rd**, and then click **Yes.**

4. To see the partitions for your virtual machine, double-click **Storage,** and then double-click **Disk Management.**

5. Locate the Unallocated area for Disk 1.

If you do not see the Unallocated area on Disk 1, inform your instructor.

6. To start the New Simple Volume wizard, right-click the **Unallocated** area on Disk 1 and then click **New Simple Volume.**

7. After reading the Welcome message, click **Next.**

8. In the Specify Volume Size dialog box, accept the recommended partition size by clicking **Next.**

9. To retain the default drive letter, click **Next.**

10. In the Format Partition dialog box, click **Format this volume with the following settings** and then type **Second NTFS** to replace the default value in the **Volume label** text box. Leave the other settings and click **Next.**

11. Review the setting information, and then click **Finish.**

12. Wait for the simple volume to format.

If you do not see the word *Healthy* in the area that was created, inform your instructor.

13. To change the drive letter, right-click the **CD-ROM 0** button and then click **Change Drive Letter and Paths**.

If you cannot locate the CD-ROM 0 button, inform your instructor.

5

14. To change the drive letter, click the **Change** button, click the **Assign the following drive letter** list box, click **R** (or the next available letter after R), and then click **OK**.
15. Read the confirmation message, and click **Yes.**
16. Verify that the drive letter has changed for the **CD-ROM 0** drive.
17. To remove the volume, right-click the **Second NTFS** area, click **Delete Volume**, and then click the **Yes** button.
18. Close the Computer Management window.
19. Leave the virtual machine logged on for future activities.

CentOS 7 File System Creation

File systems are used for storing both system configurations and data for CentOS 7. When you install CentOS 7, you are initially required to define the "/" directory and the **swap file**, a hidden file on the hard drive used to hold parts of programs and data files that do not fit in memory. The OS moves data from the swap file to memory as needed, and moves data out of memory to the swap file to make room for new data. After the "/" directory and swap file are defined, you can add files and directories. Table 5-2 lists the default directories created during installation.

The Disks utility from GNOME Desktop allows you to create partitions and put a file system on the created partition. The Disks utility shows all of the connected hard drives. To begin partitioning a hard drive, you select the drive, which shows that it has not been formatted. Figure 5-12 shows the contents as unknown. To format the disk or volume, click the two gears under the Volumes box, which brings up the menu shown in Figure 5-13. Select Format, which brings up a Format Volume menu. Enter a name for the drive without changing any of the default settings in the other lines. Before the formatting can take place, you must enter the administrative password.

After the disk is formatted, the information changes in the Contents field to display how the volume is formatted. It also displays that the volume is not mounted. To mount the volume, click the Play arrow that now appears next to the two gears under the Volumes box. You will need to enter the administrative password again. The Contents field will again change to display how the volume is formatted and where the volume is mounted. The default

Default Directory	Description
/	This directory contains the main file system. Every file system is attached, or "grafted," into this hierarchical "tree"; the root directory is the main node, or "root," of the file system tree.
/bin	The bin directory contains binary of helpful commands that are used by system users.
/boot	This directory contains the kernel and boot files.
/dev	This directory contains all the devices installed on the system, including CD-ROM and USB devices. Devices look like files, but they are actually physical or virtual hardware devices.
/etc	This directory contains the system configuration files.
/home	This folder contains all of the home directories of the users on the system.
/lib and /lib64	These directories contain the shared program libraries.
/lost+found	This directory contains damaged or disconnected files.
/media	This directory functions as a temporary mount directory for removable devices, such as CD-ROMs, DVDs, and USB drives.
/mnt	This directory contains various mount points for user file systems.
/opt	This directory contains optional add-on applications.
/proc	This virtual directory contains status information. "Virtual" means that no actual disk space is associated with the file system; it is entirely contained in memory.
/root	This is the home directory of the superuser (the system administrator). It is not to be confused with the system root "/," which is the directory at the highest level in the file system.
/sbin	This directory contains system binaries, which are typically used by the system in the background or by system administrators.
/srv	This directory contains service-related data.
/sys	This directory provides device and driver information.
/tmp	This directory contains temporary files.
/usr	This directory contains binaries, libraries, documentation, and source code for second-level programs.
/var	This directory contains files that normally vary in size, such as log files, spool files, and miscellaneous dynamic files.

Table 5-2   CentOS 7 default directories

system setting is to automatically mount the drive where the system wants it, but you can configure this setting using the advanced options of the mount command.

The parted utility is another option you can use to format and partition the disk. This command-line utility has an interactive menu for readying hard drives. From a command prompt in a terminal window, type sudo parted to start the utility. Inserting sudo prior to the parted command allows you to run the utility as a superuser. The parted menu is shown in Figure 5-14. To create a partition, you need to label it first by typing – mklabel

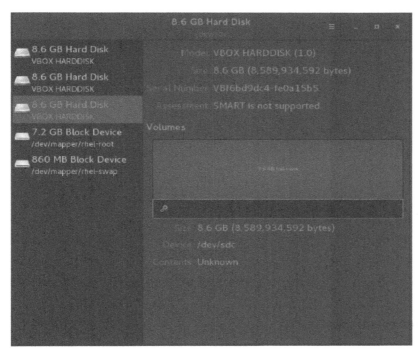

Figure 5-12 Formatting a disk in the Disks utility

Source: CentOS 7

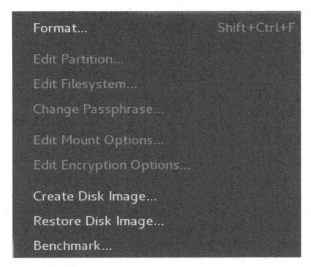

Figure 5-13 Format menu in the Disks utility

Source: CentOS 7

Figure 5-14 Creating a partition

Source: CentOS 7

msdos. If prompted to overwrite, enter y for yes. After creating the label, partition the first part of the drive by typing – mkpart primary 1 250.

Another option to format the disk is to use the fdisk command in the terminal window. The fdisk program is called a *partition table manipulator*; it shows the partition table with the corresponding file systems. The command has the following syntax:

fdisk [-l] [-v] [-s partition] [device]

-v	Prints the version number of the fdisk program
-l	Lists the partition tables for /dev/sda, /dev/sdb, /dev/sdc, /dev/sdd, /dev/sde, /dev/sdf, /dev/sdg, and /dev/sdh, and then exits
-s partition	The size of the partition is displayed in the terminal window

To use fdisk, you need to be a "super" user—simply insert sudo prior to running the command.

After formatting the volume with either the parted or fdisk command, you need to create a file system on the volume using the mkfs command. This enables the file system to store files. For example, you could use the following mkfs command to create a file system on any partition on any hardware that is connected to the computer. The command defines the file system as ext4, but you can choose any file system supported by the current OS, as listed in the earlier section on CentOS 7 file systems. The -t option specifies the file system type, and /dev/sdc1 names the target device.

mkfs -t ext4 /dev/sdc1

In the next command, the -c option tells the OS to mark bad blocks and avoid writing to them.

```
mkfs -t ext3 -c /dev/hdb1
```

After the volume is formatted with the fdisk command and a file system is created with the mkfs command, the volume needs to be mounted so the OS can use it. To mount the volume from a terminal window, use the mount command. The volume is mounted "on" an existing directory.

With the mount command, you attach a file system to a partition via a mount point directory. The syntax and options for the mount command are:

mount [-l] [-t type]	Lists all mounted file systems of the type you specify; the –l option adds ext2 mount and ext3 labels in this listing
-t	Specifies the file system type
-h	Prints a help message
–V	Prints a version string

An example of a mount command is:

```
mount /dev/sdb/ /home/user1/tmp
```

If the directory does not exist, it must be created using the mkdir command, as shown in the following example:

```
mkdir /home/User01/mydirectory
```

After you mount the file system, it can be used.

To perform Activity 5-4 and create partitions on your virtual machine, you must have free space on your hard drive. Two additional hard drives—sdb and sdc—are provided by your instructor for this activity.

Activity 5-4: Creating a CentOS 7 File System from the Command Window

Time Required: 15 minutes

Objective: Manually create a file system in CentOS 7.

Description: In this activity, you use the fdisk and mkfs commands to create a file system in CentOS 7. This activity is useful, for example, if you need to create a new partition and file system and then set aside a storage area for data.

1. If necessary, start your virtual machines using the appropriate instructions in Activity 1-1.
2. To open a terminal window, right-click the desktop and select **Open in Terminal**.
3. To start the fdisk utility, type **sudo fdisk /dev/sdb** and then press **Enter**.
4. Type **Pa$$w0rd** as the password for User1.

5. To begin creating a new partition, press **n** and then press **Enter**.

6. To specify a primary partition, press **p** and then press **Enter**.

7. To specify the second partition, press **2** and then press **Enter**.

8. To specify the starting cylinder, press **Enter** to accept the default selection of 2048.

9. To create a 2-GB disk, type **+2G**.

10. To save the changes, press **w** and then press **Enter**.

11. To create the file system, type **sudo mkfs -t ext4 -c /dev/sdb2** and then press **Enter**.

12. If necessary, type **Pa$$w0rd** as the password for User01. Notice the program working as it writes the file system to the drive.

13. To close the terminal console, type **exit** and then press **Enter**.

14. Leave the CentOS 7 virtual machine logged on for future activities.

Activity 5-5: Creating a CentOS 7 File System Using the Disks Utility

Time Required: 15 minutes

Objective: Manually create a file system in CentOS 7.

Description: In this activity, you use the Disks utility to create a file system in CentOS 7. This activity is useful, for example, if you need to create a new partition and file system and then set aside a storage area for data.

1. If necessary, start your virtual machines using the appropriate instructions in Activity 1-1.

2. To open the Disks utility, click **Applications**, click **Utilities**, and then click **Disks**.

3. Click each drive until the drive with /dev/sdc is listed for Device.

4. Click the two gears under the Volumes box.

5. Click **Format** in the menu list.

6. Enter **test** for the name of the drive, and then click **Format**.

7. Click **Format** again in the next window. Click **Format** again when prompted.

8. Type **Pa$$w0rd** and press **Enter**.

9. Note the status circle next to the drive in the left column. When the formatting is finished, notice that the information changes in the Contents line under the volume.

10. Leave the CentOS 7 virtual machine logged on for future activities.

Mounting a File System

Windows 10 and CentOS 7 have different approaches to mounting a file system, but each approach has merit. Windows 10, as previously discussed, assigns drive letters for various partitions, volumes, and CD-ROM drives. These "premounted" storage items, with the exception of removable drives, are routinely available to PC users without user intervention.

To understand the difference between approaches, imagine the lights in various rooms of a house. In a Windows 10 house, the lights would turn on in every room when you entered the front door. Windows 10 optimizes user convenience at the expense of PC performance by making all of the storage areas available. In a CentOS 7 house, you would turn on the lights of each room as you entered it, and turn off the lights when you left. CentOS 7 optimizes performance at the expense of user convenience by making only the needed storage area(s) available.

This section explains how to access storage areas in both operating systems.

Mounting a Windows 10 File System

Recall that Windows 10 assigns drive letters to each partition, logical drive, and CD-ROM drive. These storage areas are premounted and are available without any action by the user.

However, there is an exception. Removable drives, such as USB drives, are mounted by Windows 10 upon insertion into the USB port. Prior to removal, you must notify Windows 10 that you want to remove (dismount) the USB drive; you cannot remove the drive until Windows 10 has completed writing data to it. If you remove the USB drive too soon, you may interrupt the transfer of data to the USB drive.

Windows 10 supports mounted drives, as does CentOS 7. You can create a mounted drive in Windows 10 by using the Disk Management console. A mounted drive is a drive that is mapped to an empty folder on a volume that uses NTFS. Mounted drives function like any other drives, but they are assigned drive paths instead of drive letters. To access a mounted drive, you click the drive icon located on the other drive.

Mounted drives make your data storage more accessible and give you the flexibility to manage data storage based on your PC usage. For example, when space starts to run low on drive C, you can move the Documents folder to another drive with more available disk space, and then mount it as C:\Documents.

To create a mounted drive, start with the drive that you want to mount in the Disk Management console. For example, if you were mounting the G drive, you would start with the G drive. For a full description of how to create a mounted drive, see Activity 5-6.

Activity 5-6: Mounting a Windows File System

Time Required: 20 minutes

Objectives: In Windows 10, create a mount point to another drive and remove a mount point.

Description: In this activity, you open the Computer Management program and mount a drive. As a check, you will open Windows 10 File Explorer, locate the mount point icon that you created, and open the mounted drive. You will also dismount a drive. This activity is useful if you want to create or remove a mount point in Windows 10. For example, you may want to move a folder to a new drive to increase the available storage on the first drive and more effectively manage storage areas.

1. If necessary, start your virtual machines using the appropriate instructions in Activity 1-1.

2. To check the contents of the E drive, click the **Start** button, click **File Explorer**, click **This PC** in the left pane, and double-click the **NTFS (E:)** drive.

3. To create a new text document, right-click a blank area in the right pane, point to **New**, and then click **Text Document**.

4. To create the new file, type *your name* (where *your name* is your first name) over "New Text Document," and press **Enter**.

5. Close the File Explorer window.

6. To add a mount point, right-click the **Start** button and then click **Control Panel**.

7. To open the Administrative tools, click the **System and Security** link and then click the **Administrative Tools** link.

8. To run Computer Management as an administrator, right-click **Computer Management**, click **Run as administrator**, type **Pa$$w0rd**, and then click **Yes**.

9. To see the partitions for your virtual machine, click **Storage** in the right pane, and then click **Disk Management**.

10. Right-click the **NTFS (E:)** area, and then click **Change Drive Letter and Paths**.

11. To add the mount point, click the **Add** button. The Add Drive Letter or Path dialog box appears, as shown in Figure 5-15.

12. Click the **Browse** button and then expand the **C:** drive, which is where you want to create the empty folder. See Figure 5-16.

13. To specify the mount point, click the **New Folder** button. Type **Mount Drive E** over "New Folder," press **Enter**, and then click **OK** twice.

14. To open Windows 10 File Explorer again, right-click the (**C:**) area and then click **Open**.

15. To open the mounted drive and link to the other drive, double-click the gray **Mount Drive E** icon.

16. Verify that the address changed to C:\Mount Drive E.

17. Verify that the text file you created in step 3 is shown in this view.

18. Close the File Explorer window.

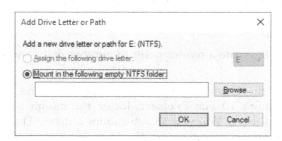

Figure 5-15 Add Drive Letter or Path dialog box

Source: Windows 10/New Volume Wizard

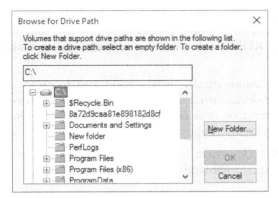

Figure 5-16 Browsing for a location to create an empty folder

Source: Windows 10/New Volume Wizard

 If you do not see the contents of the drive, inform your instructor.

19. In Computer Management under Disk Management, right-click the **NTFS (E:)** area and then click **Change Drive Letter and Paths**.

20. To remove the mount point, click **(C:)\Mount Drive E,** click the **Remove** button, and then click **Yes**.

21. To open Windows 10 File Explorer, right-click the **(C:)** area and then click **Open**.

22. To remove the folder for the previously mounted drive, right-click the **Mount Drive E** folder, and click **Delete**.

23. Close all the windows you opened in this activity.

24. Leave the virtual machine logged on for the next activity.

Mounting a CentOS 7 File System

Recall that in CentOS 7, mounting is the process by which a file system becomes available for use. After mounting, your files are accessible at the mount point. Under normal conditions, you must have superuser access to mount a file system.

Certain partitions are created and mounted by default at installation. These same partitions are automatically mounted when the OS boots. If you want to mount another partition automatically when the OS boots, you must type an entry line in the /etc/fstab file for that partition.

As in Windows 10, mounted drives make your data storage more accessible in CentOS 7 and give you the flexibility to manage data storage based on your usage. For example, when space starts to run low on drive /dev/sba1, you can move directories to another formatted physical drive with more available disk space, and then mount it as /dev/sba2.

Mounted partitions appear to be part of the local directory structure, whether they are actually located locally or on another machine across a network. Thus, mounting CentOS 7 on another partition makes no difference to the OS.

A script in /etc/rc.d executes the mount -a command, which automatically mounts all file systems listed in /etc/fstab unless a noauto option is specified. As a result, these file systems—including hard drives and CD-ROM drives—will be mounted and available when the PC starts.

If your CD-ROM drive is not mounted automatically, it is a good idea to create a special directory such as /cdrom and mount the device there. The /mnt directory is a generic mount point under which you mount file systems or devices; it is normally used to temporarily mount file systems such as CD-ROM drives and floppy drives.

With the mount command, you attach a file system to a partition via a mount point directory. The syntax and options for the mount command are:

```
mount -t type device mount-point
```

mount [-l] [-t type]	Lists all mounted file systems of the type you specify
-r	Mounts the file system as read-only; a synonym is -o ro
-w	Mounts the file system as read/write (the default selection); a synonym is -o rw
-t vfstype	The argument following the -t indicates the file system type
-h	Prints a help message
-V	Prints a version string

The currently supported file system types are ext4, ext2, ext3, iso9660 (the default), msdos, ntfs, ufs, umsdos, and vfat. If you do not use the -t option with the mount command to indicate the file system type, or if you specify the auto type, the **superblock** is probed for the file system type. The superblock contains a number that identifies it as a UFS file system and includes other numbers that describe the file system's geometry, statistics, and behavioral parameters.

Normally, only a superuser can mount a file system, but if the following line is in /etc/fstab:

```
/dev/cdrom /mnt/cdrom iso9660 ro,user,noauto,unhide 0 0
```

you can mount the system even if you are not a superuser. Use the following command:

```
mount /dev/cdrom or mount /mnt/cdrom
```

 If you want to mount a file system on a writable medium, such as a memory stick, first format and apply the file system, then mount the device, copy the files to it, and unmount the memory stick using the umount command.

The umount command detaches the specified file system(s) from the file hierarchy. A file system is specified using the directory where it has been mounted.

The umount command has the following syntax:

umount [-l] [-t type]	Lists all mounted file systems of the type you specify
-h	Prints a help message

-V	Prints a version string
-v	Verbose mode
-l	"Lazy" unmount; detaches the file system from the file system hierarchy immediately and cleans up all references to the file system as soon as it is not busy anymore (requires kernel 2.4.11 or later)

A file system cannot be unmounted when it is "busy"—for example, when files are open on it, when some process has its working directory there, or when a swap file on the file system is in use. If you have the mounted directory active in a terminal window or GNOME GUI, the drive cannot be unmounted because it is active.

Activity 5-7: Mounting a CentOS 7 File System

Time Required: 10 minutes

Objective: Create a mount point to another drive in CentOS 7.

Description: In this activity, you use the mount command to mount a CD-ROM drive. Next, you will unmount the CD-ROM drive. This activity is useful if you need to use a CD-ROM drive in CentOS 7.

1. If necessary, start your virtual machines using the appropriate instructions in Activity 1-1.
2. To open a terminal console, right-click the desktop and select **Open in Terminal**.
3. To make a directory to access the CD-ROM drive, type **sudo mkdir /mnt/cdrom** and then press **Enter**.
4. Place the CD in the CD/DVD ROM drive.

If there is no CD in the CD/DVD ROM drive, the mount will fail.

5. To mount the CD-ROM drive, type the following command:

    sudo mount -t iso9660 /dev/sdc /mnt/cdrom and then press Enter.
6. To view the mounted file systems, type **sudo mount** and then press **Enter**.
7. Locate your mounted file system.
8. To unmount the CD-ROM drive, type **sudo umount /mnt/cdrom** and then press **Enter**.
9. To view the mounted file systems, type **sudo mount** and then press **Enter**.
10. Note your unmounted file system.
11. To close the terminal console, type **exit**, press **Enter**, type **exit** again, and press **Enter**.
12. Leave CentOS 7 logged on for the next activity.

Managing File Systems

This section shows you how to manage file systems in Windows 10 and CentOS 7. In Windows 10, you can use the Local Disk Properties dialog box to assist in file system management. In CentOS 7, you can use the `free` command to manage swap space.

Managing Windows 10 File Systems

Windows 10 provides a number of tools to help you manage the day-to-day operation of your file systems. Open the Computer console and use the Local Disk Properties dialog box of the selected drive as your starting point (see Figure 5-17).

You need administrative rights to view and change information in the Sharing and Quota tabs. The tools in the Local Disk Properties dialog box are grouped under several tabs, as explained in the following sections.

General Tab The General tab (see Figure 5-17) provides the following useful information and options for managing the available disk space of a given drive:

- Type—A local disk is a hard drive on the PC.
- File system—Indicates the file system type on the drive.
- Used space—Displays the amount of used space on the drive.

Figure 5-17 Local Disk Properties dialog box

Source: Windows 10

- Free space—Displays the amount of unused space on the drive.
- Capacity—Displays the total capacity of the disk drive.
- Disk Cleanup—Click this button to remove temporary and Internet files.
- Compress this drive to save disk space—Decreases the amount of space used by the files and folders stored on the drive.
- Allow files on this drive to have contents indexed in addition to file properties—Enables you to rapidly search documents for keywords; you can control the information included in the indexes.

Tools Tab The Tools tab (see Figure 5-18) provides two tools to keep your drives tuned. You will be prompted for an administrative account password to perform error checking and defragmentation.

- Error checking—Scans the volume for damage; the volume is not available during the scan, which could take a long time if the drive has a large number of files.
- Defragmentation—Analyzes drives for **fragmentation** (parts of files scattered across a hard drive); the **defragmentation** tool locates fragmented files and folders and arranges them in order to improve disk performance.

You can use the error-checking tool to check for file system errors and bad sectors on your hard drive. If the drive is currently in use, you will be asked if you want to reschedule the

Figure 5-18 Tools tab of Local Disk Properties dialog box

Source: Windows 10

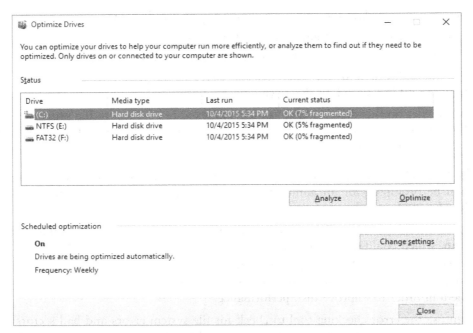

Figure 5-19 Disk defragmenting and optimization

Source: Windows 10/Disk Optimization

disk checking for the next time you restart your system. You should analyze drives regularly to keep them free of errors.

You can use the Disk Defragmenter (see Figure 5-19) to analyze local drives and to locate and consolidate fragmented files and folders. After defragmenting, each file and folder on your computer's hard drive will occupy a single, contiguous space on the volume. As a result, Windows 10 can access your files and folders more efficiently and save new ones more efficiently as well. Click the Analyze button to determine if your PC will benefit from defragmentation. After the analysis, a dialog box reports the percentage of fragmented files and folders on the drive and recommends whether to defragment the volume. You should analyze volumes regularly and defragment them only when the Disk Defragmenter recommends it. To encourage the routine analysis and defragmentation of volumes, the Disk Defragmenter provides a scheduler that is on by default.

Hardware Tab The Hardware tab (see Figure 5-20) provides access to information and settings for all drives on a PC. You can use the following options on the Hardware tab to view information about your hard drives and keep them running efficiently:

- Name and Type—Display the drives' model names and types.
- Properties button—Provides access to the Disk Properties dialog box for a selected device.

Sharing Tab From the Sharing tab (see Figure 5-21), you can share the entire contents of a drive, and other users can access the shared drive from other computers. If you have

Figure 5-20 Hardware tab of Local Disk Properties dialog box

Source: Windows 10

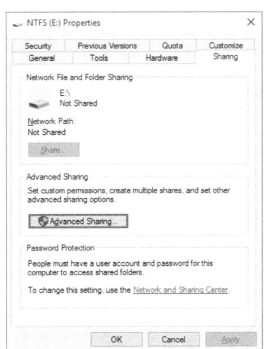

Figure 5-21 Sharing tab of Local Disk Properties dialog box

Source: Windows 10

administrative privileges, you can create additional shares for the entire contents of the local disk (E). To do so, click the Advanced Sharing button, click the Share this folder check box, type the name of the share in the Share name text box, click the Permissions button, check the appropriate Allow check boxes, and then click OK twice. You need to know about these settings because an administrator can create a share to your hard drive so that other users can access your files. You will be prompted for an administrative account password when you click the Advanced Sharing button. You will learn more about sharing in Chapter 11.

When you share a drive, anyone who has user access to the network can read the drive's contents unless it is protected by NTFS permissions.

Security Tab From the Security tab (see Figure 5-22), you can set the NTFS permissions that control access to data on the hard drive. If you have administrative privileges, you can manage the NTFS permissions for groups of users on your PC. To modify NTFS permissions, set the Allow check box for each group of users and then click OK. You need to know about these settings because an administrator can modify the NTFS permissions so that other users can access your files. You will be prompted for an administrative account password when you click the Edit button. You will learn more about security settings in Chapter 11.

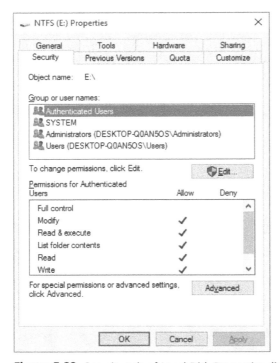

Figure 5-22 Security tab of Local Disk Properties dialog box

Source: Windows 10

Figure 5-23 Quota settings

Source: Windows 10

Quota Tab The Quota tab tracks and controls disk space usage for NTFS volumes. Administrators can configure Windows 10 to prevent excessive use of disk space. See Figure 5-23 for an example of quota settings. You will be prompted for an administrative account password when you click the Quota Entries button. You will learn more about disk quotas in Chapter 11.

The Quota tab contains the following options:

- Enable quota management—This option toggles quotas on or off. When turned on, the OS can configure disk quotas.

- Deny disk space to users exceeding quota limit—If this option is selected, a user who exceeds the limit receives an "insufficient disk space" error from Windows 10 and cannot write additional data to the drive without first deleting or moving some files from it. To affected programs, it appears that the drive is full.

- Do not limit disk usage—If this option is selected, the OS tracks disk usage. It may create a log entry when a user exceeds the limits, but it does not limit usage.

- Limit disk space to—This option specifies the amount of disk space that a user is allowed and the amount of disk space that has to be used before an event is written to the system log.

- Set warning level to—This option is similar to "Limit disk space to," but it only establishes a warning condition. A warning entry is placed in the system log when the warning level is exceeded; however, the user is not notified.

- Log event when a user exceeds their quota limit—This option places an entry in the system log whenever you exceed your quota limit.

- Log event when a user exceeds their warning level—This option places an entry in the system log whenever you exceed the quota warning level.

Activity 5-8: Defragmenting and Optimizing a Drive

Time Required: 20 minutes to two hours, depending on the size of the hard drive and the speed of the computer.

Objective: Determine whether a drive is fragmented in Windows 10, and optimize the drive if necessary.

Description: In this activity, you analyze a drive for fragmentation and optimize the drive. For example, this activity is useful if you want information about the free space on your drive and if you want to determine whether the drive needs defragmenting.

1. If necessary, start your virtual machines using the appropriate instructions in Activity 1-1.
2. To open the Control Panel, click the **Start** button, type **Defragment and Optimize Drives** in the search box, and click **Defragment and Optimize Drives** in the search results.
3. To analyze a drive for fragmentation, click a drive under the **drive** column to select it, and then click the **Analyze** button.
4. If prompted, type **Pa$$w0rd** and click **Yes**.
5. Wait for the analysis to complete.
6. To defragment the drive, click the **Optimize** button. If prompted, type **Pa$$w0rd** and click **Yes**.
7. Close all the windows within the Windows 10 virtual machine.
8. Leave the PC logged on for the next activity.

Managing CentOS 7 File Systems

This section shows you how to manage file systems in CentOS 7.

File System Checking and Repair Sometimes, power losses or abrupt shutdowns can cause file corruption and OS errors because the OS cannot synchronize the file system buffer cache with the contents of the disk. A **buffer cache** is a special memory region used for quick access to stored data items. To check for file system errors and repair them, use the fsck command.

CentOS 7 automatically checks the file systems at boot time, as Windows 10 does with the chkdsk utility, but you should also use the fsck command to check CentOS 7 file systems and correct any problems. The fsck command has syntax similar to the mkfs command, which you used earlier in the chapter. The syntax of the command is:

```
fsck [-sAVRTMNP] [-C [fd]] [-t fstype] [filesys...]
fsck -t ext3 /dev/sda2
```

You should only run the `fsck` command on unmounted or read-only file systems.

The exit code returned by the `fsck` command is the sum of the conditions shown in Table 5-3. For example, if you get an exit code of 3, the file system errors were corrected and the PC needs to be rebooted.

Disk Usage Management You can use the `df` command to report the disk space usage of a file system. Typical output is shown in Figure 5-24. The syntax of the command is:

```
df [OPTION]... [FILE]...
```

`-t, --type=TYPE`	Limits the listing to file systems of the type specified
`-T, --print-type`	Prints the file system type
`-x, --exclude-type=TYPE`	Excludes specified file systems from the list
`–help`	Prints a help message
`–version`	Prints a version string

Exit Code	Description
0	No errors
1	File system errors corrected
2	PC should be rebooted
4	File system errors left uncorrected
8	Operational error
16	Usage or syntax error
128	Shared library error

Table 5-3   Exit codes for the `fsck` command

```
                                    user01@centos7:/etc
 File  Edit  View  Search  Terminal  Help
[user01@centos7 etc]$ df
Filesystem      1K-blocks     Used Available Use% Mounted on
/dev/sda1        49410708  4723772  42153972  11% /
devtmpfs           371032        0    371032   0% /dev
tmpfs              379556      236    379320   1% /dev/shm
tmpfs              379556     5424    374132   2% /run
tmpfs              379556        0    379556   0% /sys/fs/cgroup
tmpfs              379556      844    378712   1% /tmp
/dev/sr0            57416    57416         0 100% /run/media/user01/VBOXADDITIONS_5.0.4_102546
/dev/sdd          8125880    36852   7653216   1% /run/media/user01/Logs
[user01@centos7 etc]$ ▮
```

Figure 5-24 `df` output screen

Source: CentOS 7

You can use the du command to specify disk usage of each file or recursively for directories. The syntax of the command is:

```
du [OPTION]... [FILE]...
```

-a, --all	Writes counts for all files, not just directories
-c, --total	Produces a grand total
-h, --human-readable	Creates readable output
–help	Prints a help message
–version	Prints a version string

Figure 5-25 displays a small output of the du command.

Swap Space Management You can use the free command to display the amount of free and used memory in the system and to manage swap space.

Swap space is used to implement paging, a process in which memory pages are written to disk when physical memory is low and read back into physical memory when needed. This process helps PC performance, enabling a number of programs to run simultaneously when they would not otherwise fit into physical memory.

This type of space was called a *swap file* or *swap partition* in the "File System Creation" sections earlier in this chapter. A swap partition can yield better performance because the disk blocks are guaranteed to be contiguous. To find out how much swap space you have, type free at a command prompt. This command reports memory usage, including both memory and swap space totals, along with the amount of space that is used, free, shared, buffered, and cached. All the numbers are reported in 1024-byte blocks. The syntax is:

```
free [-b | -k | -m] [-o] [-s delay ] [-t] [-l] [-V]
```

-b   Displays the amount of memory in bytes; the –k option (the default) reports the amount in kilobytes, and the –m switch displays the amount in megabytes

-t   Displays a line that contains totals

Figure 5-25 du output screen

Source: CentOS 7

Figure 5-26 `free` output screen

Source: CentOS 7

`-s` Activates a continuous polling delay, in seconds

`-V` Prints a version string

Use the `free` command to display free space for memory and swap file systems in CentOS 7, as shown in Figure 5-26.

Activity 5-9: Analyzing a Windows Paging File

Time Required: 10 minutes

Objective: Find memory and paging file information for Windows 10.

Description: In this activity, you find paging file information. This activity is useful if you need virtual memory and page file information.

1. If necessary, start your virtual machines using the appropriate instructions in Activity 1-1.
2. Click the **Start** button, click **File Explorer**, right-click **This PC** in the right pane, and click **Properties**.
3. Under the System section, notice the amount of Installed memory (RAM).
4. Click the **Change Settings** button. If prompted, type **Pa$$w0rd** and click **Yes**.
5. Click the **Advanced** tab, click **Settings** under Performance, click the **Advanced** tab, and then click **Change** under the Virtual memory section.
6. Verify that the **Automatically manage paging file size for all drives** option is checked.
7. Close all the windows within the Windows 10 virtual machine.
8. To shut down the virtual machine, click the **Start** button, click **Power**, and then click **Shut down**.
9. Wait a moment for the Windows 10 virtual machine to shut down completely.

Activity 5-10: Analyzing Available Swap Space in CentOS 7

Time Required: 10 minutes

Objective: Use the free command to see memory and swap space information for a CentOS 7 OS.

Description: In this activity, you use the free command. This activity is useful if you need memory and swap space information.

1. If necessary, start your virtual machines using the appropriate instructions in Activity 1-1.
2. To open a terminal console, right-click the desktop and select **Open in Terminal**.
3. To view memory and swap space information, type **free –bt** and then press **Enter**.
4. Note the information shown for memory and swap space in the resulting output.
5. To exit the terminal window, type exit and then press **Enter**.
6. To shut down the virtual machine, click **User01** in the upper-right corner, click **Power Off**, and then click **Power Off** again.
7. Wait a moment for the CentOS 7 virtual machine to shut down completely.
8. Close any remaining open windows, log off, and shut down your PC.

Disk Quota Similar to the way Windows 10 supports disk quotas, CentOS 7 can restrict disk space by implementing disk quotas, which alert a system administrator before a user consumes too much disk space or a partition becomes full.

Security Administrators can configure CentOS 7 data security by adding permissions to directories and the objects they contain.

Chapter Summary

- Storage areas on hard drives are used to store programs and data. Storage areas can be implemented as primary partitions or logical drives within extended partitions. Windows 10 supports the FAT32, exFAT, and NTFS file systems. CentOS 7 supports many different file systems, but defaults to the ext4 file system.

- NTFS provides options for journalizing, compression, encryption, security, auditing, and quotas for Windows 10.

- Windows 10 uses the Disk Management console to manage storage areas and assigns drive letters to storage areas.

- CentOS 7 uses partitions on a hard drive to store information. The naming conventions indicate the device name and partition number. The partitions are formatted for the type of file system needed. These partitions are either automatically mounted at boot time or manually mounted when needed, which allows users to manage their data storage.

- Windows 10 and CentOS 7 take two different approaches to mounting drives on their systems. In Windows 10, you do not need to worry about mounting the drives because the OS handles it. In CentOS 7, you can mount devices when they are needed, which allows you to have more memory available.

- Tools are available to manage file systems in Windows 10 and CentOS 7. Management tasks include reporting information about disk space availability, cleaning up temporary files, managing the disk space quota, and determining the file type of the drive.

Key Terms

auditing The process an OS uses to detect and log security-related events.

basic disk A disk that contains basic volumes, such as primary partitions, extended partitions, and logical drives.

binary search A programming technique for quickly locating an item in a sequential list.

buffer cache A region of memory that holds frequently used data values.

cluster A disk storage unit that consists of a fixed number of sectors.

compression A means of reducing the amount of space needed to store a block of data.

decompression The opposite of compression; restoring the contents of a compressed file to its original form.

defragmentation The process of writing parts of a file to contiguous sectors on a hard drive to speed access and retrieval.

dynamic disk A disk that contains dynamic volumes, such as simple volumes. Dynamic disk storage is divided into volumes instead of partitions.

encryption The process of encoding data to prevent unauthorized access.

exFAT The Extended File Allocation Table is a Microsoft file system optimized for flash drives.

FAT32 A file system first used by Windows 95 OSR 2 that uses 32-bit sector addresses (of which 28 bits are currently used).

file allocation table (FAT) A table that an operating system maintains to provide the cluster locations of a file.

file system The overall structure in which files are named, stored, and organized. A file system consists of files, directories (or folders), and the information needed to locate and access these items.

formatting Preparing a file system so that a disk can be used to store programs and data.

fragmentation The scattering of parts of the same file over different areas of a hard drive.

master file table (MFT) A special file that contains the attributes of each file created using NTFS; the MFT is used to locate a file on a hard drive.

NTFS (New Technology File System) The default file system for new installations of Windows 10; first used by Windows NT.

partition A logical storage area on a drive.

primary partition   A portion of a drive that functions as a physically separate allocation unit.

quota   A restriction on users' ability to exceed limits placed on file system resources. It allows administrators to effectively manage disk space shared by multiple users.

sector   The smallest unit of space on a disk; typically 512 bytes.

storage area   An area on a disk that can be allocated and formatted for a file system.

subdirectory   A logical grouping of related files in Windows 10.

superblock   Part of a UFS file system that contains an identifying number and other numbers that describe the file system's geometry, statistics, and behavioral parameters.

swap file   A hidden file on a hard drive that is used to hold parts of programs and data files that do not fit in memory. The OS moves data from the swap file to memory as needed and moves data out of memory to the swap file to make room for new data.

terabyte   A measurement of high-capacity storage. A terabyte is about 1 trillion bytes.

volume   A fixed amount of storage on a hard drive.

Review Questions

1. You can allocate up to _____ primary partitions on a hard drive.

   a. 1

   b. 2

   c. 3

   d. 4

2. When you allocate storage areas for hard drives in Windows 10, each storage area _____. (Choose all that apply.)

   a. is dynamically available

   b. receives the next available drive letter

   c. requires a file system

   d. must be formatted

3. The FAT32 file system supports up to _____ on installation.

   a. 2 GB

   b. 16 GB

   c. 32 GB

   d. 2 terabytes

4. The NT file system supports up to _____ on installation.

   a. 2 GB

   b. 16 GB

   c. 32 GB

   d. 2 terabytes

5. Which options are available with NTFS? (Choose all that apply.)

    a. compression

    b. encryption

    c. auditing

    d. quotas

6. Which options can you use to create a storage area in Windows 10? (Choose all that apply.)

    a. free space on a hard drive

    b. unallocated area on a hard drive

    c. free space on a CD-ROM

    d. unallocated area on a CD-ROM

7. Which tool can be used to manage disks and partitions in Windows 10?

    a. Computer Management

    b. Defragment and Optimize

    c. Disk Cleanup

    d. Task Manager

8. In Windows 10, a _____ is mapped to an empty folder on a volume that uses the NT file system.

    a. drive point

    b. drive folder

    c. mounted drive

    d. mounted folder

9. Which items can you view from the General tab of the Local Disk Properties dialog box? (Choose all that apply.)

    a. used space

    b. free space

    c. unallocated space

    d. capacity

10. Which items can you select from the Tools tab of the Local Disk Properties dialog box? (Choose all that apply.)

    a. formatting

    b. error-checking

    c. space allocation

    d. partition resizing

11. The `mkfs` command is used to _____.

    a. make a file system for Windows 10

    b. build a CentOS 7 file system on a device

    c. manage partitions in Windows 10

    d. do nothing; it is not a valid command

12. In CentOS 7, if you want to automatically mount another partition when the OS boots, you must include an entry line in _____ for that partition.

    a. /dev/hba1

    b. /dev/hba2

    c. /etc/partition

    d. /etc/fstab

13. In CentOS 7, you use the _____ command to create partitions.

    a. `mkfs`

    b. `fsdk`

    c. `dkfs`

    d. `fdisk`

14. CentOS 7 needs at least _____ partition(s) for its root file system.

    a. one

    b. two

    c. three

    d. four

15. Which of the following is a benefit of mounting your own drives in CentOS 7? (Choose all that apply.)

    a. provides flexibility in data storage

    b. makes your data storage less accessible

    c. makes your data storage more accessible

    d. provides inflexible data storage

16. Which options are available with the ext2 file type? (Choose all that apply.)

    a. compression

    b. encryption

    c. journalizing

    d. quotas

17. Which parameters do you interactively enter when creating a new partition with the `fdisk` command? (Choose all that apply.)

    a. n

    b. q

    c. p

    d. c

18. What information is reported by the `free` command? (Choose all that apply.)

    a. memory space used

    b. memory space free

    c. CPU cycles

    d. storage capacity

19. Which storage types can be allocated in CentOS 7? (Choose all that apply.)

    a. directories

    b. free space on a CD-ROM

    c. unallocated area on a CD-ROM

    d. primary partitions

20. Which of the following are valid file types for a CD-ROM device? (Choose all that apply.)

    a. ext3

    b. UDF

    c. ISO 9660

    d. ext2

Case Projects

Case 5-1: File Systems in Windows 10

Your boss has asked you to analyze the file system types that are available in Windows 10. She expects to see a summary table with the three file types as columns and the file system attributes as rows. Also, she expects you to make a recommendation. Create a short report that includes the summary table; state and justify your recommendation in the report.

Case 5-2: Adding a Second File System in CentOS 7

Your client has outgrown her system and wants you to add more space to it. She needs you to design an additional file system to be accessible by Windows 10 and CentOS 7. Also, she expects you to make recommendations about the new file system. Create a short report in which you state and justify your recommendation.

Case 5-3: Explaining NTFS Options

Your boss has accepted your recommendation to use the NT file system. Prepare a report that lists and explains the options available in NTFS. Your target audience is company management, so the report should be relatively free of technical jargon. Create a short report with a bulleted list of options. Provide an explanation for each option in the list.

Case 5-4: Fast Data Recovery in CentOS 7

Your boss has committed you to setting up and maintaining a CentOS 7 system for a new project. Fast file recovery and data integrity are of the utmost importance. Create a short report in which you recommend which CentOS 7 file system types to use, and justify your recommendations.

Case 5-5: Creating Storage Areas in Windows 10

Prepare a procedure for your company's desktop technicians to allocate storage areas in Windows 10. Your company has a standard that permits only one primary drive allocation on the two hard drives. The procedure must enable the desktop technicians to create the following drive assignments:

- C—Boot/system partition
- D—Data
- R—CD-ROM

Provide a set of numbered instructions using the format of the activities in this chapter.

## chapter 6

Directory Commands

After reading this chapter and completing the exercises, you will be able to:

- Describe directory structures
- Display directory structures
- Navigate directory structures
- Work with directories
- Work with file management commands
- Use removable drives for the storage of application data

You should learn to use directory structures to exploit the underlying technology of file systems. Knowing how to navigate directories provides great insight into how to organize files on your virtual machine. In this chapter, you will use various commands and techniques to work with directories, learn file management techniques to keep your directory structures up to date, and learn to use USB drives to store and transport data.

Directory Structures

To begin the discussion of directories, consider the example of a campus map. You probably used one when you first arrived on campus. The map in Figure 6-1 shows the buildings on a fictional campus; it is probably much more basic than the map of your school, but it demonstrates how information can be organized.

What happens to the layout when departments are added to the map? For example, what if you need to gather more information about multiple departments in each building? As you can see in Figure 6-2, your campus map becomes cluttered with the additional information. As you look closer, you may also find that not all of the departments have been listed. Campus maps often have legends with obscure letters and cryptic acronyms to distinguish buildings from each other. Also, if you needed information about courses offered by the departments, the map format would not provide the necessary information.

To store detailed information about the departments, a better approach is needed. One alternative could be a file cabinet, in which each drawer represents a building. Within the drawers, manila folders would need to be separated by dividers to keep department information from being misplaced. Many office departments still use this method to organize information.

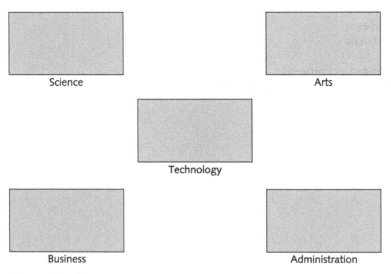

Figure 6-1 Campus map

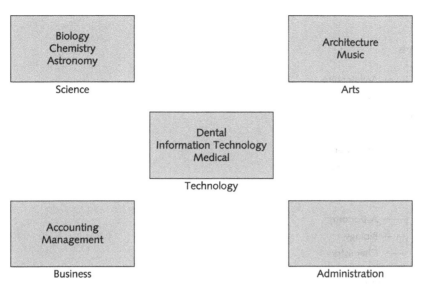

Figure 6-2 Departments on campus

However, this system may not work for you, especially if you need access to the information at home or on a computer in the school lab.

For a computer solution to be effective, campus information needs to be organized into a list, commonly referred to as a directory structure. This structure is fairly common; for example, it is similar to that of a telephone directory, where information in the yellow pages is organized alphabetically in categories, such as "Pizza" or "Restaurants." Categorizing the information makes it easier to find. When you look at Figure 6-1 again, you see that the campus map has the first group you need to begin organizing information into a directory.

In Figure 6-3, the outline of your directory begins to take shape. "Campus" is the main directory, to be followed by the buildings in alphabetical order. This ordering makes it easier to isolate information about each department when the next set of information is added.

By adding the information you gathered in Figure 6-2, you can place the departments within the correct building. In Figure 6-4, you can see that the departments have also been alphabetized for easier searching. When you need to add, delete, or modify course sections for each of the departments, you can work with the specific department or building without affecting the

Figure 6-3 Beginning of the Campus directory

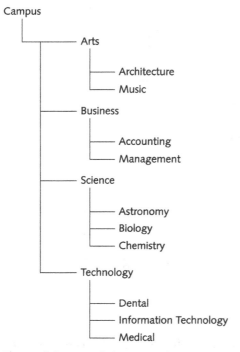

Figure 6-4 Expanded Campus directory structure

other stored information. The directory structure enables you to access your information efficiently.

You have many options for working with well-organized information in a computer system. Once the information is in a directory structure in Windows 10 and CentOS 7, you can use various tools and commands to access specific areas of your stored information. The following sections show you how to work with stored information.

Displaying Directory Structures

Your OS uses directory structures, or trees, to organize files on your virtual machine. You can display the structure as well as change your focal point in it. If needed, you can display the names of files in the directory structure. The following sections address these topics.

Displaying Directory Structures in the Windows 10 CLI

From the **command-line interface (CLI)**, you can issue commands to view the directory structure and execute other tasks. Using a CLI, the user responds to a text prompt by typing a command on a specified line, receives a response back from the OS, enters another command, and so on. In Windows 10, the **command prompt** is the line area in the CLI window where the cursor is blinking.

Figure 6-5 Command prompt console

Source: Microsoft Windows 10/Command Prompt

You can choose between two commands (TREE and DIR) when you view a directory structure. When you need to locate a single file or a set of files, you can specify which characters your search must match. These topics are explained in the following sections.

Windows Command Prompt In Windows 10, you can open the command prompt console (see Figure 6-5) by clicking Start and then clicking All apps. Scroll down, click Windows System, and then click Command Prompt.

Using the TREE Command to Display the Directory Structure To view a graphical representation of the directories on a disk, you use the **TREE** command. Figure 6-6 displays the example directory structure explained previously in this chapter.

The TREE command shows the current directory and all the subdirectories below it. The command has the following syntax:

TREE *[drive:] [path]* [/F] [/A]

/F   Displays the names of files in each folder

/A   Uses ASCII characters instead of extended characters

If you omit the path, the TREE command displays the directory structure indicated by the path in the command prompt. To specify the directory structure, type the location of the directory. For example, to display the structure of the Documents folder for User01, type C:\Users\User01\Documents instead of *[drive:] [path]*. Because the

```
Command Prompt                                          —  □  ×

E:\>tree
Folder PATH listing for volume NTFS
Volume serial number is 000000B5 A011:99FD
E:.
└──User01
    └──College
        ├──Arts
        │   ├──Architecture
        │   └──Music
        ├──Business
        │   ├──Accounting
        │   └──Management
        ├──Science
        │   ├──Astronomy
        │   ├──Biology
        │   └──Chemistry
        └──Technology
            ├──Dental
            ├──Information Technology
            └──Medical

E:\>_
```

Figure 6-6 Directory structure displayed with the TREE command

Source: Microsoft Windows 10/Command Prompt

directory is a **long filename**—a name that can contain lowercase and uppercase letters, spaces, and more than 200 characters—you may choose to enclose the drive and path in quotation marks.

Because Windows 10 does not treat spaces as delimiters, the following two commands create the same results:

```
TREE C:\Users\User01\Documents
TREE "C:\Users\User01\Documents"
```

To include filenames in the structure shown by the TREE command, you can add the /F switch. Using the /A switch, you can exclude extended characters—European characters and others that are not part of the standard ASCII set.

To page through a listing of the directories and files on a disk (or any listing that is too long for a one-screen display), use the MORE command. To pass the output of the TREE command, use the **pipe symbol** (|), as shown below.

```
TREE | MORE
```

When you use the MORE command, you can page through a listing line by line if you press Enter, and you can move through the listing page by page if you press the Spacebar.

Remember that commands are not case sensitive in Windows 10. For example, you could type the TREE command as tree or Tree.

Activity 6-1: Creating the Directory Structure in the Windows 10 CLI

Time Required: 10 minutes

Objective: Create the example directory structure in the Windows 10 CLI.

Description: In this activity, you open a command prompt and run a program file to create the example directory structure you will use in the remaining activities.

The Windows 10 activities in this chapter require the CMD files that are available at *www.cengage.com*. For further details, see the appendix for your virtualization software.

1. Start your virtual machines using the appropriate instructions in Activity 1-1.
2. Click **Start**, select **All apps**, scroll down to click **Windows System**, and then click **Command Prompt**.
3. To run the program file that creates the directories and files you need for the Windows 10 examples in this chapter, type **MakeDS** at the command prompt and press **Enter**.

Contact your instructor if you see the following message: "MakeDS is not recognized as an internal or external command, operable program or batch file."

4. Verify that the directory tree structure appears. See Figure 6-7.
5. Leave the virtual machine logged on for the next activity.

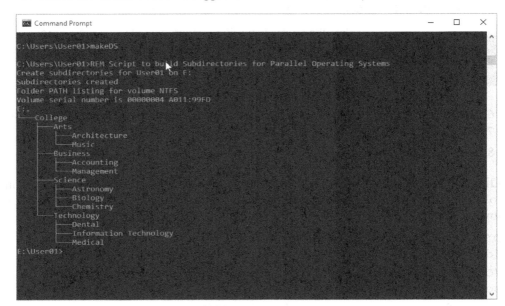

Figure 6-7 Directory structure displayed with the makeDS command

Source: Microsoft Windows 10/Command Prompt

Activity 6-2: Displaying the Directory Structure in the Windows 10 CLI

Time Required: 15 minutes

Objective: Display a directory structure in the Windows 10 CLI.

Description: In this activity, you open a command prompt and review the directory tree for the example directory structure provided with this book. This activity is useful if you want to review the directory structure on your hard drive.

If you started a new virtual session since the last time you completed Activity 6-1, you must run Activity 6-1 again before you can complete the following activity.

1. If necessary, start your virtual machines using the appropriate instructions in Activity 1-1.

2. Click **Start**, select **All apps,** scroll down to click **Windows System,** and then click **Command Prompt.**

3. To go to the drive that contains the College directory structure, type **E:** and then press **Enter.**

4. To display the example directory structure, type **TREE** and then press **Enter.**

If you do not see the example directory tree, inform your instructor.

5. Review the information in the command prompt window.

To clear the screen of previous entries, type **CLS** and press **Enter.**

6. To see the User01 directory structure with filenames, type **TREE /F** and press **Enter.**

7. Close the command prompt window.

8. Leave the virtual machine logged on for the next activity.

Displaying Filenames in the Windows 10 CLI Use the DIR (directory) command to display the names of files and subdirectories in the CLI. The DIR command has the following syntax:

`DIR [drive:] [path] [filename] [/O[[:]sortorder]] [/P] [/S] [/W]`	
`[drive:] [path] [filename]`	Specifies the drive, directory, and files to list
`/O`	Lists files in sorted order
`sortorder N`	Sorts alphabetically by name
`sortorder S`	Sorts by size (smallest first)

sortorder E	Sorts alphabetically by extension
sortorder D	Sorts by date and time (oldest first)
sortorder G	Groups directories first
sortorder -	Adds a prefix to reverse the order
/P	Pauses after each screen of information
/S	Displays files in the specified directory and all subdirectories
/W	Uses wide list format

To list information about a file, type DIR followed by the location and filename. For instance, to list information about the example file homework.doc, you would type:

DIR C:\Users\User01\Documents\homework.doc

Using the /W switch, you can list the filenames in three columns across the screen. To pause the screen as each group of filenames is listed, use the /P switch. To control the sort order, use the /O switch. For example, to sort the files by file size, you would type the sort switch as /O:S. If you do not specify a sort order, directories are listed first, and then files, in alphabetical order.

Using Wildcard Characters in the Windows 10 CLI

You may sometimes play poker or another card game that employs wild cards. If you hear "Deuces are wild!" you know that the "2" cards can be substituted for any other card in the deck.

The Windows 10 CLI uses wildcards, too. When you are entering commands, you can use two **wildcard characters** to identify groups of files: the question mark (?) and the asterisk (*, or star).

In commands, the question mark represents any single character that you want to match. For example, the following command produces a list of any files in the current directory whose name begins with "mem," followed by up to three characters.

DIR mem???.txt

This command would match any of the following filenames: memo.txt, memory.txt, mem49.txt, and memsey.txt.

The * represents any string of unknown characters. For example, *.* represents all filenames with an extension and is the default scope of the DIR command. (You may be aware that *.* is pronounced *star dot star*.) For example, the following command lists all files that have a .doc extension in the current directory:

DIR *.DOC

To list all the .doc files on drive C, sorted by date, you would type:

DIR *.DOC /S /O:D

Table 6-1 presents additional examples of how to use wildcard characters. To speed access when looking for files, you should learn to use wildcard characters.

Wildcard	Explanation
.	All files with any extension or no extension
*.txt	All files with a .txt extension
M.	All files starting with "M" or "m" (case does not matter)
H*.rpt	All files starting with "H" or "h" (case does not matter) and ending with an .rpt extension
?gop.*	All files starting with any character and followed by "gop"
Year??04.xls	Any file starting with "Year" and followed by two optional characters, then the digits "04," and then an .xls extension
Bud19??.xls	Any file starting with "Bud" and followed by any year in the twentieth century and an .xls extension

Table 6-1 Examples of using wildcard characters

Activity 6-3: Displaying Filenames in the Windows 10 CLI

Time Required: 15 minutes

Objective: Display the filenames within a directory structure in the Windows 10 CLI.

Description: In this activity, you open a command prompt and review the files within the directory structure. This activity is useful if you want to review the directory structure and file information on a hard drive.

If you started a new virtual session since the last time you completed Activity 6-1, you must run Activity 6-1 again before you can complete the following activity.

1. If necessary, start your virtual machines using the appropriate instructions in Activity 1-1.
2. Click **Start**, select **All apps**, scroll down to click **Windows System**, and then click **Command Prompt**.
3. To display the User01 directory structure, type **DIR /S /P E:\User01\.** and press **Enter**.

If you do not see the User01 files, inform your instructor.

4. Review the information in the command prompt window and press the **Spacebar**.
5. Repeat Step 4 until the message "Press any key to continue" no longer appears.
6. To display the sorted User01 directory structure, type **DIR /S /P /O:N E:\User01\.** and press **Enter**.
7. Review the information in the command prompt window and press the **Spacebar**.

8. Repeat Step 7 until the message "Press any key to continue" no longer appears.

9. Repeat Steps 6 through 8 using the **/O:S** switch.

10. Close the command prompt window.

11. Leave the virtual machine logged on for the next activity.

Displaying the Directory Structure with File Explorer

File Explorer is a part of Windows 10 that provides a graphical user interface for accessing file systems. To open File Explorer, click the Start button and then click File Explorer.

File Explorer uses two panes, as shown in Figure 6-8. The left pane is the Navigation pane, which can display the directory structure of one or more drives. The right pane displays the structure and files for the selected entry in the left pane.

To display the available drives on your virtual machine, expand This PC. To see the directory structure that you used earlier in this chapter, expand NTFS (E:), expand User01, and then click College in the left pane. The results are shown in Figure 6-9.

File Explorer provides several ways for you to arrange and identify files when viewing them in the right pane. When a folder is open, you can access these options by right-clicking the

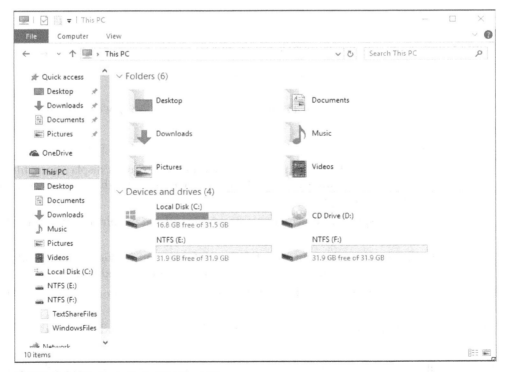

Figure 6-8 File Explorer in Windows 10

Source: Microsoft Windows 10/File Explorer

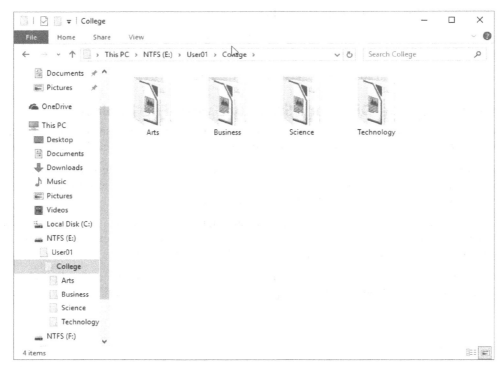

Figure 6-9 Directory structure displayed in File Explorer

Source: Microsoft Windows 10/File Explorer

white space in the right pane and pointing to View. The **white space** is any blank area of a window.

With the view options, you can control how files and folders are displayed:

- The four icon views (Extra Large, Large, Medium, and Small) display your files and folders as icons of varying sizes. The filename appears under the icon; however, sort information does not appear.

- The List view displays a folder's contents as a list of file or folder names preceded by small icons.

- The Details view lists the contents of the open folder and provides detailed information about your files, including their name, type, size, and date modified.

- The Tiles view displays the files and folders with a medium icon and includes the file size.

- The Content view uses medium icons and includes the date and time modified with the file size.

To locate files and folders more easily in Explorer, you can right-click the white space and use the Sort By options. You can arrange or sort the contents of the right pane using the following options:

- Name—Sort by file or folder name
- Date Modified—Sort by the date that the file was last accessed and modified
- Type—Sort by file type, as determined by the extension
- Size—Sort by the size of the file in bytes

You have two options for the sort order:

- Ascending—Arrange files and folders in an ascending collating sequence (0–9, A–Z, a–z).
- Descending—Arrange files and folders in a descending collating sequence (z–a, Z–A, 9–0).

A number of advanced options are available when you click the More submenu in the Sort By options. For example, you can include more tags, such as Album, Business address, and Description, for your sort.

To more easily locate files and folders by groups, you can right-click the white space in Explorer and then click Group By. Think of grouping as adding headings and placing the files under the headings. Figure 6-10 shows files and folders grouped by type. The grouping options work like the Sort By options, with one additional choice (None), which turns off grouping.

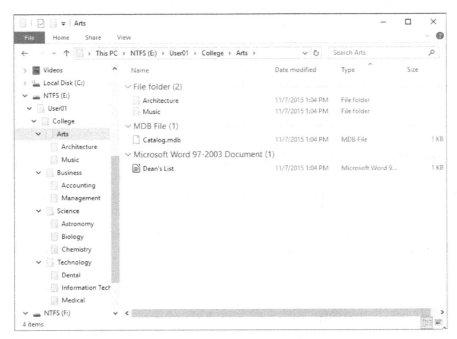

Figure 6-10 Directory structure displayed in File Explorer with grouping

Source: Microsoft Windows 10/File Explorer

Activity 6-4: Displaying the Directory Structure in the Windows 10 GUI

Time Required: 15 minutes

Objective: Display the directory structure in the Windows 10 GUI.

Description: In this activity, you open File Explorer and review the directory structure. This activity is useful if you want to review the structure before completing other activities.

 You must complete Activity 6-1 before you can complete the following activity.

1. If necessary, start your virtual machines using the appropriate instructions in Activity 1-1.
2. Click **Start** and then click **File Explorer**.
3. To go to the drive that contains the example directory structure, expand **This PC** and then double-click **NTFS (E:)**.
4. To display the example directory structure in the left pane, expand the following folders in the order shown: **User01, College, Arts, Business, Science,** and **Technology.**
5. To review files in the right pane, double-click **Arts.**
6. To change the way files are displayed in the right pane, right-click the white space in the right pane, point to **View**, and then click **Extra large icons.**
7. Repeat Step 6 for the remaining view options.
8. To change the order in which files are displayed in the right pane, right-click the white space in the right pane, point to **Sort By**, and then click **Name.**
9. Repeat Step 8 for the remaining sort options.
10. Close File Explorer.
11. Leave the virtual machine logged on for future activities.

Displaying the Directory Structure in CentOS 7

As with Windows 10, CentOS 7 directories and files are organized in a hierarchical directory structure. As the superuser, you can arrange information anywhere in this structure. As a regular user, you can manipulate directories and files in your own "branch" of the directory tree.

CentOS 7 might be configured to open to the command line. Otherwise, if the system opens to a graphical user interface (by default, GNOME), you can open a terminal console by clicking Applications and then clicking Terminal.

When you first log on to CentOS 7, you are automatically positioned in the directory tree of your home directory (for example, /home/User01). The **home** directory is the conventional starting directory for all regular users who only have permission to manipulate directories and files within their own directory. However, you can display information in the system directories if system administration permissions allow it.

The paths in CentOS 7 contain forward slashes (/) as opposed to the backslashes (\) used in the Windows 10 CLI.

CentOS 7 Command Syntax Every operating system has a general logic, or syntax, for entering commands. Consider the following command:

ls -l (the *l* is a lowercase L)

The result of the command is a detailed list of directories, files, and any errors. The ls command is explained in detail in the next section.

The general syntax for CentOS 7 commands is:

command [options] [parameter1] [parameter2] [parameter3]

The items between brackets, such as [options], are not required. You may need to enter one or more options and parameters. As an example, the following command provides a list of files in the Documents directory:

ls -l Documents

Remember that commands are case sensitive in CentOS 7. For example, you must type the ls command in lowercase. CentOS 7 does not recognize an LS command because it has the wrong case. A command's options and parameters must also have the proper case. If you type a command that does not work in CentOS 7 and you are sure that you used the right syntax, check the case.

Displaying Directories and Files in the CentOS 7 CLI To view a list of directories and files on a disk, use the **ls** command. By default, the command displays the current directory's contents and sorts the list alphabetically by filename. The following line shows the ls command syntax.

ls [options] [location]

The ls command has the following options:

- -a   Shows hidden files; does not ignore entries starting with a period (.)
- -C   Lists entries by columns
- -d   Lists directory entries instead of contents
- -F   Appends a file type indicator to the filename; for example, "" represents an executable program, "/" represents a directory, and "@" is a symbolic link
- -i   Displays the inode number (index number) of each file; in CentOS 7, an inode is used to store an application's file and directory attributes
- -l   Uses a long-listing format
- -r   Lists entries in reverse sort order
- -R   Lists subdirectories recursively

-s   Sorts by file size

-t   Sorts by modification time with the newest listed first

To page through a list of directories and files on a disk (or any list that is too long for a one-screen display), use the more command. When you use this command, you can page through a list line by line if you press Enter, and you can move through the list page by page if you press the Spacebar.

To list your directory tree, use the ls command (see Figure 6-11):

ls –Rl /etc | more

To list the size (in blocks) and inode number of the hosts file, type the following command:

ls –iS /etc/hosts

To list detailed information about a file or directory, type the following command:

ls –l /etc/hosts

```
                          User01@CentOS7:~                    _  □  ✕

 File  Edit  View  Search  Terminal  Help
[User01@CentOS7 ~]$ ls -Rl /etc | more
ls: cannot open directory /etc/audisp: Permission denied
ls: cannot open directory /etc/audit: Permission denied
ls: cannot open directory /etc/cups/ssl: Permission denied
/etc:
total 1692
drwxr-xr-x.  3 root root       97 Jan 11 11:21 abrt
-rw-r--r--.  1 root root       16 Nov 13 17:36 adjtime
drwxr-xr-x.  2 root root      112 Nov 13 17:27 akonadi
-rw-r--r--.  1 root root     1518 Jun  7  2013 aliases
-rw-r--r--.  1 root root    12288 Jan 11 11:41 aliases.db
drwxr-xr-x.  2 root root       49 Nov 13 17:21 alsa
drwxr-xr-x.  2 root root     8192 Jan 11 11:35 alternatives
drwxr-xr-x.  3 root root       43 Nov 13 17:28 amanda
-rw-------.  1 root root      541 Jul 27 05:57 anacrontab
-rw-r--r--.  1 root root      391 Jan 22  2014 ant.conf
drwxr-xr-x.  2 root root        6 Jun 10  2014 ant.d
-rw-r--r--.  1 root root       55 Mar  5  2015 asound.conf
-rw-r--r--.  1 root root        1 Nov 19 22:52 at.deny
drwxr-xr-x.  2 root root       31 Nov 13 17:24 at-spi2
drwxr-x---.  3 root root       41 Nov 13 17:21 audisp
drwxr-x---.  3 root root       79 Nov 13 18:25 audit
-rw-r--r--.  1 root root    12706 Nov 20 09:29 autofs.conf
-rw-------.  1 root root      232 Nov 20 09:29 autofs_ldap_auth.conf
-rw-r--r--.  1 root root      795 Nov 20 09:29 auto.master
drwxr-xr-x.  2 root root        6 Nov 20 09:29 auto.master.d
-rw-r--r--.  1 root root      524 Nov 20 09:29 auto.misc
-rwxr-xr-x.  1 root root     1260 Nov 20 09:29 auto.net
-rwxr-xr-x.  1 root root      687 Nov 20 09:29 auto.smb
drwxr-xr-x.  4 root root       94 Jan 11 11:28 avahi
drwxr-xr-x.  2 root root     4096 Jan 11 11:34 bash_completion.d
-rw-r--r--.  1 root root     2835 Aug 12 09:21 bashrc
--More--
```

Figure 6-11 Directory tree displayed with the ls –Rl /etc | more command in CentOS 7

Source: CentOS 7/Terminal

Column (used with the sort command)	Description
File type	The first character in the first column denotes the file type (for example, "d" = directory, "-" = file, and "l" = link).
Access permissions	The first column also displays the permissions of a file or directory, owner, group, and any other user.
Number of links	The second column displays either the number of files linked to the file or the number of subdirectories in the directory. A directory always contains entries for "." (current directory) and ".." (parent directory). The parent directory contains the current directory and is one step higher in the directory tree structure. These notations are known as **standardized channels**.
Owner	The third column shows the owner of the file or directory.
Group	The fourth column shows the group that owns the file or directory.
Size	The fifth column shows the size of the file or directory.
Date	The sixth column displays the file's creation date or last modified date.
Time	The seventh column shows the time of creation or last modified time.
Name	The eighth column shows the directory or filename.

Table 6-2 Long-list column definitions using the `ls -Rl` command

Table 6-2 summarizes the long-list column definitions when using the `-Rl` option with the `ls` command.

The `ls` command offers many useful options. For example, to list hidden files along with files that are not hidden, you would type:

`ls -a /etc/ | more`

To list a directory's files in alphabetical order using a long-listing format with the inode number, you would type:

`ls -iSl /etc/hosts`

If you do not specify a sort order, files are listed alphabetically. To sort in reverse order, you should use the `r` option. Type the following:

`ls -riSl /etc/hosts`

To page through the screen as each page of filenames is listed, you pipe the output of the `ls` command to a `more` command. For example:

`ls -l /etc | more`

To control the order in which items appear in a list, you pipe the output of the `ls` command to a **sort** command. The first `sort` command below sorts the items by the ninth field in the `ls` listing, making it the alphabetic filename. The second `sort` command reverses that sort.

`ls -l /etc | sort -k9`
`ls -l /etc | sort -rk9`

The `sort` command has many other options. Its syntax is:

```
sort [options] [files]
```

You can use the following switches with the `sort` command:

`-b`	Ignores leading blanks
`-d`	Considers only blanks and alphanumeric characters in a sort, as opposed to special and nonprinting characters
`-f`	Ignores case when sorting
`-r`	Reverses the result of comparisons
`-o [filename]`	Writes the result to a file instead of standard output

To display the full path filename of the current directory, use the `pwd` (print working directory) command. This command, along with the `more` command, has page definition options that are beyond the scope of this book. The syntax for the `pwd` and `more` commands is:

```
pwd [options]
more [options]
```

Using the `tree` Command to Display the Directory Structure in the CentOS 7 CLI

The `tree` program is a recursive directory listing program that produces an indented listing of files. Like Windows 10, the CentOS 7 CLI uses the `tree` command to list contents of directories in a tree-like format. The `tree` program is not installed by default in CentOS 7. To add the `tree` command in CentOS 7, first you need to verify that its package is in the base repository by entering `yum list tree`. You will see that the `tree .86_64` line is displayed. Switch to the root user by typing `su –` and enter Pa$$w0rd as the password (see Figure 6-12). Type `yum install tree` to install the `tree` utility. If necessary, type `y` to confirm your intention, and then press Enter.

The `tree` command itself shows the files in the current directory and its subdirectories. When directory information is given, `tree` lists all the files and subdirectories found in the given directories in turn. Figure 6-13 shows how to display the College directory structure in the CentOS 7 terminal for User01.

Using Wildcard Characters in the CentOS 7 CLI

Like Windows 10, the CentOS 7 CLI uses wildcards. When entering commands, you can use wildcards to specify groups of files.

CentOS 7 uses the same two wildcard characters as Windows 10: the question mark (?) and the asterisk (*, or star). In commands, the ? represents any single character that you want to match. For example, the following command produces a list of any files in the current directory that have a filename beginning with "host," followed by four unknown characters.

```
ls host????
```

This command would match any of the following filenames: hostuser, hosthome, hostname, and host1234.

Figure 6-12 Preparation for the `tree` command in CentOS 7 using yum

Source: CentOS 7/Terminal

The * wildcard represents any string of characters. Use *.* to represent all filenames with any extension (note that the resulting list will not show the file extensions).

 Linux filenames can contain extensions, but they are not used to make the same file type associations and identifications as they do in Windows 10.

GNOME Files is the official file browser for the GNOME desktop environment, which supports browsing local file systems. The Files file manager uses bookmarks, window backgrounds, emblems, notes, and add-on scripts. To start Files, click Applications and then click Files in the right panel.

The Files file manager uses two panes (see Figure 6-14). You use the left pane to browse to different places, devices, and networks. The right pane displays directory and file

Figure 6-13 Tree-style directory structure in the CentOS 7 terminal

Source: CentOS 7/Terminal

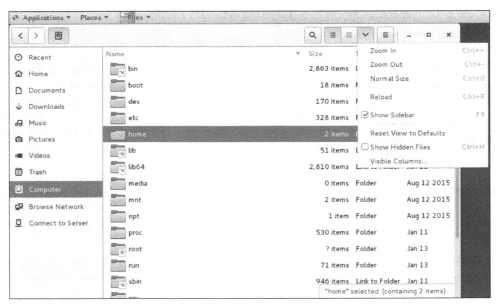

Figure 6-14 Files file manager in CentOS 7

Source: CentOS 7/Files

information for the selected entry in the left pane. You can choose an Icon or List view, and you have the option to change the view features.

Activity 6-5: Creating the Directory Structure in CentOS 7

Time Required: 10 minutes

Objective: Create the example directory structure in CentOS 7.

Description: In this activity, you open a terminal console and run a script file to create the example directory structure you will use in the remaining activities.

The CentOS 7 activities in this chapter require the script files that are available at *www.cengage.com*. For further details, see the appendix for your virtualization software.

1. Start your virtual machines using the appropriate instructions in Activity 1-1.
2. To run the program file that creates the directories and files you need for the CentOS 7 examples in this chapter, click **Applications**, and then click **Terminal**.
3. To create the directory structure with the **makeds** script, type **su -**, enter **Pa$$w0rd** at the password prompt, type **cd /usr/local/bin**, and press **Enter**. Type **makeds** and press **Enter**, and then type **su – User01** and press **Enter**.
4. Leave the virtual machine logged on for the next activity.

Contact your instructor if you see the following messages: "makeds is not recognized as an internal or external command, operable program or batch file" or "... cannot execute binary file." Also, contact your instructor if you do not see the following message when running the script: "All the directories and/or files were created successfully."

Activity 6-6: Displaying the Files in a Directory Structure in the CentOS 7 CLI Using the `ls` Command

Time Required: 10 minutes

Objective: Locate information about files and directories in CentOS 7.

Description: In this activity, you use the `ls` command to find information about the file systems on a CentOS 7 system. This activity is useful if you want to review the directory structure of a hard drive.

You must complete Activity 6-5 before you can complete the following activity.

1. If necessary, start your virtual machines using the appropriate instructions in Activity 1-1.

2. To open a terminal console, click **Applications,** and then click **Terminal.**

3. Type **ls /etc | more,** and then press **Enter.**

> To advance the paging enabled by the more command, either press the **Spacebar** to review a whole page or press **Enter** to review one line at a time.

4. To close the CentOS 7 terminal window, type **exit** and then press **Enter.**

5. Leave the virtual machine logged on for the next activity.

Activity 6-7: Displaying the Directory Structure in the CentOS 7 CLI Using the tree Command

Time Required: 10 minutes

Objective: Locate information about files and directories in the CentOS 7 CLI.

Description: In this activity, you use the tree command to find information about the file systems on a CentOS 7 system. This activity is useful if you want to review the directory structure of a hard drive.

1. If necessary, start your virtual machines using the appropriate instructions in Activity 1-1.

2. To open a terminal console, click **Applications,** and then click **Terminal.**

3. To change the path to the partition on sdb1, type **cd /mnt/sdb1/User01,** type **pwd,** and then press **Enter.**

4. Verify that the path is **/mnt/sdb1/User01.**

5. Type **tree,** and then press **Enter** (see Figure 6-15).

> If you do not see the tree structure shown in Figure 6-15, contact your instructor.

6. Type **pwd,** and then press **Enter.**

7. Type **ls –la,** and then press **Enter.** You should see Figure 6-16.

8. To close the terminal window, type **exit** and press **Enter.**

9. Leave the virtual machine logged on for the next activity.

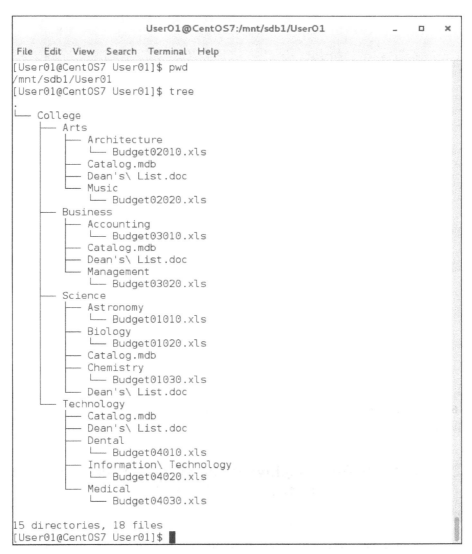

Figure 6-15 Example of directory structure displayed with `pwd` and `tree` commands

Source: CentOS 7/Terminal

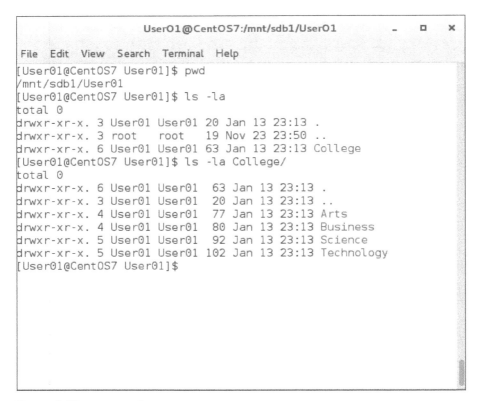

```
UserO1@CentOS7:/mnt/sdb1/UserO1          _  □  ✕

File  Edit  View  Search  Terminal  Help
[User01@CentOS7 User01]$ pwd
/mnt/sdb1/User01
[User01@CentOS7 User01]$ ls -la
total 0
drwxr-xr-x. 3 User01 User01 20 Jan 13 23:13 .
drwxr-xr-x. 3 root    root   19 Nov 23 23:50 ..
drwxr-xr-x. 6 User01 User01 63 Jan 13 23:13 College
[User01@CentOS7 User01]$ ls -la College/
total 0
drwxr-xr-x. 6 User01 User01  63 Jan 13 23:13 .
drwxr-xr-x. 3 User01 User01  20 Jan 13 23:13 ..
drwxr-xr-x. 4 User01 User01  77 Jan 13 23:13 Arts
drwxr-xr-x. 4 User01 User01  80 Jan 13 23:13 Business
drwxr-xr-x. 5 User01 User01  92 Jan 13 23:13 Science
drwxr-xr-x. 5 User01 User01 102 Jan 13 23:13 Technology
[User01@CentOS7 User01]$
```

Figure 6-16 Example of directory listing with the ls -la command

Source: CentOS 7/Terminal

Activity 6-8: Displaying the Files in a Directory Structure in the CentOS 7 GUI

Time Required: 15 minutes

Objective: Locate information about files and directories in CentOS 7.

Description: In this activity, you use the File Browser to find information about the file systems on a CentOS 7 system. This activity is useful if you want to review the directory structure of a hard drive.

You must complete Activity 6-5 before you can complete the following activity.

1. If necessary, start your virtual machines using the appropriate instructions in Activity 1-1.
2. Click **Places** on the Top Bar, and then click **Computer**.

3. To go to the disk that contains the example directory structure, click the **View** chevron, and check **Side Pane** if necessary.

4. To display the example directory structure in the right pane, click the following directories in the order shown: **File System, mnt, sdb1, User01,** and **College.**

5. To review the Arts directory files in the right pane, click **Arts.**

6. To change the default display order by name in the right pane, click the chevron next to the **Name** column.

7. To change the default appearance of files in the right pane in Icon view, press the **List View** button on the upper-right toolbar.

8. Close the file manager.

9. Leave the virtual machine logged on for future activities.

Navigating the Directory Structure

Navigating the directory structure is a bit like climbing a tree. Before climbing, you view the limbs. You can climb from limb to limb, move to smaller limbs, and retrace your steps to return to a limb. You use similar techniques to view or navigate the directory structure on your virtual machine's hard drives. The following sections explain these techniques in Windows 10 and CentOS 7.

Navigating the Directory Structure in the Windows 10 CLI

At any given time, you are working within a particular directory of the directory structure. This location is called the **working directory** or the **current directory.** You can use either the CHDIR or **CD** (change directory) command to change the location of the working directory. The CD command has the following syntax:

```
CD [/D] [drive:] [path]
CD .        Specifies that you want to change to the parent directory
CD drive    Displays the current directory in the specified drive
CD          Displays the current drive and directory
/D          Changes the current drive and the current directory
```

As long as the CLI remains open, the **command-line interpreter** maintains a current directory for each drive on your virtual machine. The current drive and path are shown in the command prompt. When you specify the path, you are changing the working directory's location for the current drive. If you include the /D switch, you change both the drive and the path that appear. You can also use the CD command without parameters to show the current drive and path, which is useful if they are not shown in the command prompt.

To change the current directory with the CD command, you have three choices:

•   CD ..—Backs up one subdirectory from the current location in the directory structure.

•   CD *path*—Changes to the relative location from the current location; when navigating to a **relative path,** the current directory path is implied. A relative path does not begin with a backward slash, and its starting address is the current directory.

Figure 6-17 Using the CD command to change the directory location

Source: Microsoft Windows 10/Command Prompt

- CD *path*—Changes to the absolute location from the current location; to navigate to an **absolute path,** you must provide the drive and the full path name, beginning with a backward slash (\ ). The CD \ command changes to the root of the current drive.

These three choices are best illustrated by the example directory structure you used earlier in the chapter.

To change the relative location to College, you would use the CD College command. The command prompt changes from E:\users\User01 to E:\users\User01\College, as shown in Figure 6-17.

To change the absolute location to Technology\Information Technology, you would type the following command:

CD \User01\College\Technology\Information Technology

The command prompt changes from E:\User01\College to the path shown above.

To back up from one subdirectory to the next higher level of the tree, use the CD . . command. The command prompt changes from E:\User01\College\Technology\Information Technology to E:\User01\College\Technology.

Activity 6-9: Changing the Current Location in the Windows 10 CLI

Time Required: 15 minutes

Objective: Change the current location within a directory structure in the Windows 10 CLI.

Description: In this activity, you open a command prompt and change the current location within a directory structure. This activity is useful if you want to change locations before completing other activities. For example, you can change from one directory level to another before listing the filenames in a subdirectory.

 You must complete Activity 6-1 before you can complete the following activity.

1. If necessary, start your virtual machines using the appropriate instructions in Activity 1-1.

2. Click **Start**, select **All apps**, scroll down to click **Windows System**, and then click **Command Prompt**.

3. To go to the example directory structure, type **CD /D E:\User01** and press **Enter**.

4. To display the example directory structure, type **TREE** and press **Enter**.

5. To change the location relative to the User01 directory structure, type **CD College** and press **Enter**.

6. Verify that the prompt is E:\User01\College.

7. To change the absolute location within the College directory structure, type the following and then press **Enter**.

   `CD \User01\ College\Technology`

8. Verify that the prompt is E:\User01\College\Technology.

9. To back up one directory, type **CD ..** and press **Enter**.

10. Verify that the prompt is E:\User01\College.

11. To change the relative location within the current directory, type **CD Technology** and press **Enter**.

12. Verify that the prompt is E:\User01\College\Technology.

13. To back up one directory, type **CD ..** and press **Enter**.

14. To navigate the directory, type **CD Business** and press **Enter**, then type **CD Management** and press **Enter**.

15. Verify that the prompt is E:\User01\College\Business\Management.

16. Close the command prompt window.

17. Leave the virtual machine logged on for the next activity.

Navigating Directory Structures in File Explorer

To navigate the example directory structure illustrated earlier, you can click a folder in the left pane of File Explorer. The location changes and the right pane is refreshed. For example, to make Science the current folder, click Science in the left pane, as shown in Figure 6-18.

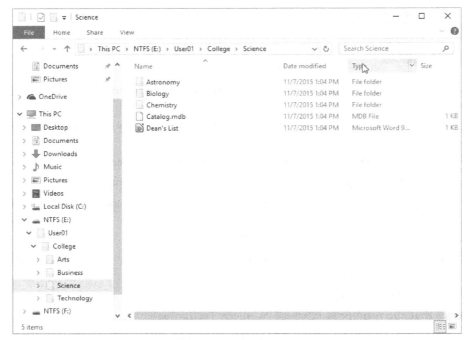

Figure 6-18 Navigating to the Science folder in File Explorer

Source: Microsoft Windows 10/File Explorer

Activity 6-10: Navigating the Directory Structure in the Windows GUI

Time Required: 15 minutes

Objective: Change the current location within a directory structure in the Windows 10 GUI.

Description: This activity is similar to Activity 6-9, except that you use File Explorer instead of the Windows 10 CLI.

You must complete Activity 6-1 before you can complete the following activity.

1. If necessary, start your virtual machines using the appropriate instructions in Activity 1-1.
2. Click **Start,** and then click **File Explorer.**

3. To go to the drive that contains the example directory structure, expand **This PC** and then expand **NTFS (E:)**.

4. To display the example directory structure in the left pane, expand the following folders in the order shown: **User01, College, Arts, Business, Science,** and **Technology**.

5. To change the location relative to the User01 directory structure, click **College** in the left pane.

6. Verify that the address is E:\User01\College.

7. To change the absolute location within the College directory structure, click **Technology** in the left pane.

8. Verify that the address is E:\User01\College\Technology.

9. To back up one directory, click **College** in the left pane.

10. Verify that the address is E:\User01\College\.

11. To navigate the directory in the left pane, expand **Business** and then click **Management**.

12. Verify that the address is E:\User01\College\Business\Management.

13. Close the File Explorer window.

14. Leave the virtual machine logged on for future activities.

Navigating Directory Structures in CentOS 7

As with Windows 10, you can use the cd command to change the location of the working (current) directory in the CentOS 7 CLI. The cd command has page definition options that are beyond the scope of this book. The command syntax is:

```
cd [options] [location path]
```

Using Absolute and Relative Paths in the CentOS 7 CLI As with Windows 10, you can change your current directory in the directory structure using either the absolute path method or the relative path method. Each directory also contains a "." entry that points to the current directory and a ".." entry that points to the parent directory. (Refer back to Figure 6-16.)

For example, if your current directory is College/Technology/Dental/ and you want to change directories to College/Business/Accounting/, as shown back in Figure 6-15, you have two options. First, you could refer to the directory structure and use the absolute path method to type the following command:

```
cd /mnt/sdb1/User01/College/Business/Accounting
```

Second, you could refer to the previous directory structure and use the relative path method by typing the following command:

```
cd ../../Business/Accounting
```

To back up one subdirectory and move one level higher in the structure, you would type:

```
cd ..
```

Activity 6-11: Navigating the Directory Structure in CentOS 7

Time Required: 15 minutes

Objective: Change the current directory in CentOS 7.

Description: In this activity, you use the cd command to change the current directory in a CentOS 7 directory tree. This activity is useful if you want to change levels in the directory structure before listing filenames in a subdirectory.

1. If necessary, start your virtual machines using the appropriate instructions in Activity 1-1.
2. To open a terminal console, click **Applications**, and then click **Terminal**.
3. To change to the /mnt/sdb1/User01 path, type **cd /mnt/sdb1/User01** and press **Enter**. Type **pwd**, and then press **Enter**.
4. To list the contents of the User01 directory, type **ls -l** and then press **Enter**.
5. To change to the College directory, type **cd College** and then press **Enter**.
6. To list the college departments as directories, type **ls -l** and then press **Enter**.
7. To change to the Technology directory, type **cd Technology** and then press **Enter**.
8. To display the /mnt/sdb1/User01/College/Technology path, type **pwd** and then press **Enter**.
9. To list the contents in the Technology directory, type **ls** and press **Enter**.
10. Verify that Catalog.mdb and Dean's List.doc are displayed.
11. To move back up one directory, type **cd ..** and press **Enter**.
12. To display /mnt/sdb1/User01/College, type **pwd** and then press **Enter**.
13. To close the CentOS 7 terminal window, type **exit** and then press **Enter**.
14. Leave the virtual machine logged on for future activities.

Working with Directories

As your requirements for data storage expand, you create new directories within the structure to accommodate new files. For example, if you have enrolled in a new course or undertaken a new project at work, you might want to separate these files from the existing directory structure. Of course, you can also remove a directory when you no longer need it. The following sections explain how to create and remove directories.

Creating Directories in the Windows 10 CLI

Use the MD (make directory) command to create a subdirectory in the CLI. You may also use the MKDIR command. The MD command has the following syntax:

```
MD [drive:]pathmd Phydir
```

The MD command syntax interprets the drive and path like the CD command described earlier. To create a subdirectory, you have two choices:

- MD *path*—Creates the subdirectory in a relative location
- MD *path*—Creates the subdirectory in an absolute location

Figure 6-19 Using the MD command to make a Physics subdirectory

Source: Microsoft Windows 10/Command Prompt

For example, to create a Physics subdirectory relative to Science, you would first navigate to Science with the CD command and then type MD Physics, as shown in Figure 6-19. To create a Physics subdirectory using the absolute path, you would type MD \User01\College \Science\Physics.

Recall that Windows 10 CLI commands are not case sensitive. Typing MD, md, Md, or mD will produce the same results. Likewise, file or folder names such as College, college, and COLLEGE are the same.

Activity 6-12: Creating Directories in the Windows 10 CLI

Time Required: 15 minutes

Objective: Create directories within a directory structure in the Windows 10 CLI.

Description: In this activity, you open a command prompt and create directories within a directory structure.

1. If necessary, start your virtual machines using the appropriate instructions in Activity 1-1.
2. Click **Start**, select **All apps**, scroll down to click **Windows System**, and then click **Command Prompt**.
3. If you are not at the example directory structure, type **CD /D E:\User01** and press **Enter**.
4. To display the example directory structure, type **TREE** and press **Enter**.
5. To change the location in the directory structure, type **CD \User01\College** and press **Enter**.
6. Verify that the prompt is E:\User01\College.
7. To create a new college directory, type **MD "Liberal Arts"** and press **Enter**.

When creating a directory name at the command prompt, use quotation marks to enclose names that include spaces.

8. To change the location to the new college directory, type **CD "Liberal Arts"** and press **Enter**.

9. Verify that the prompt is E:\User01\College\Liberal Arts.

10. To create the English Department directory, type **MD English** and press **Enter**.

11. To create the French Department directory, type **MD French** and press **Enter**.

12. To create the German Department directory, type **MD German** and press **Enter**.

13. To create the Spanish Department directory, type **MD Spanish** and press **Enter**.

14. To back up to College in the directory structure, type **CD ..** and press **Enter**.

15. To view the new directory structure, type **TREE** and then press **Enter**.

16. Verify that Liberal Arts and the four new language departments are present.

17. Close the command prompt window.

18. Leave the virtual machine logged on for the next activity.

Creating Directories in the Windows 10 GUI

To create a folder in the example directory structure using the Windows 10 GUI, navigate to the parent folder Science in the left pane, click Science, and then right-click the white space in the right pane. Point to New, and then click Folder. Type the name over "New Folder" and press Enter. For example, the new folder in Figure 6-20 is named Physics.

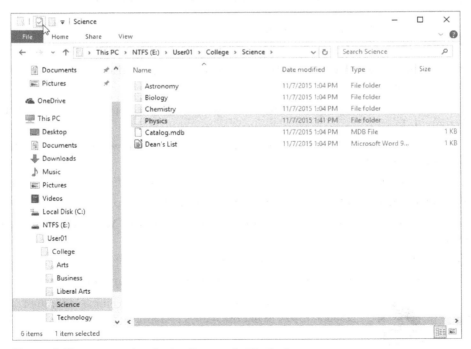

Figure 6-20 Creating the Physics directory in File Explorer

Source: Microsoft Windows 10/File Explorer

Activity 6-13: Creating Directories in the Windows 10 GUI

Time Required: 15 minutes

Objective: Create directories within a directory structure in the Windows 10 GUI.

Description: In this activity, you open File Explorer and create directories within a directory structure.

1. If necessary, start your virtual machines using the appropriate instructions in Activity 1-1.

2. Click **Start,** select **All apps,** scroll down to click **Windows System,** and then click **Command Prompt.**

3. To restore the example directories and files you used earlier in the chapter, type **MakeDS** at the command prompt and press **Enter.**

4. Close the command prompt window.

5. Click **Start,** and then click **File Explorer.**

6. To go to the drive that contains the example directory structure, expand **This PC** and then click **NTFS (E:).**

7. To display the example directory structure in the left pane, expand the following directories in the order shown: **User01, College, Arts, Business, Science,** and **Technology.**

8. To change the location relative to the User01 directory structure, click **College** in the left pane.

9. Verify that the address is E:\User01\College.

10. To create a new college directory, right-click the white space in the right pane, point to **New,** click **Folder,** type **Liberal Arts** over "New Folder," and then press **Enter.**

11. To change the location relative to the User01 directory structure, click **Liberal Arts** in the left pane.

12. Verify that the address is E:\User01\College\Liberal Arts.

13. To create a new department directory, right-click the white space in the right pane, point to **New,** click **Folder,** type **English** over "New Folder," and then press **Enter.**

14. Repeat Step 13 to create department directories for **French, German,** and **Spanish.**

15. Close the File Explorer window.

16. Leave the virtual machine logged on for future activities.

Creating Directories in CentOS 7

As in Windows 10, you sometimes need to create directories within the CentOS 7 directory structure. For example, if your college adds a Printing Department to the Arts group, you will need to add a corresponding subdirectory to the Arts directory. You must have write permission in the parent directory or be logged on as superuser to add directories in CentOS 7.

To create a directory, use the **mkdir** (make directory) command. Its command syntax is:

```
mkdir [options] [directory name]
```

The mkdir command has the following options:

-p   Makes parent directories as needed, but does not display an error if they already exist

-v   Displays a message for each created directory

For example, if your current directory is Technology/Dental/ and you want to add a Printing directory to the Arts directory, you first need to navigate to the Arts directory. Then, use the mkdir command to create the directory.

```
cd College/Arts
mkdir Printing
```

To create a printing subdirectory using the absolute path, type either of the following commands:

```
mkdir College/Arts/Printing
mkdir ../../Arts/Printing
```

Activity 6-14: Creating Directories in CentOS 7

Time Required: 15 minutes

Objective: Create directories in CentOS 7.

Description: In this activity, you open a command prompt and use the mkdir command to create directories in a CentOS 7 directory structure.

You must repeat Activity 6-5 before you can complete the following activity.

1. If necessary, start your virtual machines using the appropriate instructions in Activity 1-1.

2. To open a terminal console, click **Applications**, and then click **Terminal**.

3. To display the path /mnt/sdb1/User01, type **cd /mnt/sdb1/User01** and press **Enter**. Type **pwd**, and then press **Enter**.

4. To list the contents of the User01 directory, type **ls -l** and then press **Enter**.

5. To create a new directory under College, first move to the College directory by typing **cd College** and then pressing **Enter**.

6. To add the Liberal Arts directory, type **mkdir "Liberal Arts"** and then press **Enter**.

7. To verify that the Liberal Arts directory is added correctly, type **ls** and then press **Enter**.

8. To make Liberal Arts the current directory, type **cd "Liberal Arts"** and then press **Enter**.

9. Type **mkdir English,** and then press **Enter**.

10. Type **mkdir French,** and then press **Enter**.

11. Type **mkdir German,** and then press **Enter**.

12. Type **mkdir Spanish,** and then press **Enter**.

13. To verify that all four departments are listed in the Liberal Arts directory, type **ls** and then press **Enter**.

14. Close the terminal window.

15. Leave the virtual machine logged on for future activities.

Removing Directories in the Windows 10 CLI

When you no longer need a directory or the files in it, you can remove the directory. Use the RMDIR or **RD** (remove directory) command to remove a subdirectory in the CLI. The RD command has the following syntax:

RD [/S] [/Q] [drive:]path

/S   Removes all directories and files in the specified directory and the directory itself; use this command to remove a directory tree

/Q   Operates in quiet mode, meaning that the system does not ask for confirmation before removing a directory tree with the /S command

The RD command syntax interprets the drive and path like the CD command described earlier. To remove a subdirectory, you have two choices:

RD path   Removes the old subdirectory from the current location using the relative method

RD \path   Removes the old subdirectory from the current location using the absolute method

If you use the /S switch to remove the indicated directory and its subdirectories, you are asked to confirm your choice by pressing the Y key. The /Q switch allows you to use the RD command in script files, where no user response is needed.

For example, to remove the Science directory, you would type the RD command shown in Figure 6-21 and press Enter. To confirm the deletion, press the Y key and then press Enter.

Just as you should never "cut off the limb" you are standing on, you cannot issue the RD command for a directory in the current path of the command prompt. If you try, an error message appears, as shown in Figure 6-22.

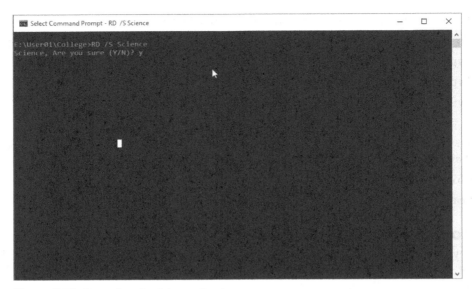

Figure 6-21 Removing the Science directory

Source: Microsoft Windows 10/Command Prompt

Figure 6-22 Error message generated from incorrect use of the RD command

Source: Microsoft Windows 10/Command Prompt

Activity 6-15: Removing Directories in the Windows 10 CLI

Time Required: 15 minutes

Objective: Remove a directory within a directory structure in the Windows 10 CLI.

Description: In this activity, you open a command prompt and remove a directory. This activity is useful if you want to remove a directory that you no longer need.

1. If necessary, start your virtual machines using the appropriate instructions in Activity 1-1.

2. Click **Start,** select **All apps,** scroll down to click **Windows System,** and then click **Command Prompt.**

3. To restore the example directories and files, type **MakeDS** at the command prompt and press **Enter.**

4. If you are not at the example directory structure, type **CD/D E:\User01** and press **Enter.**

5. To display the example directory structure, type **TREE** and press **Enter.**

6. To change the location relative to the directory structure, type **CD \User01\College** and press **Enter**.

7. Verify that the prompt is E:\User01\College.

8. To remove the Science directory and then confirm the deletion, type **RD /S Science**, press **Enter**, press the **Y** key, and then press **Enter**.

9. To see the changed directory structure, type **TREE** and then press **Enter**.

10. To remove the Business directory without confirmation, type **RD /S /Q Business** and then press **Enter**.

11. To see the changed directory structure, type **TREE** and then press **Enter**.

12. Close the command prompt window.

13. Leave the virtual machine logged on for the next activity.

Removing Directories in the Windows 10 GUI

You can navigate the directory structure by clicking a folder in the left pane of File Explorer. By doing so, the location changes and the right pane is refreshed. If you need to remove a directory, right-click its folder in the left pane and click Delete. The folder will be deleted and will no longer be visible. For example, to remove the Music folder, right-click Music in the left pane, click Delete, and then click Yes in the confirmation screen.

When you delete an item from your hard drive, Windows 10 places it in the Recycle Bin (see Figure 6-23). If you change your mind about a deletion from File Explorer, you can retrieve the deleted item from the Recycle Bin, which provides a useful safety net.

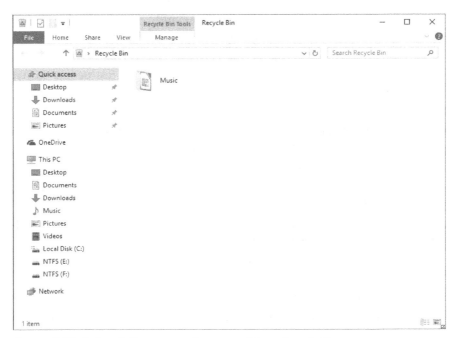

Figure 6-23 Deleted directory can be restored from Recycle Bin

Source: Microsoft Windows 10/Recycle Bin

Items that you delete from a USB drive are permanently deleted and are not placed in the Recycle Bin; neither are items you delete using the command prompt window.

If you want to "undelete"—or restore—a deleted folder back to its original location, double-click the Recycle Bin icon on the desktop, right-click the deleted folder, and click Restore.

Items remain in the Recycle Bin until you permanently delete them from your computer. However, these items still take up hard drive space. When the Recycle Bin fills up, Windows 10 automatically cleans out enough space in it to accommodate the most recently deleted files and folders.

If you are running low on hard drive space, empty the Recycle Bin. You can also restrict the size of the Recycle Bin to limit the amount of hard drive space it takes up.

Activity 6-16: Removing Directories in the Windows 10 GUI

Time Required: 15 minutes

Objective: Remove a folder within a directory structure in the Windows 10 GUI.

Description: In this activity, you open File Explorer and remove a folder within a directory structure. This activity is useful if you want to delete folders that you no longer need.

1. If necessary, start your virtual machines using the appropriate instructions in Activity 1-1.

2. Click **Start,** select **All apps,** scroll down to click **Windows System,** and then click **Command Prompt.**

3. To restore the example directories and files, type **MakeDS** at the command prompt and press **Enter.** Close the Command Prompt window.

4. Click **Start,** and then click **File Explorer.**

5. To go to the drive that contains the example directory structure, expand **This PC** and then click **NTFS (E:).**

6. To display the example directory structure in the left pane, expand **User01,** expand **College,** expand **Arts,** and then expand **Technology.**

7. To change the location relative to the User01 directory structure, click **College** in the left pane.

8. Verify that the address is E:\User01\College.

9. To remove the Arts directory, right-click the **Arts** folder in the right pane, click **Delete,** and then click **Yes.**

10. To remove the Technology directory, right-click the **Technology** folder in the right pane, click **Delete**, and then click **Yes**.

11. Close File Explorer.

12. Leave the virtual machine logged on for future activities.

Removing Directories in CentOS 7

To remove a directory from the tree in CentOS 7, you must have ownership permission or log on as superuser and then use the **rmdir** (remove directory) command. Its command syntax is:

```
rmdir [options] directory[s]
```

The rmdir command has the following options:

-p	Tries to remove each directory component in the path as needed
-v	Displays a message for each removed directory

For example, if your current directory is Technology/Dental/ and you want to delete the Printing directory from the Arts directory, you first need to navigate to the Arts directory. Then, use the rmdir command to remove the Printing directory.

```
cd College/Arts
rmdir Printing
```

 Although you can use the absolute and relative path methods, it is usually safer to navigate directly to the parent directory.

If you created several subdirectories under a directory and now need to remove the entire branch, you can use the rmdir command with the –p option. For example, if you have a directory path of /home/User01/personal/budget/ and you need to delete the personal/budget/ directories, you would type the following:

```
cd /home/User01
rmdir -p personal/budget
```

Unfortunately, this approach will not work if either of the directories contains files. For example, you might have created several files in the budget directory and now need to remove the entire branch. You will need to use the rm commands to remove specified files. The rm command actions can be modified with the following switches:

rm	Removes a file you specify
-f	Forces the system to ignore nonexistent files and does not prompt the user
-i	Interactively prompts the user before removing each file
-r or –R	Recursively removes directories and their contents
-v	Explains what is being done (the "v" stands for *verbose*)

Options can be combined. For example, -ir is a command to use both the interactive and recursive options. By default, the rm command does not remove directories. Use the recursive option (-r or -R) to remove each listed directory and all of its contents:

```
cd /home/User01
rm –ir personal or rm –iR personal
```

Because Linux does not warn against deletions, you should use the –i options so that you are prompted to confirm each file deletion, unless you are running the command in batch mode. You will learn more about the rm command later in this chapter.

Activity 6-17: Removing Directories in the CentOS 7 CLI

Time Required: 15 minutes

Objective: Remove directories in the CentOS 7 CLI.

Description: In this activity, you use the rm command to remove a directory and its files from a CentOS 7 directory tree. This activity is useful if you want to remove a directory you no longer need.

You must repeat Activity 6-5 before you can complete the following activity.

1. If necessary, start your virtual machines using the appropriate instructions in Activity 1-1.
2. To open a terminal console, click **Applications**, and then click **Terminal**.
3. To display the /mnt/sdb1/User01 path, type **cd /mnt/sdb1/User01** and press **Enter**. Type **pwd**, and then press **Enter**.
4. To list the contents of the User01 directory, type **ls -l** and then press **Enter**.
5. To change to the College directory, type **cd College** and press **Enter**.
6. To remove the Arts directory and its files, type **rm –rf Arts** and press **Enter**.
7. To verify that the Arts directory was removed, type **ls Arts** and press **Enter**.

If you do not see a message similar to "ls: cannot access Arts: No such file or directory," contact your instructor.

8. Repeat Steps 6 and 7 to remove the **Technology** directory and verify its successful removal.

The rmdir command does not work if the target directories contain files; you cannot delete the directories without first deleting the files. Therefore, the rm –rf command is used here.

9. Type **ls**, and then press **Enter**.

If you see either the Arts or Technology directory, contact your instructor.

10. To close the CentOS 7 terminal window, type **exit** and then press **Enter**.

11. Leave the virtual machine logged on for the next activity.

Activity 6-18: Removing Directories in the CentOS 7 GUI

Time Required: 15 minutes

Objective: Remove directories in the CentOS 7 GUI.

6

Description: In this activity, you remove directories from a CentOS 7 directory tree. This activity is useful if you want to remove a directory you no longer need.

You must repeat Activity 6-5 before you can complete the following activity.

1. If necessary, start your virtual machines using the appropriate instructions in Activity 1-1.

2. Click **Places** on the Top Bar, and then click **Computer**.

3. To go to the disk that contains the example directory structure in the right pane, click the following directories in the order shown: **mnt**, **sdb1**, **User01**, and then **College**.

4. Right-click the **Arts** directory, and click **Move to Trash**.

5. To move the Technology directory to the trash, right-click the **Technology** directory and click **Move to Trash**.

6. Close the GNOME file browser.

7. Leave the virtual machine logged on for future activities.

Working with Files

You can perform four tasks to keep your files up to date:

- Copy one or more files to an alternative location.
- Move files or directories from one folder to another or from one drive to another.
- Rename files and directories.
- Delete files from the computer.

The following sections explain how to perform these tasks in Windows 10 and CentOS 7.

Working with Files in the Windows 10 CLI

This section explains how to use the Windows 10 CLI to copy, move, rename, and delete files.

Copying Files in the Windows 10 CLI When copying files in the Windows 10 CLI, you can use either the **COPY** command to copy one or more files to an alternative location, or you can use the **XCOPY** command—a more powerful version of the COPY command. This section explains both commands.

Using the COPY Command in the Windows 10 CLI Use the COPY command to copy the contents of a file to a new location. The command has the following syntax:

```
COPY [/V] source [destination]
```

Source	Specifies the file(s) to be copied
Destination	Specifies the directory and/or filename for the new file(s)
/V	Verifies that new files are written correctly

For example, to copy the Budget.xls file from \Science to \Science\Chemistry, you would type:

```
COPY \Science\Budget.xls \Science\Chemistry
```

Although recording errors rarely occur with the COPY command, the /V switch lets you verify that critical data has been recorded correctly and that the new file can be read. This switch also slows down the COPY command because the OS must check each sector recorded on the disk.

Using the XCOPY Command in the Windows 10 CLI Use the XCOPY command when you need more control over what you copy. The XCOPY command is like the COPY command, except that it has more switches. Use this powerful command to copy files in bulk from one directory or drive to another, or to copy whole directories to a new destination. The XCOPY command has the following syntax:

```
XCOPY source [destination] [/P] [/S] [/E] [/V] [/Q] [/F] [/L]
```

Source	Specifies the file(s) to copy
Destination	Specifies the location and/or name of new files
/P	Prompts you before creating each destination file
/S	Copies directories and subdirectories except empty ones
/E	Copies directories and subdirectories, including empty ones
/V	Verifies each new file
/Q	Does not display filenames while copying
/F	Displays full source and destination filenames while copying
/L	Displays filenames of the selected files, but does not copy them

For example, if you needed to make a backup of the College subdirectories and files, you would type the following command, assuming that you had already created the Backup subdirectory:

```
XCOPY /S \User01\College \User01\Backup
```

If you had not already created the Backup subdirectory, you would receive this message:

```
Does \User01\Backup specify a file name
or directory name on the target
(F = file, D = directory)?
```

In this instance, you would respond by entering the letter D.

If you wanted to copy the files, duplicate the directory structure, and verify that the files were successfully copied, you would type:

```
XCOPY /E /V \User01\College \User01\Backup
```

Moving Files in the Windows 10 CLI Use the MOVE command to move the contents of a file to a new location and to rename files and directories. If you want to move one or more files, the command has the following syntax:

```
MOVE [/Y | /-Y] [drive:] [path]filename1 [,...] [destination]
```

If you want to rename a directory, the MOVE command has the following syntax:

```
MOVE [/Y | /-Y] [drive:] [path]dirname1 dirname2
```

[/Y]	Suppresses confirmation prompting
[/-Y]	Causes confirmation prompting
[drive:] [path] filename1	Specifies the location and name of the file(s) you want to move
[destination]	Specifies the new file destination, which can include a drive letter and colon, a directory name, or a combination; if you are moving only one file, you can include a filename to rename the file as you move it
[drive:] [path] dirname1	Specifies the new name of the directory
dirname2	Specifies the directory you want to rename

The MOVE command and syntax are similar to the COPY command, with one exception: The source file is always removed from the disk with the MOVE command.

The MOVE command has the ability to move subdirectories, which is useful if you want to reorganize a directory structure. For example, to move the Architecture Department from Arts to Science, you would type:

```
MOVE \User01\College\Arts\Architecture \User01\College\Science
```

One more use for the MOVE command is to rename subdirectories. For example, to change the name of the Dental subdirectory to Dental Assistant, you would type:

```
MOVE  \User01\College\Technology\Dental  \User01\College\Technology
\Dental Assistant
```

Because "Dental Assistant" contains a space, you may want to use quotation marks.

Renaming Files in the Windows 10 CLI Use the REN (or RENAME) command to rename a file. The command has the following syntax:

```
REN [drive:] [path] filename1 filename2
RENAME [drive:] [path] filename1 filename2
```

Note that you cannot specify a new drive or path for your destination file.

For example, to rename the Budget.xls file, you would type:

```
REN Budget.xls Budget2006.xls
```

You can use wildcards such as * and ? when only part of a name is changed in a series of files, but the lengths of the old and new names must be the same. For example, to change the ".txt" extensions of all filenames in the current directory to ".bak," you would type:

```
REN *.txt *.bak
```

Deleting Files in the Windows 10 CLI Use the DEL (or **ERASE**) command to remove a file or files. The command has the following syntax:

```
DEL [/P] [/S] [/Q] names
ERASE [/P] [/S] [/Q] names
```

Names   Specifies a list of one or more files or directories to delete; you can use wildcards to delete multiple files. If you specify a directory, all files in it are deleted.

/P   Prompts for confirmation before deleting each file

/S   Deletes specified files from all subdirectories

/Q   Operates in quiet mode, meaning that the system does not ask for confirmation before making a deletion using a global wildcard

You can delete one or more files with the DEL command. For example, to remove the homework.doc file, you would type:

```
DEL \User01\homework.doc
```

To remove all of the .doc files from the \User01 subdirectory, you would type:

```
DEL /S \User01\*.doc
```

Activity 6-19: Working with Files in the Windows 10 CLI

Time Required: 15 minutes

Objective: Work with files within a directory structure in the Windows 10 CLI.

Description: In this activity, you open a command prompt and work with files within the directory structure. This activity is useful if you copy, move, rename, and delete files.

1. If necessary, start your virtual machines using the appropriate instructions in Activity 1-1.

2. Click **Start**, select **All apps**, scroll down to click **Windows System**, and then click **Command Prompt**.

3. To restore the example directories and files, type **MakeDS** at the command prompt and press **Enter**.

4. If you are not at the example directory structure, type **CD/D E:\User01** and press **Enter**.

5. To back up the directory structure, type the following, press **Enter**, and then press the **D** key.

   ```
   XCOPY College\*.* /S /E User01\Backup
   ```

6. To view the files within the directory structure, type **TREE /F \User01\User01\Backup** and then press **Enter**.

7. To change the location relative to the directory structure, type **CD \User01\College\Arts** and press **Enter**.

8. Verify that the prompt is E:\User01\College\Arts.

9. To copy the catalog database to the Architecture subdirectory, type the following and then press **Enter**.

   ```
   COPY catalog.mdb Architecture
   ```

10. To move the budget file to the Arts subdirectory, type the following and then press **Enter**.

    ```
    MOVE Architecture\ budget02010.xls
    ```

11. To change the location relative to the directory structure, type the following and press **Enter**.

    ```
    CD \User01\College\Science\Chemistry
    ```

12. Verify that the prompt is E:\User01\College\Science\Chemistry.

13. To rename the budget file, type **REN Budget01030.xls BudgetChemistry.xls** and press **Enter**.

14. To change the location relative to the directory structure, type the following and press **Enter**.

    ```
    CD \User01\College\Science\Biology
    ```

15. Verify that the prompt is E:\User01\College\Science\Biology.

16. To delete a budget file, type **DEL Budget01020.xls** and press **Enter**.

17. To view the files within the directory structure, type **TREE /F \User01\College** and then press **Enter**.

18. Close the command prompt window.

19. Leave the virtual machine logged on for the next activity.

Working with Files in the Windows 10 GUI

You use File Explorer to work with files. For example, the right pane of File Explorer displays important file information. The following sections explain how to copy, move, rename, and delete files using File Explorer.

Copying Files in the Windows 10 GUI
You can copy files from one location to another using File Explorer. For example, to copy the homework.txt file, you would

navigate to the subdirectory that contains the file, right-click homework.txt, and then click Copy, as shown in Figure 6-24. Next, you would navigate to the new location in the left pane, right-click the white space in the right pane, and then click Paste.

Moving Files in the Windows 10 GUI The steps to move files are similar to those for copying files in File Explorer. For example, to move the homework.txt file, you would navigate to the subdirectory that contains the file, right-click homework.txt, and then click Cut. Next, you would navigate to the new location in the left pane, right-click the white space in the right pane, and then click Paste.

Renaming Files in the Windows 10 GUI You can rename files using File Explorer. For example, to rename the homework.txt file, you would navigate to the subdirectory that contains the file, right-click homework.txt, click Rename, type a new name over homework.txt, and press Enter to save it.

If you attempt to change the file extension when renaming a file, you will receive a warning message. If you are sure that the new file extension is acceptable, click Yes.

Deleting Files in the Windows 10 GUI You can delete files using File Explorer. For example, to delete the homework.txt file, you would navigate to the subdirectory that contains the file, right-click homework.txt, and click Delete. No warning message appears before the file is deleted.

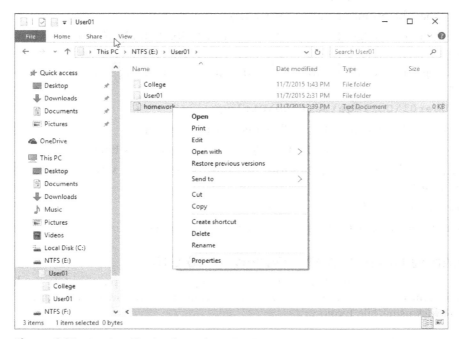

Figure 6-24 Copying files in File Explorer

Source: Microsoft Windows 10/File Explorer

ACTIVITY

Activity 6-20: Working with Files in the Windows 10 GUI

Time Required: 15 minutes

Objective: Work with files within a directory structure in the Windows 10 GUI.

Description: In this activity, you open File Explorer and work with files within the directory structure. This activity is useful if you copy, move, rename, and delete files.

1. If necessary, start your virtual machines using the appropriate instructions in Activity 1-1.

2. Click **Start**, select **All apps**, scroll down to click **Windows System**, and then click **Command Prompt**.

3. To restore the example directories and files, type **MakeDS** at the command prompt and press **Enter**. Close the Command Prompt window.

4. Click **Start**, and then click **File Explorer**.

5. To go to the drive that contains the example directory structure, expand **This PC** and then click **NTFS (E:)**.

6. To display the example directory structure in the left pane, expand the following directories in the order shown: **User01, College, Arts, Business, Science,** and **Technology**.

7. To change the location to the User01 directory structure, click **User01** in the left pane.

8. Verify that the address is E:\User01\.

9. To create a Backup folder, right-click the white space in the right pane, point to **New**, click **Folder**, and then type **Backup** over "New Folder." Press **Enter** when you finish.

10. To copy the College folder to the Backup folder, right-click the **College** folder, click **Copy**, right-click the **Backup** folder, and then click **Paste**.

11. To change the location relative to the directory structure, click **Arts** in the left pane.

12. Verify that the address is E:\User01\College\Arts.

13. To copy the catalog database to the Architecture folder, right-click **Catalog.mdb**, click **Copy**, right-click the **Architecture** folder, and click **Paste**.

14. To move the budget file to the Arts folder, click the **Music** folder, right-click **Budget02020.xls**, click **Cut**, right-click the **Arts** folder, and then click **Paste**.

15. To rename a budget file, click the **Management** folder, right-click **Budget03020.xls**, click **Rename**, enter **BudgetManagement.xls**, and then press **Enter**.

16. To delete a budget file, click **Biology**, right-click **Budget01020.xls**, and then click **Delete** to delete the file.

17. Close File Explorer.

18. Leave the virtual machine logged on for future activities.

Working with Files in CentOS 7

You can use the CentOS 7 CLI to copy, move, rename, and delete files.

Copying Files in the CentOS 7 CLI To copy files or directories in the directory tree, use the **cp** command. Its command syntax is:

```
cp [options] [source path] [target path]
cp [options] [source path] [target directory]
cp [options] [source directory] [target directory]
```

The cp command has the following options:

-f, --force	If an existing destination file cannot be opened, this command removes it and tries again
-i	Prompts before overwriting; this option is recommended to prevent destructive mistakes
-l	Links files instead of copying them
-R or -r	Copies directories recursively
-s	Makes symbolic links instead of copying files
-v	Displays command activity as it occurs

For example, if you want to copy a Budget.xls file from College/Science/Chemistry to College/Arts/Music, type the following command:

```
cp College/Science/Chemistry College/Arts/Music
```

If you have several Budgetxxx.xls files that you want to copy, type the following command:

```
cp College/Science/Chemistry/* College/Arts/Music
```

If you are copying a branch in a directory tree that contains several deep, nested directories, you can use either the -R or the -r option:

```
cp -r College/Science/Chemistry/* College/Arts/
```

Moving Files in the CentOS 7 CLI The command to move a file or directory in CentOS 7 is very similar to the Windows 10 command. You can use the **mv** command to move the contents of a file or directory to a new location. While doing so, you can also use the command to rename files. The mv command syntax is:

```
mv [options] [source] [target]
mv [options] [source] [target directory]
```

The mv command has the following options:

-f	Displays a prompt before overwriting; this command is used in batch processing to provide instructions for users
-i	Also displays a prompt before overwriting, but this command is normally used in interactive processing as a safety measure to prevent mistakes
-v	Displays command activity as it occurs

The mv command is similar to the cp command, with one exception: The source file is always removed from its directory with the mv command. The syntax is also like that of the cp command, as you must always enter a target destination. Even if you are already in the directory where you want to move the file, you must still type the directory name.

You may use the "." (the current directory metacharacter) as a relative path reference for the current location.

You can also use the mv command to move subdirectories, which is useful for reorganizing a directory structure. For example, to move the Architecture Department from Arts to Science, you would type:

```
mv /mnt/sdb1/User01/College/Arts/Architecture /mnt/sdb1/User01/College
/Science
```

Renaming Files in the CentOS 7 CLI
You can use the mv command to rename a file or directory. For example, to change the name of the Dental Department to Dental Assistant, you would type:

```
mv /mnt/sdb1/User01/College/Technology/Dental /mnt/sdb1/User01/College
/Technology/"Dental Assistant"
```

Because "Dental Assistant" contains a space, quotation marks are required. Unlike Windows 10, which interprets spaces within filenames, CentOS 7 requires quotation marks to enclose filenames that contain spaces.

Deleting Files in the CentOS 7 CLI
To remove files and directories in the directory tree, use the rm command. The syntax for the rm command is:

```
rm [options] file[s]
```

The rm command has the following options:

-i	Prompts before removing a file; this option is highly recommended for interactive program runs
-I	Prompts once before removing more than three files or when removing recursively
-R or -r	Removes the contents of directories recursively
-v	Displays command activity as it occurs

You can delete one or more files with the rm command. For example, to remove the homework.doc file, you would type:

```
rm /mnt/sdb1/User01/homework.doc
```

To remove all of the .doc files from the /User01 subdirectory, you would type:

```
rm /mnt/sdb1/User01/*
```

Because Linux does not warn against deletions, you should use the -i or -I option so that you are prompted to confirm the file deletion, unless you are running the command in batch mode (for example, rm -i /User01/*).

Activity 6-21: Working with Files in the CentOS 7 CLI

Time Required: 15 minutes

Objective: Copy, move, rename, and remove files in the CentOS 7 CLI.

Description: In this activity, you use the cp, mv, and rm commands in a CentOS 7 directory tree. This activity is useful if you need to copy, move, rename, and delete files.

You must repeat Activity 6-5 before you can complete the following activity.

1. To open a terminal console, click **Applications**, and then click **Terminal**.
2. To display the /mnt/sdb1/User01 path, type **cd /mnt/sdb1/User01** and press **Enter**. Type **pwd**, and then press **Enter**.
3. To create a Backup directory, type **mkdir Backup** and press **Enter**.
4. To list the contents of the College and Backup directories, type **ls -l** and then press **Enter**.
5. To copy the College directory to the Backup directory, type **cp –r College Backup** and then press **Enter**.
6. To list the directories, type **ls Backup/College** and press **Enter**.
7. Repeat Step 2 of this activity to make sure that your directory path is **/mnt/sdb1 /User01**.
8. To display the /mnt/sdb1/User01/College path, type **cd College** and press **Enter**. Type **pwd**, and press **Enter**.
9. To copy the catalog database file from the Arts directory to the Architecture directory, type the following and then press **Enter**.

   `cp Arts/Catalog.mdb Arts/Architecture`

10. To list the Catalog.mdb file, type **ls Arts/Architecture** and press **Enter**.
11. To move the budget file from the Music directory to the Arts directory, type the following and then press **Enter**.

    `mv Arts/Music/ Budget02020.xls Arts`

12. To list the Budget02020.xls file, type **ls Arts** and press **Enter**.
13. Type **ls Arts/Music**, and press **Enter**.

If files are listed, contact your instructor.

14. To rename the budget file in the Management directory, type the following as one command line and then press **Enter**.

```
mv Business/Management/Budget03020.xls
Business/Management/BudgetManagement.xls
```

15. To list the BudgetManagement.xls file, type **ls Business/Management** and then press **Enter**.

If the Budget03020.xls file is listed, contact your instructor.

16. To delete the budget file from the Biology directory, type the following and then press **Enter**.

```
rm Science/Biology/ Budget01020.xls
```

17. To close the CentOS 7 terminal window, type **exit** and then press **Enter**.

18. Leave the virtual machine logged on for future activities.

Activity 6-22: Working with Files in the CentOS 7 GUI

Time Required: 15 minutes

Objective: Copy, move, rename, and remove files in the CentOS 7 GUI.

Description: In this activity, you open the GNOME file manager in the desktop environment of CentOS 7 and work with files within the directory structure. This activity is useful if you copy, move, rename, and delete files.

You must repeat Activity 6-5 before you can complete the following activity.

1. If necessary, start your virtual machines using the appropriate instructions in Activity 1-1.

2. To display the GNOME file manager, click **Places** on the Top Bar, and then click **Computer**.

3. To go to the disk that contains the example directory structure in the right pane, click the following directories in the order shown: **mnt**, **sdb1**, and then **User01**.

4. To create a Backup directory in the /mnt/sdb1/User01 folder, right-click the blank space in the right pane and then click **New Folder**. Type **Backup** in the highlighted **Untitled Folder** text box under the folder icon, and then press **Enter**.

If you do not see that the Backup directory is added to the /mnt/sdb1 tree, contact your instructor.

5. To copy the College directory to the Backup directory, right-click the **College** directory in the right pane in the User01 directory, click **Copy**, right-click the **Backup** directory in the same directory, and then click **Paste Into Folder**.

6. To see the copied College directory, click the **Backup** directory. To see the content of the College directories, click the **College** directory.

7. To copy the catalog database file to the Arts/Architecture directory from the Arts directory, double-click the **College** directory under the User01 directory in the right pane. Double-click the **Arts** directory. Right-click **Catalog.mdb**, click **Copy To**, double-click the **Architecture** directory in the Select Destination screen, and then press the **Select** button.

8. To see the **Catalog.mdb** file listed in the Architecture directory, double-click the **Architecture** directory icon in the right pane.

9. To move the budget file from the Arts/Music directory to the Arts directory, click the **Arts** directory in the top path list, double-click the **Music** directory icon, right-click **Budget02020.xls** in the right pane, click **Move to**, click **College** in the top path list of the Select Destination screen, double-click the **Arts** directory in the right pane, and then press the **Select** button.

10. To verify that **Budget02020.xls** is listed in the Arts directory, click **Arts** in the top path list.

11. To rename the budget file in the Business/Management directory, click **College** in the top path list, double-click the **Business** directory in the right pane, and then double-click the **Management** directory. Right-click **Budget03020.xls**, click **Rename**, replace Budget03020 with **BudgetManagement**, and then press **Enter**. You should see the BudgetManagement.xls file in the right pane.

12. To delete the budget file from the Science/Biology directory, click **College** in the top path list, double-click the **Science** directory in the right pane, and then double-click the **Biology** directory. Right-click **Budget01020.xls**, and then click **Move to Trash**. The Budget01020.xls file should be deleted.

13. Close the GNOME File Browser window.

14. Leave the virtual machine logged on for future activities.

Using Removable Drives for Application Data Storage

You use removable drives to store and transport data. For example, your instructor might want you to submit programming assignments on USB drives.

Normally, removable media are preformatted, but you should reformat them if you need to reuse them or if you work with two operating systems.

Using Removable Drives in the Windows 10 CLI

Before using a disk, you may want to format it to remove any existing files and improve the odds that the USB drive will accept new files without write errors. You might also want to change the file system. After formatting, you can copy files to the drive from the hard drive.

Refer to the appendix for your virtualization software for specific instructions to set up your virtual machines to use USB drives.

Formatting Removable Drives in the Windows 10 CLI To format a disk for use with Windows 10, use the FORMAT command. The command has the following syntax when you format disks:

FORMAT volume [FS:exFAT] [/V:label] [/Q]

Volume	Specifies the drive letter (followed by a colon)
FS:exFAT	Uses the exFAT file system
/V:label	Specifies the volume label
/Q	Performs a quick format

For example, to format a USB drive as the H drive, type FORMAT H: and press Enter. To specify the portable exFAT file system, add FS:exFAT to the command. You can specify a volume label of up to 11 characters by using the /V switch. You can use the /Q switch to perform a quick format, which removes files from the disk without scanning it for bad sectors. Use this option only if the disk has been previously formatted and you are sure it is not damaged.

Copying Files to a Removable Drive in the Windows 10 CLI You can copy files to a formatted disk with the COPY command or the XCOPY command. For example, to copy the homework.txt file, you would navigate to the subdirectory that contains the file and then use the command COPY homework.txt H:.

Activity 6-23: Using Removable Drives in the Windows 10 CLI

Time Required: 15 minutes

Objective: Use a removable drive with the Windows 10 CLI.

Description: In this activity, you open a command prompt and use a removable drive. This activity is useful if you use removable drives to transport and store data files. For example, you might need to provide the answers to class exercises on removable drives.

1. If necessary, start your virtual machines using the appropriate instructions in Activity 1-1.

2. Click **Start**, select **All apps**, scroll down to click **Windows System**, and then click **Command Prompt**.

Windows 10 will assign the next available drive letter when the USB drive is inserted. The following steps use H as the assigned drive letter, but you might use a different letter.

3. Place a USB drive in a USB port.

4. To format the disk, type **FORMAT H: FS:exFAT /V** and press **Enter**. When prompted, type **Y** to proceed and then press **Enter**.

Be sure to include the drive letter. If you do not, you might format a different hard drive by mistake.

5. When prompted to enter the volume label, type **Homework** and then press **Enter**.

6. When asked if you want to format another disk, press the **N** key, and then press **Enter**.

7. To copy a file to the disk, type the following and then press **Enter**.

```
COPY e:\User01\College\Arts\Catalog.mdb H:
```

8. To verify that the file was copied, type **DIR H:** and press **Enter**.

9. Close the command prompt window.

10. Leave the virtual machine logged on for the next activity.

Using Removable Drives in the Windows 10 GUI

As with the Windows 10 CLI, you can format a USB drive using the Windows 10 GUI. After formatting, you can copy files from the hard drive to a USB drive or store files directly to the USB drive from an application.

Formatting Removable Drives in the Windows 10 GUI To format a USB drive, place it in the USB port. From File Explorer, right-click the USB option and then click Format. The Format USB dialog box appears. If you are sure that the disk is good, click the Quick Format check box. To start the format, click the Start button.

Copying Files to a Removable Drive in the Windows 10 GUI You can copy files to a formatted disk using File Explorer. For example, to copy the homework.txt file, you would navigate to the subdirectory that contains the file, right-click homework.txt, and then click Copy. Next, you would navigate to the USB drive in the left pane, right-click the white space in the right pane, and then click Paste.

Storing Files from an Application As an alternative to copying files from the hard drive to a USB drive, you can save files directly to the USB drive. For example, to save a file that you typed in Notepad, click the File menu, click Save As, click the Save in list box, click the USB drive, type the filename in the text box, and then click Save.

Activity 6-24: Using Removable Drives in the Windows 10 GUI

Time Required: 15 minutes

Objective: Use a removable drive with the Windows 10 GUI.

Description: In this activity, you use File Explorer to work with a removable drive. This activity is useful if you use removable drives to transport and store data files. For example, you might need to provide the answers to class exercises on removable drives.

1. If necessary, start your virtual machines using the appropriate instructions in Activity 1-1.
2. Click **Start,** and then click **File Explorer.**

 Windows 10 will assign the next available drive letter when the USB drive is inserted. The following steps use H as the assigned drive letter, but you might use a different letter.

3. Place a USB drive in a USB port.
4. To format the disk, click **Start,** click **File Explorer,** expand **This PC,** right-click **USB Drive (H:),** click **Format,** and then click the **Start** button. Click **OK** when prompted.
5. To copy a file to the disk, click **NTFS (E:),** expand **User01,** expand **College,** click **Arts,** right-click **Catalog.mdb,** click **Copy,** right-click **USB Drive (H:),** and click **Paste.**
6. To verify that the file was copied, click **USB** and review the right pane.
7. Close any open windows in the virtual machine.
8. To shut down the Windows virtual machine, click **Start,** and then click the **Shut Down** button.
9. Wait a moment for the Windows 10 virtual machine to shut down completely.

Using Removable Drives in the CentOS 7 CLI

As with Windows 10, you can use removable drives in CentOS 7 to store and transport data. Before using a disk, you must **unmount** and format it. Next, you **mount** the disk drive and copy the files from the hard drive. Refer to Chapter 5 for directions on using the mount and unmount commands.

Formatting Removable Drives in the CentOS 7 CLI
To perform a low-level format of a disk, use the floppy command. Normally, you do not need to format disks because they are preformatted. The floppy command has the following syntax when you format disks:

```
floppy [options] [target device]
```

The floppy command has the following options:

--probe, -p	Probes for available drives; the floppy command creates and displays a list of all detected drives
--showrc	Lists drives configured in /etc/floppy
--capacity, -c	Shows the available format capacities of the drive; options are C, which shows the number of cylinders; B, which shows the number of blocks per cylinder; and S, which shows the block size, in bytes
--format, -f	Formats the disk in the floppy drive

--ext2 -	Creates an ext2 (Linux) file system on the formatted disk
--fat -	Creates a FAT (DOS) file system on the formatted disk
--noprompt, -n	Prevents the display of verbose process messages produced by the --capacity and --format commands; these messages normally appear by default
--eject	Ejects the disk from the drive (IDE drives only)

Copying Files to a Removable Drive in the CentOS 7 CLI You can copy files to a formatted disk or a USB drive with the cp command. For example, to copy a file called homework.doc, you would navigate to the subdirectory that contains the file and then use one of the following commands:

```
cp homework.doc /dev/fd0
cp homework.doc /dev/sda0
```

Activity 6-25: Using Removable Drives in CentOS 7

Time Required: 30 minutes

Objective: Use a removable drive with CentOS 7.

Description: In this activity, you use CentOS 7 to work with a USB drive. You use the fdisk and mkfs commands to format removable disks and copy files from the sample directory tree. This activity is useful if you use removable drives to transport and store data files. For example, you might need to provide the answers to class exercises on removable drives.

You must repeat Activity 6-5 before you can complete the following activity.

1. If necessary, start your virtual machines using the appropriate instructions in Activity 1-1.

2. To open a terminal console, click **Applications** and then click **Terminal**. Plug in your USB drive.

3. To list the file system's disk space usage, type **df -h** and press **Enter**.

If you do not see /run/media in the Mounted on column, contact your instructor.

4. To switch to superuser, type **su** and press **Enter**, then type **Pa$$w0rd** and press **Enter**.

5. To unmount the device and get ready for the partition and format commands, type the following and then press **Enter**.

umount /dev/sdd1

If /dev/sdd1 is not the only file system associated with your USB drive when you run the df -h command, unmount them all now. For example, type umount /dev/sde.

6. To partition the disk, type **fdisk /dev/sdd** and press **Enter**.

 Make sure to include only the disk name without any digit after it. For example, it would be incorrect to use /dev/sde1 here. Optionally, if the partition to delete is already defined, you can delete it before adding it again by typing **d** and pressing **Enter**.

7. To create a new partition, type **n** at the command prompt and press **Enter**.

8. To create a primary partition, type **p** and press **Enter**.

9. To create the first primary partition, type **1** and press **Enter**.

10. Press **Enter** at the First cylinder prompt.

11. Press **Enter** at the Last cylinder prompt.

12. To save the changes and go back to the superuser prompt, type **w** and then press **Enter**.

13. To format the disk, type **mkfs.fat -F 32 -n learnusb /dev/sdd1** and then press **Enter**.

14. To switch back to the User01 user, type **su – User01** and then press **Enter**.

15. Make sure that all file systems associated with your USB drive are unmounted. Unplug the USB drive and then plug it back in. Wait a few seconds for the system to pick up the USB drive.

16. To verify that the learnusb name is listed, type **ls /run/media/User01** and press **Enter**.

17. Type **ls /run/media/User01/LEARNUSB** and press **Enter**. Verify that nothing is listed under this directory. Take note of the **/run/media/User01/LEARNUSB** directory; you will use the directory name when you use the cp command later.

18. To display /mnt/sdb1/User01 as the current working directory, type **pwd** and then press **Enter**.

19. If you are not at the directory, type **cd /mnt/sdb1/User01** and press **Enter**.

20. To copy the Catalog.mdb file, type the following and then press **Enter**.

```
cp College/Arts/Catalog.mdb /run/media/User01/LEARNUSB
```

21. To list the Catalog.mdb file, type **ls /run/media/User01/LEARNUSB** and then press **Enter**.

22. To unmount the disk, type **umount /run/media/User01/LEARNUSB** and then press **Enter**.

23. To shut down the virtual machine, click **Parallel OS Student** in the top-right corner of the desktop screen, click **Power Off**, and then click the **Power Off** button.

24. Wait a moment for the CentOS 7 virtual machine to shut down completely.

25. Close any remaining open windows, log off, and shut down your PC.

Chapter Summary

- You can use directory structures to organize and maintain information in files and folders. Knowing how to manage directories enables you to perform a variety of tasks with files and increases the portability of the information you store. The organization of the directory structure is similar in Windows 10 and CentOS 7.

- To help you display the contents of a directory, you can use a command-line interface (CLI). The commands you enter at the command line are executed by a command-line interpreter. You can use wildcard characters to help identify filenames in a directory, and you can add options to commands to produce more specific file lists.

- You can manage the directory structure by creating new directories to categorize folder information and by removing directories that are obsolete.

- Each operating system has its own syntax when you navigate directory structures. When navigating the absolute path, you must provide the drive and the full path name. When navigating with a relative path, the current directory path is implied.

- You can use a command prompt or a GUI to copy, move, rename, and delete files.

- Removable drives provide portability for file management and processing. In both Windows 10 and CentOS 7, you need to format a disk for reuse. You also need to mount and unmount an external storage device with CentOS 7.

Key Terms

absolute path   A path to a file that begins with the drive identifier and root directory or with a network share and ends with the complete filename.

CD   The command that changes the current directory. The command must be lowercase in Linux or UNIX.

command-line interface (CLI)   A form of interface in which the user types commands using a special command language.

command-line interpreter   A program that accepts typed commands from the keyboard and performs tasks as directed. The command-line interpreter, which is usually part of the operating system, is responsible for loading applications and directing the flow of information between them.

command prompt   A line area within the command window, usually indicated by a blinking cursor, where you type Windows or Linux commands.

COPY   A Windows command used to duplicate files from one disk or directory to another.

cp   The Linux command used to copy files, similar to the COPY command in Windows.

current directory   The disk directory at the end of the active directory path; it is the directory that is searched first for a requested file, and the directory in which a new file is stored unless another directory is specified.

DEL   A Windows command used to permanently remove a file. The file remains stored and is recoverable until the system reuses the storage space taken by the file.

DIR   A Windows command that displays a list of files and subdirectories in the current directory.

ERASE   A Windows command used to permanently remove a file or folder.

home   The conventional starting directory for all regular users in CentOS 7.

long filename   A plain text name assigned to a file that can be 200 characters or more; it can include uppercase and lowercase letters as well as spaces.

`ls`   The Linux command that displays a list of files and subdirectories in the current directory or the directory specified in the command.

`mkdir`   The Linux command that creates a directory or subdirectory in the current directory of a folder.

mount   To make a physical disk accessible to a computer's file system.

`MOVE`   The Windows command used to transfer a file or folder from one directory to another.

`mv`   The Linux command used to transfer a file or folder from one directory to another; similar to the `MOVE` command used in Windows.

pipe symbol   The vertical line symbol (|) that appears on a virtual machine keyboard as the shift character on the backslash key (\). This symbol is used in Windows and Linux to transfer the output of one command to the input of a second command.

`RD`   The Windows command to remove a directory.

relative path   A path that is implied by the current working directory. If a user enters a command that refers to a file and the full path name is not entered, the current working directory becomes the path of the file to which the user referred.

`REN`   The Windows command to rename a file.

`rmdir`   The Linux command used to remove a directory. All folders need to be removed from the directory before it can be removed.

`sort`   The Linux command used to organize files in a particular order. Files can be organized in ascending or descending alphabetized order.

standardized channel   A path or link through which information passes between two devices.

`TREE`   The command used in Windows to produce a graphical view of files in a directory or subdirectories.

unmount   To remove a disk or device from active use.

white space   Blank areas of a page or window that contribute to its balance and visual appeal.

wildcard character   A character you can use in a command to represent one or more unknown characters. Wildcards are useful, for example, to specify multiple filenames.

working directory   Another term for *current directory*.

`XCOPY`   A more powerful version of the Windows `COPY` command, with additional features.

Review Questions

1. A directory structure is used to _____.

   a. organize information on your virtual machine

   b. create maps that help students navigate between campus buildings

   c. find manila files in a file cabinet

   d. provide detailed information about file contents

2. CLI is the acronym for _____.

    a. core language interpreter

    b. content line interpreter

    c. command-line interface

    d. command-line interpreter

3. The TREE command is used to _____.

    a. display the contents of a single file

    b. list the directories and subdirectories on a disk

    c. organize the files on a disk

    d. list the files in a directory

4. When you use a long name for a file, you may _____. (Choose all that apply.)

    a. use lowercase letters

    b. use uppercase letters

    c. have spaces between words

    d. have no more than 200 characters in the filename

5. The DIR command is used to _____. (Choose all that apply.)

    a. display the contents of a single file

    b. list the directories and subdirectories on a disk

    c. organize the files on a disk

    d. list the files in a directory

6. Wildcard characters are used in commands to _____. (Choose all that apply.)

    a. match single characters to specify groups of files

    b. match strings of characters to specify groups of files

    c. match files with the same extension

    d. speed the process of accessing files

7. Which of the following can you use to display directory structures in Windows 10? (Choose all that apply.)

    a. File Explorer

    b. Directory Manager

    c. Windows console or command prompt

    d. Windows directory viewer

8. You can open a _____ to access the CLI in CentOS 7.

   a. Windows console

   b. terminal window

   c. directory viewer

   d. command prompt

9. Conventional users who log on to CentOS 7 are automatically placed in the _____ directory.

   a. systems

   b. root

   c. home

   d. user

10. The _____ command in CentOS 7 displays your directories and files.

   a. dir

   b. cd

   c. show

   d. ls

11. When you use the more command with the ls command in CentOS 7, _____.

   a. all information about files and directories appears at the same time

   b. you can scroll through the listing page by page

   c. nothing happens; you need to use the less command

   d. you are prompted for additional file information

12. To change the directory in Windows 10, you can use which of the following commands? (Choose all that apply.)

   a. cddir

   b. changeDIR

   c. CD

   d. CHDIR

13. The relative path _____. (Choose all that apply.)

   a. is implied to be the current working directory when a directory path is not listed in a command prompt

   b. begins with the backslash symbol (\) before the directory path in Windows

   c. begins with the forward slash symbol (/) before the directory path in Linux

   d. requires no symbol before the directory path

6

14. The absolute path _____. (Choose all that apply.)

   a. is a path to a file that begins with the drive identifier and root directory and ends with the complete filename

   b. begins with the backslash symbol (\) before the directory path in Windows

   c. begins with the forward slash symbol (/) before the directory path in Linux

   d. requires no symbol before the directory path

15. In CentOS 7, the command to change a directory is _____. (Choose all that apply.)

   a. the same as the command in Windows 10, and case does not matter

   b. the same as the command in Windows 10, but it must be lowercase

   c. complicated and not widely used

   d. able to use standardized channels to move up and down in the directory tree structure

16. White space is _____. (Choose all that apply.)

   a. used to help distinguish objects and text in a window

   b. used to provide files with longer, more meaningful names

   c. used to access menus in a window

   d. not accessible by moving your arrow cursor onto it

17. To create a directory in CentOS 7, use the _____ command.

   a. cddir

   b. dir

   c. makedir

   d. mkdir

   e. chdir

18. Which of the following commands can you use in Windows 10 to remove a directory and its files? (Choose all that apply.)

   a. RM

   b. RDDIR

   c. RD

   d. RMDIR

19. To remove a directory in CentOS 7, _____.

   a. the directory cannot contain any files

   b. you need to use the rm command

   c. you use the same command that is used in Windows 10

   d. you need to use the rmdir command

20. The MOVE command in Windows 10 and the mv command in CentOS 7
    _____.

    a. copy the contents of one file to another location, leaving the original intact

    b. can be used interchangeably

    c. move a file to another location

    d. automatically rename the file as it is processed

Case Projects

Case 6-1: Explaining Relative versus Absolute Paths

You have been stopped by a peer with a question: "What is the difference between relative and absolute paths when using the CD command?" What do you tell your peer? Write a short report that clearly answers the question and includes examples to clarify your points.

6

Case 6-2: Copying Files

You have been asked to prepare a short presentation on copying files at the next technical users meeting. Prepare a handout for your audience that explains at least eight uses of the COPY and XCOPY commands.

Case 6-3: Using the ls Command in CentOS 7

You are given a file system to clean up at work. You must delete all of the files related to the Cramden Project. A prefix of "CP" is part of the standard filename for these project files. Write a ls command that displays every directory name and filename that begins with "CP"; be sure to include hidden files.

Case 6-4: Moving Directory Tree Branches in CentOS 7

You are in charge of the data in one of your extracurricular clubs. You need to move the "Program Meeting" files from one chairperson to another in your file system. Each chairperson has a branch in the directory tree of the club's file system. List the steps and commands you would use to move the files.

## chapter 7

Files and File Attributes

After reading this chapter and completing the exercises, you will be able to:

- Describe the contents of files and identify the application that created a particular file
- Describe the use of file attributes
- Find files based on their name or content

Files are used as part of the computer file system as a way to store information under a given name. The name given to a file is known simply as a **filename**. Filenames allow you to save data or documents for later retrieval and use. Files can be of different types, and they can store executable programs or data files.

Contents of Files

When using applications, you work with files. You need to know how to recognize the contents of files and the actions a particular OS takes when opening a file. Double-clicking a data file of a certain file type may determine which application the operating system will try to use to open the file. **File type** may be determined by the filename's extension or the file's metadata. Metadata is information about a file contained within the file. The metadata used for file identification is often contained in the beginning of the file or header, and is called the *file signature* or *magic number*.

File attributes are settings related to a file; they determine how the operating system allows processes or users to perform some functions. As an example, an operating system will disallow writing to a file marked with a read-only attribute in Windows 10 or read-only file permissions in CentOS 7. Files with the system attribute are used by the operating system. You will learn more about attributes and file permissions later in this chapter.

This chapter also explains how to search for files by their filenames or contents. Searches are useful when you need information from a file but are not sure of its filename, or when you do not know a filename but know something about the file's contents.

The following sections explain the contents of files in Windows 10 and CentOS 7.

Contents of Files in Windows 10

Filenames in Windows include the base filename followed by an **extension**. The extension is an optional part of the filename. When included, the extension usually contains three letters that are separated from the base filename by a period. When you save a file, you or a Windows 10 application appends an extension to the end of the filename. File extensions typically suggest the type of data stored in a file. For example, in default.htm, the file extension is .htm, which identifies the file as an HTML document. The OS uses the extension to determine which program can process the file.

Thousands of file extensions are associated with programs in Windows. To view a Web site that identifies these extensions, try *www.file-extensions .org*.

In the days when MS-DOS was dominant, base filenames were limited to eight characters and file extensions could not exceed three characters. This filename convention is known as an 8.3 (eight dot three) filename or short filename, and is still included in Windows for backward compatibility. Conversely, filenames in modern versions of Windows may be referred to as long filenames. While the three-character extension limitation no longer holds, it is still common practice; extensions that adhere to this traditional limit are commonly called *short extensions*. A long extension has more than three characters; for example, the short extension for an HTML document is .htm, and the long extension is .html.

Short filenames can be viewed using the /x parameter with the dir directory command by typing dir /x at the command prompt.

Contents of Files in CentOS 7

Linux OS systems such as CentOS 7 view files and directories in ways that are not dependent on file extensions. For example, CentOS 7 allows you to open any file as a text file, even if it is not a text file. File extensions help users distinguish different types of files, but they are not necessary for the OS. The CentOS 7 GNOME desktop uses the file extensions to display icons and to allow for easy access within the GNOME environment.

When a file is created in CentOS 7, it is assigned both a name and an **inode** number, which is an integer that is unique within the file system. The filenames and corresponding inode numbers are stored as entries in a directory that appears to the user to contain the files. That is, the directory associates filenames with inodes. As you access files in CentOS 7, it is helpful to determine a file's contents before you try to view it, as CentOS 7 lets you open any file with a text editor, even if it is a binary executable. The **file** command is useful in this situation; you can use it to examine a file and determine its file type. The syntax for the file command is:

```
file[filename(s)]
```

For example, if you want to examine a plain text file named boot.log, you can type the following in a terminal window:

```
file boot.log
```

The terminal window file then displays the output, as shown in Figure 7-1.

If you use the file command on a file that is an executable, such as parted:

```
file parted
```

The OS lets you know that the file is an executable and reports its version number and how it is used within the system. The SHA1 hash, which ensures that the data has not changed due to accidental corruption, allows you to verify whether the file is the correct executable released from CentOS 7.

Viewing File Extensions in Windows 10 Windows tracks the extensions that your virtual machine uses. To view the file extensions registered in Windows 10, click Start, click All apps, scroll down if necessary, click Windows System, click Default Programs, and then click "Associate a file type or protocol with a program" (see Figure 7-2). For example, Microsoft WordPad documents have an extension of .rtf. File extensions are hidden from view for known file types. To turn on file extension viewing, click Start, click File Explorer, click the View tab, click the Options icon on the Ribbon, click the View tab, and then click to uncheck "Hide extensions for known file types" (see Figure 7-3). Other options allow the display of hidden files and folders and hidden system files. You will learn more about hidden files later in this chapter.

7

Figure 7-1 Using the `file` command

Source: Red Hat CentOS 7/Terminal

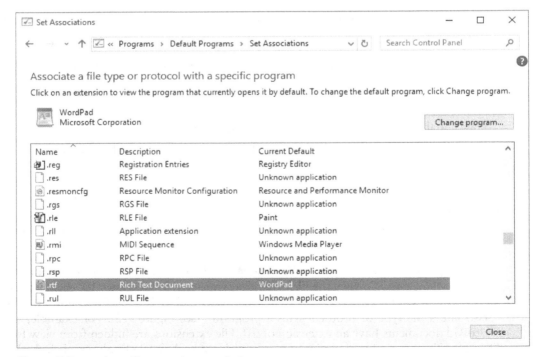

Figure 7-2 Windows file extension associations

Source: Microsoft Windows 10/Control Panel

Figure 7-3 Windows folder options

Source: Microsoft Windows 10/Control Panel

Viewing File Extensions in CentOS 7 CentOS 7 and other Linux-based OSs do

not really need file extensions, but use them as a way to distinguish files for the user.
File extensions can be used within the GNOME desktop to associate files to programs
that can open the files. The GNOME desktop also uses file extensions to change the
icon displayed by the GNOME File viewer. To change the program associated with a
particular extension within the GNOME desktop, you can make the change for just one
of the files, which will change it for all. To begin, right-click a file with the extension
whose association you want to change, select Properties, and change the window to the
"Open With" view. A list of programs is displayed. The first program listed is the default
program used to open the file. The next set of programs are the ones the OS recommends
using to open the file. The last set of programs listed are the remaining programs
installed in the operating system, as shown in Figure 7-4. To change the default program
for all the files with the same extension, select a different program than the current
default program and click "Set as default."

Using a terminal window to see whether a particular file extension has an associated program is a bit more complicated. In the following example, the extension .pdf is used to
check for associated programs. At the command prompt, type the following command:

```
cat /usr/share/mime/packages/freedesktop.org.xml | grep pdf
```

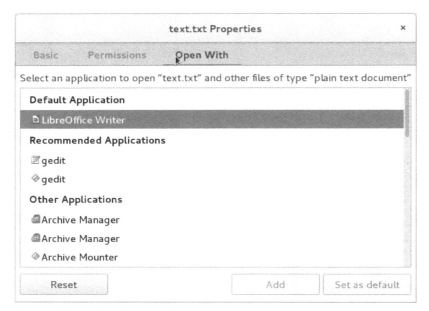

Figure 7-4 Setting the default application

Source: Red Hat CentOS 7

Next, look at the output shown in Figure 7-5. Changing or adding a file association in a terminal window is an advanced activity that will not be covered in this book.

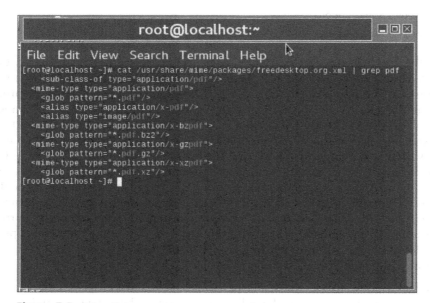

Figure 7-5 Using the cat and grep commands

Source: Red Hat CentOS 7/Terminal

File Associations Windows 10 and the CentOS 7 GNOME desktop use file extensions to identify file associations. A file association also helps to specify how the OS treats different file types. These associations include:

- Which icon appears for a file in Windows File Explorer in Windows 10 or File Explorer in CentOS 7
- Which commands appear in a file's shortcut menu
- Which application opens when a user double-clicks a file icon

Commands in a File's Shortcut Menu in Windows 10 When you right-click a file icon, a shortcut menu appears. The menu usually includes a list of actions that are appropriate to the object you clicked, as shown in Figure 7-6. Some menu choices appear on all shortcut menus; for example, you always have the option of creating a shortcut, deleting a file, renaming a file, or viewing its properties. However, the Open and Print menu options are specific to such files as word-processing documents. Also, notice in Figure 7-6 that the Open option is bold, which means it is the default option when you double-click the filename. Your virtual machine might have different options on the context menu.

Commands in a File's Shortcut Menu in CentOS 7 Like Windows, CentOS 7 also has a shortcut menu that appears when you right-click a file icon in the GNOME desktop

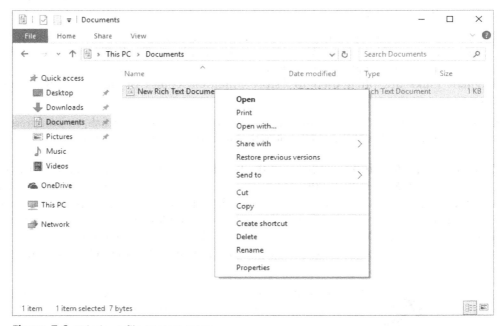

Figure 7-6 Windows file context menu

Source: Microsoft Windows 10/File Explorer

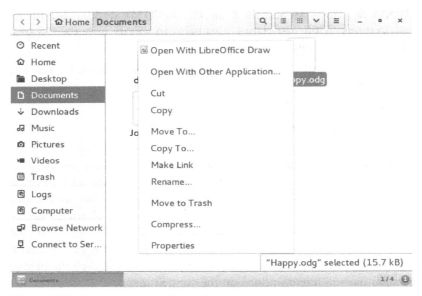

Figure 7-7 Shortcut menu of file options

Source: Red Hat CentOS 7

(see Figure 7-7). The menu allows you to open the file with the default program associated with the file or choose another application to open the file. You can also move or copy the file to another location.

With the Make Link option, you can create a symbolic link—a special kind of file that points to another file, much like a shortcut in Windows. Symbolic links are used to link libraries and ensure that files are in consistent locations without moving or copying the original. Links are often used to "store" multiple copies of the same file in different places.

Other menu options allow you to rename the file, move it to the trash, or compress it from the shortcut menu. Finally, you can view the properties of the selected file.

Opening Applications When you double-click a file icon in Windows 10 and the CentOS 7 GNOME desktop, the file opens in its associated application. For example, in Windows 10, if the user double-clicks the WordPad file Homework.rtf, the OS opens the file in WordPad because WordPad is associated with .rtf files on the system and the default action is defined as Open. In CentOS 7, double-clicking an .rtf file opens the file in gedit, because gedit is associated with .rtf files on the system and is the default program used to open them.

If Microsoft Office is installed, Windows will open files with an .rtf extension in Microsoft Word because the file type association was changed from WordPad.

Figure 7-8 Opening a file in an application

Source: Microsoft Windows 10/File Explorer

To change the default program for a given file type, right-click the file icon, and then click Open with. From the dialog box that appears, browse for the application to use with the selected file type (see Figure 7-8) and then click to select it. If you want this file type to be associated with the program you choose, retain the check next to "Always use this app to open .rtf files."

Applications in Windows 10 and CentOS 7 You should know the common file extensions that you might encounter. For example, if you receive an e-mail message with an attached file from a colleague and you recognize its extension, you might be able to assess the value of the file before you open the attachment. Or, if a co-worker gives you a removable drive, you can identify the applications used to create the files on it.

Table 7-1 lists common file extensions for business applications, including brief descriptions of the extensions and the application associated with each file. With this information, you can determine whether you have the application needed to read and update a file.

Table 7-2 identifies the programming language for a particular source file, which helps you use the right compiler. Computer programming students should find this table particularly helpful.

Category	Extension	Description	Application
Database	.myd/.myi/.frm, .accdb/.mdb	MySQL table data/index/format, MS Access database	MySQL, Access
E-mail	.pab, .pst	Personal Address Book, Post Office Box Data	Outlook, Outlook Express
Desktop publishing/ graphics	.xcf, .pub	eXperimental Computing Facility, Desktop publishing	GNU Image Manipulation Program, Publisher
Drawings/charts	.odg, .vsd	OpenOffice drawing, Visio drawing	OpenOffice, Visio
Presentations/graphics	.odp, .pptx/.ppt, .pez	OpenOffice presentation, PowerPoint presentation, Prezi	Open Office Impress, PowerPoint, Prezi Desktop
Spreadsheet	.ods, .xlsx/.xls	Open Office spreadsheet, Excel worksheet	Open Office Calc, Excel
Word processing	.odt, .docx, .doc, .dotx, .rtf	Open Office text, Microsoft Word, Rich Text Format	Open Office Write, Microsoft Word

Table 7-1 Common business applications and their file extensions

Extension	Description
.asc, .txt	ASCII text
.c	C source
.cbl	COBOL program
.cpp	C++ source
.cs	C# source
.java	Java source
.js	Javascript
.pl	PERL script
.py	Python script
.vb	VBScript

Table 7-2 Common programming source files

Table 7-3 lists some of the many Internet file extensions and formats you may encounter. This information helps you troubleshoot Internet browser problems related to particular file types. For example, you may have a file that uses **compression** to package one or more files together and use less file space.

Table 7-4 lists the files you are most likely to encounter when working with Windows 10. This table could be helpful if you need to talk to a vendor about a problem with a Windows 10 application.

Table 7-5 lists common Linux file extensions for system configuration files, installation packaging files, programming files, and compressed files.

Extension	Description
.aspx	Active Server Pages
.gif	CompuServe Graphic Interchange Format
.htm or .html	Hypertext Markup Language
.iso	CDFS/ISO 9660 disk image
.jpg or .jpeg	Joint Photographic Experts Group compression
.mov	QuickTime Movie
.mp3	Moving Picture Experts Group audio, layer 3
.mp4 or .mpg or .mpeg	Moving Picture Experts Group Video
.pdf	Adobe Acrobat Reader
.png	Portable Network Graphic
.torrent	BitTorrent file

Table 7-3 Common Internet files

Extension	Description
.bat	Batch file—runs executable scripts
.bmp	Bitmap graphic
.cfg	Configuration
.cmd	Command—runs executable scripts
.com	Executable
.dll	Dynamic link library
.drv	Device driver
.exe	Executable
.hlp	Help
.ico	Icon
.ini	Initialization/program configuration
.lnk	Shortcut
.log	Program log
.msc	Common console
.sys	System files
.ttf	Windows True Type Font
.wav	Windows sound
.zip	Zip compressed folder

Table 7-4 Common Windows 10 files

Extension	Type
.conf	A configuration file
.rpm	A Red Hat Package Manager file used to install software
.c	A C program language source code file
.pl	A PERL script
.sh	A shell script
.bz2	A file compressed with bzip2
.gz	A file compressed with gzip
.tar	A file archived with **tar** (short for "tape archive"), also known as a tar file
.zip	A file compressed with **Zip**, which is commonly found in Windows applications; most compressed files in Linux use gzip compression, so finding a Zip archive for Linux files is rare
.tgz	A tarred and gzipped file

Table 7-5 Common Linux files

Viewing the Contents of Text Files in a Windows Command Prompt

In Windows 10, you can view the contents of text files by using a Windows command prompt. For example, you might need to review the contents of a text file provided by your instructor. This technique is particularly useful when debugging computer programs.

The **TYPE** command displays the contents of a text file line by line. For example, the following command lists the contents of the Pgm1Data.txt file, which was created in Notepad:

```
TYPE Pgm1Data.txt
```

If you have a larger text file to review, the MORE command is a better choice because it displays text data files one screen at a time:

```
TYPE Pgm1Data.txt | MORE
```

 On most keyboards, the pipe character (|) is located above the Enter key.

The MORE command has the following syntax:

```
MORE [/E [/C] [/P] [/S] [/Tn] [+n]] < drive:] [path]filename
```

`[drive:] [path]filename`	Specifies a file to display one screen at a time
`/E`	Enables extended features
`/C`	Clears the screen before displaying the page
`/P`	Expands FormFeed characters
`/S`	Squeezes multiple blank lines into a single line

| /T*n* | Expands tabs to *n* spaces (the default is 8 spaces) |
| +*n* | Starts displaying the first file at line *n* |

If extended features are enabled with /E, the following commands are accepted at the -- More -- prompt:

P *n*	Displays next *n* lines
S *n*	Skips next *n* lines
F	Displays next file
Q	Quits
=	Shows line number
?	Shows help

After one page of the text is displayed, you can press the Spacebar to display the next page or press Enter to display the next line.

To use the MORE command to display the contents of the Pgm1Data.txt file, you would type the following at a command prompt and then press Enter:

```
MORE < Pgm1Data.txt
```

The < is a required redirection symbol; it tells the OS to redirect the file into the MORE command.

Activity 7-1: Viewing File Contents with the Windows 10 Command-Line Interface

Time Required: 15 minutes

Objective: Use the MORE and TYPE commands to view the contents of a text file.

Description: In this activity, you work from the User01 directory, which is the default directory when opening the command prompt as User01. You will copy a file and then display its contents using the more command and again using the type command.

1. Start your virtual machines using the appropriate instructions in Activity 1-1.
2. To open a command prompt, right-click **Start**, and then click **Command Prompt**.
3. To copy a file to work with, type the following and then press **Enter**.

   ```
   copy c:\windows\system32\drivers\etc\services MyServices.txt
   ```

The previous command should be typed as one continuous string of characters. The formatting for this book broke the lines.

4. To verify that the file was copied, type **dir** and look for the **MyServices.txt** file.
5. To display the contents of the MyServices.txt file, type the following and then press **Enter**.

   ```
   more < MyServices.txt
   ```

6. To view the next line of content, press the **Enter** key.

7. To view the next page of content, press the **Spacebar**.

8. Continue to press the **Spacebar** until you reach the end of the file and the command prompt returns.

9. To display the short filename, type the following and then press **Enter**.

    `dir /s MyServices.txt`

10. To display the contents of the file using the `type` command and the short filename, type the following and then press **Enter**.

    `type myserv~1.txt | more`

11. Continue to press the **Spacebar** until you reach the end of the file and the command prompt returns.

12. Close the command prompt window.

13. Leave the virtual machine logged on for future activities.

Viewing the Contents of Files in CentOS 7

As with Windows 10, filenames in CentOS 7 can contain file extensions, and applications in the OS contain associations that open a file in a format you can use. For example, if you open a file with an .sxw extension, OpenOffice Writer is probably the offered application that appears. However, because CentOS 7 automatically reads file headers to check a file's type, an extension is not required to open a file from the command-line interface (CLI).

More and more graphical user interfaces (GUIs) in CentOS 7 are evolving to use extensions for certain types of files and associations, as in Windows 10. Listing the default extensions for all file types is beyond the scope of this chapter.

Unlike Windows 10, when you save a file in CentOS 7, the application stores file and directory attributes in an inode. The inode contains the file type (see Table 7-6) and other information about a file or directory, except its name and its actual data. A filename does not require an extension in CentOS 7 when you use a command to list, view, or execute the file.

Recall that when a file is created in CentOS 7, it is assigned both a name and an inode number. The filenames and corresponding inode numbers are stored as entries in a directory that appears to the user to contain the files.

Symbol	Type
-	Regular file
d	Directory
l	Link
c	Special file
s	Socket
p	Named pipe

Table 7-6 CentOS 7 file types

Another option you can use to determine the file type in CentOS 7 is the `ls` command with the `-l` option. To view a list of files in the devices folder, use `ls /dev`. If you use the `| more` command, the output is displayed one screen at a time; the number of lines varies depending on the size of the console window:

`ls -l /dev | more`

Be aware that filenames can contain files and pointers to files, not just text and multimedia.

File types you might see after running the `ls` command are listed in Table 7-7.

Type	Description
Text	An ASCII character file
Executable	A binary executable program
Data	All other types

Table 7-7 CentOS 7 `file` command types

You can use several commands to view the contents of a CentOS 7 file, including the **cat** command (see Figure 7-9), which is short for *concatenate*. The original purpose of the `cat` command is to join two or more files and concatenate them into one file. When you view the contents of the file, it is concatenated to standard output.

```
                          user1@localhost:~/Desktop

File  Edit  View  Search  Terminal  Help
[user1@localhost Desktop]$ cat  /var/log/boot.log
[  OK  ] Started Show Plymouth Boot Screen.
[  OK  ] Reached target Paths.
[  OK  ] Reached target Basic System.
[    5.165841] dracut-initqueue[252]: Scanning devices sda2 for LVM logical vol
umes rhel/root rhel/swap
[    5.210861] dracut-initqueue[252]: inactive '/dev/rhel/swap' [820.00 MiB] inh
erit
[    5.211605] dracut-initqueue[252]: inactive '/dev/rhel/root' [6.67 GiB] inher
it
[  OK  ] Found device /dev/mapper/rhel-root.
         Starting File System Check on /dev/mapper/rhel-root...
[  OK  ] Started dracut initqueue hook.
[  OK  ] Reached target Remote File Systems (Pre).
[  OK  ] Reached target Remote File Systems.
[  OK  ] Started File System Check on /dev/mapper/rhel-root.
         Mounting /sysroot...
[  OK  ] Mounted /sysroot.
[  OK  ] Reached target Initrd Root File System.
         Starting Reload Configuration from the Real Root...
[  OK  ] Started Reload Configuration from the Real Root.
[  OK  ] Reached target Initrd File Systems.
[  OK  ] Reached target Initrd Default Target.
         Starting dracut pre-pivot and cleanup hook...
```

Figure 7-9 Output of the `cat` command

Source: Red Hat CentOS 7/Terminal

For example, to view the contents of a file, you can type:

```
cat -bsT /var/log/boot.log
```

The `more` command also allows you to view file contents. Sometimes, it can be easier to use than the `cat` command because the output does not run off the page before you can read it. The `more` command stops after a page and then lets you proceed page by page by pressing the Spacebar when you are ready to see more.

The `more` command has the following basic syntax and formatting options:

```
more [-dlfpcsu] [file ...]
```

-num   Specifies an integer that is the screen size (in lines)

-d   Displays *[Press 'h' for instructions]* after the `more` command prompts you to continue or quit

-l   Prevents the `more` command from treating ^L (form feed) as a special character and pausing after any line that contains a form feed

-f   Causes the `more` command to count logical lines rather than screen lines (long lines are not folded)

-p   Does not scroll, but instead clears the screen and then displays the text

-c   Does not scroll, but instead draws each screen from the top, clearing the remainder of each line as it is displayed

-s   Squeezes multiple blank lines into one

-u   Suppresses underlining

+num   Starts at line number *num*

For example, you can type the following command to display the contents of `myfile`:

```
more -dfs myfile
```

Activity 7-2: Viewing Files in CentOS 7

Time Required: 15 minutes

Objective: Use the `more`, `file`, and `cat` commands to view information about a file and its contents.

Description: In this activity, you display information about a file. This activity is useful if you need to view file information.

The CentOS 7 activities in this chapter require the script files that are available at *www.cengage.com*. For further details, see the appendix for your virtualization software.

1. Start your virtual machines using the appropriate instructions in Activity 1-1.

2. To open a terminal console, right-click the desktop and select **Open in Terminal**.

3. To create the directory structure with the makeHRS script, type the following lines, pressing **Enter** after each line.

cd /usr/local/bin

sh makeHRS

Contact your instructor if you see the following message: "makeHRS is not recognized as an internal or external command, operable program or batch file."

4. To display the file type of file001, type **file Level1/File001** and then press **Enter**.

Contact your instructor if you see the following message: "file001 is not an ASCII file."

5. To display the contents of file001, type **cat Level1/File001** and then press **Enter**.

6. To verify that file002 appears, type **more /Level1/Level2/File002** and then press **Enter**.

7. Close the terminal console.

8. Leave the virtual machine logged on for future activities.

File Attributes

Windows 10 maintains certain attributes that are associated with every file. File attributes are restrictive labels attached to a file that describe and regulate its use. These attributes are mostly maintained by various components of Windows 10 and are handled automatically, so you can use Windows 10 without manipulating attributes. However, manipulating some file attributes is not difficult and can be useful at times. The following sections explain common techniques associated with file attributes.

Using File Attributes in the Windows 10 CLI

Every file in Windows has attributes that determine how the file is treated by the operating system in certain cases. Each file has attribute information in the master file table.

Some common Windows file attributes are:

- **Read-only**—When set, you can read the contents of a file, but you cannot modify it.
- **Archive**—The archive bit is set to on when a file is created and then set to off when it is backed up. If the file is modified, the archive bit is turned back on so that the backup software can look at the archive bit on each file and determine if it needs to be backed up.
- **System**—The system attribute marks a file as a system file that is used only by the operating system.

- **Hidden**—The hidden attribute prevents a file from being seen by other commands. By default, the DIR command does not list files when the hidden attribute is set to on.

Viewing Windows File Attributes   You can use the **ATTRIB** command to view file attributes and determine how to access a particular file. The ATTRIB command has the following syntax when you display file attributes:

ATTRIB [drive:] [path] [filename] [/S [/D] [/L]]

[drive:] [path] [filename]	Specifies a file or files for the ATTRIB command to process
/S	Processes matching files in the current folder and all subfolders
/D	Processes folders in addition to matching files
/L	Operates on the symbolic link instead of the target of the symbolic link

The syntax of the ATTRIB command is similar to that of the DIR command. For example, to view the attributes of the \Users\User01\Documents directories, you would type:

ATTRIB /S C:\Users\User01\Documents*.*

Because the ATTRIB command processes matching files, you must use the wildcard characters (see Figure 7-10). Without them, no files will match.

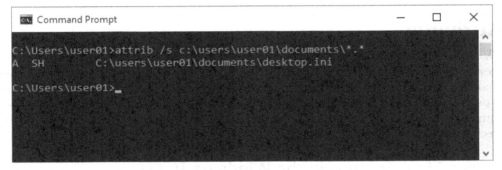

Figure 7-10 Using the attrib command

Source: Microsoft Windows 10/Command Prompt

Activity 7-3: Viewing Windows File Attributes

Time Required: 15 minutes

Objective: Display file attributes in the Windows 10 CLI.

Description: In this activity, you open the command prompt and then view file attributes. This activity is useful if you want to view file attributes.

1. If necessary, start your virtual machines using the appropriate instructions in Activity 1-1.

2. To open a command prompt, right-click **Start,** and then click **Command Prompt.**

3. To view the file attributes for the files in the Windows directory, type **attrib c:\windows*.*** and then press **Enter.**

4. Note the number and name of the system file(s) with the S attribute set.

5. Note the number and name of hidden file(s) with the H attribute set.

6. Note the number and name of read-only file(s) with the R attribute set.

7. Note the number of files that are listed.

> You can use the find command to count lines by typing the following and then pressing Enter:
>
> attrib c:\windows*.* | find /c /i "C:"

You will learn more about the find command later in this chapter.

8. To show the number of files listed by the dir command, type the following and then press **Enter.**

   dir c:\windows*.*

9. Note the number of files in the total at the end of the dir listing. By default, hidden and system files are not included in the dir command.

10. To exit the command prompt, type **exit** and then press **Enter.**

11. Leave the virtual machine logged on for the next activity.

File Attributes in CentOS 7

File attributes in Linux OSs have a different connotation than they do in Windows. Linux OSs do not respect Windows attributes; if you have a "read-only" file attribute set in Windows, the file can be read in a Linux environment. In a Linux OS, you make a file "read-only" by setting permissions on the file. These file permissions, which include all files and folders, are set at three different levels—owner, group, and everyone else. Each level has read, write, and execute options. Each choice is independent of the other; for example, a file can be writable but not readable, or it can be executed but not readable or writable. If you type ls -l, the beginning of each line shows the permission for each file or folder, as shown in Figure 7-11.

Table 7-8 explains what each field means in Figure 7-11. The permissions are shown in columns 2–10.

The permissions determine what can be done with the file or folder. Also, the read, write, and execute permissions have different meanings for files and folders, as shown in Table 7-9.

You learn about file and directory permissions in Chapter 11.

Hidden files are easy to create in CentOS 7 and in all Linux OSs. The file simply needs to have a period as the first character in the filename. To see these hidden files, use the command ls -a. Note the difference between using the ls and ls -a commands

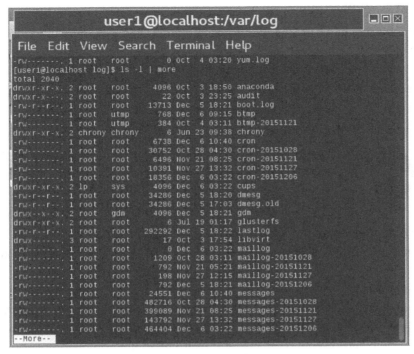

Figure 7-11 Using the `ls` and `more` commands

Source: Red Hat CentOS 7/Terminal

Column	Definition	Options
1	Type of file	- Regular file d Directory l Symbolic link p Named pipe s Socket c or b Device file
2	Owner permissions to read	- Not readable r Readable
3	Owner permissions to write	- Not writable w Writable
4	Owner permissions to execute	- Not executable x Executable
5	Group permissions to read	- Not readable r Readable
6	Group permissions to write	- Not writable w Writable
7	Group permissions to execute	- Not executable x Executable

Table 7-8 Results of the `ls -l` command

Column	Definition	Options
8	Everyone has permissions to read	- Not readable r Readable
9	Everyone has permissions to write	- Not writable w Writable
10	Everyone has permissions to execute	- Not executable x Executable t Sticky bit set with execution T Sticky bit set without execution
11	Number of links	
12	Owner of the file	
13	Group name the file is part of	
14	Size of the file	
15	Date and time the file was last accessed	
16	Filename	

Table 7-8 Results of the `ls -l` command (*continued*)

Condition	File	Folder
Read	Read	Ignored
Write	Write	Allowed to create files in the directory
Execute	Execute	Allowed to view files in the directory

Table 7-9 Read, write, and execute permissions for files and folders

(see Figure 7-12) when the commands are run in a home directory for a user. You can now see files like .bashrc and .bash_profile, which are used to set the user's environment, as well as hidden directories.

Activity 7-4: Viewing CentOS 7 File Permissions

Time Required: 15 minutes

Objective: Use the `ls -l` command to view permissions for files and folders and the `ls -a` command to view hidden files.

Description: In this activity, you display information about a file. This activity is useful if you need to view file permissions and hidden files.

1. Start your virtual machines using the appropriate instructions in Activity 1-1.
2. To open a terminal console, right-click the desktop and select **Open Terminal**.
3. To change to the user's home directory, type **cd /home/user01** and press **Enter**.
4. To see the names of files, type **ls -l** and press **Enter**.

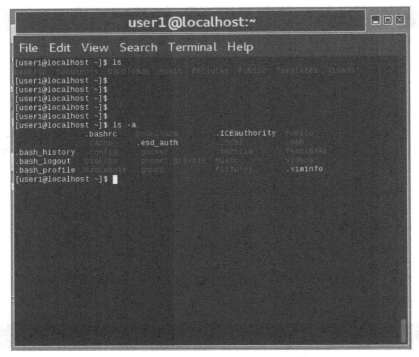

Figure 7-12 Viewing hidden files

Source: Red Hat CentOS 7/Terminal

If you have not created any new files in your home directory, only folders will appear. See the d at the beginning of each row; only the owner of the directory can create files in this directory.

5. To see files, including hidden files, type **ls –a** and press **Enter**.

6. To see all the files, including the hidden files and their permissions, type **ls –la** and press **Enter**.

7. Close the terminal console.

8. Leave the virtual machine logged on for future activities.

Setting Windows File Attributes

You can use the ATTRIB command to display or change file attributes. For example, you might need to reset a file attribute when working with a file. When setting the file attributes, the ATTRIB command has the following syntax:

ATTRIB [+R | -R] [+A | -A] [+S | -S] [+H | -H] [drive:] [path] [filename] [/S [/D]]

+   Sets an attribute

-                                      Clears an attribute

R	Read-only file attribute
A	Archive file attribute
S	System file attribute
H	Hidden file attribute
[drive:] [path] [filename]	Specifies a file or files for the ATTRIB command to process
/S	Processes matching files in the current folder and all subfolders
/D	Processes folders as well as files

You can use wildcard characters with the filename parameter to change the attributes for a group of files. If a file's system or hidden attribute is set, you must clear it before you can change any other file attributes.

You can also set the file attributes on a directory. For example, to hide a directory named Secret, you would type:

ATTRIB +H Secret

When you list the directory using the DIR command, the contents of the directory entry are listed, but not the individual directory.

Using the DIR Command with File Attributes You can use the DIR command when you want to view filenames with specified file attributes. When using file attributes, the DIR command has the following syntax:

DIR [drive:] [path] [filename] [/A[[:]attributes]]

[drive:] [path] [filename]	Specifies the drive, directory, and files to list
/A	Displays files with specified attributes
attributes	D is for directories, R is for read-only files, H is for hidden files, A is for files ready for archiving, S is for system files, I is for files that are not indexed for content, and "-" is a prefix meaning *not*

Figure 7-13 shows files with the hidden file attribute.

Activity 7-5: Setting Windows Attributes

Time Required: 15 minutes

Objective: Use the ATTRIB command to set file attributes and use the DIR command with file attributes in the Windows CLI.

Description: In this activity, you open the command prompt and then set file attributes and view file information while selecting files with specific file attributes. This activity is useful if you want to set attributes or view hidden or system files on a hard drive.

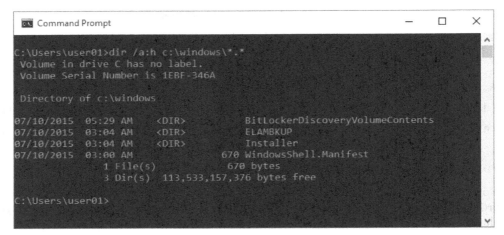

Figure 7-13 Using the `dir` command to show hidden files

Source: Microsoft Windows 10/Command Prompt

1. If necessary, start your virtual machines using the appropriate instructions in Activity 1-1.
2. To open a command prompt, right-click **Start,** and then click **Command Prompt.**
3. If necessary, copy the services file to work with. Type the following command and press **Enter.**

   ```
   copy c:\windows\system32\drivers\etc\services MyServices.txt
   ```
4. If prompted to overwrite the file, type **y** and then press **Enter.** To verify that the file was copied, type **dir** and then press **Enter.** (Look for the **MyServices.txt** file.)
5. To view the file attributes, type **attrib MyServices.txt** and then press **Enter.**
6. To hide the file, type **attrib +h MyServices.txt** and then press **Enter.**
7. To verify the hidden flag, type **attrib MyServices.txt** and then press **Enter.**
8. To verify that the file is hidden, type **dir** and then press **Enter.**
9. To list the hidden files, type **dir /ah** and then press **Enter.**
10. To "unhide" the file, type **attrib -h MyServices.txt** and then press **Enter.**
11. To verify that the file is no longer hidden, type **dir** and then press **Enter.**
12. To mark the file as read-only, type **attrib +r MyServices.txt** and then press **Enter.**
13. To verify that the file is read-only, type **attrib MyServices.txt** and then press **Enter.**
14. To list the read-only files, type **dir /ar** and then press **Enter.**
15. To verify that you cannot delete the read-only file, type **del MyServices.txt** and then press **Enter.**
16. To mark the file as a system file, type **attrib +s MyServices.txt** and then press **Enter.**
17. To verify that the file is read-only and a system file, type **attrib MyServices.txt** and then press **Enter.**
18. To list the system files, type **dir /as** and then press **Enter.**

19. Try to remove the read-only flag by typing **attrib -r MyServices.txt,** and then press **Enter.** The command should fail because the file is still marked as a system file.

20. To remove the system and read-only flags, type the following and then press **Enter.**

    ```
    attrib -s -r MyServices.txt
    ```

21. To verify the file attributes, type **attrib MyServices.txt** and then press **Enter.**

22. To exit the command prompt, type **exit** and then press **Enter.**

23. Leave the virtual machine logged on for the next activity.

Using the XCOPY Command with File Attributes

You can use the XCOPY command with file attributes. This command is useful when you want to copy filenames with specified file attributes. When using the XCOPY command with .txt file attributes, the command has the following syntax:

XCOPY source	[destination] [/A | /M] [/H] [/R] [/K]
source	Specifies the file(s) to copy
destination	Specifies the location and/or name of new files
/A	Copies only files with the archive attribute set; does not change the attribute
/M	Copies only files with the archive attribute set; turns off the archive attribute
/H	Copies hidden and system files
/R	Overwrites read-only files
/K	Copies attributes; normally, XCOPY resets read-only attributes

Figure 7-14 shows files with the hidden file attribute that are copied by the XCOPY command. You can copy selected files that need to be backed up by using the /A or /M switch.

NOTE

Remember that commands are not case sensitive in Windows 10. For example, the XCOPY command is shown in uppercase in Figure 7-14, but you can also use lowercase.

Figure 7-14 Using the XCOPY command with file attributes

Source: Microsoft Windows 10/Command Prompt

When you use the /A switch, the system copies only files with the archive attribute set. The archive attribute is not reset, and the next system archive is called a *differential backup* because the system backs up everything that has changed since the last full backup.

As with the /A switch, when you use the /M switch, the XCOPY command copies only files with the archive attribute set. However, when you use the /M switch, the archive attribute is reset; the next system archive is called an *incremental backup* because it only backs up files modified since the most recent backup.

Activity 7-6: Using XCOPY with File Attributes

Time Required: 15 minutes

Objective: Use the XCOPY command with file attributes in the Windows 10 CLI.

Description: In this activity, you open the command prompt and copy files while selecting them with file attributes. This activity is useful if you want to copy files based on the settings of file attributes.

1. If necessary, start your virtual machines using the appropriate instructions in Activity 1-1.
2. To open a command prompt, right-click **Start,** and then click **Command Prompt.**
3. To change to the User01 Documents folder, type the following and then press **Enter.**

   `cd /d C:\users\user01\Documents`
4. To create a simple file, type **echo hello > SampleFile01.txt** and then press **Enter.**
5. To create a second file, type **echo bye > SampleFile02.txt** and then press **Enter.**
6. To make the second file hidden, type **attrib +h SampleFile02.txt** and then press **Enter.**
7. To copy the text files, including hidden files, to the backup folder, type **xcopy *.txt backup /h** and then press **Enter.** If necessary, type **D** for directory.
8. To make the backup files read-only, type **attrib +r backup*.txt** and then press **Enter.** (The hidden files will not be reset to read-only.)
9. To modify the first file, type **echo world >> SampleFile01.txt** and then press **Enter.**
10. To copy the text file to the backup folder, type **xcopy *.txt backup** and then press **Enter.** This operation should fail because the file is read-only.
11. To copy the file backup folder with overwrite read-only files enabled, type the following command and then press **Enter.**

    `xcopy *.txt backup /r`
12. When the message "Overwrite C:\Users\user01\Documents\backup\SampleFile01.txt (Yes/No/All)?" appears, press the **A** key.
13. Verify that the files are copied.
14. To exit the command prompt, type **exit** and then press **Enter.**
15. Leave the virtual machine logged on for the next activity.

Using File Attributes in the Windows 10 GUI

In addition to the previously listed attributes, Windows 10 offers the following attributes:

- **Index**—When set, the folder or file is indexed by the Windows Indexing Service on an NTFS volume. The Indexing Service extracts information from a set of documents and organizes it for easy access through the Windows 10 Search function. After the index is created, you can query it for documents that contain key words or phrases.

- **Compression**—When set, the folder or file is compressed on an NTFS volume.

- **Encryption**—When set, the folder or file is encrypted on an NTFS volume. Files with encryption are encoded so that only authorized users who have the encryption key can read the contents of the file.

The compression and encryption attributes for disk files are mutually exclusive. For example, you must uncompress a compressed disk file before it can be encrypted.

These options appear as check boxes in the Advanced Attributes dialog box, as shown in Figure 7-15. See Activity 7-7 for directions on accessing this dialog box.

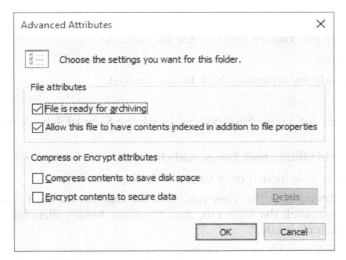

Figure 7-15 Windows advanced attributes

Source: Microsoft Windows 10/File Explorer

Compression and encryption are described in more detail in the following sections.

Activity 7-7: Viewing and Setting File Attributes in the Windows 10 GUI

Time Required: 15 minutes

Objective: View and set the attributes for files in the Windows 10 GUI.

Description: In this activity, you open Windows File Explorer and view the Windows 10 attributes for a file. This activity is useful if you want to view file attributes using the properties dialog box.

1. If necessary, start your virtual machines using the appropriate instructions in Activity 1-1.
2. Right-click **Start,** and then click **Command Prompt.**
3. To change to the User01 Documents folder, type the following and then press **Enter.**

    `cd /d C:\users\user01\Documents`
4. To create a simple file, type **echo hello > SampleFileA.txt** and then press **Enter.**
5. To create a second file, type **echo bye > SampleFileB.txt** and then press **Enter.**
6. To exit the command prompt, type **exit** and then press **Enter.**
7. Click **Start,** click **File Explorer,** and then click **Documents** in the Navigation pane.
8. To view the file attributes for SampleFileA.txt, right-click the **SampleFileA** file and then click **Properties.**

 The .txt file extension will not be visible if the "Hide extensions for known file types" system setting is on.

9. Verify that the **Read-only** and **Hidden** check boxes are unchecked.
10. Click the **Advanced** button.
11. Verify that the **File is ready for archiving** check box is checked.
12. Click **Cancel** twice.
13. To view the file attributes for SampleFileB.txt, right-click the **SampleFileB** file and then click **Properties.**
14. Check the **Read-only** and **Hidden** check boxes, and click **OK.**
15. Verify that **SampleFileB** is now hidden from view in File Explorer.
16. On the File Explorer Ribbon, click the **View** tab, click the **Options** button to open the Folder Options dialog box, click the **View** tab, click the **Show hidden files, folders and drives** check box, and then click **OK.**
17. Verify that the **SampleFileB** text file is now visible.
18. Close Windows File Explorer.
19. Leave the virtual machine logged on for future activities.

Using Compression in Windows 10 Compressing files decreases their size and reduces the amount of space they use on your drives. Folder compression decreases the amount of space used by all of the files stored within a folder. Note that some files do not work as expected when compressed.

 Windows 10 includes Zip compression in the form of Compressed Folders you can use to compress files on your hard disk. This utility uses different techniques than the file compression attribute.

Activity 7-8: Compressing Files in Windows 10

Time Required: 20 minutes

Objective: Compress a file in the Windows 10 GUI.

Description: In this activity, you open Windows File Explorer and compress files. This activity is useful if you want to save space on your hard drive.

1. If necessary, start your virtual machines using the appropriate instructions in Activity 1-1.
2. To open a command prompt, right-click **Start**, and then click **Command Prompt**.
3. To change to the User01 Documents folder, type the following and then press **Enter**.

   `cd /d C:\users\user01\Documents`
4. To copy the services file, type the following and then press **Enter**.

   `copy c:\windows\system32\drivers\etc\services MyServices.txt`
5. To exit the command prompt, type **exit** and then press **Enter**.
6. Click **Start**, click **File Explorer**, and then click **Documents** in the Navigation pane.
7. To view the file attributes for MyServices.txt, right-click the **MyServices** file and then click **Properties**.
8. Note the file size and the file size on disk for future reference.
9. Click the **Advanced** button, check the **Compress contents to save disk space** check box, click **OK**, and then click **Apply**.
10. Note the file size and the file size on disk. Verify that the size on disk is now smaller.
11. Click **OK**.
12. Verify that the filename has changed from black to blue.
13. To create a folder, click **New Folder** on the Quick Access Toolbar, type **compressed**, and then press **Enter** to rename the new folder.
14. To copy the MyServices file, right-click the **MyServices** file and then click **Copy**.
15. Move to the new folder by double-clicking the **compressed** folder.
16. Copy the file from the clipboard by clicking the **Home** tab and then clicking **Paste**. Note that the pasted file is not compressed.
17. Navigate back to the Documents folder by clicking **Documents** in the navigation pane of File Explorer.
18. To view the file attributes for the folder, right-click the **compressed** folder and then click **Properties** on the context menu.
19. Note the size on disk for future reference.
20. Click the **Advanced** button, check the **Compress contents to save disk space** check box, click **OK**, and then click **Apply**.
21. Verify that the option button **Apply changes to this folder, subfolders and files** is selected, and then click **OK**.
22. Note the file size on disk. Verify that the size on disk is now smaller.

7

23. Click **OK**.

24. Verify that the folder name has changed from black to blue.

25. Close File Explorer.

26. Leave the virtual machine logged on for the next activity.

Using Encryption in Windows 10 Encryption is provided by the **Encrypting File System (EFS)**, which is installed automatically in Windows 10. Encryption prohibits unauthorized users from viewing the contents of files. Only the user who encrypted the file or an administrator can decrypt encrypted files. The administrator account is called a *recovery agent* because it has a global key that can decrypt any files.

The compression and encryption attributes are mutually exclusive. For example, if disk files are compressed, they must be uncompressed before encryption.

Activity 7-9: Encrypting Files in Windows 10

Time Required: 15 minutes

Objective: Encrypt the files in a folder in the Windows 10 GUI.

Description: In this activity, you open Windows File Explorer and encrypt files within the directory structure. This activity is useful if you want to protect the contents of data files.

1. If necessary, start your virtual machines using the appropriate instructions in Activity 1-1.

2. Right-click **Start**, and then click **Command Prompt**.

3. To create a folder to work on, type **md e:\encrypt** and then press **Enter**.

4. To create a file in the folder, type the following and then press **Enter**.

   ```
   echo secret data > e:\encrypt\secret.txt.
   ```

5. To exit the command prompt, type **exit** and then press **Enter**.

6. Click **Start**, and then click **File Explorer**.

7. To go to the folder that contains the example directory structure, expand **This PC**, and then click **NTFS(E:)**.

8. To view the advanced properties for the encrypt folder, right-click the **encrypt** folder and then click **Properties**.

9. Click the **Advanced** button, check the **Encrypt contents to secure data** check box, click **OK**, and then click **Apply**.

10. Verify that the option **Apply changes to this folder, subfolders, and files** is selected, and then click **OK**.

11. Verify that the folder changed from black to green.

12. Double-click the **encrypt** folder.

13. Verify that the secret file changed from black to green.

14. Close Windows File Explorer.

15. Leave the virtual machine logged on for future activities.

Using File Attributes in CentOS 7

Like Windows 10, the file systems in CentOS 7 have file attributes, but they are rarely used and do not mean the same thing as they do in Windows.

Using the `lsattr` Command to View CentOS 7 File Attributes

You can view the file attributes on a CentOS 7 extended file system using the `lsattr` command. You can only set these attributes on directories and regular files:

a   ("no Access time")—When you access a file or directory that has this attribute, either for reading or writing, its last access time is not updated.

A   ("append only")—If this attribute is set for a file and it is open for writing, the only operation you can perform is to append data to the previous contents. If this attribute is set for a directory, you can only add files to it; you cannot rename or delete an existing file.

d   ("no dump")—Dump is the standard utility for backups. When a dump is in progress, files or directories that have this attribute are not taken into account.

i   ("immutable")—You cannot modify a file or directory that has this attribute.

s   ("secure deletion")—When you delete a file or directory that has this attribute, the blocks it occupied on the disk are overwritten with zeroes.

S   ("Synchronous mode")—When a file or directory has this attribute, all modifications are synchronous and are written to the disk immediately.

The syntax and options for the `lsattr` command are:

`lsattr [options] [file(s)]`

-R   Recursively lists attributes of directories and their contents

-V   Displays the program version

-a   Lists all files in directories, including files that start with '.'

-d   Lists directories like other files, rather than listing their contents

-v   Lists the file's version/generation number

To display the attributes of files in a directory, type:

`lsattr`

Using the `ls` Command to Find Hidden Files

You can use the `ls` command to view filenames with specified CentOS 7 file type attributes. The `ls` command has the following syntax:

`ls [OPTION]... [FILE]...`

-a, --all   Does not hide entries starting with "." (hidden files)

-l   Uses a long listing format

```
                    user1@localhost:/etc              _ □ ×

 File  Edit  View  Search  Terminal  Help
[user1@localhost etc]$ ls -lpa
total 1492
drwxr-xr-x. 140 root root    8192 Jan  1 14:09 /
dr-xr-xr-x.  17 root root    4096 Oct  3 18:45  /
drwxr-xr-x.   3 root root      97 Oct  3 17:49 .../
-rw-r--r--.   1 root root      16 Oct  3 18:45 adjtime
-rw-r--r--.   1 root root    1518 Jun  7 2013  aliases
-rw-r--r--.   1 root root   12288 Oct  3 23:26 aliases.db
drwxr-xr-x.   2 root root      49 Oct  3 17:52 alsa/
drwxr-xr-x.   2 root root    4096 Oct  3 18:21 alternatives/
-rw-------.   1 root root     541 Apr 21 2015  anacrontab
-rw-r--r--.   1 root root      55 Sep 16 2014  asound.conf
-rw-r--r--.   1 root root       1 Jun 22 2015  at.deny
drwxr-xr-x.   2 root root      31 Oct  3 18:01 at-spi2/
drwxr-x---.   3 root root      41 Oct  3 17:52 audisp/
drwxr-x---.   3 root root      79 Oct  3 23:25 audit/
-rw-r--r--.   1 root root   12706 Jul  6 21:07 autofs.conf
-rw-------.   1 root root     232 Jul  6 21:07 autofs_ldap_auth.conf
-rw-r--r--.   1 root root     795 Jul  6 21:07 auto.master
drwxr-xr-x.   2 root root       6 Jul  6 21:07 auto.master.d/
-rw-r--r--.   1 root root     524 Jul  6 21:07 auto.misc
-rwxr-xr-x.   1 root root    1260 Jul  6 21:07 auto.net
-rwxr-xr-x.   1 root root     687 Jul  6 21:07 auto.smb
drwxr-xr-x.   4 root root      94 Oct  3 18:12 avahi/
```

Figure 7-16 Using the `ls` command

Source: Red Hat CentOS 7/Terminal

`-p, --file-type`   Appends an indicator of /, =, @, or | to entries to indicate types of files

The results of entering the following command are shown in Figure 7-16.

`ls -lpa`

Activity 7-10: Using the `ls` and `lsattr` Commands with CentOS 7 File Attributes

Time Required: 15 minutes

Objective: Use the `ls` and `lsattr` commands to find the hidden file attribute in the CentOS 7 CLI.

Description: In this activity, you open the command prompt and view file information while selecting files with the hidden file attribute. This activity is useful if you want to list hidden files on a hard drive. You will also list the Linux file attributes.

The CentOS 7 activities in this chapter require the script files that are available at *www.cengage.com*. For further details, see the appendix for your virtualization software.

1. If necessary, start your virtual machines using the appropriate instructions in Activity 1-1.

2. To open a terminal console, click **Applications**, point to **Utilities**, and then click **Terminal**.

3. To create the directory structure with the makeABC script, type **cd /usr/local/bin**, press **Enter**, type **sh MakeABC**, and press **Enter**.

Contact your instructor if you see the following message: "makeABC is not recognized as an internal or external command, operable program or batch file."

4. To display the hidden files in the directory, type **ls -la** and then press **Enter**.

5. Verify that all the files in the directory appear, including the files preceded with a ".".

6. To display the attributes of the files in the directory, type **lsattr** and then press **Enter**.

7. Verify that all the files in the directory list their attributes.

8. To display the filename additions, further indicating the file types in the directory, type **ls -lpa /dev** and then press **Enter**.

9. Verify that all the files in the directory appear, including the filenames, further illustrating the file type.

10. Close the terminal console.

11. Leave the virtual machine logged on for future activities.

Using Compression in CentOS 7 As in Windows 10, compressing files decreases their size and reduces the amount of space they use on your drives. Folder compression decreases the amount of space used by all of the files stored in a folder. Note that some files do not work as expected when compressed.

Zip compression utility extensions correspond with the file types listed in Table 7-5.

A commonly used GNU compression utility is **gzip**. The GNU software is the largest single component of the CentOS 7 source code, and it includes some of the major components required by the system.

By default, gzip deletes the ASCII file it compresses, and the new file contains the default extension of .gz. To decompress files, you can use a utility called **gunzip**. The gzip command is the basis for gunzip and zcat; both utilities are simply links to gzip.

The **zcat** utility is identical to using the gunzip −c command. By default, gzip keeps the original filename and stamp in the compressed file.

The commands have the following syntax:

```
gzip [ -acdfhlLnNrtvV19 ] [-S suffix] [ filename ... ]
gunzip [ -acfhlLnNrtvV ] [-S suffix] [ filename ... ]
zcat [ -fhLV ] [ filename ... ]
```

You can use the following switches with the preceding commands:

-a -ascii   In ASCII text mode, use this switch to convert end-of-line characters across operating system platforms using local conventions. This option is supported only on some non-UNIX systems. For Windows, the CR LF character is converted to LF when compressing, and LF is converted to CR LF when decompressing. This conversion is crucial to ensuring cross-platform ASCII text compatibility.

`-c --stdout --to-stdout` Writes output to standard output and keeps the original files unchanged. If there are several input files, `gzip` concatenates them before compressing to achieve the best compression.

`-d --decompress –uncompress` Decompresses a file.

`-f –force` Forces compression or decompression even if the file has multiple links, the corresponding file already exists, or the compressed data is read from or written to a terminal.

`-h –help` Displays a help screen and quits.

`-l –list` Lists information about the files and the compression; used in conjunction with the verbose and name switches.

`-L –license` Displays the license and quits.

`-n --no-name` When compressing, does not save the original filename and time stamp. This option is the default setting when decompressing.

`-N –name` When compressing, always saves the original filename and time stamp; this is the default setting. When decompressing, restores the original filename and time stamp if present. This option is useful on systems that have a limit on filename lengths and when the time stamp has been lost after a file transfer.

`-q –quiet` Suppresses all warnings.

`-r –recursive` Traverses a directory structure recursively. If a directory is specified on the command line, `gzip` will compress all the files in it. If you are using the `gunzip` command, this switch decompresses the files in the specified directory.

`-S .suf --suffix .suf` Applies the suffix .suf instead of .gz to the compressed file. You can use any suffix, but you should avoid suffixes other than .z and .gz to avoid confusion when files are transferred to other systems.

`-t –test` Checks the compressed file's integrity.

-v –verbose	Displays the name and percentage reduction for each compressed or decompressed file.
-V –version	Displays the version number and compilation options, then quits.
-# --fast –best	Regulates the speed of compression; -1 or --fast creates the fastest and least compression, and -9 or --best creates the slowest and best compression. The default setting is -6.

To compress a file using the gzip command, type:

gzip myfile

The results are shown in Figure 7-17.

The gzip utility also decompresses files created by the gzip and zip utilities.

To decompress a file using the gzip command, type:

gzip –d myfile

The results are shown in Figure 7-18.

The gunzip utility decompresses files created by the gzip, zip, and compress utilities. The utility automatically detects the input format.

To decompress a file using the gunzip command, type:

gunzip myfile

Figure 7-17 Compressing a file using the gzip command

Source: Red Hat CentOS 7/Terminal

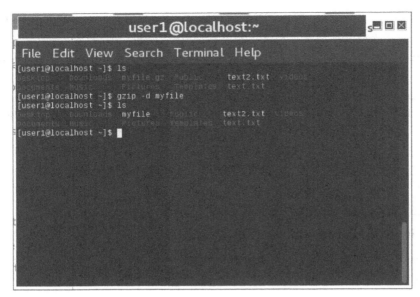

Figure 7-18 Decompressing a file using the `gzip` command

Source: Red Hat CentOS 7/Terminal

The results are shown in Figure 7-19.

The `zcat` utility decompresses files created by `gzip` and `zip` and sends the results to standard output. The utility automatically detects the input format. The compressed file is only decompressed for the display.

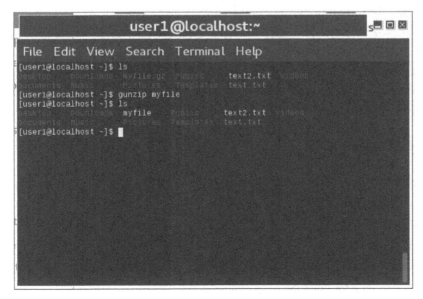

Figure 7-19 Decompressing a file using the `gunzip` command

Source: Red Hat CentOS 7/Terminal

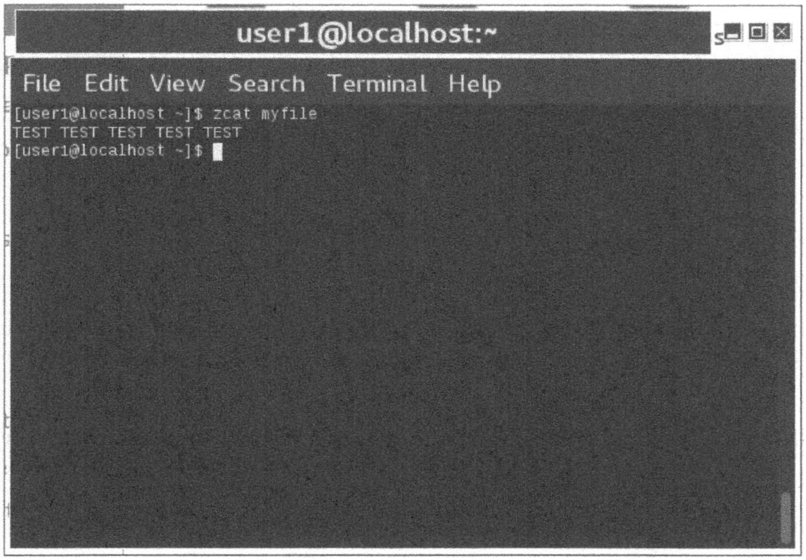

Figure 7-20 Using the zcat command on a compressed text file

Source: Red Hat CentOS 7/Terminal

To decompress a file and display its contents in ASCII form to standard output using the zcat command, you would type:

zcat myfile

The results are shown in Figure 7-20.

Compression is often used in conjunction with archiving utilities. One such utility is tar, which works in conjunction with gzip to package multiple files into one file.

The tar command has the following syntax:

tar [flags] archive-file-name files-to-archive

You must use one of the following options with the tar command:

-a, --catenate, --concatenate	Appends tar files to an archive
-c, --create	Creates a new archive
-d, --diff, --compare	Finds differences between the archive and file system
--delete	Deletes files from the archive (do not use this command on magnetic tapes!)
-r, --append	Appends files to the end of an archive
-t, --list	Lists the contents of an archive
-u, --update	Only appends files that are updated versions of the copy in the archive

`-x, --extract, --get`	Extracts files from an archive
`-f, --file [HOSTNAME:]F`	Uses archive file or device F (the default selection is "-", which means standard input/output)
`-recursion`	Recurses into directories (the default selection)
`-v, --verbose`	Verbosely lists files processed
`-z, --gzip, --gunzip, --ungzip`	Filters the archive through gzip

The `tar` utility is used mainly for backups and needs many different types of filters. Other options for filtering were omitted from the preceding list for the sake of simplicity.

For example, if you enter `gzip myfile.tar` at the command line, you create a file named myfile.tar.gz. If you enter `tar czvf myfile1.tgz myfile1` at the command line, you create a file named myfile1.tgz (see Figure 7-21).

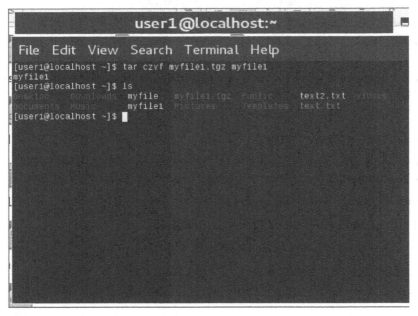

Figure 7-21 Using the `tar` command

Source: Red Hat CentOS 7/Terminal

Activity 7-11: Compressing Files in CentOS 7

Time Required: 15 minutes

Objective: Use the `gzip`, `gunzip`, and `zcat` utilities to compress and decompress files.

Description: In this activity, you will use several utilities to compress and decompress files. This activity is useful if you need to compress files before transmitting them or to save space on your hard drive.

The CentOS 7 activities in this chapter require the script files that are available at *www.cengage.com*. For further details, see the appendix for your virtualization software.

1. If necessary, start your virtual machines using the appropriate instructions in Activity 1-1.
2. To open a terminal console, right-click the desktop and click **Open in Terminal**.
3. To create the directory structure with the makeQUOTE script, type **cd /usr/local/bin,** press **Enter,** type **sh MakeQUOTE** at the prompt, and then press **Enter.**

Contact your instructor if you see the following message: "makeQUOTE is not recognized as an internal or external command, operable program or batch file."

4. Type **ls -l Quote0012,** press **Enter,** and note the file size.
5. Type **gzip Quote0012** and press **Enter.**
6. Type **ls -l Quote0012*,** press **Enter,** and note the difference in file size.
7. Type **gunzip Quote0012** and press **Enter.**
8. Type **ls -l Quote0012*,** press **Enter,** and note the difference in filename and size.
9. Type **cat Quote0012,** press **Enter,** and inspect the file contents displayed on the screen.
10. Type **gzip Quote0012** and press **Enter.**
11. Type **ls -l Quote0012*** and press **Enter.**
12. Type **zcat Quote0012,** press **Enter,** and inspect the file contents displayed on the screen.
13. Type **ls -l Quote0012*,** press **Enter,** and inspect the output.
14. Close the terminal console.
15. Leave the virtual machine logged on for future activities.

Using Encryption in CentOS 7 As with Windows 10, encryption in CentOS 7 prohibits other users from viewing the contents of files. Only the user who encrypted the file or an administrator can decrypt encrypted files.

Files must be encrypted and then compressed. Likewise, they must be uncompressed before decryption.

Entire file systems are designed for encryption, but the most popular encryption utility is gpg. If you encrypt an ASCII file, the extension is .asc; if you encrypt a binary file, the extension is .gpg.

The gpg command has the following syntax:

gpg [--homedir name] [--options file] [options] command [args]

-c	Encrypts with a symmetric cipher.
-decrypt [file]	Decrypts the file and writes it to standard output (or the file specified with --output).
-o, --output file	Writes output to a file.
-v, --verbose	Provides more information during processing. If used twice, the input data is listed in detail.
-q, --quiet	Limits the amount of detail displayed.
quit	Quits the program without updating the key rings.

If you forget your password or passphrase, you cannot recover the data, as the utility uses very strong encryption.

The gpg utility has many more switches and is used with key exchange, encryption, signature validation, and trust relationships. These topics are beyond the scope of this text.

Finding Files

When working on your computer, you need to locate files quickly. For example, you might need to prepare a report for a class. You recall that you wrote a similar report last year, and you want to use its format for your new report. Unfortunately, you have 12,000 files on your hard drive, and you cannot remember where you stored the report file. You think the filename contained the word *privacy* or *private*, but you are not sure.

You can search for files using the DIR, FIND, and FINDSTR commands in the Windows 10 CLI and using the ls + grep and find commands in CentOS 7, as described in the following sections.

Finding Files in the Windows 10 CLI

The Windows 10 CLI includes commands that enable you to locate files quickly and efficiently. You can base your search on part of a filename or the contents of a file. When searching the contents of files, you can employ powerful pattern-matching techniques.

Finding Files with the DIR Command
Recall that the DIR command supports wildcards. You use two wildcard characters for searches: the question mark (?) and the asterisk (*, or star). Use the question mark to represent a single unknown character, and use the star to stand for multiple unknown characters. Use a period to extend the search to include all file extensions. Table 7-10 lists examples of multiple character substitutions using the * wildcard.

Table 7-11 lists examples of single character substitution using the ? wildcard.

In Figure 7-22, the DIR command is used with the ab*.* string to find all files that start with the characters *ab* and have any extension.

Expression	Explanation
DIR *.cpp	Lists all files that have a .cpp extension in the current directory
DIR b*	Lists all filenames that begin with a *b* in the current directory
DIR b*.t*	Lists all filenames that begin with a *b* and have an extension that begins with a t
DIR *.*.	Lists all files in the current directory
DIR *.* /S .	Lists all files in the current and nested directories

Table 7-10 Multiple character substitutions for searches

Expression	Explanation
DIR ?.cpp	Lists all filenames that contain one letter and have a .cpp extension in the current directory
DIR b??	Lists all filenames that begin with a *b* followed by one or two other letters (and that have no extension) in the current directory
DIR b?.t?	Lists all filenames that begin with a *b* followed by one other letter, and that have an extension beginning with a *t* followed by one other letter
DIR ???.*	Lists all filenames that contain one, two, or three letters in the current directory
DIR /S ???.*	Lists all filenames that contain one, two, or three letters in the current and nested directories

Table 7-11 Single character substitutions for searches

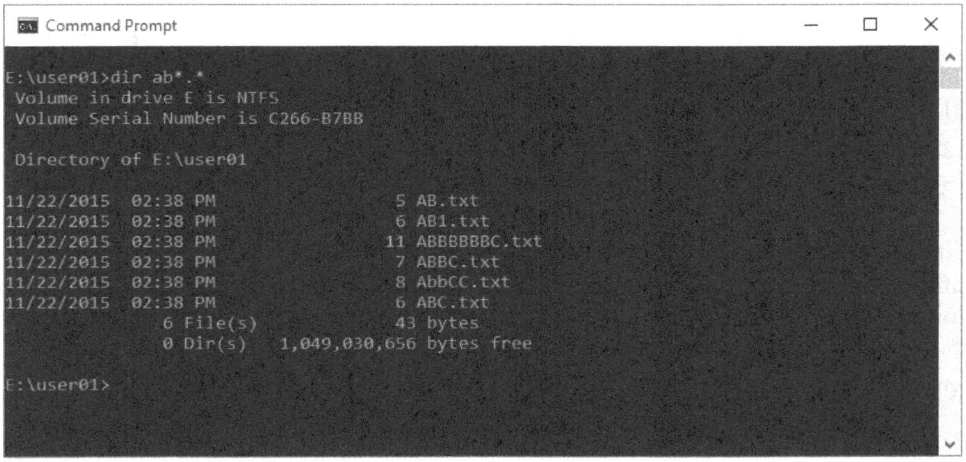

Figure 7-22 Using the dir command with wildcards

Source: Microsoft Windows 10/Command Prompt

Activity 7-12: Finding Files with the DIR Command and Wildcard Characters

Time Required: 15 minutes

Objective: Use the DIR command with wildcard characters in the Windows 10 CLI.

Description: In this activity, you open the command prompt and find files using wildcard characters. This activity is useful if you want to locate files when you know a portion of a filename.

1. If necessary, start your virtual machines using the appropriate instructions in Activity 1-1.
2. Right-click **Start,** and then click **Command Prompt.**
3. To create the example files for the search activities, type **MakeABC** at the command prompt and then press **Enter.**

Contact your instructor if you see the following message: "MakeABC is not recognized as an internal or external command, operable program or batch file."

4. To view filenames that start with *ab*, type **DIR ab*.txt,** and then press **Enter.**
5. Verify that six files are listed.
6. To view filenames that contain a *b* as the third character, type **DIR ??b*.txt** and then press **Enter.**
7. Verify that four files are listed.
8. To view filenames that contain three characters, with *a* as the first character, type **DIR a??.txt** and then press **Enter.**
9. Verify that six files are listed.
10. To view filenames that contain 9 as the second character, type **DIR ?9*.txt** and then press **Enter.**
11. Verify that two files are listed.
12. Close the command prompt window.
13. Leave the virtual machine logged on for the next activity.

Finding Files with the FIND Command
Use the FIND command to locate a specific text string in an ASCII file and then send the line that contains the information to the console or a file. This command is most useful for finding single-line data in lists; it reduces the list to a file that contains only the information you want to view.

When you are searching for files, the FIND command has the following syntax:

```
FIND [/V] [/C] [/N] [/I] [/OFF[LINE]] "string" [[drive:][path]filename[...]]
```

/V   Displays only the count of lines that contain the string

/C	Displays all lines that do not contain the specified string
/N	Displays line numbers with the displayed lines
/I	Ignores the case of characters when searching for the string
/OFF[LINE]	Does not skip files with the offline attribute set
"string"	Specifies the text string to find
[drive:][path]filename	Specifies a file or files to search

The text string for the search must be enclosed in quotation marks. The command is case sensitive unless used with the /I switch. The command finds the exact text as specified, so you can use it to search for partial words.

For example, to find files that contain *Good*, use the following command:

FIND /I "Good" *.*

The results are shown in Figure 7-23.

The greater-than and less-than signs (> and <) are used with the FIND command to redirect output and input. Recall that most command prompt commands send their output to a standard output device or command prompt window. The > and < signs redirect the input or output to places other than the default standard output (the screen) or default standard input (the keyboard).

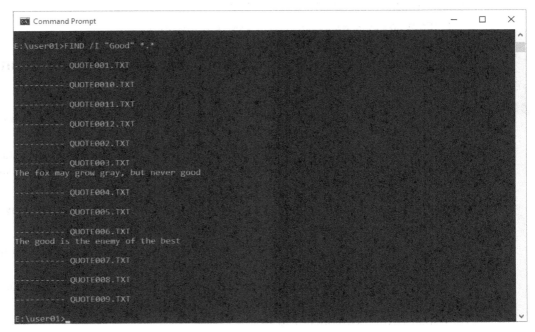

Figure 7-23 Search results using the find command

Source: Microsoft Windows 10/Command Prompt

Use the > sign to redirect the output of a program. For example, consider the following command:

```
FIND /i "Good" *.* > dirfile
```

The output of the command is sent directly to the file named dirfile, overwriting anything that is already in the file. To append the redirected output to an existing file, use the "much greater than" operator (>>). If necessary, the operating system creates the destination file.

Use the < sign to redirect input to a command, and use the more command to view blocks of output one screen at a time. Thus, if the DIR *.* /S command produces a long list of files that scrolls off the screen, you can use the following commands:

```
DIR *.* /S > dirlist
MORE < dirlist
```

The first command creates a file called dirlist that contains the directory listing; the second command, **MORE**, displays one screen of information, and then pauses by displaying the following line at the bottom of the screen:

```
- - More - -
```

You then press any key to see another screen of information. (You can do the same thing with the DIR /P command, but MORE has other uses.)

The redirection operators greatly enhance the flexibility of the FIND command. For example, the following command finds all lines that contain *Football* in a file named Winners.txt and stores the output in a file named FootballWinners.txt:

```
FIND /I "Football" < Winners.txt > FootballWinners.txt
```

Activity 7-13: Finding Files with the FIND Command

Time Required: 15 minutes

Objective: Use the FIND command to locate files by finding specified characters within the files in the Windows 10 CLI.

Description: In this activity, you open the command prompt and find files that contain specific characters. This activity is useful if you want to locate files when you know a word or part of a word contained in the files.

1. If necessary, start your virtual machines using the appropriate instructions in Activity 1-1.
2. Right-click **Start**, and then click **Command Prompt**.
3. To refresh the example files for the search activities, type **MakeABC** at the command prompt and then press **Enter**.
4. To view the names of files that contain the case-sensitive characters *ab*, type FIND **"ab"** *.* and then press **Enter**.
5. Verify that two files are identified.
6. To view the names of files that contain the uppercase or lowercase characters *ab*, type FIND **/I "ab"** *.* and then press **Enter**.

7. Verify that seven files are identified.

8. To view the names of files that contain the case-sensitive characters *bbb*, type **FIND "bbb" *.*** and then press **Enter**.

9. Verify that no file is identified.

10. To view the names of files that contain the uppercase or lowercase characters *bbb*, type **FIND /I "bbb" *.*** and then press **Enter**.

11. Verify that one file is identified.

12. To view the names of files that contain the characters *123*, type the following and then press **Enter**.

    ```
    FIND "123" *.*
    ```

13. Verify that two files are identified.

14. To view the names of files that contain the uppercase or lowercase characters *bc*, type **FIND /I "bc" *.*** and then press **Enter**.

15. Verify that five files are identified.

16. To close the command prompt window, type **exit** and then press **Enter**.

17. Leave the virtual machine logged on for the next activity.

Finding Files with the `FINDSTR` Command You may find the `FINDSTR` command more useful than the `FIND` command because it offers more control over the search process. When used to find text strings in files, the `FINDSTR` command has the following syntax:

```
FINDSTR [/B] [/E] [/L] [/R] [/S] [/I] [/X] [/V] [/N] [/M] [/O] [/P]
[/C:string] strings [[drive:] [path]filename[ ...]]
```

/B	Matches the pattern at the beginning of a line
/E	Matches the pattern at the end of a line
/L	Uses search strings literally
/R	Uses search strings as regular expressions
/S	Searches for matching files in the current directory and all subdirectories
/I	Specifies that the search is not case sensitive
/X	Prints lines that match exactly
/V	Prints only lines that do not contain a match
/N	Prints the line number before each line that matches
/M	Prints only the filename if a file contains a match
/O	Prints the character offset (the location of the character) before each matching line
/P	Skips files with nonprintable characters

/C: string	Uses a specified string as a literal search string
strings	Specifies the text to search for
[drive:] [path] filename	Specifies a file or files to search

For example, to find files that contain *good* or *fool*, use the following command:

FINDSTR /I "good fool" *.*

The results are shown in Figure 7-24.

Table 7-12 shows more examples of using the FINDSTR command to find files.

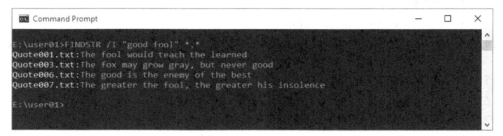

Figure 7-24 Finding files using the FINDSTR command

Source: Microsoft Windows 10/Command Prompt

Expression	Explanation
FINDSTR "hello there" Greeting.txt	Searches for the word *hello* or the word *there* in the Greeting.txt file
FINDSTR /c: "hello there" Greeting.txt	Searches for the phrase *hello there* in the Greeting.txt file
FINDSTR Windows Proposal.txt	Searches for the word *Windows* (with a capital *W*) in the Proposal.txt file
FINDSTR /s /i Windows *.*	Searches every file in the current directory and all subdirectories for all occurrences of the word *Windows*, regardless of case

Table 7-12 Examples of using the FINDSTR command

Activity 7-14: Finding Files with the FINDSTR Command

Time Required: 15 minutes

Objective: Use the FINDSTR command with wildcard characters in the Windows 10 CLI.

Description: In this activity, you open the command prompt and find files that contain specific characters. This activity is useful if you want to locate files when you know a word or part of a word contained in the files.

1. If necessary, start your virtual machines using the appropriate instructions in Activity 1-1.
2. Right-click **Start**, and then click **Command Prompt**.
3. To create the example files for the search activities, type **MakeQUOTE** at the command prompt and then press **Enter**.

 Contact your instructor if you see the following message: "MakeQUOTE is not recognized as an internal or external command, operable program or batch file."

4. To view the names of files that contain *The*, type **FINDSTR "The" *.*** and then press **Enter**.
5. Verify that 11 files are identified.
6. To view the count of lines that contain *The*, type the following and then press **Enter**.

    FINDSTR "The" *.* | find /v /c ""

    (This should match the count from the previous step.)
7. To view the names of files that contain *never* and/or *good*, type the following and then press **Enter**.

    FINDSTR "never good" *.*
8. Verify that two files are identified.
9. To view the names of files that contain the phrase *never good*, type the following and then press **Enter**.

    FINDSTR /C: "never good" *.*.
10. Verify that one file is identified.
11. To view only the names of files that contain *rocks* and/or *rules*, type the following and then press **Enter**.

    FINDSTR /M "rocks rules" *.*
12. Verify that one file is identified.
13. Close the command prompt window.
14. Leave the virtual machine logged on for the next activity.

Using the FINDSTR Command with Regular Expressions

The FINDSTR command can find the exact text you are looking for in any ASCII file or files. However, sometimes you only know part of the information that you want to match. For example, you might need to find a file that contains the characters *TEX*. In such cases, the FINDSTR command has the powerful ability to search for patterns of text using regular expressions.

Regular expressions are a notation for specifying patterns of text as opposed to exact strings of characters. The notation uses literal characters and **metacharacters**. Every character that does not have special meaning in the regular expression syntax is a literal character and matches an occurrence of that character. For example, letters and numbers are literal characters. A metacharacter is a symbol with special meaning (an operator or delimiter) in the regular expression syntax.

Table 7-13 lists the metacharacters that FINDSTR accepts.

The special characters in regular expression syntax are most powerful when you use them together. Table 7-14 lists examples of regular expressions and explanations for each.

For example, to find lines from files containing words that start with the characters *Work*, as shown in Figure 7-25, use the following command:

```
FINDSTR /R "\<Work" *.*
```

Character	Value
.	A wildcard for any character
*	Repeats zero or more occurrences of the previous character or class
^	Line position: beginning of line
$	Line position: end of line
[class]	A character class that matches a single character out of all the possibilities offered; for example, *[abcd]* matches *a, b, c,* or *d*
[^class]	Inverse class; all characters except the listed special characters
[x-y]	Specifies a range of characters; for example, *[a-zA-Z0-9]* matches any letter or digit
\x	Specifies a metacharacter that is used as a literal character; for example, to use the metacharacter *$* as a literal character, enter *\$*
\<xyz	Specifies characters that match the beginning of the word; for example, *\<Win* would match words that start with the characters *Win*
xyz\>	Specifies characters that match the end of the word; for example, *dows\>* would match words that end with the characters *dows*

Table 7-13   Regular expressions and metacharacters with the FINDSTR command

Expression	Explanation
.*	Matches any string of characters
w.*ing	Matches any string that begins with *w* and ends with *ing*
fox*	Matches any string that begins with *fo* followed by zero or more *x*s
[ABC]	Matches any occurrence of *A, B,* or *C*
[^ABC]	Matches any text that does not start with *A, B,* or *C*
[A-C]	Matches only the characters *A, B,* or *C*

Table 7-14   Regular expression examples for the FINDSTR command

Figure 7-25 Finding files using the FINDSTR command with a regular expression

Source: Microsoft Windows 10/Command Prompt

Activity 7-15: Finding Files with FINDSTR and Regular Expressions

Time Required: 15 minutes

Objective: Use the FINDSTR command with regular expressions in the Windows 10 CLI.

Description: In this activity, you open the command prompt and find files using regular expressions. This activity is useful for locating files when you know patterns contained within the file.

1. If necessary, start your virtual machines using the appropriate instructions in Activity 1-1.

2. Right-click **Start**, and then click **Command Prompt**.

3. To create the example files for the search activities, type **MakeQuote** at the command prompt and then press **Enter**.

4. To view the lines from files that contain the characters *x*, *y*, or *z*, type the following and then press **Enter**.

   FINDSTR /R " [xyz] " *.*

5. Verify that four files are identified.

6. To view the lines from files that do not contain the characters *x*, *y*, or *z*, type the following and then press **Enter**.

   FINDSTR /R "^[^xyz]*$" *.*

7. Verify that eight files are identified.

8. To view the lines from files containing words that end in *r*, type the following and then press **Enter**.

   FINDSTR /R "r\>" *.*

9. Verify that seven files are identified.

10. To view the lines from files containing words that begin with *r*, type the following and then press **Enter**.

    FINDSTR /R "\<r" *.*

11. Verify that one file is identified.

12. To view the lines from files that contain the characters *oo*, type the following and then press **Enter**.

    FINDSTR /R "oo" *.*

13. Verify that four files are identified.

14. To view the lines from files that contain the character *g*, followed by zero or more *o* characters and followed by a *d*, type the following and then press **Enter**.

    FINDSTR /R "go*d" *.*

15. Verify that four files are identified.

16. Close the command prompt window.

17. Leave the virtual machine logged on for the next activity.

Finding Files in Windows 10 with Windows Search

The Windows Search feature in Windows 10 might be the most direct way to locate a file. You first learned about Windows Search in Chapter 3. Windows will also search the Web for possible matches. This can sometimes lead to extra results to sift through when looking for local files. While this feature is often the quickest way to find what you are looking for, the next section explains another option for finding files on the system.

 Windows 10 also includes Cortana, a digital personal assistant, which can aid searches.

Finding Files in Windows 10 File Explorer with Windows Search

In this section, you will learn about features for Windows Search from File Explorer. To open the search tool, click Start and then click File Explorer. The search box appears in the upper-right corner of File Explorer, as shown in Figure 7-26, with the word *Quote* typed as a search term. As you start to type the search term, Windows 10 displays the items that meet the initial characters of your request. As you type additional characters, Windows 10 narrows the displayed results. In addition to filename searches, you can search by specifying a word or phrase within a file.

Using Quotation Marks with Windows Search If you want to search on more than one word, place the phrase in quotation marks. For example, you might have searched your files for documents related to an old project called the Dallas Project and got a large number of results because many files contained just the word *Dallas* or just *Project*. Searching with *"Dallas Project"* would provide the file list that you need.

Using Wildcards with Windows Search Windows Search can use the wildcards that you learned to use with the command-line interface commands. Add an asterisk (*) to a search term to represent an unknown string of letters or numbers, and use a question mark (?) as a single-character wildcard.

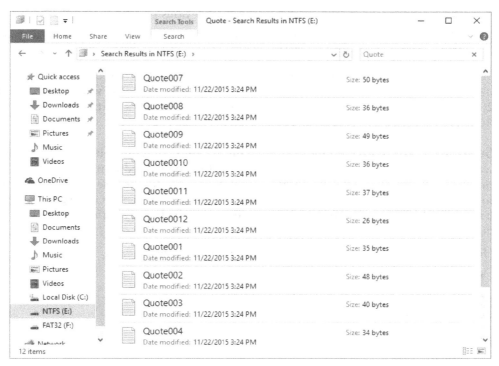

Figure 7-26 Searching for files in Windows File Explorer

Source: Microsoft Windows 10/File Explorer

Unfortunately, Windows Search does not support the regular expressions that you learned to use with the FINDSTR command.

Using File Sizes with Windows Search When you know the approximate size of a file, you can include the file's size in your search by using the keyword size:. For example, to find a file that is less than 100 kilobytes (KB) and that contains the word *resume*, enter the command resume size:<100KB. Windows 10 will display a pop-up menu of options for common file sizes, but you can still enter a custom size.

To specify ranges, use the following operators:

- <   less than
- <= less than or equal to
- >   greater than
- >= greater than or equal to
- ..   range of file sizes

Using Dates and Date Ranges with Windows Search You can use relative dates such as today, tomorrow, or yesterday in a search. You can also combine words such as *this*, *last*, *past*, and *coming* with *week*, *month*, and *year* to create search terms such as *thisweek*, *nextmonth*, *pastmonth*, and *comingyear*. To find a file you created last week, for example, enter created:lastweek or created:pastweek.

To specify ranges, use the operators listed in the previous section.

To find a file that you created in 2013, enter `datecreated:<1/1/2014`. The date format is mm/dd/year or mm/dd/yy.

To find a file created between June 3, 2010 and February 2, 2013, use `datecreated:>6/03/2010..<2/2/2013`. Note that this search excludes files that were created on June 3, 2010 or February 2, 2013. To find those files as well, enter `datecreated: >=6/03/2010..<=2/2/2013` or `datecreated: 6/03/2010..2/2/2013`.

Searching by Kind   Suppose you want to find all your photos that contain the word *vacation* in the filename, but you have documents and e-mails that contain *vacation* as well. Simply entering *vacation* is not very useful, so use the `kind:` command to narrow your search results. For example, enter `vacation kind:photo` or `vacation kind:pictures` to find only pictures that include *vacation* somewhere in their description.

Here is a list of possible kinds that you can use in searches:

- Calendar
- Communications (e-mails and appointments)
- Contacts (also person)
- Documents
- E-mail
- Folder
- Instant message (also im)
- Journal
- Link
- Meetings
- Movie
- Music (also song)
- Notes
- Picture (also pics or photo)
- Playlist
- Program
- Tasks
- Videos
- Web history

You can enter the search command `kind:music` to find all your mp3 files, wma files, wav files, and so on. You need to use Microsoft Outlook or Windows Live Mail to search with the following kinds: e-mail, journal, meetings, notes, or tasks.

Searching by Type You can use the `type:` command to narrow the search if you use the `kind:` command and receive results that are too broad. For example, if you have a large music collection and you want to find only mp3 files, but not wma files, type `rock type:mp3`. If you have many photos and you want to find only files that have a .jpg extension, enter `type:jpg.?`.

Searching by File Properties Windows Search indexes the filename and metadata for every file type and indexes the entire contents of many file types. You can search the metadata by specifying a file property. For example, suppose you want to find the song *Canon in D* by Johann Pachelbel; you know you have the song both in mp3 and wma formats, and that the wma format sounds better. But, the file has a cryptic filename, similar to 00jpcd.wma. Enter `artist:pachelbel title:canon type:wma` to find the file.

To find Word documents created by Bill Jones, enter `type:doc author:BillJones`. Another useful search would be for e-mails sent to a specific person. To find these e-mails, you could enter a command such as `type:eml to:billJones@alamo.edu`.

Here is a selection of file properties that you might find useful in searches:

- album
- artist
- author
- bitrate
- cameramake
- cameramodel
- cc
- created
- date
- datetaken
- firstname
- genre
- lastname
- modified
- rating
- size
- subject
- title
- tag
- to
- track
- year

7

Activity 7-16: Finding Files with the Windows Search Utility in File Explorer

Time Required: 20 minutes

Objective: Use the Windows Search utility to find files in Windows 10.

Description: In this activity, you search for files using the Windows Search utility. This activity is useful if you want to locate files and you know characters contained within the files.

1. If necessary, start your virtual machines using the appropriate instructions in Activity 1-1.

2. Right-click **Start,** and then click **Command Prompt.**

3. To refresh the example files for the search activities, type **MakeQuote** at the command prompt and then press **Enter.**

4. Close the command prompt.

5. To open File Explorer, click **Start** and then click **File Explorer.**

6. In the navigation pane on the left side of the window, click **This PC** and then double-click the **NTFS (E:)** drive in the right pane.

7. To try to view the names of files that contain *good*, type **good** over "Search NTFS (E:)" in the search box in the upper-right corner of File Explorer.

8. Note your results, if there are any. The previous search fails with default settings. You will fix this in the next steps.

9. Click the search box to display the search tab on the File Explorer Ribbon, click **Advanced options,** and then click **Change indexed locations.**

10. To add the location to the index, click the **Modify** button, click the **NTFS (E:)** check box to select it, click **OK,** and then click **Close.**

11. To view the files that contain *good*, type **good** in the search box in File Explorer.

12. Verify that two files are returned by the search.

13. Click the **X** on the right side of the search box to clear the search filter.

14. To view files that contain *lab*, type **lab** in the search box.

15. Verify that two files are returned by the search.

16. Click the **X** on the right side of the search box to clear the search filter.

17. To view files that contain the word *fool*, type **fool** in the search box in File Explorer.

18. Verify that two files are listed.

19. To view files that contain the word *fool* and that were created today, click **fool** in the search box, click **Date modified,** and then click **Today.**

20. Verify that two files are located.

21. To change the search date, click the word **today** just after datemodified: in the search box, and then click another date other than today on the calendar that appears.

22. Verify that no files are located.

23. Close any open windows in the virtual machine.

24. To shut down the Windows virtual machine, click **Start,** click **Power,** and then click the **Shut Down** button.

25. Wait a moment for the Windows 10 virtual machine to shut down completely.

Finding Files in CentOS 7

You have several options for finding files in CentOS 7. For example, you can find files in a specific directory using the `ls` command. You can also use the **`find`** command in a terminal window or use the GNOME desktop search function. As with most things in Linux, the CLI's `find` utility is much more robust and versatile than the comparable tool in the GNOME GUI. The `find` utility can search for files by name, size, or date from any directory.

Finding Files with the `ls` Command in CentOS 7
The `ls` command is a very simple way of searching for files in a specific directory. The `ls` command supports the same basic wildcards you use in Windows. Refer to Tables 7-10 and 7-11 for examples of how to use the asterisk and question mark wildcards.

For example, to find files using the `ls` command and a wildcard expression, you would type:

`ls m*`

or

`ls –l mcopy`

The results are shown in Figure 7-27.

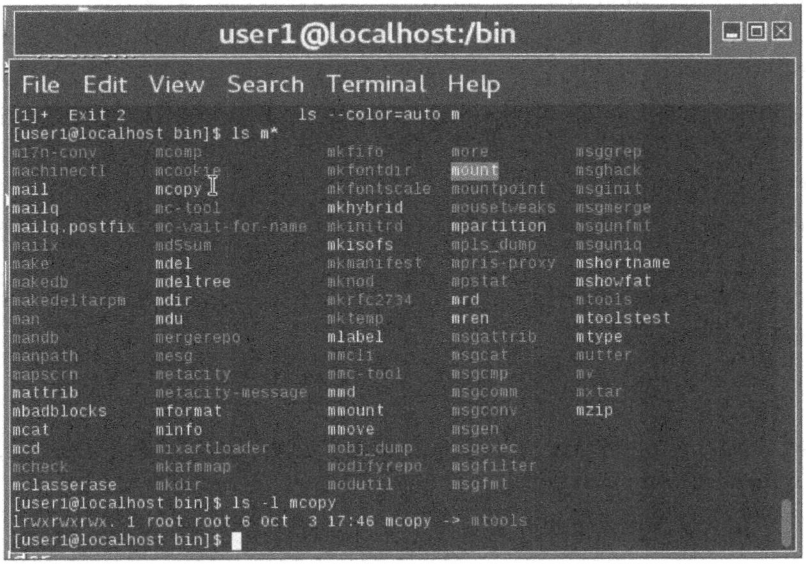

Figure 7-27 Finding files using the `ls` command

Source: Red Hat CentOS 7/Terminal

Activity 7-17: Finding Files with the `ls` Command and Wildcard Characters in CentOS 7

Time Required: 15 minutes

Objective: Use the `ls` command with wildcard characters to find files in CentOS 7.

Description: In this activity, you open the terminal console and find files with the help of wildcard characters. This activity is useful if you want to locate files when you know a portion of a filename.

1. If necessary, start your virtual machines using the appropriate instructions in Activity 1-1.
2. To open a terminal console, right-click the desktop and select **Open in Terminal**.
3. To create the directory structure, type the following and then press **Enter**.

   `cd /usr/local/bin`

4. Type **sh makeABC**, and then press **Enter**.

Contact your instructor if you see the following message: "makeABC is not recognized as an internal or external command, operable program or batch file."

5. To view filenames that start with *ab*, type **ls ab*** and then press **Enter**.
6. Verify that two files are listed.
7. To view filenames that contain a *b* as the third character, type **ls –a ??b*** and then press **Enter**.
8. Verify that two files are listed.
9. To view filenames that contain three characters, with *a* as the first character, type **ls a??** and then press **Enter**.
10. Verify that three files are listed.
11. To view filenames that contain *9* as the second character, type **ls ?9*** and then press **Enter**.
12. Verify that two files are listed.
13. Close the terminal console.
14. Leave the virtual machine logged on for the next activity.

Finding Files with the `find` Command in CentOS 7
The `find` utility can search based on the following criteria:

- Name
- Links
- Time

- Size
- Type
- Owner
- Mode bits
- Contents
- Directories
- File systems
- Combining primaries with operators

The find command searches the directory tree by evaluating a search expression from left to right, according to the rules of precedence, and then lists the files that match the test expression. The find command returns a status of 0 if all files are processed successfully, and a status of greater than 0 if errors occur. The search expression consists of the following elements:

- Options—These elements affect overall operation rather than the processing of a specific file, and always return a true value.
- Tests—These elements return a true or false value.
- Actions—These elements have side effects and return a true or false value.

These elements are separated by operators. The -and operator is assumed when an operator is omitted. Table 7-15 lists the order of precedence for expressions in the CentOS 7 find command, in ascending order.

Table 7-16 contains the test syntax used with the CentOS 7 find command.

Table 7-17 contains file types you can use with the CentOS 7 find command.

Expression	Description
(expr) parentheses	The parentheses work as they do in mathematical expressions, forcing precedence and changing the order in which operations are performed
! expr	The ! symbol means that the inverse of the expression returns a true value; in other words, "if expr is false"
-not expr	Same as ! expr
expr1 expr2	expr2 is not evaluated if expr1 is false (in other words, an implied AND operation)
expr1 -a expr2	Same as expr1 expr2
expr1 -and expr2	Same as expr1 expr2
expr1 -o expr2	expr2 is not evaluated if expr1 is true (an OR expression)
expr1 -or expr2	Same as expr1 -o expr2
expr1 , expr2	Both expr1 and expr2 are always evaluated (a LIST expression); the value of expr1 is discarded, and the value of the list is the value of expr2

Table 7-15 Order of precedence for expressions in the CentOS 7 find command

Test syntax	Description
+n	For greater than *n*
-n	For less than *n*
N	For exactly *n*

Table 7-16 Test syntax used with the CentOS 7 `find` command

Type	Description
c	Character
b	Block
d	Directory
p	Named pipe
f	Regular file
l	Symbolic link
s	Socket

Table 7-17 File types used with the CentOS 7 `find` command

The syntax and options for the `find` command are:

-daystart	Measures times (for -amin, -atime, -cmin, -ctime, -mmin, and -mtime) from the beginning of the day rather than from 24 hours ago
-depth	Processes each directory's contents before the directory itself
-maxdepthlevels	Descends at the specified number of directory *levels* (a non-negative integer) below the command-line arguments
-mindepthlevels	Does not apply any tests or actions beyond the specified number of *levels* (a non-negative integer)
-xdev	Does not descend into directories on other file systems
-aminn	File was last accessed *n* minutes ago
-atimen	File was last accessed *n* hours ago
-cminn	File's status was last changed *n* minutes ago
-cnewer file	File's status was last changed more recently than file was modified
-ctimen	File's status was last changed *n* hours ago
-empty	File is empty and is either a regular file or a directory
-fstypetype	File is on a file system of *type*; accepted types are DOS, Fat, NTFS, ext2, and ext3; use the -printf option to see the available types of file systems

-gidn	File's numeric group ID is *n*
-inamepattern	Searches for files with common name patterns; similar to -name, but the match is case insensitive
-inum n	File has inode number *n*
-links n	File has *n* links
-name *pattern*	Looks for a certain pattern in a filename; uses the metacharacters , ?, and []
-size n[bckw]	File uses *n* units of space; the units are 512-byte blocks by default
-type c	The type of file, where *c* represents the type
-user uname	File is owned by user *uname* (numeric user ID allowed)
-print True	Prints the full filename on the standard output device, followed by a newline character
-prune	If -depth is not given, true; does not descend into the current directory

For example, to locate directories using the find command, you can type:

find /etc –type d | more

The results are shown in Figure 7-28. The CentOS 7 **more** command functions like the Windows 7 MORE command by displaying one page at a time.

To locate links using the find command, you can type:

find /etc -maxdepth 1 -type l | more

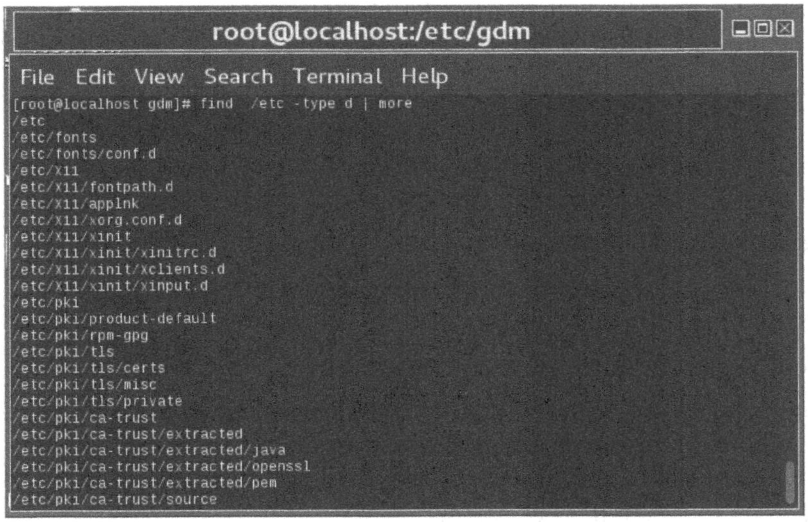

Figure 7-28 Locating directories using the find command

Source: Red Hat CentOS 7/Terminal

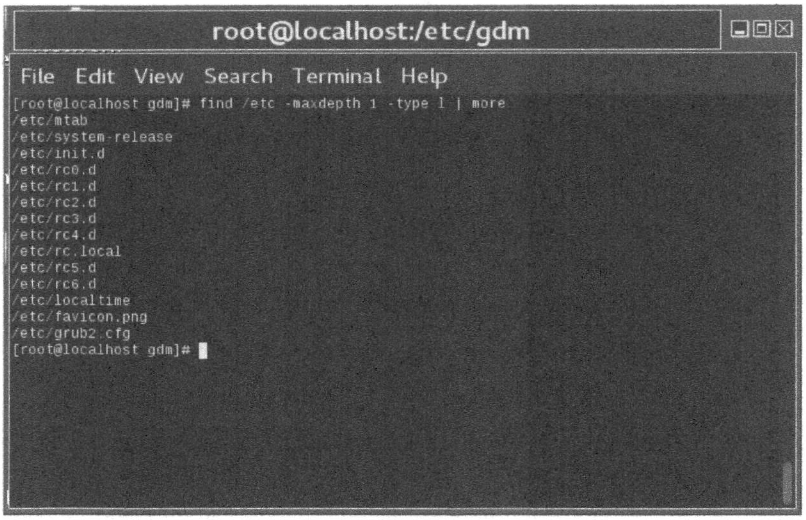

Figure 7-29 Locating links using the `find` command

Source: Red Hat CentOS 7/Terminal

The results are shown in Figure 7-29.

The **xargs** command is often piped with the `find` command to construct an argument list using standard input from the `find` command. The `xargs` command has the following syntax:

```
xargs [options] [command]
```

In the following example, `xargs` executes a command once for each piped record. The `find` command searches the entire directory structure for filenames that contain a specified string. The `xargs` command processes the resulting list of files and executes the `grep` command for each.

For example, to systematically locate files that include a certain string pattern, you can type:

```
find . -name 'myfile*' -print | xargs -n2 grep 'compression'
find . -name 'myfile*' -print | xargs -n2 grep 'compression6'
find . -name 'myfile*' -print | xargs -n2 grep 'compression[46]'
```

The results are shown in Figure 7-30.

The **grep** utility finds character or string patterns in an ASCII file. The `grep` CLI utility has the following syntax:

```
grep [options] [-e PATTERN | -f FILE] [FILE...]
```

The `grep` utility searches the named input files for lines that contain a match of the given pattern. By default, the `grep` command prints the matching lines. The `grep` utility can also be used with the `ls` utility.

The `grep` command has the following options:

`-a -text`   Does not suppress output lines that contain binary data. Normally, the first few bytes of a file indicate that the

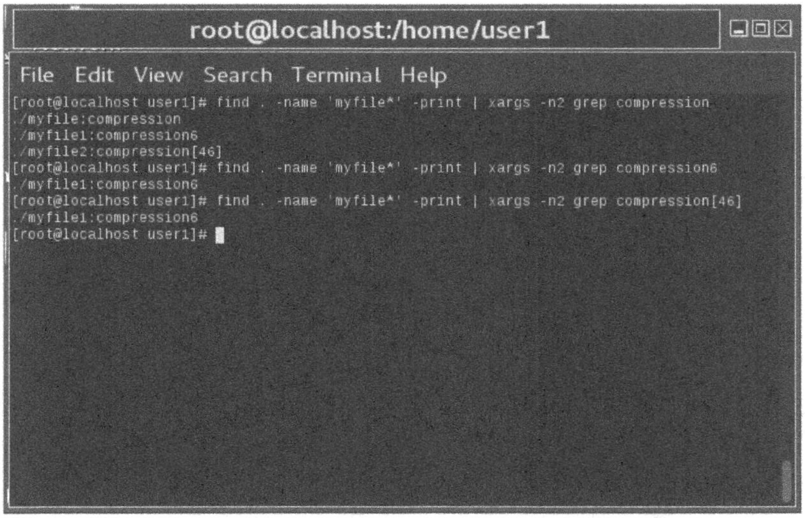

Figure 7-30 Using the `find` command with `xargs` and `grep`

Source: Red Hat CentOS 7/Terminal

file contains binary data. This option causes `grep` to treat the file like a text file, even if it would otherwise be treated as binary. Note that the result might be binary garbage printed to the terminal, which can create problems if the terminal driver interprets some of it as commands.

`-c –count`	Suppresses normal output; instead prints a count of matching lines for each input file.
`-e PATTERN --regexp=PATTERN`	Uses *PATTERN* as the pattern; this option is useful for protecting patterns that begin with a `-`.
`-f FILE --file=FILE`	Obtains patterns from *FILE*, one per line.
`-H --with-filename`	Prints the filename for each match.
`-r –recursive`	For each directory mentioned in the command line, reads and processes all files in the directories recursively.
`-v --invert-match`	Reverses the matching to select nonmatching lines.
`-V -version`	Prints the `grep` version number to the standard output stream.

You can use the `grep` command to select files that contain certain string patterns. The next two commands show either every line in the file that contains the pattern looked for or the number of lines in which the pattern appears:

```
grep root messages
grep –c root messages
```

Figure 7-31 Output of the `grep` command

Source: Red Hat CentOS 7/Terminal

The `grep` utility can be very helpful in looking at log files. The previous command tells you how many times root has been used on the system to perform actions.

The results are shown in Figure 7-31.

Activity 7-18: Finding Files in CentOS 7

Time Required: 15 minutes

Objective: Use the `find`, `xargs`, and `grep` commands to find files.

Description: In this activity, you open the terminal console and find files with the help of wildcard characters and a string (pattern) search. This activity is useful if you want to locate files when you know a portion of a filename or a string of characters in a file.

1. If necessary, start your virtual machines using the appropriate instructions in Activity 1-1.

2. To open a terminal console, right-click the desktop and select **Open in Terminal**.

3. To create the directory structure with the **makeHRS** script, type the following and press **Enter**.

   `cd /usr/local/bin`

4. Type **sh makeHRS** at the prompt, and press **Enter**.

Contact your instructor if you see the following message: "makeHRS is not recognized as an internal or external command, operable program or batch file."

5. To display symbolic links, type **find /etc type l | more** and press **Enter**.
6. To display directories, type **find /etc type d | more** and press **Enter**.
7. To find files that contain certain filename strings, type **find /etc –name cro*** and press **Enter**.
8. Verify that 11 files are listed.
9. To find files that contain certain strings, type **find /rc | xargs grep mode*.** and press **Enter**.
10. Verify that the rc file includes two lines that contain the word *mode*.
11. To close the terminal window, type **exit** and then press **Enter**.
12. To shut down the virtual machine, click **User01**, click **Power Off**, and then click the **Power Off** button.
13. Wait a moment for the CentOS 7 virtual machine to shut down completely.
14. Close any remaining open windows, log off, and shut down your PC.

7

Chapter Summary

■ Files can have different types of contents. You can determine file types by their extensions in Windows 10 or by their file header information in CentOS 7. Knowing the contents of a file helps with error processing, application selection, troubleshooting, and other file processing. You can view a file's contents as a whole or in sections, on a standard display, or within another file.

■ File attributes provide information about a file's access privileges. Files in Windows 10 and CentOS 7 have different file attributes. The most common Windows 10 file attributes are archive, read-only, hidden, compression, and encryption.

■ As directories are built, more files are added. Many options are available to help you locate these files quickly. For example, when you do not know the exact name of a file you need, you can use wildcards to represent unknown characters in the filename or file type. You can search for files by their name, type, or content. Use the FIND and FINDSTR commands to locate needed information in a file. Regular expressions permit pattern searching of file contents.

■ Using the File Explorer Search feature in Windows 10, you can locate files by their contents, as you can with the FINDSTR command. You can also search for files by their type, kind, size, and date.

■ File compression saves disk space by removing duplicated data in files. In Windows 10, the compression attribute indicates that the file has been compressed. In CentOS 7, the gzip and gunzip commands are used to compress and uncompress files.

Key Terms

archive   A Windows 10 file attribute that indicates a file is available for archiving or backup.

ATTRIB   A command used to view Windows file attributes from the command line.

cat   A command used to display file contents by directing the entire contents of a compressed file to an output device in one pass.

compression   A Windows 10 file attribute that indicates a file is compressed.

Encrypting File System (EFS)   A system that Windows 10 uses to store data using file encryption.

encryption   A Windows 10 file attribute that indicates a file is protected using the Encrypting File System.

extension   A set of characters that a user or program adds to a filename to help describe or categorize a file.

file   A command used in CentOS 7 to examine a file and determine its file type.

file   A basic unit of storage that enables a computer to distinguish one set of information from another.

file attribute   A restrictive label attached to a file that describes and regulates its use; examples include hidden, system, read-only, and archive.

file type   A classification that indicates the kind of information contained within a file; usually indicated by the filename extension or file header.

filename   The set of letters, numbers, and allowable symbols assigned to a file to distinguish it from all other files in a particular directory on a disk. A filename is the label under which a user saves and requests a block of information.

FIND   A CLI command used in Windows to locate a specific text string in an ASCII file. The information is sent either to the console or a file.

find   A command used in CentOS 7 to search the root directory for files.

FINDSTR   A command used at the Windows command prompt to locate an exact text string in any ASCII file. The information is sent either to the console or a file.

grep   A command used to find string patterns in files.

gunzip   The sister utility to gzip that decompresses gzip files.

gzip   A command used to compress CentOS 7 files.

hidden   A Windows 10 file attribute that indicates a file is hidden from directory commands.

index   A Windows 10 file attribute that indicates a file should be indexed.

inode   A place where CentOS 7 applications store file and directory attributes. The inode contains information about a file or directory, including its type.

lsattr   A command used in CentOS 7 to view file attributes.

metacharacter   A character embedded in a program source or a data stream that conveys information about characters other than itself.

MORE   A Windows command that displays text files one screen at a time.

more   A command used in CentOS 7 to display text one screen at a time.

read-only   A Windows 10 file attribute that indicates a file cannot be modified.

regular expression   A combination of symbols, identifiers, values, and operators that yields a result upon evaluation.

system   A Windows 10 file attribute that indicates a file belongs to the operating system.

tar   An archive or backup utility that selects and packages files according to filters and is often used in conjunction with the gzip compression utility.

TYPE   A Windows 10 command used to display the text contained in files.

xargs   A command often piped with the find command to construct an argument list using standard input from the find command.

zcat   A utility that decompresses gzip files and redirects the output to standard output.

Zip   A format for compressed data files in Windows.

Review Questions

1. A file extension _____. (Choose all that apply.)

   a.   is required in both the Windows 10 and CentOS 7 operating systems

   b.   is usually three letters and comes after the comma

   c.   is usually three letters and comes after the period

   d.   typically suggests the type of data in the file

   e.   is used by the OS to determine which program could be used to process the file

2. File associations _____.

   a.   specify certain aspects of the operating system's treatment of different directories

   b.   specify the operating system you are using

   c.   refer to left-over information that does not help you

   d.   specify certain aspects of the operating system's treatment of different file types

   e.   are only used in the Windows 10 OS

3. When working with files, knowing the file extension helps you _____.
   (Choose all that apply.)

   a.   determine if you need to load the application to read or update the file

   b.   determine the value of the file before you begin working with it

   c.   determine the correct compiler to use

   d.   troubleshoot problems you may encounter with downloaded files from the Internet

   e.   in no way; it is only for decorative purposes

4. In CentOS 7, file extensions _____. (Choose all that apply.)

   a.   are required

   b.   are not necessary because the OS can read the file header to check for the file type

   c.   are identical to those used in the Windows 10 OS

   d.   do not help in determining the contents of the file

5. To view the contents of a file in CentOS 7, use the _____ command. (Choose all that apply.)

    a. FIND

    b. cat

    c. find

    d. more

6. The cat command displays a file's contents _____. (Choose all that apply.)

    a. by concatenating them to the standard output device or another file

    b. and requires a file operand to do so

    c. and can use the redirection symbol >

    d. one page at a time when the more command is also used

7. Every file in Windows has at least _____ attributes.

    a. one

    b. two

    c. three

    d. four

8. Use the more command to _____.

    a. copy file contents

    b. determine file attributes

    c. view file contents

    d. view hardware configuration

9. The hidden attribute _____. (Choose all that apply.)

    a. causes your files to become invisible to the OS

    b. cannot be seen unless you use the DIR UNHIDE command

    c. is used to prevent a file from being seen by other commands

    d. is not listed by the DIR command by default

10. Use the _____ command to view attributes in a Windows command prompt.

    a. VIEW

    b. FIND

    c. ATTRIB

    d. FILE_ATTRIB

11. Setting the compression attribute _____. (Choose all that apply.)

    a. decreases a file's size

    b. decreases the amount of space used by all the files stored within a folder

    c. may result in a loss of performance

    d. is not recommended and should not be considered

    e. cannot be done prior to encryption

12. Setting the encryption attribute of Windows 10 files _____. (Choose all that apply.)

    a. will remove the compression attribute

    b. is the same as compression

    c. prohibits other users from viewing the contents of encrypted files

    d. is not available in Windows 10

    e. is used to decrease file size

13. File attributes in CentOS 7 _____. (Choose all that apply.)

    a. are different from those in Windows 10

    b. are seldom used

    c. can be viewed with the `lsattr` command

    d. are the same as those in Windows 10

14. A regular expression _____. (Choose all that apply.)

    a. uses literal characters and metacharacters

    b. is a notation for specifying patterns of text, as opposed to exact strings of characters

    c. is helpful when searching for exact text matches in an ASCII file

    d. example is `[A-C]`

15. Use the _____ command to search for exact text matches in an ASCII file.

    a. `ATTRIB`

    b. `SEEK`

    c. `SEARCH`

    d. `FIND`

16. The `DIR` command in Windows 10 is similar to the _____ command in CentOS 7.

    a. `find`

    b. `more`

    c. `file`

    d. `ls`

17. Which search criteria can you use with the Windows File Explorer Search feature? (Choose all that apply.)

    a. all of a filename

    b. part of a filename

    c. date modified

    d. date deleted

18. You use the FINDSTR command in Windows to search for _____.

    a. text within a file

    b. directories

    c. links

    d. files based on file type

19. You use the find command in CentOS 7 to search for _____. (Choose all that apply.)

    a. text within a file

    b. directories

    c. symbolic links

    d. files based on file type

20. You use the grep command in CentOS 7 to search for _____.

    a. text within a file

    b. directories

    c. links

    d. files based on file type

Case Projects

CASE PROJECTS

Case 7-1: Copying Files for an Associate with Windows 10

You want to give an associate a disk that contains a copy of all the files in the default directory, except files with the .bak extension. The disk is in drive A. Your virtual machine also has a B drive. You plan to use the XCOPY command to copy only the files you have marked with the archive attribute. Describe the steps to achieve this objective. Provide examples of the commands you plan to use.

Case 7-2: Preparing for a Presentation on Windows File Attributes

You have been asked to give a short presentation on Windows file attributes. The presentation should include handouts that provide definitions of the file attributes and at least three examples of setting them.

Case 7-3: Selecting Files for a Forensics Investigation with CentOS 7

Your law firm is investigating a company's files and inventories. The company is suspected of doctoring its inventory records. Your firm asks you to find and display all inventory files that were last modified after a certain date. You must also keep the directory structure intact. List and explain the steps you need to perform, and include plausible commands to do the job. Keep in mind that you may find many directories full of files and that you must consider resource efficiencies.

7

The Command Line

After reading this chapter and completing the exercises, you will be able to:

- Describe the shell environment
- Customize the shell environments
- Use the Windows 10 and CentOS 7 shells
- Access Help files
- Display the contents of files

Depending on your level of technical expertise, you may have experience using a command-line interface (CLI). As computers evolved, many users moved away from the CLI and began depending on the graphical user interface (GUI). Although GUIs allow you to control an operating system without memorizing commands and key combinations, there are still many reasons to learn to work "under the hood" of the PC. With Windows 10, Microsoft has added new features for both shells—the Command Prompt and PowerShell—which allow users to work faster and efficiently. The shells have many similarities, but their underlying technology is not the same.

You have used the CLI in previous chapters. This chapter fills in many of the remaining details for using the CLI and provides comparable commands for PowerShell.

Describing the Shell Environment

The command shell is a separate software program that provides direct communication between you and the operating system. When you enter a command, the command interpreter executes it, requests that the operating system perform the task for you, and displays text output on the screen.

A **command interpreter** is the part of a computer operating system that understands and executes commands entered by a user or from a program. The command interpreter is called the **shell**.

To visualize what happens in a command console, whether it is a Command Prompt in Windows 10 or a terminal console in CentOS 7, consult Figure 8-1 and the following steps:

1. Type a command on your keyboard. After passing through the **STDIN** (standard input), the characters are echoed on the console.

2. When you press Enter, the command processor takes over and performs the appropriate action.

3. If the command produces errors when processed, the error message is passed through the **STDERR** (standard error) for display on your monitor. Other output passes through the **STDOUT** (standard output) for display on your monitor.

You can redirect input or output—for example, you can type commands in a text file and use it for input to the command processor by passing the file through standard input. Likewise, you can redirect output from the command processor and have a text file accept the standard output. Redirection is explained later in this chapter.

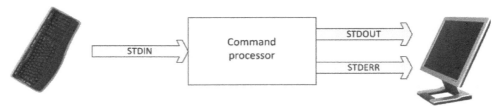

Figure 8-1 Consoles

PowerShell is a new Windows shell. Unlike the Command Prompt, which accepts and returns text, PowerShell accepts and returns objects. **Objects** allow PowerShell to work with the .NET Framework. The **.NET Framework** (pronounced *dot net*) is a software environment that runs primarily in Windows.

As an example of an object, consider a bicycle. All real-world objects share two characteristics: state and behavior. A bicycle's state includes current gear ratio, current pedal cadence, current speed, and current direction. Bicycles also have behaviors, such as changing gear ratio, changing pedal cadence, applying brakes, and rotating handle bars. The state of an object is its data, and the behavior of an object is its methods. When you use an object, you pass along the data and the methods that can be used to transform the data.

Reasons to Learn Command Prompt and PowerShell

You may have asked yourself, "Why should I be proficient with the Command Prompt and PowerShell?" Here are reasons to consider:

- Using the CLI often offers a faster way to perform a task, such as renaming multiple files or folders.
- Working from the CLI uses fewer resources than working from the GUI.
- PowerShell is here to stay. It helps you automate routine tasks.
- Many GUIs are PowerShell front ends—Microsoft has been designing GUIs for various products that are actually front-end interfaces to PowerShell.
- Virtually all current Microsoft products can be managed through PowerShell.
- If you become proficient in PowerShell, you can manage most of Microsoft's newer products.

Customizing the Windows Shells

Windows 10 allows you to customize the look of Windows shells. In this section, you learn to change the appearance of these shells.

Using the Command Line Shell with the Windows 10 CLI

You can use the Windows 10 CLI to configure your Command Prompt, copy and paste text using the Command Prompt, explore the command history, and complete filenames and directory names. Windows 10 provides word wrap capability, drag and select capability, and the keyboard shortcuts Ctrl+C and Ctrl+V for copying and pasting in the CLI. The following sections explain these topics.

Customizing the CLI Window You can use the CLI menu in the Command Prompt to customize the window. To access this menu, right-click the title bar of the Command Prompt (see Figure 8-2). From this menu, you have the following options for customizing the CLI:

- Restore—Restore the Command Prompt from the taskbar.
- Move—Move the Command Prompt with the arrow keys.

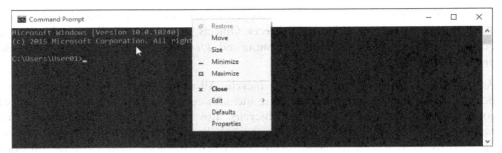

Figure 8-2 Command prompt menu

Source: Microsoft Windows 10/Command Prompt

- Size—Resize the Command Prompt with the arrow keys.
- Minimize—Minimize the Command Prompt to the taskbar.
- Maximize—Maximize the Command Prompt.
- Close—Close the Command Prompt.
- Edit—Edit lines in the Command Prompt; the options in the Edit submenu are explained in "Using the Command Prompt and PowerShell Edit Menu in Windows 10" later in this chapter.
- Defaults—Permanently change the default settings in the Command Prompt; the changes do not appear in the current window, but do in subsequent Command Prompts.
- Properties—Use the Properties dialog box to change settings for the current window only; however, you can subsequently choose to make your changes permanent for any Command Prompt you open from the same shortcut.

You can click the Defaults menu option to open the Console Windows Properties dialog box and change default settings that affect all future Command Prompts. For example, this dialog box is helpful if you need to increase the vertical size of the Command Prompt.

From the Options tab of the Console Windows Properties dialog box, you can set the following options:

- Cursor Size—Changes the cursor size to Small, Medium, or Large.
- Display Options—Chooses a window to share text with other programs or a full screen to run DOS programs that display graphics; press Alt+Enter to toggle between the window and full-screen modes.
- Buffer Size—Indicates the number of commands that can be stored in the buffer. (Recall that a buffer is a memory location that holds data while it is being moved or copied from one place to another.)
- Number of Buffers—Specifies how many processes can have distinct buffers.
- Discard Old Duplicates—Eliminates duplicate commands in the buffer to conserve buffer space.
- **QuickEdit Mode**—Uses the mouse to mark text without using the Mark tool on the Edit menu.

- Insert Mode—Enables text to be inserted at the cursor as you type instead of using Overtype mode.

- Ctrl key Shortcuts—Enables the keyboard shortcuts to be used in the CLI.

- Filter clipboard content on paste—If this setting is enabled, a couple of unsupported characters are removed or changed when content is pasted from the Clipboard to the Command Prompt. In particular, tabs are removed and smart quotes are converted to regular quotation marks.

- Enable line wrapping selection—This option enables you to copy and paste text from the Clipboard to the command-line window. Using this option preserves the wrapping lines that are copied and pasted in the CLI.

- Extended text selection keys—Enables the keyboard shortcuts for cutting and pasting.

- Use Legacy Console—If this setting is enabled, administrators can restrict new features in Windows 10 from being used.

Click the Properties option from the Command Prompt menu to open the Command Prompt Properties dialog box (see Figure 8-3) and make changes that affect only the current Command Prompt. For example, from the Font tab of this dialog box, you can select the display font's pixel size and shape and then verify your selection in the Selected Font window.

8

Figure 8-3 Command prompt properties

Source: Microsoft Windows 10/Command Prompt

From the Layout tab, you can select the screen buffer and window sizes of the Command Prompt. You have the following choices:

- Screen Buffer Size–Width—Set the number of characters stored in a line in the buffer.

- Screen Buffer Size–Height—Set the number of lines stored in memory; if the height of the screen buffer size is smaller than the current window size, scroll bars appear.

- Window Size–Width—Set the number of characters that can fit in a line on the screen.

- Window Size–Height—Set the number of lines that can fit on the screen.

- Window Position–Left and Top—Indicate the pixel position of the Command Prompt if you check the "Let system position window" check box.

- Let system position window—Allow the operating system to automatically position the window.

From the Colors tab of the Command Prompt Properties dialog box, you can select colors for screen text, the screen background, pop-up text, and the pop-up background. You can also set the transparency within a range of 100 percent to 30 percent by using the opacity slider.

Windows PowerShell Figure 8-4 shows that all the preceding options are also available when using PowerShell. You configure these options in Activity 8-2.

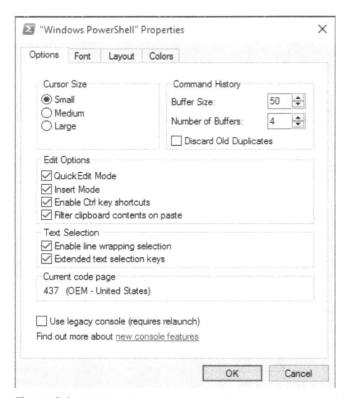

Figure 8-4 Windows PowerShell properties

Source: Microsoft Windows 10/PowerShell

To access the Command Prompt and PowerShell quickly, place a shortcut on the taskbar:

- To pin the Command Prompt to the Start menu, click Start, click All apps, click Window Systems, right-click Command Prompt, and then click Pin to Start.

- To pin the Windows PowerShell to the Start menu, click Start, type PowerShell, right-click Windows PowerShell, and then click Pin to Start.

Activity 8-1: Customizing the Command Prompt in Windows 10

Time Required: 15 minutes

Objective: Customize the Command Prompt in Windows 10.

Description: In this activity, you log on to your virtual machine, pin the Command Prompt to the Start menu, open the Command Prompt, and customize its look and behavior. This activity is useful if you want to modify the Command Prompt for your own needs.

1. Start your virtual machines using the appropriate instructions in Activity 1-1.

2. To add the Command Prompt as a tile on the Start menu, click **Start,** click **All apps,** click **Windows System,** right-click **Command Prompt,** and then click **Pin to Start.**

3. To open the Command Prompt, click **Start** and then click **Command Prompt.**

4. To display the Command Prompt Properties dialog box, right-click the title bar of the Command Prompt and then click **Properties.**

5. To change the cursor size, click the **Options** tab if necessary and then click the **Medium** or **Large** option button.

6. To increase the buffer size for the command history, click the **Buffer Size** up arrow until 60 is displayed.

7. To enable use of the mouse for copy-and-paste operations, verify that the **QuickEdit Mode** check box is checked.

8. To enable the use of Insert mode rather than Overtype mode for typing, verify that the **Insert Mode** check box is checked.

9. To enable the use of Ctrl key shortcuts and keyboard shortcuts, verify that the **Enable Ctrl key shortcuts** and **Extended Text selection keys** check boxes are checked.

10. To set the previous selections for the current window only, click **OK.**

11. To display the Command Prompt Properties dialog box again, right-click the title bar of the Command Prompt and then click **Properties.**

12. To change the font size, click the **Font** tab, click the desired font size in the Size list box, and then view the size in the Selected Font preview box. Adjust the **Size** list box until you find a suitable font size.

13. To increase the screen buffer size, click the **Layout** tab, and increase the appropriate Height value by clicking the **up arrow**. Adjust the height until 60 is displayed.

14. To increase the window size, increase the appropriate Height value by clicking the **up arrow**, and then view the size in the Window Preview box. Adjust the height until you find a suitable size.

15. To change the color scheme for the screen text in the Command Prompt, click the **Colors** tab, click the **Screen Text** option button, click the **black** box, click the **Screen Background** option button, and then click the **white** box. If these colors are not suitable, repeat this step and try other combinations.

16. To change the color scheme for the pop-up text in the Command Prompt, click the **Colors** tab, click the **Popup Text** option button, click the **red** box, click the **Popup Background** option button, and then click the **white** box. If these colors are not suitable, repeat this step and try other combinations. When the colors are suitable, click **OK**.

17. At the Command Prompt, type **exit** and then press **Enter**.

18. Leave the virtual machine logged on for the next activity.

Activity 8-2: Customizing PowerShell in Windows 10

Time Required: 15 minutes

Objective: Customize PowerShell in Windows 10.

Description: In this activity, you pin PowerShell to the Start menu, open PowerShell, and customize its look and behavior. This activity is useful if you want to modify PowerShell for your own needs.

1. Start your virtual machines using the appropriate instructions in Activity 1-1.

2. To add PowerShell as a tile on the Start menu, click **Start**, type **PowerShell** in the "Search the web and Windows" box, right-click **Windows PowerShell**, and then click **Pin to Start**.

3. To open Windows PowerShell, click **Start** and then click **Windows PowerShell**.

4. To display the Windows PowerShell Properties dialog box, right-click the title bar of Windows PowerShell and then click **Properties**.

5. To change the cursor size, click the **Options** tab if necessary and then click the **Medium** or **Large** option button.

6. To increase the buffer size for the command history, click the **Buffer Size** up arrow until 100 is displayed.

7. To enable use of the mouse for copy-and-paste operations, verify that the **QuickEdit Mode** check box is checked.

8. To enable the use of Insert mode rather than Overtype mode for typing, verify that the **Insert Mode** check box is checked.

9. To enable the use of Ctrl key shortcuts and keyboard shortcuts, verify that the **Enable Ctrl key shortcuts** and **Extended Text selection keys** check boxes are checked.

10. To set the previous selections for the current window only, click **OK**.

11. To display the PowerShell Properties dialog box again, right-click the title bar of the PowerShell window and then click **Properties**.

12. To change the font size, click the **Font** tab, click the desired font size in the **Size** list box, and then view the size in the Selected Font preview box. Adjust the **Size** list box until you find a suitable font size.

13. To increase the window size until the maximum value is available to enter cmdlets, click the **Layout** tab and increase the Window Size value by clicking the **up arrow** until the scroll bar appears in the Window Preview. Click the Window Size **down arrow** until the scroll bar disappears.

14. To increase the screen buffer size, increase the Width value by clicking the **up arrow**. Adjust the height until the Screen Buffer Size value matches the Window Size value in Step 13. To increase the window size, increase the appropriate Height value by clicking the **up arrow**, and then view the size in the Window Preview box. Adjust the height until you find a suitable size.

15. To change the color scheme for the screen text in PowerShell, click the **Colors** tab, click the **Screen Text** option button, click the **blue** box, click the **Screen Background** option button, and then click the **yellow** box. If these colors are not suitable, repeat this step and try other combinations.

16. To change the color scheme for the pop-up text in PowerShell, click the **Colors** tab, click the **Popup Text** option button, click the **black** box, click the **Popup Background** option button, and then click the **white** box. If these colors are not suitable, repeat this step and try other combinations. When the colors are suitable, click **OK**.

17. In PowerShell, type **exit** and then press **Enter**.

18. Leave the virtual machine logged on for the next activity.

Using the Windows 10 and CentOS 7 Shells

In this section, you put the Windows 10 and CentOS 7 shells to work. Windows provides two shells: Command Prompt and PowerShell.

Using the Command Prompt and PowerShell Edit Menu in Windows 10

To display the Edit menu of the Command Prompt or PowerShell (see Figures 8-5 and 8-6), right-click its title bar and then click Edit.

You can perform the following tasks with the Edit menu:

- Mark—Mark text in the Command Prompt using the Shift key and cursor movement keys.
- Copy—Copy marked text to the Windows Clipboard.
- Paste—Paste copied text from the Windows Clipboard.
- Select All—Mark all of the text in the Command Prompt.

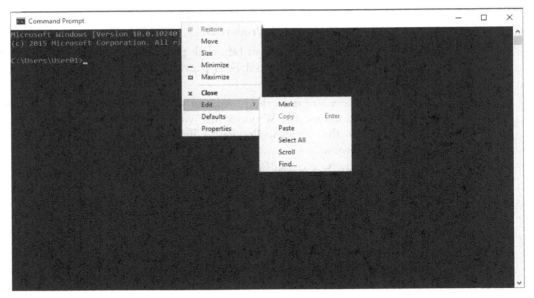

Figure 8-5 Command Prompt Edit menu

Source: Microsoft Windows 10/Command Prompt

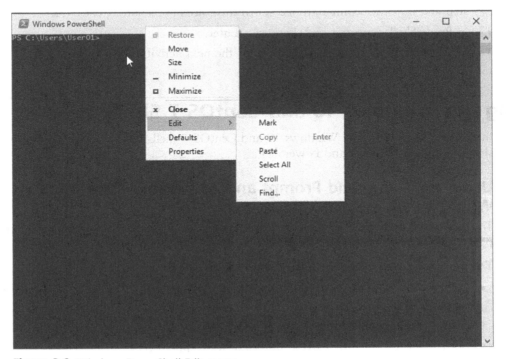

Figure 8-6 Windows PowerShell Edit menu

Source: Microsoft Windows 10/PowerShell

- Scroll—Turn on scrolling; when *Scroll Command Prompt* appears in the title bar, use the arrow keys to scroll within the window. Press the Esc key to turn off scrolling.
- Find—Display a dialog box to find a text string within the Command Prompt.

When using the Command Prompt default settings, you cannot cut text from a Command Prompt.

If you want to use a mouse in the Command Prompt, check the QuickEdit Mode check box, as discussed earlier in this chapter. To copy text when you have enabled QuickEdit mode, drag your mouse to select the text and then press Enter to place it in the Windows Clipboard. To paste text in a Command Prompt, position your cursor at the insertion point and then right-click.

If you want to copy text and you have not enabled QuickEdit mode, right-click the title bar of the Command Prompt, choose Edit, and then click Mark. Position your cursor at the beginning of the text you want to copy and hold down the Shift key while repeatedly pressing the arrow keys. Press Enter to place the selected text in the Windows Clipboard. To paste text in the Command Prompt, position your cursor where you want to insert the text, right-click the Command Prompt's title bar, and then select Paste from the menu that appears.

Use the Find option to locate text in the Command Prompt. Right-click the title bar of the Command Prompt, choose Edit, and then click Find. Type the text string in the Find what text box and then click the Find Next button. If you need to locate other occurrences of the text, repeatedly click the Find Next button. Click Cancel when you finish.

Activity 8-3: Using the Command Prompt Edit Menu in Windows 10

Time Required: 15 minutes

Objective: Use the Command Prompt Edit menu to copy text to the Windows 10 Clipboard.

Description: In this activity, you open the Command Prompt, copy text to the Clipboard, and then view the copied text by pasting it into Notepad. In Notepad, create a command and copy it to the Windows Clipboard, then return to the Command Prompt and paste the command there. This activity is useful if you want to practice copying and pasting text in the Command Prompt.

You must complete Activity 8-1 before starting this activity.

1. If necessary, start your virtual machines using the appropriate instructions in Activity 1-1.
2. Click **Start** and then click **Command Prompt**.
3. To fill the text window with sample text, type **DIR** and then press **Enter**.
4. Right-click the title bar of the Command Prompt, click **Edit**, and then click **Mark**.
5. Use the mouse to highlight five lines of text in the Command Prompt.

6. Right-click the title bar of the Command Prompt, click **Edit,** and then click **Copy.**

7. To open the Notepad text editor, click **Start,** click **All apps,** click the arrow to open **Windows Accessories,** and then click **Notepad.**

8. To paste the contents of the Clipboard, click the **Edit** menu in Notepad and then click **Paste.**

9. To open a second window in Notepad, click the **File** menu and then click **New.** If prompted to save the window as Untitled, click **Don't Save.**

10. To create a command line in the second Notepad window, type **DIR** and then press **Enter.**

11. To copy the command to the Clipboard, click the **Edit** menu, click **Select All,** click the **Edit** menu, and then click **Copy.**

12. Close all the Notepad windows. If necessary, click **Don't Save.**

13. Return to the Command Prompt. To clear everything from the CLI screen, type **CLS** and then press **Enter.**

14. To paste the command from the Windows Clipboard, right-click the title bar of the Command Prompt, click the **Edit** menu, and then click **Paste.**

15. Verify that the DIR command displayed a directory listing.

16. At the Command Prompt, type **exit** and then press **Enter.**

17. Leave the virtual machine logged on for future activities.

Working with the Terminal Window in CentOS 7

As with the Windows 10 Command Prompt, you can choose how you want to work with the terminal window in CentOS 7. For example, to scroll through previous commands and output, use one of the following methods:

- Use the scroll bar, which is usually displayed on the right side of the terminal window.

- Press the Shift+Page Up, Shift+Page Down, Shift+Home, or Shift+End keys.

You can select text in any of the following ways:

- To select a group of characters, click the first character that you want to select and drag the mouse to the last character you want to select.

- To select a group of words, double-click the first word that you want to select and drag the mouse to the last word you want to select. Symbols are selected individually.

- To select a line or lines, triple-click the first line that you want to select and drag the mouse to the last line you want to select.

For all text selections, the terminal window copies the selected text into the clipboard when you release the mouse button. Of course, you could also highlight text with your mouse, right-click the selected text, and then click Copy.

After you have copied text to the clipboard, you can paste the text into a terminal window by clicking the middle mouse button at the command prompt. If you do not have a middle mouse button, press both the left and right mouse buttons at the same time. Of course, you could also right-click at the command prompt and then click Paste.

To change the size of text in the terminal window, click View and then click Zoom Out or Zoom In. To restore characters to their default size, click View and then click Normal Size.

Figure 8-7 Terminal window title change in CentOS 7

Source: CentOS 7.2/Terminal

If you are using multiple terminal window sessions, you might want to change the title of the currently displayed terminal window. In previous CentOS releases, you can click Terminal, click Set Title, type the new title, and then close the dialog box. In CentOS 7, however, this feature is not supported. To change the title of the current terminal window in CentOS 7, use the following command with bash:

PROMPT_COMMAND='echo –ne "\033]0;*[TARGET TITLE HERE]*\007"' .

Figure 8-7 shows three terminal windows; note that two have titles. Other changes, such as changes to colors, require that you edit window preferences. To access these preferences, click the Edit menu, click Profile Preferences, and then click Colors.

Activity 8-4: Working with the Terminal Window in CentOS 7

Time Required: 10 minutes

Objective: Use terminal window commands and tailor the terminal window.

Description: In this activity, you open the terminal window and practice using copy and paste commands. You also will customize the appearance of the terminal window.

1. Start your virtual machines using the appropriate instructions in Activity 1-1.

2. To open a console, click **Applications** and then click **Terminal**.

3. To display directories, type **ls** and then press **Enter**.

4. To copy the word *Public*, double-click **Public**. Right-click, and then click **Copy**.

5. To change to the public directory, type **cd** and point to a location that is at least one space from the cd command. If you have a middle mouse button, click it; otherwise, press the left and right mouse buttons at the same time, and then press **Enter**.

6. To make the displayed characters larger, click **View** and then click **Zoom In**.

7. To make the displayed characters smaller, click **View** and then click **Zoom Out**.

8. To change the colors used in the window, click **Edit**, click **Profile Preferences**, click the **Colors** tab, and clear the **Use Colors from system theme** check box.

9. Experiment with the text color and background colors.

10. To see the new color scheme, click **Close**.

11. If you are not satisfied with your color choices, go back to Step 8.

12. To close the terminal window, type **exit** and then press **Enter**.

13. Leave the virtual machine logged on for future activities.

Using the Command History in Windows 10

Both Windows 10 and CentOS 7 allow the reuse of commands. By reusing existing commands in the command history, you can save time when entering many commands in a Command Prompt or terminal session. You will learn how to use the Windows 10 command history (see Figure 8-8) in this section, and you will learn how to use the CentOS 7 command history later in this chapter.

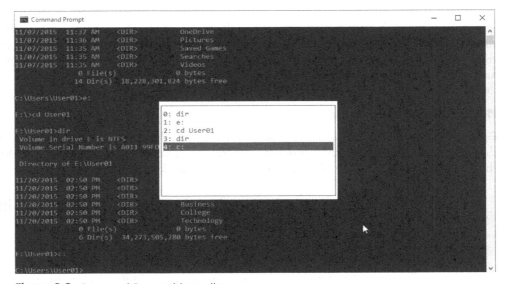

Figure 8-8 Command Prompt history list

Source: Microsoft Windows 10/Command Prompt

If you want to reuse a command that you used in the current session in the Command Prompt, click within the window and then press the up arrow. The first press displays the previous command, the second the command before that, and so on. If you go back too far, press the down arrow to go back through the list.

To review a list of previous commands, press F7 (see Figure 8-8). Use the arrow keys to move up and down the list and then press Enter to copy the highlighted command to the prompt. Press the Esc key to close the window.

Using Shortcut Keys in Windows 10

As you improve your skills with the Command Prompt, you can use function keys to speed the entry of commands. Table 8-1 lists the function keys you can use at the Command Prompt and the actions they perform.

Key	Action
F1	Brings back the last command one character at a time (same as the right arrow)
F2	Copies the current command from the history buffer to the Command Prompt, up to the character you specify
F3	Brings back the last command
F4	Deletes characters to the right of the cursor, up to the character you specify
F5	Shows the previous command in the history buffer and stops at the top of the list (same as the up arrow)
F6	Inserts the end-of-file character (^Z)
F7	Shows the command history list and executes the highlighted command
Alt+F7	Clears the command history
F8	Shows the previous command in the history buffer and cycles from the bottom when it reaches the top; also searches for matching commands in the history buffer if you enter the first few characters of a command
F9	Retrieves commands by number from the history buffer
Esc	Clears the command line
Insert	Toggles Insert mode on and off
Home	Moves the cursor to the beginning of the line
End	Moves the cursor to the end of the line
Delete	Deletes characters above the cursor
Backspace	Deletes the character to the left of the cursor
Up arrow	Shows the previous command in the history buffer and stops at the top of the list (same as F5)
Down arrow	Shows the next command in the history buffer and stops at the bottom of the list
Right arrow	Brings back the last command one character at a time (same as F1)
Left arrow	Moves the cursor to the left one character at a time

Table 8-1 Command prompt shortcut keys

As an example of using shortcut keys, consider F2, which is handy for repeating parts of lengthy or complex command lines. You can use F2 to copy the current command in the history buffer to the Command Prompt, up to the first occurrence of the character you specify.

For example, suppose that the current command in the history buffer is CD \Program Files\Internet Explorer and you want to move one directory level up to the Program Files directory. Directories with spaces in their names are cumbersome to type because they require quotation marks. To save time, press F2 and type *I* to copy the line up to but not including the *I*, as shown in Figure 8-9. The command line then contains CD \Program Files\. Press Enter to execute the command.

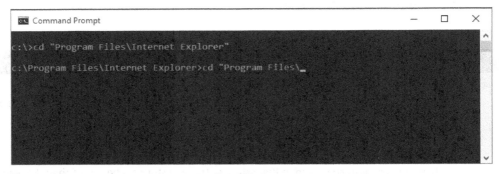

Figure 8-9 Command Prompt command completion

Source: Microsoft Windows 10/Command Prompt

Activity 8-5: Using the Command History in Windows 10

Time Required: 15 minutes

Objective: Use the command history to locate, modify, and reuse previously entered commands.

Description: In this activity, you open the Command Prompt and then practice using the command history. This activity is useful if you want to reuse commands.

1. If necessary, start your virtual machines using the appropriate instructions in Activity 1-1.

2. Click **Start**, and then click **Command Prompt**.

3. Type each of the lines in Table 8-2 at the Command Prompt, pressing **Enter** at the end of each line.

CD /D E:\User01
MD Accounting
CD Accounting
ECHO Budget 2010 > Budget10.txt
ECHO Budget 2011 > Budget11.txt
ECHO Sales 2010 > Sales10.txt
ECHO Sales 2011 > Sales11.txt
ECHO Expenses 2010 > Expense10.txt
ECHO Expenses 2011 > Expense11.txt
DIR Sales*.txt

Table 8-2   Commands to practice using the command history

The redirection operator (>) is explained in the section on console redirection later in this chapter. Also, the **ECHO** command is used to display text to the console, as explained later in this chapter.

4. To obtain a listing of the sales files, press the **up arrow** until the DIR Sales*.txt command appears, and then press **Enter**.

5. To find the files that contain information on 2010 expenses, press the **down arrow** until the FIND 10 exp*.* command appears, and then press **Enter**.

6. To find the files that contain sales information, press the **down arrow** until the FINDSTR Sales *.* command appears, and then press **Enter**.

7. To recall the last command, press **F3**.

8. To change the FINDSTR command to a FIND command, repeatedly press **F1** until Sales *.* appears, and then press **Enter**. To view the command history and select a command, press **F7**, use the arrow keys to locate FINDSTR Sales *.*, and then press **Enter**.

9. Leave the Command Prompt open for the next activity.

If you close the Command Prompt window, you will need to re-enter the information in Table 8-2 before continuing with Activities 8-6, 8-10, and 8-12.

Completing Filenames and Directory Names in Windows 10

A helpful feature at the command line and in PowerShell is filename and directory name completion. You can use it when you enter a command and are unsure of the directory name or filename that you need.

The completion feature is not enabled by default, but you can type the following command to use it during an editing session:

`CMD /F:ON`

After you execute the command, the title bar changes to indicate that filename and directory name completion is active, as shown in Figure 8-10.

To use the completion feature, type a partial directory name or filename and then a key combination at a Command Prompt; the system automatically completes the entry. Press Ctrl+D to complete a directory entry and Ctrl+F to complete a filename entry.

For example, you can type the following partial command:

`CD \pro`

and then press Ctrl+D to supply the Program Files directory (see Figure 8-10).

If multiple directory names or filenames match the characters you enter, press the key combination again to move to the next instance. When you find the file or directory you want, press Enter to complete the command. If you do not find a match, the system sounds a beep.

PowerShell works the same way as the Command Prompt. Figure 8-11 shows the directory completion from the C:\ prompt to the Program Files folder.

Figure 8-10 Command Prompt directory name completion

Source: Microsoft Windows 10/Command Prompt

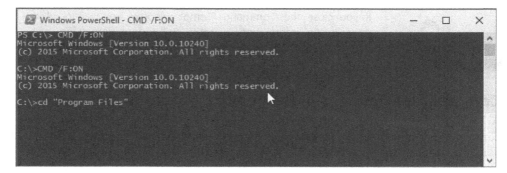

Figure 8-11 Windows PowerShell directory name completion

Source: Microsoft Windows 10/PowerShell

Activity 8-6: Using Filename and Directory Name Completion in Windows 10

Time Required: 10 minutes

Objective: Use the filename and directory name completion feature to locate files and directories.

Description: In this activity, you open the Command Prompt and practice using the filename and directory name completion feature. This activity is useful if you need help completing directory names and filenames.

You must complete Activity 8-5 before starting this activity. If you closed the Command Prompt, repeat Steps 2 and 3 in Activity 8-5.

1. Return to the Command Prompt you used in Activity 8-5.
2. To turn on filename and directory name completion for the current session, type **CMD /F:ON** and then press **Enter**.
3. To change the directory to E:\User01, type **CD ..** and then press **Enter**.
4. To see the files in the Accounting directory, type **DIR Acc**, press **Ctrl+D**, and then press **Enter**.
5. To change to the Accounting directory, type **CD Acc**, press **Ctrl+D**, and then press **Enter**.
6. Leave the Command Prompt open for activities later in this chapter.

Using the Command History in CentOS 7

It does not take long before typing the same command over and over in CentOS 7 becomes unappealing. One solution is to use the command line history. By scrolling with the up and down arrow keys, you can find previously typed commands and reuse them.

Activity 8-7: Using the Command History in CentOS 7

Time Required: 15 minutes

Objective: Use the command history to locate, modify, and reuse previously entered commands.

Description: In this activity, you open the terminal window and practice using the command history and completion keys. This activity is useful if you want to learn to use the command history.

1. If necessary, start your virtual machines using the appropriate instructions in Activity 1-1.
2. To open a console, click **Applications,** and then click **Terminal**.
3. Type each of the lines in Table 8-3 at the command prompt, pressing **Enter** at the end of each line.

```
mkdir accounting
cd accounting
echo Budget 2010 > budget10
echo Budget 2011 > budget11
echo Sales 2010 > sales10
echo Sales 2011 > sales11
echo Expenses 2010 > expense10
echo Expenses 2011 > expense11
cat budget10
echo Update 2010 >> budget10
cat budget10
ls
ls exp*
ls s*
```

Table 8-3 Commands to illustrate command history

4. To obtain a listing of all the files created, press the **up arrow** until the `ls` command appears, and then press **Enter**.

5. To find the files that begin with an *s*, press the **up arrow** until the `ls s*` command appears, and then press **Enter**.

6. To see the first entered command, press the **up arrow** until the `mkdir accounting` command appears.

7. To view the contents of the **budget10** file, press the **down arrow** until the `cat budget10` command appears, and then press **Enter**.

8. To begin a command, type **cat b** and then press **Tab**.

9. To view a list of all the files that begin with a *b*, press **Tab** again.

10. To complete the command and display the contents of the file, type 0 and then press **Enter**.

11. To close the terminal window, type **exit** and then press **Enter**.

12. Leave the virtual machine logged on for future activities.

Comparing Command Prompt Commands and PowerShell Cmdlets

PowerShell introduces the concept of a **cmdlet** (pronounced *command-let*) or small command. These single-function command-line tools are built into PowerShell. You can use each cmdlet separately, but their power is realized when you chain them in sequence to perform complex tasks. PowerShell includes more than 400 basic cmdlets.

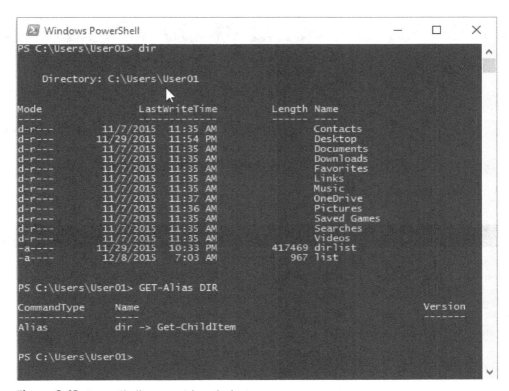

Figure 8-12 PowerShell command equivalents

Source: Microsoft Windows 10/PowerShell

Many common commands for the command line work in PowerShell. For example, most common commands, such as CD, DIR, ECHO, and CLS, will work in both shells.

PowerShell also allows you to create aliases to represent cmdlets in case you have trouble remembering some of their names. Alias commands are already built into PowerShell for easy transition from the Command Prompt to PowerShell. Figure 8-12 shows how Power-Shell interprets these commands. Type DIR and press Enter to review the listing of the current directories. Next, type Get-Alias DIR and then press Enter. You will see that PowerShell uses Get-ChildItem to produce the output for the DIR command.

To see the alias for other familiar commands, type **Get-Alias** followed by the command. For example, to see the alias for the copy command, type Get-Alias COPY. To see the alias for CLS, type Get-Alias CLS. The get-alias command is a quick way to learn equivalent PowerShell commands for commands that you learned when working with other shells.

PowerShell cmdlets are named as a verb/noun pair. The verb and noun are separated by a hyphen. As in any language, a verb conveys action. For example, consider the cmdlet Get-Date; the cmdlet is constructed from a verb (Get) and a noun (Date). Table 8-4 describes some common verbs that you might encounter when working with PowerShell. Table 8-5 lists common verb/noun pairs in PowerShell.

Verb	Description
Get	Retrieves a resource
Set	Creates or replaces data for a resource
Copy	Copies a resource to another container; also renames a resource
Out	Sends data out of the environment
New	Creates an empty resource that is not associated with any content
Add	Adds a resource to a container; paired with Remove
Remove	Deletes a resource from a container; paired with Add

Table 8-4   Standard PowerShell verbs

Noun	Cmdlet	Description
Alias	Get-Alias	Returns alias names for cmdlets
ChildItem	Get-ChildItem	Gets child items, which are contents of a folder or registry key
Command	Get-Command	Retrieves basic information about a command
Computer	Stop-Computer	Stops (shuts down) a computer
Content	Get-Content	Gets the content of the item at the specified location
Date	Set-Date	Sets the system date on the host system
History	Clear-History	Deletes entries from the session history
Item	New-Item	Creates a new item in a namespace
Location	Set-Location	Sets the current working directory
Object	New-Object	Creates a new .NET object
Path	Test-Path	Returns true if the path exists; otherwise, returns false
Process	Stop-Process	Stops a running process
Service	Start-Service	Starts a stopped service

Table 8-5   Common verb/noun pairs in PowerShell

Activity 8-8: Exploring Windows 10 PowerShell Cmdlets

Time Required: 15 minutes

Objective: Explore PowerShell in Windows 10.

Description: In this activity, you open PowerShell and explore various PowerShell aliases. This activity is helpful if you want to transition to using PowerShell.

1. Start your virtual machines using the appropriate instructions in Activity 1-1.

2. To open Windows PowerShell, click **Start** and then click **Windows PowerShell**.

3. To view the files in the current folder with a Windows directory command, type **DIR** and press **Enter**.

4. To view the files in the current folder with a Linux directory command, type **ls** and press **Enter**.

5. To view the files in the current folder with a cmdlet, type **Get-ChildItem** and press **Enter**.

6. Verify that the directory listings are the same.

7. To view the alias for the DIR command, type **Get-Alias DIR** and press **Enter**.

8. To view the alias for the ls command, press the **up arrow**, change DIR to ls, and press **Enter**.

9. To see the current date and time, type **DATE** and press **Enter**.

10. To clear the screen, type **CLS** and press **Enter**.

11. To see the PowerShell alias for CLS, type **Get-Alias CLS** and press **Enter**.

12. To create a new folder called TryMD, type **MD TryMD** and press **Enter**.

13. To see the PowerShell alias for MD, type **Get-Alias MD** and press **Enter**.

14. To change to the TryMD folder, type **CD TryMD** and press **Enter**.

15. To see the PowerShell alias for CD, type **Get-Alias CD** and press **Enter**.

16. To change to the User01 folder, type **CD ..** and press **Enter**.

17. To remove the TryMD folder, type **RD TryMD** and then press **Enter**.

18. To see the PowerShell alias for RD, type **Get-Alias RD** and press **Enter**.

19. Leave PowerShell open for a later activity in this chapter.

20. Leave the virtual machine logged on for future activities.

Environment Variables

Environment variables have long been used in computer operating systems and are present in Windows 10 and CentOS 7. In this context, *environment* refers to various features of the computer system and certain basic system data.

The environment exists in memory during program execution. Some of the environment can be tweaked or adapted by the running programs (with permission, of course) through the use of commands within the programs.

Picture a parent who teaches a child to ride a bicycle. The parent (administrator) provides an environment of a driveway (space), custom instruction (input), practice assistance (processing), standard instruction (libraries), doctor phone numbers, first aid, street monitoring, steadying the bike (security), and letting go (output). The parent might need to adapt this environment, perhaps by using an empty street instead of a steeply sloped driveway or by using training wheels. The parent could also schedule the lesson on a sunny, clear day, or increase the amount of emotional support.

Using Environment Variables in the Windows 10 Command Prompt

Environment variables are strings that contain information, such as drives, paths, or filenames. They control the behavior of various programs. For example, the TEMP environment variable specifies the location in which programs place temporary files.

Variable	Typical value
%COMPUTERNAME%	{computername}
%DATE%	Current date
%HOMEDRIVE%	C:
%HOMEPATH%	\Users\{username}
%PATH%	Varies, but can include C:\Windows\System32\, C:\Windows\, and C:\Windows\System32\Wbem
%PROMPT%	Code for the current Command Prompt format; usually PG
%PUBLIC%	C:\Users\Public
%TEMP% and %TMP%	C:\Users\{Username}\AppData\Local\Temp
%TIME%	Current time
%USERNAME%	{username}

Table 8-6   Useful Windows 10 environment variables

Values for some environment variables are established at login; these variables are sometimes called *predefined variables*. They include such parameters as the path and the name of the current user; a **parameter** is a variable that has a specific value for the operating system. Table 8-6 shows some of the more useful variables for Windows 10. The variables are enclosed by percent signs when used in scripts or at the command line, as shown in the table. Although the variables are shown in uppercase, they are not case sensitive in Windows 10.

In Windows 10, you can use the **set** command without any arguments to display all environment variables along with their values.

To see the current value of a particular variable, use the following format:

SET VARIABLE

where VARIABLE is a variable name or the initial characters of one or more variables.

For example, the SET P command shows the current setting for environment variables that start with *p*.

To set a variable to a particular value, use the following format:

SET VARIABLE=value

For example, to create a variable for your school name, you would type:

SET SCHOOL=XYZ

This value will remain stored in SCHOOL until you log out from the virtual machine or exit the current command session.

To delete the SCHOOL variable, type:

SET SCHOOL =

Activity 8-9: Viewing Environment Variables in Windows 10

Time Required: 10 minutes

Objective: Display the contents of environment variables.

Description: In this activity, you open the Environment Variables dialog box, display the current user variables, create an environment variable, and display the contents. Also, you view the environment variables available in PowerShell. This activity is useful if you want to view environment variables in Windows 10.

1. If necessary, start your virtual machines using the appropriate instructions in Activity 1-1.

2. Type **Computer** in the search box on the taskbar. Right-click **This PC**, click **Properties**, click the **Advanced system settings** link, and then click **Environment Variables**. Scroll and view the user variables for User01.

3. To add an environment variable, click the **New** button under User variables for User01, type **Mascot** in the Variable name text box, type a mascot name in the Variable value text box, and then click **OK** three times.

4. Close the open window.

5. Return to the PowerShell window.

6. To view the environment variables, type **Get-ChildItem env:** and press **Enter**. Verify that Mascot and Value are present. Leave PowerShell open for a later activity in this chapter.

7. Leave the virtual machine logged on for the next activity.

Activity 8-10: Using Environment Variables in Windows 10

Time Required: 10 minutes

Objective: Create and display the contents of environment variables.

Description: In this activity, you open the Command Prompt, create new environment variables, and display their contents. Also, you work with the environment variables available in PowerShell. This activity is useful if you want to practice working with environment variables.

1. Return to the Command Prompt you used in Activity 8-6.

2. To create an environment variable for your first name, type **SET FNAME=***John* and then press **Enter**. Type your own first name instead of *John*.

3. To create an environment variable for your last name, type **SET LNAME=***Doe* and then press **Enter**. Type your own last name instead of *Doe*.

4. To display a message with environment variables, type the following:

   ECHO %FNAME% %LNAME% is %USERNAME% on computer %COMPUTERNAME%

   Press **Enter** when you finish.

5. Leave the Command Prompt open for a later activity in this chapter.

6. Return to the PowerShell window you used in Activity 8-8.

7. To create an environment variable for your first name, type **$FNAME = *"John"*** and then press **Enter**. Type your own first name instead of *John*.

8. To create an environment variable for your last name, type **$LNAME5 = *"Doe"*** and then press **Enter**. Type your own last name instead of *Doe*.

9. To display a message with environment variables, type the following as one line:

   ECHO $FNAME $LNAME is $env:USERNAME on computer $Env:COMPUTERNAME

   Press **Enter** when you finish.

10. Leave PowerShell open for a later activity in this chapter.

11. Leave the virtual machine logged on for future activities.

The CentOS 7 Shell and Environment Variables In CentOS 7, the shell interprets the commands in a terminal session. The default shell for CentOS 7 is bash—the Bourne Again shell. Bash is an extension of the original UNIX Bourne shell.

As with Windows 10, CentOS 7 supports environment variables (see Tables 8-7 and 8-8). Most default environment variables can be read-only, changed, or added.

As an example of manipulating a shell environment variable, consider the following command syntax to temporarily set the value of the **shell variable** VARNAME:

VARNAME="ABC Company"

This value will remain stored in VARNAME until you log out from the virtual machine or exit from the current shell session. In other words, it is shell session-based.

If you type the following command and press Enter, other programs that use the variable are made aware of the new value:

export VARNAME

To delete the variable, use the unset command:

unset VARNAME

Variable	Description
SHELL	Returns the location where applications store data by default
PS1	The primary prompt string
PATH	A colon-separated list of directories in which the shell looks for commands
HOME	The current user's home directory; the default for the cd built-in command

Table 8-7 Some predefined Bourne shell environment variables

Variable	Description
BASH	The full path name used to execute the current instance of bash
BASH_VERSION	The version number of the current instance of bash
EDITOR	The name of the default text editor
HISTFILE	The name of the file to which the command history is saved; the default value is ~ /.bash_history
HISTFILESIZE	The maximum number of lines contained in the history file. When this variable is assigned a value, the history file is truncated if necessary by removing the oldest entries to contain no more than the specified number of lines. The history file is also truncated to this size after it is saved when an interactive shell exits. The default value is 500.
HISTSIZE	The maximum number of commands to remember in the history list; the default value is 500
HOSTNAME	The name of the current host
LINES	A variable used by the selected built-in command to determine the column length for printing selection lists
PWD	The current working directory as set by the cd built-in command
RANDOM	Each time this parameter is referenced, a random integer between 0 and 32767 is generated; assigning a value to this variable seeds the random number generator
SECONDS	This variable expands to the number of seconds since the shell was started
SHELL	The full path name to the shell is kept in this environment variable; if it is not set when the shell starts, bash assigns it the full path name of the current user's login shell
UID	The numeric real user ID of the current user; this variable is read only

Table 8-8   **Some predefined bash shell environment variables**

Activity 8-11: Using Environment Variables in CentOS 7

Time Required: 10 minutes

Objective: Use the shell environment variables.

Description: In this activity, you open the terminal window and practice using the shell environment variables. This activity is useful if you want to learn to use shell environment variables.

1. If necessary, start your virtual machines using the appropriate instructions in Activity 1-1.
2. To open a console, click **Applications,** and then click **Terminal.**
3. To display the current user's home directory, type **echo $HOME** and then press **Enter.**
4. To display the computer name, type **echo $HOSTNAME** and then press **Enter.**
5. To establish a variable called CITY, type **CITY="San Antonio"** and then press **Enter.**
6. To display the city, type **echo $CITY** and then press **Enter.**
7. To remove the city variable, type **unset CITY** and then press **Enter.**
8. Type **echo $CITY** and then press **Enter.** You should see a blank line before the next prompt.

9. Close the terminal window.

10. Leave the virtual machine logged on for future activities.

Console Redirection

Instead of displaying the output of a command on the screen, you can **redirect** the output to a file or printer. The following sections explain how to redirect output in Windows 10 and CentOS 7.

Console Redirection in Windows 10 Command Prompt For example, you can redirect the output of the DIR command to a file named `dirlist` with a > switch, as shown in the following command:

```
DIR /S *.* > dirlist
```

You can use this technique when you need to document the files in a directory. Using a text editor, you can then read the contents of the redirected file. Or, you can use the output to produce a report.

To send the output to a local printer, use a printer port in your command:

```
DIR /S *.* > prn
```

You can use the local printer ports (such as PRN, LPT1, LPT2, and LPT3) or a network printer in your redirection command. To redirect the output to a network printer, specify the printer using the **UNC (Universal Naming Convention) format** of `\\servername \printername`, in which you substitute the actual server name and printer name, respectively:

```
DIR /S *.* > \\Windows99\Printer
```

You can just as easily redirect input by using an < after the command.

Console Redirection in Windows 10 Using PowerShell By default, Windows PowerShell sends all command output to the Windows PowerShell console. You can use Windows PowerShell redirection operators to send output to a file. For example, the following cmdlets will redirect the folder listing to a file and display the directory listing:

```
Get-ChildItem > dirlist
Get-Content dirlist
```

With **Get-Content**, you can read and display the contents of a text file. In this example, the `dirlist` is read and placed in an object. Then the contents of the object are displayed.

Console Redirection in CentOS 7 As with Windows 10, you can redirect output to a file or printer in CentOS 7 instead of displaying the output of a command on the screen. You might be creating a report, a printout of the contents of a directory, or a printout of an ASCII file. For example, you can redirect the output of the `ls` command to a file named `myReport` with a > symbol, as shown in the following command:

```
ls -l *.* > myReport
```

If you need to append subsequent reports to this same file each day, you can redirect the output using an append (>>) redirection symbol. For example, you can redirect the output of the `ls` command and append it to the file named `myReport` with a >> symbol, as shown in the following command:

```
ls -l *.* >> myReport
```

If `myReport` does not exist, it will be created depending on the user's directory permissions.

To quickly create a text file, type:

```
echo "I am creating a new file on the fly." > newFile
```

You can use both input and output redirection with the same command, as you will see later in this chapter.

Using Filter Commands for Redirection in Windows 10 Command Prompt

Filter commands take input from a file, change the input in some way, and send the output to a file or the standard output device. They are called *filter commands* because they work like physical filters, removing unnecessary material and returning the material you need. You learned about the FIND and MORE commands in Chapter 7.

- **FIND**—Searches for a string of characters
- MORE—Temporarily pauses display output to give you time to read the lines
- **SORT**—Arranges lines in ascending or descending order

Recall that to find all of the lines containing the .txt extension, you can use the FIND filter with the input from a file called `dirlist` that you used earlier:

```
FIND "txt" dirlist
```

You can also find the lines that do not contain a particular string by including the /V switch. For example, the following command finds lines that do not contain the string *txt*:

```
FIND /V "txt" dirlist
```

Using the SORT Filter

The SORT filter arranges, or sorts, lines of input and sends the sorted output to the standard output device unless you redirect it. The SORT filter has the following syntax:

```
SORT [/R] [/+n] [[drive1:] [path1] filename1]
```

The simplest use of the SORT filter is to sort a file in ascending order starting in the first column:

```
SORT < dirlist
```

The sorted output is displayed on the standard output device. To sort the output in descending (reverse) order on column 40, for example, you would type the following command:

```
SORT /+40 /R < dirlist
```

If you want to redirect both input and output, follow the filter name with < and the name of the input file, and then type > followed by the name of a file or a printer.

```
SORT < dirlist > prn
```

Connecting Commands with a Pipe A filter is useful for redirecting the output of a command as input to a filter command. In effect, the two commands are connected, with the output of one command routed directly into a filter command. This connection is called a **pipe** (|).

Type a pipe symbol between two commands to form the connection between them. Recall that you use the MORE filter with a pipe.

Recall that the MORE filter displays one screen (24 lines) of information at a time followed by -- More --. After reviewing the screen, press the Spacebar to see another screen. For example, to display the files in a directory one screen at a time, use the following command:

```
DIR *.* | MORE
```

You can combine filter commands—for example, one technique is to feed the output of one FIND filter into another FIND filter. Because you know that the /V switch selects lines that do not contain a specified string, you could use the following series of piped filters to display filenames and omit lines that contain *<DIR>* or *File(s)* or *Total*:

```
FIND /V <DIR>dirlist | FIND /V File(s) | FIND /V Total
```

The first FIND command removes the lines that contain the *<DIR>* characters and passes the remaining lines to the next FIND command. The second FIND command removes the lines that contain *File(s)*. The third FIND command acts on the output of the second FIND command, removes the lines that contain Total, and displays the resulting lines.

Using Filter Commands in Windows 10 PowerShell

Windows PowerShell has many built-in cmdlets. Each cmdlet is specialized and is used for a specific operation. To get the most out of PowerShell, you need to understand how to direct a specific output from a command and pipe it to another cmdlet, thus refining the final output. The pipe is typically used with the following types of commands in PowerShell:

- Sorting—Arranges items in a particular order
- Filtering—Selects items to remain in a table after filtering out unwanted items using the Where-Object cmdlet
- Formatting—Makes the output look more pleasing
- Redirecting—Sends output to a file

The **Sort-Object** cmdlet sorts objects in ascending or descending order based on specified property values. You can specify a single property or multiple properties. For example, consider the following:

```
Get-Childitem |sort-object –property LastWriteTime
```

These cmdlets create a folder listing and then pass it to sort-object, where the object contents are sorted by LastWriteTime.

In case the output is more than one page, you can manage the output by piping it with the more command to the end of the previous command. If you want to sort with more than one property, make sure to separate each property with a comma. For example:

```
Get-Childitem |sort-object –property LastWriteTime, Name | More
```

Operator	Definition
-eq	Equals, which is used for finding identical values
-ne	Not equals, which includes values that are not identical
-gt	Greater than
-ge	Greater than or equal to
-lt	Less than
-le	Less than or equal to
-like	Matching operator that uses the * wildcard operator
-match	Allows you to find the values of a string that do match
-contains	Allows you to see whether an identical value exists in a list of values
-In	Returns a Boolean value
-notlike	Allows you to identify the value that does not match
-notmatch	Allows you to find the values of a string that do not match
-notcontains	Allows you to find the values in a list that do not match
-NotIn	Returns a Boolean value
-Replace	Changes the specified elements of a value

Table 8-9   Comparison operators used with `Where-Object`

The **`Where-Object`** cmdlet filters objects passed down the pipeline based on specified criteria included with the cmdlet. To use this filter more effectively, it is important to know the comparison operators in Table 8-9.

For example, if you want to include only directories that specify a *D* as the Mode (see the first column of the `Get-ChildItem` listing), add `Where-Object` (shown in bold) to the following command.

```
Get-Childitem | Where-Object Mode –Like "D*" | Sort-Object -property
LastWriteTime, Name | More
```

Using Format Cmdlets for Filtering
The most commonly used format cmdlets include `Format-List`, `Format-Wide`, and `Format-Table`.

The **`Format-List`** cmdlet displays an object in the form of a listing, with each property labeled and displayed on a separate line (see Figure 8-13). For example:

```
Get-ChildItem | Format-List –property Name, LastWriteTime
```

The **`Format-Wide`** cmdlet, by default, displays only the default property of an object. The information associated with each object is displayed in a single column. For example:

```
Get-ChildItem | Format-Wide
```

If you use the **`Format-Table`** cmdlet with no property names specified to format the output of the `Get-ChildItem` command, you get exactly the same output as you do without performing any formatting. The reason is that directories are usually displayed in a tabular format, as are most Windows PowerShell objects. For example:

```
Get-ChildItem | Format-Table
```

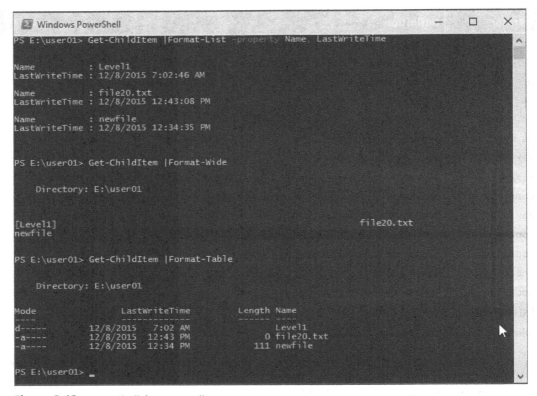

Figure 8-13 PowerShell format cmdlets

Source: Microsoft Windows 10/PowerShell

Activity 8-12: Using the Filters in Windows 10

Time Required: 20 minutes

Objective: Use the Windows 10 filters with redirection and piping.

Description: In this activity, you open the Command Prompt and practice using common filters. Also, you use the filters available in PowerShell. This activity is useful if you want to learn to use the Windows 10 filters.

You must complete Activity 8-10 before starting this activity. If you closed the Command Prompt, repeat Steps 2 and 3 in Activity 8-10.

1. Return to the Command Prompt you used in Activity 8-10.
2. To redirect the directory listing to a file, type **DIR > list** and then press **Enter**.
3. To redirect and display the contents of the list file, type **MORE < list** and then press **Enter**.

4. To eliminate the lines that contain *<DIR>* and pipe the results, type **FIND** **/V** **",DIR." list | MORE** and then press **Enter**.

The string for the FIND command is case sensitive. Type DIR, not dir.

5. To eliminate the lines that contain *<DIR>* and sort on the filenames, type **FIND /V ",DIR." list | SORT | MORE** and then press **Enter**.

6. To eliminate the lines that contain *<DIR>* and *bytes* and sort on the filenames, type **FIND /V ",DIR." list | FIND /V "bytes" | SORT /140 | MORE** and then press **Enter**.

7. At the Command Prompt, type **exit** and then press **Enter**.

8. Return to the PowerShell window you used in Activity 8-7.

9. Enter the following command on one line and then press **Enter**.

```
Get-Childitem | Where-Object Mode -Like "D*" | Sort-Object -property
LastWriteTime, Name | Format-List -property Name, LastWriteTime
```

10. In PowerShell, type **exit** and then press **Enter**.

11. Leave the virtual machine logged on for future activities.

Accessing Help for Commands

As you work with the CLI, you will become more familiar with its commands and techniques. Many users might be able to type commands without turning to a reference, but others might need to refresh their memories or discover new commands to help them complete new tasks. In Windows 10, you use Help to learn command information. PowerShell has an intensive Help system that assists you in using cmdlets. In CentOS 7, Help files are called **man pages** (short for *manual*). This section describes all three help systems.

Accessing Help with the Windows 10 CLI

To see a list of available commands at the Windows 10 Command Prompt, type HELP and press Enter. The commands are listed in alphabetical order and briefly described (see Figure 8-14).

You can display Help information for a specific command by typing the command followed by /?. For example, type DATE /? and press Enter to produce the output shown in Figure 8-15.

In addition to describing the form of the command, Help also shows tips for using the command.

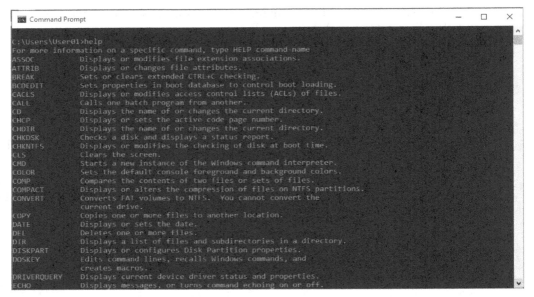

Figure 8-14 Command Prompt Help

Source: Microsoft Windows 10/Command Prompt

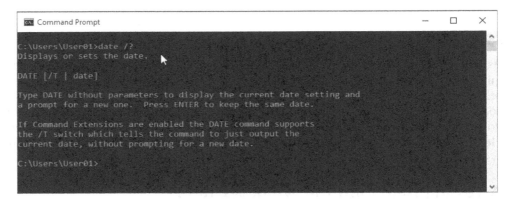

Figure 8-15 Command Prompt `date` command

Source: Microsoft Windows 10/Command Prompt

Accessing Help with Windows 10 PowerShell

Windows PowerShell includes minimal help files, but you can use the **Update-Help** cmdlet to bring your help files up to date and then use the **Get-Help** cmdlets to display the help information. You can use the Update-Help-Force cmdlet to download new help files as they are released.

The Get-Help cmdlet displays help about Windows PowerShell cmdlets and concepts. To download and install these help files on your computer:

1. Start Windows PowerShell with the "Run as administrator" option.

2. Type update-help and press Enter.

To get help about a particular command, type Get-help <*cmdlet-name*>. For example, the cmdlet Get-help Get-Date displays help for the cmdlet Get-Date. If you learn better by seeing examples, you can add the –examples switch and run the cmdlet.

Get-Help Get-Date –example

A switch controls the action of the cmdlet. Using the –example switch provides real examples and helps reduce the learning curve for PowerShell.

You can also use Get-Help to display online help for cmdlets and functions:

Get-help <*cmdlet-name*> -online

To get help for a concept or language element, type:

Get-Help About_<*topic-name*>

For example, the cmdlet Get-Help About_Modules displays help about Windows Power-Shell modules.

To search for a word or phrase in all help files, type:

Get-Help <*search-term*>

For example, use the Get-help Child cmdlet to search help topics for the word *Child*.

PowerShell is not case sensitive, but it does require proper syntax and spelling. For example, GET-DATE, get-date, and Get-Date will all produce the same result. When you enter a cmdlet in the wrong syntax or misspell a word, a message appears in red and indicates that something is wrong.

Activity 8-13: Using Windows 10 Help

Time Required: 15 minutes

Objective: Use the Windows 10 Help.

Description: In this activity, you open the Command Prompt and explore Help. Also, you will explore the PowerShell Get-Help cmdlet. This activity is useful if you want to get help using Windows 10 commands and PowerShell cmdlets.

1. If necessary, start your virtual machines using the appropriate instructions in Activity 1-1.

2. Click **Start** and then click **Command Prompt**.

3. To see a list of commands, type **HELP | MORE** and then press **Enter**.

4. To advance through the Help listing, repeatedly press the **Spacebar**.

5. To see information about the XCOPY command, type **XCOPY /? | MORE** and then press **Enter.**

6. If necessary, press the **Spacebar** to see the remaining information.

7. To scroll through the commands, click and drag the slider on the right scroll bar.

8. To see help information for additional commands, repeat Steps 5 through 7 for the commands of your choice: COPY, DATE, DEL, DIR, FIND, FINDSTR, MD, MOVE, PRINT, RD, RENAME, RMDIR, SORT, TIME, TREE, TYPE, and VER.

9. At the Command Prompt, type **exit** and then press **Enter.**

10. To start Windows PowerShell with elevated privileges, click **Start**, right-click **Windows PowerShell**, and then click **Run as administrator**. Click **Yes.**

11. To update the contents of the PowerShell Help, type **Update-Help** and press **Enter.**

12. Wait for the update to complete.

13. To see the Help for the DIR command, type **Get-Help DIR -examples** and press **Enter.**

14. To see the Help for the Get-Date cmdlet, type the following and then press **Enter.**

    Get-Help Get-Date -examples

15. At the prompt, type **exit** and then press **Enter.**

16. Leave the virtual machine logged on for future activities.

Accessing the Man Pages in CentOS 7

The man pages (short for *manual*) are the Help files you use to reference commands in CentOS 7. The man pages are structured differently from the Help files you work with in Windows 10. The man pages can be a little overwhelming at first; however, once you understand their structure and what you need to look for, the man pages become very helpful.

The man pages display the following information for a command:

- Name—The name of the command
- **Synopsis**—The syntax of the command
- Description—The description or use of the command
- Options—The variety of switches you can use with the command
- Specific definitions—The regular expressions or environment variables
- Diagnostics—The return codes associated with the command
- Bugs—Links to or descriptions of any known errors associated with the command

The number of available command options can be intimidating at first. For example, Figure 8-16 shows the list of information that appears when you type man man at the command prompt.

```
                                    Ranran                        _  □  ×
File  Edit  View  Search  Terminal  Help
MAN(1)                        Manual pager utils                      MAN(1)

NAME
      man - an interface to the on-line reference manuals

SYNOPSIS
      man [-C file] [-d] [-D] [--warnings[=warnings]] [-R encoding] [-L
      locale] [-m system[,...]] [-M path] [-S list] [-e extension] [-i|-I]
      [--regex|--wildcard]    [--names-only]   [-a]  [-u]  [--no-subpages]  [-P
      pager] [-r prompt] [-7] [-E encoding] [--no-hyphenation] [--no-justifi-
      cation]  [-p  string]  [-t]  [-T[device]]  [-H[browser]]  [-X[dpi]]  [-Z]
      [[section] page ...] ...
      man -k [apropos options] regexp ...
      man -K [-w|-W] [-S list] [-i|-I] [--regex] [section] term ...
      man -f [whatis options] page ...
      man -l [-C file] [-d] [-D] [--warnings[=warnings]] [-R  encoding]  [-L
      locale]  [-P  pager]  [-r  prompt]  [-7]  [-E encoding] [-p string] [-t]
      [-T[device]] [-H[browser]] [-X[dpi]] [-Z] file ...
      man -w|-W [-C file] [-d] [-D] page ...
      man -c [-C file] [-d] [-D] page ...
      man [-?V]

DESCRIPTION
      man is the system's manual pager. Each page argument given  to  man  is
      normally  the  name of a program, utility or function. The manual page
      associated with each of these arguments is then found and displayed.  A
      section,  if  provided,  will  direct  man to look only in that section of
      the manual.  The default action is to search in all  of  the  available
      sections, following a pre-defined order and to show only the first page
      found, even if page exists in several sections.

      The table below shows the section numbers of the manual  followed by the
      types of pages they contain.

      1    Executable programs or shell commands
      2    System calls (functions provided by the kernel)
      3    Library calls (functions within program libraries)
      4    Special files (usually found in /dev)
      5    File formats and conventions eg /etc/passwd
      6    Games
      7    Miscellaneous  (including  macro  packages  and  conventions), e.g.
Manual page man(1) line 1 (press h for help or q to quit)
```

Figure 8-16 CentOS 7 Man page information

Source: CentOS 7.2/Terminal

Activity 8-14: Using the CentOS 7 Man Pages

Time Required: 15 minutes

Objective: Use the man pages to research the grep command and its −c, −l, −m, −n, and −v switches. (You will learn more about using the grep command and its switches later in this chapter.)

Description: In this activity, you open the terminal window and use the man command with a switch to view the descriptions, syntax, and options of the grep command. This activity is useful if you need to access the man pages and research different commands and their options.

1. If necessary, start your virtual machines using the appropriate instructions in Activity 1-1.

2. To open a console, click **Applications**, and then click **Terminal**.

3. To access the man pages for the grep command, type **man grep** and then press **Enter**.

4. To find information about one of the command switches, press **Page Down** until you find the -c switch and then read what it does.

5. Repeat Step 4 for the -l, -m, -n, and -v switches.

6. To exit the man pages, type **q**.

7. To close the terminal window, type **exit** and then press **Enter**.

8. Leave the virtual machine logged on for future activities.

Displaying the Contents of Files

This section discusses some of the commands you can use to display a file's contents in Windows 10 and CentOS 7. You can use the PRINT and TYPE commands to display file contents in Windows 10. In CentOS 7, you can use the less, cut, head, tail, and grep commands.

Displaying the Contents of Files in the Windows 10 Command Prompt and PowerShell

The Windows 10 Command Prompt has two additional commands—PRINT and TYPE. With the **PRINT** command, you can output the contents of a text file to a printer. The command has the following syntax:

PRINT [/E:device] [[drive:] [path]filename [...]]

/E:device   Specifies a print device

You can use the local printer ports (such as PRN, LPT1, LPT2, and LPT3) or a network printer as the output device. To redirect the output to a network printer, specify the printer using the UNC format of *servername\printername*, where you substitute the actual server name and printer name, respectively.

Use the **TYPE** command to display the contents of a text file on the standard output device. The command has the following syntax:

TYPE [*drive:*] [*path*]*filename*

Using Windows 10 PowerShell to Display File Contents Use the Get-Content cmdlet to show the contents of the item at the location specified by the path. The cmdlet reads the content one line at a time.

The command has the following syntax:

Get-Content [-*path*] <*String*[ ] >

To see Help examples for this command, you can also type:

Get-Help Get-Content -examples

Figure 8-17 Windows PowerShell cmdlets

Source: Microsoft Windows 10/PowerShell

You can pipe the output of this command to another storage location for later evaluation (see Figure 8-17).

If you do not want to read the whole file, but just want to retrieve part of a large file, add the parameter '-totalcount' to the Get-Content command and specify the number of lines that should be retrieved.

Activity 8-15: Displaying the Contents of Files in Windows 10

ACTIVITY

Time Required: 10 minutes

Objective: Create new files and display their contents.

Description: In this activity, you open the Command Prompt and PowerShell window and explore techniques for creating and displaying the contents of a text file. This activity is useful if you want to evaluate alternatives for viewing a text file's contents.

1. If necessary, start your virtual machines using the appropriate instructions in Activity 1-1. To open the Command Prompt, click **Start** and then click **Command Prompt**.
2. To create a file with a first line of text, type the following on one line and then press **Enter**.

   `ECHO "This is a test to add content to this new file" > newfile1`
3. To add more text to the file, type the following on one line and then press **Enter**.

   `ECHO "This is a test to add content to this new file" >> newfile1`
4. To view the contents, type **TYPE newfile1** and press **Enter**.
5. At the Command Prompt, type **exit** and then press **Enter**.

6. To start Windows PowerShell with elevated privileges, click **Start**, right-click **Windows PowerShell**, and then click **Run as administrator**. Click **Yes**.

7. To change the directory to the E: drive, type **CD E:\user01** and then press **Enter**.

8. To create a new file in this directory, type **New-Item –path e:\user01\newfile2** and press **Enter**.

9. To add content to this new file, type the following as one line and then press **Enter**.

   Add-Content –path e:\user01\newfile2 "This is a test to add content to this new file"

10. To see the content of the file, enter the following as one line and then press **Enter**.

    Get-Content –path E:\user01\newfile2

11. To add more content to the file, repeat Step 9 with new text to be added to the file.

12. Review the newly added content by repeating Step 10.

13. To view only part of the file, type the following and then press **Enter**.

    Get-content –totalcount 1 –path e:\user01\newfile2

    You will see only the first line of the content in the new file.

14. At the PowerShell prompt, type **exit** and then press **Enter**.

15. To shut down the virtual machine, click **Start**, click **Power**, and then click the **Shut Down** button.

16. Wait a moment for the Windows 10 virtual machine to shut down completely.

Displaying the Contents of Files in CentOS 7

The `cat` command displays the contents of an ASCII file to the standard output device. The command has the following syntax:

```
cat [FILE] filename [-n] [-b] [-u] [-s] [-v] [-e] [-t]
```

Some of the options for using the `cat` command are:

-n   Precede each line of output with its line number

-b   Number the lines, as with the -n option, but omit numbers from blank lines

-u   The output is not buffered (the default is buffered output)

-v   Nonprinting characters except for tabs, new lines, and form feeds are printed visibly. ASCII control characters (octal 000-037) are printed as ^n, where *n* is the corresponding ASCII character in the range octal 100-137

-e   A $ character will be printed at the end of each line (prior to the new line)

-t   A tab will be printed as ^I and a form feed will be printed as ^L

The -e and -t switches will be ignored if used with the –v switch.

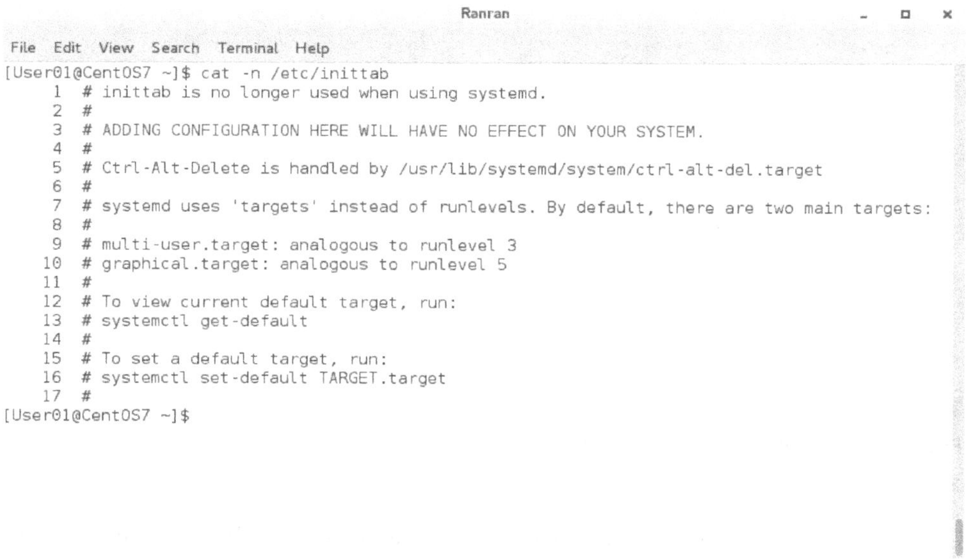

```
                                    Ranran                                    _  □  ×

 File  Edit  View  Search  Terminal  Help
[User01@CentOS7 ~]$ cat -n /etc/inittab
     1  # inittab is no longer used when using systemd.
     2  #
     3  # ADDING CONFIGURATION HERE WILL HAVE NO EFFECT ON YOUR SYSTEM.
     4  #
     5  # Ctrl-Alt-Delete is handled by /usr/lib/systemd/system/ctrl-alt-del.target
     6  #
     7  # systemd uses 'targets' instead of runlevels. By default, there are two main targets:
     8  #
     9  # multi-user.target: analogous to runlevel 3
    10  # graphical.target: analogous to runlevel 5
    11  #
    12  # To view current default target, run:
    13  # systemctl get-default
    14  #
    15  # To set a default target, run:
    16  # systemctl set-default TARGET.target
    17  #
[User01@CentOS7 ~]$
```

Figure 8-18 CentOS 7 `cat` command results

Source: CentOS 7.2/Terminal

Figure 8-18 illustrates the results of using the following `cat` command to display the contents of an ASCII file and precede each line of output with its line number:

`cat -n /etc/inittab`

The **less** command is like the `more` command, which you learned about in Chapter 6. Use the `more` command to move forward through a file and the `less` command to move backward through a file. Because the `less` command does not have to read the entire file, you can access larger files faster. The command has the following syntax:

`less [-[+]NpsS] [FILE]`

Options for using the `less` command include:

`-p pattern`	Causes the file to be read starting at the first occurrence of the matched pattern
`-s`	Causes multiple blank lines to be compressed into a single blank line for display
`-S`	Causes the excess of a long line to be discarded
`-N`	Displays the line number

Figure 8-19 illustrates the results of using the following `less` command to display the contents of a file starting at the first occurrence of a pattern:

`less -Np runlevel /etc/inittab`

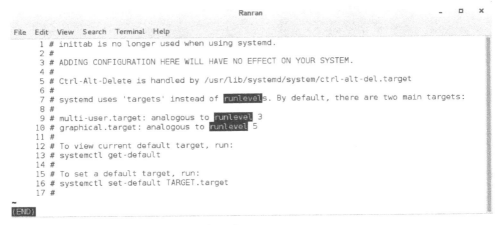

Figure 8-19 CentOS 7 less command results

Source: CentOS 7.2/Terminal

Use the **cut** command to extract fields from a file line (record). The command mainly uses the −d and −f options and prints the extracted fields to standard output unless redirected. The syntax for the cut command is:

cut [OPTION]… [FILE]…

You can use the following options with the cut command:

-c   Defines the cut by the line's starting character and length; for example, cut −c1-30 outputs the first 30 characters of each line

-d   Specifies the delimiter to use; the default selection is Tab

-f   Designates the field number, counting from left to right; the output is the field only, as opposed to the entire line

For example, Figure 8-20 shows the results of using the following cut command to print the third field (delimited by the : symbol) of the lines in the /etc/passwd file:

cut −d: -f3-6 /etc/passwd | more -10

Figure 8-21 shows the results of using the following cut command to print the first 15 characters of the lines in the /etc/passwd file:

cut −c1-15 /etc/passwd | more -10

The **head** command prints the first 10 lines from a file to standard output. The syntax and options for the head command are:

head [OPTION]… [FILE]…

-n   Prints the first *n* lines instead of the first 10; to change the default setting of 10, type a different number after -n

For example, Figure 8-22 shows the results of using the following head command to print the first 15 lines from the /etc/passwd file:

head −n15 /etc/passwd

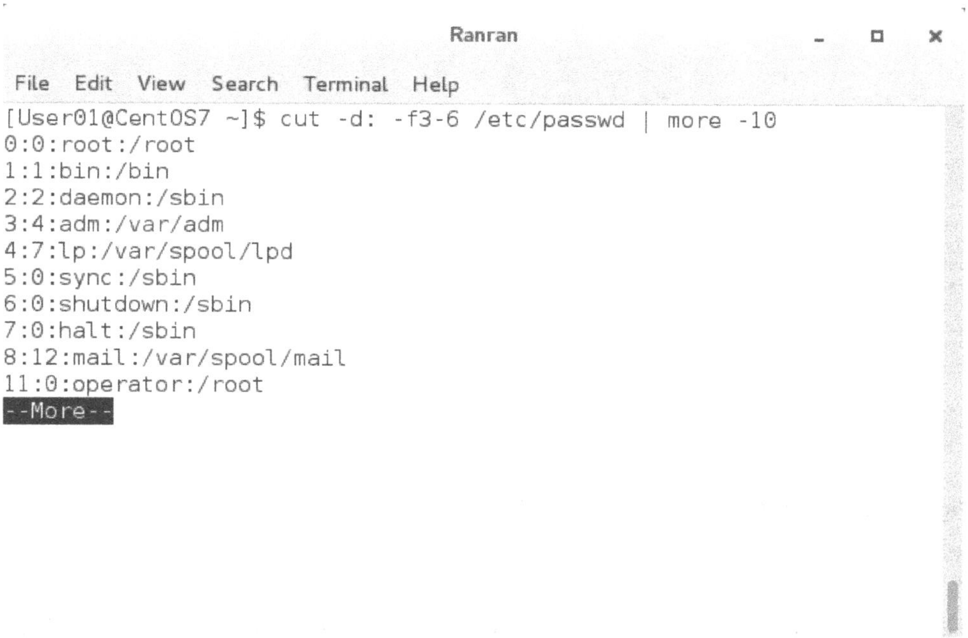

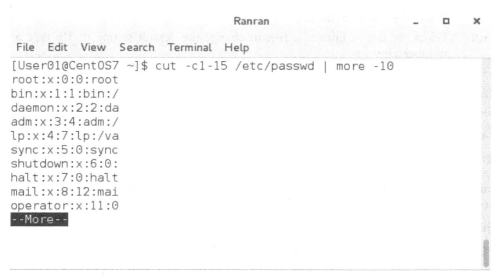

Figure 8-20 Using the CentOS 7 cut command to print a specific field

Source: CentOS 7.2/Terminal

Figure 8-21 Using the CentOS 7 cut command to print specific characters

Source: CentOS 7.2/Terminal

Figure 8-22 CentOS 7 head command results

Source: CentOS 7.2/Terminal

The `tail` command prints a specified number of lines or bytes at the end of a file and allows you to move backward through the file. Because the `tail` command does not have to read the entire file, you can access larger files faster. The syntax and options of the `tail` command are:

`tail [OPTION] … [FILE] …`

-c*N*   Prints the last *N* bytes in a file

-n*N*   Prints the last *N* lines of a file; to change the default setting of 10, type a different number after –n

-v   Prints headers that list the filenames involved

For example, Figure 8-23 shows the results of using the following `tail` command to print the last 20 lines of the `/etc/passwd` file:

`tail –n20 –v /etc/passwd | more`

You can use the **grep** command to search a file and then print all the lines that match your search. You can also list line numbers and counts to summarize your search results. If necessary, you can use wildcard metacharacters such as * and ? to refine your search. The syntax and options for the grep command are:

`grep [options] PATTERN [FILE…]`

-C N   Prints *N* lines from the file; used for formatting

-c   Suppresses normal output and instead prints a count of matching lines for each input file

-I   Ignores case in both the search pattern and input files

-L	Suppresses normal output and instead prints the name of each file from which there is no match
-l	Suppresses normal output and instead prints the name of each file from which there is at least one match; the command stops after one match
-m N	Stops processing the file after *N* matches
-n	Adds the line number to the beginning of each matching line
-o	Prints only the matching part of the line
-R or -r	Reads all files under each directory recursively; you can use this option to process an entire branch of a file system
--include=PATTERN	Indicates the pattern a file must contain before it can be searched
--exclude=PATTERN	Indicates the pattern a file must contain so it will *not* be searched
-v	Inverts the match pattern
-x	Selects only exact matches of whole lines

For example, Figure 8-24 shows the results of a grep command that prints the line numbers, count, and actual lines of text that contain the "root" pattern in the /etc/ passwd file:

```
grep −n root /etc/passwd
```

Figure 8-23 CentOS 7 tail command results

Source: CentOS 7.2/Terminal

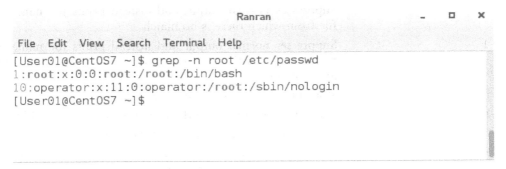

Figure 8-24 CentOS 7 `grep` command results

Source: CentOS 7.2/Terminal

When many lines will be displayed as a result of the `grep` command, you may want to use the `more` command to help display the information. Figure 8-25 shows that you can pipe the two commands together to view the information without it scrolling past:

`grep -n nologin /etc/passwd | more -10`

Notice that `-- More --` is highlighted at the end of the displayed information. You can press the Spacebar and view the information 10 lines at a time.

Figure 8-25 Results of using the `grep` command with a pipe

Source: CentOS 7.2/Terminal

Activity 8-16: Listing and Viewing Files in CentOS 7

Time Required: 10 minutes

Objective: List all files in a CentOS 7 directory, including hidden files, and view the contents of the hidden files.

Description: In this activity, you open the terminal window and practice using the `ls` command with a switch to view all the files in a directory. You also use the `cat` command with a pipe symbol to view the contents of hidden files and become acquainted with the bash history and profile files. This activity is useful if you need to view hidden files and use a pipe symbol to help control large scrolling displays of file contents.

1. If necessary, start your virtual machines using the appropriate instructions in Activity 1-1.
2. To open a console, click **Applications**, and then click **Terminal**.
3. To list all files in the home directory, including the hidden files, type **ls –a** and then press **Enter**.
4. To view the contents of the bash history file, type **cat .bash_history** and then press **Enter**.

The bash history file records all the commands entered at the command line. If you need to duplicate a command, you can do so using the bash history file with special commands. Becoming familiar with the history file can save you time.

5. To view the contents of the bash history file one line at a time, type **cat .bash_history | more**.
6. Keep pressing the **Spacebar** until you reach the command prompt.
7. To view the contents of the bash history file one page at a time, type **cat .bash_history | less** and then press **Enter**. Next, press **Page Down** until *END* appears at the bottom of the list.
8. To return to the Command Prompt, type **q**.
9. To view the bash profile file, type **cat .bash_profile** and then press **Enter**.

The bash profile file allows you to set up the shell environment, which includes the command prompt and shortcuts for frequently used command combinations.

10. To close the terminal window, type **exit** and then press **Enter**.
11. Leave the virtual machine logged on for the next activity.

Activity 8-17: Displaying the Contents of Files in CentOS 7

Time Required: 10 minutes

Objective: Display the contents of files using a variety of commands.

Description: In this activity, you open the Vim editor and then use several commands to display the contents of a text file. This activity is useful if you want to evaluate alternatives for displaying a text file's contents.

1. If necessary, start your virtual machines using the appropriate instructions in Activity 1-1.
2. To open a console, click **Applications**, and then click **Terminal**.
3. To open the Vim editor without displaying the introductory text, type **vim courselist** at the command prompt and then press **Enter**.
4. To begin Insert mode, type **i** and then type the text from Table 8-10, pressing **Enter** at the end of each line.

botany
biology
accounting
finance
chemistry
english
programming
engineering
art
calculus
networking

Table 8-10   **Text of the courselist file**

5. To save the file, press **ESC**, type **:wq**, and then press **Enter**.
6. To display the contents of the courselist file with the cat command, type **cat courselist** and then press **Enter**.
7. To display the contents of the courselist file with the less command, type **less < courselist** and then press **Enter**.
8. To quit the less command and return to the command line, type **q**.
9. To display the file contents sorted in ascending order, type **sort -f courselist** and then press **Enter**.
10. To display the file contents sorted in descending order, type **sort -r courselist** and then press **Enter**.
11. To close the terminal window, type **exit** and then press **Enter**.
12. Leave the virtual machine logged on for the next activity.

Activity 8-18: Displaying the Contents of Files Using grep in CentOS 7

Time Required: 10 minutes

Objective: Display the contents of files using the grep command.

Description: In this activity, you use the `grep` command and switches to select text from a previously created file. This activity is useful if you want to learn to use the `grep` command.

1. If necessary, start your virtual machines using the appropriate instructions in Activity 1-1.

2. To open a console, click **Applications**, and then click **Terminal**.

3. To find course names in the file that contain a *b*, type **grep "b" courselist** and then press **Enter**.

4. To determine if case matters with the `grep` command, type **grep "B" courselist** and then press **Enter**. No courses should be listed.

5. To ignore the case of the search argument, use the –i switch with the `grep` command. Type **grep –i "B" courselist** and then press **Enter**. The course names that contain a *b* or a *B* appear.

6. To find courses in the file that contain an *a* and the lines that include those courses, type **grep –n "a" courselist** and then press **Enter**.

7. To find courses in the file that do not contain the letter *e*, type the following and then press **Enter**.

   ```
   grep -v "e" courselist
   ```

8. To find the lines in the /etc/passwd file that *do not* contain the phrase *nologin*, type **grep –nv "nologin" /etc/passwd | more** and then press **Enter**.

9. To close the terminal window, type **exit** and then press **Enter**.

10. To shut down the virtual machine, click **User01** in the top-right corner of the desktop screen, click **Power Off**, and then click the **Power Off** button.

11. Wait a moment for the CentOS 7 virtual machine to shut down completely.

12. Close any remaining open windows, log off, and shut down your PC.

Chapter Summary

- Use the command line to perform tasks quickly. Knowing how to use the command line is helpful if you cannot access the GUI and the command line is the only interface available.

- A command interpreter is the part of a computer operating system that understands and executes commands entered by a user or from a program. Environment variables are strings that contain information and control the behavior of various programs.

- Windows 10 provides two shells: the traditional Command Prompt, which works with text files, and PowerShell, which works with objects.

- The Help files in Windows 10 and the man pages in CentOS 7 provide reference information for using OS commands, including command descriptions, syntax, usage, possible errors, and other helpful links.

■ Each operating system has its own methods for displaying the contents of a file; learning to display this information becomes important when you do not need to see the entire file. You can sort the information you want to display or open files in a read-only view to help protect the original contents.

Key Terms

cat   A command in CentOS 7 that displays the contents of an ASCII file on the standard output device.

cmdlet   A small command in PowerShell.

command interpreter   A computer program that reads lines of text entered by a user and interprets them in the context of a given operating system or programming language.

cut   A command in CentOS 7 that extracts fields from a line in a file or extracts an entire record from a file.

ECHO   A command in Windows 10 that displays text to the standard output device.

environment variable   A set of dynamic named values that can affect the way running processes behave on a computer.

FIND   A command or filter in Windows 10 that provides the lines to match a prescribed pattern.

Format-List   A PowerShell cmdlet that formats the output of a command as a list of properties in which each property is displayed on a separate line.

Format-Table   A PowerShell cmdlet that formats the output of a command as a table with the selected properties of the object in each column.

Format-Wide   A PowerShell cmdlet that formats the output of a command as a wide table displaying one property of each object.

Get-Alias   A PowerShell cmdlet that gets aliases (alternate names for commands).

Get-Content   A PowerShell cmdlet that gets the content of the item at the location specified by the path, such as the text in a file.

Get-Help   A PowerShell cmdlet that displays information about Windows PowerShell concepts and commands.

grep   A command in CentOS 7 that searches a file or files by keyword.

head   A command in CentOS 7 that prints the first 10 lines (by default) from a file to standard output.

less   A command that allows backward movement when you view file contents.

man pages   The Help file documents in CentOS 7.

.NET Framework   A software framework developed by Microsoft that runs primarily on Microsoft Windows.

object   A programming entity that supports data and methods (actions on data).

parameter   A special kind of data used as input to a command.

pipe   A temporary connection between two commands, represented by the I symbol.

PowerShell   A Microsoft tool that features both a shell and a scripting language.

PRINT   A Windows 10 command that outputs text to the console.

QuickEdit Mode   An option that permits users to copy text between the Command Prompt and a Windows program.

redirect   To change the direction of command output or input from the standard location.

set   A Windows 10 command that displays, creates, or removes environment variables.

shell   An invoked interface that parses and interprets command lines and code for execution on behalf of a user interface or program process.

shell variable   In CentOS 7, a variable that is local to the shell in which it is defined for its specific feature availability and efficiencies. It is locally scoped and not available to other shells. Shell variables are usually represented in lowercase format.

SORT   A Windows command or filter that arranges lines in a directed order.

Sort-Object   A PowerShell cmdlet that sorts objects in ascending or descending order based on the values of properties of the object.

STDERR   A standard device that accepts error messages.

STDIN   A standard device that accepts input.

STDOUT   A standard device that accepts output.

synopsis   A term used in the CentOS 7 man pages to describe the syntax of commands.

tail   A command in CentOS 7 that typically prints the last 10 lines or bytes of a file. For large files, this command can provide faster access to data within the file.

TYPE   A Windows 10 command that displays the contents of a text file on the standard output device.

UNC (Universal Naming Convention) format   A string used to specify the location of resources, such as shared files or devices.

Update-Help   A PowerShell cmdlet that downloads and installs the newest help files for Windows PowerShell modules.

Where-Object   A PowerShell cmdlet that filters objects based on specified criteria.

Review Questions

1. Why should you use the CLI? (Choose all that apply.)

    a. It offers a faster way to perform a task, such as renaming multiple files.

    b. It may inspire you to stay away from computer programming.

    c. It uses fewer resources than the graphical user interface.

    d. It allows you to use powerful, multifaceted commands.

2. The command history is _____.

    a. a historical document of a virtual machine's specifications

    b. useful if you need to recall a previously used command

    c. nonexistent in CentOS 7

    d. unreliable and should be used with caution

Chapter 8   The Command Line

3. The man pages in CentOS 7 display _____. (Choose all that apply.)

   a. the synopsis of a command

   b. the description of a command

   c. the known bugs associated with a command

   d. options you can use with a command

4. Which of the following commands should you use in a CentOS 7 script to print the last bytes of a file?

   a. `tail`

   b. `last`

   c. `lastbytes`

   d. `head`

5. Use the _____ commands to locate lines with certain text in Windows 10. (Choose all that apply.)

   a. `FIND`

   b. `LOCATE`

   c. `FINDSTR`

   d. `SEARCH`

6. In its basic form, the `grep` command in CentOS 7 _____.

   a. prints to the standard output device

   b. erases data from a file

   c. searches a file for a particular pattern

   d. appends data to a file

7. Environment variables in Windows 10 are classified as _____. (Choose all that apply.)

   a. user

   b. system

   c. character

   d. fundamental

8. By default, the `head` command in CentOS 7 _____.

   a. provides a detailed description of the header record

   b. only outputs the first, or head, record

   c. outputs the first 10 lines of a file

   d. only works with the `tail` command

9. You can use the SET command in Windows 10 to _____ environment variables. (Choose all that apply.)

   a. print

   b. create

   c. remove

   d. display

10. Use the ECHO command in Windows 10 to _____. (Choose all that apply.)

   a. display messages

   b. temporarily stop the program to ask a question

   c. create text files

   d. display environment variables

11. PowerShell cmdlets used for filtering are _____. (Choose all that apply.)

   a. Find-Object

   b. Sort-Object

   c. Where-Object

   d. Format-Table

12. To display the contents of a file in Windows 10, you can use the _____ command. (Choose all that apply.)

   a. SET

   b. REM

   c. PRINT

   d. TYPE

13. To display the entire contents of a file in CentOS 7, you can use the _____ command.

   a. cat

   b. head

   c. tail

   d. less

14. Which of the following symbols do you use to redirect output from a screen display to a file in Windows 10 or CentOS 7?

   a. <

   b. >

   c. ->

   d. <>

15. Which of the following symbols do you use to redirect input from a file to a screen display in Windows 10 or CentOS 7?

    a. <

    b. >

    c. ->

    d. <>

16. Which standard output devices can you use in Windows 10?

    a. STDIN

    b. STDOUT

    c. STDERR

    d. STDCON

17. Which of the following commands can you use with PowerShell in Windows 10 to obtain help? (Choose all that apply.)

    a. Get-Help DIR

    b. Get-Help ECHO

    c. DIR /?

    d. ECHO /?

18. Which of the following commands can you use in the Windows 10 Command Prompt to obtain help? (Choose all that apply.)

    a. Get-Help DIR

    b. Get-Help ECHO

    c. DIR /?

    d. ECHO /?

19. Which of the following are considered filter commands in Windows 10? (Choose all that apply.)

    a. FOR

    b. FIND

    c. MORE

    d. SORT

20. Which of the following Windows 10 PowerShell cmdlets can be used for filtering the output? (Choose all that apply.)

    a. Sort

    b. Sort-object

    c. Where-object

    d. Format-list

Case Projects

Case 8-1: Why Learn PowerShell?

You overhear a conversation between two students. One of the students asks, "Why would I need to learn to use PowerShell? I know how to use the Command Prompt." The second student turns to you for advice. How will you answer your fellow students? Create a list of responses.

Case 8-2: Displaying System Environment Variables in Windows 10

You are making a short presentation to your classmates on the Windows 10 environment variables. Prepare a handout of Windows 10 commands that display the account of a user who logs on to a computer.

Hint: To see the environment variables, open a Command Prompt, type SET, and press Enter. Include the computer name, operating system, and processor architecture. Using the ECHO command, display the environment variables with appropriate identifying text.

Case 8-3: The Contents of a Text File in CentOS 7

You receive a file called GameWinners on a USB drive from a friend and then copy the file to the hard drive on your CentOS 7 virtual machine. What command would you use to see the first 10 lines of text? The last five lines of text? Prepare a short report that provides the commands to accomplish these two tasks.

Case 8-4: Using the PowerShell Get-Alias Cmdlet

You are asked to prepare a short presentation on the PowerShell Get-Alias cmdlet. Prepare a handout that provides three examples of equivalent Command Prompt commands and PowerShell cmdlets.

Hint: Using PowerShell, enter the chosen command after the Get-Alias cmdlet.

8

## chapter 9

Text Editors

After reading this chapter and completing the exercises, you will be able to:

- Understand the functions of common text editors
- Work with individual files and multiple files in text editors
- Work with lines of text in files using cut, copy, and paste commands
- Search for character strings in documents
- Search and replace character strings in documents

You use text editors to create and revise text files, which contain important system configuration data and program source information. In this chapter, you will learn to use three text editors: PowerShell Integrated Scripting Environment (ISE) in Windows 10, Gedit, and Vim in CentOS 7. PowerShell ISE is installed by default in Windows 10. The Vim and Gedit programs are installed by default when you install the CentOS operating system.

After a brief overview, you will begin learning to use the three text editors, including working with multiple files, searching for character strings, and replacing character strings. You will also continue to learn the power of regular expressions, to which you were introduced in Chapter 7.

Overview of Common Text Editors

This chapter starts with a brief overview of three text editors: PowerShell ISE, Vim, and Gedit. Text editors are used to edit plain text files in ASCII or Unicode format. Word processors are also used for editing textual content, but they add extra formatting characters to the document by providing options for font size, boldface, italics, underlining, and other enhancements. These additions are not needed for the purpose of general text editors, which is to work with files used by the computer system. Configuration files, programming source code, and scripts are typical textual items to be modified with a text editor.

Overview of PowerShell ISE

PowerShell ISE is an integrated development environment from Microsoft for PowerShell scripts. To make PowerShell easier to use, the ISE allows you to create, edit, save, and debug scripts in a single application. Key features in the ISE include:

- Brace Matching—Locate the closing brace if you have an opening brace selected.
- IntelliSense—Display clickable menus of potentially matching cmdlets, parameters, parameter values, files, or folders as you type.
- Snippets—Insert short sections of PowerShell code into the scripts.
- Show-Command—Compose or run a cmdlet by filling in a graphical form.
- Drag and drop text editing—Select any block of text and drag it to another location in the editor.
- Parse error display—Errors are indicated with red underlines. When you hover over an indicated error, tooltip text displays the problem that was found in the code.
- Context-sensitive Help—If you press F1 when your cursor is in a cmdlet, or you have part of a cmdlet highlighted, you see context-sensitive Help about the cmdlet.

The ISE has three panes, as shown in Figure 9-1: Script, Console, and Command Add-on. At top left is the Script pane, which provides the text editor function; you can use it to write PowerShell scripts. Because the ISE is a graphical user interface (GUI) tool, you can use the familiar cut, copy, and paste features.

At the bottom left, the Console pane is a command-line shell that allows you to enter commands for immediate execution. Also, the output of scripts appears in the Console pane as

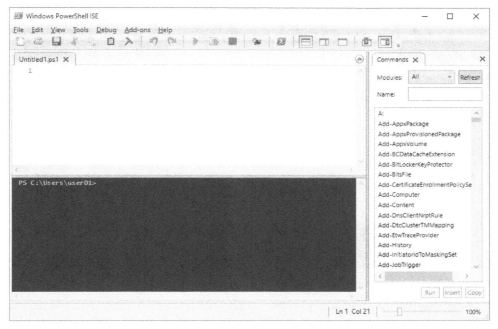

Figure 9-1 Windows PowerShell ISE application interface

Source: Windows 10/PowerShell ISE

you run them in the ISE. (You will learn to write PowerShell scripts in Chapter 10.) The version of the ISE that comes with Windows 10 merges the functionality of the Command and Output panes from previous versions into the Console pane.

On the right side is the Command Add-on pane, where you can search for cmdlets. You can also restrict your search to a particular module by selecting one from the Modules drop-down box.

Use the items from the menu bar to carry out commands, edit text, work with scripts, and specify preferences. The menu commands are explained later in the chapter.

Overview of Gedit

Gedit is a graphical text editor originally used in the graphical GNOME environment in Linux. It is now the default editor in the graphical environment for many Linux distributions. It is configurable and can highlight syntax for many programming languages, making it useful as a source code editor. Gedit also allows plugins, which can extend the functionality of the editor beyond the base application.

Gedit is a cross-platform editor, which means it can also be used in Windows. For more information, visit *https://wiki.gnome.org/Apps/Gedit*.

Figure 9-2 Gedit running in Windows 10

Source: Windows 10/Gedit

Gedit's menu bar contains many of the commands available in the editor. The default installation of Gedit in Windows 10 is shown in Figure 9-2. The basic text-editing functions of Gedit are covered in this chapter, but some advanced features and uses of Gedit are beyond the scope of this chapter.

Overview of Vim

Vim, also known as *Vi* (Vim is short for Vi Improved), is a powerful, cross-platform editor that many computer professionals use to write computer programs and text documents (see Figure 9-3). Unlike the editors you have seen so far, you do not use Vim via GUI menus. However, the same text-editing options and features are available. This editor is very helpful for Linux server administrators who are responsible for systems that do not have a desktop environment installed. Learning Vim is a challenge, but once learned, it makes system management much easier.

If you question why you need to learn yet another text editor, be aware that Vim offers some advantages and is quite different from other GUI-based editors. Vim is a purely keyboard-based editor that can be very useful in a system that does not have a type of GUI desktop installed, such as Linux Server. For example, the documents you write for your classes will be scripts, data files, and source code that a computer reads and processes, so you need an editor that allows you to do more than just "type it in." Vim offers several modes depending on your task. In Command mode, for instance, you can make minor changes to a file without having the entire document available for editing.

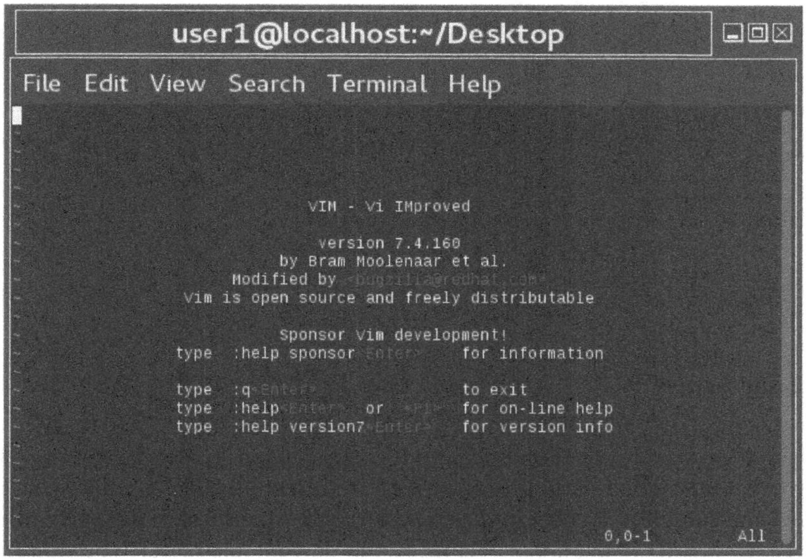

Figure 9-3 Vim running in terminal window

Source: CentOS 7/Terminal

After writing a few programs, you will discover that you do not spend all of your time typing new text, but that you frequently edit existing text. The Vim editor has two modes with distinct features that help you accomplish specific tasks during an editing session:

- **Command mode**—This is the default mode of the editor. You use Command mode to move around the file, search, and so on.

- **Edit/Insert mode**—Use this mode to enter text into the file.

To toggle between the modes, press the Esc key. This point is important to remember because you can only quit the editor from Command mode.

Working with Files

When you need to work with a file, you open it in a document editor, as shown in Figure 9-4. The editor is an application loaded into memory. It also loads the file into memory when it is opened. After you finish editing the file, you must save it—if not, your changes will be lost.

Of course, you can also start by creating a new document. Or, you may find it advantageous to open multiple files and work among them.

The editors all work with ASCII or Unicode encoded text, which includes some nonprintable characters like the newline and tab characters. While most encoded text will be the same on different systems, the characters used to signal the next line are slightly different in Windows

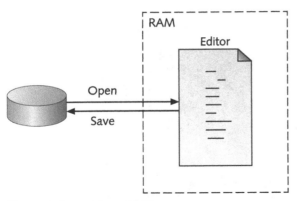

Figure 9-4 Working with files

and Linux. Linux uses the line feed character represented by ASCII decimal value 10. Windows uses a two-character combination of a carriage return followed by a line feed, or ASCII decimal value 13 followed by 10. These differences make sharing text files between systems more difficult. Text must be converted, specifically the newline character representation, or it may not be displayed properly on the other system.

Use the more command in Windows with the /P parameter to expand form feed characters to include a carriage return—for example, more /p < linuxFile > windowsFile.txt.

You will learn editing techniques using each of the three editors in the following sections.

Working with Files in PowerShell ISE

You work with files in the ISE application using a tabbed document interface in the Script pane. You can begin by creating a file or opening an existing file. To create a file, click File on the ISE menu bar, click New, and then begin typing in the script document. Press Enter when you complete a line. You can also create a new document using the Ctrl+N key combination. Each new document will open in a new tab.

To open an existing file, press the Ctrl+O key combination. As an alternative, you can select Open from the File menu. When the Open dialog box appears, as shown in Figure 9-5, type or click the name of the file you want to open. If necessary, you can select a file filter from the drop-down list, as shown in Figure 9-6. The All Files option displays files with any file extension, allowing you to open any type of file.

In many editing operations, you need access to multiple files. To open a second file, press Ctrl+O and select another file from the dialog box. The second file will appear in another tab in the Script pane.

Unless you want to reject the changes you make in a document tab, save the file before closing it. If you close a file without saving changes, a warning dialog will ask if you want to save changes. The Save option in the File menu applies to the file in the currently selected

Figure 9-5 PowerShell ISE Open dialog box

Source: Windows 10

9

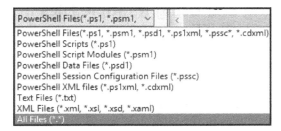

Figure 9-6 Filters in PowerShell ISE Open dialog box

Source: Windows 10

tab. To save an existing file, make sure its tab is selected, click File, and then click Save from the menu. The Ctrl+S key combination can also be used to save a file. When saving a new file, you will be prompted to enter a filename. To save a file under a new name, click File and then Save As. To perform the Save As operation using the keyboard, press Alt+F, and then press the A key. Enter the name in the File name field of the Save As dialog box and select the appropriate file type for the document in the Save as type field (see Figure 9-7). Then, click the Save button or press Enter.

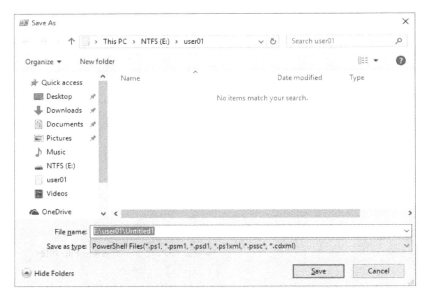

Figure 9-7 PowerShell ISE Save As dialog box

Source: Windows 10

Activity 9-1: Creating and Using Multiple Files in PowerShell ISE

Time Required: 15 minutes

Objective: Create files with the ISE editor in Windows 10.

Description: In this activity, you open PowerShell ISE and enter two short program files. This activity is useful if you want to create files in the ISE.

1. Start your virtual machines using the appropriate instructions in Activity 1-1.
2. To open PowerShell ISE, click **Start**, click **All apps,** scroll down, click **Windows Power-Shell** to expand the folder, and then click **Windows PowerShell ISE.**
3. To create a new file, click **File** on the menu bar, and then click **New.**
4. Type the statements from Table 9-1, pressing **Enter** at the end of each line.
5. To save the file, click **File,** and then click **Save As.**
6. To change to the E: drive, click **NTFS (E:).**

```
<!doctype html>

<html lang="en">
```

Table 9-1 First lines of program in HTML

7. To change the file type, click the **Save as type** drop-down menu and click **All Files** (*.*).

8. To enter the filename and save the file, type **doctype.htm** in the File name text box, and then click **Save**.

9. To start a new document in another tab, press **Alt+F** and then press the **N** key.

10. Type the statements from Table 9-2, pressing **Enter** at the end of each line.

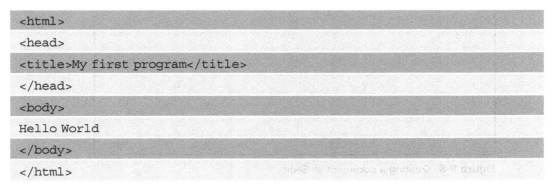

```
<html>
<head>
<title>My first program</title>
</head>
<body>
Hello World
</body>
</html>
```

Table 9-2   **Second part of program in HTML**

11. To save the file, press **Alt+F** and then press the **A** key.

12. To change to the E: drive, click **NTFS (E:)**.

13. To change the file type, click the **Save as type** drop-down menu and click **All Files** (*.*).

14. To enter the filename and save the file, type **program1.htm** in the File Name text box, and then press **Enter**.

15. To switch between windows, click the doctype.htm and program1.htm tabs in the Script pane. Note that the cursor moves to the other tab, and the filename is highlighted in the tab.

16. To close the ISE, press **Alt+F** and then press the **X** key.

17. Leave the virtual machine logged on for the next activity.

Working with Files in Gedit

To open the Gedit editor, click Applications, click Accessories, and then click Gedit. To create a new document in Gedit, click the button next to Open, as shown in Figure 9-8. Once the file is open, you can insert text in the same way you would in any other GUI-based editors. You can also change how the text is highlighted, which makes things easier when you are writing code. To change how text is highlighted, select the menu icon (which displays three horizontal lines) next to Save. Click View, click Highlight Mode, and then select the type of code being written (for example, HTML), as shown in Figure 9-9.

To open an existing file, click the Open button. By default, the most recent shortcut is opened, but you can select any file by clicking the Other Documents button at the bottom of the window, as shown in Figure 9-10. Navigate to the directory where the file is stored. Double-click the filename to open it in the editor.

Menu icon

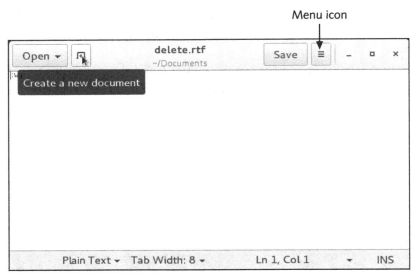

Figure 9-8 Creating a document in Gedit

Source: CentOS 7/Gedit

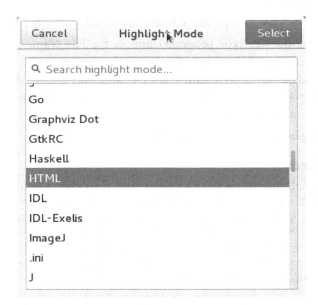

Figure 9-9 Gedit Highlight Mode selection

Source: CentOS 7/Gedit

Figure 9-10 Opening a file in Gedit

Source: CentOS 7/Gedit

9

Activity 9-2: Creating and Using Multiple Files in Gedit

Time Required: 15 minutes

Objective: Create files in Gedit.

Description: In this activity, you open Gedit and create two short program files. This activity is useful if you need to create files in Gedit.

1. If necessary, start your virtual machines using the appropriate instructions in Activity 1-1.
2. To open Gedit, click **Applications,** click **Accessories,** and then click **gedit.**
3. Type the statements from Table 9-1, pressing **Enter** at the end of each line.
4. Save the file by clicking the **menu** icon (which displays three horizontal lines) and selecting **Save As.**
5. Specify that you want to save the file in the /home/user01/Documents folder.
6. To save the file, type **doctype.html** in the File name text box and then click **Save.**

Click Replace if the following message appears:
"A file doctype.html already exists. Do you want to replace it?"

7. To open a second document, click the button to the left of Open.

8. Each open file has its own tab, so make sure that the new file you just opened is the file highlighted.

9. Type the statements from Table 9-2, pressing **Enter** at the end of each line.

10. To save the file, click the "three-line" **menu** icon and select **Save As**.

11. Browse to the directory named /home/user01/Documents.

12. Type **program1.html** in the File name text box, and then click **Save**.

13. To exit, click **X** in the upper-right corner.

14. Leave the virtual machine logged on for future activities.

Working with Files in Vim

You can open the Vim editor from the terminal window in CentOS 7 by typing the vi command. If you specify a filename with the command, the file will open. Vim always opens in Command mode. Vim is a very different type of editor; becoming completely proficient with it can take years, but it is very functional even if you know just a series of useful commands. To get started with Vim, for example, you need to use a few basic commands to open and then edit a file. Once a file is opened in Vim, notice the file information shown at the bottom of the terminal window (see Figure 9-11).

With the file open, you can start adding text using four basic methods, all of which are covered in this section (see Table 9-3). All methods use either the letter *i* or *a*. Notice that after you enter Insert or Edit mode, the message at the bottom of the window changes to *INSERT*, as shown in Figure 9-12.

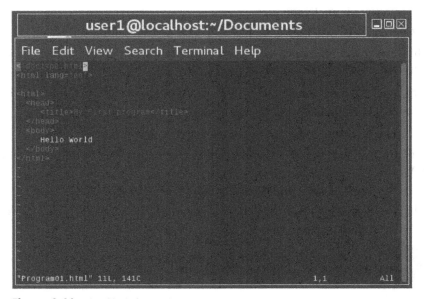

Figure 9-11 Vim file information screen

Source: CentOS 7/Terminal/Vim

Command	Results
i	Inserts text before the cursor
a	Inserts text after the cursor
I	Inserts text at the beginning of the line
A	Inserts text at the end of the line

Table 9-3   Commands for inserting text in Vim

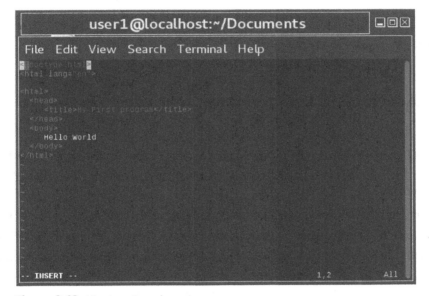

Figure 9-12   Vim Insert mode

Source: CentOS 7/Terminal/Vim

Command	Action
h	Moves cursor left
j	Moves cursor down
k	Moves cursor up
l	Moves cursor right

Table 9-4   Commands for navigating in Vim

Once you have entered text, use the Esc key to return to Command mode. When you are in Insert mode, you cannot move around in the file. So, the next important commands help you navigate the file. These commands are shown in Table 9-4.

The last set of basic commands allows you to close a file, save it, or close and save a file at the same time. These commands are shown in Table 9-5.

Command	Action
:q	Quits the file
:q!	Quits the file without saving, even if it was modified
:cq	Quits the file without saving it
:wq	Saves the current file and exits
:wq!	Saves the current file and exits
:wq (*filename*)	Saves the file under the specified filename and exits
:wq! (*filename*)	Saves the file under the specified filename and exits

Table 9-5 Commands for closing and saving files in Vim

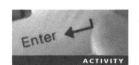

Activity 9-3: Using Vim to Create and Save a File

Time Required: 20 minutes

Objective: Open a file in Vim, enter text, save the file, and then close Vim.

Description: In this activity, you will open Vim, enter text, save the file, and then close Vim using Vim commands.

1. If necessary, start your virtual machines using the appropriate instructions in Activity 1-1.

2. To open a terminal console, click **Applications,** point to **Utilities,** and then click **Terminal.**

3. To change the directory to the /home/user01directory, type **cd /home/user01/** and press **Enter.**

4. To create your first file and open the Vim editor without seeing the introductory text, type **vi doctype.html** at the command line and then press **Enter.**

5. You are in Command mode. To begin inserting text, type **i.** The word *INSERT* appears at the bottom of the editor.

6. Type the statements from Table 9-1, pressing **Enter** at the end of each line.

7. To save the file, you must be in Command mode. Press **Esc.** The word *INSERT* disappears from the bottom of the screen.

8. To save the file and quit the editing session, type **:wq** and then press **Enter.**

9. To see the new file, type **ls** at the command prompt and then press **Enter.**

10. To create the second file, type **vi** and then press **Enter.** To begin Insert mode, type **i** and then type the text from Table 9-2, pressing **Enter** at the end of each line.

11. To save the file, press **Esc** to move from Insert mode to Command mode, type **:wq program1.html,** and then press **Enter.**

12. To view the files in your directory, type the **ls** command at the command prompt and then press **Enter.** Your two new files are listed in the directory.

13. To re-open program1.html in the Vim editor, type **vi program1.html** at the command line and then press **Enter.**

14. Instead of a blank screen, your program appears. If you accidentally enter Insert mode, press **Esc** to go back to Command mode.

15. To navigate the lines of text, press **j** to move down each line.

16. To navigate across a row, press **h**.

17. To quit, type **:q** and then press **Enter**.

18. If prompted to save changes, type **:q!** and then press **Enter**.

19. Close the terminal window.

20. Leave the virtual machine logged on for the next activity.

Working with Lines of Text

In the following sections, you learn to work with individual lines of text in the three editors. For example, you can use the cut, copy, and paste commands when working with lines of text. The principles behind these commands are similar to using physical tools like scissors and tape to cut and paste paper. Once you learn to cut and paste, your editing becomes much more productive. Of course, if you need to copy text, you can copy and paste instead.

Working with Lines of Text in PowerShell ISE

The cut, copy, and paste operations work in the ISE as shown in Figure 9-13. All three operations use a temporary holding area called an *edit buffer*. Placing an item in the buffer overwrites the previous entry in it. When working with PowerShell ISE, you can cut, copy, and paste one line of text or multiple lines. When you cut highlighted text, it is removed from the document and placed in the buffer.

A copy operation is similar to a cut. However, the copy leaves the selected text in the document and places the same text in the buffer. After you cut or copy the text, use the paste operation to insert the text from the buffer into the document at the cursor location. If you highlighted text in the document before pasting, the text from the buffer replaces the selected text.

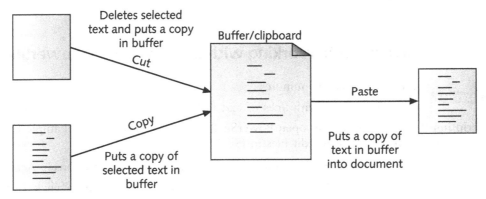

Figure 9-13 Cut, copy, and paste operations

Key	Action
Home	Moves the cursor to the beginning of the current line
End	Moves the cursor to the end of the current line
Up	Scrolls up one line
Down	Scrolls down one line
Page Up	Scrolls up one screen
Page Down	Scrolls down one screen
Ctrl+Home	Scrolls to the top of the document
Ctrl+End	Scrolls to the bottom of the document
Ctrl+Left	Moves left one word
Ctrl+Right	Moves right one word

Table 9-6   Cursor movement keys

To select text you want to cut or copy, position your mouse cursor at the first character, and then click and drag the mouse highlighting to the last character. You can also use the keyboard to select text. For example, you can hold down the Shift key while clicking the arrow keys to highlight text. Other keyboard shortcuts can be useful. For example, press Shift+End to highlight all the characters from the cursor to the end of a line. To select all text, use the Ctrl+A key combination. To cut text, type the Ctrl+X key combination. To copy text, press Ctrl+C. You can only use the Paste command to place text from the edit buffer after first using the Cut or Copy command. Indicate the new text location by moving the cursor with the arrow keys or clicking. To paste text, press the Ctrl+V key combination. Other keystrokes that will move the insertion point in Windows are shown in Table 9-6. Pressing Shift in combination with these keys will also select text.

Using the shortcut keys Ctrl+Z and Ctrl+Y will undo and redo edits in PowerShell ISE and many other Windows programs.

Activity 9-4: Working with Lines of Text in PowerShell ISE

Time Required: 15 minutes

Objective: Work with lines of text in PowerShell ISE in Windows 10.

Description: In this activity, you open PowerShell ISE and edit a pair of example files. This activity is useful if you want to edit files in ISE.

1. If necessary, start your virtual machines using the appropriate instructions in Activity 1-1.

2. To open a Command Prompt window, right-click **Start,** and then click **Command Prompt.**

3. To refresh the example files, type **makeQuote** at the command prompt and then press **Enter.** Close the command prompt window.

4. To open PowerShell ISE, click **Start,** click **All apps,** scroll down, click **Windows Power-Shell** to expand the folder, and then click **Windows PowerShell ISE.**

5. To open the Open dialog box for the first file, click **File** and then click **Open.**

6. To change to the correct path, click **This PC,** double-click **NTFS (E:),** and then double-click the **user01** folder.

7. To show the text files, click the drop-down menu of file types next to the File name field, and then click **Text Files (*.txt).**

8. To open the file, click **Quote001.txt,** and then click **Open.**

9. To open the Open dialog box for another file, press **Alt+F** and then press the **O** key.

10. To show the text files, click the drop-down menu of file types next to the File name field, and then click **Text Files (*.txt).**

11. To open the file, click **Quote002.txt,** and then click **Open.**

12. To switch to the Quote001.txt tab, press **Ctrl+Tab** until Quote001.txt is the current tab.

13. Confirm that the insertion point is at the beginning of the text.

14. To toggle to overtype mode, press the **Insert** key. In overtype mode, the cursor changes to a block.

15. To replace the line of text, type **The fool who refuses to be taught, is eager to teach others** without typing a period at the end.

16. To save the changes, click **File** and then click **Save.**

17. To switch to the other file, click the **Quote002.txt** tab.

18. Using the cursor movement keys, move to the end of the line and add a period to the end of the sentence.

19. To add a second sentence, type **A harsh word stirs up anger.**

20. To save the changes, press **Alt+F** and then press **S.**

21. To highlight all the text in the Quote002.txt file, press **Ctrl+A.**

22. To copy the highlighted text to the text buffer, press **Ctrl+C.**

23. To change to the Quote001.txt tab, click **View** and then click **Quote001.txt** on the menu.

24. To position the cursor at the end of the file, press **Ctrl+End.**

25. To paste the text from the text buffer, press **Ctrl+V.**

26. To save the file, press **Ctrl+S.**

27. To close the file, click **File** and then click **Exit.**

28. Leave the virtual machine logged on for the next activity.

9

Working with Lines of Text in Gedit

Gedit works with the Windows **Clipboard** to store or retrieve text. The cut, copy, and paste functions in Gedit are similar to those in PowerShell ISE. You must highlight text before using the Cut or Copy command. Use the arrow keys or cursor movement keys to move to the first character you want to select, and then highlight text using the arrow keys or cursor movement keys in conjunction with the Shift key. Highlighted text is shown in Figure 9-14. You can also select text for cutting or copying by dragging the mouse over it. To drag the mouse, click and hold the left mouse button while moving over the text.

To cut the highlighted text, you have the following choices:

- Right-click and then click Cut from the menu.
- Press Ctrl+X.

To copy the highlighted text, you have the following choices:

- Right-click and then click Copy from the menu.
- Press Ctrl+C.

Before issuing the Paste command, use the cursor movement keys or the mouse to move to the new text location. To paste the text from the Windows Clipboard, you have the following choices:

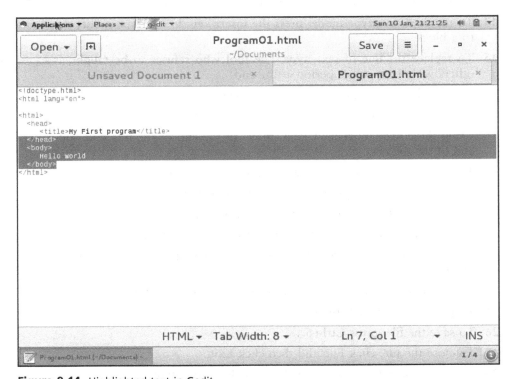

Figure 9-14 Highlighted text in Gedit

Source: CentOS 7/Gedit

- Right-click and then click Paste from the menu.
- Press Ctrl+V.

Activity 9-5: Working with Lines of Text in Gedit

Time Required: 15 minutes

Objective: Edit text using the Gedit editor.

Description: In this activity, you refresh the example files with the makeQuote script and then edit the files. This activity is useful if you want to edit files in Gedit.

1. If necessary, start your virtual machines using the appropriate instructions in Activity 1-1.

2. To open a console, click **Applications**, and then click **Terminal**.

3. To refresh the files for this activity, type **su –**, enter **Pa$$w0rd** at the password prompt, type **cd /usr/local/bin**, and press **Enter**. Type **sh makeQuote** and press **Enter**, and then type **su – User01** and press **Enter**.

4. To open the Gedit editor, click **Applications**, click **Accessories**, and then click **gedit**.

5. To open the Quote001.txt file, click **File** and then click **Open**. Browse to **/mnt/sdb1 /User01/QUOTE**.

6. Double-click **Quote001.txt**. Highlight the first line of text and then type **The fool who refuses to be taught, is eager to teach others**.

7. The original line of text should be deleted and the new line of text should appear instead.

8. Highlight the line again, and then copy it by typing **Ctrl+C**.

9. Paste the line in again by typing **Ctrl+V**. You should see two identical lines.

10. Add another line of text: **A harsh word stirs up anger**.

11. To open an additional file, Quote002.txt, click **File**, click **Open**, and then double-click **Quote002.txt**.

12. Move the cursor to the end of the file.

13. Type **Ctrl+V**. You should see another instance of the following text:

    The fool who refuses to be taught, is eager to teach others.

14. To save the files, click the **menu** icon, which displays three horizontal lines. Next, click **Save All**.

15. Close Gedit by clicking the **X** in the upper-right corner.

16. Leave the virtual machine logged on for future activities.

Working with Lines of Text in Vim

One of the Vim editor's strengths is how well it works for editing text documents. The key is to practice the variety of line-editing options that Vim provides. To cut a line from a document, for example, use the arrow keys to position the cursor anywhere on the line you want to cut and then type the dd command. If you have more than one line to cut, you can enter a number before typing dd; the number of lines you specify are cut and placed in the buffer area. For example, type 20dd to remove 20 lines of text from your document. If you make a mistake—for example, if you type 2 instead of 20—type u for undo before you move on.

Do not try to use the mouse in Vim; instead, use the arrow keys or the h, j, k, or l keys. Remember that none of these commands work in Insert mode, but only in Command mode. Before pasting lines you cut, you must first decide if you want to paste before the cursor or after it. Type a capital P to paste the text before the cursor and a lowercase p to paste the text after the cursor. Again, if you make a mistake, you can undo your action by typing u.

To place the text into the buffer, type y (which is short for *yank*); this command is like the copy command in other programs. Table 9-7 lists some examples of how to yank in Vim.

Commands	Action
yy	Copies the whole line
y(number)w	Copies *n* words
yy(number)	Copies *n* lines

Table 9-7   Yank commands in Vim

Once the text is yanked, you can paste it using p or P.

As with other editors you have already used, you can store cut or copied text in the buffer. However, it will be overwritten by the next text you cut. When you decide to cut or copy text, you should paste it immediately; otherwise, you might forget the text and then overwrite it in the buffer the next time you make a cut or copy.

Activity 9-6: Working with Lines of Text in Vim

Time Required: 20 minutes

Objective: Edit text in the Vim editor in CentOS 7.

Description: In this activity, you edit lines of text using Vim. Refresh the example file with the makeQuote script, and then use editing commands to modify lines of text and undo the modifications. This activity is useful if you need to modify text documents and undo unwanted edits.

You must complete Activity 9-5 before you start this activity.

1. If necessary, start your virtual machines using the appropriate instructions in Activity 1-1.

2. To open a terminal console, right-click the desktop and then click **Open in Terminal**.

3. To refresh the files for this activity, type **su –**, enter **Pa$$w0rd** at the password prompt, type **cd /usr/local/bin**, and press **Enter**. Type **makeQuote** and press **Enter**, and then type su – User01 and press **Enter**.

4. Navigate to **/mnt/sdb1/User01/QUOTE**.

5. To open a file in the Vim editor, type **vi Quote001.txt** at the command line and press **Enter**.

6. Verify that the name of the file, Quote001.txt, appears at the bottom of the editor window.

7. To practice cutting a line of text, type **dd** on the first line. (There should be two lines of the same text from the previous activity, but only one after the *dd*.)

8. To paste the line back into the text, move the cursor to the end of the file by pressing **j** and **l** until the cursor is on the last line. At the end of the line, press **P**.

9. To undo the edits (because the text was pasted incorrectly), press **u**.

10. To move the cursor up a line, press **k** and then press **P**.

11. To move the cursor to the first line in the file, press **k** until the cursor is on the first line.

12. To "yank" the text into the buffer, type **yy**.

13. Press **l** until the cursor is at the end of the line.

14. To paste the text, press **p**.

15. Verify that the text is pasted to the right of the cursor.

16. To undo the paste operation and then paste the text correctly, press **u** and then press **P**.

17. To save your file and quit the editor, type **:wq** and then press **Enter**.

18. Close the terminal window.

19. Leave the virtual machine logged on for the next activity.

Searching for Text Strings

A handy feature in text editors is the Search or Find command, which lets you locate a **text string** (a series of characters) in a document. Because the text may appear more than once in a document, you may have to repeat the search to find the occurrence of the text you want.

In the following sections, you learn to search for text strings in each of the three editors.

Searching for Text Strings in PowerShell ISE

To search for text strings in the ISE, press the Ctrl+F key combination. The Find dialog box appears, as shown in Figure 9-15. Type the text string that you want to search for in the Find what text box. If you are searching for a particular word, press Alt+W or click the Whole word check box to match only the whole word. If you need to search with a text string that has both uppercase and lowercase characters, press Alt+C or click the Match case check box to make the search case sensitive. Click the Find Next button to start the search, and click the Find Next button again to find the next occurrence of the search text.

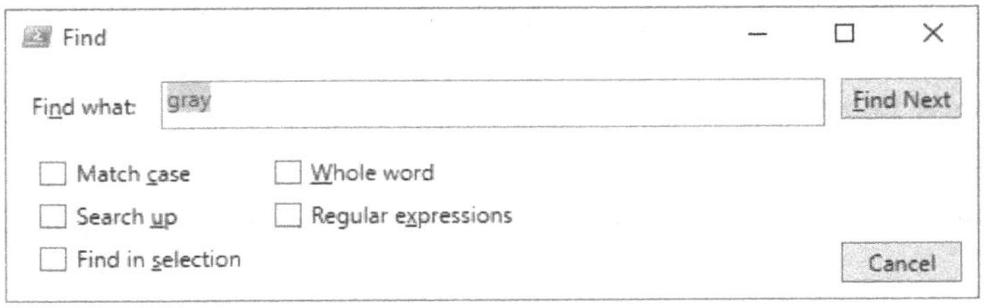

Figure 9-15 Find dialog box in PowerShell ISE

Source: Windows 10

You used the * and ? wildcard characters to search for the contents of files in Chapters 7 and 8. For example, you can search using a pattern such as [B?T], where the question mark matches any single character. This pattern matches *Bat*, *Bet*, *Bit*, *Bot*, and *But*. As you learned in Chapter 7, this is an example of a *regular expression*, in which a sequence of characters defines a search pattern, mainly for use in string matching or search-and-replace operations. Another way to express the preceding search pattern is -- B[AEIOU]T.

Activity 9-7: Searching for Text Strings in PowerShell ISE

Time Required: 15 minutes

Objective: Search for text in PowerShell ISE in Windows.

Description: In this activity, you search for text strings. This activity is useful if you want to search for text using PowerShell ISE.

1. If necessary, start your virtual machines using the appropriate instructions in Activity 1-1.
2. To open a Command Prompt window, right-click **Start,** and then click **Command Prompt.**
3. To refresh the example files, type **makeQuote** at the command prompt and then press **Enter.** Close the command prompt window.
4. To open PowerShell ISE, click **Start,** click **All apps,** scroll down, click **Windows Power-Shell** to expand the folder, and then click **Windows PowerShell ISE.**
5. To open the Open dialog box, click **File** and then click **Open.**
6. To change to the correct path, click **This PC,** double-click **NTFS (E:),** and then double-click the **user01** folder.
7. To show text files, click the drop-down menu of file types next to the File name field, and then click **Text Files (*.txt).**
8. To open the file, click **Quote007.txt,** and then click **Open.**
9. To search for the first occurrence of *greater*, click **Edit,** click **Find in script,** type **greater,** and then press **Enter.**
10. Verify that the word *greater* is highlighted.
11. To find the next occurrence, click the **Find Next** button.

12. Verify that the second occurrence of the word *greater* is highlighted.

13. Click the **Find Next** button.

14. To clear the "cannot find" error dialog box, click **OK**.

15. To find a previous match, click the **Search up** check box, and click the **Find Next** button.

16. Verify that the first occurrence of the word *greater* is highlighted.

17. Click the **Search up** check box to uncheck it.

18. To cancel the search, click the **Cancel** button.

19. To return to the start of the document, press **Ctrl+Home**.

20. To search for the first occurrence of *the*, press **Ctrl+F**, type the word **the** in the Find what text box, press **Alt+C** to check the Match case check box, and then press **Enter**.

21. Verify that the first occurrence of the word *the* in lowercase is highlighted and that the search skips the word *The* starting with an uppercase *T*.

22. To close the search dialog box, click the **Cancel** button.

23. To repeat the search for additional occurrences of *the* without reopening the search dialog box, press **F3**.

24. To find previous occurrences of *the* without reopening the search dialog box, press **Shift+F3**.

25. Exit PowerShell ISE.

26. Leave the virtual machine logged on for the next activity.

Activity 9-8: Searching for Text Strings Using Regular Expressions in PowerShell ISE

Time Required: 15 minutes

Objective: Search for text using regular expressions in the PowerShell ISE editor.

Description: In this activity, you search for text using regular expressions in PowerShell ISE. This activity is useful if you want to learn to search for text using regular expressions in ISE.

1. If necessary, start your virtual machines using the appropriate instructions in Activity 1-1.

2. To open a Command Prompt window, right-click **Start**, and then click **Command Prompt**.

3. To refresh the example files, type **makeQuote** at the command prompt and then press **Enter**. Close the command prompt window.

4. To open PowerShell ISE, click **Start**, click **All apps**, scroll down, click **Windows PowerShell** to expand the folder, and then click **Windows PowerShell ISE**.

5. To open the Open dialog box, click **File** and then click **Open**.

6. To change to the correct path, click **This PC**, double-click **NTFS (E:)**, and then double-click the **user01** folder.

7. To show text files, click the drop-down menu of file types next to the File name field, and then click **Text Files (*.txt)**.

8. To open the file, click **Quote009.txt**, and then click **Open**.

9. To search for occurrences of the letter *h* followed by a vowel, click **Edit**, click **Find in script**, type h[aeiou] in the Find what text box, click to check the **Regular expressions** check box, and then click the **Find Next** button.

10. Verify that the letter *h* followed by a vowel is highlighted.

11. To find the next occurrence, click the **Find Next** button.

12. Verify that the second occurrence of the letter *h* followed by a vowel is highlighted.

13. Continue to click the **Find Next** button until all occurrences are found.

14. To clear the "cannot find" error dialog box, click **OK**.

15. To cancel the search, click the **Cancel** button.

16. To return to the start of the document, press **Ctrl+Home**.

17. To search for a text pattern that includes the letter *r* followed by any three characters followed by the letter *s*, press **Ctrl+F**, type **r...s** in the Find what text box, verify that the **Regular expressions** check box is still checked, and then press **Enter**.

18. Verify that the word *rocks* is highlighted.

19. To find the next occurrence, click the **Find Next** button.

20. Verify that the word *rules* is highlighted.

21. Exit PowerShell ISE.

22. Leave the virtual machine logged on for the next activity.

Searching for Text Strings in Gedit

To open the Find dialog box shown in Figure 9-16, click the menu icon next to the Save button and then select Find. The Find dialog box remains on the screen until you close it. Type the text string you want to find in the Find text box. All instances of the text that match the string are highlighted. The up and down arrows allow you to move up or down through the searched strings.

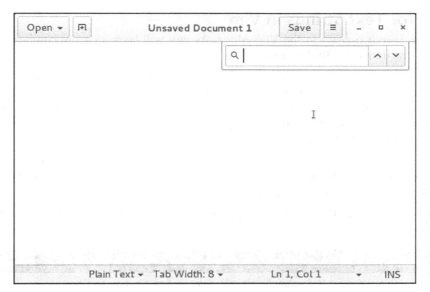

Figure 9-16 Find feature in Gedit

Source: CentOS 7/Gedit

Activity 9-9: Searching for Text Strings in Gedit

Time Required: 15 minutes

Objective: Search for text using the Gedit editor.

Description: In this activity, you open Gedit and search for text in the file you created earlier. This activity is useful if you want to learn to search for text using Gedit.

1. If necessary, start your virtual machines using the appropriate instructions in Activity 1-1.

2. To start Gedit, click **Applications**, click **Accessories,** and then click **gedit**.

3. To begin opening the program1.htm file, click **File** and then click **Open**.

4. Navigate to /home/user01/documents.

5. Double-click **program1.htm**.

6. Click the **menu** icon, click **Find**, and type **title** in the box. The word is highlighted as
   you type.

7. Verify that *title* is highlighted.

8. To being searching for the word *Hello*, click the **menu** icon, and then press **Ctrl+F**.

9. In the find box, type **Hello**.

10. Verify that *Hello* is highlighted.

11. To close all the files, click the **X** in the upper-right corner. Click **Close without Saving**.

12. Leave the virtual machine logged on for the next activity.

Searching for Text Strings in Vim

You have many search options in the Vim editor. As you will learn in an upcoming activity, Vim highlights the items you find in a successful search operation.

If you need to perform multiple searches and remove the highlighting, type either `:noh` or `:nohl` and press Enter. The `nohighlight` command is useful to remember, especially when using the Vim editor in a student lab where other students may have performed searches and left text highlighted. Highlighting is considered "sticky"; it remains from one session to the next and can be distracting if you are not doing searches.

To search for more than one word or command, use regular expressions. As with the other editors, you can substitute characters for other characters, locate the beginning and end of a line, and find special characters in programming documents.

Table 9-8 contains a partial list of expressions that you may find useful when doing text searches in the Vim editor.

Expression	Explanation
.	Finds a single character (for example, *b.t* matches *bat*, *bet*, *bit*, *bot*, and *but*)
[ ]	Finds any one of the characters in the brackets, or any of a range of characters separated by a hyphen or a character class operator (for example, *b[aeiou][a-z]* matches *bat*, *ben*, *bit*, *bop*, and *but*; *[A-Za-z]* matches any single letter; and *x[0-9]* matches *x0*, *x1*, ..., *x9*)
[^]	Finds any characters except those after the caret (^); for example, *b[^u]t* matches *bat*, *bit*, and *bot*, but not *but*
^	Finds characters at the start of a line (for example, *^the* only matches *the* when it is the first word on a line)
$	Finds characters at the end of a line, excluding line-break characters (for example, *end$* only matches *end* when it is the last word on a line)
\<	Finds the start of a word
\>	Finds the end of a word
\t	Finds the tab character
\f	Finds the page break (form feed) character
\n	Finds a newline character, which is useful for matching expressions that span line boundaries; this cannot be followed by operators such as *, +, or {}
*	Matches zero or more of the preceding characters (for example, *bo*p* matches *bp*, *bop*, and *boop*)
\{count\}	Matches the specified number of preceding characters (for example, *bo\{2\}p* matches *boop*, but not *bop*)
\{min,\}	Matches at least the specified number of preceding characters (for example, *bo\{1,\}p* matches *bop* and *boop*, but not *bp*)
\{min,max\}	Matches between the minimum and maximum numbers of the preceding characters (for example, *bo\{1,2\}p* matches *bop* and *boop*, but not *bp* or *booop*)
|	Matches either the expression to its left or its right (for example, *bop|boop* matches *bop* or *boop*)
\	"Escapes" the special meaning of the above expressions so that they can be matched as literal characters; hence, to match a literal "\", you must use "\\" (for example, "\<" matches the start of a word, but "\\<" matches "\<")

Table 9-8 Regular expressions used in Vim editor

Activity 9-10: Searching for Text Strings in Vim

Time Required: 10 minutes

Objective: Search for text strings in the Vim editor in CentOS 7.

Description: In this activity, you search documents for text strings using Vim. Open a file and search the text using complete words and single letters. Remove highlighting after your search to prepare for the next search. This activity is useful if you need to find particular words, letters, or special characters in a Vim document.

1. If necessary, start your virtual machines using the appropriate instructions in Activity 1-1.

2. Open a terminal window by right-clicking the desktop and then clicking **Open in Terminal**.

3. To refresh the files for this activity, type **su –**, enter **Pa$$w0rd** at the password prompt, type **cd /usr/local/bin**, and press **Enter**.

4. Type **makeQuote** and press **Enter**, and then type **su – User01** and press **Enter**.

5. Navigate to the **/mnt/sdb1/User01/QUOTE** directory.

6. To open the file in the Vim editor, type **vi Quote007.txt** at the command line and press **Enter**.

7. Verify that the name of the file, Quote007.txt, appears at the bottom of the editor window.

8. To find the word *Greater*, type **/Greater** and press **Enter**. To turn off the highlighting, type either **:noh** or **:nohl** and press **Enter**.

9. To search for the next instance of *Greater*, type **n**.

10. To find all instances of the letter *e* in the text, type **/e** and press **Enter**. Notice that all embedded characters are highlighted.

11. To quit the editing session, type **:q** and press **Enter**.

12. Close the terminal window.

13. Leave the virtual machine logged on for the next activity.

Activity 9-11: Searching for Text Strings Using Regular Expressions in Vim

Time Required: 15 minutes

Objective: Search for text using regular expressions in the Vim editor.

Description: In this activity, you search a text document in Vim using regular expressions. This activity helps you learn to search for text when you are not sure about exact spelling or the correct characters to use. Knowing how to work with highlighted text also helps in future text searches using Vim.

1. If necessary, start your virtual machines using the appropriate instructions in Activity 1-1.

2. To open a terminal console, right-click the desktop and click **Open in Terminal**.

3. To refresh the files for this activity, type **su –**, enter **Pa$$w0rd** at the password prompt, type **cd /usr/local/bin**, and press **Enter**.

4. Type **makeQuote** and press **Enter**, and then type **su – User01** and press **Enter**.

5. Navigate to the **/mnt/sdb1/User01/QUOTE** directory.

6. To open the file in the Vim editor, type **vi Quote009.txt** at the command line and press **Enter**.

7. To search for lines containing strings that start with an *h* and are followed by a vowel, type **:/h[aeiou]** and press **Enter**.

8. Verify that lines in the file contain the highlighted text.

9. To clear the highlighting, type either **:noh** or **:nohl** and press **Enter**.

10. To search for lines containing strings that start with an *r* and are followed by an *o* or a *u* and then a *c* or an *l*, type **:/r[ou][cl]** and press **Enter**.

11. Verify that *rocks* and *rules* have highlighted text.

12. To clear the highlighting, type either **:noh** or **:nohl** and press **Enter**.

13. To close the Vim editor, type **:q** and then press **Enter**.

14. Close the terminal window.

15. Leave the virtual machine logged on for future activities.

Searching and Replacing Text Strings

Another handy tool when you work with text strings is the search-and-replace operation, also known as *Find and Replace*. This operation lets you replace a text string with another string throughout a document. For example, if you repeatedly assigned the wrong name to an item in a document, you can use a search-and-replace operation to fix the problem quickly.

Most text editors have two search-and-replace modes. In the first mode, the text editor automatically makes all the replacements in the document. In the second mode, the text editor requires you to approve each replacement. The latter method is better when you do not want to make the change everywhere in the document.

Searching and Replacing Text Strings in PowerShell ISE

To search and replace text strings in the ISE, press the Ctrl+H key combination. The Replace dialog box appears, as shown in Figure 9-17. Type the text string you want to search for in the Find what text box, and then type the replacement text string in the Replace with text box. If you are searching for a word, press Alt+W or click the Whole word check box to match the search text to a whole word. If you need to search with a text string that has uppercase and lowercase characters, press Alt+C or click the Match case check box to match the case of the search string text. Click the Find Next button to start the search. When a match is found, click the Replace button to change the text or click the Find Next button to find the next match. To replace all occurrences of matches, click the Replace All button.

Replace	— □ ×

Fi**n**d what: gray   **F**ind Next

Re**p**lace with: grey   **R**eplace

☐ Match **c**ase   ☐ **W**hole word   Replace A**l**l

☐ Search **u**p   ☐ Regular e**x**pressions

☐ Find in **s**election   Cancel

Figure 9-17 Replace dialog box in PowerShell ISE

Source: Windows 10

Activity 9-12: Searching and Replacing Text Strings in PowerShell ISE

Time Required: 15 minutes

Objective: Search and replace text in PowerShell ISE in Windows.

Description: In this activity, you search for one text string and replace it with another. This activity is useful if you want to replace the same text several times in a file using the ISE.

1. If necessary, start your virtual machines using the appropriate instructions in Activity 1-1.

2. To open a Command Prompt window, right-click **Start**, and then click **Command Prompt**.

3. To refresh the example files, type **makeQuote** at the command prompt and then press **Enter**.

4. To open PowerShell ISE, click **Start**, click **All apps**, scroll down, click **Windows Power-Shell** to expand the folder, and then click **Windows PowerShell ISE**.

5. To open the Open dialog box, click **File** and then click **Open**.

6. To change to the correct path, click **This PC**, double-click **NTFS (E:)**, and then double-click the **user01** folder.

7. To show the text files, click the drop-down menu of file types next to the File name field, and then click **Text Files (*.txt)**.

8. To open the file, click **Quote003.txt**, and then click **Open**.

9. To open the Replace dialog box, press the **Ctrl+H** key combination.

10. In the Find what text box, type the word **gray**.

11. In the Replace with text box, type the word **grey**.

12. To search for the first occurrence of *gray*, click **Find Next**.

13. To replace the text, click **Replace**.

14. Verify that the word *gray* replaced the word *grey*.

15. If necessary, clear the "cannot find" error dialog box, and then click **OK**.

16. Exit PowerShell ISE.

17. To shut down the virtual machine, click **Start**, click **Power**, and then click the **Shut Down** button.

18. Wait a moment for the Windows 10 virtual machine to shut down completely.

Searching and Replacing Text Strings in Gedit

To open the Replace dialog box in Gedit, click the menu icon and select Find and Replace. The Replace dialog box appears (see Figure 9-18). Type the search string in the Search for box. If you want to use a previous search string, click the drop-down arrow for the box. Type the replacement text string in the Replace with text box. To use a previous replacement string, click the drop-down arrow, and then click the text string you want.

After entering the search and replacement text strings, you have a number of options for tailoring and refining your search:

- Match case
- Match entire word only
- Match as regular expression
- Search backwards
- Wrap around

To select any or all of these options, click to insert a check for each option you want.

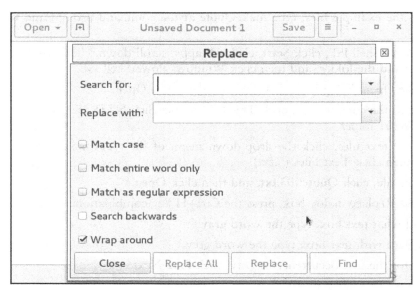

Figure 9-18 Replace window in Gedit

Source: CentOS 7/Gedit

Activity 9-13: Searching and Replacing Text Strings in Gedit

Time Required: 15 minutes

Objective: Search and replace text strings using the Gedit editor.

Description: In this activity, you search for one text string and replace it with another. This activity is useful if you want to replace the same text several times in a Gedit file.

1. If necessary, start your virtual machines using the appropriate instructions in Activity 1-1.
2. To open Gedit, click **Applications**, click **Accessories**, and then click **gedit**.
3. To open the quote003.txt file, click **File**, click **Open**, navigate to the **/mnt/sdb1/User01 /QUOTE** directory, and then double-click **quote003.txt**.
4. To replace the first instance of *bit* with *five*, first click the **menu** icon and then select **Find and Replace**.
5. Type **bit**, press **Tab** twice, type **five**, click **Find**, and then click **Replace**.
6. Verify that the first sentence changed to *I bet a five on the big red bag.*
7. To replace each occurrence of the word *bug* with *wasp*, first click the **menu** icon and select **Find and Replace**.
8. In the Search for text box, type **bug**. In the Replace with text box, type **wasp** and then click **Replace All**.
9. Verify that two occurrences of *bug* changed to *wasp*.
10. Close Gedit by clicking the **X** in the upper-right corner.
11. Leave the virtual machine logged on for the next activity.

Searching and Replacing Text Strings in Vim

In Vim, the term used for search-and-replace operations is *substitution*; you need to know this before using the Vim help manual. The placement of the cursor causes most of the frustration with the : substitution command, though some users blame the command itself. The basic command syntax used for searching and replacing a string is:

- `:%s/pattern/string`
- `:s/pattern/string`

Figure 9-19 shows a program before any changes are made. The cursor is located at the line to change. Figure 9-20 shows the effect of the search-and-replace operation without a specified range. Notice that *Starting* is replaced with *Finishing* on one line.

You might become frustrated if Vim does not find a pattern and make replacements. If so, consider whether to search the whole document or just a range of lines in it. A basic search does not encompass the entire document; it only searches for the pattern on the line that contains the cursor, and then displays an error message if the search finds nothing. To replace a word throughout the whole document, start with the cursor located at the beginning of the

Figure 9-19 Searching and replacing text strings in Vim

Source: CentOS 7/Terminal/Vim

Figure 9-20 Results of searching and replacing in Vim

Source: CentOS 7/Terminal/Vim

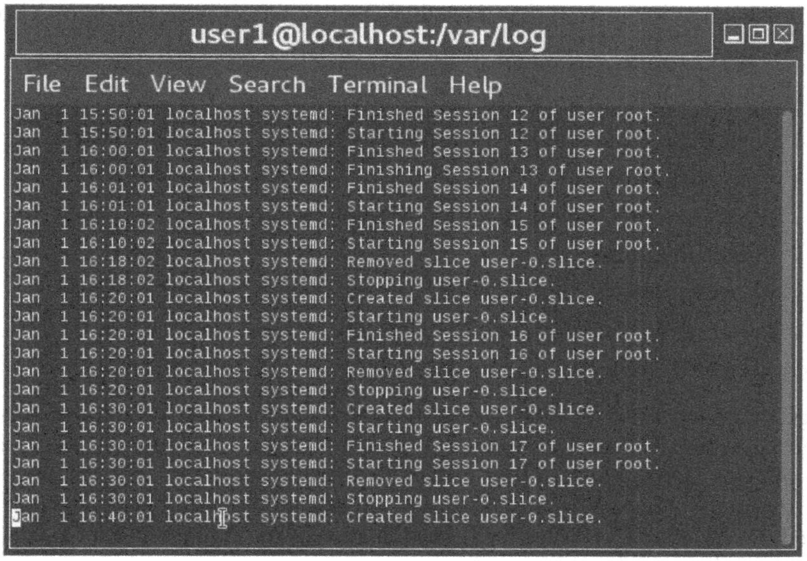

Figure 9-21 Searching and replacing text in the entire document

Source: CentOS 7/Terminal/Vim

program. Then, to perform a search-and-replace operation on the entire document, use the following syntax:

```
%s/"string"/"string"/g
```

The results are shown in Figure 9-21. To continue from the previous example, all instances of *Started* have been replaced with *Finished*.

You can use the following search-and-replace syntax and options:

```
:[range]sub /{pattern}/{string} [&] [c] [g]
```

[range]   Specifies which lines you want to search for the pattern; if you are uncertain about the range of lines to specify, use a wildcard like %, which starts the search from the beginning of the document. The following example would replace all occurrences of *bug* with *wasp*:

```
:% s/bug/wasp:
```

A few of the flags that you can use to improve a search-and-replace operation are more helpful with a little explanation:

[&]   Uses the previous search pattern; if you used flags in the previous search, the search works differently. To keep the same flags in your search, use the following command:

```
:sub &&
```

[c]   Confirms each substitution; this flag displays a question with one-letter choices:

      'y'   Yes, substitute this match

      'l'   Yes, substitute this match

      'n'   Skips this match and goes to the next match

      Esc   Quits substituting

      'a'   Substitutes this and all remaining matches

      'q'   Quits substituting

^E   Scrolls the screen up (same as Ctrl+E)

^Y   Scrolls the screen down (same as Ctrl+Y)

[g]   Performs a global replacement in a line or within a specified range

Search-and-replace operations are more effective when you use regular expressions; in fact, some advanced searches are nearly impossible without them. Learning the many combinations of these options can seem daunting at first, but eventually you will discover favorites and use them frequently. Special characters, also known as "magic" characters in the Vim editor, are used as wildcards in search patterns and strings. Table 9-9 lists some common magic characters used in regular expressions.

The following examples show you how to use some of these special characters in regular expressions to perform a search and replace:

`:s/a|b/xxx\0xxx/g`	Modifies *a b* to *xxxaxxx xxxbxxx*
`:s/\([abc]\)\([efg]\)/\2\1/g`	Modifies *af fa bg* to *fa fa gb*
`:s/abcde/abc^Mde/`	Modifies *abcde* to *abc*; *de* will be placed on the next line

Magic character	Special meaning
\0	Replaces text with the whole matched pattern
\1	Replaces text with the matched pattern in the first pair of ( )
\2	Replaces text with the matched pattern in the second pair of ( )
\n	Replaces text with the matched pattern in the *n*th pair of ( )
\9	Replaces text with the matched pattern in the ninth pair of ( )
\u	Makes the next character uppercase
\	Makes the next character lowercase
^M	Splits a line in two; to enter this command, press Ctrl+V and then press Enter
\b	Inserts a Backspace character (which may appear as ^H in the text)
\t	Inserts a Tab character
\\	Inserts a single backslash

Table 9-9 Magic characters for search-and-replace operations

Activity 9-14: Searching and Replacing Text Strings in Vim

Time Required: 20 minutes

Objective: Search and replace text strings in the Vim editor.

Description: In this activity, you search and replace a text string using the : substitution command. This activity is useful if you need to modify a text document by replacing incorrect text; it also demonstrates that you can retract changes with the undo command if you make errors during editing.

1. If necessary, start your virtual machines using the appropriate instructions in Activity 1-1.

2. To open a terminal console, right-click the desktop and click **Open in Terminal**.

3. To refresh the files for this activity, type **su –**, enter **Pa$$w0rd** at the password prompt, type **cd /usr/local/bin**, and press **Enter**. Type **makeQuote** and press **Enter**, and then type **su – User01** and press **Enter**.

4. Navigate to the **/mnt/sdb1/User01/QUOTE** directory.

5. Change the directory by typing **cd /mnt/sdb1/User01/QUOTE**.

6. To open the Quote003.txt file, type **vi Quote003.txt** at the command prompt and press **Enter**.

7. Place the cursor within the first line. To replace *gray* with *grey*, type **:s /gray/grey/c** and press **Enter**.

8. In response to the confirmation question, press **y**.

9. Verify that the instances of *gray* are now changed to *grey*.

10. To undo the search-and-replace operation, type **u**.

11. To save the file and quit the editing session, type **:wq** and press **Enter**.

12. Close the terminal window.

13. Leave the virtual machine logged on for the next activity.

Activity 9-15: Searching and Replacing Text Strings Using Regular Expressions in Vim

Time Required: 15 minutes

Objective: Search and replace text strings using regular expressions in the Vim editor.

Description: In this activity, you use the : substitution command with regular expressions in the Vim editor to search and replace text strings. This activity is useful if you want to use regular expressions to replace text in the Vim editor.

1. If necessary, start your virtual machines using the appropriate instructions in Activity 1-1.

2. To open a terminal window, right-click the desktop and then click **Open in Terminal**.

3. Type **cd /mnt/sdb1/User01/QUOTE**, and then press **Enter**.

4. To open the Quotes009.txt file, type **vi Quotes009.txt** at the command prompt and press **Enter**.

5. Type **:s/a/xxx\0xxx/g** and press **Enter**.

6. Notice that all of the letters *a* now are preceded by three *xxx*s and followed by three *xxx*s.

7. To undo the substitution, press **Enter** and then type **u**.

8. Notice that all instances of *a* now stand alone.

9. Close the terminal window.

10. To shut down the virtual machine, click **User01**, click **Power Off**, and then click the **Power Off** button.

11. Wait a moment for the CentOS 7 virtual machine to shut down completely.

12. Close any remaining open windows, log off, and shut down your PC.

Chapter Summary

- Text editors do more than allow you to edit files. For example, you can use them to create files, modify them, search for text within a file, and save files under new names. The same basic editing capabilities exist in PowerShell ISE, Gedit, and Vim.

- Each text editor discussed in this chapter allows you to work with multiple files at the same time. When working with multiple files, be careful not to inadvertently change the wrong one.

- Text editors allow you to rearrange words and lines in your text files. Use cut-and-paste operations to define text in one section of a document and move it to another section. Copy-and-paste operations are beneficial because you do not have to retype similar phrases or lines over and over. You can also move text between multiple files.

- Use a text editor's search feature to locate information quickly. You can find text in an entire document or on a particular line. Knowing how a particular editor performs a search operation helps you perform the corresponding replace operation.

- Search-and-replace operations are especially powerful when you use regular expressions. When you only know part of a text string, you can use wildcards and "magic characters" to make a search more precise, which is useful in large documents. You can also use wildcards when searching for text that contains special characters.

Key Terms

Clipboard   A data storage area for use with copy, cut, and paste functions within or across applications.

Command mode   The state in which the Vim editor accepts changes to a file.

Edit/Insert mode   A mode of operation in which the Vim editor pushes characters to the right of the screen rather than overwriting them. Use Insert mode to first enter information into a file.

Gedit   A general-purpose text editor used in Linux and Windows.

PowerShell ISE   An integrated scripting environment that includes a text editor.

text string   A sequence of characters in a file that you can display, print, or process.

Vim   A powerful, cross-platform text editor that many computer professionals use to write computer programs and text documents.

Review Questions

1. Text editors are used to _____. (Choose all that apply.)

   a. edit files

   b. create files

   c. execute files

   d. compile files

2. Common text editors include _____. (Choose all that apply.)

   a. PowerShell ISE

   b. Vim

   c. Windows 10

   d. Gedit

3. Word processors may add extra _____, which may not be desirable for working with plain text files.

   a. text

   b. formatting characters

   c. copy and paste functions

   d. "save as" functionality

4. File menu options in PowerShell ISE include _____. (Choose all that apply.)

   a. Find

   b. Save

   c. New

   d. Exit

5. Edit menu options in PowerShell ISE include _____. (Choose all that apply.)

   a. Close

   b. Copy

   c. Cut

   d. Paste

6. Copy and cut commands in Vim are executed in which mode? (Choose all that apply.)

   a. Insert Mode

   b. Command mode

   c. WildWing Mode

   d. CopyPaste Mode

7. Gedit can _____. (Choose all that apply.)

   a. be upgraded from PowerShell ISE

   b. be used as a powerful word processor

   c. be used in Linux

   d. be used in Windows 10

8. When you cut or copy text in Gedit, it is placed in _____.

   a. the Windows registry

   b. the buffer stack within the editor

   c. the Clipboard

   d. a file within your editing session

9. You can use Gedit to _____. (Choose all that apply.)

   a. create and edit text documents

   b. create and edit computer programs

   c. run Java applications

   d. compile Java programs

10. The Windows Clipboard can be used with the Copy, Cut, and Paste commands to _____. (Choose all that apply.)

    a. copy text within a text file edited in PowerShell ISE

    b. cut text within a text file edited in Gedit

    c. copy text from a text file edited in PowerShell ISE to another Windows application

    d. paste text to a text file edited in PowerShell ISE from the Clipboard

11. You can use the Vim editor to _____. (Choose all that apply.)

    a. create and edit text documents

    b. create and edit computer programs

    c. run Java applications

    d. compile Java programs

12. Which of the following is a mode in the Vim editor? (Choose all that apply.)

    a. Insert

    b. Sight

    c. Command

    d. Application

13. To save a file in the Vim editor, type _____. (Choose all that apply.)

    a. `:w`

    b. `:wq`

    c. `:s`

    d. `:wf`

14. What keys allow you to edit or add text in Vim?

    a. A

    b. E

    c. M

    d. I

    e. T

15. Which of the following editors work with Linux? (Choose all that apply.)

    a. PowerShell ISE

    b. Gedit

    c. Vim editor

    d. all of the above

16. In the Vim editor, you must first be in _____ mode before you quit.

    a. Command

    b. Help

    c. Insert

    d. The mode does not matter.

17. To move from Insert mode to Command mode in the Vim editor, press the _____ key.

    a. C

    b. Alt

    c. Ctrl

    d. Esc

18. Which keys are used to move the cursor around in the Vim editor? (Choose all that apply.)

    a. E

    b. H

    c. I

    d. G

    e. K

    f. J

    g. L

19. You can use regular expressions to _____. (Choose all that apply.)

    a. search for strings

    b. search and replace strings

    c. make mathematical calculations

    d. make complex comparisons

20. Word processors are seldom used to edit plain text files because they add extra formatting characters, such as _____. (Choose all that apply.)

    a. font size

    b. boldface

    c. italics

    d. underlines

Case Projects

CASE PROJECTS

Case 9-1: Comparing Text Editors

You are walking between classes and overhear a conversation between two of your classmates. They are discussing the advantages of the text editors they use in their Parallel Operating Systems course. One classmate asks, "Why would I ever need a text editor other than Gedit?" What would you say in reply?

Case 9-2: Using PowerShell ISE

You are preparing a short presentation to discuss the pros and cons of having network administrators in your company use PowerShell ISE as a text editor. How will you justify your decision to use or not use PowerShell ISE?

Case 9-3: Why Learn Vim?

Linux comes with many programs you can use to edit text files; two such programs are Gedit and Vim. Why might you want to learn Vim when Gedit seems easier to learn?

## chapter 10

Scripting in Windows 10 and CentOS 7

After reading this chapter and completing the exercises, you will be able to:

- Use the Windows PowerShell Integrated Scripting Environment (ISE)
- Create a PowerShell script to complete a directory tree
- Use PowerShell Help to build scripts
- Create a report with PowerShell scripting
- Troubleshoot PowerShell scripts
- Create scripts in CentOS 7

When working with operating systems, you may find yourself entering the same commands repeatedly. You could manually type the lines each time you need to accomplish a task and get the same results, but script files make this work easy. A **script** is a program that consists of a set of commands to control some function of an operating system. Rather than executing commands one by one via manual entry, the script can be set to execute in a scripting shell, such as PowerShell for Windows 10 or Bash for CentOS 7. Windows PowerShell is a task automation framework from Microsoft that consists of a command-line shell and an associated scripting language. Bash is an acronym for the CentOS 7 Bourne-again shell.

Using the Windows PowerShell Integrated Scripting Environment

To make PowerShell easier to use, Windows 10 comes with the **Integrated Scripting Environment (ISE)**. The ISE provides a rich scripting experience by enabling you to write, run, and test scripts in a graphical and intuitive environment.

Identifying ISE Panes

The ISE has three panes, as shown in Figure 10-1: Script, Console, and Command Add-on.

Starting at the bottom left is the familiar **Console pane**. This pane is similar to the PowerShell command prompt that you used to enter and execute PowerShell cmdlets in Chapter 8. Recall that PowerShell introduces the concept of a cmdlet (pronounced *command-let*), or small command. These single-function command-line tools are built into PowerShell. You

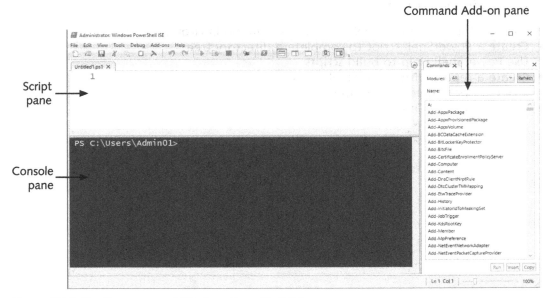

Figure 10-1 The three panes of Windows PowerShell ISE

Source: Windows 10/PowerShell ISE

can use cmdlets separately, but their power is realized when you chain them in sequence to perform complex tasks.

The output of scripts appears in the Console pane as you run them in the ISE. To the right of the Console pane is the **Command Add-on pane,** where you can search for cmdlets. You can click the arrow beside All to display all the commands that are available in PowerShell. You can also filter these commands. Above the Console pane is the **Script pane,** an editor pane in the ISE. You used the ISE to create text files in Chapter 9. Because the ISE is a GUI tool, you can use the familiar cut, copy, and paste features.

The ISE's true power is that it helps you enter and update PowerShell cmdlets easily. Although you can edit cmdlets and scripts in Notepad and then run them in PowerShell command windows, it is much easier to do everything in one place.

The ISE is an integrated development editor for PowerShell scripts. It provides key features to support the development of these scripts:

- **Brace matching**—Locates the closing brace if you have an opening brace selected.
- **IntelliSense**—Displays clickable menus of cmdlets, parameters, parameter values, files, or folders that match the characters you type.
- **Drag and drop text editing**—You can select any block of text and drag it to another location in the editor.
- **Parse error display**—Errors are indicated with red underlines.
- **Context-sensitive Help**—If you press F1 when your cursor is in a cmdlet or you have part of a cmdlet highlighted, the ISE displays context-sensitive Help about the highlighted cmdlet.

Using the ISE Toolbar

Figure 10-2 shows the multitude of buttons on the ISE toolbar. If you have used a recent Microsoft Office product, you are familiar with eight of the first nine buttons. To clear the output pane, click the Clear Console Pane button, which looks like a blue squeegee.

The next five buttons control the execution of scripts. You can launch a script directly from the PowerShell ISE by pressing F5 or clicking the icon that displays a green triangle. The tool turns green when the Script pane has commands that can be executed. In an empty Script pane, the tool is off. If you have several versions of cmdlets in the editor and you want to run some of them, highlight the portion you want to run and press F8, or click the icon that displays a book and green triangle.

If you need to stop execution, press Ctrl+Break or click the Stop Operation button.

To run a PowerShell script on a remote computer, click the New Remote PowerShell button. After you enter a computer name, username, and password, the script runs on the remote computer. To run PowerShell cmdlets in a new session on the same computer, select the Start PowerShell.exe button.

Of the remaining five buttons, the next three control the display and placement of the three panes in the ISE. If you need more information about the properties of a cmdlet, highlight the cmdlet and select Show Command Window. A pop-up window appears that shows the

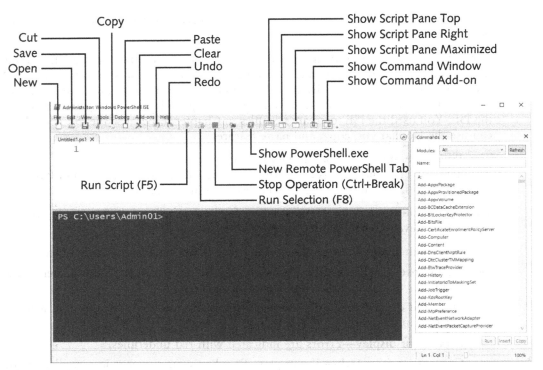

Figure 10-2 PowerShell ISE toolbar

Source: Windows 10/PowerShell ISE

properties. By highlighting a cmdlet and pressing the F1 key, you can display a Help window. The Show Command Add-on button toggles the display of the Command Add-on pane.

Why Learn PowerShell and Scripting?

You need to learn PowerShell scripting for several reasons:

- *PowerShell scripting is here to stay.* For example, PowerShell version 5 is featured in Windows 10 and Windows Server 2016.

- *Virtually all current Microsoft products, including Windows 10, can be managed through PowerShell.* If you become proficient in PowerShell, you can manage most of Microsoft's newer products.

- *Microsoft considers it important.* The single most important skill you will need as a Windows administrator in the coming years is proficiency with Windows PowerShell scripting.

- *It can make your job easier.* You can automate routine tasks. With a PowerShell script, you can complete these tasks with less effort.

- *Many GUIs are PowerShell front ends.* Microsoft has been designing GUIs for various products that are actually front-end interfaces to PowerShell scripting.

- *Microsoft certification exams contain PowerShell questions.* Microsoft has been adding questions about PowerShell to its certification exams.

- *If you do not learn it, someone else will.* Given the intense competition for IT jobs, you need every edge you can get. Your chances for advancement might improve by knowing PowerShell scripting.

Activity 10-1: Getting Familiar with ISE in Windows 10

Time Required: 10 minutes

Objective: Become familiar with the ISE window and customize the Power-Shell ISE for use.

Description: In this activity, you locate the PowerShell ISE, pin it to the taskbar for easy access, and customize it for use.

1. Start your virtual machines using the appropriate instructions in Activity 1-1.

2. To log on with administrator privileges, log on as **Admin01** with a password of **Pa$$w0rd**.

3. To create an icon on the taskbar, type **ISE** in the "Search the web and Windows" text box, right-click **Windows PowerShell ISE,** and then click **Pin to taskbar.**

There are two similar entries: Windows PowerShell ISE and Windows PowerShell ISE (x86). You want the Windows PowerShell ISE, which is the 64-bit version.

4. To open PowerShell ISE, right-click the **PowerShell ISE** icon on the taskbar, right-click **Windows PowerShell ISE,** and then click **Run as administrator.** Click **Yes.**

If you see a red message indicating that scripts are disabled, close the Windows PowerShell ISE window. Most likely, you failed to run Windows PowerShell ISE with administrator privileges. Try Step 4 again, right-clicking both the PowerShell ISE icon on the taskbar and Windows PowerShell ISE.

5. To see the available options for displaying the panes, click **View.**

6. To add the Script pane to the display, click **Show Script Pane.**

7. To remove the Command Add-on pane from the display, click **Show Command Add-on.**

8. Customize your PowerShell window panes by clicking the **Show Script Pane Top** button.

9. To customize the font of the Script and Console panes, click **Tools** and select **Options.**

10. To pick a larger font, click the **Font Size** chevron and select **12.** Click **OK.**

While you can change the themes for the Script pane, you might want to retain the default theme because PowerShell "color codes" script elements. A sample is shown in the Options window.

11. Notice that the font size increased in both the Script and Console panes.

12. To increase the width of a pane, click and hold its right border, move the mouse to the right until you like the result, and release the mouse button.

13. Review and close the ISE window. The changes will be saved across sessions.

Working with IntelliSense

Microsoft's IntelliSense is an "automatic completion" feature that helps you develop scripts more quickly. It displays clickable menus of cmdlets, parameters, and parameter values that match the characters you type.

With the addition of IntelliSense, it is easier to discover cmdlets and syntax when you use the ISE to create scripts. Double-click a suggestion from an IntelliSense menu to include it in your script.

As an example of using IntelliSense, consider the `Get-ChildItem` cmdlet that you used in Chapter 8. Typing `Get-C` tells IntelliSense to provide a list of the cmdlets that start with `Get-C`. Figure 10-3 shows an example of IntelliSense used to find `Get-ChildItem`. To include the highlighted item in the script, double-click it.

Using Profiles

The **PowerShell profile** is simply a script file that runs automatically each time the ISE starts. PowerShell profiles can be used to configure your ISE environment according to your preference. Profiles can be set to load the common modules you use every time you open the shell. By default, the modules that are loaded remain in memory for the active session only.

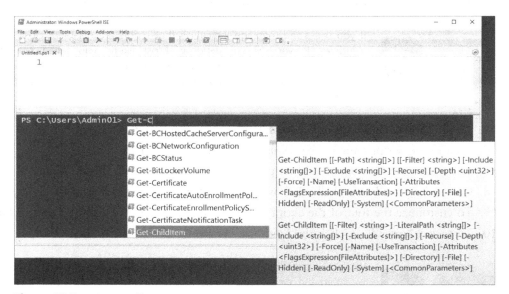

Figure 10-3 Using IntelliSense

Source: Windows 10/PowerShell ISE

Creating profiles is a way to set up your user environment to use PowerShell more easily and effectively.

Windows PowerShell execution policies let you determine the conditions under which Windows PowerShell loads configuration files and runs scripts. The Restricted policy is the default policy. The **RemoteSigned** policy requires a digital signature for scripts received from an Internet site.

Activity 10-2: Creating the ISE Profile

Time Required: 10 minutes

Objective: Create the required ISE profile.

Description: In this activity, you will create a profile in the ISE. You will also use the Intelli-Sense suggestion tool.

1. If necessary, start your virtual machines using the appropriate instructions in Activity 1-1.

2. If necessary, log on with administrator privileges using a log-on name of **Admin01** and a password of **Pa$$w0rd**.

3. If necessary, open the ISE. Right-click the **PowerShell ISE** icon on the taskbar, right-click **Windows PowerShell ISE**, and then click **Run as administrator**. Click **Yes**.

4. Type the following in the Console pane:

   $Pro

   IntelliSense will appear and provide suggestions. Double-click **Profile,** and then press **Enter**.

5. Review the result in the Console pane. A new profile is created.

6. To create a new profile file with the aid of IntelliSense in the Console pane, type **New-I** and double-click **New-Item**. Type **$P**, and then double-click **$Profile**. Type **–**, and then double-click **ItemType**. Type **File**. Type **–**, and double-click **Force**.

7. Verify that you have constructed the cmdlet on the following line, and then press **Enter**.

   New-Item $Profile –ItemType File –Force

8. The file properties for the Microsoft.PowerShellISE_profile you just created are displayed in the console window.

9. To open the Microsoft.PowerShellISE_profile, click **File**, double-click **Windows PowerShell**, click **Microsoft.PowerShellISE_profile**, and then click **Open**.

10. To set the execution policy for your script, type **Set-Ex** and double-click **Set-ExecutionPolicy**. Type **–**, and double-click **Scope**. Type **L**, and then double-click **LocalMachine**. Type **–**, and double-click **ExecutionPolicy**. Double-click **RemoteSigned**. Type **–**, and double-click **Force**.

10

11. Verify that you have constructed the following as a single line in the Script pane, and then press **Enter**.

```
Set-ExecutionPolicy -Scope LocalMachine –ExecutionPolicy
RemoteSigned -Force
```

12. Copy line 1 to line 2.

13. Change **LocalMachine** to **CurrentUser** in line 2. Press **Enter**.

14. To change to the Admin01 directory, type **Set-Location -Path C:\Users\Admin01** and press **Enter**.

15. To save the file, click the **Save** button, which looks like a blue diskette.

16. Close the PowerShell ISE window.

17. To open PowerShell ISE again, right-click the **PowerShell ISE** icon on the taskbar, right-click **Windows PowerShell ISE**, and then click **Run as administrator**. Click **Yes**.

18. To verify the execution policy, type **Get-Ex** and double-click **Get-ExecutionPolicy**. Type **–**, and double-click **List**. Press **Enter**.

19. Verify that both LocalMachine and CurrentUser are RemoteSigned.

20. Leave the ISE open for additional activities.

Creating a PowerShell Script for a Directory Tree

In Chapter 6, you created a directory tree. You used the MD command to make directories and the CD command to change the path. While these two commands will work in PowerShell, you should learn to use the equivalent native cmdlets in PowerShell as you create scripts: MKDIR and Set-Location. Figure 10-4 shows an example of a directory structure for a fictional college called STEM. You will create this directory structure in Activity 10-3.

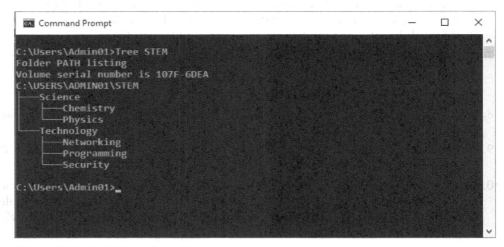

Figure 10-4 The STEM college directory structure

Source: Windows 10/Command Prompt

Activity 10-3: Creating Folders and Files

Time Required: 10 minutes

Objective: Create the directory structure for the STEM college.

Description: In this activity, you will create a PowerShell script to create the STEM college directory structure. This lab will help you work with the MKDIR and Set-Location cmdlets to create the script file.

1. If necessary, start your virtual machines using the appropriate instructions in Activity 1-1.

2. If necessary, log on with administrator privileges (enter **Admin01**) and a password of **Pa$$w0rd.**

3. If necessary, open the ISE. Right-click the **PowerShell ISE** icon on the taskbar, right-click **Windows PowerShell ISE,** and then click **Run as administrator.** Click **Yes.**

4. To create the STEM college directory structure, type **MKDIR STEM** in the Script pane and then press **Enter.**

5. To change to the STEM directory, type **Set-L** and double-click **Set-Location,** type **STEM,** and then press **Enter.**

6. To make the Science folder, type **MKDIR Science** in the Script pane and then press **Enter.**

7. To change to the Science directory, type **Set-L** and double-click **Set-Location,** type **Science,** and then press **Enter.**

8. To make the Chemistry folder, type **MKDIR Chemistry** in the Script pane and then press **Enter.**

9. Repeat Step 8 for **Physics.**

10. To change to the STEM directory, type **Set-L** and then double-click **Set-Location,** type **STEM,** and then press **Enter.**

11. Repeat Steps 6–10 for the **Technology, Networking, Programming,** and **Security** directories.

12. To save the script, click **File,** click **Save As,** type **Script1** over "Untitled1," and click **Save.**

13. To run the script, click the **Clear Console Pane** button (which looks like a blue squeegee), and then click the **Run Script (F5)** button (the green arrow).

14. To verify the results, press the **Windows** key, type **CMD,** and then double-click **Command Prompt.** Type **CD C:\Users\Admin01,** and then press **Enter.** Type **TREE STEM,** and then press **Enter.**

You can run the TREE command in the PowerShell script, but at the time this text was written, the results would display incorrectly. Running Windows commands within PowerShell is not as efficient as using an equivalent PowerShell cmdlet, because you essentially run an instance of CMD.EXE just to execute your Windows command.

15. Compare the results with those in Figure 10-4. If the tree is identical, skip the remaining steps.

16. To enter two "cleanup" statements, go to the start of line 1 and press the **Enter** key twice.

17. At line 1, type **Set-Location C:\Users\Admin01**.

18. At line 2, type **Remove-Item .\STEM -Force -Recurse**.

19. Make changes to the script as needed, and then save the script by clicking the **Save** button, which displays an icon of a blue diskette.

20. To run the script, click the **Clear Console Pane** button (which looks like a blue squeegee), and then click the **Run Script (F5)** button (the green arrow).

21. Return to the command line. Press the **up arrow** twice, and then press **Enter**. Press the **down arrow,** and then press **Enter**.

22. Compare the results with those in Figure 10-4. If the trees are not identical, go back to Step 19.

23. Leave the ISE open for additional activities.

Using PowerShell Help to Build Scripts

To be a successful builder of PowerShell scripts, you need to learn to work with the Help cmdlet, which provides information about other useful cmdlets. Learning the PowerShell Help will pay off in your future job in IT.

For example, to obtain help for the Get-ChildItem cmdlet (see Figure 10-5), type Get-Help Get-ChildItem | More in the Console pane and press Enter. To see more information, scroll down. With each Get-Help cmdlet, the NAME, SYNOPSIS (a short description for the cmdlet), and SYNTAX are displayed. The Help Get-ChildItem cmdlet is equivalent to using the Get-Help Get-ChildItem | More command.

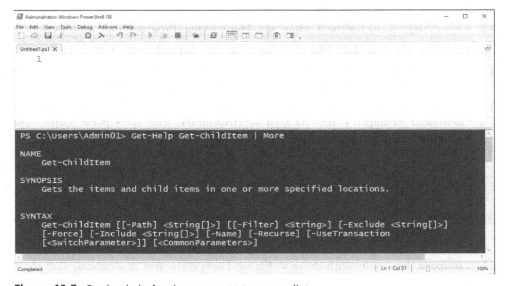

Figure 10-5 Getting help for the Get-ChildItem cmdlet

Source: Windows 10/PowerShell ISE

The cmdlet syntax is the set of rules that govern how a cmdlet can be used. Unless you know how to read the cmdlet syntax, you can't use or understand cmdlets properly or to their full potential. Here is a brief summary of the syntax characters for the Get-ChildItem cmdlet:

- A hyphen (-) indicates a parameter name. For example, -Path is the directory path.

- Angle brackets (< >) indicate placeholder text. You do not type the angle brackets or the placeholder text in a command. Instead, you replace it with the item it describes. For example, -Path C:\UsersAdmin01 would be a valid path.

- Brackets ([ ]) indicate optional items. A parameter and its value can be optional, or the name of a required parameter can be optional. For example, the [-Filter parameter <String>] and its value are enclosed in brackets because both are optional. The use of [-Force] is optional.

With the Help cmdlet, you can find information for cmdlets. For example, type Help 'Create File' to list the cmdlets that create files. Figure 10-6 shows the results. While you might not find a cmdlet with Help that exactly matches Create File, it is a good place to start your search. It appears that New-Item is probably a good choice for creating a file, so you type Help New-Item, as shown in Figure 10-7. Scanning the parameter list, you find -ItemType. You need to know if File is an acceptable option for -ItemType. PowerShell provides a -WhatIf parameter that shows what would happen if you chose to run the cmdlet.

To continue the example, type the following cmdlet with the aid of IntelliSense and then press Enter:

```
New-Item -Path C:\Tryit -ItemType file -WhatIf
```

Figure 10-8 shows that -ItemType file is acceptable. The Help cmdlet is designed to search intuitively for the information you need to build PowerShell scripts.

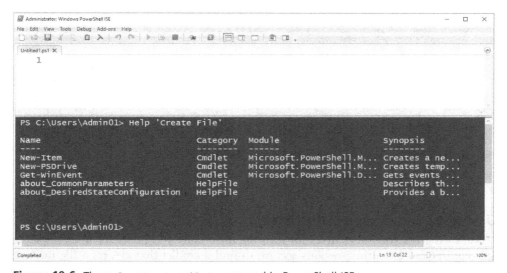

Figure 10-6 The Help 'Create File' command in PowerShell ISE

Source: Windows 10/PowerShell ISE

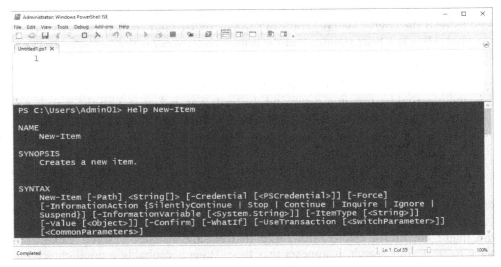

Figure 10-7   The `Help New-Item` command in PowerShell ISE

Source: Windows 10/PowerShell ISE

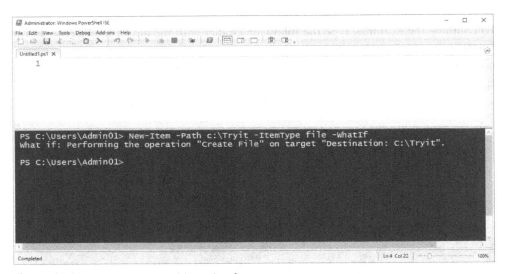

Figure 10-8   `File` is an acceptable option for `-ItemType`

Source: Windows 10/PowerShell ISE

Using `Get-Command` and Help

PowerShell gives you alternatives for locating the cmdlet you need. As an example, reconsider the requirement from the previous section to find a cmdlet that creates a file in PowerShell.

`Get-Command` is one of the more useful cmdlets. With it, you can find a cmdlet you need for the script you are writing. Figure 10-9 shows the help for `Get-Command`. The second

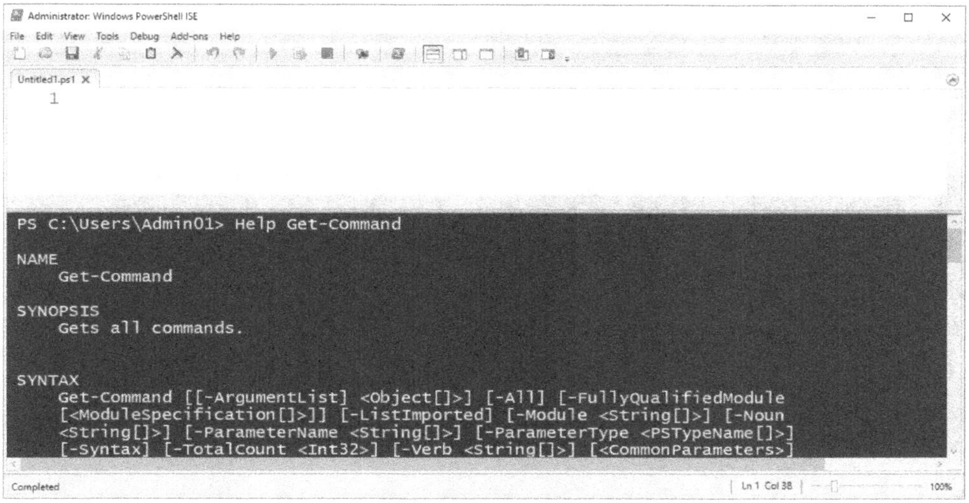

Figure 10-9 Help for the Get-Command cmdlet in PowerShell ISE

Source: Windows 10/PowerShell ISE

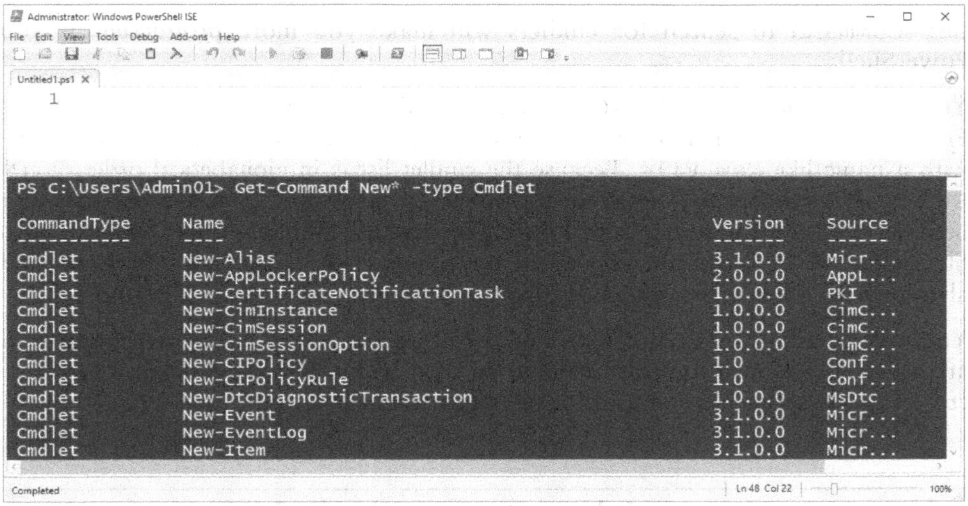

Figure 10-10 Finding a cmdlet that creates a new file

Source: Windows 10/PowerShell ISE

parameter list shows that you use a string to guide the search and the --CommandType cmdlet to focus on cmdlets.

To find a cmdlet that creates a new file, try Get-Command New* -Type cmdlet, which produces the list shown in Figure 10-10. The parameter -Type is an alias for —CommandType.

With PowerShell, you may not find a cmdlet that matches exactly what you are looking for. However, Get-Command is a good starting point for your search. Using

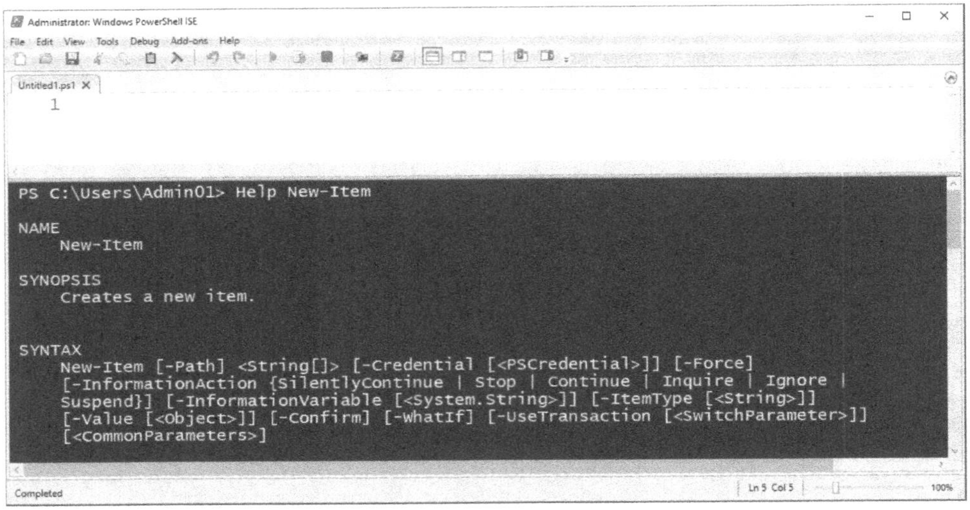

Figure 10-11 The Help New-Item command in PowerShell ISE

Source: Windows 10/PowerShell ISE

Get-Command to search for cmdlets will make you more productive as you master PowerShell.

You can practice using Get-Command to lead you to the New-Item cmdlet. Refer to Figure 10-10. You might assume at the start of your search that you are looking for a cmdlet with a name like New-File. Because the cmdlet list is in alphabetical order, you see New-Event, New-EventLog, and then New-Item. However, New-File does not appear between the New-EventLog and New-Item cmdlets. Perhaps New-Item can create a new file. Figure 10-11 shows the results for Help New-Item. The Get-Command cmdlet is an alternative to Help when you need to locate a cmdlet.

You may be asking yourself, "Why can't I just click the New File icon to create a file?" You are asking PowerShell to create a file to be used within a script. Clicking the New File icon creates a new script file, not a file to be used within the script.

Preparing a Report with a PowerShell Script

In this section, you will build a script to report memory usage by the various processes running on your Windows 10 virtual machine. While you use PowerShell to develop the report, you will develop skills that enable you to build scripts to meet other IT requirements.

Also in this section, you will see how to construct scripts using **incremental development**, a method of script development in which the script is designed, implemented, and tested incrementally, a few cmdlets at a time, until the script is finished. Again, the PowerShell Get-Command cmdlet is a good way to search for cmdlets, and the PowerShell Help features are essential in clarifying the proper use of PowerShell cmdlets. A good rule of thumb is to add cmdlets to the script only if they have a high probability of executing successfully. This technique will improve your productivity in PowerShell by reducing the time needed to discover and correct mistakes.

Obtaining Process Data

You used Task Manager earlier in this book to view the processes running on your computer. You can also find the processes that might be associated with a particular service or application. A process is a file, such as an executable file with an .exe extension, that the computer uses to start a program directly or to start other services. Figure 10-12 shows the Processes tab in Task Manager. For your report, you decide to concentrate on the top 10 Processor Memory (PM) values.

To find a cmdlet that obtains process values, use the `Get-Command -noun Process` command, which is shown in Figure 10-13. You see that `Get-Process` is a likely candidate. Figure 10-14 shows the results of using the `Help Get-Process` command. By adding the `-Examples` option, you see possible uses for the `Get-Process` cmdlet.

Task Manager			— □ ✕

File Options View

Processes | Performance | App history | Startup | Users | Details | Services

Name	2% CPU	66% Memory	0% Disk	0% Network
Apps (2)				
> Task Manager	1.1%	7.7 MB	0 MB/s	0 Mbps
> Windows PowerShell ISE	0%	65.3 MB	0 MB/s	0 Mbps
Background processes (12)				
Cortana	0%	0.1 MB	0 MB/s	0 Mbps
Host Process for Windows Tasks	0%	1.1 MB	0 MB/s	0 Mbps
InstallAgent	0%	1.1 MB	0 MB/s	0 Mbps
Microsoft Malware Protection C...	0%	0.7 MB	0 MB/s	0 Mbps
Microsoft OneDrive (32 bit)	0%	1.9 MB	0 MB/s	0 Mbps
Microsoft Skype (32 bit)	0%	2.6 MB	0 MB/s	0 Mbps
> Microsoft Windows Search Inde...	0%	4.5 MB	0 MB/s	0 Mbps
> Microsoft® Volume Shadow Co...	0%	0.4 MB	0 MB/s	0 Mbps
RDP Clipboard Monitor	0%	0.6 MB	0 MB/s	0 Mbps
Runtime Broker	0%	4.0 MB	0 MB/s	0 Mbps

⌃ Fewer details   End task

Figure 10-12 Processes in Task Manager

Source: Windows 10/Task Manager

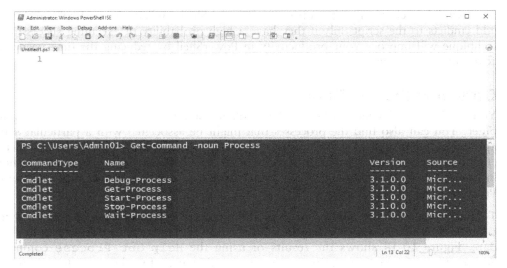

Figure 10-13 Locating a cmdlet that obtains process values

Source: Windows 10/PowerShell ISE

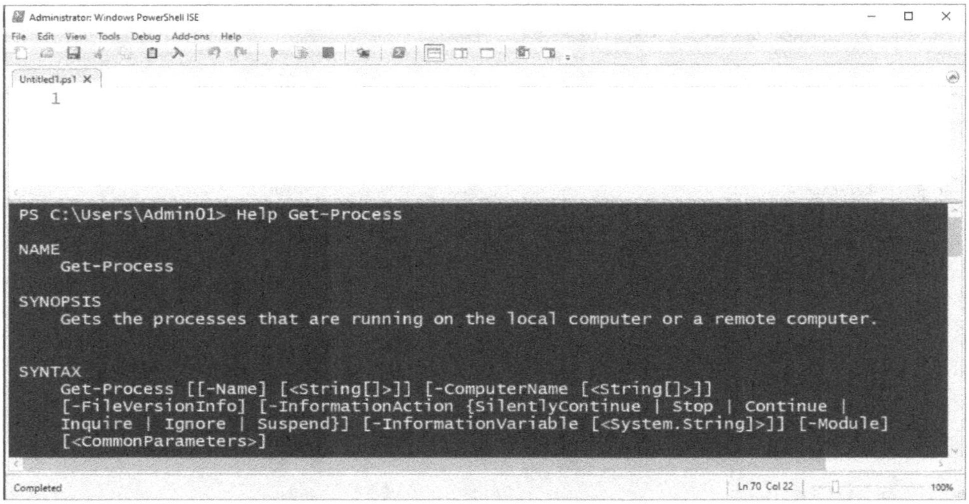

Figure 10-14 Using the `Help Get-Process` command

Source: Windows 10/PowerShell ISE

Scroll for a likely example, as shown in Figure 10-15; it looks like `Get-Process` will do the trick. Notice the Additional Notes, which provide a definition for each column. Use the `-full` option to provide these definitions. Scroll down to locate the definitions shown in Figure 10-16.

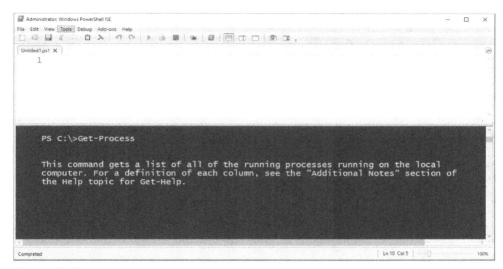

Figure 10-15 Uses for the `Get-Process` cmdlet

Source: Windows 10/PowerShell ISE

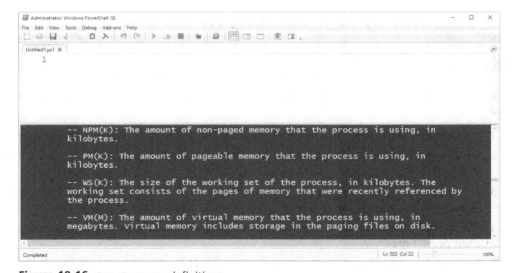

Figure 10-16 `Get-Process` definitions

Source: Windows 10/PowerShell ISE

See Figure 10-17 for an example of using `Get-Process`. You will start the report in Activity 10-4, and then complete it in Activity 10-5 after learning additional reporting techniques in the next section. Recall that the `Get-Process` cmdlet produces a table with one row for each process and its statistics. This table can be piped to additional cmdlets for further processing.

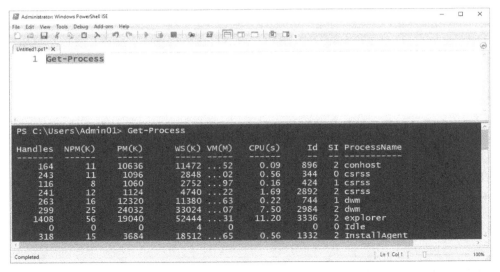

Figure 10-17 Using Get-Process

Source: Windows 10/PowerShell ISE

Activity 10-4: Obtaining Process Data

Time Required: 10 minutes

Objective: Obtain data for processes running on the Windows 10 virtual machine.

Description: In this activity, you start a PowerShell script to report on system processes. This lab will help you work with Get-Process.

1. If necessary, start your virtual machines using the appropriate instructions in Activity 1-1.

2. If necessary, log on with administrator privileges (enter **Admin01**) and a password of **Pa$$w0rd**.

3. If necessary, open the ISE. Right-click the **PowerShell ISE** icon on the taskbar, right-click **Windows PowerShell ISE,** and then click **Run as administrator.** Click **Yes.**

4. To see the process cmdlets, type **Get-Command -noun Process** in the Console pane and then press **Enter.**

5. To see the Help for Get-Process, type **Get-Help Get-Process -Examples** and press **Enter.** Review the syntax and description. Scroll down until you locate the process definitions in the Additional Notes section.

6. To see the process data, type **Get-Process** in the Script pane, click the **Clear Console Pane** button, and then click the **Run Script (F5)** button.

7. Review the process data.

8. To save the script, click **File,** click **Save As,** type **Script2** over "Untitled1," and click **Save.**

9. Leave the ISE open for future activities.

Filtering, Sorting, Selecting, and Formatting Scripts

Recall that you want only the top 10 Processor Memory (PM) values in your report. Also, the report will be more meaningful if the memory used by PowerShell is excluded, or filtered out. Also, it would be nice to have the PM values sorted in the report. This section explains how to use cmdlets to sort and filter data, and to perform other useful operations:

- **Sorting**—Arranging a table in a particular order with the `Sort-Object` cmdlet.

- **Filtering**—Selecting items to remain in a table after filtering out unwanted items using the `Where-Object` cmdlet.

- **Selecting**—Selecting items to remain in a table after removing unwanted items using the `Select -Object` cmdlet.

- **Formatting**—Making the output look more pleasing with the `Format-Table` cmdlet.

The pipe operator is typically used with all of the preceding types of commands.

Sorting Data   The only cmdlet you need to learn in order to sort tables is `Sort-Object`. You also need to know the parameters of an object to sort the table. For example, if you want help sorting a table of process data, run the cmdlets shown in Figure 10-18. With `-Descending`, the sort starts with the highest values. Because you are building a script to present Processor Memory values, you would sort based on the PM property. When a line ends in a pipe character (|), the cmdlets continue on the next line, as shown in Figure 10-18.

 To meet the formatting requirements of this textbook, cmdlets are split between lines. To split lines in PowerShell, place a pipe character (|) at the end of the line.

NOTE

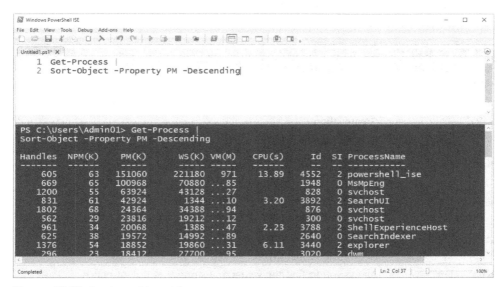

Figure 10-18 Sorting tables with `Sort-Object`

Source: Windows 10/PowerShell ISE

Filtering Data The report will be more meaningful if you eliminate the powershell _ise process, which represents the memory used by PowerShell. You can use PowerShell's filtering capabilities with the Where-Object cmdlet. Type Help Where-Object -Examples to see examples for how to use Where-Object. Figure 10-19 shows the filter that resembles what you need.

To use filtering in PowerShell, you need to know the comparison operators defined in Table 10-1.

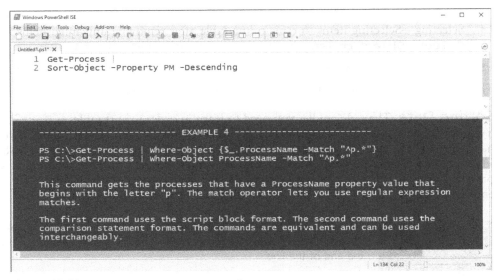

Figure 10-19 Using the Where-Object cmdlet

Source: Windows 10/PowerShell ISE

Operator	Definition
-eq	Equals, which is used for finding identical values
-ne	Not equals, which includes values that are not identical
-gt	Greater than
-ge	Greater than or equal to
-lt	Less than
-le	Less than or equal to
-like	Matching operator that uses the * wildcard operator
-match	Allows you to find the values of strings that match
-contains	Allows you to see whether an identical value exists in a list of values
-notlike	Allows you to identify the value that does not match
-notmatch	Allows you to find the values in a string that do not match
-notcontains	Allows you to find the values in a list that do not match

Table 10-1 Comparison operators used with Where-Object

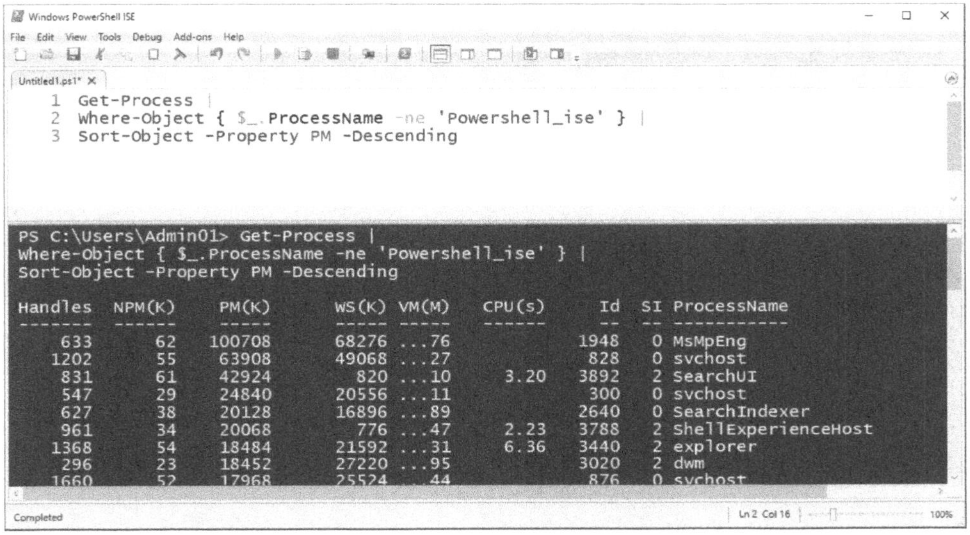

Figure 10-20 Results of adding `Where-Object`

Figure 10-18 shows that the ProcessName for the PowerShell ISE is `powershell_ise`. To eliminate the `powershell_ise` process, select all of the processes that are not equal to `powershell_ise`. Using the example as a guide, add the following cmdlet shown in bold to your script.

```
Get-Process |
Where-Object {$_.ProcessName -ne 'powershell_ise'} |
Sort-Object -Property PM -Descending
```

The characters `$_.` represent a dynamic variable that stores the current information being piped to it. In the preceding example, `$_` is a process; it is so named because the underscore character resembles a pipe character (|) lying on its side, implying that it contains whatever was piped in. Figure 10-20 shows the results of adding `Where-Object`.

Selecting Data For reporting purposes, remember that you want to include only the top 10 PM values in your report. To select this data, use `Select-Object`. Review the `Help` for `Select-Object` and examine the examples. Scroll and locate the example that appears in Figure 10-21.

The `-Last` option, shown in the figure, is documented in the `Help` file. For `Select-Object`, PowerShell also has an undocumented `-First` option, which selects the specified number of lines from the front of the cmdlet. Using the example as a guide, add the following cmdlet shown in bold to the script. Figure 10-22 shows this addition.

```
Get-Process |
Where-Object {$_.ProcessName -ne 'powershell_ise'} |
Sort-Object -Property PM -Descending |
Select-Object -First 10
```

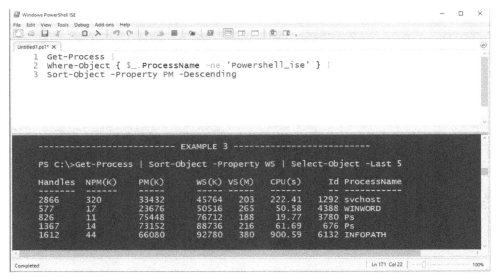

Figure 10-21 Help for `Select-Object`

Source: Windows 10/PowerShell ISE

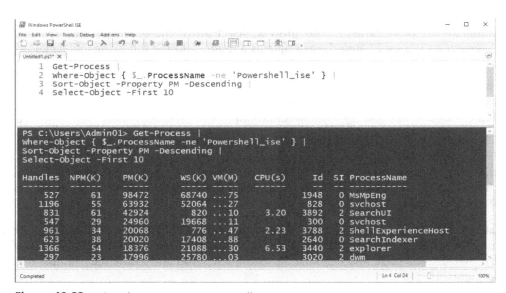

Figure 10-22 Using the `Select-Object` cmdlet

Source: Windows 10/PowerShell ISE

Formatting Data The `Format-Table` cmdlet is used to display process information. With this cmdlet, you control which property values are presented. Unless you specify the properties, the cmdlet displays the properties in the order in which they appear in the object. With the `-Property` parameter, you can select which properties you want to display and change their order of display.

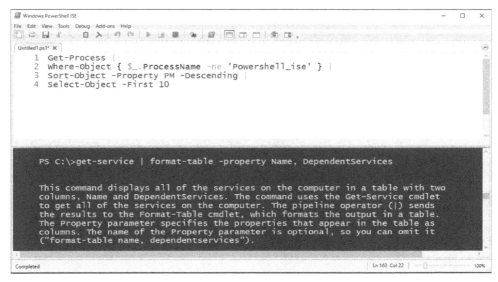

Figure 10-23 Help for Format-Table

Source: Windows 10/PowerShell ISE

Review the Help for Format-Table and locate the example that appears in Figure 10-23.

Using the example as a guide, add the following cmdlet shown in bold to your script. Figure 10-24 shows this addition.

```
Get-Process |
Where-Object {$_.ProcessName -ne 'powershell_ise'} |
Sort-Object -Property PM -Descending |
Select-Object -First 10 |
Format-Table -Property ProcessName,PM
```

Notice that PM numbers are large. Perhaps there is a way to scale these numbers, so you return to the Help for an example (see Figure 10-25). You see that you can scale the PM property with a calculation, as indicated in bold in the following example. A label is required, so you type Label="PM(1MB)". Note that PowerShell can use constants such as 1KB, 1MB, 1GB, 1TB, and 1PB. So, you can type Expression= $_.PM/1MB to divide each PM by 1 MB.

Figure 10-26 shows the results of scaling.

```
Get-Process |
Where-Object {$_.ProcessName -ne 'powershell_ise'} |
Sort-Object -Property PM -Descending |
Select-Object -First 10 |
Format-Table -Property ProcessName,
@{Label="PM(MB)";Expression={$_.PM/1MB}}
```

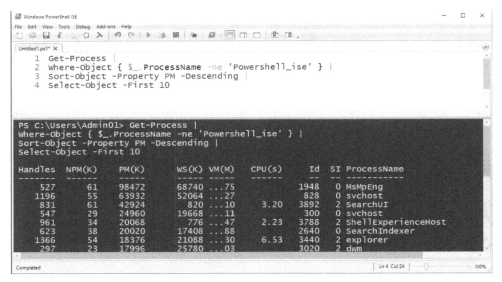

Figure 10-24 The `Format-Table` cmdlet

Source: Windows 10/PowerShell ISE

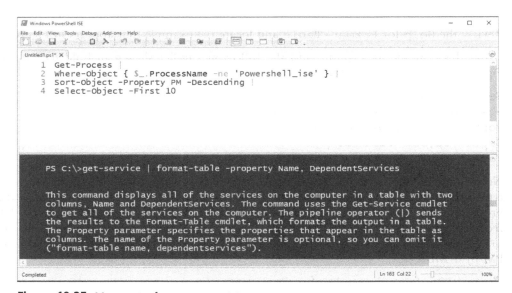

Figure 10-25 More `Help` for `Format-Table`

Source: Windows 10/PowerShell ISE

The line that was added requires further explanation. Notice that there is a lot of punctuation in the new line. All of the parentheses and brackets should be balanced—every starting bracket matches an ending bracket, and every starting parenthesis matches an ending parenthesis. The Label provides a way to customize the column heading. In this case, PM(MB)

```
Windows PowerShell ISE                                                          —  □  ×
File  Edit  View  Tools  Debug  Add-ons  Help

Untitled1.ps1* ×
   1  Get-Process |
   2  Where-Object { $_.ProcessName -ne 'Powershell_ise' } |
   3  Sort-Object -Property PM -Descending |
   4  Select-Object -First 10 |
   5  Format-Table -Property ProcessName,
   6  @{ Label="PM(MB)"; Expression={$_.PM/1MB}}

PS C:\Users\Admin01> Get-Process |
Where-Object { $_.ProcessName -ne 'Powershell_ise' } |
Sort-Object -Property PM -Descending |
Select-Object -First 10 |
Format-Table -Property ProcessName,
@{ Label="PM(MB)"; Expression={$_.PM/1MB}}


ProcessName              PM(MB)
-----------              ------
MsMpEng              96.16796875
svchost              62.421875
SearchUI             41.91796875
svchost              24.28125
ShellExperienceHost  19.59765625


Completed                                              Ln 1 Col 35              100%
```

Figure 10-26 Scaling numbers in the cmdlet

Source: Windows 10/PowerShell ISE

indicates that the values are scaled by dividing by 1 MB. The actual scaling occurs in the Expression, where the current value of the Processor Memory $_ . PM is divided by 1 MB.

Activity 10-5: Reporting on Processor Memory

Time Required: 15 minutes

Objective: Report on processor memory running on the Windows 10 virtual machine.

Description: In this activity, you start a PowerShell script to report on processes. This activity will use incremental development so that you code only as much as you can conveniently test. The goal is to develop the script with testing as you go along. You practice using the Sort-Object, Where-Object, Select-Object, and Format-Table cmdlets.

Before performing the following activity, you must complete and save the script in Activity 10-4.

1. If necessary, start your virtual machines using the appropriate instructions in Activity 1-1.

2. If necessary, log on with administrator privileges (enter **Admin01**) and with a password of **Pa$$w0rd**.

3. If necessary, open the ISE. Right-click the **PowerShell ISE** icon on the taskbar, right-click **Windows PowerShell ISE,** and then click **Run as administrator.** Click **Yes.**

4. If necessary, open the Script2 file. Click **File,** click **Script2,** and then click **Open.**

To meet the formatting requirements of this textbook, cmdlets are split between lines. To split lines in PowerShell, place a pipe character (|) at the end of the line.

5. To continue the script on the next line, add a | after `Get-Process` on line 1. Press **Enter**.

6. To sort the data by processor memory, type **Sort-Object -Property PM -Descending** on line 2.

7. Click the **Save** button, click the **Clear Console Pane** button, and then click the **Run Script (F5)** button. Verify the results, correct them as needed, and repeat this step.

8. To continue the script on the next line, add a | at the end of line 2. Press **Enter**.

9. To exclude the processes associated with the PowerShell ISE, type **Where-Object {$_.ProcessName -ne 'powershell_ise'}** on line 3.

10. Repeat Step 7.

11. To continue the script on the next line, add a | at the end of line 3. Press **Enter**.

12. To limit the report to the top 10 memory processes, type **Select-Object -First 10** on line 4.

13. Repeat Step 7.

14. To continue the script on the next line, add a | at the end of line 4. Press **Enter**.

15. To specify the properties for the report, type **Format-Table -Property ProcessName,PM** as line 5.

16. Repeat Step 7.

17. To continue the cmdlet on the next line, remove **PM** from line 5. Press **Enter**.

18. To scale the processor memory values, type the following as line 6.

    ```
    @{Label="PM(MB)" ; Expression={$_.PM/1MB}}
    ```

19. Repeat Step 7.

20. Close the PowerShell ISE window.

21. To shut down the virtual machine, click **Start**, click **Power**, and then click the **Shut Down** button.

22. Wait a moment for the Windows 10 virtual machine to shut down completely.

Troubleshooting PowerShell Scripts

When building and testing in PowerShell, you may encounter errors or be confused about how PowerShell arrived at a particular result. This section presents some tools you can use to solve your problems.

Clear Typing

Clear typing in PowerShell will save you time and frustration. Consider this: If a command is typed clearly, there is a better chance that PowerShell will interpret it correctly. Here are some suggestions that will make your script more readable by other users and reduce the chances that PowerShell will misinterpret your cmdlets:

- Capitalize the first letter of each word, and leave the other letters lowercase. For example, `Get-ChildItem` follows this convention.
- Be sure to place spaces between the cmdlet and the first property, between the property and value, and so on. Adding extra spaces seldom confuses PowerShell. Consider the formatting of the following:

```
Get-Process | Soft-Object -Property PM
```

- Continuing lines is another matter. Lines can be terminated between cmdlets by a | (pipe).
- You can break cmdlets between parameters using the backtick key (`` ` ``). The backtick character is located on the key below Esc.
- Clear typing looks professional!

Interpreting Errors

Getting errors while building and running scripts is inevitable. In PowerShell, you will see red text in the parse error display to indicate errors. PowerShell error messages indicate exactly where the problem lies in the executed command. The questionable text is reported and then followed by an explanation of the problem, as shown in Figure 10-27.

Error messages almost always include the line and char (character) number where PowerShell was unable to interpret your cmdlet. In Figure 10-27, notice that the misspelled text `wher-object` is underlined in the `Where-Object` cmdlet.

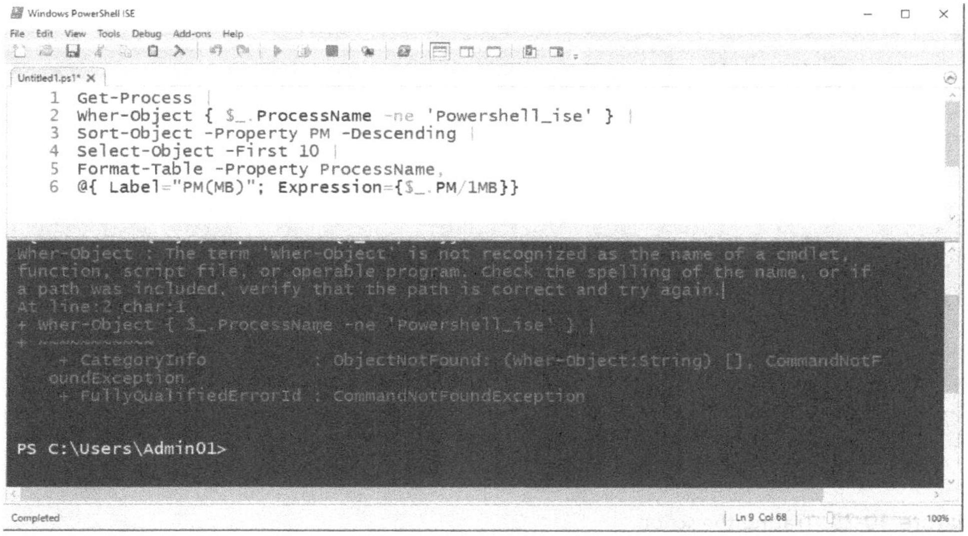

Figure 10-27 Misspelled cmdlet error

Source: Windows 10/PowerShell ISE

Here are a few rules for using PowerShell and avoiding errors:

- Cmdlet names are always a combination of a verb and noun, separated by a dash.
- Cmdlets and parameters are always separated by a space.
- When there are multiple parameters in a command, each parameter is separated by a space.
- Every parameter is preceded by a hyphen (-).

Tracing the Script

One of the simplest ways to debug a script is to use script-level tracing. When you turn on **script-level tracing**, each command that is executed is displayed in the Windows PowerShell console. **Tracing** is a method that developers use to debug and refine programs. By watching the commands as they are displayed, you can determine if a line of code is executed. To enable script tracing, you use the `Set-PSDebug` cmdlet and specify one of three levels for the `-trace` parameter:

- 0—Turns off script tracing.
- 1—Traces each line of the script as it is executed. Lines in the script that are not executed are not traced. This level does not display variable assignments.
- 2—Traces each line of the script as it is executed. Lines in the script that are not executed are not traced. This level displays variable assignments.

Figure 10-28 shows the statement from the trace where `ProcessName` was `powershell_ise`. Look for the following line:

```
Where-Object {$_.ProcessName -ne 'powershell_ise' >>>>
```

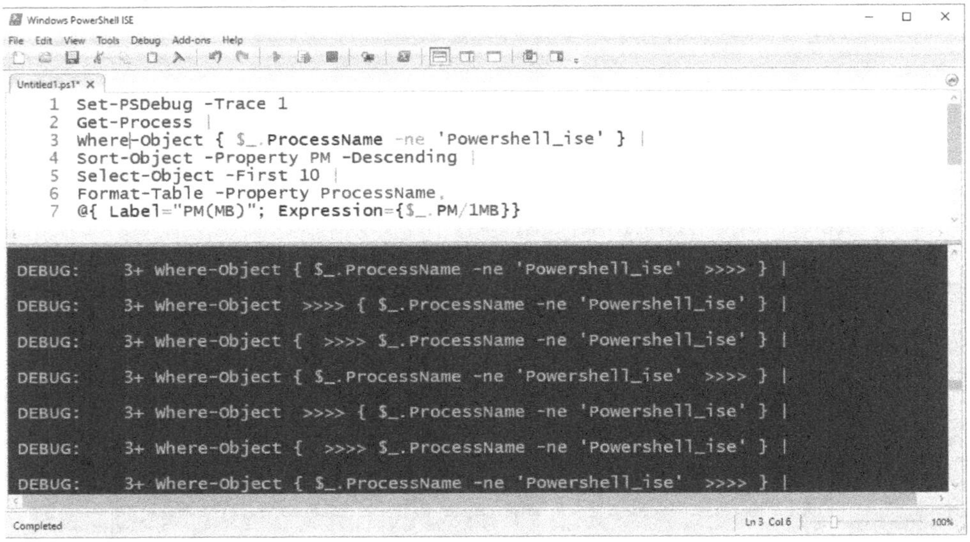

Figure 10-28 Tracing the script

Source: Windows 10/PowerShell ISE

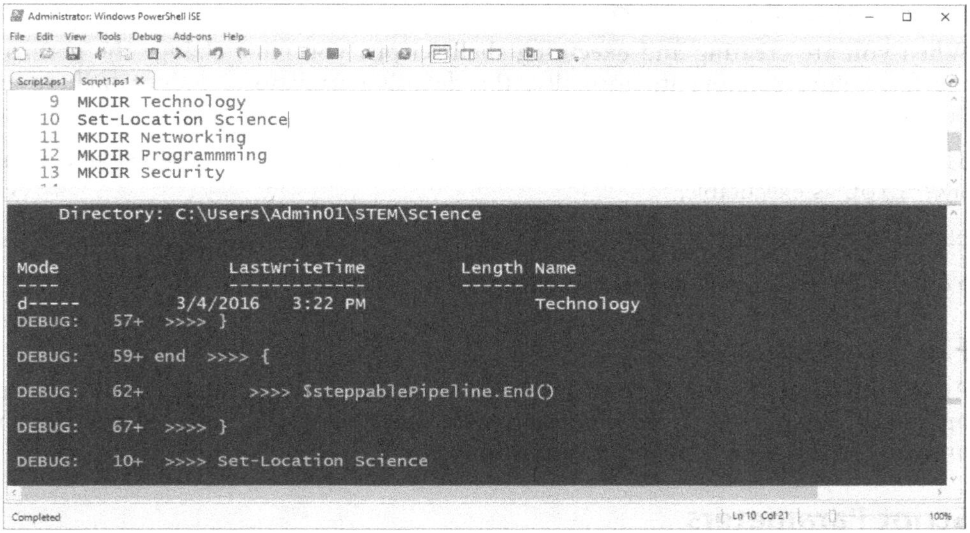

Figure 10-29 A logic error in a script

Source: Windows 10/PowerShell ISE

Figure 10-29 shows the results of a logic error. Statement 10 should be `Set-Location Technology`, but the script returned the current directory to `Science`, not `Technology`. To correct the problem, change the statement to `Set-Location Technology` in the script.

Creating Script Files in CentOS 7

In this section, you will learn to build script files and enhance them by adding decision-making capabilities and repetition to handle simple tasks in CentOS 7.

You write scripts in CentOS 7 using a text editor such as Vim. The basic design of a well-written script should include the components described in the following sections.

Header Line

The **header line** is the first line in a script. This statement indicates the type of shell environment under which the script is run. When you write a script, you should include a header line to ensure that the script is run under the correct shell. For example, the following line shows a header line for a bash script:

```
#!/bin/bash
```

Exit Return Code

The statement `exit 0` is needed to end the script if all goes well because a code must be returned from the script. A return code of zero indicates success.

Executable Permission

When you are creating and executing shell scripts, you must change the permissions on the file before running it; normally, the default permissions do not include execution permissions.

The chmod command modifies the permissions of a file. The following command sets myScript as executable:

```
chmod 755 myScript
```

You will learn more about Linux permissions in Chapter 11.

File Extensions

As with the other file types you have seen in CentOS 7, using an extension on script files is optional. However, to avoid confusion with other file types, some system administrators prefer to use an .sh extension on their scripts.

Script Parameters

Script parameters can contain any information you need to pass to a batch program when you execute it. The parameters $0 through $9 are separated by spaces, commas, or semicolons. The parameter $0 contains the name of the batch command as it appears on the command line when the batch is executed. The parameter $1 represents the first string typed after the batch command, $2 represents the second string, and so on. Table 10-2 contains a list of command-line reference parameters.

For example, to copy the contents of myFile1 to myFile2, in which $1 is replaced by the value myFile1 and $2 is replaced by myFile2, type the following cp command:

```
cp /home/myFile1 /home/myFile2
```

Conditional Execution

In CentOS 7, many programmers develop small, simple script routines that they can use generically and within multiple scripts. These scripts require structures that allow

Modifier	Description
$1, $2, . . . $n	How command-line parameters are referenced in a script
$#	Shows the command-line parameter count (used for display and iteration delimiters)
$@	Represents the list of actual command-line parameters with quotation marks around each parameter (used for display and iteration delimiters)
$*	Represents the list of actual command-line parameters (used for display and iteration delimiters)

Table 10-2 Command-line parameter reference in a CentOS 7 script

repetitive and conditional processing. The structures should have two important properties:

- Command lines that are executed multiple times should be written only once to avoid errors in consistency. This simplicity also makes scripts easy to maintain.
- Structures must provide a clear selection between command lines when conditions in a script are tested.

The following sections introduce you to three common conditional commands in CentOS 7.

if Command The `if` command enables decision making in scripts when a program contains different sets of instructions to execute based on a conditional test result. For example, if the result of the test is true, the script executes a set of instructions. Two formats are used when you need to set up decisions within scripts. The first format is sometimes referred to as the **if then...fi** construct; use it when only one decision path is needed. The construct has the following syntax:

```
if [decision placed here] ; then
[command list here]
fi
```

The other common syntax used with the `if` command is the **if else fi** construct. Use it when you need to take two distinctly different paths based on the results of a decision. The syntax for this construct is:

```
if [decision]; then
[command list here]
else
[command list here]
fi
```

With both `if` command constructs, the decision is made by testing a variable. This variable may change as the script is run.

while Command Use the `while` command to enable multiple executions of a set of instructions while a certain condition exists. The general syntax of the **while** construct is:

```
while [ loop decision ] do
done
```

The limit for the loop comes from testing a changing variable. Figure 10-30 illustrates how you can use the `while` loop in a script; the results of the script are shown in Figure 10-31.

for in Command Use the **for in** command to execute a number of instructions based on a maximum count you specify. (You will use the command in Activity 10-7.) The syntax for the command is:

```
for [somevalue] in [limitation variable] do
done
```

```
                                 User01@CentOS7:~                    _   □   ×

  File  Edit  View  Search  Terminal  Help
[User01@CentOS7 ~]$ cat while_loop.sh
#!/bin/bash
ARG_COUNT=$#
EXP_ARGS=2

if [ $ARG_COUNT -eq $EXP_ARGS ]; then
    echo "Congratulations!"
    echo "You have successfully passed $EXP_ARGS arguments to this script. "
    echo "The $EXP_ARGS arguments were $1 and $2 respectively."
else
    echo "Error: Incorrect number of command line arguments.
            Actual number of argument(s) passed: " $ARG_COUNT
            "Required number of argument(s): " $EXP_ARGS
    echo "Error#: " 60
fi

counter=1
while [ $counter -le $ARG_COUNT ]
do
    echo "Counting up to the parameter count limit: " $counter
    let "counter +=1"
done
[User01@CentOS7 ~]$ █
```

Figure 10-30 Using the `while` loop in a script

Source: CentOS 7/Terminal

```
                                 User01@CentOS7:~                    _   □   ×

  File  Edit  View  Search  Terminal  Help

[User01@CentOS7 ~]$ ./while_loop.sh Jane Doe
Congratulations!
You have successfully passed 2 arguments to this script.
The 2 arguments were Jane and Doe respectively.
Counting up to the parameter count limit:  1
Counting up to the parameter count limit:  2
[User01@CentOS7 ~]$ ./while_loop.sh Jane
Error: Incorrect number of command line arguments.
            Actual number of argument(s) passed:  1
./while_loop.sh: line 12: Required number of argument(s): : command not found
Error#:  60
Counting up to the parameter count limit:  1
[User01@CentOS7 ~]$ ./while_loop.sh Jane Mary Doe
Error: Incorrect number of command line arguments.
            Actual number of argument(s) passed:  3
./while_loop.sh: line 12: Required number of argument(s): : command not found
Error#:  60
Counting up to the parameter count limit:  1
Counting up to the parameter count limit:  2
Counting up to the parameter count limit:  3
[User01@CentOS7 ~]$
```

Figure 10-31 Output of the `while` loop in a script

Source: CentOS 7/Terminal

```
UserO1@CentOS7:~                              _  □  ×

File  Edit  View  Search  Terminal  Help
[User01@CentOS7 ~]$ cat for_in.sh
#!/bin/bash
ARG_COUNT=$#
EXP_ARGS=2

if [ $ARG_COUNT -eq $EXP_ARGS ]; then
    echo "You have passed $EXP_ARGS arguments to this script. "
    echo "The $EXP_ARGS arguments were $1 and $2 respectively."
else
    echo "Error: Incorrect number of command line arguments.
            Actual number of argument(s) passed: " $ARG_COUNT
            "Required number of argument(s): " $EXP_ARGS
    echo "Error#: " 60
fi

ct=1
while [ $ct -le $ARG_COUNT ]
do
    echo "Counting up to the parameter count limit: " $ct
    let "ct +=1"
done

ct=1
for entry in $*
do
    echo "Argument $((ct++)): $entry "
done
[User01@CentOS7 ~]$
```

Figure 10-32 Using the for in loop in a script

Source: CentOS 7/Terminal

The limitation variable for the loop can either come from a single number or operate on a list of items. The bottom of Figure 10-32 illustrates a script using the for in loop; the results of the script are shown in Figure 10-33.

The following basic steps explain how to write a bash shell script:

1. In a terminal window, open the text editor of choice, such as Vim, with the script filename:

   vim yourScriptName.sh

2. On the first line of each script, type this header line: #!/bin/bash.

3. When the coding is complete, save the script and return to the command prompt in the terminal.

4. Modify the permissions of the script to be executed using the following command:

   chmod 755 yourScriptName.sh

5. To run the script, type ./yourScriptName.sh.

```
                                 User01@CentOS7:~                      _  □  ✕

 File  Edit  View  Search  Terminal  Help
[User01@CentOS7 ~]$ ./for_in.sh Jane Doe
You have passed 2 arguments to this script.
The 2 arguments were Jane and Doe respectively.
Counting up to the parameter count limit:  1
Counting up to the parameter count limit:  2
Argument 1: Jane
Argument 2: Doe
[User01@CentOS7 ~]$ ./for_in.sh Jane
Error: Incorrect number of command line arguments.
              Actual number of argument(s) passed:  1
./for_in.sh: line 11: Required number of argument(s): : command not found
Error#:  60
Counting up to the parameter count limit:  1
Argument 1: Jane
[User01@CentOS7 ~]$ ./for_in.sh Jane Mary Doe
Error: Incorrect number of command line arguments.
              Actual number of argument(s) passed:  3
./for_in.sh: line 11: Required number of argument(s): : command not found
Error#:  60
Counting up to the parameter count limit:  1
Counting up to the parameter count limit:  2
Counting up to the parameter count limit:  3
Argument 1: Jane
Argument 2: Mary
Argument 3: Doe
[User01@CentOS7 ~]$
[User01@CentOS7 ~]$ █
```

Figure 10-33 Output of the `for in` loop in a script

Source: CentOS 7/Terminal

Activity 10-6: Creating a Script in CentOS 7 to Work with Directories and Files

Time Required: 15 minutes

Objective: Create a directory and text file with a script.

Description: In this activity, you use the Vim editor to create a script file that adds a new directory, adds a new file within the directory, and adds text to the file. This activity is useful if you want to develop skills for creating scripts in CentOS 7.

1. If necessary, start your virtual machines using the appropriate instructions in Activity 1-1.

2. To open a terminal console, click **Applications**, point to **Utilities**, and then click **Terminal**.

3. To open the Vim editor with the filename, type **vim createNew.sh** at the command prompt and press **Enter**.

4. To begin Insert mode, press the **i** key.

5. To begin the script header, type **#!/bin/bash** on the first line of the file and press **Enter**.

6. To enter program documentation, type the following as one line and then press **Enter**.

#This script creates a directory and new file.

7. To finish the program documentation, type the following as one line and then press **Enter**.

#Text is entered and appended to the new file.

8. To create the newone directory, type **mkdir newone** and press **Enter**.

9. To create a new file and enter text in it, type the following as one line and then press **Enter**.

echo "This is text entered into a new file in the new directory" > newone/testing.txt

10. To append text to the new file, type the following as one line and then press **Enter**.

echo "Another line has been added to the test file text." >> /newone/testing.txt

To add some blank lines to the file, press **Enter** three times.

11. To provide a program exit, type **exit** 0 and then press **Enter**.

12. To save the file and return to the command line, press **Esc**, type **:wq**, and then press **Enter**.

13. To change the permissions of the new script, type the following command and press **Enter**.

chmod 755 createNew.sh

14. To run the script, type **./createNew.sh** and press **Enter**.

15. To view the new directory, type **ls** and press **Enter**.

16. To select the newone directory, type **cd newone** and press **Enter**.

17. To list the files in the directory, type **ls** and press **Enter**.

18. To view the contents of the new file and verify that it contains the two lines of information, type **cat testing.txt** and press **Enter**.

19. To close the terminal window, type **exit** and then press **Enter**.

20. Leave the virtual machine logged on for the next activity.

Activity 10-7: Creating a Script in CentOS 7 to Illustrate the `for in` Construct

Time Required: 15 minutes

Objective: Create a script that uses the `for in` construct.

Description: In this activity, you open the terminal window and then use the Vim editor to create a script file. The script displays a screen listing within a `for in` loop. This activity is useful if you want to develop skills for creating scripts that use loops.

1. If necessary, start your virtual machines using the appropriate instructions in Activity 1-1.

2. To open a terminal console, click **Applications**, point to **Utilities**, and then click **Terminal**.

3. To open the Vim editor, type **vim createlist.sh** at the command prompt and then press **Enter**.

4. To begin Insert mode, press the **i** key.

5. Type the text shown in Table 10-3. Press **Enter** at the end of each line.

```
#!/bin/bash
#for arg in "$var1" "$var2" "$var3" ... "$varN"
for plant in Daisy Geranium Grass Oak Juniper Rose Fern
do
echo $plant #Each plant on a separate line.
done
exit 0
```

Table 10-3 **Text for the createlist.sh script**

6. To save the file and return to the command prompt, press **Esc**, type **:wq**, and then press **Enter**.

7. To change the permissions of the new script, type the following command and press **Enter**.

   chmod 755 createlist.sh

8. To run the script, type **./createlist.sh** and press **Enter**.

9. Verify that the seven plant names are listed.

10. To close the terminal window, type **exit** and then press **Enter**.

11. To shut down the virtual machine, click the **User01** icon in the upper-right corner of the desktop, and then click the **Power Off** button twice.

12. Wait a moment for the CentOS 7 virtual machine to shut down completely.

13. Close any remaining open windows, log off, and shut down your PC.

Chapter Summary

- The PowerShell ISE provides a rich scripting experience. It enables you to write, run, and test scripts in a graphical and intuitive environment.

- Use the MKDIR and Set-Location cmdlets to create a directory structure.

- You can use incremental development to design, implement, and test scripts. The PowerShell Help and Get-Command features are essential in clarifying the proper use of PowerShell cmdlets.

- You can prepare reports with the Where-Object, Select-Object, Sort-Object, and Format-Table cmdlets.

- Scripts and batch command files can help you automate directory and file management tasks that you need to perform often.

- Troubleshoot PowerShell scripts with the Set-PSDebug cmdlet.

Key Terms

brace matching   A feature of certain text editors and integrated development environments that highlights matching sets of braces.

clear typing   In the ISE, a technique that minimizes errors by consistently observing typing rules.

Command Add-on pane   In the PowerShell ISE, a pane that allows selection of a PowerShell cmdlet.

Console pane   In the PowerShell ISE, a pane where cmdlets are typed for execution and the script output appears.

context-sensitive Help   In the PowerShell ISE, details about a cmdlet are presented in a window when you press the F1 key at the location of the cmdlet.

drag and drop text editing   A feature of the PowerShell ISE and many other applications that allows you to select any block of text and drag it to another location in the editor.

filtering   Commands that allow you to select items to remain in your work after filtering out unwanted items. In PowerShell, filtering is accomplished with the `Where-Object` cmdlet.

for in   The CentOS 7 version of the `for` command. You can use the command without `in` and vary the syntax depending on the task the loop needs to perform.

formatting   Commands that establish a layout for data. In PowerShell, formatting is accomplished with the `Format-Table` cmdlet.

header line   A construct in CentOS 7 scripts that signals a file is an executable script.

if else fi   A command in CentOS 7 that works like the `IF` command in Windows 7 when the `ELSE` clause is included.

if then ... fi   A command in CentOS 7 that is used when only one decision path is needed.

incremental development   A method of script development in which the script is designed, implemented, and tested incrementally until it is finished.

Integrated Scripting Environment (ISE)   The Microsoft script development and testing environment.

IntelliSense   A feature in PowerShell that helps you develop scripts quickly by providing automatic-completion assistance for cmdlets, parameters, parameter values, filenames, and folder names.

parse error display   In PowerShell, the red lines in the Console pane that indicate an error has occurred.

PowerShell profile   A set of cmdlets that run as the ISE is opened. PowerShell profiles can be used to configure your ISE environment according to your preference.

RemoteSigned   In PowerShell, a policy in which a digital signature is required for scripts received from an Internet site.

script   A program that consists of a set of instructions to control some function of an application or utility program; these instructions typically use the rules and syntax of the application or utility.

script-level tracing   A PowerShell tracing technology controlled by the `Set-PSDebug` cmdlet.

Script pane   In PowerShell, the pane where cmdlets are typed to create scripts.

selecting   Commands for selecting items to remain in a table after removing unwanted items using the `Select-Object` cmdlet.

sorting   Commands for arranging data based on criteria. In PowerShell, you use the `Sort-Object` cmdlet for sorting.

tracing   A feature in PowerShell that indicates the flow of statements in an executed script.

while   A command in CentOS 7 that enables you to execute a group of statements a specified number of times.

Review Questions

1. With the PowerShell ISE, you can _____. (Choose all that apply.)
   a. write scripts
   b. run scripts
   c. test scripts
   d. create graphics

2. The PowerShell ISE provides _____. (Choose all that apply.)
   a. brace matching
   b. IntelliSense
   c. content-sensitive Help
   d. a text editor

3. The PowerShell IntelliSense feature displays potentially matching _____ as you type. (Choose all that apply.)
   a. cmdlets
   b. parameters
   c. parameter values
   d. files

4. The PowerShell ISE provides which of the following panes? (Choose all that apply.)
   a. Debug
   b. Script
   c. Console
   d. Command Add-on

5. The PowerShell ISE toolbar provides which of the following buttons? (Choose all that apply.)

    a. Clear Console Pane

    b. Run Script (F5)

    c. Windows key

    d. Save

    e. Stop Operation

6. In the PowerShell ISE toolbar, which buttons clear the Output pane? (Choose all that apply.)

    a. Clear Console Pane

    b. Run Script (F5)

    c. The button that looks like a blue squeegee

    d. Windows key

    e. Stop Operation

7. With the `Get-Process` cmdlet, you can _____.

    a. debug a process

    b. start a process

    c. stop a process

    d. none of the above

8. With the `Help` cmdlet, you can use which of the following strings? (Choose all that apply.)

    a. `Get-Command`

    b. `'Create File'`

    c. `New-Item`

    d. `Format-Table`

9. The PowerShell profile is a script that _____. (Choose all that apply.)

    a. configures your PowerShell environment

    b. runs automatically

    c. loads modules

    d. formats tables

10. To arrange data values with PowerShell, use the _____ cmdlet.

    a. `Select-Object`

    b. `Sort-Object`

    c. `Filter-Object`

    d. `Where-Object`

10

11. To filter data values with PowerShell, use the _____ cmdlet.

    a. `Select-Object`

    b. `Sort-Object`

    c. `Filter-Object`

    d. `Where-Object`

12. With PowerShell, errors are indicated by _____.

    a. pop-up messages

    b. event logs

    c. red text

    d. green text

13. In PowerShell, cmdlets are separated by _____.

    a. carriage returns

    b. pipes

    c. break characters

    d. backticks

14. In PowerShell, which of the following comparison operators can be used? (Choose all that apply.)

    a. `-eq`

    b. `-like`

    c. `-notequal`

    d. `-match`

15. In PowerShell, which of the following rules are recommended for building scripts? (Choose all that apply.)

    a. Cmdlet names are always a combination of verbs and nouns, separated by a dash.

    b. Cmdlets and parameters are always separated by a space.

    c. Each parameter is separated by a space.

    d. Every parameter is preceded by a hyphen.

16. Scripts and batch files are written to _____. (Choose all that apply.)

    a. organize commonly used commands

    b. provide complex logical statements that maintain files

    c. provide more work

    d. use specific commands

17. After a CentOS 7 script is completed and saved, which commands are required to execute the script? (Choose all that apply.)

    a. `createlist > more`

    b. `chmod 755 createlist.sh`

    c. `./createlist.sh`

    d. `vim createlist.sh`

18. In CentOS 7 scripts, which commands are required? (Choose all that apply.)

    a. `#!/bin/bash`

    b. `head`

    c. `tail`

    d. `exit 0`

19. In CentOS 7 scripts, which commands enable multiple executions of a set of instructions until a condition is met? (Choose all that apply.)

    a. `circle`

    b. `for`

    c. `while`

    d. `loop`

20. Which of the following file extensions can you use on scripts in CentOS 7?

    a. .exe

    b. .cmd

    c. .bat

    d. .sh

Case Projects

Case 10-1: Explaining Why PowerShell Skills Are Important

You are walking between classes and overhear a conversation between two of your classmates. One classmate asks, "Why would I ever need to learn PowerShell scripting?" What would you say in reply?

Case 10-2: Preparing for a Presentation

You have been asked to make a brief presentation on preparing reports using PowerShell scripting. You need to provide a one-page handout that indicates the purpose of each cmdlet. Provide an example of each cmdlet.

Case 10-3: Creating a Script in CentOS 7 to Process Files

Create a script in CentOS 7 that uses the createlist.sh script described earlier in this chapter. The revised script must write the information to a file and then display the information to the user in descending sorted order.

Case 10-4: Creating a Script in CentOS 7 to Back Up Files

Create a script in CentOS 7 to list the contents of the /etc directory and redirect the output to a file called dir_list in your home directory. List the file contents and modify the script to make changes to filenames within the dir_list file. (Note: Do not modify the actual /etc directory in this case; modify the contents of the dir_list file.)

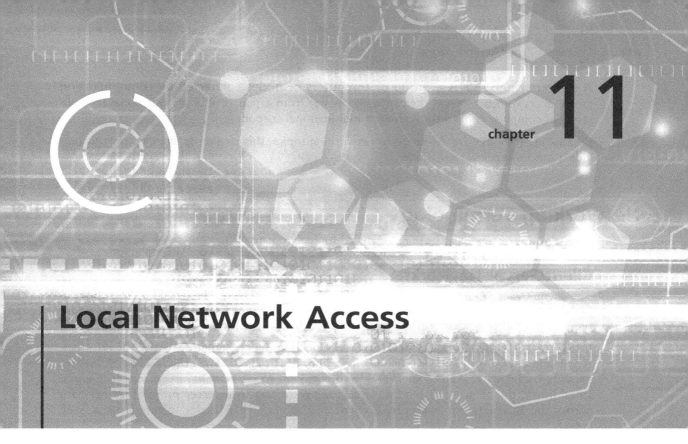

## chapter 11

Local Network Access

After reading this chapter and completing the exercises, you will be able to:

- Explain networking terminology
- View TCP/IP settings
- Access network resources
- View folder and file sharing permissions

A computer network is a group of computers or nodes connected by communication media and protocols. Networks can range in size from a pair of PCs in your home to thousands of computers linked throughout a multinational corporation.

Because entire books are dedicated to networking topics, this chapter is intended only to provide a quick overview.

Networking Terminology

This section presents basic terminology used to explain networking.

Client/Server Networks

The **client/server** model has become a central idea of networking. The term describes the relationship between two computers in which a desktop computer (the client) makes a service request of another computer (the server), which fulfills the request.

In Figure 11-1, the client is a desktop computer that accesses or uses network resources. A switch provides connectivity between the local client and the server. A server provides network resources such as files or printers to client computers and their users. In addition, the clients can send a request for resources to a server on another network across the Internet. For example, a client can request HTML documents from a Web server.

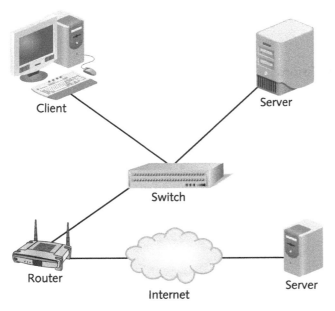

Client

Server

Switch

Router

Internet

Server

Figure 11-1 Client/server model

Peer-to-Peer Networks

You also may be familiar with **peer-to-peer networks**, which employ computers that are equally capable of being both clients and servers. An example is a small office/home office (SOHO) network, which serves the needs of small office environments and the self-employed. A typical SOHO network is shown in Figure 11-2; near the top is a router, which connects to the Internet. The router secures the local network and provides connectivity for the three local computers. Other services, such as those for file sharing, can extend the network to Internet clients.

Server Message Block (SMB) is a file sharing protocol commonly used by Windows for peer-to-peer connections. A variant of SMB, called *Common Internet Files System (CIFS)*, may also be used for file sharing. CentOS 7 provides peer-to-peer networking with **Samba**, which is based on the common client/server protocol. The name *Samba* was created by adding two *A*s to SMB. Samba is functionally identical to the protocols provided by Windows 10, which allows Windows 10 and CentOS 7 to share files.

LANs (Local Area Networks)

LANs (local area networks) are usually confined to a geographic area, such as a single building or a college campus. As shown in Figure 11-3, LANs can be small, linking as few as two or three computers, but often they link hundreds of computers used by many people. The development of standard networking protocols and media has resulted in worldwide proliferation of LANs throughout business and educational organizations.

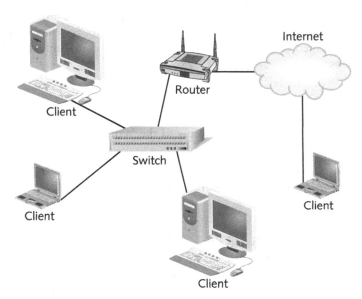

Figure 11-2 Peer-to-peer network model

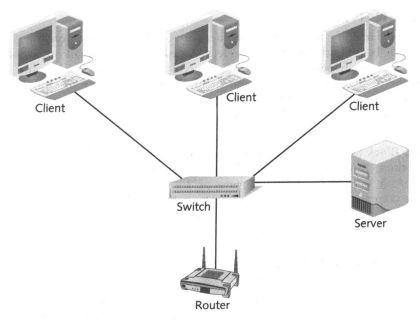

Figure 11-3 Local area network

WANs (Wide Area Networks)

Figure 11-4 shows a system that combines multiple, geographically separate LANs to form a WAN (**wide area network**). A WAN connects different LANs using services such as dedicated, leased data lines, satellite links, and data packet carrier services. Wide area networking can be as simple as a modem and remote access server for employees to dial into, or it can be as complex as hundreds of branch offices globally linked over data communication lines to send data over vast distances.

Internet

As you know, the Internet is a system of linked networks that are worldwide in scope and facilitate data communication services that permit access to the World Wide Web and e-mail.

With the rapid rise in demand for connectivity, the Internet has become a communications highway for billions of users. Social media, which include Facebook, Twitter, YouTube, and LinkedIn, could not have become popular without the Internet.

Intranet

With the advancements made in browser-based software for the Internet, many private organizations are implementing intranets. An intranet is a private network that uses Internet-type applications but is available only within a single organization. For large organizations, an intranet allows easy access to Web-based applications to provide corporate information for employees.

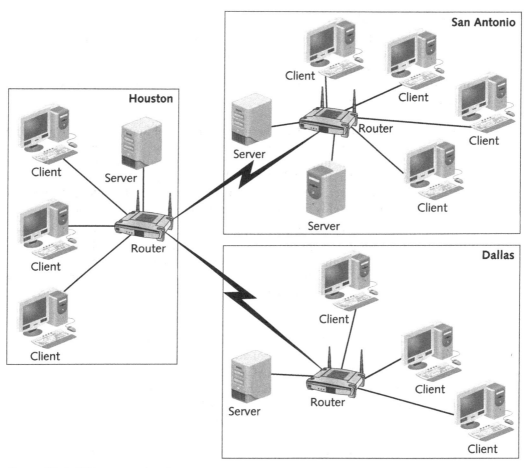

Figure 11-4 Wide area network

VPN

A **VPN** (**virtual private network**) uses a technique known as *tunneling* to transfer data securely on the Internet to a remote access server on your workplace network. Using a VPN helps you save money by using the public Internet to connect securely with your private network instead of requiring you to make long-distance dial-up calls. Data is routed over the Internet from your Internet service provider (ISP) to your organization. Encryption is used to ensure data security.

Internet Protocol

The **Internet Protocol** (**IP**) is the main networking protocol that allows for data communication across a network. Using this protocol, computers can deliver **packets**, or units of data, to other computers and devices based on their unique IP addresses. This protocol is the standard used by home and business computers and all networking software, and is the foundation of the Internet Protocol Suite.

Networking Protocols

A protocol is a set of rules that enables two computers to talk to each other. It is a computing standard that defines the syntax and regulations of a connection across a network: how to detect the other computer, how to send a message to it, how to format that message, and so on. A specific implementation may be referred to as a dialect of the protocol. For example, CIFS is a dialect of SMB.

The Internet Protocol Suite   The Internet Protocol Suite is a set of protocols used in combination for different networking tasks. IP and the Transmission Control Protocol (TCP) are the two underlying standards that all other protocols use, so the suite is commonly referred to as TCP/IP. While IP handles each transmission of each packet of data, the TCP is like an overseer, organizing data into packets and sending them to the IP. On the flip side, the TCP rebuilds files from the individual packets the IP sent.

The Internet Protocol Suite, as shown in Figure 11-5, is divided into four "layers" of communication from bottom to top: the Network (or Network Access) layer, the Internet layer, the Transport layer, and the Application layer. Very simply, the Network layer links the computers, the Internet layer allows the IP to transfer packets across the link, the Transport layer uses the TCP to organize the packets, and the Application layer consists of protocols for specific types of transfer.

Network Access   The Network Access layer specifies how data is sent as a signal over physical media. A unique media access control address, or **MAC address**, is used to identify a physical device like a network adapter. A MAC address consists of 48 bits or 6 bytes represented by a 12-digit hexadecimal number. The first half of the MAC address is assigned to the hardware manufacturer. The address resolution protocol (ARP) is used to resolve IP addresses at the next layer to MAC addresses at the Network Access layer.

Internet Layer   IP requires unique addresses, simply called **IP addresses**, to identify two computers or devices at the Internet layer. There are two standards of IP addresses. The most common is IPv4 (IP Address Version 4), which consists of 32 bits divided into four octets. Each octet is represented by a value between 0 and 255, and each value is separated by a period—192.168.0.1, for example. A newer standard, IPv6, has also emerged; it consists of 128 bits, resulting in longer addresses and more possibilities for variation. In this text, you use IP Version 4 addresses. Every networked computer is assigned an IP address, although a

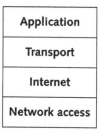

Figure 11-5 Internet Protocol Suite

Dynamic Host Configuration Protocol (DHCP) server can provide IP addresses dynamically. You learn about DHCP later in this chapter.

Transport Layer The Transport layer provides session management and a guarantee of delivery that is not available at lower levels. Protocols at this level include TCP, UDP, and others.

Application Layer While IP itself is the foundation for network communication, many other popular protocols exist in the topmost Application layer:

- HTTP (Hypertext Transfer Protocol), which allows Web users to request Web sites from remote servers
- FTP (File Transfer Protocol), which allows for the rapid transfer of files across the Web
- POP3 (Post Office Protocol 3), for sending and receiving e-mail
- SMTP (Simple Mail Transfer Protocol), for sending and receiving e-mail

There are other network models; some are similar to the Internet Protocol Suite but have slight differences, such as a Link layer instead of the Network Access layer. Another popular model is the OSI model, which contains seven layers.

Viewing TCP/IP Settings

To assist in troubleshooting TCP/IP-related problems, you need to know how to view TCP/IP settings. In this text, you will view IP Version 4 addresses. To communicate effectively on a routed network, such as a WAN, computers require four TCP/IP settings:

1. The IP address is a numerical label assigned to devices participating in a computer network that uses IP for communication between its nodes.
2. The subnetwork, or subnet, is a logically visible, distinctly addressed part of a single IP network. Subnetting is the division of a network into groups of computers that have a common, designated IP address routing prefix. The bits for the network are indicated by the subnet mask.
3. The gateway IP address is a node (a router) on a TCP/IP network that serves as an access point to another network.
4. The final item is the DNS IP address of the server that provides domain name resolution. Most importantly, this server translates domain names that are meaningful to people into numerical (binary) identifiers associated with networking equipment for the purpose of locating and addressing these devices worldwide. For example, *www.google.com* translates into IP address 74.125.227.51.

DHCP is a computer networking protocol used by hosts (DHCP clients) to retrieve IP address assignments and other configuration information. DHCP uses a client/server architecture. The client sends a broadcast request for configuration information; the DHCP server receives the request and responds with the needed information from its configuration database.

In the absence of DHCP, all hosts on a network must be manually configured with static IP addresses—a time-consuming and error-prone undertaking.

Viewing TCP/IP Settings in Windows 10

You can use Windows 10 GUI tools or execute commands from the command line to view TCP/IP settings in Windows 10.

Figure 11-6 shows the Network Connection Details window, which is a convenient way to view TCP/IP settings. To display the Network Connection Details window, right-click Start, click Network Connections, double-click a Connection link (Ethernet if available), and then click Details. A Yes value for the DHCP Enabled property means that the machine will look for a DHCP server for IP information and assignment; in this case, the DHCP server has an IP address of 192.168.227.254. All four required entries are present for the 192.168.227.0 network: an IPv4 address of 192.168.227.152, an IPv4 subnet mask of 255.255.255.0, an IPv4 default gateway of 192.168.227.2, and an IPv4 DNS server of 192.168.227.2.

The IPCONFIG /ALL command provides similar information, as shown in Figure 11-7. To access this information, right-click Start, click Command Prompt, type IPCONFIG /ALL, and then press Enter.

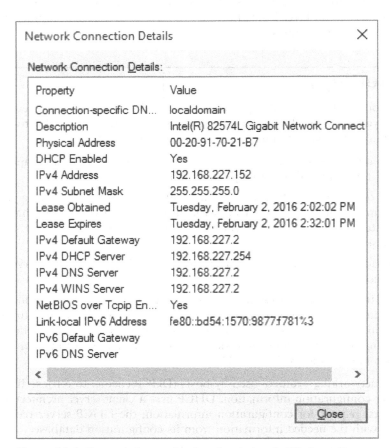

Figure 11-6 Network Connection Details window in Windows 10

Source: Windows 10/Network Connection

Figure 11-7 IP configuration in Windows CLI

Source: Windows 10/Command Prompt

Activity 11-1: Viewing TCP/IP Settings in Windows 10

Time Required: 10 minutes

Objective: View TCP/IP settings in Windows 10.

Description: In this activity, you will investigate ways to view the TCP/IP settings. First, you will use the Network Connection Details window to view the settings. Later in the activity, you will execute the IPCONFIG /ALL command. This activity is useful if you want to view your TCP/IP settings.

1. Start your virtual machines using the appropriate instructions in Activity 1-1.

2. To display the Network Connection Details window, right-click **Start,** click **Network Connections,** double-click **Ethernet** (or another connection), and then click **Details.**

3. Record your Physical Address, IPv4 address, Subnet Mask, and Default Gateway settings.

4. Close the open windows.

5. To open a command prompt, right-click **Start,** and then click **Command Prompt.**

6. To view the IP configuration, type **IPCONFIG /ALL** and then press **Enter.**

7. Compare your settings with the ones you recorded in Step 3.

8. Close the Command Prompt window.

9. Leave the virtual machine logged on for future activities.

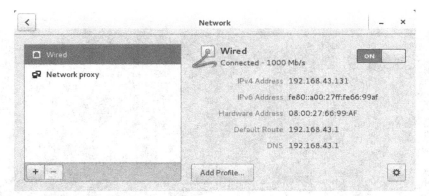

Figure 11-8 Network configuration window

Source: CentOS 7/Network

Viewing TCP/IP Parameters in CentOS 7

As in Windows 10, you can use the CentOS 7 GUI or execute commands from the terminal window to view TCP/IP settings. The Ethernet Device settings, as shown in Figure 11-8, follow the same sequence as Windows 10.

To display the Ethernet Device settings, click Applications, click System Tools, click Settings, and then click Network. When the window opens, highlight the active network connection. In Figure 11-8, the network card is set to DHCP, so the IP address is assigned by an outside computer.

Another way to view the IPv4 settings is to use the `ifconfig` or `ip` command in a terminal window. The results of using the `ifconfig` command are shown in Figure 11-9 for one network interface. The `ifconfig` command is an older command that has been deprecated in some installations (deprecated installations are tolerated or supported but not recommended). The `ifconfig` command shows all of the network adapter information except for the DNS information and gateway. Using the `ip` command requires several different commands to get the same information; for example, you can enter `ip -d addr` for the IP addresses or `ip -d route` for the default gateway. To see if a DNS lookup is set, you need to view the /etc/resolv.conf file. The DNS servers are noted in this file by the following notation: `nameserver 8.8.8.8` (Google's DNS lookup server).

Activity 11-2: Viewing TCP/IP Settings in CentOS 7

Time Required: 10 minutes

Objective: View TCP/IP settings using CentOS 7.

Description: In this activity, you will investigate ways to view the TCP/IP settings in CentOS 7. First, you will use the Ethernet Device window to view the settings. Later in the activity, you will execute the `ifconfig` command in the terminal window. This activity is useful if you want to view your TCP/IP settings.

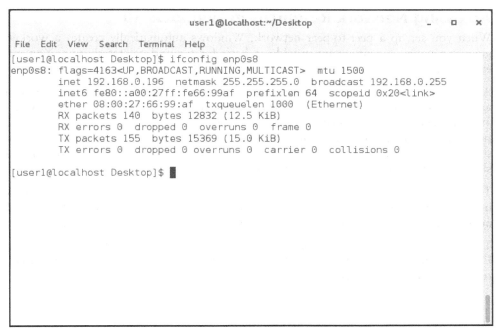

Figure 11-9 Network configuration from `ifconfig` terminal window

Source: CentOS 7/Terminal

1. If necessary, start your virtual machines using the appropriate instructions in Activity 1-1.

2. To display the Ethernet Device settings, click **Applications**, click **System Tools**, click **Settings**, and then click **Network**.

3. Highlight the active network interface.

4. Record the IP address, IP gateway, and DNS IP address for future use.

5. Close the open windows.

6. To use the `ifconfig` tool to view the TCP/IP settings, right-click the desktop and click **Open in Terminal**.

7. Type **ifconfig**, and then press **Enter**.

8. Notice that many different interfaces are displayed, but look for the interface that has an IP address that matches the one you saw in Step 3.

9. Compare your settings with the ones you recorded in Step 4.

10. Close the Command Prompt window.

11. Leave the virtual machine logged on for future activities.

Accessing Network Resources

When you speak of network resources, you are usually referring to shared folders and files on file servers, shared resources and files on other people's computers, and shared printers.

Accessing Network Resources in Windows 10

When you set up a peer-to-peer network, Windows automatically creates a workgroup and gives it a name. A **workgroup** provides a basis for file and printer sharing. You can join an existing network workgroup, by default called WORKGROUP, or you can create a new one.

Also, you can create or join a homegroup in Windows 10, which automatically turns on file and printer sharing on home networks. A **homegroup** makes it easy to share your libraries and printers on a home network. You can share pictures, music, videos, documents, and printers with other people in your homegroup. The homegroup is protected with a password, so you can always choose what you share with the group. If you have a home network, you should create or join an existing homegroup.

The Network option in File Explorer displays shortcuts to shared computers, printers, and other resources on the network. These shortcuts are created automatically in the Network area whenever you open a shared network resource, such as a printer or shared folder.

To open the Network window, click Start, click File Explorer, and then click Network. File Explorer shows the computers in the network that are participating in the shared network resources (see Figure 11-10).

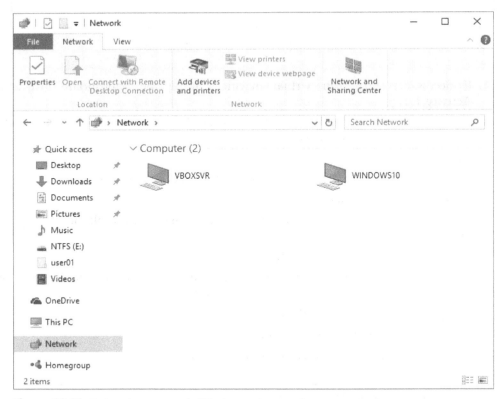

Figure 11-10 Network resources in Windows

Source: Windows 10/File Explorer

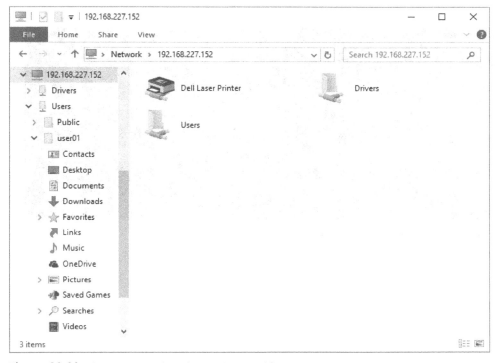

Figure 11-11 Shares on Windows host using IP address

Source: Windows 10/File Explorer

To see the shares that another computer is offering, type *servername*\ in the Windows Search text box and then click the server name. In place of *servername* in the preceding command, you can use the name of the other computer. If your computer cannot resolve the server name (which may occur on a home network), use the IP address, as shown at the top of Figure 11-11.

Also, you can type NET VIEW *servername* at a command prompt to see the shares that another computer is offering. Again, for *servername* you can use the name of the other computer. If your computer cannot resolve the server name, use the IP address (see Figure 11-12).

Windows 10 allows you to refer to network shares through the use of syntax known as **UNC (Universal Naming Convention)** notation. Using UNC notation requires that you know the name or IP address of the server and share. You can then open a folder to a network location by typing the UNC in the search box, as shown in Figure 11-13. To access the files, click one of the items displayed in the search results.

Also, you can access a network share from the command prompt by using the following syntax for the NET USE command:

```
NET USE [drive letter | *] \\computername\sharename
```

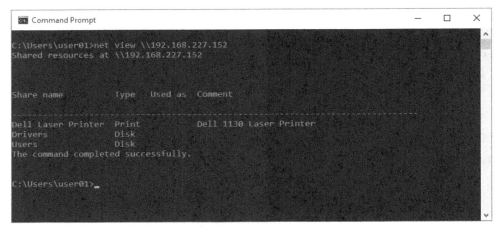

Figure 11-12 Net View command showing shares in Windows CLI

Source: Windows 10/Command Prompt

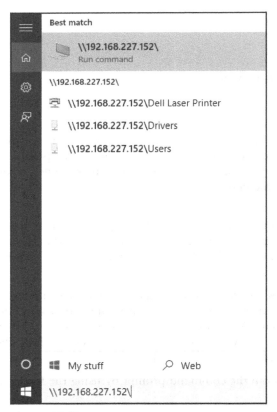

Figure 11-13 Accessing network shares from the Windows search tool

Source: Windows 10

You may specify a drive letter or permit Windows 10 to provide one. If you do not provide a drive letter, Windows 10 will assign drive letters in reverse order starting with Z:. For example, to connect the N: drive to the Windows 10 virtual machine and the Drivers share, type:

```
NET USE N: \\Windows10\Drivers
```

The N: drive is available in Windows Explorer. Of course, you can use the DIR directory command to view the files.

Activity 11-3: Connecting to a Network Share in Windows 10

Time Required: 10 minutes

Objective: Connect to a network share using Windows 10.

Description: In this activity, you will investigate ways to connect to a shared folder. First, you will need to determine the IP address for your host computer. Next, you will use the search box to locate and connect to the TextShare folder on your host computer. The TextShare folder was installed on the host computer when you followed the instructions in Appendix B, C, or D for your virtualization software. Later in the activity, you will connect to the share using a UNC. This activity is useful if you want to access network data.

1. If necessary, start your virtual machines using the appropriate instructions in Activity 1-1.

2. Perform Steps 2 through 4 in Activity 11-1 on your host computer to determine the IP address for accessing the computer.

3. Minimize your virtual machine.

4. To display the Network Connection Details window, right-click **Start** on your host computer, click **Network Connections**, double-click the **Ethernet** (or other connection) link, and then click **Details**.

5. Record the IPv4 address for your host computer.

6. Close the open windows.

7. To display the shared files for the TextShare folder on your host computer, click **Start**, type ***IPv4 Address*** in the search text box, and then click the **TextShare** folder on your host computer.

If you are unable to connect to the TextShare folder, contact your instructor.

8. Close the File Explorer window.

9. Return to the Windows 10 virtual machine. To open a command prompt, right-click **Start**, and then click **Command Prompt**.

10. To use the UNC to locate the shared files, type the following and press **Enter**:

    NET USE * \\IPv4Address\TextShare

11. Verify that Windows 10 assigned the Z: drive for the shared folder.

12. To change to the Z: drive, type **Z:** and then press **Enter**.

13. To view the filenames, type **DIR** and press **Enter**.

14. Close the Command Prompt window.

15. To view the contents of the Z: drive in Windows Explorer, click **Start**, click **File Explorer**, and then click **TextShare (*IPv4 Address*) (Z:)**.

16. To view the contents of the Article12.txt file in Notepad, double-click **Article12.txt**.

17. Close the open windows.

18. Leave the virtual machine logged on for future activities.

Checking Network Resources in CentOS 7

After setting up a network connection, it is important to check the communication between your computer and adjacent computers. To check whether a computer is able to communicate with another computer in the network, you can use the ping command. If the command is successful, a message on the screen reports how many bytes the sent packet contained and how long the message took to be requested and received. Using the ping command is very useful for checking that the network is set up correctly, especially if the network information has been entered manually.

If the network is not working or the other system cannot be found, the ping command returns a series of "Destination Host Unreachable" messages, as shown in Figure 11-14. Using the ping command is very helpful to verify that your system is connected and that it can communicate on the network. When the computer is available, the ping command returns a series of bytes, as shown in Figure 11-15. You might have noticed that in the previous examples, the ping command was used with an IPv4 IP address. In Figure 11-16, you can see the same use of the command, but an Internet routable host name is used (*www.sun.com*) instead of an IP address.

Another tool, called traceroute, is very useful for checking whether the network communication is working. Traceroute can be used to see every "hop" that a connection makes (see Figure 11-17), including all of the switches, routers, firewalls, or other computers that your communication hops across to reach the requested host. Sometimes when using traceroute, the communication stops and you see a series of *** symbols because the devices in the path are not available or a device has been configured not to respond to this type of request, as shown in Figure 11-18.

Accessing Network Resources in CentOS 7

CentOS 7's methods for accessing shared files are similar to the methods used in Windows 10. To access a share, you must mount the share. After you create a directory for the mount destination, you can type the mount command and specify the UNC for the share, the logon credentials, and the destination directory. Once the share completes, you change the directory to the mount destination and issue an ls command to view the files.

```
                    user1@localhost:~/Desktop                    _  □  ×

 File  Edit  View  Search  Terminal  Help
[user1@localhost Desktop]$ ping 12.41.71.189
PING 12.41.71.189 (12.41.71.189) 56(84) bytes of data.
From 12.41.71.248 icmp_seq=1 Destination Host Unreachable
From 12.41.71.248 icmp_seq=2 Destination Host Unreachable
From 12.41.71.248 icmp_seq=3 Destination Host Unreachable
From 12.41.71.248 icmp_seq=4 Destination Host Unreachable
From 12.41.71.248 icmp_seq=5 Destination Host Unreachable
From 12.41.71.248 icmp_seq=6 Destination Host Unreachable
^C
--- 12.41.71.189 ping statistics ---
8 packets transmitted, 0 received, +6 errors, 100% packet loss, time 7000ms
pipe 3
[user1@localhost Desktop]$
```

Figure 11-14 Unsuccessful `ping` command

Source: CentOS 7/Terminal

```
                    user1@localhost:~/Desktop                    _  □  ×

 File  Edit  View  Search  Terminal  Help
[user1@localhost Desktop]$ ping 192.168.122.1
PING 192.168.122.1 (192.168.122.1) 56(84) bytes of data.
64 bytes from 192.168.122.1: icmp_seq=1 ttl=64 time=0.058 ms
64 bytes from 192.168.122.1: icmp_seq=2 ttl=64 time=0.059 ms
64 bytes from 192.168.122.1: icmp_seq=3 ttl=64 time=0.058 ms
64 bytes from 192.168.122.1: icmp_seq=4 ttl=64 time=0.077 ms
64 bytes from 192.168.122.1: icmp_seq=5 ttl=64 time=0.058 ms
64 bytes from 192.168.122.1: icmp_seq=6 ttl=64 time=0.057 ms
64 bytes from 192.168.122.1: icmp_seq=7 ttl=64 time=0.058 ms
^C64 bytes from 192.168.122.1: icmp_seq=8 ttl=64 time=0.059 ms
64 bytes from 192.168.122.1: icmp_seq=9 ttl=64 time=0.075 ms
64 bytes from 192.168.122.1: icmp_seq=10 ttl=64 time=0.106 ms
^C
--- 192.168.122.1 ping statistics ---
10 packets transmitted, 10 received, 0% packet loss, time 8999ms
rtt min/avg/max/mdev = 0.057/0.066/0.106/0.017 ms
[user1@localhost Desktop]$
```

Figure 11-15 Successful `ping` command

Source: CentOS 7/Terminal

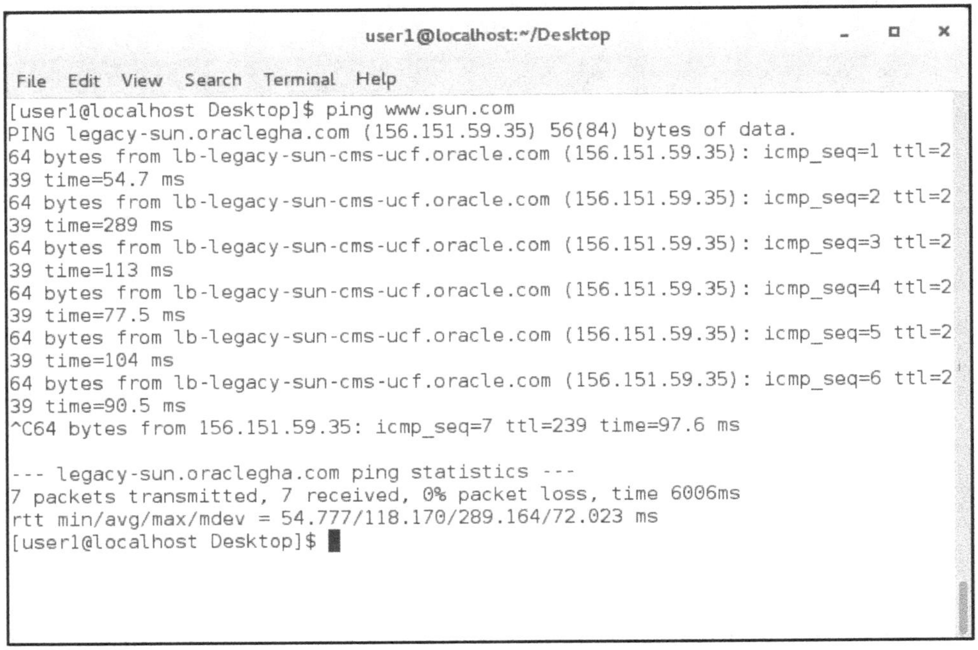

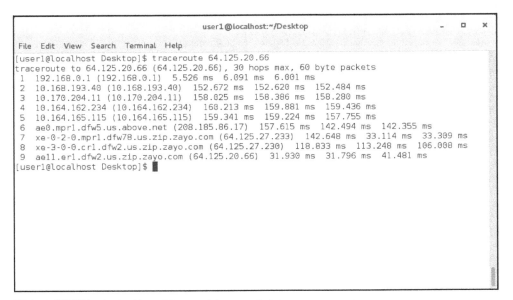

Figure 11-16 A ping command used with a host name

Source: CentOS 7/ Terminal

Figure 11-17 Output of traceroute command

Source: CentOS 7/ Terminal

```
                              user1@localhost:~/Desktop                    _  □  ×
 File  Edit  View  Search  Terminal  Help
 4  10.164.162.234 (10.164.162.234)  80.232 ms  81.866 ms  82.382 ms
 5  10.164.165.115 (10.164.165.115)  82.274 ms  99.758 ms  101.467 ms
 6  ae0.mpr1.dfw5.us.above.net (208.185.86.17)  100.995 ms  86.669 ms  86.366 ms
 7  xe-0-2-0.mpr1.dfw78.us.zip.zayo.com (64.125.27.233)  80.661 ms ae3.cr2.dfw2.us.zip.zayo.c
om (64.125.28.85)  48.508 ms  49.993 ms
 8  ae8.cr1.dfw2.us.zip.zayo.com (64.125.20.205)  48.930 ms  48.826 ms xe-3-0-0.cr1.dfw2.us.z
ip.zayo.com (64.125.27.230)  48.736 ms
 9  ae11.er1.dfw2.us.zip.zayo.com (64.125.20.66)  48.648 ms  41.052 ms  41.600 ms
10  *  *  *
11  *  *  *
12  *  *  *
13  *  *  *
14  *  *  *
15  *  *  *
16  *  *  *
17  *  *  *
18  *  *  *
19  *  *  *
20  *  *  *
21  *  *  *
22  *  *  *
23  *  *  *
24  *  *  *
25  *  *  *
```

Figure 11-18 Unsuccessful `traceroute` command

Source: CentOS 7/Terminal

Likewise, you can use File Browser to see the file entries. After a network drive has been mounted, it becomes almost transparent from a directory perspective, which can be a problem if the computer sharing the files is booted. The file system will disappear and the directory will seem empty because the file share cannot be remounted.

Activity 11-4: Connecting CentOS 7 to a Network

Time Required: 10 minutes

Objective: Verify that the system has network connectivity.

Description: In this activity, you will open a terminal session, and then use the `ping` and `traceroute` commands to verify that your system can communicate with other systems using network connections.

1. If necessary, start your virtual machines using the appropriate instructions in Activity 1-1.

2. To open a terminal session, right-click the desktop and select **Open in Terminal**.

3. To verify connectivity to the router, type **ping** and then the IP address of the default gateway you recorded in Step 4 of Activity 11-2.

4. Verify that the response is similar to that shown in Figure 11-15.

5. To end the pings, press **CTRL+C**.

6. To illustrate a scenario in which connectivity does not occur, type **ping 172.16.5.89** and press **Enter**.

7. For this ping, you should receive a negative response, "No Destination to Host," similar to that shown in Figure 11-14.

8. To end the pings, press **CTRL+C**.

9. In the terminal window, type **ping www.sun.com** or any other Internet address. (This command will work only if you are connected to the Internet.)

10. Verify that you receive a positive response, indicating a good connection.

11. To end the pings, press **CTRL+C**.

12. In the terminal window, start a trace by typing **traceroute www.sun.com** and pressing **Enter**.

13. Close any open windows.

14. Leave the virtual machine logged on for future activities.

The command in Step 12 may not travel all the way to the *www.sun .com* server because of possible restrictions in the network, but it should reveal how far your computer is able to trace. Sometimes it is interesting to note the names of the switches and routers the messages traverse and where they might be located across the world.

Accessing Network Printers

It makes good economic sense to share a printer and make it available to several users on a network. Network administrators are responsible for setting up shared printers on the network. The following activities explain how to connect and access a network printer in Windows 10 and CentOS 7, respectively.

Activity 11-5: Connecting a Network Printer in Windows 10 Using the Add Printer Wizard

Time Required: 10 minutes

Objective: Connect to a network printer using the Add Printer Wizard.

Description: In this activity, you use the Add Printer Wizard to connect to a network printer. This activity is useful if your network has a shared printer.

1. If necessary, start your virtual machines using the appropriate instructions in Activity 1-1.

2. Click **Start**, click **Settings**, click **Devices**, and click **Printers & Scanners** (if necessary), and then click the **Add printers & scanners** link.

3. Click **The printer that I want is not listed**. (You may have to wait while Windows performs an automatic search before the link appears.)

4. Click the **Select a shared printer by name** option button.

5. In the Name text box, type ***IPv4 Address**SharedPrinter*,** substituting your IP address for *IPv4 Address*. When you finish, click **Next**.

If you receive an error message, contact your instructor for assistance.

6. Wait for the printer to be detected, and then click **Next** to accept the default name.

7. To finalize the installation, click **Finish**.

8. Close any open windows.

9. Leave the virtual machine logged on for future activities.

Activity 11-6: Accessing Network Printers in CentOS 7

Time Required: 10 minutes

Objective: Connect to a Windows shared printer in CentOS 7.

Description: In this activity, you will open a terminal session, change to the superuser, and connect to the Windows shared printer on your host computer. This activity is useful if you want to connect to a Windows network printer.

1. If necessary, start your virtual machines using the appropriate instructions in Activity 1-1.

2. To open a terminal session, right-click the desktop and select **Open in Terminal**.

3. To switch to the superuser, type **su –** and press **Enter**. Type **Pa$$w0rd** and press **Enter**.

4. To open the printer dialog box, type **system-config-printer** and then press **Enter**.

5. To select the new printer, click **Add**, click **Yes**, click **Network Printer**, scroll through the list, and then click **Windows Printer via SAMBA**.

6. Type *IP address*/**SharedPrinter** in the smb:// text box, substituting your IP address for *IP address*. When you finish, click **Forward**.

7. Wait for the driver search to complete.

8. To specify the driver, click **Generic**, click **Forward**, click **Generic Text-only printer**, click **Forward**, and then click **Apply**.

9. When asked if you want to print a test page, click **Cancel**.

10. Close the open windows.

11. Leave the virtual machine logged on for future activities.

Folder and File Sharing Permissions

When administrators share files and folders with you and other computer users on the network, you can open and view those files and folders as if they were stored on your own computers. Any changes that administrators allow users to make to a shared file or folder will change the file or folder on your computer. However, administrators can restrict people to viewing shared files without having the ability to change them.

This section explains how to view file permissions in Windows 10 and CentOS 7. To troubleshoot problems related to file sharing, you need to know how to view these settings.

Managing Windows NT File System Permissions

Because system access and security are so crucial, you must be able to view folder and file permissions and make sure that only authorized users can access local and network folders and files.

NT File System Required The NTFS is required to share folders and files with other network users. Although the FAT and FAT32 file systems permit folders to be shared, they do not provide the required permissions to properly secure the files. Only NTFS permits user accounts and user groups to be linked to folder and file permissions, which are required to implement the needed security.

Using Local User Groups Administrators use local user groups to simplify the management and authorization of network resources. Groups are created to define sets of user accounts that require access to the same resources. For example, users who conduct sales activities can be placed in the Sales group, and newly hired salespeople can be added to the group as new user accounts so that all salespeople have access to the same network resources. Likewise, if a person switches jobs from sales to advertising, his or her user account permissions in the Sales group would need to be switched to the Advertising group permissions.

Activity 11-7: Viewing Local User Groups in Windows 10

Time Required: 15 minutes

Objective: View local user groups.

Description: In this activity, you view a local user group that consists of the local user accounts. This activity is useful because it will help you answer questions about local user groups.

1. If necessary, start your virtual machines using the appropriate instructions in Activity 1-1.

2. Right-click **Start**, and then click **Computer Management**.

3. Expand **Local Users and Groups** in the left pane and then click **Groups**, which displays the window shown in Figure 11-19.

User accounts have single-headed icons and user groups have two-headed icons.

4. Close any open windows.

5. Leave the virtual machine logged on for future activities.

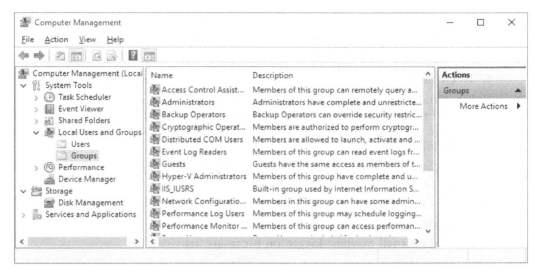

Figure 11-19 Local Users and Groups in Windows

Source: Windows 10/Computer Management

Shared folder permission	Definition
Read	Displays folders and files within a shared folder and executes programs contained in the folder
Change	Has all of the permissions associated with the Read permission; also allows you to add folders and files to the shared folder, and to append to or delete existing files
Full Control	Has all of the permissions associated with the Change permission; also allows you to change file permissions and take ownership of the file resources (if you have the proper NTFS permissions)

Table 11-1 Windows 10 shared folder permissions

Viewing Shared Folder Permissions When sharing a folder with users on a network, administrators must specify the level of access they are willing to assign to specific users. They must also balance security with functionality by allowing access to appropriate resources and prohibiting unauthorized access. To support shared access, Windows 10 provides the shared folder permissions listed in Table 11-1.

Activity 11-8: Viewing Share Permissions in Windows 10

Time Required: 15 minutes

Objective: View share permissions on a folder.

Description: In this activity, you view the share permissions on an existing folder. This activity is useful because it will help you answer users' questions about using share permissions.

1. If necessary, start your virtual machines using the appropriate instructions in Activity 1-1.

2. To view shared resources, right-click **Start,** and then click **Computer Management.**

3. Double-click **Shared Folders.** In the right pane, double-click **Shares.**

4. To create a new share, click the **Action** menu, and then click **New Share.**

5. When the share wizard starts, click **Next,** click **Browse,** expand **This PC,** navigate to the **NTFS E:** drive, click **Make New Folder,** type **Drivers,** and click **OK.** Click **Next,** verify that the default share name is Drivers, click **Next,** leave the default permissions, and click **Finish** twice.

6. Right-click the **Drivers** shared folder, click **Properties,** and then click the **Shared Permissions** tab.

7. Verify that the **Everyone** and **Read** boxes are checked. Click **Cancel.**

8. Close any open windows.

9. Leave the virtual machine logged on for future activities.

Assigning NTFS Permissions Administrators secure the folders and files on an NTFS volume. It is worth repeating that the NT file system is required to use NTFS permissions. Unless you are a member of a group with assigned permissions, you cannot access the files for that account or group.

You can view folder permissions that control access to folders and the files in them. Table 11-2 lists the NTFS permissions that can be assigned to a folder.

You assign file permissions to control access to files. Table 11-3 lists the NTFS permissions that can be assigned to a file.

Multiple NTFS Permissions Although permissions can be assigned to individual user accounts, it is more effective to assign them to user groups. Being a member of a local user group entitles a user to the same permissions as the other group members. If you have

Permission	Description
List Folder Contents	Allows you to view the names of subfolders and files
Read	Allows you to view files and subfolder names and to view folder attributes, ownership, and permissions
Read & Execute	Has all of the permissions associated with the List Folder Contents and Read permissions; also allows you to traverse folders
Write	Allows you to create files and subfolders within the folder, change folder attributes, and view ownership and permissions
Modify	Has all of the permissions associated with the Read & Execute and Write permissions; also allows you to delete folders
Full Control	Allows you to change permissions, take ownership of folders, delete subfolders and files, and perform the actions granted by the other permissions

Table 11-2   NTFS folder permissions

Permission	Description
Read	Allows you to read files and view file attributes, ownership, and permissions
Read & Execute	Allows you to run applications and perform the actions permitted by the Read permission
Write	Allows you to overwrite existing files, change file attributes, and view ownership and permissions
Modify	Has all of the permissions associated with the Read & Execute and Write permissions; also allows you to modify and delete files
Full Control	Allows you to change permissions, take ownership of folders, delete files, and perform the actions granted by the other permissions

Table 11-3   **NTFS file permissions**

memberships in multiple groups, the permissions associated with each group are combined. The exception to this rule is Deny. When Deny appears as the Read permission, for example, it overrides any other Read permission.

NTFS permissions are assigned to all of the files on the NTFS volume. When determining a user's effective permissions, you must examine the permissions assigned to particular resources. Remember that permissions assigned at the file level override those assigned at the folder level.

Permission Inheritance   When you create or copy a subfolder or a file, it inherits the permissions of the parent folder by default. This concept, known as *permission inheritance*, is illustrated in Figure 11-20. For example, after the Accounting folder was created, the

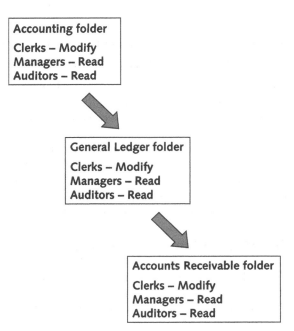

Figure 11-20 Permission inheritance

indicated permissions were assigned. When the General Ledger folder was created as a subfolder in the Accounting folder, its permissions were inherited from the Accounting folder. Likewise, Accounts Receivable inherited the permissions of the General Ledger folder.

Administrators can prevent subfolders and files from inheriting the parent's permissions if they do not want changes to the parent folder to affect its subfolders and files. When administrators elect to prevent inheritance, they must choose one of the following options:

- Copy the inherited permissions from the parent folder.
- Remove the inherited permissions and retain only the assigned permissions.

Combining Shared Folder and NTFS Permissions Administrators use share permissions to grant access to resources over a network. In a previous section, you encountered shared folder permissions, which provide limited security. Shared folder permissions provide access to an entire directory structure, from the shared folder down to the subfolders, so administrators seldom use these permissions without also using NTFS permissions.

By combining shared folder permissions and NTFS permissions, administrators gain the highest level of security and control. To effectively use these permissions together, administrators must combine them to control access to network resources. Administrators can use shared folder permissions to grant access to folders over the network and then use NTFS permissions to secure the resources in your file system. NTFS offers the most flexible level of control and can be assigned to resources on an individual basis.

To determine your effective permissions for a given network resource, you need to complete the following three steps:

1. Combine the shared folder permissions (recall that Deny prevents access and overrides other permissions).
2. Combine the NTFS folder permissions (again, Deny overrides other permissions).
3. Determine which permission is the most restrictive—this is the effective permission.

Figure 11-21 illustrates these three steps. The shared folder permissions have a combined permission of Full Control. The NTFS permissions—Read, Write, and Modify—combine as Modify. Between Full Control and Modify, the more restrictive permission is Modify.

 To demonstrate these three steps, you can write the shared folder permissions on the left side of a marker board and the NTFS permissions on the right. To indicate how shared folder permissions are combined, make a trickling motion. Repeat this motion for the NTFS permissions. To indicate the most restrictive permission, join your hands together.

Moving and Copying Files in NTFS Volumes When you use File Explorer to copy or move files and folders within or between NTFS volumes in Windows 10, the files or folders will inherit permissions from the destination folder. When you move a file or folder between NTFS volumes, it must be created on the destination volume, meaning that the moved file or folder will inherit the destination folder's permissions. When files or folders are moved within an NTFS partition using the MOVE command from the CLI, they retain their original permissions after the move.

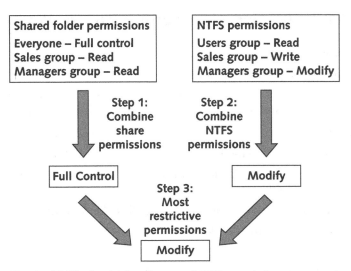

Figure 11-21 Combining Share and NTFS permissions

 If you used File Explorer prior to Windows Server 2008 or Windows Vista, recall that NTFS permissions were retained for the move on the same NTFS partition. The move behavior is different in the new version of File Explorer, in that it treats a move as a "copy, paste, delete" operation so that the file is created in the new location rather than having its pointer updated. This difference makes administration much easier and gives users less chance to accidentally create file and folder structures with incorrect permissions.

However, the MOVE command in the CLI has not changed! Regardless of the operating system, the MOVE command works the same way. That is, a move retains the original permissions if it occurs on the same partition.

Be aware that neither the FAT16 nor FAT32 file system supports NTFS permissions—only NTFS does. Likewise, NTFS permissions are removed when a file or folder is moved or copied to a FAT16- or FAT32-formatted partition.

Table 11-4 summarizes permission inheritance for move and copy actions on the same volume or different volumes when you use File Explorer or the MOVE command in the CLI. Note that the only option that retains permissions is a move on the same volume using the MOVE command in the CLI.

	File Explorer		MOVE Command in CLI	
Action	**Same Volume**	**Different Volume**	**Same Volume**	**Different Volume**
Copy	Inherit	Inherit	Inherit	Inherit
Move	Inherit	Inherit	Retain	Inherit

Table 11-4   Effects of move and copy actions on NTFS permissions

Activity 11-9: Viewing NTFS Permissions in Windows 10

Time Required: 15 minutes

Objective: View the NTFS permissions for a folder.

Description: In this activity, you view the NTFS permissions assigned to a folder. This activity is useful because it will help you answer users' questions about using NTFS permissions.

1. If necessary, start your virtual machines using the appropriate instructions in Activity 1-1.

2. Click **Start**, click **File Explorer**, click **This PC**, and then double-click **NTFS (E:)**.

3. If the Drivers folder does not exist, click **Home** on the Ribbon, click **New Folder**, and then type **Drivers** to name the folder.

4. Right-click the **Drivers** folder, click **Properties**, and then click the **Security** tab.

5. Review the NTFS permissions, and then click **OK**.

6. Close any open windows.

7. To shut down the virtual machine, click **Start**, click **Power**, and then click the **Shut Down** option.

8. Wait a moment for the Windows 10 virtual machine to shut down completely.

Activity 11-10: Analyzing Share and NTFS Permissions

Time Required: 10 minutes

Objective: Analyze share and NTFS permissions to determine the effective permissions.

Description: In this activity, you combine share permissions, combine NTFS permissions, and determine the effective permission for a given scenario. This activity is useful because it will help you answer users' questions regarding security.

1. Using Figure 11-21 and Table 11-5 as guides, specify the combined permissions and the effective permission for a scenario in which Laura is a member of the Everyone, Executive, and Finance groups.

Combined share permissions	Combined NTFS permissions	Most restrictive permission

Table 11-5   Combined permissions and effective permission

2. Using Figure 11-21 and Table 11-6 as guides, specify the combined permissions and the effective permission for a scenario in which Bob is a member of the Everyone, Executive, and Accounting groups.

Combined share permissions	Combined NTFS permissions	Most restrictive permission

Table 11-6   Combined permissions and effective permission

3. Using Figure 11-21 and Table 11-7 as guides, specify the combined permissions and the effective permission for a scenario in which Roger is a member of the Everyone, Executive, and Marketing groups.

Combined share permissions	Combined NTFS permissions	Most restrictive permission

Table 11-7   Combined permissions and effective permission

4. Using Figure 11-21 and Table 11-8 as guides, specify the combined permissions and the effective permission for a scenario in which Marie is a member of the Everyone, Accounting, Executive, and Finance groups.

Combined share permissions	Combined NTFS permissions	Most restrictive permission

Table 11-8   Combined permissions and effective permission

5. Using Figure 11-21 and Table 11-9 as guides, specify the combined permissions and the effective permission for a scenario in which George is a member of the Everyone, Finance, and Marketing groups.

Combined share permissions	Combined NTFS permissions	Most restrictive permission

Table 11-9   Combined permissions and effective permission

Viewing CentOS 7 File Permissions

When specifying CentOS 7 permissions, you basically define them by files and directories. Throughout this book, you have used the ls command with the −l option to see detailed lists of directories and files in a file system.

Each file and directory has permissions for the owner, group, and everyone else, as shown in Figure 11-22. The permissions for each group consist of three (binary) bits. The 10th bit is the sticky bit, as you will learn later. The bits are assigned as RWX.

You can view these file permissions from the Properties dialog box in File Browser (see Figure 11-23).

Use the ls command with the −l option to show the file permissions. When you type the following command, you see the output shown in Figure 11-24.

ls −l

The first character in the permissions column is the file type. The available file types are listed in Table 11-10. Table 11-11 lists some combinations of permissions for files and directories.

```
drwxr-xr-x.  2 root          root
drwx--x--x.  4 root          gdm
```

Figure 11-22 Linux permissions

Source: CentOS 7/Terminal

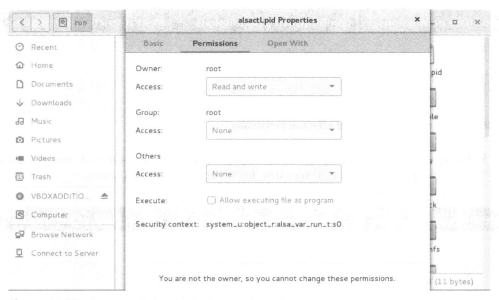

Figure 11-23 Linux permissions in GNOME Desktop GUI

Source: CentOS 7/GNOME Desktop

```
user1@localhost:/run
File  Edit  View  Search  Terminal  Help
prw-------.  1 root   root               0 Jan 31 18:27 dmeventd-server
drwxr-xr-x.  2 root   root              40 Jan 31 18:27 faillock
drwx--x--x.  4 root   gdm              120 Jan 31 18:28 gdm
-rw-------.  1 root   root               4 Jan 31 18:27 gssproxy.pid
srw-rw-rw-.  1 root   root               0 Jan 31 18:27 gssproxy.sock
drwxr-xr-x.  4 root   root             120 Jan 31 18:27 initramfs
-rw-r--r--.  1 root   root               4 Jan 31 18:27 ksmtune.pid
drwxr-xr-x.  6 root   root             160 Jan 31 18:27 libvirt
-rw-r--r--.  1 root   root               4 Jan 31 18:27 libvirtd.pid
drwxr-xr-x.  7 root   root             180 Jan 31 18:27 lock
drwxr-xr-x.  3 root   root              60 Jan 31 18:27 log
drwxrwxr-x.  3 root   libstoragemgmt    60 Jan 31 18:27 lsm
drwx------.  2 root   root              80 Jan 31 18:27 lvm
-rw-r--r--.  1 root   root               4 Jan 31 18:27 lvmetad.pid
drwx--x---.  2 root   root              40 Jan 31 18:27 mdadm
drwxr-xr-x.  3 root   root              60 Jan 31 18:28 media
drwxr-xr-x.  2 root   root              80 Jan 31 18:28 mount
drwxrwxr-x.  2 root   root              40 Jan 31 18:27 netreport
drwxr-xr-x.  2 root   root              80 Jan 31 18:27 NetworkManager
drwxr-xr-x.  2 root   root              40 Jan 31 18:28 plymouth
drwxr-xr-x.  2 root   root              40 Jan 31 18:27 ppp
drwxr-xr-x.  2 radvd  radvd             40 Jan 31 18:27 radvd
drwx------.  2 rpc    rpc               40 Jan 31 18:27 rpcbind
srw-rw-rw-.  1 root   root               0 Jan 31 18:27 rpcbind.sock
```

Figure 11-24 Linux permissions with different users and groups

Source: CentOS 7/Terminal

Character	File type
D	Directory
-	Regular file
C	Character device
B	Block device
L	Link
S	Socket
P	Named pipe

Table 11-10 CentOS 7 file types

Display	Permissions
r--	Read only
r-x	Read and execute
rw-	Read and write

Table 11-11 CentOS 7 file and directory permissions

The User Identification Attribute The file permissions bits include an execute permission bit for the file owner, the group, and others. When the execute bit is set for the owner, the SUID bit (short for *set user ID*) is set to *s*. This permission allows any users or processes that run the file to have the same access to system resources as the owner of the file. This permission is important if a program must use the same environment as the owner's. (See Figure 11-25.)

```
-rwSrw-r--. 1 user1 user1 53 Jan 31 19:12 File.txt
```

Figure 11-25 Permissions with SUID set

Source: CentOS 7/Terminal

NOTE This permission can be dangerous because the ability to run someone else's programs allows other users to enjoy the permissions for the duration of the program run. This is how hackers get superuser rights; they break out of the running program and keep the resource permissions.

The Sticky Bit Setting the **sticky bit** ensures that only the owner (and root, of course) who created a file in his or her directory can delete the file and prevent malicious or accidental deletion by others. A *t* or *T* appears as the third character of the Others permission bits when the sticky bit is set, as shown in Figure 11-26.

```
-rw-rw-r-T. 1 user1 user1 53 Jan 31 19:12 File.txt
```

Figure 11-26 The sticky bit

Source: CentOS 7/Terminal

Activity 11-11: Viewing File Permissions in CentOS 7

Time Required: 10 minutes

Objective: View the permissions for a file in CentOS 7.

Description: In this activity, you view the permissions for a file. This activity is helpful when you want to check file permissions.

1. If necessary, start your virtual machines using the appropriate instructions in Activity 1-1.

2. To open a terminal console, right-click the desktop and select **Open in Terminal**.

3. To change the directory to the home directory, type : **cd /var/log/** and then press **Enter**.

4. To view the file permissions for the message file, type **ls –l message** and then press **Enter**.

5. Look at the file list that is returned and notice the permissions on the file.

6. Close the terminal window.

7. To shut down the virtual machine, click **User01**, click **Power Off,** and then click the **Power Off** button.

8. Wait a moment for the CentOS 7 virtual machine to shut down completely.

9. Close any remaining open windows, log off, and shut down your PC.

Chapter Summary

- A network is a series of computers interconnected by communication paths. Common network organizations are client/server, peer-to-peer, LANs, and WANs. The Internet Protocol Suite is the de facto standard for network communications.

- To enable communications in a routed network, a computer must have an IP address, subnet mask, gateway IP address, and DNS IP address.

- Network resources, folders, files, and printers are shared on the network. In Windows 10, you can access these resources from File Explorer and the Add Printer Wizard. In CentOS 7, network resources are accessed using the `mount` command and the `system-config-printer` command.

- File permissions enable users to access needed files and enable groups to share project files and folders. A file's owner and the system administrator determine a file's level of access. Be careful not to give blanket permissions to users who may not need access to your files.

Key Terms

client/server   A network architecture in which each computer or process on the network is either a client or a server.

Dynamic Host Configuration Protocol (DHCP)   An autoconfiguration protocol used on IP networks.

homegroup   A feature available in Windows 10 that permits a simple password-protected network with other Windows systems (versions 7 and up) through which you can easily share printers and folders.

Internet Protocol (IP)   The principal communications protocol used for relaying packets across the Internet.

IP address   A numeric label assigned to each computer, printer, and other device in a computer network.

LAN (local area network)   A network that is usually confined to a small geographic area.

MAC address   The media access control address uniquely identifies a physical device like a network adapter.

network   A series of computer devices or nodes interconnected by communication paths.

packets   Units of data traveling over a network.

peer-to-peer network   A type of network in which each workstation has equivalent capabilities and responsibilities.

Samba   The CentOS 7 implementation of peer-to-peer networking.

Server Message Block (SMB) A network protocol used by Windows 10 and CentOS 7 computers that allows systems within the same network to share files.

sticky bit An access flag that you can assign to files and directories on UNIX systems. When the sticky bit is set for a directory, users can only modify and delete files and subdirectories in the directories they own.

UNC (Universal Naming Convention) A naming convention used primarily to specify and map network drives.

VPN (virtual private network) A secured private network connection built on top of publicly accessible infrastructure.

WAN (wide area network) Two or more LANs. Computers connected to a WAN are often connected through public networks.

workgroup A collection of computers on a LAN that share common resources and responsibilities.

Review Questions

1. A _____ employs computers that are capable of being both clients and servers.

   a. client/server network

   b. peer-to-peer network

   c. LAN

   d. WAN

   e. VPN

2. The four layers of the Internet Protocol Suite are arranged in which of the following orders from top to bottom?

   a. Application, Internet, Transport, Network Access

   b. Application, Transport, Internet, Network Access

   c. Network Access, Internet, Transport, Application

   d. Application, Link, Transport, Network Access

3. TCP/IP normally requires which of the following settings to communicate on a routed network using a computer host name like *www.sun.com*? (Choose all that apply.)

   a. IP address

   b. Subnet mask

   c. Default gateway address

   d. DNS IP address

   e. Web server address

4. _____ is a computer networking protocol used by hosts to retrieve IP address assignments.

   a. DNS

   b. Workgroup

   c. DHCP

   d. Homegroup

5. In Windows 10, the _____ command displays TCP/IP settings.

   a. DHCP

   b. DNS

   c. IPCONFIG -A

   d. IPCONFIG /ALL

6. In CentOS 7, the _____ command displays TCP/IP settings. (Choose all that apply.)

   a. DHCP

   b. DNS

   c. ifconfig –a

   d. IPCONFIG

   e. IPCONFIG /ALL

7. In Windows 10, the _____ makes it easy to share libraries with a single password.

   a. peer-to-peer network

   b. client/server

   c. homegroup

   d. workgroup

8. In Windows 10, the NET USE command maps a _____ to a shared folder.

   a. user

   b. drive letter

   c. homegroup

   d. computer

9. In Windows 10, the correct format for the UNC is _____.

   a. *driveletter**sharename*

   b. *servername**sharename*

   c. *servername**driveletter*

   d. *sharename**servername*

10. To securely share folders and files with required permissions in Windows 10, use the _____ file system.

    a. NT

    b. FTS

    c. FAT32

    d. FAT

11. Folder permissions are used to _____.

    a. keep paging at a minimum

    b. control access to folders and their files

    c. maintain processors

    d. control memory usage

12. Which of the following statements is true of NTFS? (Choose all that apply.)

    a. It is required to support NTFS permissions.

    b. Some of its permissions are not supported by FAT16 and FAT32 file systems.

    c. Some of its permissions are removed when a file or folder is moved or copied to a FAT16- or FAT32-formatted partition.

    d. Its permissions are supported by FAT16 and FAT32 file systems.

13. In CentOS 7, the file type is a _____ when the first bit in the permissions column is a "-".

    a. directory

    b. socket

    c. link

    d. regular file

14. In CentOS 7, the file type is a _____ when the first bit in the permissions column is a d.

    a. directory

    b. socket

    c. link

    d. regular file

15. To switch to the superuser in CentOS 7, use the _____ command.

    a. su –

    b. SU–

    c. SUPERUSER

    d. Superuser

16. In Windows 10, the shared folder permissions are _____. (Choose all that apply.)

    a. Read

    b. Write

    c. Change

    d. Full Control

17. In Windows, the NTFS file permissions are _____. (Choose all that apply.)

    a. Read

    b. Write

    c. Change

    d. Full Control

18. When a file is moved to an existing folder on the same partition with File Explorer, permissions _____.

    a. are retained

    b. are inherited

    c. must be reentered by the administrator

    d. are ignored

19. CentOS 7 has permissions for _____. (Choose all that apply.)

    a. the owner

    b. the user

    c. the group

    d. everyone

20. In CentOS 7, the r-x file permissions represent _____.

    a. Read only

    b. Read and change

    c. Read and execute

    d. Read and write

Case Projects

CASE PROJECTS

Case 11-1: Accessing File Shares

You have been asked to give a short presentation on accessing file shares from Windows 10 and CentOS 7. Prepare a one-page handout to support your presentation.

Shared folder permissions	NTFS folder permissions
Everyone – Full control	Everyone – Read
Accounting – Deny all	Accounting – Modify
Executive – Read	Executive – Read
Finance – Change	Finance – Modify
Marketing – Read	Marketing – Write

Figure 11-27 Combined Share and NTFS permissions activity

Case 11-2: Using Share and NTFS Permissions

You are interviewing for a summer job as a desktop support technician. All client computers at the company run Windows 10. Before moving to the Finance Department, Upali was a member of the Accounting Department. He is a member of the Accounting and Finance groups, and is attempting to gain access to the Schedules folder, which has the share and NTFS permissions shown in Figure 11-27. How will you give Upali access to the Schedules folder?

Case 11-3: Investigating a User Access Problem

Your company's Programming Department installed a new client notes system last weekend. You get a call from Janey, who cannot use the new system. She can log on and access the initial screen, but when she clicks the calendar, she gets an error message that reads "No calendar found." Your associate tells you that the calendar module is installed on the server and that all interfaces have been tested by the Development Department. How will you investigate this access problem using the `ls` command?

## chapter 12

Operating System Management

After reading this chapter and completing the exercises, you will be able to:

- Manage tasks
- Monitor performance
- Monitor reliability

Operating system management is the general area of information technology that deals with the configuration and management of computer resources. In this chapter, you will learn to manage the processes that are executed on your virtual machine and measure the virtual machine's performance. Also, you will monitor your virtual machine's reliability.

Managing Tasks

Sometimes your computer might seem slow and unresponsive for reasons you do not understand. Using the task management tools in Windows 10 and CentOS 7, you can explore the factors that affect your virtual machine's performance.

Managing Tasks in Windows 10

As you learned in Chapter 2, the Windows 10 Task Manager provides information about the programs and processes running on your computer and displays common performance measurements for these processes. The following section provides a more comprehensive explanation of Task Manager.

Before you learn to use Task Manager, you will learn a technique for running a system tool when you do not have the administrative privileges to execute it.

Using the Run As Feature You can use the Run As feature to access system tools that require administrative privileges and determine the cause of a problem. This feature works like the sudo command in CentOS 7. Knowing the cause of a problem might help you resolve it. See Activity 12-1 for details on using the Run As feature.

Activity 12-1: Running a Computer Management Tool without Administrative Privileges

Time Required: 15 minutes

Objective: Run a program that requires administrative privileges from an account with limited rights.

Description: In this activity, you practice using the Run As feature to run a program that requires administrative privileges. This activity is useful for troubleshooting problems without disturbing users by having them log off their user accounts.

1. Start your virtual machines using the appropriate instructions in Activity 1-1.

2. To open the administrative tools, right-click **Start** and then click **Control Panel**. If necessary, click **View By** and then click **Small icons**. Click **Administrative Tools**.

3. In the Administrative Tools folder, right-click **Computer Management** and then click **Run as administrator**. Click the **The following user** option button. If necessary, type **Administrator** in the User name text box, type **Pa$$w0rd** in the Password text box, and then click **OK**.

4. Click **Device Manager**.

5. Click **View**, click **Resources by type**, and then expand **Interrupt request (IRQ)**.

6. Review the IRQs.

7. Close the Computer Management window and any other open windows.

8. Leave the virtual machine logged on for the next activity.

Using Task Manager Use Task Manager to monitor active applications and processes on your computer. You can also stop a hung application or process, which helps your computer run better. You can start Task Manager on your virtual machine (see Figure 12-1) in one of two ways:

- Right-click an empty area of the taskbar, and click Task Manager.

- Press the Windows and X keys at the same time, and then select Task Manager.

If you need to access Task Manager from a native installation of Windows 10, you have another alternative: Press Ctrl+Shift+Esc.

Consult your virtualization software for the actions needed to key the Ctrl+Alt+Delete sequence.

By default, Task Manager opens to the same Fewer details or More details view it displayed when it was last closed (see Figure 12-2).

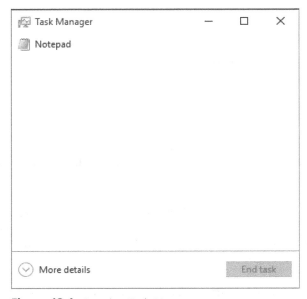

Figure 12-1 Opening Task Manager

Source: Microsoft Windows 10/Task Manager

		2% CPU	54% Memory	0% Disk	0% Network
Name	Status				
Apps (5)					
> ⊞ Microsoft Management Console		0%	3.7 MB	0 MB/s	0 Mbps
> ⊞ Task Manager		0%	12.7 MB	0 MB/s	0 Mbps
> ⊞ Windows Explorer (4)		0%	25.6 MB	0 MB/s	0 Mbps
> ⊞ Windows PowerShell		0%	3.2 MB	0 MB/s	0 Mbps
> ⊞ Windows PowerShell ISE		0%	12.2 MB	0 MB/s	0 Mbps
Background processes (11)					
⊞ Application Frame Host		0%	1.7 MB	0 MB/s	0 Mbps
◉ Cortana		0%	46.1 MB	0 MB/s	0 Mbps
⊞ Device Association Framework ...		0%	1.9 MB	0 MB/s	0 Mbps
⊞ Host Process for Windows Tasks		0%	2.1 MB	0 MB/s	0 Mbps
☁ Microsoft OneDrive (32 bit)		0%	1.6 MB	0 MB/s	0 Mbps
⧗ Microsoft Windows Search Filte...		0%	0.8 MB	0 MB/s	0 Mbps
> ⧗ Microsoft Windows Search Inde...		0%	7.6 MB	0 MB/s	0 Mbps

Task Manager — □ ×
File   Options   View
Processes   Performance   App history   Startup   Users   Details   Services

⌃ Fewer details   End task

Click to toggle between more details and fewer details

Figure 12-2 Detailed view of Task Manager

Source: Microsoft Windows 10/Task Manager

Use the six tabs in Task Manager to control and examine information about processes, performance, application history, startup programs, details, and services. The following sections describe each tab.

Another tab called *Users* is available in Task Manager if your computer is in a Windows workgroup or is a stand-alone system with no networking capabilities installed. This tab is not available to computer systems in a domain network.

Using the Processes Tab in Task Manager The Processes tab is shown by default when you open Task Manager (see Figure 12-3). There are two primary components: Currently running processes are shown on the left side, and a "heat map" of resource

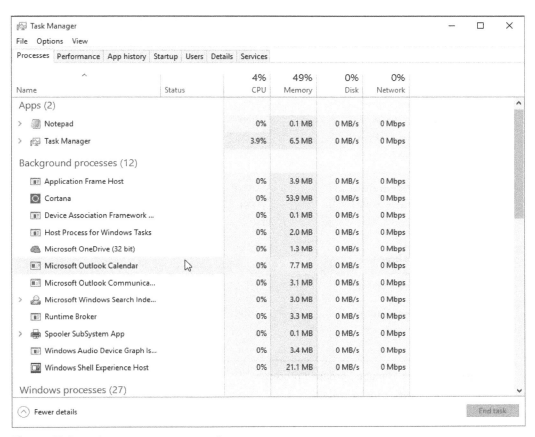

Figure 12-3 Task Manager, Processes tab

Source: Microsoft Windows 10/Task Manager

utilization is shown on the right side. Running processes are sorted by applications at the top of the window, non-Windows background processes, and then Windows processes. Applications are listed at the top of the window for easy monitoring and managing. The heat map displays resources like CPU, memory, network, and disk utilization sorted by processes. The color coding helps you better visualize resource utilization. Low resource utilization is shown in pale yellow, while darker shades of yellow and orange represent greater resource utilization. If the utilization reaches critical levels, values will be shown with a red background. Color coding makes it easy to pinpoint where high resource utilization is taking place.

If the program is not behaving as expected or is taking too many resources, you can kill the program by selecting it and clicking the End task button.

In addition to killing applications, you can stop background and Windows processes from the Processes tab. Background processes, as the name implies, run in the background. Windows processes are run by the Windows operating system. Similar processes are usually

Task Manager				1%	46%	0%	0%	
File Options View								
Processes Performance App history Startup Users Details Services								
Name		Status		CPU	Memory	Disk	Network	
Client Server Runtime Process				0%	0.4 MB	0 MB/s	0 Mbps	
Desktop Window Manager				0%	21.8 MB	0 MB/s	0 Mbps	
> Local Security Authority Process...				0%	2.2 MB	0 MB/s	0 Mbps	
> Microsoft Network Realtime Ins...				0%	2.5 MB	0 MB/s	0 Mbps	
> Service Host: DCOM Server Proc...				0%	3.5 MB	0 MB/s	0 Mbps	
> Service Host: Local Service (9)				0%	4.4 MB	0 MB/s	0 Mbps	
⌄ Service Host: Local Service (Net...				0%	5.1 MB	0 MB/s	0 Mbps	
DHCP Client								
HomeGroup Provider								
Security Center								
TCP/IP NetBIOS Helper								
Windows Audio								
Windows Connection Manager								
Windows Event Log								
> Service Host: Local Service (No I...				0%	0.8 MB	0 MB/s	0 Mbps	
> Service Host: Local Service (No...				0%	8.7 MB	0 MB/s	0 Mbps	
⌃ Fewer details							End task	

Figure 12-4 Task Manager, grouped processes

Source: Microsoft Windows 10/Task Manager

grouped under a parent process. To view a set of these subprocesses, click the appropriate chevron to expand a parent process (see Figure 12-4). Right-click any process to display a context menu that provides more details about the process. The menu also lets you end a task, search online, open the file location for a process, and create a dump file for troubleshooting (see Figure 12-5).

To view all grouped applications in Task Manager, click the View menu and then click Expand All.

Using the Performance Tab in Task Manager From the Performance tab (see Figure 12-6), you can get a quick view of your computer's CPU, memory, disk, and network usage. The left side of the tab displays live, miniature performance graphs and the right side displays a detailed view of the selected metric. Double-click the left side of the tab to display a live graph summary of all performance categories. Double-click the right side to display a full-sized graph for a selected category. Double-click the graph to return to the normal display. You can also highlight a metric to display more detailed metrics for that category. For

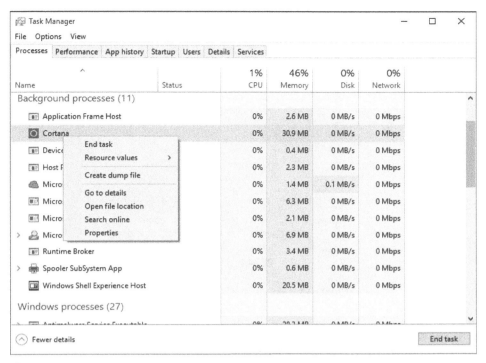

Figure 12-5 Task Manager context menu

Source: Microsoft Windows 10/Task Manager

example, selecting CPU displays more details about the CPU on the lower-right side of the tab, along with the amount of time the computer has been on (the "Up" time, as shown in Figure 12-6). You can also open Resource Monitor to see more performance data. The graphs for each category are color coded for easy reading.

Select the Memory performance category to show statistics for memory usage and memory composition, including total memory and memory in use (see Figure 12-7). Select a disk to see details about its total capacity, as shown in Figure 12-8, as well as read and write speeds and a notification of whether a page file is in use. Select a network, such as Ethernet in Figure 12-9, to see details about the connection type and your IP address. In Windows 10, these graphic views are dynamically scaled to reflect current utilization of resources.

Using the App History Tab in Task Manager As the name suggests, this tab shows metrics for historical application usage (see Figure 12-10). By default, the tab shows utilization for Windows Store applications only. To view details for all applications, click the Options menu, and then check the option for "Show history for all processes," as shown in Figure 12-11. To delete the usage history and reset all metrics to show zero usage, you can click the Delete usage history link just under the row of tabs.

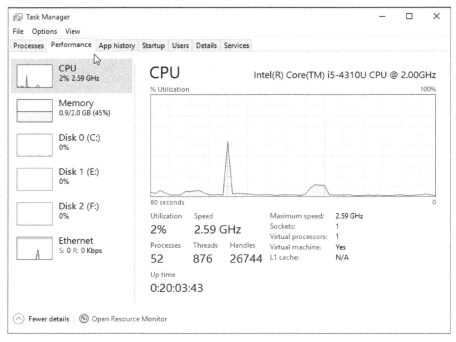

Figure 12-6 Task Manager, Performance tab (CPU)

Source: Microsoft Windows 10/Task Manager

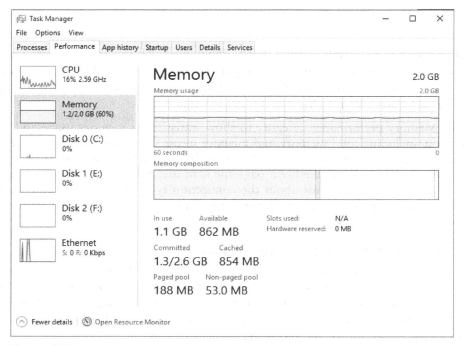

Figure 12-7 Task Manager, Performance tab (Memory)

Source: Microsoft Windows 10/Task Manager

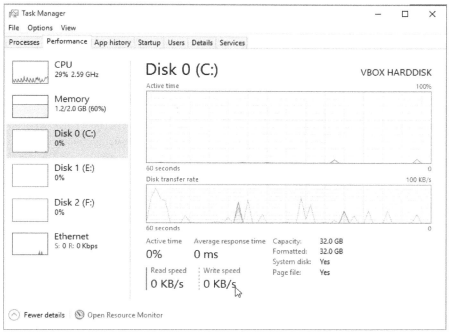

Figure 12-8 Task Manager, Performance tab (Disk)

Source: Microsoft Windows 10/Task Manager

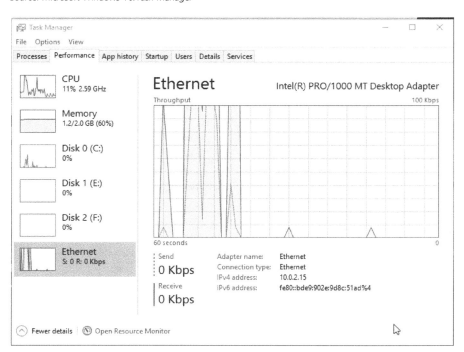

Figure 12-9 Task Manager, Performance tab (Network)

Source: Microsoft Windows 10/Task Manager

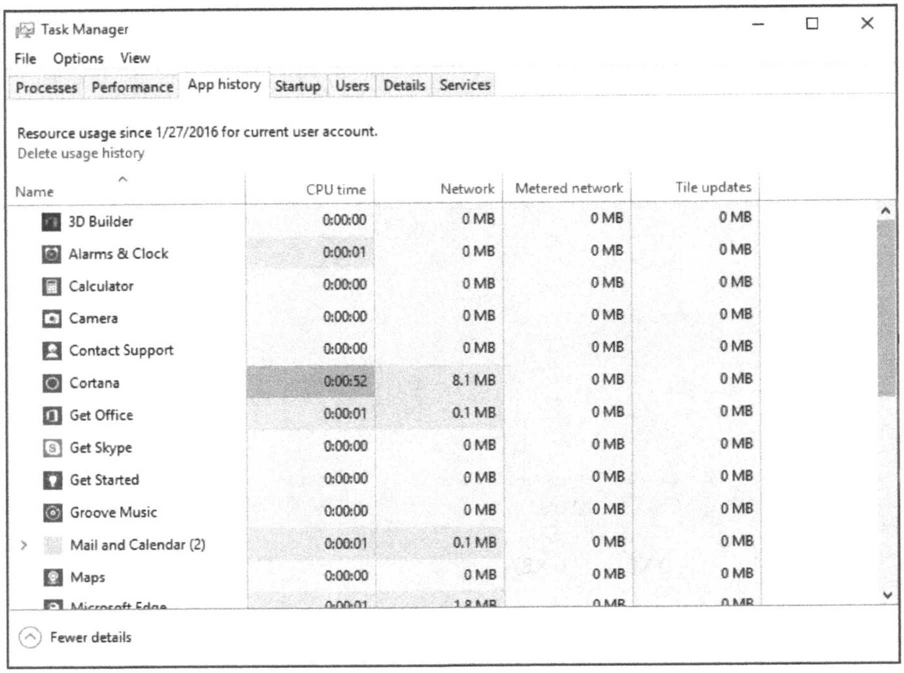

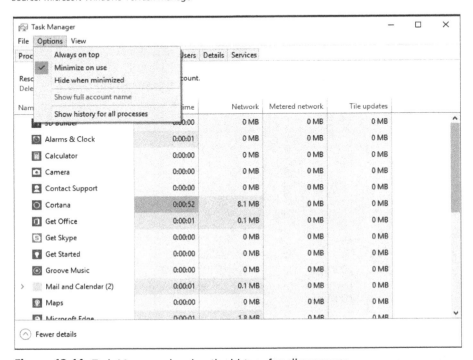

Figure 12-10 Task Manager, App history tab

Source: Microsoft Windows 10/Task Manager

Figure 12-11 Task Manager showing the history for all processes

Source: Microsoft Windows 10/Task Manager

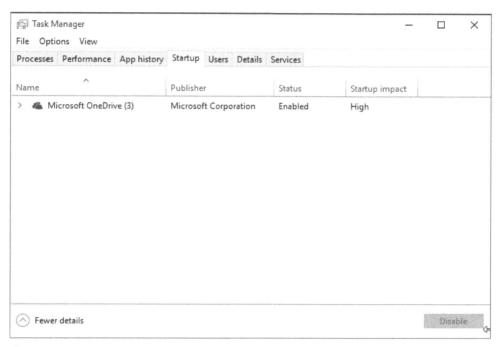

Figure 12-12 Task Manager, Startup tab

Source: Microsoft Windows 10/Task Manager

Using the Startup Tab in Task Manager The Startup tab shown in Figure 12-12 displays which programs start automatically during system log-in. Windows 10 also measures and reports the impact these programs have during boot time in the Startup impact column. Not all columns are activated by default. To analyze the impact rating that Windows assigned a program, you may want to view columns such as Startup type, Disk I/O at startup, CPU at startup, Running now, Disabled time, and Command line (see Figure 12-13). You can display these columns by right-clicking a column heading.

The Startup tab is useful for troubleshooting slow performance or unknown behavior for certain processes. The tab also helps you see a summary of the computer's startup performance and tune startup behavior, all in one place. To prevent a program from running at startup, select the program and click Disable.

Using the Users Tab in Task Manager Figure 12-14 shows the resources that your account is using. It also shows other users on the system and allows you to switch to other user sessions or to disconnect them.

Using the Details Tab in Task Manager The Details tab displays more information about all the processes that are running on the PC (see Figure 12-15). A process can be an

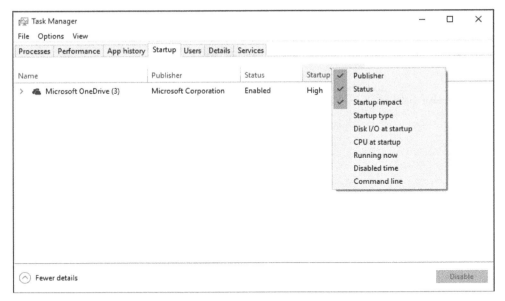

Figure 12-13 Task Manager, displaying more information in the Startup tab

Source: Microsoft Windows 10/Task Manager

User	Status	99% CPU	56% Memory	0% Disk	0% Network
∨ ⊞ User01 (18)		0.5%	90.3 MB	0 MB/s	0 Mbps
⊞ Task Manager		0.5%	8.3 MB	0 MB/s	0 Mbps
⊞ Desktop Window Manager		0%	17.5 MB	0 MB/s	0 Mbps
⊞ Windows Explorer		0%	11.7 MB	0 MB/s	0 Mbps
⊞ Runtime Broker		0%	2.1 MB	0 MB/s	0 Mbps
⊜ Internet Explorer		0%	39.9 MB	0 MB/s	0 Mbps
⊞ Client Server Runtime Proc...		0%	0.3 MB	0 MB/s	0 Mbps
⊜ Microsoft OneDrive (32 bit)		0%	1.5 MB	0 MB/s	0 Mbps
⊞ Application Frame Host		0%	2.4 MB	0 MB/s	0 Mbps
⊞ Notepad		0%	0.3 MB	0 MB/s	0 Mbps
⊞ Calendar		0%	0.1 MB	0 MB/s	0 Mbps
⊙ Cortana		0%	0.1 MB	0 MB/s	0 Mbps
⊞ Host Process for Windows ...		0%	1.5 MB	0 MB/s	0 Mbps

Figure 12-14 Task Manager, Users tab

Source: Microsoft Windows 10/Task Manager

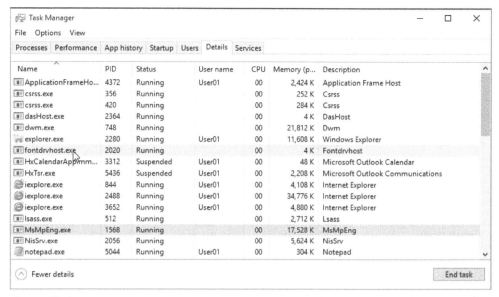

Name	PID	Status	User name	CPU	Memory (p...	Description
▣ ApplicationFrameHo...	4372	Running	User01	00	2,424 K	Application Frame Host
▣ csrss.exe	356	Running		00	252 K	Csrss
▣ csrss.exe	420	Running		00	284 K	Csrss
▣ dasHost.exe	2364	Running		00	4 K	DasHost
▣ dwm.exe	748	Running		00	21,812 K	Dwm
▣ explorer.exe	2280	Running	User01	00	11,608 K	Windows Explorer
▣ fontdrvhost.exe	2020	Running		00	4 K	Fontdrvhost
▣ HxCalendarAppImm...	3312	Suspended	User01	00	48 K	Microsoft Outlook Calendar
▣ HxTsr.exe	5436	Suspended	User01	00	2,208 K	Microsoft Outlook Communications
◉ iexplore.exe	844	Running	User01	00	4,108 K	Internet Explorer
◉ iexplore.exe	2488	Running	User01	00	34,776 K	Internet Explorer
◉ iexplore.exe	3652	Running	User01	00	4,880 K	Internet Explorer
▣ lsass.exe	512	Running		00	2,712 K	Lsass
▣ MsMpEng.exe	1568	Running		00	17,528 K	MsMpEng
▣ NisSrv.exe	2056	Running		00	5,624 K	NisSrv
▣ notepad.exe	5044	Running	User01	00	304 K	Notepad

Figure 12-15 Task Manager, Details tab

Source: Microsoft Windows 10/Task Manager

application that you start or services that are managed by Windows. Right-click any process to view the available advanced options. You also have the option to end any process—just select it and click End task at the bottom of the window.

Using the Services Tab in Task Manager The Services tab is the last one in Task Manager, as shown in Figure 12-16. Services are system programs that run in the background; they provide the core system functionality. The Services tab in Task Manager provides a convenient way to quickly view and manage the services that are running while you troubleshoot your virtual machine. You can start, stop, or restart a service by right-clicking it. You can also open services by clicking the Open Services link at the bottom of the window.

If you want to investigate whether a running service is tied to a particular process, you can right-click the service name and select the Open Services command to open the services window. Double-click the service, and click the Dependencies tab to view the dependencies.

You can invoke new processes in Task Manager by clicking the File menu and selecting Run new task, just like a Run command.

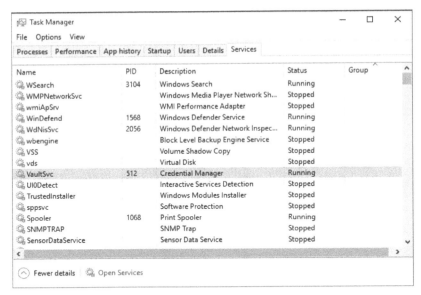

Figure 12-16 Task Manager, Services tab

Source: Microsoft Windows 10/Task Manager

Activity 12-2: Controlling Processes in Windows 10

Time Required: 15 minutes

Objective: Manage processes with Windows Task Manager.

Description: In this activity, you practice controlling processes with Task Manager. You view running programs, verify that they are responding, and check the performance of the processor and RAM. This activity is useful for troubleshooting problems related to applications, processes, and performance.

1. If necessary, start your virtual machines using the appropriate instructions in Activity 1-1. Click **Start**, click **All apps**, scroll down and click **Windows Accessories**, and then click **WordPad**.

2. Right-click an empty spot on the taskbar, and then click **Task Manager**.

3. If necessary, click **More details**, click the **Processes** tab, and view the running programs.

4. Click the **File** menu, click **Run new task**, type **notepad** in the Open list box, click **OK**, and then minimize the Notepad window.

5. Open Microsoft Edge, and go to *www.google.com*. Search for **Win 16 programs on Windows 10**, and press **Enter**. Minimize Microsoft Edge.

6. View the **Processes** tab to see the active processes in Task Manager and verify that applications are running.

7. Locate the WordPad, Notepad, and Microsoft Edge apps under the Apps heading.

8. Click the **Details** tab, and locate wordpad.exe, notepad.exe, and MicrosoftEdge.exe.

9. Locate and right-click the **wordpad.exe** process, click **End task**, read the caution message, and then click **End process**. Note that the wordpad.exe process is removed.

10. Repeat Step 9 for the notepad.exe and MicrosoftEdge.exe processes. Verify that you cannot locate the above processes in the Details tab.

11. To view the process statistics, click the **Processes** tab and then click **Status** to sort the metrics in ascending or descending order.

12. To see which program is using the most CPU (processor cycles), click **CPU**. To see which program is using the most memory, click **Memory**.

13. Click the **Performance** tab, and view the CPU and Memory Usage graphs.

14. Click the **Options** menu, and then select **Show history for all processes**.

15. Click the **Windows Task Manager** title bar, and drag the window to another location.

16. Observe the CPU spike that occurred when you moved the Task Manager window.

17. Close all open windows.

18. Leave the virtual machine logged on for future activities.

Managing Tasks in CentOS 7

The task management tool in CentOS 7 is called *GNOME System Monitor*, as you learned in Chapter 2. It provides essential system information and monitors system processes running on the computer. The following sections provide a more comprehensive explanation of System Monitor.

Using System Monitor You use System Monitor to monitor current system processes, view graphs, and manipulate the running applications on your computer. System Monitor also displays information about memory usage on your system (see Figure 12-17). You can access System Monitor in one of two ways: Either access it from the desktop by clicking Applications, pointing to System Tools, and then clicking System Monitor, or access the program at a shell prompt in a terminal window by typing gnome-system-monitor and then pressing Enter.

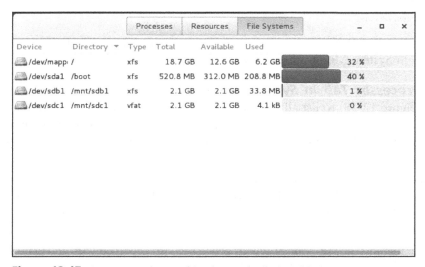

Figure 12-17 System Monitor and its three tabs in CentOS 7

Source: CentOS 7/System Monitor

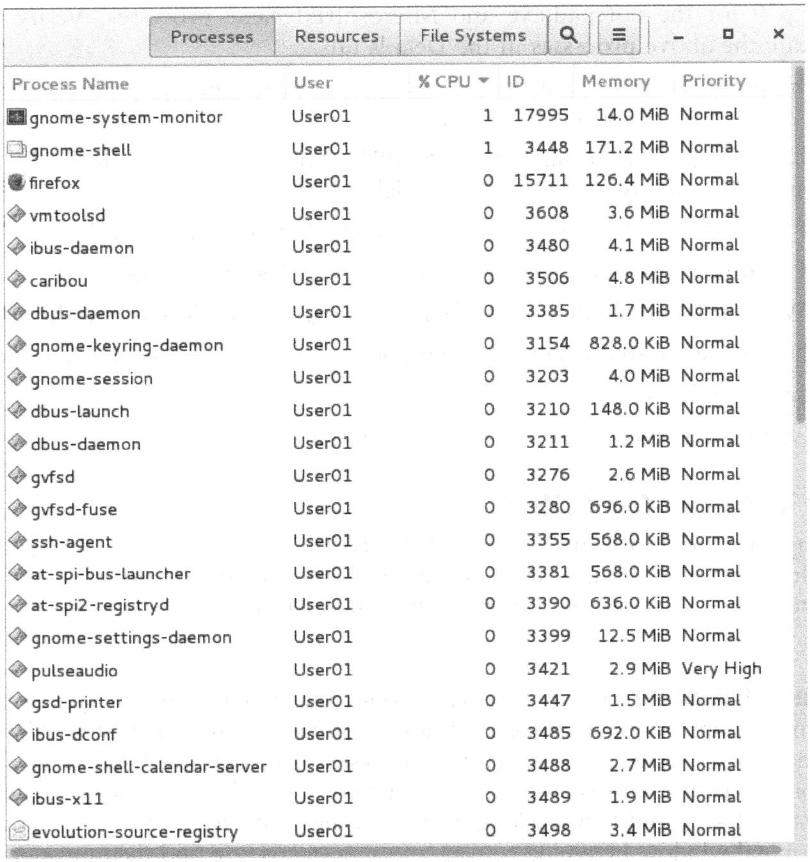

Figure 12-18 System Monitor, Processes tab

Source: CentOS 7/System Monitor

The three tabs in System Monitor are Processes, Resources, and File Systems.

Using the Processes Tab in System Monitor You use the Processes tab in System Monitor (see Figure 12-18) to list all the processes that are running on your computer. Information is shown for each process. To sort the information by a specific column in ascending order, click the name of the column. To toggle the sort between ascending and descending order, click the column name again.

Two items on the Processes tab are worth notice: the End Process button and View menu. To stop a process, highlight it and then click the End Process button that appears (see Figure 12-19). Alternatively, you can right-click a process row and select End. To kill a process, right-click the process row and select Kill.

From the View menu, you can control which processes are displayed (All Processes, My Processes, or Active Processes). See Figure 12-20 for more details. If you select the Dependencies

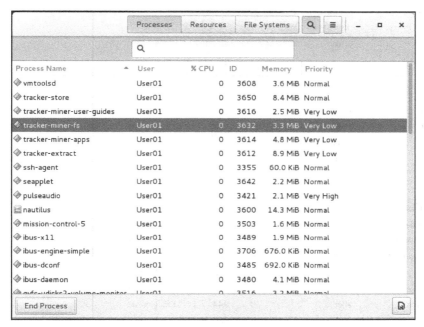

Figure 12-19 End Process button on the Processes tab

Source: CentOS 7/System Monitor

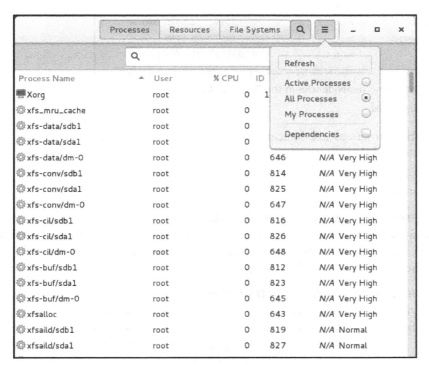

Figure 12-20 View menu on the Processes tab

Source: CentOS 7/System Monitor

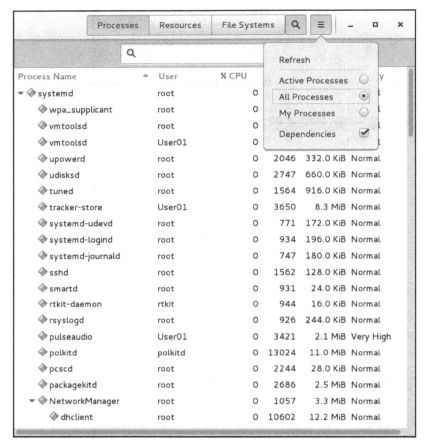

Figure 12-21 Displaying dependencies in the Processes tab

Source: CentOS 7/System Monitor

option, the parent processes are indicated by a diamond symbol to the left of the process name (see Figure 12-21).

The commands to display the information for system processes are ps and top. You will see more details for these commands later in this chapter.

Using the Resources Tab in System Monitor The Resources tab displays the usage history of your CPU, memory, swap memory, and network in graphical format (see Figure 12-22). The corresponding command for the Resources tab is free, which is covered in more detail later in this chapter.

Using the File Systems Tab in System Monitor The File Systems tab displays information about your file systems, including where they are mounted and what their types are. The tab also shows how much disk space is being used and how much is free. The Device, Directory, and Type columns are displayed alphabetically. The Total, Available, and Used columns can be listed in ascending or descending order.

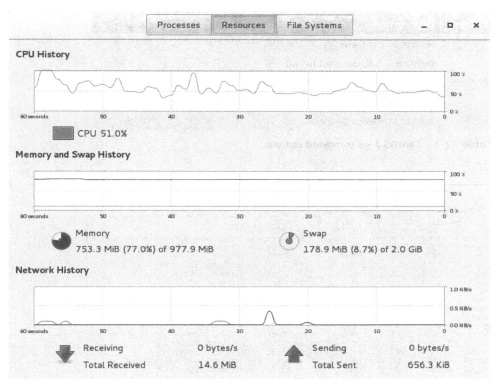

Figure 12-22 System Monitor, Resources tab

Source: CentOS 7/System Monitor

12

The next sections explain a number of commands you can use to manage tasks in CentOS 7, including ps and `kill`.

Using the Process Command The **ps** command lists the system processes that are running, identifies who owns them, and shows the amount of system resources being used. You can control these processes at the command line. Whenever a program or command is executed, the kernel assigns an identification number called a **PID** (process ID) to the process. The syntax for the ps command is:

ps *[options]*

Table 12-1 lists the options you can use with the ps command.

Figure 12-23 shows how to access the processes for your ID when you type the following command:

ps -fu User01

Parent processes spawn child processes. The first number in the ps display indicates the child PID, and the second number indicates the parent PID. The 3355, 3399, and 3448

Entry	Description
e	Selects all processes
f	Displays a full, detailed listing
P	Selects specific processes by PID
t	Selects processes associated with a particular tty (physical terminal)
u	Selects processes by user

Table 12-1 CentOS 7 ps command options

```
                              User01@CentOS7:~              _  □  ×

 File  Edit  View  Search  Terminal  Help
[User01@CentOS7 ~]$ ps -fu User01
UID        PID  PPID  C STIME TTY       TIME CMD
User01     3154     1  0 11:36 ?     00:00:00 /usr/bin/gnome-keyring-daemon --daemo
User01     3203  3144  0 11:36 ?     00:00:00 gnome-session --session gnome-classic
User01     3210     1  0 11:36 ?     00:00:00 dbus-launch --sh-syntax --exit-with-s
User01     3211     1  0 11:36 ?     00:00:00 /bin/dbus-daemon --fork --print-pid 4
User01     3276     1  0 11:36 ?     00:00:00 /usr/libexec/gvfsd
User01     3280     1  0 11:36 ?     00:00:00 /usr/libexec/gvfsd-fuse /run/user/100
User01     3355  3203  0 11:36 ?     00:00:00 /usr/bin/ssh-agent /bin/sh -c exec -l
User01     3381     1  0 11:36 ?     00:00:00 /usr/libexec/at-spi-bus-launcher
User01     3385  3381  0 11:36 ?     00:00:05 /bin/dbus-daemon --config-file=/etc/a
User01     3390     1  0 11:36 ?     00:00:00 /usr/libexec/at-spi2-registryd --use-
User01     3399  3203  0 11:36 ?     00:00:05 /usr/libexec/gnome-settings-daemon
User01     3421     1  0 11:36 ?     00:00:01 /usr/bin/pulseaudio --start --log-tar
User01     3447     1  0 11:36 ?     00:00:00 /usr/libexec/gsd-printer
User01     3448  3203  1 11:36 ?     00:05:38 /usr/bin/gnome-shell
User01     3480  3448  0 11:36 ?     00:00:00 ibus-daemon --xim --panel disable
User01     3485  3480  0 11:36 ?     00:00:00 /usr/libexec/ibus-dconf
User01     3488     1  0 11:36 ?     00:00:00 /usr/libexec/gnome-shell-calendar-ser
User01     3489     1  0 11:36 ?     00:00:00 /usr/libexec/ibus-x11 --kill-daemon
User01     3498     1  0 11:36 ?     00:00:00 /usr/libexec/evolution-source-registr
User01     3503     1  0 11:36 ?     00:00:00 /usr/libexec/mission-control-5
User01     3506     1  0 11:36 ?     00:00:06 /usr/libexec/caribou
User01     3516     1  0 11:36 ?     00:00:00 /usr/libexec/gvfs-udisks2-volume-moni
```

Figure 12-23 User01's processes

Source: CentOS 7/Terminal

child processes have been forked out of the 3203 parent process. Figure 12-24 displays the list of child processes from the 3203 parent process.

Using the `kill` Command Use the `kill` command to end processes that you need to stop. The command works by sending one of many signals to a process or processes; you must be specific (and very careful) about which processes, users, or terminals you want to stop.

The basic syntax of the `kill` command is:

`kill option PID`

One common use of the `kill` command is with the process ID. Type the following command to stop the process with the associated PID:

`kill PID`

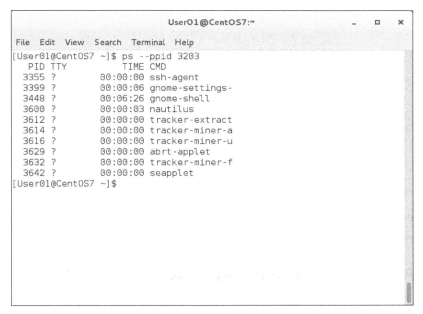

Figure 12-24 Parent and child processes

Source: CentOS 7/Terminal

When you use −9, the `kill` command is considered stronger. Its associated signal name is SIGKILL. Use the following command if the preceding `kill` command doesn't work:

`kill −9 PID`

Another `kill` command, `SIGHUP`, is the signal to "hang up," or stop, a process. Its associated signal number is −1. It is cleaner than the −9 SIGKILL signal because it cleans up all associated processes as well.

`kill -SIGHUP PID`

As you become proficient at process control and job control, you will understand the usefulness of a number of `kill` options. You can find a full list of signal options on the signal man page.

To display the User01 associated processes, as shown in Figure 12-25, type the following command:

`ps −ef | grep User01 | more −d20`

Refer back to Figure 12-24, which shows a screen of User01's associated processes. Note the 3355, 3399, and 3448 child processes listed after User01 at the top of the figure. All of them were "spawned" by the parent process 3203; this PID is listed after its child PIDs in Figure 12-25.

You must be very careful with `kill` commands that use PIDs. If you kill processes using a PID, you also kill the processes it has spawned. For example, if you kill the gnome-session (PID 3203), you also kill PIDs 3355, 3399, 3448, and all the other PIDs listed in Figure 12-24; in this case, the user will log out from the current session.

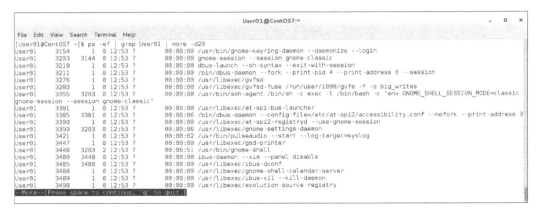

Figure 12-25 The first screen of the User01 process display

Source: CentOS 7/Terminal

Activity 12-3: Displaying Processes in CentOS 7

Time Required: 20 minutes

Objective: Display and trace processes in CentOS 7.

Description: In this activity, you display system processes using the ps command. This activity is useful when you need to view system processes running in CentOS 7.

1. Start your virtual machines using the appropriate instructions in Activity 1-1.

2. To open a console, click **Applications,** and then click **Terminal.**

3. Type **ps –ef | more –d20,** and press **Enter.**

4. Take notes on the processes, their child PIDs, and their parent PIDs.

5. Press the **Spacebar** to scroll through the list of processes, and trace the spawning of child processes. Notice the pattern and sequence of which processes create others.

6. To find your own processes, type **ps** at the command prompt and trace the relationships of the processes attached to your PID.

7. Close any open windows.

8. Leave the virtual machine logged on for the next activity.

Activity 12-4: Killing Processes in CentOS 7

Time Required: 15 minutes

Objective: Kill system processes in CentOS 7.

Description: In this activity, you kill system processes using the ps and kill commands.

1. If necessary, start your virtual machines using the appropriate instructions in Activity 1-1. To open a console, click **Applications,** and then click **Terminal.**

2. To spawn another bash shell within your original bash shell, type **bash** and then press **Enter**. Type **ps –ef**, and then press **Enter**.

3. Note the two bash shell processes. Note the child PID on the latest bash shell and how it is attached to your PID and the `ps -ef` process.

4. To kill the latest bash shell process you spawned, type **kill -9** *child_PID_value*, substituting the correct PID for *child_PID_value* in the command, and then press **Enter**.

5. Verify that the message *Killed* appears on the screen.

6. To verify that the later bash process is gone, type **ps –ef** and press **Enter**. Note that only one bash process is displayed.

7. Close any open windows.

8. Leave the virtual machine logged on for future activities.

Monitoring Performance

By using the performance-monitoring tools in Windows 10 and CentOS 7 for real-time and periodic observation, you can acquire important information about the health of your virtual machine. In general, acceptable performance is a subjective judgment that can vary significantly from one virtual machine to another. To use the tools efficiently, you need to know how data is collected, what types of data are collected, and how to use the data to keep your system performing at its best.

Routine performance monitoring starts with establishing a default set of counters to track. You can use these counters to establish a performance **baseline**—the level of performance you can reliably expect during typical usage and workloads.

A **bottleneck** is anything that slows down a virtual machine's performance. A systematic approach to investigating bottlenecks is important in determining the correct solution.

12

Monitoring System Performance in Windows 10

Use Performance Monitor in Windows 10 to collect and view real-time data about a system's memory, disk, processor, network, and other activities. You can view these activities as a graph, histogram, or report. To open Performance Monitor, right-click Start and then click Control Panel. If necessary, click View By and then click Small icons. Click Administrative Tools, double-click Performance Monitor, and then click Performance Monitor. By default, Performance Monitor shows the % Processor Time (see Figure 12-26).

The % Processor Time measures how much time the processor actually spends working on productive threads versus how often it is busy servicing requests; if this counter's value continually exceeds 85 percent, you might need to upgrade the processor.

To add a counter, click the + button on the toolbar. The Add Counters dialog box appears, as shown in Figure 12-27. The dialog box contains options for the following items:

- Computers—Use the controls at the top of the dialog box to specify the source virtual machine of the item you select as the performance object; you can select the local

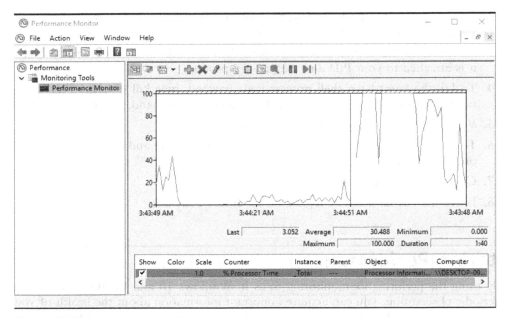

Figure 12-26 Performance Monitor

Source: Microsoft Windows 10/Performance Monitor

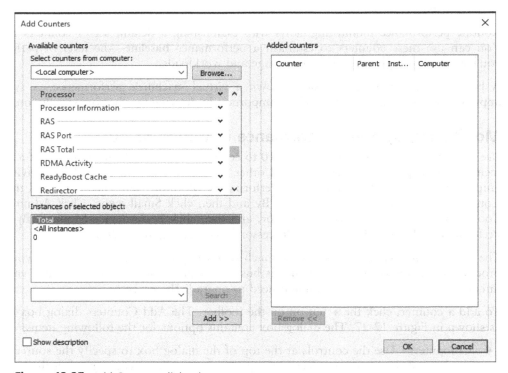

Figure 12-27 Add Counters dialog box

Source: Microsoft Windows 10/Performance Monitor

computer or another computer on your network by typing the computer name in the appropriate box.

- Performance object—From this list, select the area of the virtual machine that you want to monitor. You can select Memory, Processor, or Physical Disk. Click the chevron to expand the performance object and view its counters.

- Counters—Select all counters or select particular counters for the performance object you choose for monitoring; the counters depend on the performance object you select.

- Instances—Select all instances or the specific instance to measure when multiple objects of the same type exist on a single system; for example, if you select the Processor performance object, the instances list displays all the active processors on the specified computer. If you have multiple processors, you will see *Total, 0, 1* in the list.

To view a description for each individual counter during the selection steps, check the Show description check box.

When you have completed your selection for a counter, click the Add button. Your choice appears in the right pane. If you change your mind about a counter, click the Remove button. After you have added the last counter, click OK.

Monitoring Disk Performance Disk usage statistics help you balance the workload of your virtual machine. Performance Monitor provides physical disk counters for troubleshooting and measuring activity on a physical volume. Microsoft recommends using the following physical disk counters, which you can access and set in Activity 12-5:

- % Disk Time—A general indicator of how busy the disk is; if the value of the counter exceeds 90 percent, check the Current Disk Queue Length.

- Disk Reads/sec—The number of reads that the disk can accomplish per second; this count should not exceed the manufacturer's specifications for the disk drive.

- Disk Writes/sec—The number of writes that the disk can accomplish per second; again, this count should not exceed the manufacturer's specifications.

Activity 12-5: Monitoring Disk Performance in Windows 10

Time Required: 12 minutes

Objective: Manage disk performance with Performance Monitor.

Description: In this activity, you add recommended counters to practice monitoring disk performance using Performance Monitor.

 Because the peaks on the graphs are limited by the amount of disk activity, you may see only limited activity on the graphs.

1. If necessary, start your virtual machines using the appropriate instructions in Activity 1-1.

2. Right-click **Start**, click **Control Panel**, click **System and Security**, click **Administrative Tools**, double-click **Performance Monitor**, and then click **Performance Monitor**.

3. To open the Add Counters dialog box, click the green plus button on the Performance Monitor toolbar.

4. To view the counter descriptions, check the **Show description** check box at the bottom of the dialog box.

5. To add a counter, scroll down and expand **Physical Disk**. Scroll again and click **% Disk Time**. Click **All instances** in the instances list, read the explanation for the counter, and then click **Add**.

6. To add the next counter, scroll and then click **Disk Reads/sec**. Click **All instances** in the instances list, read the explanation for the counter, and then click **Add**.

7. Repeat Step 5 for **Disk Writes/sec**.

8. Click **OK**, and observe the changes in the counters.

9. To simulate activity, click **Start**, click **All apps**, scroll, click **Windows Accessories**, and then click **WordPad**.

10. To view the counter statistics, click the **Highlight** button, which is just to the right of the + and X buttons in the toolbar shown in Figure 12-26. Click the **Disk Reads/sec** counter, and observe the changes in the statistics. Note that the line for Disk Reads/sec is highlighted on the graph.

11. Repeat Step 10 for Disk Writes/sec.

12. Close all open windows.

13. Leave the virtual machine logged on for the next activity.

Managing Memory If your virtual machine is paging frequently, it may have a memory shortage. Paging occurs when the virtual machine accesses the hard drive to store or retrieve a memory page. Although some paging activity is acceptable because it enables Windows 10 to use more memory than actually exists, constant paging is a drain on performance. Therefore, you can reduce paging to significantly improve your virtual machine's responsiveness. The following counters are recommended for monitoring memory and paging; you can access and set them using Performance Monitor in Activity 12-6:

- Available MBytes—Indicates the amount of memory that is left after operating system allocations; if the value drops below 4 MB or 5 percent of RAM for several minutes at a time, your computer may have a memory shortage.

- Cache Bytes—Monitors the number of bytes used by the file system cache; use this counter in association with the Available MBytes counter. If the value exceeds 4 MB, you may need to add more RAM.

- Pages/sec—A general indication of how often a virtual machine uses the hard drive to store or retrieve memory-associated data; if the value exceeds 20, you need to analyze paging activity. A high degree of page file activity indicates that more RAM is required.

- Page Faults/sec—Gives you a general idea of how often requested information must be retrieved from another memory location or the page file; although a sustained value might indicate trouble, you should be more concerned with hard page faults that represent actual reads or writes to the disk. Remember that disk access is much slower than RAM.

Activity 12-6: Monitoring Memory Performance in Windows 10

Time Required: 12 minutes

Objective: Manage memory performance with Performance Monitor.

Description: In this activity, you add recommended counters to practice monitoring memory performance with Performance Monitor.

Because the peaks on the graphs are limited by the amount of memory activity, you may see only limited activity on the graphs.

1. If necessary, start your virtual machines using the appropriate instructions in Activity 1-1.

2. Right-click **Start**, click **Control Panel**, click **System and Security**, click **Administrative Tools**, double-click **Performance Monitor**, and then click **Performance Monitor**.

3. To open the Add Counters dialog box, click the green plus button on the Performance Monitor toolbar.

4. If necessary, check **Show description** to view the counter descriptions.

5. To add a counter, scroll down and click **Memory**. Scroll again and click **Available MBytes**. Read the explanation for the counter, and then click **Add**.

6. To add the next counter, scroll and then click **Cache Bytes**, read the explanation for the counter, and then click **Add**.

7. Repeat Step 5 for **Pages/sec** and **Page Faults/sec**.

8. Click **OK**, and observe the changes in the counters.

9. To simulate activity, click **Start**, click **All apps**, scroll, click **Windows Accessories**, and then click **WordPad**.

12

10. To view the counter statistics, click the **Highlight** button, which is just to the right of the + and X buttons in the toolbar shown in Figure 12-26. Click the **Cache Bytes** counter, and observe the displayed changes in the statistics.

11. Repeat Step 10 for Pages/sec and Page Faults/sec.

12. Close all open windows.

13. Leave the virtual machine logged on for the next activity.

Monitoring Processor Use The Processor and System object counters provide valuable information about the use of your processors. You need this information to effectively tune your virtual machine. You should monitor the following counters; to access and set them in Performance Monitor, see Activity 12-7.

- % Processor Time—Measures how much time the processor actually spends working on productive threads versus how often it is busy servicing requests; if this counter's value continually exceeds 85 percent, you might need to upgrade the processor.

- Interrupts/sec—The average rate, in incidents per second, at which the processor receives and services hardware interrupts.

- Processor Queue Length—The number of threads in the processor queue that are ready to be executed; this counter is located under the System object. A sustained processor queue of less than 12 threads per processor is normally acceptable.

Activity 12-7: Monitoring Processor Use in Windows 10

Time Required: 12 minutes

Objective: Manage processor use with Performance Monitor.

Description: In this activity, you add recommended counters to analyze and monitor processor use with Performance Monitor.

Because the peaks on the graphs are limited by the amount of processor activity, you may see only limited activity on the graphs.

1. If necessary, start your virtual machines using the appropriate instructions in Activity 1-1.

2. Right-click **Start**, click **Control Panel**, click **System and Security**, click **Administrative Tools**, double-click **Performance Monitor**, and then click **Performance Monitor**.

3. To open the Add Counters dialog box, click the green plus button on the Performance Monitor toolbar.

4. If necessary, check **Show description** to view the counter descriptions.

5. To add a counter for % Processor Time, scroll and expand **Processor**, then scroll and click **% Processor time**. Read the explanation for the counter, and then click **Add**.

6. To add the next counter, scroll through the counters list, click **Interrupts/sec**, read the explanation for the counter, and then click **Add**.

7. Collapse the **Processor** list.

8. To add the last counter, scroll down and expand **System**. Scroll again and click **Processor Queue Length**, read the explanation for the counter, and then click **Add**.

9. Click **OK**, and observe the changes in the counters.

10. To simulate activity, click **Start**, click **All apps**, scroll, click **Windows Accessories**, and then click **WordPad**.

11. To view the counter statistics, click the **Highlight** button, which is just to the right of the + and X buttons in the toolbar shown in Figure 12-26. Click the **Interrupts/sec** counter, and observe the changes in the statistics.

12. Repeat Step 11 for the **Processor Queue Length** counter.

13. Close all open windows.

14. Leave the virtual machine logged on for future activities.

Monitoring System Performance in CentOS 7

When you monitor performance, you typically look at such statistics as memory usage, CPU usage, input/output usage, delay times, and queuing. The commands in the following sections describe these statistics and provide an introduction to monitoring system performance.

CentOS 7 contains a command-line reporting and control information system known as the **/proc file system**. To access this information, use the cat command and different kernel parameters. The kernel, or system, information is contained in files in the /proc directory. The /proc file system is known as a **pseudo-file system**, which directly interfaces with the kernel and is stored in memory.

This chapter covers only a few of the many kernel parameters; see Table 12-2 for a partial list of kernel values. To see a complete list and descriptions of the available kernel values, consult the proc man page.

Entry	Description
iomem	Memory input/output statistics
mounts	Mounted file system statistics
stat	Process status in readable format
diskstats	Disk statistics
swaps	Swap file statistics (swap files are used in the way that virtual memory is used in Windows 10)
loadavg	The average number of processes ready to run during the last 1, 5, and 15 minutes

Table 12-2   Kernel system values

You can use the /proc file system for the following types of system-related tasks:

- Viewing performance and memory information
- Viewing and modifying run-time parameters
- Viewing hardware information
- Viewing and modifying network parameters
- Viewing statistical information

You can see the available kernel value statistics, as shown in Figure 12-28, by changing to the /proc directory and typing `ls`:

```
cd /proc
ls
```

To see performance information for system and mounted file system statistics, as shown in Figures 12-29 and 12-30, type the following commands:

```
cd /proc
cat stat
cat mounts
```

To see performance information for the disk statistics, as shown in Figure 12-31, type the following commands:

```
cd /proc
cat diskstats
```

Figure 12-28 List of /proc directory contents

Source: CentOS 7/Terminal

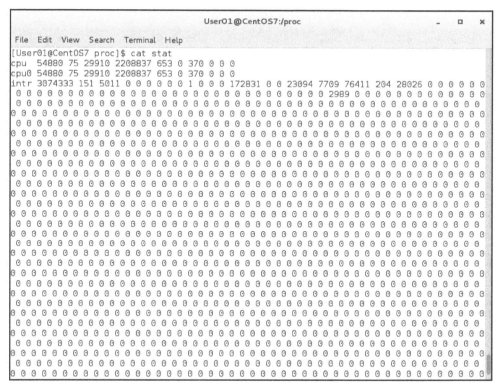

Figure 12-29 System statistics and mounted file system statistics

Source: CentOS 7/Terminal

To see performance information for swap statistics, average load, and input/output memory usage, as shown in Figure 12-32, type the following commands:

```
cd /proc
cat swaps
cat loadavg
cat iomem
```

Using the `top` Command The `top` command displays system statistics continuously in real time, with a five-second delay by default. The command constantly updates console-based output for the most CPU-intensive processes that are running. The basic syntax of the `top` command is:

```
top - display top CPU processes
```

The basic fields for the `top` command are:

- uptime—The amount of time the system has been up and the system's three average loads: the average number of processes ready to run during the last 1, 5, and 15 minutes

```
User01@CentOS7:/proc
File Edit View Search Terminal Help
[User01@CentOS7 proc]$ cat mounts
rootfs / rootfs rw 0 0
sysfs /sys sysfs rw,seclabel,nosuid,nodev,noexec,relatime 0 0
proc /proc proc rw,nosuid,nodev,noexec,relatime 0 0
devtmpfs /dev devtmpfs rw,seclabel,nosuid,size=485316k,nr_inodes=121329,mode=755 0 0
securityfs /sys/kernel/security securityfs rw,nosuid,nodev,noexec,relatime 0 0
tmpfs /dev/shm tmpfs rw,seclabel,nosuid,nodev 0 0
devpts /dev/pts devpts rw,seclabel,nosuid,noexec,relatime,gid=5,mode=620,ptmxmode=000 0 0
tmpfs /run tmpfs rw,seclabel,nosuid,nodev,mode=755 0 0
tmpfs /sys/fs/cgroup tmpfs ro,seclabel,nosuid,nodev,noexec,mode=755 0 0
cgroup /sys/fs/cgroup/systemd cgroup rw,nosuid,nodev,noexec,relatime,xattr,release_agent=/u
sr/lib/systemd/systemd-cgroups-agent,name=systemd 0 0
pstore /sys/fs/pstore pstore rw,nosuid,nodev,noexec,relatime 0 0
cgroup /sys/fs/cgroup/cpu,cpuacct cgroup rw,nosuid,nodev,noexec,relatime,cpuacct,cpu 0 0
cgroup /sys/fs/cgroup/blkio cgroup rw,nosuid,nodev,noexec,relatime,blkio 0 0
cgroup /sys/fs/cgroup/devices cgroup rw,nosuid,nodev,noexec,relatime,devices 0 0
cgroup /sys/fs/cgroup/memory cgroup rw,nosuid,nodev,noexec,relatime,memory 0 0
cgroup /sys/fs/cgroup/cpuset cgroup rw,nosuid,nodev,noexec,relatime,cpuset 0 0
cgroup /sys/fs/cgroup/perf_event cgroup rw,nosuid,nodev,noexec,relatime,perf_event 0 0
cgroup /sys/fs/cgroup/hugetlb cgroup rw,nosuid,nodev,noexec,relatime,hugetlb 0 0
cgroup /sys/fs/cgroup/net_cls cgroup rw,nosuid,nodev,noexec,relatime,net_cls 0 0
cgroup /sys/fs/cgroup/freezer cgroup rw,nosuid,nodev,noexec,relatime,freezer 0 0
configfs /sys/kernel/config configfs rw,relatime 0 0
/dev/mapper/centos-root / xfs rw,seclabel,relatime,attr2,inode64,noquota 0 0
selinuxfs /sys/fs/selinux selinuxfs rw,relatime 0 0
systemd-1 /proc/sys/fs/binfmt_misc autofs rw,relatime,fd=28,pgrp=1,timeout=300,minproto=5,m
axproto=5,direct 0 0
debugfs /sys/kernel/debug debugfs rw,relatime 0 0
mqueue /dev/mqueue mqueue rw,seclabel,relatime 0 0
sunrpc /var/lib/nfs/rpc_pipefs rpc_pipefs rw,relatime 0 0
hugetlbfs /dev/hugepages hugetlbfs rw,seclabel,relatime 0 0
nfsd /proc/fs/nfsd nfsd rw,relatime 0 0
/dev/sdb1 /mnt/sdb1 xfs rw,seclabel,relatime,attr2,inode64,noquota 0 0
```

Figure 12-30 System statistics and mounted file system statistics (continued)

Source: CentOS 7/Terminal

- processes—The total number of processes running at the time of the last update
- CPU states—The percentage of CPU time in user mode, system mode, niced tasks, iowait, and idle (a niced task is a task run with a modified scheduling priority); time spent in niced tasks is also counted in system and user time, so the total will be more than 100 percent
- Mem—Statistics on memory usage, including total available memory, free memory, used memory, shared memory, and memory used for buffers
- Swap—Statistics on swap space, including total swap space, available swap space, and used swap space
- PID—The process ID of each task
- PPID—The parent process ID of each task
- UID—The user ID of the task's owner
- USER—The user name of the task's owner
- SHARE—The amount of shared memory used by the task

To start the `top` utility with five iterations and a delay of 10 seconds (see Figure 12-33), type the following command with the default abbreviated field names:

```
top -n5 -d10.00
```

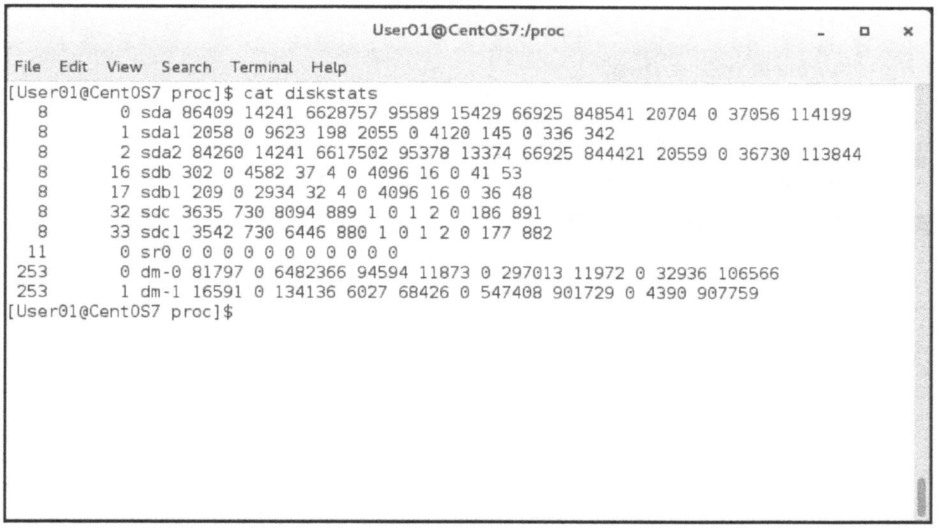

```
                                UserO1@CentOS7:/proc                    _  □  ×

 File  Edit  View  Search  Terminal  Help
[User01@CentOS7 proc]$ cat diskstats
    8      0 sda 86409 14241 6628757 95589 15429 66925 848541 20704 0 37056 114199
    8      1 sda1 2058 0 9623 198 2055 0 4120 145 0 336 342
    8      2 sda2 84260 14241 6617502 95378 13374 66925 844421 20559 0 36730 113844
    8     16 sdb 302 0 4582 37 4 0 4096 16 0 41 53
    8     17 sdb1 209 0 2934 32 4 0 4096 16 0 36 48
    8     32 sdc 3635 730 8094 889 1 0 1 2 0 186 891
    8     33 sdc1 3542 730 6446 880 1 0 1 2 0 177 882
   11      0 sr0 0 0 0 0 0 0 0 0 0 0 0
  253      0 dm-0 81797 0 6482366 94594 11873 0 297013 11972 0 32936 106566
  253      1 dm-1 16591 0 134136 6027 68426 0 547408 901729 0 4390 907759
[User01@CentOS7 proc]$
```

Figure 12-31 Disk statistics

Source: CentOS 7/Terminal

```
                                UserO1@CentOS7:/proc                    _  □  ×

 File  Edit  View  Search  Terminal  Help
[User01@CentOS7 proc]$ cat swaps
Filename                              Type        Size      Used    Priority
/dev/dm-1                             partition   2097148   71860   -1
[User01@CentOS7 proc]$ cat loadavg
0.14 0.16 0.14 3/609 33650
[User01@CentOS7 proc]$ cat iomem
00000000-00000fff : reserved
00001000-0009ebff : System RAM
0009ec00-0009ffff : reserved
000a0000-000bffff : PCI Bus 0000:00
000c0000-000c7fff : Video ROM
000ca000-000cafff : Adapter ROM
000cc000-000cffff : PCI Bus 0000:00
000d0000-000d3fff : PCI Bus 0000:00
000d4000-000d7fff : PCI Bus 0000:00
000d8000-000dbfff : PCI Bus 0000:00
000dc000-000fffff : reserved
  000f0000-000fffff : System ROM
00100000-3fedffff : System RAM
  01000000-0164a17a : Kernel code
  0164a17b-01a74b7f : Kernel data
  01c13000-01f30fff : Kernel bss
3fee0000-3fefefff : ACPI Tables
3feff000-3fefffff : ACPI Non-volatile Storage
3ff00000-3fffffff : System RAM
c0000000-febfffff : PCI Bus 0000:00
  c0000000-c0007fff : 0000:00:0f.0
  c0008000-c000bfff : 0000:00:10.0
  e5b00000-e5bfffff : PCI Bus 0000:22
  e5c00000-e5cfffff : PCI Bus 0000:1a
  e5d00000-e5dfffff : PCI Bus 0000:12
  e5e00000-e5efffff : PCI Bus 0000:0a
  e5f00000-e5ffffff : PCI Bus 0000:21
  e6000000-e60fffff : PCI Bus 0000:19
```

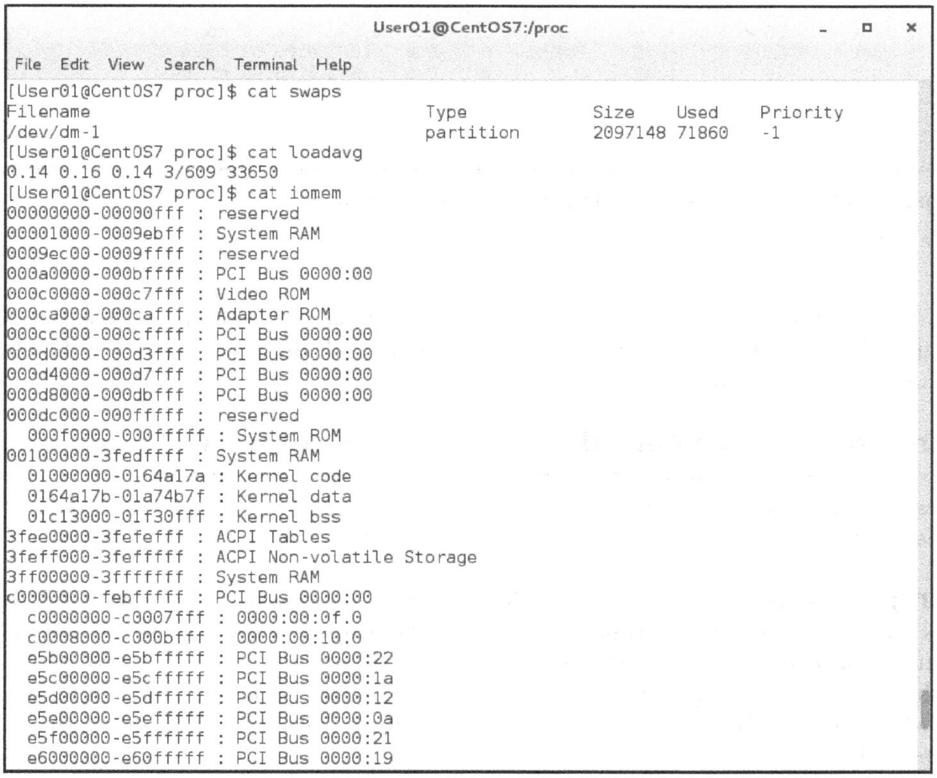

Figure 12-32 Swap statistics, average load, and input/output memory usage

Source: CentOS 7/Terminal

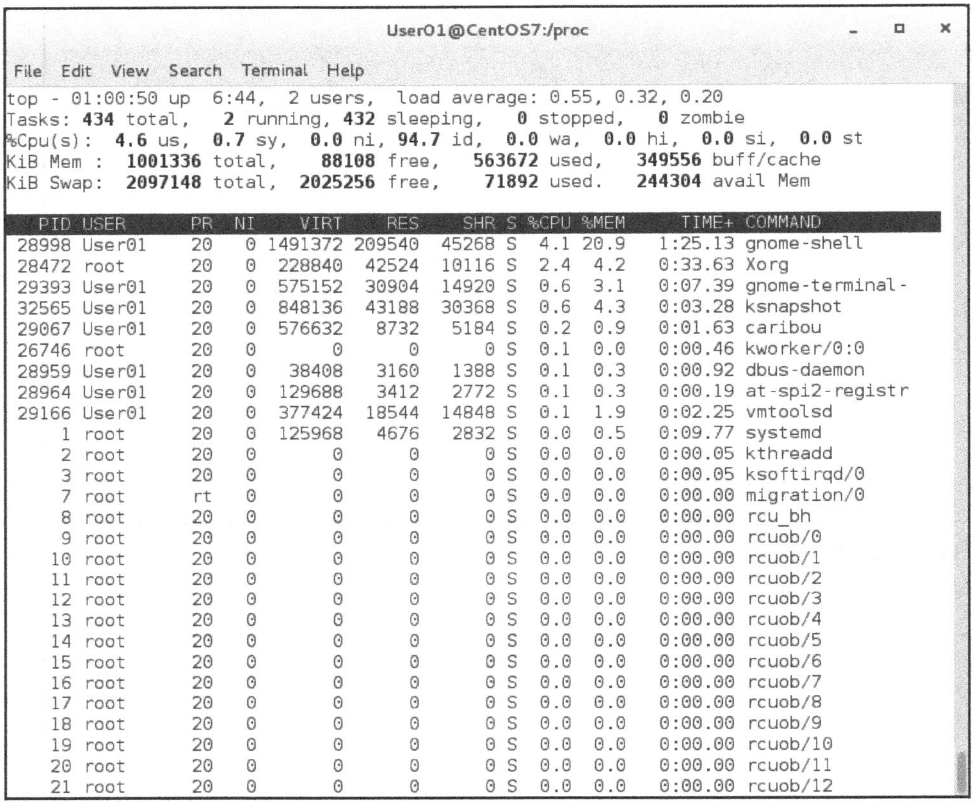

Figure 12-33 The `top` command with delay and iteration defined

Source: CentOS 7/Terminal

The `top` command uses a large amount of memory, so you should only use the command for troubleshooting and tuning; don't keep it running all the time. When you finish, press q to quit the `top` display.

Using the `free` Command The `free` command indicates the amounts of free, used, and swap memory in the system. The amounts of free and used memory are shown in kilobytes; use the −m option with `free` if you want to see the readings in megabytes. To use the `free` command, as shown in Figure 12-34, simply type `free`.

Using the `watch free` Command Line The `watch free` command repeatedly runs `free` to produce real-time statistics for the amount of free space in the system. By default, you can view updated output every two seconds. You can control the frequency of the output by setting the interval time, and you can terminate the output by pressing Ctrl+C. To use the command line, as shown in Figure 12-35, type the following command:

```
watch free
```

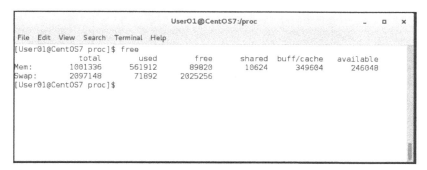

Figure 12-34 Output of the `free` command

Source: CentOS 7/Terminal

```
                               UserO1@CentOS7:/proc              _   □   ✕

 File  Edit  View  Search  Terminal  Help
Every 2.0s: free                                   Sun Mar 13 01:03:56 2016

              total        used        free      shared  buff/cache   available
Mem:        1001336      564980       84340       10624      352016      242980
Swap:       2097148       71892     2025256
```

Figure 12-35 Output of the `watch free` command

Source: CentOS 7/Terminal

Using the `vmstat` Command

The `vmstat` command reports on process status, memory consumption, paging activity, I/O operations, and CPU usage. It typically provides an average since the last reboot, or it can report usage for a current period of time if you specify the time interval in seconds and the number of iterations you need. The command continues reporting until you interrupt it.

The basic fields for the `vmstat` command are:

- procs—Number of processes running and sleeping
- swap—Amount of memory paged for input and output
- us—Percentage of total processor time consumed by user space
- sy—Percentage of total processor time consumed by the kernel
- wa—Percentage of total processor time spent in I/O wait
- id—Percentage of total processor time spent idle

Figure 12-36 shows how the `vmstat` command begins to execute with a delay of five seconds and 10 iterations after you type the following command:

`vmstat 5 10`

Figure 12-37 shows the results of the `vmstat` command after a delay of five seconds.

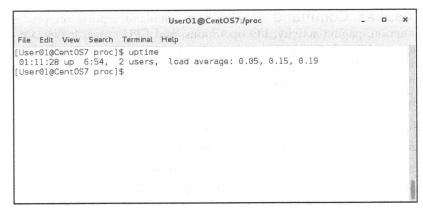

Figure 12-36 The `vmstat` command with a five-second delay and 10 iterations

Source: CentOS 7/Terminal

```
                              User01@CentOS7:/proc                    _  □  ×
File  Edit  View  Search  Terminal  Help
[User01@CentOS7 proc]$ vmstat 5 10
procs ----------memory---------- ---swap-- -----io---- -system-- ------cpu-----
 r  b   swpd   free   buff  cache   si   so    bi    bo   in    cs us sy id wa st
 3  0  71892  88476    20 352588    3   11   138    18  139   251  3  1 96  0  0
 0  0  71892  88404    20 352536    0    0     0     1  290   650  7  1 92  0  0
 0  0  71892  72764    20 352536    0    0     0    11  356   686 13  5 82  0  0
 0  0  71892  77916    20 352536    0    0     0     1  404  1137 17  5 78  0  0
 0  0  71892  84596    20 352524    0    0     2     0  358   691 11  2 88  0  0
 0  0  71892  83976    20 352536    0    0     0     0  340   645 13  2 85  0  0
 0  0  71892  83976    20 352536    0    0     0     0  134   215  2  0 98  0  0
 0  0  71892  83976    20 352536    0    0     0     0  150   231  2  0 97  0  0
 0  0  71892  79692    20 355836    0    0   651    14  366   709 10  3 86  1  0
 0  0  71892  79692    20 355836    0    0     0     0  183   434  8  2 90  0  0
[User01@CentOS7 proc]$
```

Figure 12-37 The `vmstat` command after a five-second delay

Source: CentOS 7/Terminal

```
                              User01@CentOS7:/proc                    _  □  ×
File  Edit  View  Search  Terminal  Help
[User01@CentOS7 proc]$ uptime
 01:11:28 up  6:54,  2 users,  load average: 0.05, 0.15, 0.19
[User01@CentOS7 proc]$
```

Figure 12-38 Output of the `uptime` command

Source: CentOS 7/Terminal

Using the `uptime` Command The **uptime command** displays the amount of time since the last system reboot, shows the CPU average load for the past 1, 5, and 15 minutes, and shows how many users are logged on (see Figure 12-38). To use the command, simply type uptime.

Activity 12-8: Displaying Free Memory Statistics in CentOS 7

Time Required: 5 minutes

Objective: Display free memory statistics.

Description: In this activity, you display free memory statistics using the `free` command. The activity is useful if you need to view and monitor the memory on your CentOS 7 system.

1. If necessary, start your virtual machines using the appropriate instructions in Activity 1-1.
2. To open a console, click **Applications**, and then click **Terminal**.
3. To display memory statistics, type **free** and then press **Enter**.
4. Note the system's average loads for the past 1, 5, and 15 minutes.
5. Close all open windows.
6. Leave the virtual machine logged on for the next activity.

Activity 12-9: Real-Time Monitoring of System Performance in CentOS 7

Time Required: 5 minutes

Objective: Display real-time, continuous system statistics.

Description: In this activity, you display system processes using the `top` command. The system statistics are updated every five seconds for 10 iterations. This activity is useful if you need to establish a real-time system monitor for statistics.

1. If necessary, start your virtual machines using the appropriate instructions in Activity 1-1.
2. To open a console, click **Applications**, and then click **Terminal**.
3. Type **top –n5 –d10.00**, and then press **Enter**.
4. Note the different system statistics and how they change as the display iterates.
5. Close any open windows.
6. Leave the virtual machine logged on for the next activity.

Activity 12-10: Viewing System Statistics Straight from the Kernel in CentOS 7

Time Required: 10 minutes

Objective: Display up-to-date system statistics straight from the kernel.

Description: In this activity, you display system processes using the cat command with /proc files. This activity is useful if you want to view statistics on swap files, average CPU load, and memory input/output.

1. If necessary, start your virtual machines using the appropriate instructions in Activity 1-1.

2. To open a console, click **Applications,** and then click **Terminal.**

3. To change to the /proc directory, type **cd /proc** and then press **Enter.**

4. To view swap file statistics, type **cat swaps** and then press **Enter.**

5. To view average CPU load statistics, type **cat loadavg** and then press **Enter.**

6. To view memory input/output statistics, type **cat iomem** and then press **Enter.**

7. Close all open windows.

8. To shut down the virtual machine, click **User01** in the upper-right corner of the desktop, click **Power Off,** and then click the **Power Off** button.

9. Wait a moment for the CentOS 7 virtual machine to shut down completely.

Monitoring Reliability

The following sections introduce you to two tools that help you check the reliability of your system: the Reliability Monitor in Windows 10 and the Automatic Bug Reporting Tool in CentOS 7.

Using the Reliability Monitor in Windows 10

The Windows 10 Reliability Monitor (shown in Figure 12-39) is an advanced tool that measures hardware and software problems and other changes to your computer. It provides a stability index that ranges from 1 to 10, where 10 is most stable. You can use the index to help evaluate the reliability of your computer. Any change you make to your computer and any problem that occurs on it affects the stability index. To open the Reliability Monitor, type *reliability* in the "Search the web and Windows" box on the taskbar, and then click View reliability history.

The main goal of the Windows 10 Reliability Monitor is to keep track of "reliability events," which are changes to your system that could alter its stability or other events that might indicate system instability.

Events monitored include:

- Windows updates
- Software installations and uninstalls
- Device driver installations, updates, rollbacks, and uninstalls
- Application hangs and crashes
- Device drivers that fail to load or unload
- Disk and memory failures
- Windows failures, including boot failures, system crashes, and sleep failures

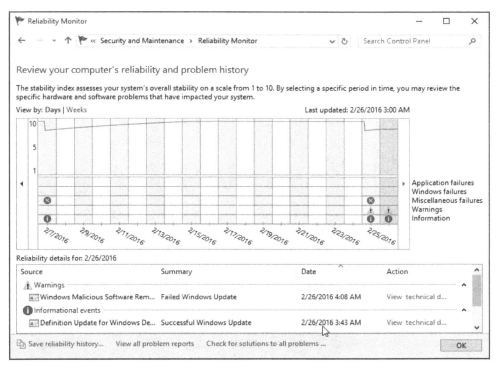

Figure 12-39 Reliability Monitor

Source: Microsoft Windows 10/Reliability Monitor

The Stability Index rating gives you a visual indication of how reliably your system performs over time. You are given an overall Stability Index score. Ten is a perfect score, and one is the lowest. The Reliability Monitor retains data for up to a year so you can see how your system has been performing over time. Recent events will only be displayed in the Reliability Monitor after 24 hours have passed.

If you see a drop in stability for your virtual machine, you can check the date that the drop began and then see if the decline was due to one of the following issues:

- Application failures
- Windows failures
- Miscellaneous failures
- Warnings

Figure 12-40 shows an informational event, which is indicated by a blue circle that contains the letter *i*. Warning messages are indicated by a yellow triangle that contains a black exclamation mark. Error messages appear as red circles with a white X. To see information about a warning message, click the day that the warning occurred. Figure 12-40 shows summary information about the events on the chosen day.

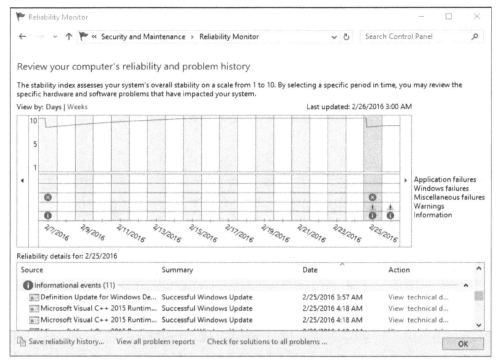

Figure 12-40 Reliability Monitor showing information for events

Source: Microsoft Windows 10/Reliability Monitor

Activity 12-11: Viewing the Reliability History for Windows 10

Time Required: 12 minutes

Objective: View the reliability history of your virtual machine.

Description: In this activity, you will open the Reliability Monitor and view the history of your virtual machine. This activity is useful if you want to view recent changes to your virtual machine and the possible consequences of these changes.

1. If necessary, start your virtual machines using the appropriate instructions in Activity 1-1.

2. To open the Reliability Monitor, right-click **Start,** and then click **Control Panel.** Click **System and Security,** click **Security and Maintenance,** and then expand **Maintenance.** Under "Check for solutions to problem reports," click **View reliability history.**

There is a 24-hour delay for the display of events in the Reliability Monitor. For this reason, you may not see warnings or other failures.

3. Examine the information. When you finish, close any open windows in the virtual machine.

4. To shut down the virtual machine, click **Start,** click **Power,** and then click **Shut Down**.

5. Wait a moment for the Windows 10 virtual machine to shut down completely.

Automatic Bug Reporting in CentOS 7

Automatic Bug Reporting Tool (ABRT) is a set of small utilities in CentOS for end users to report software problems by providing comprehensive information for the developers (see Figure 12-41). It also provides useful crash statistics for prioritization and self-support. The ABRT daemon resides in the background and watches for application crashes. Automatic bug reporting can be accomplished from either the command-line interface or a graphical user interface (CLI and GUI, respectively). The following section introduces the GUI approach.

When a crash occurs, the ABRT daemon collects the crash-related data and an alert appears in the bottom panel on the desktop (see Figure 12-42). When you click the Bug Report alert, the Automatic Bug Reporting Tool screen appears. If the alert disappears, go to Applications, point to Sundry, and then click Automatic Bug Reporting Tool to invoke the ABRT GUI (see Figure 12-43). After you click the button that displays a

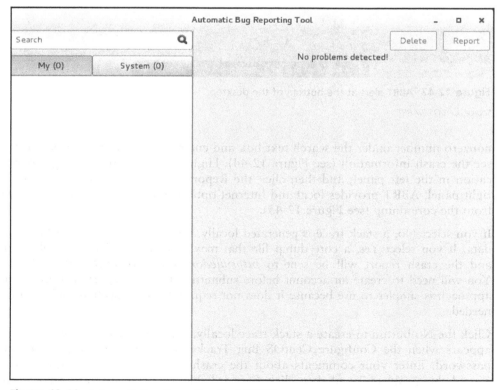

Figure 12-41 Automatic Bug Reporting Tool (ABRT)

Source: CentOS 7/Automatic Bug Reporting Tool (ABRT)

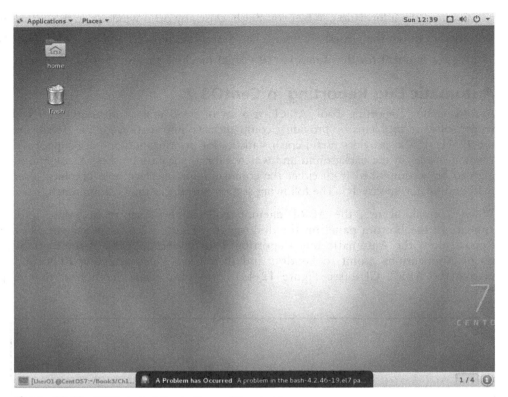

Figure 12-42 ABRT alert at the bottom of the desktop

Source: CentOS 7/ABRT

nonzero number under the search text box and enter the Admin user's password, you will see the crash information (see Figure 12-44). Highlight the corresponding reported application in the left panel, and then click the Report button in the top right corner of the right panel. ABRT provides local and Internet options for where to generate the backtrace from the core dump (see Figure 12-45).

If you select No, a stack trace is generated locally, which may download a huge amount of data. If you select Yes, a core dump file that may contain sensitive data will be uploaded and the crash report will be sent to *https://fedorahosted.org/abrt/wiki/AbrtRetraceServer*. You will need to create an account before submitting the bug report. The local stack trace approach is simpler to use because it does not require login credentials and no follow-up is needed.

Click the No button to create a stack trace locally. The user crash description input screen appears when the Configure CentOS Bug Tracker is enabled and after you enter your password. Enter your comments about the crash or simply check "I don't know what caused this problem," and then click Forward. Figure 12-46 displays the corresponding stack trace analysis interface with the backtrace tab selected. Click Forward to move to the summary list screen. Double-click the items that display "(click here to view/edit)," as

Figure 12-43 ABRT in the Applications Sundry submenu

Source: CentOS 7/ABRT

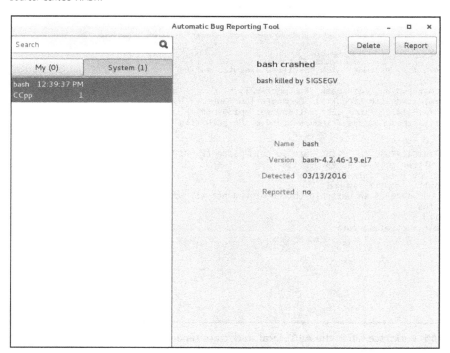

Figure 12-44 Crash information in the ABRT graphical interface

Source: CentOS 7/ABRT

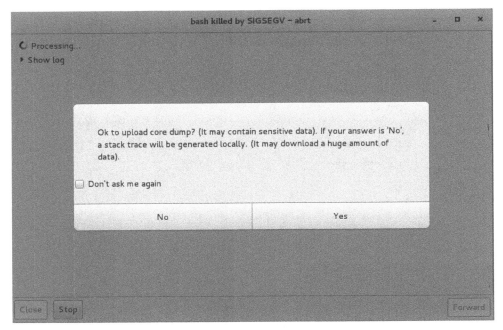

Figure 12-45 ABRT local or Internet report option

Source: CentOS 7/ABRT

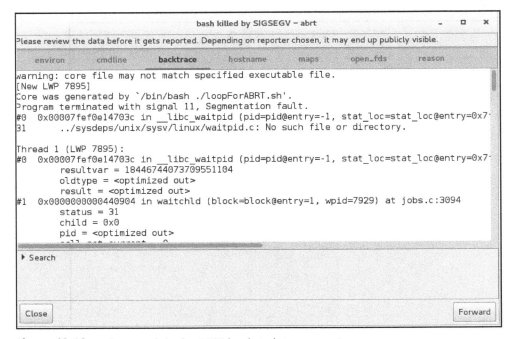

Figure 12-46 Backtrace tab in the ABRT local stack trace report

Source: CentOS 7/ABRT

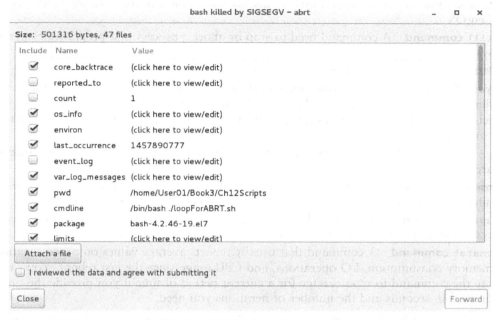

Figure 12-47 Detailed analysis in the ABRT local stack trace report

Source: CentOS 7/ABRT

shown in Figure 12-47. You can also attach files if their submission is needed. To submit, check "I reviewed the data and agree with submitting it," and then click Forward. Enter your account information, and then submit the data.

Chapter Summary

- Use the Windows 10 Task Manager to maintain your computer system and monitor the processes that are running. If Task Manager indicates a problem, you can correct it so that other tasks can use necessary resources. In CentOS 7, you use the ps and kill commands to manage tasks.

- Monitoring system performance can help you run processes more efficiently and quickly, and can help determine if you need more memory or a faster processor for tasks that are not working properly.

- To check the reliability of your system, you can use the Reliability Monitor in Windows 10 and the Automatic Bug Reporting Tool in CentOS 7.

Key Terms

baseline   The level of performance that you can expect during typical usage and workloads.

bottleneck   A performance problem that occurs when multiple processes are competing for resources and all of them converge on the same resource at once.

free command   A command used to display the amount of free and used memory in CentOS 7.

kill command   A command used to stop or abort a process in a program or operating system.

PID   A number used by CentOS 7 to uniquely identify a process.

/proc file system   A command-line reporting and control information system in CentOS 7 that directly interfaces with the kernel and is stored in memory. It is used for such system-related tasks as performance, memory information, and viewing and modifying run-time parameters.

ps command   A command used in CentOS 7 to provide a "snapshot" of the processes that are running.

pseudo-file system   A system that acts like a file system but is specially constructed to interface with specific areas in a system; it is maintained by the system, not a user.

uptime command   A command that displays the amount or percentage of time a computer system or associated hardware is functioning and available for use.

vmstat command   A command that usually reports average values on process status, memory consumption, I/O operations, and CPU usage since the last reboot. You can also use the command to report usage for a current period of time if you provide the time interval in seconds and the number of iterations you need.

watch free command   A command used in CentOS 7 to run a command repeatedly. When you combine `watch` with another command, such as `free`, you can view output on the terminal screen every two seconds by default.

Review Questions

1. Use Windows 10 Task Manager to _____. (Choose all that apply.)
   a. install Windows 10 applications
   b. provide information about programs running on your computer
   c. display common performance measurements for processes running on your computer
   d. provide information about processes running on your computer

2. The Run As feature in Windows 10 is similar to the _____ command in CentOS 7.
   a. `run`
   b. `go`
   c. `sudo`
   d. `runs`

3. You can use the Run As feature in Windows 10 to _____. (Choose all that apply.)

   a. access system tools that require administrative privileges for execution

   b. run an administrative tool to determine what caused a problem

   c. run all applications in Windows 10

   d. resolve problems

4. Use the Processes tab in Task Manager to view _____. (Choose all that apply.)

   a. the names of applications running on the computer

   b. the processor

   c. the memory usage

   d. conflicts that are occurring

5. In CentOS 7, you use the _____ command to list the running processes.

   a. view

   b. kill

   c. ps

   d. top

6. In CentOS 7, you use the _____ command to stop processes.

   a. ps

   b. kill

   c. top

   d. stop

7. In Windows 10, disk usage statistics help _____.

   a. determine which applications cannot run on your system

   b. determine whether upgrades are necessary

   c. balance uploading to your virtual machine

   d. balance the workload of your virtual machine

8. You can use the /proc file system in CentOS 7 to _____. (Choose all that apply.)

   a. view and modify run-time parameters

   b. view performance and memory information

   c. view hardware information

   d. view statistical information

9. In CentOS 7, the `top` command _____. (Choose all that apply.)

    a. monitors system statistics and displays them in real time

    b. constantly updates console-based output for the most CPU-intensive processes that are running

    c. is used to kill processes

    d. is used to monitor processes

10. In CentOS 7, the `top` command _____. (Choose all that apply.)

    a. uses a large amount of memory

    b. is mainly used for troubleshooting and tuning

    c. is very efficient for viewing processes

    d. should be kept running all the time

11. Frequent paging _____.

    a. is a normal occurrence

    b. indicates that you may have a memory shortage

    c. indicates that you have a lot of memory available

    d. does not drain performance

12. High CPU usage is _____. (Choose all that apply.)

    a. indicated by a value that is consistently greater than 85 percent

    b. an indication that the processor speed is inadequate

    c. an indication that your system needs more RAM

    d. indicated by a high rate of page file activity

13. A high rate of page file activity is _____.

    a. indicated by a value that is consistently greater than 85 percent

    b. an indication that the processor speed is inadequate

    c. an indication that your system needs more RAM

    d. indicated by high CPU usage

14. The GUI task management tool in CentOS 7 is called _____.

    a. Task Management

    b. System Monitor

    c. GNOME System Tool

    d. KDE System Monitor

15. Which of the following displays CPU-related system information in System Monitor?

    a. System tab

    b. Resources tab

    c. Processes tab

    d. Both the System and Resources tabs

    e. Both the System and Processes tabs

16. If you want to report a bug when using the Automatic Bug Reporting Tool, which of the following should you use?

    a. Bugzilla

    b. Logger

    c. Either Bugzilla or Logger

    d. None of the above

17. By default, the Windows 10 Performance Monitor displays the _____.

    a. % Disk Time

    b. % Processor Time

    c. Disk Reads/Sec

    d. Disk Writes/Sec

18. The Windows 10 Reliability Monitor tracks _____. (Choose all that apply.)

    a. hardware problems

    b. software problems

    c. changes to the computer

    d. user errors

19. Events monitored in the Windows 10 Reliability Monitor include _____. (Choose all that apply.)

    a. Windows updates

    b. software installations and uninstalls

    c. application hangs and crashes

    d. disk and memory failures

20. Reporting of events in the Windows 10 Reliability Monitor is delayed _____ hours.

    a. 8

    b. 24

    c. 48

    d. 168

Case Projects

CASE PROJECTS

Case 12-1: Observing Performance with Task Manager

You are interning for a local firm and respond to a user's complaint about the performance of her Windows 10 computer, which she says seems "sluggish." Which features will you use in Task Manager to research her problem? Explain each of your choices in detail.

Case 12-2: Investigating a Performance Problem in CentOS 7

You are working for a company that provides financial services to clients. An employee tells you that his CentOS 7 computer is running slowly. Explain how you would investigate this performance problem.

Case 12-3: Investigating System Reliability

You are interning for a local firm and respond to a user's complaint about the stability of his Windows 10 computer. How will you use the Reliability Monitor to research the problem? Explain each of your choices in detail.

Numbering Systems and Data Representation

After reading this appendix and completing the exercises, you will be able to:

- Convert numbers from one base to another (decimal, binary, and hexadecimal)
- Use an ASCII reference table to see the decimal and hexadecimal equivalents for a specified character
- Describe the data types for Boolean, character, integer, and floating-point data

Probably the biggest stumbling block that beginning programmers encounter is the common use of binary and hexadecimal numbering systems in programming languages. Most people have used the decimal numbering system all their lives, so using systems with different "base" numbers can be disconcerting. Knowing the binary and hexadecimal systems can simplify other complex topics, including Boolean algebra, signed numeric representation, and character codes.

This appendix explains the relationships among decimal, binary, and hexadecimal numbering systems, and explains how to convert numbers from one base to another. It also provides information about the ASCII character set.

Numbering Systems

PCs do not represent numeric values using the well-known decimal system. Instead, PCs typically use a binary numbering system and represent large binary values using hexadecimal numbers. When programming for the PC, you should be familiar with the three numbering systems listed in Table A-1. These numbering systems are described in the following sections.

Name	Base	Symbol
Decimal	Base 10	none or D
Binary	Base 2	B
Hexadecimal	Base 16	H or 0x

Table A-1   Numbering systems

Decimal Numbers

You've been using the decimal numbering system for so long that you probably take it for granted. In the decimal system (base 10), there are 10 different symbols to represent values: 0, 1, 2, 3, 4, 5, 6, 7, 8, and 9. Because the "base" of the system is 10, you can represent all values of less than 10 with single numbers. Once you reach 10, however, you need a second column of numbers to represent the value. When you reach 100, you need a third column, and so on. Each column is distinguished by a greater power of 10, which is why the decimal system is called base 10.

The only real difference between the decimal, binary, and hexadecimal systems is that a different base is used to distinguish these columns. Throughout this appendix, the values of these columns are called *positional values*.

The values for each base 10 position are shown in the following columns. The caret symbol (^) represents an exponent—for example, 10^2 is 10 to the 2nd power, or 10×10, which equals 100.

10^4	10^3	10^2	10^1	10^0
10000	1000	100	10	1

When you see a number like 123, you probably don't think much about the composition of the value. Remember from elementary school, however, that 1 is the value in the hundreds position, 2 is the value in the tens position, and 3 is the value in the ones position. A new column or position is required each time the numeric value surpasses a power of 10:

```
1 * 10^2 + 2 * 10^1 + 3 * 10^0 =
1 * 100 + 2 * 10 + 3 * 1 =
100 + 20 + 3 =
123
```

The asterisk (*) is the common representation for multiplication on computer systems. The forward slash (/) represents division.

In the United States and other countries, every three decimal digits are separated with a comma to make larger numbers easier to read. For example, the number 123,456,789 is much easier to read and comprehend than 123456789.

Binary Numbers

The binary numbering system (base 2) has only two symbols to represent values: 0 and 1. Because the hardware for modern digital computers uses electronic circuits called gates, which represent information using only the two values of On and Off, binary is a convenient numbering system for computers to use.

The values for each binary column position are shown in Table A-2. Note that these positions operate on the same principle as those in base 10; the only difference is that a new column or position is required each time the numeric value surpasses a power of 2.

2^7	2^6	2^5	2^4	2^3	2^2	2^1	2^0
128	64	32	16	8	4	2	1

Table A-2   Powers of 2

Just as commas are used to separate decimal numbers and make them more readable, spaces are added after every fourth number in the binary system. For example, the following binary value:

```
1010111110110010
```

is written:

```
1010 1111 1011 0010
```

Hexadecimal Numbers

Because binary numbers use only two values, representing large amounts in binary quickly becomes unwieldy. To represent the value 911, for example, you need 10 binary digits. The hexadecimal numbering system solves this problem. In the hexadecimal system (base 16), there are 16 different symbols to represent values instead of just two: 0, 1, 2, 3, 4, 5, 6, 7, 8, 9, A, B, C, D, E, and F. Because hexadecimal has a much larger "base" number than binary, you can represent a value like 911 with just three symbols (38F) instead of 10 binary digits.

Notice that hexadecimal uses the letters A through F to represent single digits of more than 9—specifically, the numbers 10 through 15.

Table A-3 shows relationships between the binary, decimal, and hexadecimal numbering systems. The table shows all the conversions for the decimal values of 0 to 15 into binary and hexadecimal.

Binary	Decimal	Hexadecimal
0000B	00	00H
0001B	01	01H
0010B	02	02H
0011B	03	03H
0100B	04	04H
0101B	05	05H
0110B	06	06H
0111B	07	07H
1000B	08	08H
1001B	09	09H
1010B	10	0AH
1011B	11	0BH
1100B	12	0CH
1101B	13	0DH
1110B	14	0EH
1111B	15	0FH

Table A-3   Number conversions

In programming, most compilers require the first digit of a hexadecimal number to be 0 and require an H at the end to denote the use of hexadecimal.

As with binary numbers, programmers make hexadecimal numbers more readable by adding a space every four digits. For example, the hexadecimal value 3287092778E3 is written 3287 0927 78E3.

Converting Between Numbering Systems

Students of programming are expected to be able to convert between the decimal, binary, and hexadecimal numbering systems. The following sections show you how.

Converting Binary Numbers to Decimal Numbers

To begin converting a binary number to a decimal number, simply separate the number into columns and write the positional value of each column above each binary digit. The positional values are calculated using the powers of 2 that you saw in Table A-2. Keep in mind that the equivalent positional values in the decimal system are ones, tens, hundreds, and so on; because the binary system uses a smaller base number, its positional values are ones, twos, fours, and so on.

For example, take the following binary number:

   1001B =

Disregard the B, which merely represents a binary number, and write the positional value above each binary digit:

Column Value (Binary)	8	4	2	1
Number	1	0	0	1

Discard the positional values that result in zero and add the positions that have 1s; in other words, $8 + 1 = 9$. The conversion of 1001 results in a decimal value of 9.

When you think about this operation, keep in mind that binary and decimal systems operate on the same principle—only the base is different. For example, in decimal, a 1 in the thousands column plus a 1 in the ones column equals 1001.

Column Value (Decimal)	1000	100	10	1
Number	1	0	0	1

Activity A-1: Converting Binary Numbers to Decimal Numbers

Time Required: 10 minutes

Objective: Convert binary numbers to decimal numbers.

Description: In this activity, you practice converting binary numbers to decimal numbers. To perform this conversion, simply separate the binary number into columns and write the positional value of each column above each binary digit. Next, add the positional values wherever a binary 1 appears.

Complete Table A-4 by providing the decimal equivalents for each binary number. Use scratch paper for your calculations.

Binary	Decimal
1011B	
1100B	
0011B	
0110B	
1001 1110B	
1011 0111B	

Table A-4   **Answers for binary to decimal conversions**

Keep in mind that the B merely represents a binary number; it does not play a part in the conversion.

Converting Decimal Numbers to Binary Numbers

One way to convert decimal numbers to binary numbers is to use long division, as demonstrated in Figure A-1. Follow these steps:

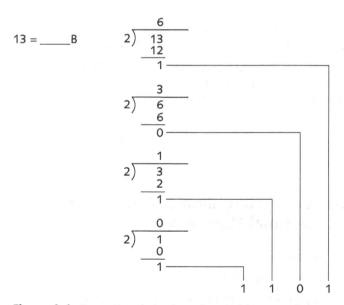

Figure A-1 Converting decimal numbers to binary numbers

1. Repeatedly divide the decimal number by 2, using the remainder of each division operation as part of your binary answer. Record the remainders from right to left.

2. Each quotient becomes the dividend of the next division operation. For example, dividing 13 by 2 produces a quotient of 6, which becomes the dividend for the next step. Dividing 6 by 2 produces a quotient of 3, and so on.

3. Continue dividing until you get a quotient of zero, which will yield the last (far left) digit of your binary answer.

Study this procedure thoroughly; you will use a similar procedure later in this appendix for decimal to hexadecimal conversions.

Activity A-2: Converting Decimal Numbers to Binary Numbers

Time Required: 10 minutes

Objective: Convert decimal numbers to binary numbers.

Description: In this activity, you practice converting decimal numbers to binary numbers. To perform this conversion, you repeatedly divide the decimal number by 2, using the procedure explained in the previous section.

Complete Table A-5 by providing the binary equivalents for each decimal number. Use scratch paper for your calculations.

Decimal	Binary
5	
10	
16	
25	
31	
49	

Table A-5   Answers for decimal to binary conversions

Converting Hexadecimal Numbers to Decimal Numbers

To begin converting from hexadecimal to decimal, simply separate the hexadecimal number into columns and write the positional value of each column above each hexadecimal digit. Because the hexadecimal system uses a base number of 16, the positional values are calculated using powers of 16, as shown in Table A-6.

16^6	16^5	16^4	16^3	16^2	16^1	16^0
16,777,216	1,048,576	65,536	4,096	256	16	1

Table A-6   Powers of 16

Take the following number:

0239H =

Disregard the H at the end and write the positional value above each hexadecimal digit:

256	16	1
2	3	9

Multiply each digit by its column value and then add the products for each position:

$2 \times 256 + 3 \times 16 + 9 \times 1$

$512 + 48 + 9 = 569$

Activity A-3: Converting Hexadecimal Numbers to Decimal Numbers

Time Required: 10 minutes

Objective: Convert hexadecimal numbers to decimal numbers.

Description: In this activity, you practice converting hexadecimal numbers to decimal numbers. To perform this conversion, write the positional value of each column above each hexadecimal digit, multiply each digit by its column value, and add the products.

Complete Table A-7 by providing the decimal equivalents for each hexadecimal number. Use scratch paper for your calculations.

Hexadecimal	Decimal
5H	
10H	
1AH	
2EH	
31H	
4BH	

Table A-7   Answers for hexadecimal to decimal conversions

Converting Decimal Numbers to Hexadecimal Numbers

One way to convert decimal numbers to hexadecimal numbers is to use long division, as demonstrated in Figure A-2 and explained in the following steps. You used a similar method to convert decimal numbers to binary numbers.

A

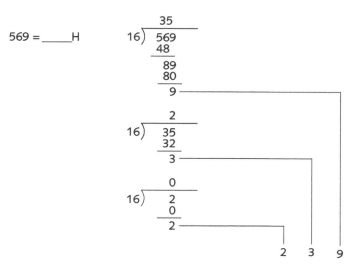

Figure A-2 Converting decimal numbers to hexadecimal numbers

1. Divide the decimal number by 16, using the hexadecimal remainder of each division operation as part of your answer. Record the remainders from right to left.

2. Each quotient becomes the dividend of the next division operation. For example, dividing 569 by 16 provides 35, which becomes the next number to divide by 16.

3. Continue dividing until you get a quotient of zero, which will yield the last (far left) digit of your hexadecimal answer.

If a remainder is between 10 and 15, you must convert it to the corresponding hexadecimal value between A (10) and F (15) in your answer. For another example of converting decimal numbers to hexadecimal numbers, as well as a helpful conversion chart, see Figure A-3. The remainder for the first division is 10, which is represented by the hexadecimal number A.

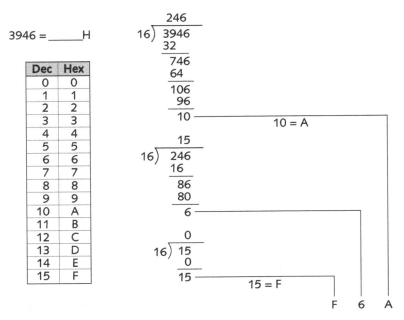

$3946 = \underline{}H$

Dec	Hex
0	0
1	1
2	2
3	3
4	4
5	5
6	6
7	7
8	8
9	9
10	A
11	B
12	C
13	D
14	E
15	F

Figure A-3 Another example of converting decimal numbers to hexadecimal numbers

Activity A-4: Converting Decimal Numbers to Hexadecimal Numbers

Time Required: 10 minutes

Objective: Convert decimal numbers to hexadecimal numbers.

Description: In this activity, you practice converting decimal numbers to hexadecimal numbers. To perform this conversion, repeatedly divide the decimal number by 16, using the remainder of each division as part of your hexadecimal answer. Record the remainders from right to left.

Complete Table A-8 by providing the hexadecimal equivalents for each decimal number. Use scratch paper for your calculations.

Decimal	Hexadecimal
5	
10	
75	
88	
126	
500	

Table A-8   Answers for decimal to hexadecimal conversions

Converting Binary Numbers to Hexadecimal Numbers

A bit is a binary digit—either a zero or a one. To make a binary number more readable, place a blank between each set of four bits, as shown in Figure A-4. Group the bits from right to left. If you are left with a group of less than four bits, pad the group with zero bits on the left. For example, the bit pattern 111 is padded as 0111.

When converting binary numbers to hexadecimal numbers, there is a simple rule: Each group of four bits is converted to one hexadecimal character, as shown in the conversion chart in Figure A-4. For example, to convert the binary number 0101, scan the conversion table to find the equivalent hexadecimal number: 5.

0111 1010 0101B = _____ H

Bin	Hex
0000	0
0001	1
0010	2
0011	3
0100	4
0101	5
0110	6
0111	7
1000	8
1001	9
1010	A
1011	B
1100	C
1101	D
1110	E
1111	F

Figure A-4 Converting binary numbers to hexadecimal numbers

Activity A-5: Converting Binary Numbers to Hexadecimal Numbers

Time Required: 10 minutes

Objective: Convert binary numbers to hexadecimal numbers.

Description: In this activity, you practice converting binary numbers to hexadecimal numbers. To perform this conversion, use the procedure explained in the previous section and the conversion table in Figure A-4.

Complete Table A-9 by providing the hexadecimal equivalents for each binary number. Use scratch paper for your calculations.

Binary	Hexadecimal
1100B	
1000 0111B	
0110 0100B	
0001 0011 0110B	
1001 1101 1000B	
1111 0011 1100B	

Table A-9   **Answers for binary to hexadecimal conversions**

Converting Hexadecimal Numbers to Binary Numbers

To accomplish this conversion, use the inverse of the rule in the previous section. Each hexadecimal character can be converted to four bits, as shown in Figure A-5. For example, to convert the hexadecimal character A, scan the conversion table to find the equivalent binary number: 1010. Repeat the search for the remaining hexadecimal characters.

9BAH = _____ B

Bin	Hex
0000	0
0001	1
0010	2
0011	3
0100	4
0101	5
0110	6
0111	7
1000	8
1001	9
1010	A
1011	B
1100	C
1101	D
1110	E
1111	F

```
 9    B    A
 |    |    |
 |    |    |
1001 1011 1010
```

Figure A-5   Converting hexadecimal numbers to binary numbers

Activity A-6: Converting Hexadecimal Numbers to Binary Numbers

Time Required: 10 minutes

Objective: Convert hexadecimal numbers to binary numbers.

Description: In this activity, you practice converting hexadecimal numbers to binary numbers. To perform this conversion, use the procedure explained in the previous section and the conversion table in Figure A-5.

Complete Table A-10 by providing the binary equivalents for each hexadecimal number. Use scratch paper for your calculations.

Hexadecimal	Binary
05H	
1CH	
75H	
8FH	
126H	
500H	

Table A-10 Answers for hexadecimal to binary conversions

Converting Numbers Using the Windows 10 Calculator

You can use the calculator (see Figure A-6) in Windows 10 to check your answers. To open the calculator, click Start, click All apps, and then click Calculator. In the Standard view, you can perform decimal calculations.

Figure A-6 Calculator in Standard view

Source: Windows 10/Calculator

When checking number conversions, the Programmer view is more useful. To switch to this view, click the Menu button with the three horizontal lines and then click Programmer (see Figure A-7).

Figure A-7 Calculator in Programmer view

Source: Windows 10/Calculator

Start by selecting the base of the number you want to convert. Choose from HEX (base 16), DEC (base 10), or BIN (base 2) near the top of the calculator. Octal (base 8) is not covered in this appendix but is also available in Calculator. Next, enter the number you want to convert. (If you're more comfortable entering numbers with the numeric keypad on your keyboard, press NUM LOCK and then enter the number.) The conversion will be displayed next to the base name. To convert the number in the main area, click the HEX, DEC, or BIN button.

Activity A-7: Converting Numbers Using the Windows 10 Calculator

Time Required: 10 minutes

Objective: Convert numbers from one base to another using the Windows 10 calculator.

A

Description: In this activity, you enter a decimal number into the calculator and convert it to a hexadecimal or binary number.

1. Start your virtual machines using the appropriate instructions in Activity 1-1.

2. Click **Start,** click **All apps,** and then click **Calculator.**

3. To turn on the Programmer view, click the **Menu** button with the three horizontal lines, and then click **Programmer.**

4. Click the **DEC** button.

5. To enter the decimal number 2007, press the **2** key, press the **0** key twice, and then press the **7** key.

6. Click the **HEX** button.

7. Click the **BIN** button.

8. Close any open windows.

9. Leave the PC logged on for the next activity.

Using ASCII Characters

Because a computer can only understand numbers, it requires a code to translate text characters such as *a* or @ and certain actions into numbers. The most common of these codes is ASCII (pronounced *ask-key*), which stands for American Standard Code for Information Interchange. ASCII was finalized in 1968 by the American National Standards Institute (ANSI). The standard ASCII character set consists of 128 decimal numbers from 0 to 127, which are assigned to letters, numbers, punctuation marks, and the most common special characters.

The ASCII characters were assigned codes using the following guidelines:

- The first 32 characters, ASCII codes 0 through 31, form a special set of nonprinting characters called the control characters. These control characters, now obsolete, once controlled how text was printed.

- The second group of 32 codes comprises various punctuation symbols, special characters, and numbers.

- The third group of 32 codes is reserved for uppercase alphabetic characters and six special symbols.

- The fourth and final group of 32 codes is reserved for lowercase alphabetic symbols, five additional special symbols, and another control character (delete).

Table A-11 shows the ASCII character codes with their equivalent decimal and hexadecimal values. The obsolete control characters are not included.

Character	Dec	Hex	Character	Dec	Hex	Character	Dec	Hex
(space)	32	0x20	@	64	0x40	`	96	0x60
!	33	0x21	A	65	0x41	a	97	0x61
"	34	0x22	B	66	0x42	b	98	0x62
#	35	0x23	C	67	0x43	c	99	0x63
$	36	0x24	D	68	0x44	d	100	0x64
%	37	0x25	E	69	0x45	e	101	0x65
&	38	0x26	F	70	0x46	f	102	0x66
'	39	0x27	G	71	0x47	g	103	0x67
(	40	0x28	H	72	0x48	h	104	0x68
)	41	0x29	I	73	0x49	i	105	0x69
*	42	0x2a	J	74	0x4a	j	106	0x6a
+	43	0x2b	K	75	0x4b	k	107	0x6b
,	44	0x2c	L	76	0x4c	l	108	0x6c
-	45	0x2d	M	77	0x4d	m	109	0x6d
.	46	0x2e	N	78	0x4e	n	110	0x6e
/	47	0x2f	O	79	0x4f	o	111	0x6f
0	48	0x30	P	80	0x50	p	112	0x70
1	49	0x31	Q	81	0x51	q	113	0x71
2	50	0x32	R	82	0x52	r	114	0x72
3	51	0x33	S	83	0x53	s	115	0x73
4	52	0x34	T	84	0x54	t	116	0x74
5	53	0x35	U	85	0x55	u	117	0x75
6	54	0x36	V	86	0x56	v	118	0x76
7	55	0x37	W	87	0x57	w	119	0x77
8	56	0x38	X	88	0x58	x	120	0x78
9	57	0x39	Y	89	0x59	y	121	0x79
:	58	0x3a	Z	90	0x5a	z	122	0x7a
;	59	0x3b	[	91	0x5b	{	123	0x7b
<	60	0x3c	\	92	0x5c	|	124	0x7c
=	61	0x3d	]	93	0x5d	}	125	0x7d
>	62	0x3e	^	94	0x5e	~	126	0x7e
?	63	0x3f	_	95	0x5f	(delete)	127	0x7f

Table A-11   ASCII characters and equivalent decimal and hexadecimal values

Table A-11 uses the alternative symbol 0x for hexadecimal values.

Because most modern computers work with 8-bit bytes, which can represent 256 different values, the ASCII character set now offers an additional 128 characters known as extended ASCII. These extended character sets are platform- and locale-dependent, so more than one set is available. One example of an extended ASCII character set is available in Windows, as you will see in Activity A-9.

Activity A-8: Using ASCII Character Codes

Time Required: 10 minutes

Objective: Look up the character codes for ASCII characters.

Description: In this activity, you practice looking up the decimal and hexadecimal codes for ASCII characters. Use the conversions in Table A-11 to fill in the appropriate codes in Table A-12 for the given ASCII characters.

Character	Decimal	Hexadecimal
*		
4		
Q		
f		
(space)		

Table A-12 Decimal and hexadecimal codes for ASCII characters

Activity A-9: Entering ASCII Characters in WordPad

Time Required: 10 minutes

Objective: Enter ASCII characters into a document using WordPad.

Description: In this activity, you enter ASCII characters in WordPad.

1. Start your virtual machines using the appropriate instructions in Activity 1-1.
2. Click **Start,** click **All apps,** scroll down and click **Windows Accessories,** and then click **WordPad.**
3. Press the " key.
4. To enter the ¡ character (ASCII 173), type **Alt+173.**

Hold down the Alt key while typing the ASCII code. You must use the numeric keypad to type the numbers. The number at the top of the keyboard will not work.

5. Type **Cuidado! grit.**

6. To type the ó character (ASCII 162), type **Alt+162.**

7. Type **." "Careful!" he shouted.** and then press **Enter.**

8. Review the text and make any necessary corrections. The WordPad window should look like Figure A-8.

Figure A-8 Entering ASCII characters in WordPad

Source: Windows 10/WordPad

9. Close any open windows, click **Start,** click **Power,** and then click the **Shut Down** button.

10. Wait a moment for the Windows 10 virtual machine to shut down completely.

Representing Data Types

In a PC, the hardware stores data items and software applications perform operations on them. The values of these data items are called bits (short for *binary digits*); each bit represents a discrete piece of information.

Bits are grouped together, and the pattern of values within the group is used to represent a symbol. For example, a group of 8 bits (called a byte) can have 256 different patterns and can therefore represent 256 different symbols. In modern computers, groupings of 2 or 4 bytes, called words, can represent larger "chunks" of information.

Understanding internal binary representation is not required for programming, but it is helpful to know. The following sections explain common data types.

Character Type

You learned previously about the representation of ASCII characters. Two types of character data are defined:

- Signed characters—These characters store integers in the range of –128 to +127.

- Unsigned characters—These characters store whole integers in the range of 0 to 255; they are also used to store ASCII characters.

Boolean Type

The Boolean type can have only one of two values: true or false. (In some cases, the two values are 0 or non-0.)

Integer Type

The integer data type is used for storing whole numbers. You can use signed integers, which can hold positive or negative values, or unsigned integer values, which can hold only positive values.

The most common source of confusion when discussing an integer type is its size and the range of values it can hold. The confusion stems from the fact that languages leave many features of integer types for particular implementations to define themselves, meaning that each program compiler can determine its own exact specifications. The C and C++ compilers do set minimum requirements for each integer type, but the implementation is free to exceed these limits.

The g++ compiler included with CentOS 7 provides the integer sizes listed in Table A-13.

Type	Length	Minimum value	Maximum value
char	1 byte	–128	127
unsigned char	1 byte	0	255
short	2 bytes	–32,768	32,767
short unsigned	2 bytes	0	65,535
long	4 bytes	–2,147,483,648	2,147,483,647
long unsigned	4 bytes	0	4,294,967,295

Table A-13   Integer sizes

Floating-Point Type

A floating-point number is a number that can contain a fractional part. For example, floating-point numbers can contain decimal values, such as 3.14, 0.18, or –0.087. The term *floating point* means that there is no fixed number of digits before or after the decimal point; that is, the decimal point can float. In general, floating-point calculations are slower and less accurate than fixed-point (integer) calculations, but they can handle a larger range of numbers.

Floating-point representation is similar to scientific notation, which is a useful way to represent numbers that are very large or very small. The following are examples of scientific notation:

$$47,300 = 4.73 \times 10^4$$

$$0.000000021 = 2.1 \times 10^{-8}$$

Floating-point numbers come in two sizes: float (single-precision) and double (double-precision). The g++ compiler included with CentOS 7 provides the floating-point sizes listed in Table A-14.

Type	Length	Maximum
float	4 bytes	3.40282E ± 38 (7 digits)
double	8 bytes	1.79769E ± 308 (15 digits)

Table A-14   **Floating-point sizes**

Activity A-10: Providing a Data Type

Time Required: 10 minutes

Objective: Given example data, provide the proper data type to store it.

Description: In this activity, you practice specifying data types for example data by completing Table A-15.

Data example	Data type
A	
1024	
66	
1023.996	
#	
−32700	
−88888.778	
65000	
−2,000,000,000	
777777789	

Table A-15   **Answers for data types**

Working with Hyper-V Virtualization

Getting Started with Hyper-V Virtualization

Many versions of Windows include the Hyper-V virtualization technology, which enables you to run virtualized computer systems on top of a physical host. You use and manage these systems just as if they were physical computer systems; however, they exist in a virtualized and isolated environment. This feature in Windows 10 is called Client Hyper-V, which is the same technology used in Windows Server 2012 Hyper-V.

X86 virtualization allows multiple operating systems to simultaneously share processor resources safely and efficiently. This virtualization is used to simulate a complete hardware environment, or virtual machine, in which an unmodified guest operating system executes. Virtualization was added to most x86 processors (Intel VT-x or AMD-V) in 2006.

To use hardware virtualization, the VT-x or AMD-V option must be enabled in the BIOS. You can access the BIOS settings menu by pressing the appropriate key (F2 or Delete) as the startup flash screen is displayed. The BIOS settings for Intel VT or AMD-V are usually available in the Chipset or Security menu.

Configuring the Host Computer

To enable two virtual machines to communicate with the Internet and with each other, you will install the Hyper-V Hypervisor and Internet Connection Sharing (ICS). Next, you connect the existing network adapter in your Host01 computer to the Internet. Next, you create an external virtual switch, which has a separate connection to the virtual machines. You will enable ICS on the Internet connection to share the Internet with the internal virtual switch.

Complete the following steps to prepare the host computer running Windows 10 to support the virtual environment.

1. Log on to your host PC as the user account with administrative privileges.
2. Type **Windows Features** over "Search the web and Windows" on the taskbar.
3. To install the Hyper-V Hypervisor, click **Turn Windows features on or off**, check **Hyper-V**, and then click **OK**.
4. Wait for Windows to complete the requested changes, and then click **Restart now**.

5. Wait for the changes to be applied.

6. Log on to the Windows 10 desktop as the user account with administrative privileges.

7. To start the Hyper-V Manager, type **Hyper-V Manager** over "Search the web and Windows" on the Start screen.

8. Double-click **Hyper-V Manager**.

9. Click the name for the host computer under Hyper-V Manager.

10. To create a network connection for the virtual machines, click **Virtual Switch Manager** in the Actions pane.

11. Click **Create Virtual Switch**. Type **External Network Connection** over "New Virtual Switch." Click **OK**. Click **Yes**.

12. Wait for the changes to be applied.

13. To enable enhanced session mode for the virtual machine connection, click **Hyper-V Settings** in the right pane, click **Enhanced Session Mode Policy**, and then click **Allow enhanced session mode**. Under User, click **Enhanced Session Mode**, and then click **Use enhanced session mode**. Click **OK**.

14. Keep the Hyper-V Manager window open for future activities.

15. To configure ICS, right-click the **Network** icon on the taskbar, click **Open Network and Sharing Center**, and then click **Change adapter settings**. Right-click the **Ethernet** adapter, click **Properties**, click the **Sharing** tab, and then click **Allow other network users to connect through this computer's Internet connection**. Click **OK**. Close the Network Connection windows.

16. To create the folder for the .iso operating system files, click **Start**, click **File Explorer**, click **This PC**, and double-click **Local Disk (C:)**. Right-click the white space, point to **New**, click **Folder**, type **ISOFiles** over "New folder," and then press **Enter**.

Refer to the book's preface to find the sources for the operating system files. For example, if you downloaded the Windows 10 .iso file from DreamSpark, copy the .iso file to the C:\ISOFiles folder.

17. To create the folder for the virtual machine files, click the **File Explorer** icon on the taskbar, double-click **Local Disk (C:)**, right-click in the white space, point to **New**, click **Folder**, type **VirtualMachines** over "New folder," and then press **Enter**. Close the File Explorer window.

18. To create the TextShare folder on the host computer, click **Start**, click **Computer**, and double-click **Local Disk (C:)**. Note that your operating system drive might have a different name. Right-click the white space in the right pane, point to **New**, click **Folder**, type **TextShare**, and press **Enter**. Right-click **TextShare**, click **Properties**, click the **Sharing** tab, and click **Share**. Type **Everyone**, click **Add**, click **Share**, and click **Done**. When asked if you want to turn on network discovery and file sharing for all public networks, click **Yes**, and then click **Close**. Close the Local Disk (C:) window.

19. To share a printer on the Host01 computer, right-click **Start**, click **Control Panel**, click the **View by** chevron, and click **Small icons**. Click **Devices and Printers**, click **Add a printer**,

click **The printer that I want isn't listed,** click **Add a local printer or network printer with manual settings,** and click **Next** twice. Scroll the Manufacturer list, click **Generic,** click **Generic/Text Only,** and click **Next.** Type **SharedPrinter** in the Printer name text box, click **Next** twice, and then click **Finish.** Close the Devices and Printers window.

Visit *www.cengagebrain.com* and log on to access student-specific resources on the Student Companion Site. If you are not a registered user, you can create a new account.

20. To access student resources on the Cengage Learning Web site, open your Web browser, type **www.cengagebrain.com/** in the address bar, and press **Enter.** Type **carswell** over "Enter ISBN, Author or Title," and then click the **Search** button, which looks like a magnifying glass.

21. To download the student data files, click **Guide to Parallel Operating Systems with Windows 10 and Linux,** click the **Free Materials** tab, click **Save to MyHome,** and click **Open.** Click the **Data Files for Students (TextShareFile)** link on the left, and then click the entry after **Download Now.** Click **Run** twice. If your Web browser automatically downloads files from the Internet, they should be downloaded and saved in your Downloads folder. Find the file you downloaded and copy it to the **TextShare** folder. If prompted for a location to download your files, click **Browse,** click **Local Disk (C:),** double-click **TextShare,** and click **OK.** Click **Unzip,** click **OK,** and then click **Close.** If you are unable to download your student data files, contact your instructor for assistance.

22. To download the host file, click the **Data Files for Students (Host File)** link on the left, click the entry after **Download Now,** and click **Run** twice. Click **Browse,** click **Local Disk (C:),** double-click **VirtualMachines,** click **OK,** click **Unzip,** click **OK,** and then click **Close.** Close your Web browser.

23. To create a shortcut on the desktop to start the virtual machines, right-click the desktop, point to **New,** click **Shortcut,** and then click **Browse.** Navigate to **C:\VirtualMachines.** Click **RunScript.cmd,** click **OK,** and then click **Next.** Type **Manage Virtual Machines** as the shortcut name. Click **Finish.**

24. To specify an icon for the shortcut, right-click the **Manage Virtual Machines** icon and then click **Properties.** Click **Change Icon,** and then click **OK.** Scroll and click the multiple-screen icon. Click **OK.**

25. Leave the Hyper-V Manager open for future activities.

Installing Operating Systems in Hyper-V

In the following sections, you will create virtual machines and virtual hard drives, and you will configure network adapters. When you finish, you will be ready to install a guest operating system. Recall that the virtual machines look like physical machines to the operating system installers.

Creating the First Virtual Machine for Windows 10

Because each chapter in the text starts with Windows 10 activities first, you will create a virtual machine for Windows 10 first. With the following steps, you will use the features of Hyper-V Manager to create the virtual machine for Windows 10.

1. To create a virtual hard disk to store a new virtual machine, click **New** in the Actions pane. Click **Hard Disk.**

2. Review the Before You Begin page. Click **Next** three times.

3. Type **Windows 10 – Disk0** over "New Virtual Hard Disk.vhdx." Click **Browse**, click **Windows (C:\)**, scroll and click **VirtualMachines**, and then click **Select Folder.** Click **Next** twice.

4. Click **Finish.**

5. To create a virtual hard disk for student use, click **New** in the Actions pane. Click **Hard Disk.**

6. Review the Before You Begin page. Click **Next** twice, and then click **Fixed Size.** Click **Next.**

7. Type **Windows 10 – Disk1** over "New Virtual Hard Disk.vhdx." Click **Browse**, click **Windows (C:\)**, scroll and click **VirtualMachines**, and then click **Select Folder.** Click **Next.** Enter 4 for the Size, and then click **Next.** Click **Finish.**

8. Repeat Steps 5 through 7 for **Windows 10 – Disk2.**

9. To create a virtual machine, click **New** in the Actions pane. Click **Virtual Machine.**

10. Review the Before You Begin page. Click **Next.**

11. Type **Windows 10** over "New Virtual Machine." Check **Store the virtual machine in a different location.** Click **Browse**, click **Windows (C:\)**, scroll and click **VirtualMachines**, click **Select Folder**, and then click **Next.**

12. To specify a virtual machine with the newer virtualization features, click **Generation 2.** Click **Next.**

13. To specify memory, enter **1024** for the Startup Memory, click **Use Dynamic Memory for this virtual machine**, and then click **Next.**

14. To configure networking, click the **Connection** chevron and then click **External Network Connection.** Click **Next.**

15. To delay the connection of the virtual hard disk, click **Attach a virtual hard disk later.** Click **Next.**

16. Review the summary and click **Finish.**

17. Wait for the virtual machine to be created.

18. To view the virtual machine settings, click **Windows 10** in the middle pane and then click **Settings** in the Actions pane.

19. To add the hard drive created in Steps 1–4, click **SCSI Controller** and then click **Add.**

20. Click **Browse**, click **Windows (C:\)**, scroll and double-click **VirtualMachines**, click **Windows 10 – Disk0.vhdx**, and then click **Open.** Click **Apply.**

21. To add the hard drive created in Steps 5–7, click **SCSI Controller** and then click **Add**.

22. Click **Browse**, click **Windows (C:\)**, scroll and double-click **VirtualMachines**, click **Windows 10 – Disk1.vhdx**, and then click **Open**. Click **Apply**.

23. Repeat Steps 21 and 22 for **Windows 10 – Disk2.vhdx**.

24. To add the Windows 10 .iso file, click **SCSI Controller**, click **DVD Drive**, and then click **Add**. Click **Image File**.

25. Click **Browse**, navigate to **C:\ISOFiles**, click the Windows 10 .iso file, and then click **Open**. Click **Apply**.

 Refer to the book's preface to find the name of the specific .iso file you are using. If you downloaded the .iso file from DreamSpark, the filename is en_windows_10_education_x64_6848120.iso.

26. To change the boot order, click **Firmware**, click **DVD Drive**, and then click **Move Up** until the DVD drive is the first item listed. Click **Network Adapter**, and then click **Move Down** until the network adapter is the last item listed.

27. Verify that the Firmware window lists the DVD drive as the first item in the boot order.

28. To add Guest services, click **Integration Services**, click **Guest services**, and then click **OK**.

29. Leave the Hyper-V Manager window open for future activities.

Installing Windows 10

Installing Windows 10 on a virtual machine is not fundamentally different from installing it on a physical machine. Perform the following steps to install the Windows 10 virtual machine, which ensures that your virtual environment corresponds to the environment used throughout the text.

1. If necessary, log on to your host PC with the user account, which has administrative privileges.

2. If necessary, type **Hyper-V Manager** over "Search the web and Windows" on the Start screen. Double-click **Hyper-V Manager**.

3. To connect to the Windows 10 virtual machine, right-click **Windows 10** in the center pane of Hyper-V Manager. Click **Connect**.

4. To start the Windows 10 virtual machine, click the **Action** menu, and click **Start**. Click in the **Virtual Machine Connection** window.

5. When "Press any key to boot from CD or DVD" appears, immediately press the **Spacebar**.

6. Verify and correct the language and other settings as needed, and then click **Next**.

7. To continue with the installation of Windows 10, click the **Install now** button when prompted.

8. Wait for the Setup program to start.

9. When the "Enter the product key to activate Windows" screen appears, enter the product key and then click **Next**.

10. When the license terms appear, click **I accept the license terms**, and then click **Next**.

11. When asked to select the type of installation you want, click **Custom (advanced)**, click **Drive 0 Unallocated Space**, and then click **Next**.

12. Wait for the files to be copied and expanded.

13. When the Get going fast window appears, click **Use Express settings**.

14. When prompted to choose a user name for your account, type **Admin01** in the "Who's going to use this PC" text box.

15. Type **Pa$$w0rd** over "Enter password," press **Tab**, type **Pa$$w0rd** over "Re-enter password," type **It's a Microsoft password** over "Password hint," and then click **Next**.

16. Wait for Windows to set up the desktop.

17. To release the Windows 10 .iso file, click the **Media** menu, click **DVD drive**, and then click **Eject**.

18. To change the computer name, type **control** in the "Search the web and Windows" text box, click **Control Panel**, click **System and Security**, click **System**, click the **Change settings** link, click **Change**, and type **Windows10** for the Computer name. Click **OK** twice, click **Close**, and then click **Restart Now**.

19. To sign in as Admin01, click the **Action** menu, and then click **Ctrl-Alt-Delete**. Click **Admin01** in the lower-left corner, enter **Pa$$w0rd** for the password, and press **Enter**.

20. Wait for the user setup to complete.

21. To extend the Path Environment variable for the scripts, type **control** in the "Search the web and Windows" text box, and then click **Control Panel**. Click **System and Security**, click **System**, click **Advanced system settings**, and then click **Environment variables**. Click **Path** and then click **Edit**. Press the **right arrow** key, type **Scripts**, and click **OK** three times.

22. To verify that the Path Environment variable was added correctly, type **cmd** in the "Search the web and Windows" text box, click **Command Prompt**, type **ECHO %PATH%**, and then press **Enter**.

23. Close the open windows in the Windows 10 virtual machine.

24. To download the scripts to the Windows 10 virtual machine, log in to *www.cengage brain.com* with your student account. Type **carswell** over "Enter ISBN, Author or Title," and then click the **Search** button, which looks like a magnifying glass. Click **Guide to Parallel Operating Systems with Windows 10 and Linux**, click the **Free Materials** tab, click **Save to MyHome**, and click **Open**. Click the **Data Files for Students (Windows Files)** link on the left, click the entry after **Download Now**, and click **Run** twice. Click **Browse**, click **Local Disk (C:)**, double-click **Scripts**, click **OK**, click **Unzip**, click **OK**, and then click **Close**. If you are unable to download your student data files, contact your instructor for assistance.

25. To allocate and format the partitions for student use, type **computer** in the "Search the web and Windows" text box, double-click **Computer Management**, double-click **Disk Management**, click **MBR (Master Boot Record)**, and then click **OK**.

26. To create the first volume on Disk1, right-click the unallocated area, click **New Simple Volume**, click **Next**, enter **2048** for the Simple volume size in MB, and then click **Next** twice. Type **NTFS** over "New Volume," click **Next**, and then click **Finish**.

27. To create the first volume on Disk2, right-click the unallocated area, click **New Simple Volume,** click **Next,** enter **2048** for the Simple volume size in MB, and then click **Next** twice. Type **FAT32** over "New Volume," click **Next,** and then click **Finish.**

28. To create the User01 user account, reopen **Computer Management,** expand **Local Users and Groups,** click **Users,** right-click in the white space, and then click **New User.**

29. Enter **User01** for the User name, enter **Pa$$w0rd** for the password, press **Tab,** and then enter **Pa$$w0rd** for the Confirm password. Clear the **User must change password at first logon** check box, click **Password never expires,** and then click **Create.** Click **Close.**

30. To set the password for the Administrator account, right-click **Administrator,** click **Set Password,** and then click **Proceed.** Enter **Pa$$w0rd** for the password, press **Tab,** enter **Pa$$w0rd** for the Confirm password, and then click **OK** twice. Right-click **Administrator,** click **Properties,** clear the **Account is disabled** check box, and then click **OK.**

31. For the changes to take effect, you must restart your Windows 10 virtual machine. Press the **Windows** key, click **Power,** and then click **Restart.**

32. To sign in as User01, click **User01** in the lower-left corner, enter **Pa$$w0rd** for the password, and then press **Enter.**

33. Wait for the user setup to complete.

Using the USB Drive with Windows 10

To use a USB drive with the Windows 10 virtual machine, complete these steps:

1. Prior to starting the virtual machines, insert the USB drive in the host computer.

2. Double-click **Manage Virtual Machines** on the desktop.

3. Go to the Windows 10 window, click the **Show Options** chevron, click the **Local Resources** tab, click **More,** expand **Drives,** click the check box for your USB drive, and then click **OK.** Click **Connect.**

4. To sign in as Admin01, click the **Action** menu, and then click **Ctrl-Alt-Delete.** Click **Admin01** in the lower-left corner, enter **Pa$$w0rd** for the password, and press **Enter.**

5. To view the files on your USB drive, press the **Windows** key, click **File Explorer,** and double-click your USB drive.

Creating a Second Virtual Machine for CentOS 7

Creating a CentOS 7 virtual machine is not fundamentally different from creating a Windows 10 virtual machine. Perform the following steps to install the CentOS 7 virtual machine, which ensures that your virtual environment corresponds to the environment used throughout the text.

1. If necessary, log on to your host PC as **Admin01** with a password of **Pa$$w0rd.**

2. If necessary, start the Hyper-V Manager by typing **Hyper-V Manager** over "Search the web and Windows" on the Start screen. Double-click **Hyper-V Manager.** Click the name of the host computer under Hyper-V Manager.

3. To create a virtual hard disk to store a new virtual machine, click **New** in the Actions pane. Click **Hard Disk.**

4. Review the Before You Begin page. Click **Next** three times.

5. Type **CentOS7 – sda** over "New Virtual Hard Disk.vhdx." Click **Browse**, click **Windows (C:\)**, scroll and click **VirtualMachines**, and then click **Select Folder** Click **Next** twice.

6. Click **Finish**.

7. To create a virtual hard disk for student use, click **New** in the Actions pane. Click **Hard Disk**.

8. Review the Before You Begin page. Click **Next** twice, click **Fixed Size**, and then click **Next**.

9. Type **CentOS7 – sdb** over "New Virtual Hard Disk.vhdx." Click **Browse**, click **Windows (C:\)**, scroll and click **VirtualMachines**, and then click **Select Folder**. Click **Next**. Enter **4** for the Size, and then click **Next**. Click **Finish**.

10. Repeat Steps 7 through 9 for **CentOS7 – sdc**.

11. To create a virtual machine, click **New** in the Actions pane. Click **Virtual Machine**.

12. Review the Before You Begin page. Click **Next**.

13. Type **CentOS 7** over "New Virtual Machine." Click **Browse**, click **Windows (C:\)**, scroll and click **VirtualMachines**, click **Select Folder**, and then click **Next** twice.

14. To specify memory, enter **1024** for the Startup Memory, click **Use Dynamic Memory for this virtual machine**, and then click **Next**.

15. To configure networking, click the **Connection** chevron and then click **External Network Connection**. Click **Next**.

16. To delay the connection of the virtual hard disk, click **Attach a virtual hard disk later**. Click **Next**.

17. Review the summary and click **Finish**.

18. Wait for the virtual machine to be created.

19. To view the virtual machine settings, click **CentOS 7** in the middle pane and then click **Settings** in the Actions pane.

20. To add the hard drive created in Steps 3–6, click **IDE Controller 0**, click **Hard Drive**, and then click **Add**.

21. Click **Browse**, click **Windows (C:\)**, scroll and double-click **VirtualMachines**, click **CentOS7 – sda.vhdx**, and then click **Open**. Click **Apply**.

22. To add the hard drive created in Steps 7–9, click **SCSI Controller** and then click **Add**.

23. Click **Browse**, click **Windows (C:\)**, scroll and double-click **VirtualMachines**, click **CentOS7 – sdb.vhdx**, and then click **Open**. Click **Apply**.

24. Repeat Steps 22 and 23 for **CentOS 7 – sdc.vhdx**.

25. To add the CentOS 7 .iso file, click **IDE Controller 1**, click **DVD Drive**, and then click **Image File**.

26. Click **Browse**, navigate to **C:\ISOFiles**, click the CentOS 7 .iso file, and then click **Open**. Click **Apply**.

27. To add Guest services, click **Integration Services**, click **Guest services**, and then click **OK**.

28. Leave the Hyper-V Manager window open for future activities.

Installing CentOS 7

Installing CentOS 7 on a virtual machine is not fundamentally different from installing it on a physical machine. Perform the following steps to install the CentOS 7 machine, which ensures that your virtual environment corresponds to the environment used throughout the text.

1. If necessary, log on to your host PC as **user01** with a password of **P@ssw0rd**.

2. If necessary, type **Hyper-V Manager** over "Search the web and Windows" on the Start screen. Double-click **Hyper-V Manager**.

3. To connect to the CentOS 7 virtual machine, right-click **CentOS 7** in the center pane of Hyper-V Manager. Click **Connect**.

4. To start the CentOS 7 virtual machine, click the **Action** menu, and click **Start**. Click in the **Virtual Machine Connection** window.

5. When the next window prompts you to install or test, press the **up arrow** to select **Install CentOS 7**. Press **Enter**.

6. When the Welcome to CentOS 7 window appears, verify that **English (United States)** is selected and then click **Continue**.

7. In the next window, click **INSTALLATION DESTINATION**.

8. Click the **sda** disk and then click **Done** in the upper-left corner.

9. To specify the GNOME desktop, click **SOFTWARE SELECTION**. Click **GNOME Desktop** on the left side. On the right side, click **GNOME Applications, Internet Applications, Office Suite and Productivity, Development Tools,** and **Security Tools**. Click **Done**.

10. To set the date and time, click **Date and Time** and then change the setting to match your time zone. Click **Done**.

11. To start the installation, click **Begin Installation** in the lower-right corner.

12. To set the root password, click **ROOT PASSWORD**, type **P@ssw0rd**, press **Tab**, type **P@ssw0rd**, and then click **Done** twice.

13. To create the user01 user account, click **USER CREATION**. Enter User01 as the Full Name and **User01** as the User Name. Check **Make this user administrator**. Enter **Pa$$w0rd** for the password twice.

14. Click **Done** twice.

15. The installation can take up to an hour. When it finishes, click **Reboot**.

16. If the installation starts again, click **Action**, and then click **Turn Off** twice. Click **File**, click **Settings**, check the boot order, and make sure the IDE Disk is first.

17. When the system reboots, accept the license agreement by entering a **1**, a **2**, and then **c**. The login page appears and the previous user (user01) is available to be selected for login.

18. Log on to CentOS 7 as **User01** with a password of **Pa$$w0rd**.

Completing CentOS 7 Configuration

Perform the following steps to finish configuring the CentOS 7 virtual machine, which ensures that your virtual environment corresponds to the environment used throughout the text. You will prepare two hard disks (sdb and sdc) for use in the text activities by partitioning and formatting them.

1. If necessary, log on to your host PC as **User01** with a password of **Pa$$w0rd**.

2. If necessary, double-click **Manage Virtual Machines** on the desktop.

3. Log on to CentOS 7 as **User01** with a password of **Pa$$w0rd**.

4. Verify that **English** is the selected language and click **Next** twice.

5. Click **Start using CentOS Linux**. Close the Getting Started window.

6. To verify that the Ethernet adapter is available, click the down arrow in the upper-right corner of the screen. If Wired is Off, click the arrow and select **Connect**.

7. To disable the screensaver, click **Applications**, click **System Tools**, click **Settings**, click **Power**, click the **Blank screen** chevron, and then click **Never**. Close the Power window.

8. To open a terminal window, right-click the desktop and click **Open in Terminal**.

9. Type **sudo yum install samba**, type **Pa$$w0rd**, and press **Enter**. Type **y** in response to any prompts during the installation, and then press **Enter**.

10. To start partitioning the sdb disk, type **sudo fdisk /dev/sdb** and press **Enter**. Enter **Pa$$w0rd** for the password and press **Enter**.

11. Ignore the warning messages.

12. To create the first primary partition on sdb, wait until "Command (m for help)" appears, type **n** and press **Enter**, type **p** and press **Enter**, and then type **1** and press **Enter** three times.

13. To review the partition and write to the partition table, type **p** and press **Enter**, and then type **w** and press **Enter**.

14. To format the partition as Ext4, type **sudo mkfs /dev/sdb1** and press **Enter**. Enter **Pa$$w0rd** for the password and press **Enter**.

15. To label the partition, type **sudo e2label /dev/sdb1 Ext4** and then press **Enter**. If necessary, enter **Pa$$w0rd** for the password and press **Enter**.

16. To start partitioning the sdc disk, type **sudo fdisk /dev/sdc** and press **Enter**. If necessary, enter **Pa$$w0rd** for the password and press **Enter**.

17. Ignore the warning message.

18. To create the first primary partition on sdc, wait until "Command (m for help)" appears, type **n** and press **Enter**, type **p** and press **Enter**, and then type **1** and press **Enter** three times.

19. To review the partition and write to the partition table, type **p** and press **Enter**, and then type **w** and press **Enter**.

20. To format the partition, type **sudo mkfs –t vfat /dev/sdc1** and press **Enter**. Enter **Pa$$w0rd** for the password and press **Enter**.

21. To label the partition, type **sudo e2label /dev/sdc1 vFat** and then press **Enter**. If necessary, enter **Pa$$w0rd** for the password and press **Enter**.

22. To position the partition to the /mnt directory, type **cd /mnt** and press **Enter**.

23. To make the directory for sdb1, type **sudo mkdir sdb1** and press **Enter**. If necessary, enter **Pa$$w0rd** for the password and press **Enter**.

24. To mount the sdb1 partition, type **sudo mount /dev/sdb1 –t ext4 /mnt/sdb1** and press **Enter**. If necessary, enter **Pa$$w0rd** for the password and press **Enter**.

25. To make the directory for sdc1, type **sudo mkdir sdc1** and press **Enter**. If necessary, enter **Pa$$w0rd** for the password and press **Enter**.

26. To mount the sdc1 partition, type **sudo mount /dev/sdc1 –t vfat /mnt/sdc1** and press **Enter**. If necessary, enter **Pa$$w0rd** for the password and press **Enter**.

27. To return to the root folder, type **cd ..** and press **Enter**.

28. To open the /etc/fstab file for editing, type **sudo nano /etc/fstab** and press **Enter**. Enter **Pa$$w0rd** for the password and press **Enter**.

29. Move the arrow down to a new line.

30. To add the mount line for sdb1, type the following and then press **Enter**.

    ```
    /dev/sdb1 /mnt/sdb1 ext4 defaults 0 0
    ```

31. To add the mount line for sdc1, type the following and then press **Enter**.

    ```
    /dev/sdc1 /mnt/sdc1 vfat defaults,dmask=000,fmask=111 0 0
    ```

32. To write the file to disk, press **Ctrl+O** and then press **Enter**.

33. To exit nano, press **Ctrl+X**.

34. To remount the devices, type **sudo mount –a** and press **Enter**. If necessary, enter **Pa$$w0rd** for the password and press **Enter**.

35. To verify that the mount worked, return to the desktop, click the **Places** arrow, click **Computer**, double-click **mnt**, verify that the sdb1 and sdc1 folders appear, and then close the open windows.

36. Go to *www.cengagebrain.com* and log in with your student account. Type **carswell** over "Enter ISBN, Author or Title," and then click the **Search** button, which looks like a magnifying glass.

37. To download the CentOS 7 student data files, click **Guide to Parallel Operating Systems with Windows 10 and Linux,** click the **Free Materials** tab, click **Save to MyHome,** and click **Open.** Click the **Data Files for Students (CentOSFiles)** link on the left, click the entry after **Download Now,** and then click **Run** twice. Click the **Data Files for Students (CentOSFiles)** link on the left. Right-click the **tgz** entry, click the **Save link as** option, and then click **Save.**

38. When the download is complete, right-click the **tar.gz** file, click **Open Containing Folder**, and verify that the file was downloaded into the Downloads directory.

39. To open a terminal window, right-click the desktop and click **Open in Terminal**.

40. Type **cd Downloads**, and then press **Enter**.

41. To decompress the file to the /mnt/sdb1/ directory, type the following line and then press **Enter**. If necessary, enter **Pa$$w0rd** for the password and press **Enter**.

    ```
    sudo tar -zxvf makes.tar.gz -C /mnt/sdb1/
    ```

42. Type **cd /mnt/sdb1** and press **Enter**.

43. Type **chmod 555 [mM]ake[dAHQ]*** and press **Enter**.

44. To log out, click the **down** chevron in the upper-right corner, click **User01**, and then click **Log Out** twice.

45. To shut down the virtual machine, click the **Action** menu, and then click **Shut Down** twice.

Working with VirtualBox

Getting Started with VirtualBox

Oracle VirtualBox is an x86 virtualization software package that was originally created by the German software company innotek GmbH. VirtualBox was purchased by Sun Microsystems and is now developed by Oracle Corporation as part of its family of virtualization products. It is installed on an existing host operating system; within this application, additional guest operating systems can be loaded and run, each with its own virtual environment.

VirtualBox includes the following features:

- The full VirtualBox package comes under a proprietary Personal Use and Evaluation License (PUEL), which allows use of the software free of charge for personal and educational purposes and for product evaluation.

- Several guest operating systems can be loaded. Each can be started, paused, and stopped independently. The host operating system and guest operating systems can communicate with each other through a common clipboard or using the network facility provided.

- X86 virtualization allows multiple operating systems to simultaneously share processor resources safely and efficiently. This virtualization is used to simulate a complete hardware environment, or virtual machine, in which an unmodified guest operating system executes. Virtualization was added to most x86 processors (Intel VT-x or AMD-V) in 2006.

- Hard disks are emulated in a disk image format called Virtual Disk Image (VDI).

- Both ISO images and host-connected physical devices can be mounted as CD/DVD drives. For example, the DVD image of a Linux distribution can be downloaded and used directly by VirtualBox.

- By default, VirtualBox provides graphics support through a custom virtual graphics card that is VESA compatible. The Guest Additions for Windows and Linux come with a special video driver that allows for better performance and features such as dynamic adjustment of the guest resolution when the VM window is resized.

- When used with an Ethernet network adapter, VirtualBox virtualizes a variety of network interface cards. Network Address Translation (NAT) is the default networking mode in VirtualBox.

- When used with a sound card, VirtualBox virtualizes an Intel ICH AC'97 device or a SoundBlaster 16 card.

Configuring the Host Computer

To enable future activities, you will share and populate the TextShare folder with files from the Cengage Learning Web site. In addition, you will set up a shared generic printer.

Complete the following steps to prepare the host computer running Windows 10 to support the virtual environment.

1. Log on to your host PC as **Admin01** with a password of **P@ssw0rd**.

2. To share a printer on the Host01 computer, click **Start**, click **Control Panel**, click the **View by** chevron, and click **Small icons**. Click **Devices and Printers**, click **Add a printer**, click **Add a local printer**, and then click **Next**. Scroll the Manufacturer list and click **Generic**, click **Generic/Text Only**, and then click **Next** twice. Type **SharedPrinter** in the Printer name text box, click **Next** twice, and then click **Finish**.

3. To create the TextShare folder on the host computer, click **Start**, click **Computer**, and double-click **Local Disk(C:)**. Note that your operating system drive might have a different name. Right-click the white space in the right pane, point to **New**, and click **Folder**. Type **TextShare**, press **Enter**, right-click **TextShare**, click **Properties**, and click the **Sharing** tab. Click **Share**, type **Everyone**, click **Add**, click **Share**, click **Done**, and then click **Close**.

Visit *www.cengagebrain.com* and log on to access student-specific resources on the Student Companion Site. If you are not a registered user, you can create a new account.

4. To access student resources on the Cengage Learning Web site, open your Web browser, type **www.cengagebrain.com/** in the address bar, and press **Enter**. Type **carswell** over "Enter ISBN, Author or Title," and then click the **Search** button, which looks like a magnifying glass.

5. To download the student data files, click **Guide to Parallel Operating Systems with Windows 10 and Linux**, click the **Free Materials** tab, click **Save to MyHome**, and click **Open**. Click the **Data Files for Students (TextShareFile)** link on the left, and then click the entry after **Download Now**. Click **Run** twice. If your Web browser automatically downloads files from the Internet, they should be downloaded and saved in your Downloads folder. Find the file you downloaded and copy it to the **TextShare** folder. If prompted for a location to download your files, click **Browse**, click **Local Disk (C:)**, double-click **TextShare**, and click **OK**. Click **Unzip**, click **OK**, and then click **Close**. If you are unable to download your student data files, contact your instructor for assistance.

Downloading VirtualBox

Complete the following steps to download the current version of VirtualBox from the Oracle Web site.

1. Log on to your host PC as **Admin01** with a password of **P@ssw0rd**.

2. To start the Microsoft Edge browser, click **Start**, click **All apps**, scroll, and then click **Microsoft Edge**. Download the current version of VirtualBox for Windows from the following link:

   https://www.virtualbox.org/wiki/Downloads

3. In the Download VirtualBox screen, under the VirtualBox platform packages, click **x86/amd64** to download the current VirtualBox version for Windows hosts.

4. After downloading the .exe file, find it in your downloads folder, and then double-click it and select all of the default settings in the window installer screens. (The installation will disconnect your network connections, but they will be restored after the installation.)

5. Click **Finish** when the installation is done, and then launch **VirtualBox**.

Installing Operating Systems in VirtualBox

In the following sections, you will create virtual machines, create virtual hard drives, and configure network adapters. When you finish, you will be ready to install a guest operating system. Recall that the virtual machines look like physical machines to the operating system installers.

Creating the Virtual Machine for Windows 10

Complete the following steps to create a virtual machine for Windows 10:

1. To start VirtualBox, double-click **Oracle VM VirtualBox** on the desktop.

2. To open the Create Virtual Machine Wizard for Windows 10, click **New**.

3. Enter **Windows 10** for the Name, click the **Version** chevron, and then scroll and select **Windows 10 (64-bit)**. Click **Continue**.

4. Enter **1024** for the memory size. Click **Continue**.

5. For the operating system hard disk, select **Create a virtual hard disk now**, and then click **Create**. Click **Continue** twice. Type **Windows 10 – Disk0** over "NewVirtualDisk1." Click **Create**.

6. To create a second hard disk, click **Windows 10**, click **Settings**, click **Storage**, and click **Controller: SATA**. Click the + icon over the diskette, click **Add Hard Disk**, click **Create a new disk**, and then click **Continue** twice. Type **Windows 10 – Disk1** over "NewVirtualDisk1." Change the size to **4096 MB** and then click **Create**.

7. Repeat Step 6 for **Windows 10 – Disk2**.

8. Click **Network** and verify that **Enable Network Adapter** is checked. Click **OK**.

Installing Windows 10

Installing Windows 10 on a virtual machine is not fundamentally different from installing it on a physical machine. Perform the following steps to install the Windows 10 virtual machine, which ensures that your virtual environment corresponds to the environment used throughout the text.

Complete the following steps to create the first virtual machine for Windows 10.

1. Place the Windows 10 DVD in the DVD drive. Click **Windows 10**, click **Settings**, and then click **Storage**. Click **Empty**, click the optical drive icon next to SATA Port 1, and click **Host Drive 'D:'**. Click **OK**. If you are instead using the Windows 10 ISO for installation, navigate to the location and select the ISO.

2. To start the Windows 10 virtual machine, highlight **Windows 10** and click the green arrow labeled **Start**.

3. If any messages appear about the "auto capture keyboard" or mouse pointer integration, close the message windows.

4. Verify and correct the language and other settings as needed, and then click **Next**.

5. To continue with the installation of Windows 10, click the **Install now** button when prompted.

6. Wait for the Setup program to start.

7. When prompted to enter the product key to activate Windows, enter the product key and then click **Next**.

8. When the license terms appear, click **I accept the license terms**, and then click **Next**.

9. When asked to select the type of installation you want, click **Custom: Install Windows only (advanced)**, click **Drive 0 Unallocated Space**, and then click **Next**.

10. Wait for the files to be copied and expanded.

11. When the Get going fast window appears, click **Use Express settings**.

12. If the **Choose how you'll connect** window appears, click **Join a domain**, and then click **Next**.

13. When prompted to choose a user name for your account, type **Admin01** in the "Who's going to use this PC" text box

14. Type **Pa$$w0rd** over "Enter password," press **Tab**, type **Pa$$w0rd** over "Re-enter password," type **It's a Microsoft password** over "Password hint," and then click **Next**.

15. Wait for Windows to set up the desktop. It will not take long. If the Networks window appears, click **No**.

16. To release the Windows 10 .iso file, click the **Devices** menu, point to **Optical Drives**, and then remove the disk from the virtual drive.

17. To change the computer name, type **control** in the "Search the web and Windows" text box, click **Control Panel**, click **System and Security**, click **System**, click the **Change settings** link, click **Change**, and type **Windows10** for the Computer name. Click **OK** twice, click **Close**, and then click **Restart Now**.

18. To sign in as user Admin01, click anywhere on the Windows 10 screen. On the Admin01 login screen, enter **Pa$$w0rd** for the password, and then press **Enter**.

19. Wait for the user setup to complete.

20. To extend the Path Environment variable for the scripts, type **control** in the "Search the web and Windows" text box, click **Control Panel**, click **System and Security**, click **System**, click **Advanced system settings**, and then click **Environment variables**. Under System variables, click **Path** and then click **Edit**. Press the **right arrow** key, type **Scripts**, and click **OK** three times.

21. To verify that the Path Environment variable was added correctly, type **cmd** in the "Search the web and Windows" text box, click **Command Prompt**, type **ECHO %PATH%**, and then press **Enter**.

22. Close the open windows in the Windows 10 virtual machine.

23. To download the scripts to the Windows 10 virtual machine, log in to *www.cengagebrain .com* with your student account. Type **carswell** over "Enter ISBN, Author or Title," and then click the **Search** button, which looks like a magnifying glass. Click **Guide to Parallel Operating Systems with Windows 10 and Linux,** click the **Free Materials** tab, click **Save to MyHome,** and click **Open**. Click the **Data Files for Students (Windows Files)** link on the left, click the entry after **Download Now,** and click **Run** twice. Click **Browse,** click **Local Disk (C:),** double-click **Scripts,** click **OK,** click **Unzip,** click **OK,** and then click **Close**. If you are unable to download your student data files, contact your instructor for assistance.

24. To allocate and format the partitions for student use, type **computer** in the "Search the web and Windows" text box, double-click **Computer Management,** double-click **Disk Management,** click **MBR (Master Boot Record),** and then click **OK**.

25. To create the first volume on Disk1, right-click the unallocated area, click **New Simple Volume,** click **Next,** enter **2048** for the Simple volume size in MB, and click **Next** twice. Type **NTFS** over "New Volume," click **Next,** and then click **Finish**.

26. To create the first volume on Disk2, right-click the unallocated area, click **New Simple Volume,** click **Next,** enter **2048** for the Simple volume size in MB, and click **Next** twice. Type **FAT32** over "New Volume," click **Next,** and then click **Finish**. Keep the Computer Management window open.

27. To create the User01 user account, expand **Local Users and Groups,** click **Users,** right-click in the white space, and then click **New User**.

28. Enter **User01** for the User name, enter **Pa$$w0rd** for the password, press **Tab,** and then enter **Pa$$w0rd** for the Confirm password. Clear the **User must change password at first logon** check box, click **Password never expires,** and then click **Create**. Click **Close**.

29. To set the password for the Administrator account, right-click **Administrator,** click **Set Password,** and then click **Proceed**. Enter **Pa$$w0rd** for the password, press **Tab,** enter **Pa$$w0rd** for the Confirm password, and then click **OK** twice. Right-click **Administrator,** click **Properties,** clear the **Account is disabled** check box, and then click **OK**. Close the Computer Management window.

30. To sign out, press the **Windows** key, click **Admin01** at the top of the Start menu, and then click **Sign out**.

31. To sign in as User01, click anywhere on the Windows 10 screen. Click **User01** in the lower-left corner, enter **Pa$$w0rd** for the password, and press **Enter**.

32. Wait for the user setup to complete, and then sign out as User01.

33. To sign in as Admin01, click anywhere on the Windows 10 screen. Click **Admin01** in the lower-left corner, enter **Pa$$w0rd** for the password, and then press **Enter**.

34. To start installing the Guest Additions, click **Devices** on the virtual machines menu, and then select **Insert Guest Additions CD Image**.

35. When the CD DRIVE (D:) VirtualBox Guest Additions window appears, click the message, click **Run VBoxWindowsAdditions.exe**, click **Yes**, click **Next** twice, and then click **Install**.

36. If asked if you want to install the software's display adapters, click **Install**.

37. If asked if you want to install the software's system devices, click **Install**.

38. When the Completing the Oracle VM VirtualBox Guest Additions window appears, click **Finish**. The system reboots.

39. To sign in as Admin01, click anywhere on the Windows 10 screen. Click **Admin01** in the lower-left corner, enter **Pa$$w0rd** for the password, and press **Enter**.

40. When the mouse pointer integration information appears, click the **Do not show this message again** check box and then click **OK**.

41. To force updates to be installed, click **Start**, click **Settings**, click **Update and Security**, click **Windows Update**, and then click **Check for updates**.

42. Wait for the downloads and for a response from Windows Update.

43. Wait for the updates to install and then click the **Restart now** button.

44. Wait for the remaining updates to be installed. The system will then restart.

45. Log on with the **User01** account and a password of **Pa$$w0rd**.

46. Wait for the desktop to be prepared.

47. Close any open windows in the virtual machine.

48. To shut down the virtual machine, click **Start**, click **Power**, and then click the **Shut Down** button.

49. Wait a moment for the Windows 10 virtual machine to shut down completely.

 The remaining steps in this section must be completed from the Host01 computer. After these steps are completed, all changes to the Windows 10 operating environment will be discarded on each launch of the Windows 10 virtual machine. This includes all virtual disks (Disk 0, Disk 1, and Disk 2).

50. To open the Storage link and disconnect the virtual drives, highlight the **Windows 10 virtual machine** entry, click **Settings**, and then click **Storage**. Click **Windows 10 – Disk 0.vdi**, click the – disk icon, click **Windows 10 – Disk 1.vdi**, click the – disk icon, click **Windows 10 – Disk2.vdi**, click the – disk icon, and then click **OK**.

51. Close the Oracle VM VirtualBox window.

52. To open a Command Prompt window, type **cmd** in the "Search the web and Windows" text box, and then click **Command Prompt**.

53. To change to the VirtualBox folder where the .vdi drives are stored, navigate to **C:\User\Student\VirtualBox VMs\Windows 10**.

54. To mark Disk0 as immutable, type the following command as one line and then press **Enter**.

```
C:\Program Files\Oracle\VirtualBox\vboxmanage.exe "modifyhd Win-
dows 10 - Disk0.vdi" -type immutable
```

The command must be typed on one line. The quotation marks are very important in this command.

55. Repeat Step 54 for **Windows 10 – Disk1.vdi.**

56. Repeat Step 54 for **Windows 10 – Disk2.vdi.**

57. Type **exit** and then press **Enter.**

58. To start the VirtualBox console, double-click the **Oracle VM VirtualBox** icon on the desktop.

59. To reconnect the Windows 10 – Disk0.vdi file, click **Windows 10,** click **Settings,** and then click **Storage.**

60. Highlight **Controller: SATA** and click the + disk icon.

61. Select **Choose Existing Disk** and then browse to **Windows 10 – Disk0.vdi.**

62. Repeat Step 61 for **Windows 10 – Disk1.vdi.**

63. Repeat Step 61 for **Windows 10 – Disk2.vdi.**

If an entry appears more than once, right-click one of the duplicate entries and click Remove Attachment.

64. Verify that the disks are in the following order: Windows 10 – Disk0.vdi, Windows 10 – Disk1.vdi, and Windows 10 – Disk2. Click **OK.**

65. To start the Windows 10 virtual machine, click the green **Start** arrow.

All changes made to the virtual hard drives will be discarded when you start the Windows 10 virtual machine.

66. Log on with the **User01** account and a password of **Pa$$w0rd.**

67. Continue with the lab activities in the text.

Creating a Virtual Machine for CentOS 7

Here is a brief overview of the tasks required to create a virtual machine for CentOS 7:

1. Start VirtualBox.

2. Create the CentOS 7 virtual machine, which will use sda.

3. Create two virtual disks (sdb and sdc) for future lab activities.

4. Connect the network adapter to the virtual machine.

Complete the following steps to create the virtual machine for CentOS 7.

1. If necessary, log on to your host PC as **Admin01** with a password of **P@ssw0rd**.

2. If necessary, double-click the **Oracle VM VirtualBox** icon on the desktop.

3. To open the Create Virtual Machine Wizard for CentOS 7, click **New**.

4. Enter **CentOS 7** for the Name, click the **Type** chevron and select **Linux**, click the Version chevron, and then scroll and select **Red Hat(64-bit)**. Click **Continue**.

5. Enter **1024** for the memory size. Click **Continue**.

6. For the operating system hard disk, select **Create a virtual hard disk now**, and then click **Create**. Click **Continue** twice. Type **CentOS 7 – sda** over "NewVirtualDisk1." Click **Create**.

7. To create a second hard disk, click **CentOS 7**, click **Settings**, click **Storage**, and then click **Controller: SATA**. Click the **+** icon over the diskette, click **Add Hard Disk**, click **Create a new disk**, and then click **Continue** twice. Type **CentOS 7 – sdb** over "NewVirtualDisk1." Change the size to **4096 MB**, and then click **Create**.

8. Repeat Step 7 for **CentOS 7 – sdc**.

9. Click **Network**, and verify that **Enable Network Adapter** is checked. Click **OK**.

10. Leave the machine logged on for the next activity.

Installing CentOS 7

Installing CentOS 7 on a virtual machine is not fundamentally different from installing it on a physical machine. Pay careful attention to the following steps to install the CentOS 7 machine, which ensures that your virtual environment corresponds to the environment used throughout the text.

1. If necessary, log on to your host PC as **user01** with a password of **P@ssw0rd**.

2. If necessary, double-click the **Oracle VM VirtualBox** icon on the desktop.

3. Insert the CentOS 7 DVD in the DVD/CD drive.

4. To mount the DVD, click **Settings**, click **Storage**, click **Empty** under IDE Controller, click the **CD/DVD Device** arrow, click **Host Drive 'D:'**, and then click **OK**. If you are instead using the CentOS 7 ISO for installation, navigate to the location and select the ISO.

5. To start the CentOS 7 virtual machine, click the green **Start** arrow.

6. When the next window prompts you to install or test, use the up arrow key to select **Install CentOS 7**, and then press **Enter**. Close the capture messages displayed by VirtualBox.

7. Verify that **English (United States)** is selected as the language. To proceed with the installation, click **Continue**.

8. In the next window, click **INSTALLATION DESTINATION**.

9. Select the first .vdi disk (sda) created for the installation of the operating system. (There should be a checkmark beside it.) Click **Done** in the upper-left corner.

10. Click **SOFTWARE SELECTION**. Click **GNOME Desktop** on the left side. On the right side, click **GNOME Applications, Internet Applications, Office Suite and Productivity, Development Tools,** and **Security Tools.** Click **Done** when you finish.

11. To set the date and time, click **Date and Time** and then change the setting to match your time zone. Click **Done.**

12. To start the installation, click **Begin Installation** in the lower-right corner.

13. To set the root password, click **ROOT PASSWORD**, type **P@ssw0rd**, press **Tab**, type **P@ssw0rd**, and then click **Done** twice.

14. To create the user01 user account, click **USER CREATION**. Enter **User01** as the Full Name and **User01** as the User Name. Check **Make this user administrator.** Enter **Pa$$w0rd** for the password twice.

15. Click **Done** twice.

16. The installation can take up to an hour. Click **Reboot** when it finishes. If the installation starts again, check the boot order and make sure Hard Disk is first.

17. When the system reboots, click **License Information**. Accept the license agreement and click **Done.** Click **Finish Configuration.** At the next prompts, enter a **1**, a **2**, and then **c**. The login page appears and the previous user (User01) is available to be selected for login.

18. Log on to CentOS 7 as **User01** with a password of **Pa$$w0rd**. Press **Enter.**

19. When the CentOS 7 desktop appears, click **Next** twice, and then click **Start using CentOS Linux.** Close the GNOME Help window.

Completing CentOS 7 Configuration

Next, you prepare two hard disks (sdb and sdc) for use in the text activities by partitioning and formatting them. Also, you will install the VirtualBox Guest Additions, which is special software for Windows and Linux virtual machines that improves performance and makes integration much more seamless. The Guest Additions provide features such as mouse pointer integration and screen resizing.

Finally, you will configure your hard disks to be immutable, which means that you can repeat the lab activities because the changes will be discarded every time you start your virtual machines.

Perform the following steps to configure the CentOS 7 virtual machine, which ensures that your virtual environment corresponds to the environment used throughout the text.

1. If necessary, log on to your host PC as **User01** with a password of **P@ssw0rd**.

2. If necessary, double-click the **Oracle VM VirtualBox** icon on the desktop.

3. If you need to start the CentOS 7 virtual machine, double-click the **CentOS 7 Virtual Machine** icon.

4. To attach the CentOS 7 – sdb disk, click **CentOS 7**, click **Settings**, click **Storage**, click **Controller: SATA**, click the **+** icon, and then select **Add Hard Disk**. Next, select **Create New Disk**. Select the **.vdi** option, click **Dynamically allocate**, and then click **Next** twice. The new drive should be configured.

5. Repeat the preceding steps to attach the CentOS 7 – sdc disk.

6. To start the CentOS 7 virtual machine, double-click the **CentOS 7 Virtual Machine** icon.

7. Log on to CentOS 7 as **User01** with a password of **Pa$$w0rd**.

8. To verify that the Ethernet adapter is available, click the down arrow in the upper-right corner of the screen. If the Wired setting is Off, click the arrow and select **Connect**.

9. Close the configuration window.

10. To open a terminal window, right-click the desktop and click **Open in Terminal**.

11. Type **sudo yum install samba**, type **Pa$$w0rd,** and press **Enter**. Type **y** in response to any prompts during the installation.

12. To start partitioning the sdb disk, type **sudo fdisk /dev/sdb** and press **Enter**. Enter **Pa$$w0rd** for the password and press **Enter**.

13. Ignore the warning message.

14. To create the first primary partition on sdb, wait until "Command (m for help)" appears, type **n** and press **Enter**, type **p** and press **Enter**, type **1** and press **Enter** twice, and then type **+2G** and press **Enter**.

15. To review the partition and write to the partition table, type **p** and press **Enter**, and then type **w** and press **Enter**.

16. To format the partition as Ext4, type **sudo mkfs /dev/sdb1** and press **Enter**. Enter **Pa$$w0rd** for the password and press **Enter**.

17. To label the partition, type **sudo e2label /dev/sdb1 Ext4** and press **Enter**. If necessary, enter **Pa$$w0rd** for the password and press **Enter**.

18. To start partitioning the sdc disk, type **sudo fdisk /dev/sdc** and press **Enter**. If necessary, enter **Pa$$w0rd** for the password and press **Enter**.

19. Ignore the warning message.

20. To create the first primary partition on sdc, wait until "Command (m for help)" appears, type **n** and press **Enter**, type **p** and press **Enter**, type **1** and press **Enter** twice, and then type **+2G** and press **Enter**.

21. To review the partition and write to the partition table, type **p** and press **Enter**, and then type **w** and press **Enter**.

22. To format the partition, type **sudo mkfs –t vfat /dev/sdc1** and press **Enter**. Enter **Pa$$w0rd** for the password and press **Enter**.

23. To label the partition, type **sudo e2label /dev/sdc1 vFat,** and then press **Enter**. If necessary, enter **Pa$$w0rd** for the password and press **Enter**.

24. To position the partition to the /mnt directory, type **cd /mnt** and press **Enter**.

25. To make the directory for sdb1, type **sudo mkdir sdb1** and press **Enter**. If necessary, enter **Pa$$w0rd** for the password and press **Enter**.

26. To mount the sdb1 partition, type **sudo mount /dev/sdb1 –t ext4 /mnt/sdb1** and press **Enter**. If necessary, enter **Pa$$w0rd** for the password and press **Enter**.

27. To make the directory for sdc1, type **sudo mkdir sdc1** and press **Enter**. If necessary, enter **Pa$$w0rd** for the password and press **Enter**.

28. To mount the sdc1 partition, type **sudo mount /dev/sdc1 –t vfat /mnt/sdc1** and press **Enter**. If necessary, enter **Pa$$w0rd** for the password and press **Enter**.

29. To return to the root folder, type **cd ..** and press **Enter**.

30. To open the /etc/fstab file for editing, type **sudo nano /etc/fstab** and press **Enter**. Enter **Pa$$w0rd** for the password and press **Enter**.

31. Move the arrow down to a new line.

32. To add the mount line for sdb1, type the following and then press **Enter**.

    `/dev/sdb1 /mnt/sdb1 ext4 defaults 0 0`

33. To add the mount line for sdc1, type the following and then press **Enter**.

    `/dev/sdc1 /mnt/sdc1 vfat defaults,dmask=000,fmask=111 0 0`

34. To write the file to disk, press **Ctrl+O** and then press **Enter**.

35. To exit nano, press **Ctrl+X**.

36. To remount the devices, type **sudo mount –a** and press **Enter**. If necessary, enter **Pa$$w0rd** for the password and press **Enter**.

37. To verify that the mount worked, double-click **Home**, double-click **Computer**, double-click **mnt**, verify that the sdb1 and sdc1 folders appear, and then close the open windows.

38. Go to *www.cengagebrain.com* and log in with your student account. Type **carswell** over "Enter ISBN, Author or Title," and then click the **Search** button, which looks like a magnifying glass.

39. To download the CentOS 7 student data files, click **Guide to Parallel Operating Systems with Windows 10 and Linux,** click the **Free Materials** tab, click **Save to MyHome,** and click **Open**. Click the **Data Files for Students (CentOSFiles)** link on the left, click the entry after **Download Now,** and then click **Run** twice. Click the **Data Files for Students (CentOSFiles)** link on the left. Right-click the **tgz** entry, click the **Save link as** option, and then click **Save**.

40. When the download is complete, right-click the **tar.gz** file, click **Open Containing Folder,** and verify that the file was downloaded into the Downloads directory.

41. To open a terminal window, right-click the desktop and click **Open in Terminal**. Type **cd Downloads,** and then press **Enter**.

42. To uncompress the file to the /mnt/sdb1/ directory, type the following line and then press **Enter**. If necessary, enter **Pa$$w0rd** for the password and press **Enter**.

    `sudo tar –zxvf makes.tar.gz –C /mnt/sdb1/`

43. Type **cd /mnt/sdb1** and press **Enter**. Type **chmod 555 [mM]ake[dAHQ]*** and press **Enter**.

44. To install the VBOXADDITION, click the **Devices** menu, and then click **Insert Guest Additions CD Image**.

45. On the desktop, a CD image will appear—VBOXADDITIONS_(version)—and run automatically.

46. When asked to run software, click **Run.** Enter **Pa$$w0rd** for the password and click **Authenticate.** Keep the default settings and continue through all the screens until the software is installed. Click **Finish.**

47. To close the virtual machine, click **User01,** click **Power Off,** and then click **Power Off.**

The following steps will set all of the virtual disks to discard any changes that students make. This will be helpful when multiple classes use the same computers. The following steps must be completed from the Host01 computer.

48. To open the Storage link and disconnect the virtual drives, click **CentOS 7 – sda.vdi,** click the – disk icon, click **CentOS 7 – sbd.vdi,** click the – disk icon, click **CentOS 7 – sdc.vdi,** click the – disk icon, and then click **OK.**

49. Close the Oracle VM VirtualBox window.

50. To open a Command Prompt window, click **Start,** type **CMD** in the "Search programs and files" box, and then double-click **CMD.**

51. Navigate to the VirtualBox VM folder that contains the CentOS 7 drives.

52. To mark the sda drive as immutable, type the following command as one line and then press **Enter.**

    ```
    C:\Program Files\Oracle\VirtualBox\vboxmanage.exe "modifyhd CentOS
    7 - sda.vdi" -type immutable
    ```

The command must be typed on one line. The quotation marks are very important in this command.

53. Repeat the previous step for **CentOS 7 – sdb.vdi.**

54. Repeat the previous step for **CentOS 7 – sdc.vdi.**

55. Type **Exit** and then press **Enter.**

56. To start the VirtualBox console, double-click the **Oracle VM VirtualBox** icon on the desktop.

57. To reconnect the CentOS 7 – sda.vdi file, highlight the CentOS 7 virtual image and then click **Settings,** click **Storage,** click **SATA Controller,** and click the + disk icon. Select **Create Hard Drive,** and then click **Existing disk.** Browse to the folder that contains the CentOS 7 virtual hard disks and click **CentOS 7 – sda.vdi.**

58. Repeat the previous step for the **CentOS 7 – sdb.vdi** file and **CentOS 7 – sdc.vdi** file.

If an entry appears more than once, right-click one of the duplicate entries and click Remove Attachment.

59. Verify that the disks are in the following order: CentOS 7 – sda.vdi, CentOS 7 – sdb.vdi, and CentOS 7 – sdc.vdi. Click **OK**.

60. To start the CentOS 7 virtual machine, click the green **Start** arrow.

61. To show the CentOS 7 virtual machine, click the green **Show** arrow.

 All previous changes to the virtual hard drives will be discarded when you start the CentOS 7 virtual machine.

62. Log on to the CentOS 7 virtual machine with a password of **Pa$$w0rd**.

63. Continue with the lab activities in the text.

Working with VMware

Getting Started with VMware

VMware Inc. is a company that provides x86 virtualization software; it is a subsidiary of EMC Corporation with headquarters in Palo Alto, California. VMware Workstation, a virtual machine software suite for x86 and x86-64 computers, is one of VMware's products. It is installed on an existing host operating system and allows the physical machine to run multiple operating systems simultaneously.

Note the following points about VMware's products:

- You need a license to use a VMware product. VMware offers full working versions of its software for evaluation purposes with an evaluation license.
- Several guest operating systems can be loaded. Each can be started, paused, and stopped independently. The host operating system and guest operating systems can communicate with each other through a common clipboard or the provided network facility.
- VMware virtual machines do not directly support FireWire.
- The Virtual Machine Disk (VMDK) file format, a type of virtual appliance, is used in VMware Workstation.
- ISO images and host-connected physical devices can be mounted as CD/DVD drives. For example, the DVD image of a Linux distribution can be downloaded and used directly by VMware.

Configuring the Host Computer

To enable future activities, you will share and populate the TextShare folder with files from the Cengage Learning Web site. In addition, you will share a generic printer.

Complete the following steps to prepare the host computer running Windows 10 to support the virtual environment.

1. Log on to your host PC as **Admin01** with a password of **Pa$$w0rd**.
2. To share a printer on the Host01 computer, type **Control** in the "Search the web and Windows" text box, click **Control Panel**, click the **View by** chevron, and click **Small**

icons. Click **Devices and Printers**, click **Add a printer**, click **Add a local printer**, and then click **Next**. Scroll the Manufacturer list, click **Generic**, click **Generic/Text Only**, and then click **Next** twice. Type **SharedPrinter** in the Printer name text box, click **Next** twice, and then click **Finish**.

3. To create the TextShare folder on the host computer, click the **File Explorer** icon on the taskbar, and then double-click **Local Disk(C:)**. Note that your operating system drive might have a different name. Right-click the white space in the right pane, point to **New**, click **Folder**, type **TextShare**, and press **Enter**. Right-click **TextShare**, click **Properties**, click the **Sharing** tab, and click **Share**. Type **Everyone**, click **Add**, click **Share**, click **Done**, and then click **Close**.

Visit *www.cengagebrain.com* and log on to access student-specific resources on the Student Companion Site. If you are not a registered user, you can create a new account.

4. To access student resources on the Cengage Learning Web site, open your Web browser, type **www.cengagebrain.com/** in the address bar, and press **Enter**. Type **carswell** over "Enter ISBN, Author or Title," and then click the **Search** button, which looks like a magnifying glass.

5. To download the student data files, click **Guide to Parallel Operating Systems with Windows 10 and Linux**, click the **Free Materials** tab, click **Save to MyHome**, and click **Open**. Click the **Data Files for Students (TextShareFile)** link on the left, and then click the entry after **Download Now**. Click **Run** twice. If your Web browser automatically downloads files from the Internet, they should be downloaded and saved in your Downloads folder. Find the file you downloaded and copy it to the **TextShare** folder. If prompted for a location to download your files, click **Browse**, click **Local Disk (C:)**, double-click **TextShare**, and click **OK**. Click **Unzip**, click **OK**, and then click **Close**. If you are unable to download your student data files, contact your instructor for assistance.

6. Close all open windows.

Downloading VMWare

Obtain a copy of VMware Workstation 11 or 12 with the appropriate license key. You can obtain a 30-day trial version from the Softonic Web site. Open your Web browser and search for "Softonic download VMware Workstation."

Installing VMware

The installation of VMware uses the VMware Workstation Installer. Complete the following steps to install VMware.

1. To start the VMware Workstation Setup wizard, double-click **Vmware-workstation-full-x.x.x**. (The value *x.x.x* is the product version number.)

2. In the User Access Control window, click **Yes**. Click **Next**. Click **I accept the terms of the license agreement**. Click **Next**. Click **Typical**. Click **Next** four times. Click **Install**. Wait for the installation to complete, then click **Skip** and click **Finish**.

 The following two steps (3 and 4) apply only to a VMware software update. Skip these steps if no update is involved.

3. If the Software Updates screen appears, click **Download and Install**, click **Continue**, click **Uninstall** to remove the current VMware workstation, and then click **Restart Now**.

4. After restarting the system, click **Next** on the Vmware Workstation Setup screen, click **Typical**, accept the default settings by clicking through the wizard, and then click **Restart Now**. Repeat Step 1.

5. To start VMware Workstation, double-click **VMware Workstation** on the desktop.

6. If required, enter an e-mail address and click **Next**.

7. To enter a license key, click **Enter License Key**, enter the license key, click **OK**, and then click **Close**.

8. Click **Edit** and then click **Virtual Network Editor**. Click **Change Settings** and then click **Yes**.

9. Click the **VMnet8** entry. Click **NAT settings**, and then enter **1** for the fourth octet of the Gateway IP Address. Click **OK**.

10. Click the **DHCP Settings** tab, and then verify that an entry for **VMnet8** exists. Click **OK** twice.

Installing Operating Systems in VMware

In the following sections, you will create virtual machines, create virtual hard disks, and configure network adapters. When you finish, you will be ready to install a guest operating system. Recall that the virtual machines look like physical machines to the operating system installers.

Creating the Virtual Machine for Windows 10

Here is a brief overview of the tasks required to create a virtual machine for Windows 10:

1. Start VMware.

2. Create the Windows 10 virtual machine, which will use Disk0. Install the Windows 10 operating system with the disk image file (.iso).

3. Install VMware tools to improve the performance of the guest operating system.

4. Create two virtual disks (Disk1 and Disk2) and attach them to the virtual machine for future activities.

5. Connect the network adapter to the virtual machine.

Complete the following steps to create the first virtual machine:

1. If necessary, log on to your host PC as **Admin01** with a password of **Pa$$w0rd**.

2. If you are using the Windows 10 DVD, insert the Windows 10 (64 bit) Installer disc image file in the CD/DVD drive.

You can also choose to install the Windows 10 operating system files, which is not fundamentally different from installing to a physical machine instead of using the .iso file.

3. If necessary, start VMware by double-clicking the **VMware Workstation** icon on the desktop.

4. Click **File**, and then click **New Virtual Machine**. Select **Typical** and then click **Next**.

5. In the Install from window, select a method of installation. Either click **Installer disc to install from CD/DVD** or click **Install disk image file (iso)** to install from the ISO file located on your local hard drive. Click **Next** twice and click **Yes**. You will also be able to enter your license key and create an Admin01 user account later.

6. Type **Windows 10** as the Virtual machine name. Click **Next**. Enter 20 as the Maximum disk size (GB), click **Next**, and then click **Finish**. Wait for the disk to be created.

7. If the virtual machine did not start, click **Windows 10** in the VMware Workstation window under My Computer. Click **Windows 10**, and then click the **Power on this virtual machine** link.

8. If the Windows 10 setup fails to automatically start and install, click in the Windows 10 VM window and then click **Next** in the Windows Setup screen. Click **OK**. Click **Install Now**.

9. Wait for the Setup program to start.

10. When the "Enter the product key to activate Windows" screen appears, enter the product key and then click **Next**.

11. When the license terms appear, click **I accept the license terms**, and then click **Next**.

12. When asked to select the type of installation you want, click **Custom (advanced)**, click **Drive 0 Unallocated Space**, and then click **Next**.

13. Wait for the files to be copied and expanded.

14. When the Get going fast window appears, click **Use Express settings**. Click **I Finished Installing**.

15. Wait for the critical updates to install.

16. When the "Choose how you'll connect" window appears, click **Join a local Active Directory domain**, and then click **Next**.

Local Active Directory domains are used to centralize user account administration. By selecting this option, you can continue to log on with your local user account. The Azure Active directory exists in the Microsoft cloud.

17. When prompted to choose a user name for your account, type **Admin01** in the "Who's going to use this PC" text box.

18. Type **Pa$$w0rd** over "Enter password," press **Tab**, type **Pa$$w0rd** over "Re-enter password," type **It's a Microsoft password** over "Password hint," and then click **Next**.

19. Wait for Windows to set up the desktop.

20. When asked if you want to allow your PC to be discoverable by other devices on this network, click **Yes**.

21. In the VMware Workstation window, click the **VM** menu, and then click **Install VMware Tools**. Follow the wizard by accepting the default settings. Wait for the tools installation to complete, and then restart the Windows 10 virtual machine.

If this setup fails, press Windows +R, enter D:\Setup, and then click OK.

22. Log on with the **Admin01** account and a password of **Pa$$w0rd**.

23. To shut down the Windows 10 virtual machine, press the **Windows** key, click **Power**, and then click **Shut Down**.

24. To release the Windows 10 .iso file, click the **VM** menu, click **Settings**, click **CD/DVA(SATA)**, uncheck **Connect at power on**, click **Use physical drive**, and then click **OK**.

25. To add a virtual hard disk, click **VM**, click **Settings**, click **Hard Disk**, click **Add**, and then click **Yes**. Click **Next** three times. Type **4** as the Maximum disk size (GB). Click **Next**. Type **Windows 10 – Disk1.vmdk** as the Disk file, and then click **Finish**.

26. Repeat Step 25 for **Windows 10 – Disk2.vmdk**. Click **OK** to close the Virtual Machine Settings window.

Completing Configuration

In this section, you will prepare the two hard disks (Disk1 and Disk2) for use in the text activities by partitioning and formatting them. As part of disk creation, you will copy and paste a set of script files to Disk1 from the TextShare folder that is created in the host machine, and extend the Path Environment variable for the scripts.

Next, you will create the User01 Standard user account, which is used by some activities in the text. It is not a good practice to use the Administrator accounts for day-to-day computer use.

Next, you will perform Windows Update.

Finally, you will configure your hard disks to be nonpersistent, which means that you can repeat the lab activities because the changes will be discarded every time you start your virtual machines.

Perform the following steps to configure the Windows 10 virtual machine, which ensures that your virtual environment corresponds to the environment used throughout the text. After these steps are completed, all changes to the operating environment for Windows 10 will be discarded on each launch of Windows 10. This includes all virtual disks (Disk 0, Disk 1, and Disk 2).

1. In the VMware Workstation window for Windows 10, click the **Power on this virtual machine** link. Log on with the **Admin01** account and a password of **Pa$$w0rd**.

2. To start Disk Management, type **Control** in the "Search the web and Windows" text box, press **Enter**, and then click **Control Panel**. Click the **System and Security** link, scroll to **Administrative Tools**, double-click **Computer Management**, and then click **Disk Management**.

3. When the Initialize Disk dialog box appears, review the settings and then click **OK**.

In the following steps, you will create disk volumes for future activities. For other future activities, you will need unallocated space on these two disks. It is important that you do not create the volume over the entire disk.

4. To create and format an NTFS volume, scroll the bottom pane until Disk 1 appears, right-click the **4.00 GB Unallocated** box, click **New Simple Volume**, and then click **Next**. Type **2048** over the 4093 in the "Simple volume size MB" spinner box, click **Next** twice, type **NTFS** over "New volume label," click **Next**, and then click **Finish**.

5. Go back to Disk Management.

6. To create and format a FAT32 volume, scroll the bottom pane until Disk 2 appears, right-click the **4.00 GB Unallocated** box, click **New Simple Volume**, and then click **Next**. Type **2048** over the 4093 in the "Simple volume size MB" spinner box, click **Next** twice, click the **Format the volume with the following settings** arrow, click **File system**, click **FAT32**, type **FAT32** over "New Volume label," click **Next**, and then click **Finish**.

7. Close the Computer Management window in the virtual machine. Close all remaining windows.

8. To extend the Path Environment variable for the scripts, type **control** in the "Search the web and Windows" text box, click **Control Panel**, click **System and Security**, click **System**, click **Advanced system settings**, and then click **Environment variables**. Click **Path** and then click **Edit**. Press the **right arrow** key, type **Scripts**, and then click **OK** three times.

9. To verify that the Path Environment variable was added correctly, type **cmd** in the "Search the web and Windows" text box, click **Command Prompt**, type **ECHO% PATH%**, and then press **Enter**.

10. Close the open windows in the Windows 10 virtual machine.

11. To download the scripts to the Windows 10 virtual machine, log in to *www.cengage brain.com* with your student account. Type **carswell** over "Enter ISBN, Author or Title," and then click the **Search** button, which looks like a magnifying glass. Click **Guide to Parallel Operating Systems with Windows 10 and Linux**, click the **Free Materials** tab, click **Save to MyHome**, and click **Open**. Click the **Data Files for Students (Windows Files)** link on the left, click the entry after **Download Now**, and click **Run** twice. Click **Browse**, click **Local Disk (C:)**, double-click **Scripts**, click **OK**, click **Unzip**, click **OK**, and then click **Close**. If you are unable to download your student data files, contact your instructor for assistance.

12. To open User accounts management, type **Control** in the "Search the web and Windows" text box, and click **Control Panel**. Click **Small icons** from the View by menu in the upper-right corner. Click **Administrative Tools**, double-click **Computer Management**, expand **Local Users and Groups**, click **Users**, right-click the white space in the right panel, and then click **New User**.

13. Enter **User01** for the User name, enter **Pa$$w0rd** for the Password, press **Tab**, and enter **Pa$$w0rd** for the Confirm password. Clear the **User must change password at first logon** check box. Click **Password never expires** and then click **Create**. Click **Close**.

14. To set the password for the Administrator account, right-click **Administrator**, click **Set Password**, and then click **Proceed**. Enter **Pa$$w0rd** for the Password, press **Tab**, enter **Pa$$w0rd** for the Confirm password, and then click **OK** twice. Right-click **Administrator**, click **Properties**, clear the **Account is disabled** check box, and then click **OK**. Close all open windows.

15. To force updates to be installed, type **update** in the "Search the web and Windows" text box, and then click **Check for updates**.

16. Wait for the updates to install and for the virtual machine to restart.

17. Log on with the **User01** account and a password of **Pa$$w0rd**.

18. Wait for the desktop to be prepared.

19. To shut down the Windows 10 virtual machine, click **Start**, click **Power**, and then click **Shut down**.

20. Highlight **Windows 10** in the left panel. Click **VM**, click **Settings**, click **Hard Disk (SCSI)** under the Hardware tab, and then click **Advanced**. Check **Independent** mode and then click the **Nonpersistent** radio button. Click **OK**.

21. Repeat the preceding step for Hard Disk 2 (Windows 10 – Disk1.vmdk) and Hard Disk 3 (Windows 10 – Disk2.vmdk).

22. Click **OK** to exit the virtual machine settings and save the changes.

23. To start the Windows 10 virtual machine, click **Power on this virtual machine**.

All changes made to the virtual hard drives will be discarded when you start the Windows 10 virtual machine.

24. Log on with the **User01** account and a password of **Pa$$w0rd**.

25. Continue with the lab activities in the text.

Creating a Virtual Machine for CentOS 7

Here is a brief overview of the required tasks to create a virtual machine for CentOS 7:

1. Start the VMware workstation.

2. Create the CentOS 7 virtual machine, which will use sda. Install the CentOS 7 operating system with the disk image file (.iso).

3. Create two virtual disks (sdb and sdc) and attach them to the virtual machine for future activities.

Installing CentOS 7 Complete the following steps to create the virtual machine and install CentOS 7. Also, you will install the VMware Tools, which is special software for Windows and Linux virtual machines that improves performance and makes integration much more seamless. The VMware Tools provide features such as mouse pointer integration and screen resizing. (Skip this step if VMware Tools installation is included in the process of creating the CentOS 7 virtual machine.)

1. If necessary, log on to your host PC as **Admin01** with a password of **Pa$$w0rd**.

2. Insert the CentOS 7 Installer disc image file in the CD/DVD drive. If necessary, double-click the **VMware** icon on the desktop.

You can also choose to install the CentOS 7 operating system. Installing CentOS 7 to a virtual machine is not fundamentally different from installing it to a physical machine. Pay careful attention to the following steps to install the CentOS 7 machine, which ensures that your virtual environment corresponds to the environment used throughout the text.

3. Click **File**, and then click **New Virtual Machine**.

4. Select **Typical**, and then click **Next**.

5. In the Install from window, select a method of installation. Either click **Installer disc to install from CD/DVD** or click **Install disk image file (iso)** to install from the ISO file located on your local hard drive. Click **Next**. Enter **CentOS 7** as the Full name. Enter **user01** (lowercase only) as the User name, and then enter **Pa$$w0rd** as the Password. Enter **Pa$$w0rd** again to confirm the password, and then click **Next**. Type **CentOS 7** as the Virtual machine name, and then click **Next**. Enter **20** as the Maximum disk size (GB). Click **Next** and then click **Finish**.

6. Wait for CentOS 7 to install.

7. Log on to CentOS 7 as **user01** with a password of **Pa$$w0rd**.

8. Click **English**, click **Next** twice, and then click **Start using CentOS Linux**.

9. Close the Getting Started window.

10. To shut down the CentOS 7 virtual machine, right-click the CentOS 7 desktop, and then click **Open in Terminal**. Type **shutdown -h now** and then press **Enter**.

Configuring CentOS 7

You will want to prepare two hard disks (sdb and dsc) for use in the text activities by partitioning and formatting them. You will also configure your hard disks to be nonpersistent, which means that you can repeat the lab activities because the changes will be discarded every time you start your virtual machines.

Pay careful attention to the following steps to configure the CentOS 7 virtual machine, which ensures that your virtual environment corresponds to the environment used throughout the text.

1. If necessary, log on to your host PC as **Admin01** with a password of **Pa$$w0rd**.

2. If necessary, double-click the **VMware** icon on the desktop. Highlight **CentOS 7 Virtual Machine** under Favorites.

3. To attach the CentOS 7 – sdb disk, click the **VM** menu, click **Settings**, click **Add**, select **Hard Disk**, click **Next**, check **Independent**, and then click **Next** twice. Type **4** as the Maximum disk size (GB), and click **Next**. Type **CentOS 7 – sdb.vmdk** as the Disk file, and then click **Finish**.

4. Repeat Step 3 for **CentOS 7 – sdc.vmdk**. Click **OK** to close the Virtual Machine Settings window.

5. To start the CentOS 7 virtual machine, click **Power on this virtual machine**.

6. Log on to CentOS 7 as **user01** with a password of **Pa$$w0rd**.

7. To verify that the Ethernet adapter is available, click the down arrow in the upper-right corner of the screen. If Wired is off, click **Off** to connect.

8. To open a terminal session, click **Applications**, and then click **Terminal**.

9. Type **su –** and press **Enter**. Type **Pa$$w0rd** and press **Enter**.

10. Type **visudo** and press **Enter**.

11. To insert the group, press the **A** key, press **Enter**, type **user01 ALL=(ALL) ALL**, press the **ESC** key, type **:wq**, and then press **Enter**.

Leave out the # in the statement or the entry will be treated as a remark.

12. Type **Exit** at the root prompt, and then press **Enter**.

13. To open a terminal window, right-click the desktop and click **Open in Terminal**.

14. Type **yum search lshw** and press **Enter**. If you receive an error message, check your network adapter and make sure you are connected to VMnet8.

15. Type **sudo yum install lshw**, and press **Enter**. Enter **Pa$$w0rd** when prompted for the password.

16. When "Is this ok [y/N]" appears, press **y** and press **Enter**. Wait for the download to begin and for the installation to complete.

17. Repeat Steps 14 through 16 for **nm-connection-editor**, **system-config-printer**, and **gnome-disk-utility**.

18. To start partitioning the sdb disk, type **sudo fdisk /dev/sdb** and press **Enter**.

19. Type **Pa$$w0rd** at the password prompt.

20. To create the first primary partition on sdb, type **n** and press **Enter**, type **p** and press **Enter**, type **1** and press **Enter**, type **2048** and press **Enter**, and then type **+2G** and press **Enter**.

21. To review the partition and write to the partition table, type **p** and press **Enter**, and then type **w** and press **Enter**.

22. To format the partition as XFS, type **sudo mkfs /dev/sdb1** and press **Enter**. Type **Pa$$w0rd** at the password prompt.

23. To label the partition, type **sudo e2label /dev/sdb1 xfs label** and press **Enter**.

24. To start partitioning the sdc disk, type **sudo fdisk /dev/sdc** and press **Enter**.

25. Type **Pa$$w0rd** at the password prompt.

26. To create the first primary partition on sdc, type **n** and press **Enter**, type **p** and press **Enter**, type **1** and press **Enter**, type **2048** and press **Enter**, and then type **+2G** and press **Enter**.

27. To review the partition and write to the partition table, type **p** and press **Enter**, and then type **w** and press **Enter**.

28. To format the partition, type **sudo mkfs.vfat –F 32 /dev/sdc1** and press **Enter**.

29. To label the partition, type **sudo dosfslabel /dev/sdc1 VFAT** and press **Enter**.

30. To position the partition to the /mnt directory, type **cd /mnt** and press **Enter**.

31. To make the directory for sdb1, type **sudo mkdir sdb1** and press **Enter**.

32. To mount the sdb1 partition, type **sudo mount /dev/sdb1 –t ext4 /mnt/sdb1** and press **Enter**.

33. To make the directory for sdc1, type **sudo mkdir sdc1** and press **Enter**.

34. To mount the sdc1 partition, type **sudo mount /dev/sdc1 –t vfat /mnt/sdc1** and press **Enter**.

35. To return to the home folder, type **cd ..** and press **Enter**.

36. To open the /etc/fstab file for editing, type **sudo nano /etc/fstab** and press **Enter**.

37. Use the arrow keys to move down to a new line.

38. To add the mount line for sdb1, type **/dev/sdb1 /mnt/sdb1 ext4 defaults 0 0** and press **Enter**.

39. To add the mount line for sdc1, type **/dev/sdc1 /mnt/sdc1 vfat defaults,dmask=000, fmask=111 0 0** and press **Enter**.

40. To write the file to disk, press **Ctrl+O** and then press **Enter**.

41. To exit nano, press **Ctrl+X**.

42. To remount the devices, type **sudo mount –a** and press **Enter**.

43. To verify that the mount worked, click the **Places** arrow, click **Computer**, double-click **mnt**, verify that the sdb1 and sdc1 folders appear, and then close the open windows.

44. Go to *www.cengagebrain.com* and log in with your student account. Type **carswell** over "Enter ISBN, Author or Title," and then click the **Search** button, which looks like a magnifying glass.

45. To download the CentOS 7 student data files, click **Guide to Parallel Operating Systems with Windows 10 and Linux,** click the **Free Materials** tab, click **Save to MyHome,** and click **Open.** Click the **Data Files for Students (CentOSFiles)** link on the left, click the entry after **Download Now,** and then click **Run** twice. Click the **Data Files for Students (CentOSFiles)** link on the left. Right-click the **tgz** entry, click the **Save link as** option, and then click **Save.**

46. When the download is complete, right-click the **tar.gz** file, click **Open Containing Folder,** and verify that the file was downloaded into the Downloads directory.

47. In the CentOS 7 virtual machine, right-click the desktop and click **Open in Terminal.** Type **cd Downloads** and then press **Enter.**

48. To uncompress the file to the /mnt/sdb1/ directory, type the following line and then press **Enter.** If necessary, enter **Pa$$w0rd** for the password and press **Enter.**

    ```
    sudo tar -zxvf makes.tar.gz -C /mnt/sdb1/
    ```

49. Type **cd /usr/local/bin/** and press **Enter.** Type **chmod 555 [mM]ake[dAHQ]*** and then press **Enter.**

NOTE

The following steps will set all of the virtual disks to discard any changes that students make, which will be helpful when multiple classes use the same computers. Steps 50 and 51 must be completed from the Host01 computer.

50. Highlight **CentOS 7 Virtual Machine** in the left panel. Click **VM,** click **Settings,** click **Hard Disk (SCSI)** under the Hardware tab, and then click **Advanced.** Check **Independent** mode and then click the **Nonpersistent** radio button. Click **OK.**

51. Repeat the preceding step for Hard Disk 2 (CentOS 7 – sdb.vmdk) and Hard Disk 3 (CentOS 7 – sdc.vmdk).

52. Click **OK** to exit the virtual machine settings and save the changes.

53. To start the CentOS 7 virtual machine, click **Power on this virtual machine** in the CentOS 7 tab.

54. Log on to the CentOS 7 virtual machine with a password of **Pa$$w0rd.**

55. Continue with the lab activities in the text.

D

Index